CW01081917

SOCIAL CONTROL IN LATE ANTIQUITY

Social Control in Late Antiquity: The Violence of Small Worlds explores the small-scale communities of late antiquity – households, monasteries, and schools – where power was a question of personal relationships. When fathers, husbands, teachers, abbots, and slave-owners asserted their own will, they saw themselves as maintaining the social order, and expected law and government to reinforce their rule. Naturally, the members of these communities had their own ideas, and teaching them to 'obey their betters' was not always a straightforward business. Drawing on a wide variety of sources from across the late Roman Mediterranean, from law codes and inscriptions to monastic rules and hagiography, the book considers the sometimes conflicting identities of women, slaves, and children and asks how they found opportunities for agency and recognition within a system built on the unremitting assertion of the rights of the powerful.

KATE COOPER is Professor of History at Royal Holloway, University of London. She writes and teaches about Roman history and early Christianity with a special interest in daily life, gender, and the household. Her publications include *Band of Angels: The Forgotten World of Early Christian Women* (2013), *The Fall of the Roman Household* (2007), and *The Virgin and the Bride: Idealized Womanhood in Late Antiquity* (1996). Kate has been awarded numerous grants and prizes, including the Rome Prize of the American Academy in Rome, an RCUK Global Uncertainties Fellowship, and a Leverhulme Trust Major Research Fellowship.

JAMIE WOOD is Associate Professor of History at the University of Lincoln. He works on late antique and early medieval history, with particular interests in the religious and social history of the Iberian Peninsula. He has published widely on the writings of Isidore of Seville, including: *The Politics of Identity in Visigothic Spain* (2012),

A Companion to Isidore of Seville (co-edited, 2019), and *Isidore of Seville and His Reception in the Early Middle Ages* (co-edited, 2016). Jamie's postdoctoral research was funded by a Leverhulme Trust Early Career Fellowship and he has received grants from the British Academy and the Gulbenkian Foundation, among others. He is currently writing a book about the Byzantine presence in the Iberian Peninsula in the sixth and seventh centuries.

SOCIAL CONTROL IN LATE ANTIQUITY

The Violence of Small Worlds

EDITED BY

KATE COOPER

Royal Holloway, University of London

JAMIE WOOD

University of Lincoln

CAMBRIDGE
UNIVERSITY PRESS

University Printing House, Cambridge CB2 8BS, United Kingdom

One Liberty Plaza, 20th Floor, New York, NY 10006, USA

477 Williamstown Road, Port Melbourne, VIC 3207, Australia

314–321, 3rd Floor, Plot 3, Splendor Forum, Jasola District Centre, New Delhi – 110025, India

79 Anson Road, #06–04/06, Singapore 079906

Cambridge University Press is part of the University of Cambridge.

It furthers the University's mission by disseminating knowledge in the pursuit of education, learning, and research at the highest international levels of excellence.

www.cambridge.org
Information on this title: www.cambridge.org/9781108479394
DOI: 10.1017/9781108783491

First published 2020

A catalogue record for this publication is available from the British Library.

Library of Congress Cataloging-in-Publication Data
NAMES: Cooper, Kate, 1960- editor. | Wood, Jamie, 1978- editor.
TITLE: Social control in late antiquity : the violence of small worlds / edited by Kate Cooper, Royal Holloway, University of London, Jamie Wood, University of Lincoln.
DESCRIPTION: Cambridge, United Kingdom ; New York, NY : Cambridge University Press, 2020. | Includes bibliographical references and index.
IDENTIFIERS: LCCN 2020014089 (print) | LCCN 2020014090 (ebook) | ISBN 9781108479394 (hardback) | ISBN 9781108742696 (paperback) | ISBN 9781108783491 (epub)
SUBJECTS: LCSH: Social control–Rome–History–To 1500. | Violence–Rome–History–To 1500. | Social structure–Rome–History–To 1500. | Roman provinces–Administration. | Rome–History–Empire, 284-476.
CLASSIFICATION: LCC HN10.R7 S623 2020 (print) | LCC HN10.R7 (ebook) | DDC 303.3/70945632–dc23
LC record available at https://lccn.loc.gov/2020014089
LC ebook record available at https://lccn.loc.gov/2020014090

ISBN 978-1-108-47939-4 Hardback

Contents

Contributors

KATE COOPER, Professor of History, Royal Holloway, University of London

JAMES CORKE-WEBSTER, Senior Lecturer in Roman History, King's College London

CHRIS L. DE WET, Associate Professor of Biblical and Ancient Studies, University of South Africa, Pretoria

THOMAS DIMAMBRO, Financial Planning and Analysis Manager, National Grid, Warwick

MARIA CHIARA GIORDA, Professore Associato in Studi Umanistici, Università Roma Tre

JULIA HILLNER, Professor of Medieval History, University of Sheffield

AARON P. JOHNSON, Associate Professor of Humanities, Lee University

LILLIAN I. LARSEN, Professor of Religious Studies, University of Redlands

BLAKE LEYERLE, Associate Professor of Theology, University of Notre Dame

VASILIKI LIMBERIS, Professor of Religion, Temple University

MELISSA MARKAUSKAS, Departmental Support Administrator, School of Environment, Education and Development, University of Manchester

DAVID NATAL, Lecturer in History, Royal Holloway, University of London

BLOSSOM STEFANIW, Heisenberg Fellow, Martin-Luther-Universität, Halle-Wittenberg

JONATHAN TALLON, Tutor in Biblical Studies, Northern Baptist College

JAMIE WOOD, Associate Professor of History, University of Lincoln

Preface and Acknowledgements

This volume has its roots in a collaborative research project on religion and violence in late antiquity, the RCUK-funded Constantine's Dream: Belonging, Deviance, and the Problem of Violence in Early Christianity, which was hosted by the University of Manchester from 2009 to 2012. One of the most important insights of that project was the critical importance of the 'small worlds' of the household, the monastery, and the schoolroom as the places where social change either did or did not happen, depending on whether or not the men (and women) tasked with maintaining the social order were successful in doing their job. We became fascinated by the problem of social reproduction and the reciprocal relationship between 'big ideas' and the 'small worlds' in which people lived out their lives. Of course, the very nature of our sources – fragmentary, allusive, frustratingly focused on the viewpoint of elites – posed a significant barrier to making sense of the problem. We were fortunate that Manchester was buzzing with young people who were keen to think 'outside the box' – postgraduates and postdoctoral fellows who have become colleagues to reckon with. (Though our own paths have eventually led us elsewhere, this volume is among other things a tribute to a university that shaped a generation of historians by fostering both independent thinking and creative collaboration.) In 2011–12 we were fortunate to receive a British Academy Small Grants Scheme Award for a project entitled Cognitive Violence and Social Reproduction in Late Ancient Christianity: A Preliminary Study.

The idea – and the crowd – kept growing. A workshop, 'Violence, Education and Social Reproduction in Late Antiquity', was organised to coincide with the XVI International Conference on Patristic Studies in August 2011. (We are grateful to Worcester College, Oxford, for hosting this memorable symposium.) Since Oxford, we have picked up several further conversation-partners, a number of whom have become contributors to the present volume. So our first vote of thanks goes to the friends and colleagues who have lent their energy to the conversation – one that has made an immeasurable difference to our way of seeing the ancient world.

The chapters represent a collective effort to view the changing landscape of the fourth and fifth centuries from the perspective of lived experience. Wherever possible we have tried to bring forward the experience of people whose voices have largely been passed over by the historical record. Many of the sources on which our contributors draw – laws, hagiographies, and theological tracts by superstar bishops (many of them later saints) – have traditionally been understood to offer a 'top-down' point of view, so we have made every effort to read these texts against the grain. Rather than assuming that elite bishops were transparently accurate spokesmen for their communities, we have tried to assess their efforts to influence audiences who saw things from a point of view very different to their own.

A number of chapters in our collection demonstrate how social reproduction functioned in small-scale social contexts, and thus go some way to explaining how the late Roman social order perpetuated itself across time and space. This order was maintained as much through quotidian microaggressions as much as it was through the weight of the state and its legal system. Yet our constant interest has been in the point of view of the disempowered – women, children, and the enslaved, both how they were treated and how they resisted the worst excesses of their oppressors. It is in the contexts of small worlds that some individuals whose social power was modest or minimal were nonetheless able to carve out opportunities to exercise agency. In these contributions we gain insights into the resilience of individuals and social structures on a small, everyday scale.

In addition to the contributors, we would like thank our institutions – the Universities of Manchester and Lincoln, and Royal Holloway, University of London, along with the British Academy and Research Councils UK – for the support that has made this work possible. We must also acknowledge the acute and generous work of Michael Sharp at Cambridge University Press and the anonymous peer reviewers, whose comments have done so much to sharpen our thinking. (Any errors that remain are, of course, our own.)

Finally, we must thank our families, whose bewildering power to charm, distract, and even educate us has made all the difference.

Abbreviations

AA	Auctores Antiquissimi
ACW	Ancient Christian Writers
Adv. Jud.	John Chrysostom, *Against the Jews*
Alph.	Alphabetical collection of *Apophthegmata Patrum*
Ambrose, *Ep.*	Ambrose, *Epistulae*
Ambrose, *Ep. extra coll.*	Ambrose, *Epistulae extra collectionem*
AP	*Apophthegmata Patrum*
can.	Canon
CCSL	Corpus Christianorum Series Latina
c.Marc.	Eusebius, *Contra Marcellum*
Cod. Iust.	Codex Justinianus
CSEL	Corpus Scriptorum Ecclesiasticorum Latinorum
Cod. Theod.	*Codex Theodosianus*
Dig.	*Digesta*
Ep.	*Epistula*
Ep. Ant.	*Epistulae Antonii*
Euphemia	*Euphemia and the Goth*
Exp. Ps.	John Chrysostom, *Commentary on the Psalms*
Field	F. Field, ed., *Ioannis Chrysostomi interpretatio omnium epistularum Paulinarum*, 7 vols. (Oxford: J. H. Parker, 1854–62)
Foerster	Richard Foerster, ed., *Libanii opera*. Vols. I–IV (Leipzig: Teubner, 1903–8)
FOTC	Fathers of the Church
GCS	Griechischen Christlichen Schriftsteller
Gregory of Tours, *Hist.*	Gregory of Tours, *Libri historiarum X*
Hab. eun. spir.	John Chrysostom. *Homily on 'Those Who Have the Same Spirit of Faith' (2 Cor. 4:13)*

Hist. Laus.	Palladius, *Historia Lausiaca*
Hom. acta apost.	John Chrysostom, *Homilies on the Acts of the Apostles*
Hom. Col.	John Chrysostom, *Homilies on Colossians*
Hom. 1 Cor.	John Chrysostom, *Homilies on 1 Corinthians*
Hom. 2 Cor.	John Chrysostom, *Homilies on 2 Corinthians*
Hom. Eph.	John Chrysostom, *Homilies on Ephesians*
Hom. Gen.	John Chrysostom, *Homilies on Genesis*
Hom. Heb.	John Chrysostom, *Homilies on Hebrews*
Hom. Jo.	John Chrysostom, *Homilies on John*
Hom. Laz.	John Chrysostom, *Homilies on Lazarus*
Hom. Matt.	John Chrysostom, *Homilies on Matthew*
Hom. Phlm.	John Chrysostom, *Homilies on Philemon*
Hom. Philip.	John Chrysostom, *Homilies on Philippians*
Hom. Rom.	John Chrysostom, *Homilies on Romans*
Hom. 1 Thess.	John Chrysostom, *Homilies on 1 Thessalonians*
Hom. 2 Thess.	John Chrysostom, *Homilies on 2 Thessalonians*
Hom. 1 Tim.	John Chrysostom, *Homilies on 1 Timothy*
Hom. Tit.	John Chrysostom, *Homilies on Titus*
Illum. catech.	John Chrysostom, *Instructions to Catechumens*
Inan.	John Chrysostom, *On Vainglory and the Education of Children*
John of Ephesus, *Vit.*	John of Ephesus, *Lives of the Eastern Saints*
Laud.	John Chrysostom, *In Praise of Saint Paul the Apostle*
LCL	Loeb Classical Library
Leges	Leges nationum Germanicarum
Lib. grad.	*Book of Steps*
Libanius, *Ep.*	Libanius, *Epistulae*
Libanius, *Or.*	Libanius, *Orationes*
Macrina	Gregory of Nyssa, *Vita Macrinae*
MGH	Monumenta Germaniae Historica
N	Anonymous collection of *Apophthegmata*
Nov. Iust.	*Novellae*
NPNF	Nicene and Post-Nicene Fathers of the Christian Church
Or.	Oratio
PE	Eusebius, *Praeparatio Evangelica*
Pelagius, *Ep.*	Pelagius I, *Epistulae*
Perf. carit.	John Chrysostom, *Homily on 'Concerning Perfect Love'*

PG	Patrologia Graeca
PL	Patrologia Latina
PLRE	Prosopography of the Later Roman Empire
PO	Patrologia Orientalis
Propt. fornic.	John Chrysostom, *Homily on 'For Fear of Fornication, Let Each Man Have His Own Wife' (1 Cor. 7:2)*
PS	Patrologia Syriaca
Rhet.	Aristotle, *Rhetorica*
Sacr.	John Chrysostom, *On the Priesthood*
SC	Sources chrétiennes
Serm. Gen.	John Chrysostom, *Sermons on Genesis*
SRM	Scriptores Rerum Merovingicarum
Stat.	John Chrysostom, *On the Statues*
TCH	Transformation of the Classical Heritage
Thecla	*Acts of Paul and Thecla*
Theodoret, *Hist. mon.*	Theodoret, *History of the Monks of Syria*
TTH	Translated Texts for Historians
VA	*Vita Antonii*
Vidi Dom.	John Chrysostom, *Homilies on 'I Saw the Lord' (Isa 6:1)*
Virg.	John Chrysostom, *On Virginity*
Zos.	Zosimus, *New History*

Introduction

The Violence of Small Worlds: Rethinking Small-Scale Social Control in Late Antiquity

Kate Cooper and Jamie Wood

Historians have tended to see the great cultural, social, and political conflicts of late antiquity through the lens of institutions: the movements of armies, the speeches of senators, the bizarre effervescence of urban violence that so often resulted from the deliberations of church councils. And yet a revolution has taken place in the wider historical discipline across the last generation, which has much to offer the study of late antiquity.

Beginning in the 1970s, historians of later periods began to explore 'large questions in small places'[1] under the banner of microhistory, using inquisition documents to support sustained discussion of small-scale communities and socially disadvantaged protagonists who had otherwise left little trace in the historical record. Emmanuel Le Roy Ladurie's *Montaillou* illuminated the social world of a village in the Pyrenees around the end of the thirteenth century,[2] while Carlo Ginzburg reconstructed the experience and world-view of the Italian miller Domenico Scandella, known as Menocchio, who was burned at the stake as a heretic in 1599.[3]

Another branch of the microhistory movement has explored the 'small worlds' of rural estates and settlements from archives and legal disputes, considering how small-scale social technologies of power affected the relationship between landowners and their dependents. For example, Wendy Davies' study of Medieval Brittany and Stephanie McCurry's *Masters of Small Worlds* on the antebellum South Carolina low country have changed how we understand the vertical relationships between

[1] The phrase 'large questions in small places' is that of Charles Joyner; see C. Joyner, 'From Here to There and Back Again: Adventures of a Southern Historian', in J. B. Boles, ed., *Shapers of Southern History: Autobiographical Reflections* (Athens, GA: University of Georgia Press, 2004), 137–63.

[2] E. Le Roy Ladurie, *Montaillou, Village occitan de 1294 à 1324* (Paris: Gallimard, 1975).

[3] C. Ginzburg, *Il formaggio e i vermi. Il cosmo di un mugnaio del Cinquecento* (Turin: Einaudi, 1976); on the history of the term 'microhistory', see C. Ginzburg, 'Microhistory: Two or Three Things That I Know about It', *Critical Inquiry*, 20 (1993), 10–35.

peasant and lord or slave and master.[4] It is in this sense that the essays which follow have taken the idea of 'small worlds' as a starting point.[5]

Our focus in what follows is on the 'little big men'[6] of the Roman provinces – and of course the women as well – the prosperous but unglamorous individuals who had inherited or managed to commandeer control of a petty kingdom, in the form of a household, a church, a school, or a monastery. We know these men and women better than we knew their predecessors, thanks to a new kind of source material surviving from the fourth century onward: the letters, sermons, and essays of Christian bishops and, to a lesser extent, ascetics. (A smattering of similar material survives from the third century, but it is with the conversion of Constantine that churches and monasteries began to preserve the writings of their leaders on a large scale.)

Jaclyn Maxwell has drawn attention to the systematic efforts of fourth-century Christian preachers to improve public morality among their congregations, the impulse which drove the production of our source material. In comparison to even the most ambitious proposals for collective moral formation elsewhere in the late Roman world, such as those of the orator Themistius (d. 387), Christian efforts were far more effective:

> there was something new in the intensity with which speakers attempted to convey information to their listeners and in the regularity of the assemblies. The relationship between Christian preacher and layperson was more structured and more rigorous than someone like Themistius would have even hoped for. This meant that people came to listen, even when moral rules were not their favorite topic, and that preachers had to try to explain their teachings in ways that people would understand.[7]

[4] See, e.g., W. Davies, *Small Worlds: The Village Community in Early Medieval Brittany* (Berkeley, CA: University of California Press, 1988), and S. McCurry, *Masters of Small Worlds: Yeoman Households, Gender Relations, and the Political Culture of the Antebellum South Carolina Low Country* (Oxford: Oxford University Press, 1995).

[5] The term 'small worlds' carries a different connotation among social scientists, for whom it evokes the work of psychologist Stanley Milgram, whose 1967 'small world' experiment influenced the development of modern Social Network Analysis; see S. Milgram, 'The Small World Problem', *Psychology Today*, 22 (1967), 61–7, and subsequent publications.

[6] The phrase is Peter Brown's, *Through the Eye of a Needle: Wealth, the Fall of Rome, and the Making of the Christian West, 350–550 AD* (Princeton, NJ: Princeton University Press, 2013), 398.

[7] J. L. Maxwell, *Christianization and Communication in Late Antiquity: John Chrysostom and his Congregation in Antioch* (Cambridge: Cambridge University Press, 2009), 86–7. For religious and moral formation in late antique cities, see also I. Sandwell, *Religious Identity in Late Antiquity: Greeks, Jews and Christians in Antioch* (Cambridge: Cambridge University Press, 2007).

Themistius envisaged a law requiring the entire population to listen to moral precepts, but it was the Christians who established a channel for getting a substantial portion of the population to actually do so.

A brilliant recent study of North Africa by Leslie Dossey offers an insight into the kinds of social disruptions that challenged contemporaries and resulted in calls for moral instruction. Dossey characterised the fourth century as an age when prosperity was accompanied by a profound social uneasiness:

> This uneasiness was displayed in a variety of ways: gently mocking small farmers for building bathhouses on their tiny plots of land ... polemics against the circumcellions for pitching landlords off their carriages and hurling themselves into a suicidal frenzy against the imperial military. Because of the crossing of boundaries – economic, communal, and mental – the world seemed to be spinning out of control.[8]

Christian writers were intensely interested in the moral lives of peasants and townsmen, so even if that interest was often critical or even sarcastic, the efforts of these men and women to keep their small worlds from spinning out of control are far more visible in the historical record than they would have been in previous centuries, and it is on this record that many of the chapters in the present volume focus.

Part of the genius of Roman rule had always been the habit of aligning the interest of local and regional authorities with that of the ruling power wherever possible. Trying to understand how this worked in practice has given rise to one of the most vital seams of writing by Roman historians in recent decades, beginning with Fergus Millar's *The Emperor in the Roman World.*[9] Millar reconsidered the lines of communication between the imperial administration and regional elites, suggesting that the constant production of rescripts to petitions by local and regional elites allowed imperial policy-making, and thus Roman government in the provinces, to evolve in a way that was less programmatic than responsive. Subsequent studies by Greg Woolf and J. E. Lendon developed Millar's insights into the nature of interaction between the empire and provincial elites. Lendon documented the importance of informal relationships and favour-trading among the governing class, while Woolf traced the 'Romanisation' of a conquered province as a complex and mutually beneficial on-the-ground

[8] L. Dossey, *Peasant and Empire in Christian North Africa* (Berkeley, CA: University of California Press, 2010), 200.

[9] F. Millar, *The Emperor in the Roman World* (London: Duckworth, 1977), which builds on the same author's 'Emperors at Work', *Journal of Roman Studies*, 57 (1967), 9–19.

negotiation between local elites – who were often able to make inspired use of the resources and mechanisms introduced by Roman governors – and the governors or other representatives of the capital.[10]

Ritual and culture played a central role in articulating and negotiating the relationship between local elites and the imperial centre. The alignment between larger and smaller systems was very much in the interest of the middle men. In an influential study of the imperial cult in Roman Asia Minor, Simon Price traced how cult practices previously understood as 'top-down' initiatives were in fact engineered by regional elites, who wanted to be seen both by their local subordinates and by Roman governors as indispensable brokers mediating the relationship between the central authority and regional manpower.[11] James Rives has documented a similar dynamic in Roman Africa;[12] here, it is inscriptions that allow us to gain a glimpse of the ambitions of regional elites.

It is in legal sources that the balance of agency involved in the relation between local elites and representatives of the imperial administration is most visible.[13] In a much-cited study of legal *tabellae* Elizabeth Meyer has shown that legal instruments were widely understood as a public and ritually visible ratification of already-existing power relations and commitments.[14] But close examination of court records in Egypt reveals how landowners and *patresfamilias* promoted their own interests in their dealings with the central administration, and used their position as brokers of communication between the centre and the localities as an opportunity to enhance their position in local networks. Ari Bryen characterises this tireless self-promotion as seen from above:

> From the perspective of a Roman governor . . . the Greek-speaking world was composed of difficult, demanding, overlapping, needling populations each claiming the rights granted to them through their particular citizen statuses while simultaneously demanding that Roman governors often change or augment these rights.[15]

10 G. Woolf, *Becoming Roman: The Origins of Provincial Civilization in Gaul* (Cambridge: Cambridge University Press, 1998); J. E. Lendon, *Empire of Honour: The Art of Government in the Roman World* (Oxford: Clarendon Press, 1997).

11 S. R. F. Price, *Rituals and Power: The Roman Imperial Cult in Asia Minor* (Cambridge: Cambridge University Press, 1983).

12 J. B. Rives, *Religion and Authority in Roman Carthage* (Oxford: Clarendon Press, 1995).

13 See especially C. Ando, *Law, Language, and Empire in the Roman Tradition* (Philadelphia, PA: University of Pennsylvania Press, 2011), with the response of A. Z. Bryen, 'Judging Empire: Courts And Culture in Rome's Eastern Provinces', *Law and History Review*, 30 (2012), 771–811.

14 E. A. Meyer, *Legitimacy and Law in the Roman World: Tabulae in Roman Belief and Practice* (Cambridge: Cambridge University Press, 2004).

15 Bryen, 'Judging Empire', 779.

Local elites could be expected to make active and strategic use of the imperial presence in the provinces to foster their own ambitions.

A particularly valuable thread of inquiry in recent years has focused on the settlement of disputes, especially in late Roman Egypt, where the papyrus sources make it possible to assess how opportunities for agency were shaped by specific and contingent circumstances. The mechanisms for validating the actions and claims of parties to a dispute were framed by legal and religious institutions. But factors such as gender or access to networks of support often coloured the availability of those mechanisms. At the same time, in the multicultural environment of Roman Egypt disputants sometimes had access to parallel structures sponsored by alternative institutions.

There is good evidence in late Roman Egypt for what legal anthropologists call 'forum shopping', individuals and families channelling claims and disputes in light of the specific opportunities for dispute resolution available in a given locality. What was the prospective balance of cost to benefit, for example, if a Christian sought a judgment through the proconsular assize or through the local episcopal court? Seeking resolution of a dispute involved an on-the-ground assessment of which forum could offer the most promising balance of likeliness to help and ability to do so.[16] Contingency played an important role here. A guess about which judge or arbiter might be more sympathetic could have far-reaching consequences.

Studies of petitions and affidavits from civil and criminal cases have shed light on the dynamics of violence and intimidation in Egyptian towns and settlements. For example, Benjamin Kelly has shown that across the Roman period, formal litigation often went hand in hand with private violence and other forms of intimidation,[17] while Ari Bryen has argued that surviving petitions to the Roman provincial administration evidence a strategic and proactive use of the legal system by plaintiffs both to articulate and sometimes to challenge the balance of power.[18] Of special interest for the present volume, Sabine Hübner has shown that the papyri allow unprecedented insight into power and conflict at a more intimate

[16] On legal pluralism and 'forum shopping', see C. Humfress, 'Thinking through Legal Pluralism: "Forum Shopping" in the Later Roman Empire', in J. Duindam, J. Harries, C. Humfress, and N. Hurvitz (eds.), *Law and Empire: Ideas, Practices, Actors* (Leiden: Brill, 2013), 225–50, along with her monograph, *Multi-Legalism in Late Antiquity* (212–565 CE) (Oxford: Oxford University Press, forthcoming).

[17] B. Kelly, *Petitions, Litigation, and Social Control in Roman Egypt* (Oxford: Oxford University Press, 2011).

[18] A. Z. Bryen, *Violence in Roman Egypt: A Study in Legal Interpretation* (Philadelphia, PA: University of Pennsylvania Press, 2013).

scale level, that of household and family.[19] Though the focus of the present volume is on the long arc of development from Constantine (d. 337) to Justinian (d. 565), these studies of Roman rule in the provinces of earlier periods have laid crucial groundwork. What emerges from this literature is an exciting but somewhat unruly set of interpretative questions. How did the everyday exercise of power and social control in small-scale communities align with the wide-scale exercise of power by civic and other institutions?

If law notionally protected the agency of women in these small-scale settings – at least in the case of citizen women – it was constrained by all-too-real relationships of power and intimidation. Consider, for example, the case of Aurelia Artemis, a small-scale landowner in the Egypt of Diocletian who found to her distress that a powerful neighbour's offer of assistance had in fact been a stratagem to annex her property. The surviving papyri related to her case show her carrying a complaint up and down the system of criminal justice, an expensive, time-consuming, and at best frustrating process whose outcome is sadly not documented.[20] Within her own household and even her neighbourhood, the widow Artemis may have ruled with an iron will, and yet in her dealings with government officials she adopts a pose of something very like helplessness. Can we hope to assess the balance of perception and reality in such a case?

And can we begin to assess the process by which a widow like Artemis herself might hope to elicit help from magistrates, friends and relatives, or religious practitioners of various kinds, or choose between sources of assistance, especially in a context in which the legal system was so skewed in favour of male dominance? Another papyrus, P. Oxyrhynchus VI.903, preserves a fourth-century deposition by an unnamed wife, giving evidence that when a male protector – in this case a husband – turned hostile, it was

[19] S. R. Hübner, *The Family in Roman Egypt: A Comparative Approach to Intergenerational Solidarity and Conflict* (Cambridge: Cambridge University Press 2013). It is also worth mentioning the work of legal historians not as deeply engaged with papyri, for example, J. Evans Grubbs, 'Parent–Child Conflict in the Roman Family: The Evidence of the Code of Justinian', in M. George (ed.), *The Roman Family in the Empire: Rome, Italy, and Beyond* (Oxford: Oxford University Press, 2005), 92–128.

[20] The key inscriptions are P. Sakaon 31, 7 and P. Thead. 15, 18; for discussion, see C. Kotsifou, 'A Glimpse into the World of Petitions: The Case of Aurelia Artemis and her Orphaned Children', in A. Chaniotis (ed.), *Unveiling Emotions: Sources and Methods for the Study of Emotions in the Greek World* (Stuttgart: Franz Steiner Verlag, 2012), 317–27. The case is also discussed by S. Connolly, *Lives behind the Laws: The World of the Codex Hermogenianus* (Bloomington; Indianapolis, IN: Indiana University Press, 2010), 19–20, and J. Evans Grubbs, *Women and Law in the Roman Empire: A Sourcebook on Marriage, Divorce and Widowhood* (London; New York, NY: Routledge, 2002), 257–60.

invaluable for women and children to have access to systems of support that were more immediate than that offered by a distant governor.[21] Within the domestic and village setting, the support offered by religious networks – in this case by a Christian bishop – was often essential. Gatekeepers of supernatural power could offer a focus of grievance against the powerful in the here and now.

Social Control in the Small Worlds of Late Antiquity

Our aim in the present volume has been to consider a wide variety of social relationships in households, estates, and other small-scale communities. These power relationships – between slaves and masters, children and parents, monks and abbots, bishops and their congregations, pupils and teachers – created the skeleton of the social order. Since small-scale social structures were aligned to the wider social and political fabric, disruption or instability at this comparatively intimate social plane could have a knock-on effect on larger and more visible social structures. The success or failure of these relationships could tip the social balance toward stability or change.

In recent years, both Peter Brown and Kyle Harper have called attention to the growing importance of the 'middling sort' across the fourth and fifth centuries.[22] Recent demographic work makes a distinction between 'elite' households – the top 1 per cent that included the curial class – and the next 10 per cent identified as the middling stratum: bourgeois and agricultural households with up to five slaves.[23] Our sources tend to blur the distinction between the lower part of the 1 per cent – the locally based elites of the curial class – and the middling stratum, satirising and

[21] P. Oxy. VI.903 is discussed by P. Clark, 'Women, Slaves and the Hierarchies of Domestic Violence: The Family of St Augustine', in S. R. Joshel (ed.), *Women and Slaves in Greco-Roman Culture* (London: Routledge, 1998), 109–29, and L. Dossey, 'Wife Beating and Manliness in Late Antiquity', *Past & Present*, 199 (2008), 2–40; see also K. Cooper, 'Closely Watched Households: Visibility, Exposure, and Private Power in the Roman *Domus*', *Past & Present*, 197 (2007), 3–33, at 29–31, and literature cited there.

[22] Brown, *Through the Eye of a Needle*, 21–3 (at 22): 'In the society of the fourth century West, the future lay . . . with landowners of the provinces', and Kyle Harper, *Slavery in the Late Roman World, AD 275–425* (Cambridge: Cambridge University Press, 2011), 16, 25, 32, and 41, for discussion of the 'middling' classes in the late and post-Roman worlds.

[23] Harper, *Slavery in the Late Roman World*, 40–1, citing W. Scheidel and S. J. Friesen, 'The Size of the Economy and the Distribution of Income in the Roman Empire', *Journal of Roman Studies*, 99 (2009), 61–91. At 56–8 Harper suggests that the 'middling' orders represented between 6 and 12 per cent of a fourth-century population of roughly 50 million, with the higher end of the scale more likely.

sympathising with the troubles and moral weaknesses of the prosperous peasant and the cash-strapped decurion fairly indiscriminately. In what follows we will often consider regional elites alongside the 'middling' orders, but it is the latter that will come into focus most clearly.

We shall see in what follows that Christian sources of the fourth, fifth, and sixth centuries offer a distinctive insight into the concerns of this group. These sources tend to be written from the point of view of those responsible for maintaining small worlds: the masters and teachers, and of course the bishops. In one sense this is regrettable, since we would like to know more about those further down the social scale. Yet there is still much to be discovered about this layer of the social order – the layer of the 'middling sort'. These were powerful individuals, but their power had limits.

Power was always vulnerable to challenge. In order to maintain their position, elites had to focus their attention downward as well as upward, spending considerable energies engaging with those below them in the social ladder. In the 'small world' of the town, estate, monastery, or household, the *dominus* or *domina* might claim to rule, but the effectiveness of that claim depended on a thousand incremental successes in negotiating relationships. It was necessary to curb the will of subordinates, on the understanding that one's position – and even the social order itself – depended on being seen to keep others in line with a firm hand. Sometimes, the appearances were as important – and as effort-consuming – as the reality.

But the mere presence of ideals and identities is never self-evidently sufficient to bring about social cohesion. Symbolic systems nearly always require human agents to animate them. Modern fieldwork-based studies have found that, however deeply they are felt, identities and values depend on social bonds and emotional motivations for their momentum and staying power.[24] When they are at their most effective, human agents pour their energies into interlocking roles which reinforce each other reciprocally, allowing members of small-scale units like families, schools, and villages to experience social control as part of the 'natural' order of things.

[24] J. Lofland and R. Stark, 'Becoming a World-Saver: A Theory of Conversion to a Deviant Perspective', *American Sociological Review* 30 (1965), 862–75. For an application of this work to interpreting the spread of early Christianity, see R. Stark, *The Rise of Christianity: A Sociologist Reconsiders History* (Princeton, NJ: Princeton University Press, 1996).

Foucault and Bourdieu have charted the close relationship between punishment and the mechanisms of social control which subject individuals are trained to internalise in a successful social system; in what follows we will return frequently to the evidence for such a relationship in the 'small worlds' of late antiquity.[25] Stable power relations require the management of subjectivities. The perceptions of subject individuals must be encouraged to dovetail with a material system of discipline and punishment.

The stability of a community thus relied on the willingness of its members to internalise norms and to watch one another for signs of nonconformity. Modern research confirms that reminding people that they are being watched can be a strong driver towards conformity to social norms.[26] The desire for social recognition is an especially powerful tool when it is integrated into a pattern of cultural expectations – a point that was obvious to late ancient writers and preachers, who made expert use of the impulse to conformity and the desire for belonging, and even the human readiness to find fault in others.

For those who sought to impose authority, then, the aim was to cultivate an almost instinctive responsiveness in subordinates: a spectrum of attitudes ranging from obedience, dependence, and loyalty to reciprocal obligation. Lords and masters could not retain their position indefinitely unless they could display evidence of assent to their position by those they claimed to rule.[27] This was true for emperors and governors, but equally for parents, husbands, teachers, abbots, bishops, and slaveholders.

A useful concept drawn from Pierre Bourdieu's work on the sociology of education and social reproduction is that of 'misrecognition': in order to remain in power, elites must persuade those below them in the social pyramid that the shape of the social order is natural and inevitable, rather than the contingent outcome of a struggle for power.[28] The inevitability of the powers-that-be becomes a social fiction which must repeatedly be reasserted and reformulated. The perceptions of social participants must repeatedly be channelled to 'recognise' the collective social fiction as truth.

25 M. Foucault, *Discipline and Punish: The Birth of the Prison*, A. Sheridan (trans.) (New York, NY: Vintage, 1977).

26 M. Bateson, D. Nettle, and G. Roberts, 'Cues of Being Watched Enhance Cooperation in a Real World Setting', *Biology Letters*, 2 (2006), 412–14; K. J. Haley and D. M. T. Fessler, 'Nobody's Watching? Subtle Cues Affect Generosity in an Anonymous Game', *Evolution of Human Behaviour*, 26 (2005), 245–56.

27 Cooper, 'Closely Watched Households', 7–8.

28 P. Bourdieu, *Pascalian Meditations*, R. Nice (trans.) (Cambridge: Polity Press, 2000).

And of course, social control in late antiquity was also asserted through violence. We should not understand violence in a narrow sense, as referring only to physical acts such as beating unruly pupils or recalcitrant slaves, but rather as a continuum exerted across a spectrum of action and discourse. The World Health Organization's 2002 *World Report on Violence and Health* identifies four modes of violence: physical, sexual, psychological, and privative.[29] Privative violence, for instance, is defined as denying, or neglecting to provide, access to resources and functions as a form of social control. Although violence, domination, and control can take explicit and physical forms, the intimate connection between concrete and symbolic forms of violence comes into focus in the chapters that address the rhetorical uses to which late ancient authors put violent imagery. In late antiquity, power relations were articulated not only through the control of material resources and the assertion of physical dominance but also through the display, exchange, and withholding of social and cultural capital. Then, as now, symbolic and implicit violence had their own specific power.

Schools, monasteries, and churches played a pivotal role in enforcing and reproducing the social order, and their work of cultivating obedient subjects often involved symbolic or actual violence. These chapters offer a number of different ways of thinking about how a range of violent practices contributed to the making of individuals and communities. We have sought to understand how leaders used every tool at their disposal – from displays of rhetorical virtuosity to scare tactics and even physical violence – to draw members into their communities and to intensify the commitment of new members once they had joined, drawing them into alignment as sharers of an interdependent subjectivity.

The effectiveness of such practices in destabilising individuals and initiating processes of self-reinvention and integration into a social role is borne out by recent Anglophone work on social reproduction, which has shown that harsh physical treatment, regulation, and surveillance can play a pivotal role in the process of cultivating the subjectivity of initiates into a community.[30] These disciplinary practices often generate strong horizontal relationships among participants alongside the formal vertical hierarchies

[29] World Health Organization, *World Report on Violence and Health* (2002), www.who.int/violence_injury_prevention/violence/world_report/en/, last accessed August 11 2017.

[30] A. T. Chappell and L. Lanza-Kaduce, 'Police Academy Socialization: Understanding the Lessons Learned in a Paramilitary-Bureaucratic Organization', *Journal of Contemporary Ethnography*, 39 (2010), 205; B. S. Turner, 'Warrior Charisma and the Spiritualization of Violence', *Body & Society*, 9 (2003), 103–5; D. Levine, 'Martial Arts as a Resource for Liberal Education: The Case of Aikido',

that they are intended to reinforce.[31] Late antique teachers and preachers used related techniques to similar effect, simultaneously reinforcing their authority, promoting group coherence, and inculcating acquiescence in the membership.

Bourdieu argued that schools play a critical role in cultivating tractable social subjects. His repurposing of Aristotle's idea of *habitus* as the implicit, non-discursive, aspects of culture and its knowledge that are anchored in the daily practices of life, and particularly the body, can shed light on how schools and monasteries socialised members of their communities in late antiquity.[32] Physical practices and shared routines of interaction created an identity-enhancing stream of lived experience in the schools and monasteries. Monastic rules prescribed that monks should engage their senses almost constantly – listening to preaching, reciting the psalms, discussing scripture, and listening to edifying literature during mealtimes.

Yet in late antiquity such processes of individual and social formation could have a particularly hard edge. It has long been recognised that the schoolrooms of the late ancient world were violent places, and that the infliction of pain was integral to the process of instruction. Pupils were often beaten to discipline them into learning, while teachers were sometimes subject to attacks by students.[33] It is worth remembering too that narratives of pain often figured in the 'content' of teaching in late antiquity.[34] From Virgil's *Aeneid* to accounts of the sufferings of the Christian martyrs explored in Part IV of this volume, violent stories played a central part role in the grammatical and moral formation of individuals and communities. The chapters in this volume demonstrate collectively that bodily discipline, physical punishment, and meditation on heroic endurance abetted the internalisation and reproduction of the social order. Such strategies operated across the social spectrum, from the schoolroom to the monastery, the church and the Christian household and beyond.

in M. Featherstone, M. Hepworth, and B. S. Turner (eds.), *The Body: Social Process and Cultural Theory* (London: Sage, 1991), 209–24.

31 Chappell and Lanza-Kaduce, 'Police Academy Socialization', 190, 196–7, 202–5.

32 In the France of Bourdieu's day, the explicitly articulated function of schools as vehicles for social mobility was in tension with their implicit, often unrecognised, role as the vehicle through which, by shaping the perceptions of the young, the dominant elite could not only reproduce the existing social order but also reinforce inequality; see P. Bourdieu and J.-C. Passeron, *Reproduction in Education, Society and Culture*, R. Nice (trans.) (London: Sage, 1990); P. Bourdieu, *The State Nobility: Elite Schools in the Field of Power*, L. C. Clough (trans.) (Stanford, CA: Stanford University Press, 1996).

33 R. Cribiore, *Gymnastics of the Mind: Greek Education in Hellenistic and Roman Egypt* (Princeton, NJ: Princeton University Press, 2001), 67–72.

34 R. A. Kaster, 'Controlling Reason: Declamation in Rhetorical Education at Rome', in Y. L. Too (ed.), *Education in Greek and Roman Antiquity* (Leiden: Brill, 2001), 317–37.

Religion and the Small Worlds of Late Antiquity

The present volume plays special, but not exclusive, attention to the distinctive sources surviving from Christian religious communities: sermons, biographies, manuals of order, letters of instruction, and biblical exegesis. These sources offer a particularly rich source of insight into quotidian practices of social reproduction. They allow us to consider how individuals struggled to manipulate social processes in a variety of small-scale contexts – in households and churches, schools and monasteries – in order to assert, maintain, and reproduce their authority over subordinates.

It is worth noting that the technologies of control deployed by Christian leaders in the small worlds which they inhabited were not particularly unusual when viewed in context. This point bears emphasis because often when scholars look at the religious and cultural conflicts of late antiquity, an assumption is in play that the working of ideals and identities is not susceptible to social analysis; either developments were governed by the logic of a theological progress – depending on the point of view of the writer this is seen as either as necessary and pre-ordained, guided by divine intervention, or as the product of 'misguided belief' and therefore essentially inexplicable.[35] In either case, conflicts and pressures involving religion are imagined as taking place in a parallel universe not accountable to the human rules of social reality. It is suggested here that ideas and ideals were harnessed to a wider system of power and knowledge.[36]

What is particularly interesting to us is that these processes occurred while the self-same provincial elites were subject to the power of more exalted members of the imperial elite. The chapters in this volume demonstrate collectively that the Christian writings of late antiquity can shed an especially bright light on the means by which the leaders of such small worlds strove to maintain their standing across the generations in the face of a pressure from above and below.

[35] 'The principal actors were moved by the logical, if fulfilling, credulities of religious faith and by not much more'; B. D. Shaw, *Sacred Violence: African Christians and Sectarian Hatred in the Age of Augustine* (Cambridge: Cambridge University Press, 2011), 1.

[36] For an argument that functional analysis is by no means necessarily reductionist, see K. Cooper, 'Ventriloquism and the Miraculous: Conversion, Preaching, and the Martyr Exemplum in Late Antiquity', in K. Cooper and J. Gregory (eds.), *Signs, Wonders, Miracles: Representations of Divine Power in the Life of the Church*, Studies in Church History 41 (Woodbridge: Boydell & Brewer, 2005), 22–45.

PART I

Women and Children First
Autonomy and Social Control in the Late Ancient Household

In thinking about how social control was reproduced over time and space, the problem of agency comes into focus – especially when we consider the position of women. Women had distinctive problems of access to rights and resources in the late ancient world. The constraints imposed on wives and daughters meant that their autonomy in domestic environments was compromised both domestically and in the public sphere. Women had distinctive problems of access to rights and resources, and yet it was a well-known fact that they had their own way of seeing things, and sometimes of helping each other behind the scenes.

Roman law protected women's rights to property and to some extent their freedom from violence, but it was not always easy to gain access in practice to rights enjoyed in principle. In this section Julia Hillner explores the 'hard edge' of masculine control of female dependents in her survey of domestic imprisonment of 'disobedient' women, while Vasiliki Limberis shows that within the household women could command surprisingly threatening resources as dispensers of discipline, and their actions often lived on in memory, preserved by later generations.

Yet one of the insights of the papers in Part I is that the exercise of power in ancient household offered no room for complacency; it was a matter of constantly reasserting a *status quo* that might or might not hold firm. The power of the *paterfamilias* is a case in point. The sermons of John Chrysostom offer an invaluable frame for exploring how the authority of the master was given theological support within the slave-owning household. Rather than rejecting the institution of slavery, Jonathan Tallon suggests, Chrysostom sought to mitigate its excesses by aligning it with the household's other relationships of faithful obedience.

Tallon shows how the asymmetrical bonds of faith between the *pater* and his household were reinforced through Christian preaching. Ideas, perceptions, and material realities were brought into alignment in order to reinforce one another, so that the obedience of wives could find its place alongside that of sons and slaves. Yet, as Kate Cooper suggests, an alternative vision of the *pater*'s relations with women was on the horizon. In the writings of Augustine of Hippo we can glimpse a tentative but nonetheless radical sexual ethics, in which the dominant male's entitlement to pleasure, previously limited only by the need to avoid damaging the property or compromising the honour of other *patresfamilias*, began to be tempered by a new concern for moral symmetry.

CHAPTER 1

Female Crime and Female Confinement in Late Antiquity

Julia Hillner

In the spring of 326, the emperor Constantine interrupted his journey from Nicomedia to Rome, where he was headed to celebrate his *vicennalia*, to deal with a family crisis. He summoned his eldest son Crispus from Trier to Northern Italy and had him executed at Pola in Istria.[1] The emperor then allegedly also put to death his wife Fausta, Crispus' stepmother, by suffocation in a hot bath.[2] From the fifth century on, it was suggested that Fausta had had a sexual relationship with her stepson or had plotted against him.[3]

Historians have traditionally assumed that Fausta, like Crispus, also died in 326. Yet the only ancient source to offer a date for her death, Jerome's *Chronicle*, places the event two years after Crispus' death, in 328. Other sources remain vague, referring to Fausta's death as 'a short while later' than Crispus' (*mox* according to Eutropius; *dehinc* according to the anonymous author of the *Epitome de Caesaribus*; both writing in the second half of the fourth century).[4] What is more certain is that Fausta disappeared

I would like to thank Kate Cooper, the Late Antiquity Reading Group at the University of Sheffield (John Drinkwater, Katie Hemer, Simon Loseby, Máirín MacCarron, Harry Mawdsley, Dirk Rohmann, Mary Young), and the anonymous readers of Cambridge University Press for invaluable comments on earlier drafts of this contribution. All remaining errors are my own.

1 Aurelius Victor, *Liber de Caesaribus* 41.11, F. Pichlmayr and R. Gruendel (eds.), *Sexti Aurelii Victoris De caesaribus liber* (Leipzig: Teubner, 1970).

2 *Epitome de Caesaribus* 41.11–12, F. Pichlmayr and R. Gruendel (eds.) (Leipzig: Teubner, 1961); Eutropius, *Breviarium*, 10.6.3, C. Santini (ed.), *Eutropii Breviarium ab urbe condita* (Leipzig: Teubner, 1979); murder in the bath: Philostorgius, *Historia ecclesiastica* 2.4.4a, F. Winkelmann (ed.), *Philostorgius, Kirchengeschichte. Mit dem Leben des Lucian von Antiochien und den Fragmenten eines arianischen Historiographen* (Berlin: Akademie Verlag, 1981, 3rd edn.); Sidonius Apollinaris, *Ep.* 5.8.2, A. Loyen (ed.), *Sidonius Apollinaris, Epistulae et carminae*, 3 vols. (Paris: Les Belles Lettres, 1960–70); Zos. 2.29.2.

3 John Chrysostom, *Hom. Philip.* 4.15.5; Philostorgius, *Historia ecclesiastica* 2.4.4a; Zos. 2.29; Zonaras, *Epitome Historiarum* 13.2.38–41, L. Dindorf (ed.) *Ioannis Zonarae epitome historiarum*, 6 vols. (Leipzig: Teubner, 1868–75).

4 Jerome, *Chronicon* 2340.22, R. Helm (ed.), *Die Chronik des Hieronymus*, GCS 47 (Eusebius Caesariensis, Werke Vol. VII) (Berlin: De Gruyter, 1956): *Constantinus uxorem suam Faustam*

from public view in 326; this is confirmed by the abrupt termination of coins struck with her portrait, and of references to her activities in contemporary sources, after this date.[5] It is therefore reasonable to assume, as suggested by our later witnesses, that the actions Crispus and Fausta were punished for had been somehow linked.[6] This should not mean, however, that they also died at the same time. In his recent biography of Constantine, David Potter has argued, building on Jerome's dating, that in 326 Constantine did not murder Fausta, but rather submitted her to informal confinement, a form of 'internal exile'.[7] Two years into this 'exile' she died, whether by murder or, more likely, of natural causes.[8]

Constantine's treatment of his son was altogether more formal and public. Crispus was executed after a formal judicial process that Aurelius Victor called *iudicium patris*, suggesting that Constantine exercised, in addition to his role as imperial judge, the legal right over life and death of a son under *patria potestas*.[9] Evidently Constantine deemed formal and lethal punishment of his son as imperative to the restoration of his honour as emperor and the head of his family. The same may not have been true in the case of his wife.

It is beyond the scope of this essay, and perhaps altogether impossible, to resolve the mystery of what really happened in 326–328 in Constantine's family. Yet we will see that the interpretation of events as reflecting differentiated treatment of Crispus and Fausta – a formal process against Crispus leading to execution by contrast to a strategy of concealment where Fausta was concerned – is in tune with a wider pattern of gendered customs structuring criminal justice in the ancient and late antique world. Seen in this light Constantine's action may have not been dissimilar to other family practices during, after, and in lieu of criminal procedure in the period.

interficit. On the customary assumption about the temporal proximity of Crispus' and Fausta's death see e.g. J. W. Drijvers, 'Flavia Maxima Fausta: Some Remarks', *Historia*, 41 (1992), 506.

5 K. Longo, *Donne di potere nella tarda antichità. Le Augustae attraverso le immagini monetali* (Reggio Calabria: Falzea, 2009), 107–16.

6 T. D. Barnes, *Constantine: Dynasty, Religion and Power in the Late Roman Empire* (Oxford: Wiley-Blackwell, 2014), 149.

7 D. Potter, *Constantine the Emperor* (Oxford: Oxford University Press, 2013), 245. Also note that the earliest reference to Crispus' death (Aurelius Victor, *Liber de Caesaribus* 41.11) does not link it to Fausta's.

8 The murder-in-the-bath story may be a trope: J. Harries, 'The Empresses' Tale, AD 300–360', in C. Harrison, C. Humfress and I. Sandwell (eds.), *Being Christian in Late Antiquity* (Oxford: Oxford University Press, 2014), 206.

9 W. V. Harris, 'The Roman Father's Power of Life and Death', in R. S. Bagnall and W. Harris (eds.), *Studies in Roman Law in Memory of A. Arthur Schiller* (Leiden: Brill, 1986), 81–96.

As I will argue, during the Roman empire and into late antiquity high-ranking female criminal defendants were often treated differently, although not necessarily more leniently, from men, in order to safeguard the honour of their families. Yet, some families chose to evade public criminal process altogether when it came to remedying the unwanted behaviour of their womenfolk. Whether this was to maximise control over their women, or in order to protect against the shame of public law enforcement, it testifies to the tensions between everyday exercises of power within households and large-scale acts of social control pursued by the late Roman state that are at the heart of this volume. Always a possibility in the accusatory criminal system of the Roman world, these strategies of evasion became increasingly formalised during late antiquity with the rise of ecclesiastical mediation. Such extrajudicial redress could result in women's confinement, not least because female domestic seclusion was held as an ideal across the ancient world, although as a spatial practice it was by no means uncontroversial.

The final part of this chapter will discuss how, towards the end of antiquity, female confinement was moved from the extrajudicial to the judicial sphere, with the introduction of the penalty of forced residence in a monastery. I have discussed the slow emergence of this penalty in detail elsewhere.[10] Here, I will further explore its function within the small-scale power relations underpinning the late antique household up to the end of the sixth century. Both in theory and in practice, forced residence in a monastery was seen as applicable to both male and female offenders. Nonetheless, when applied to women, forced monastic residence had distinct advantages, which, as I will argue, eased the pressures exerted by Roman law's interference with intimate family affairs described in the first part of this chapter. In this way, the monastery became a locus of intersection between small-scale and large-scale acts of social control, a theme also explored elsewhere in this volume.

Female Criminals and Late Antique Criminal Justice

While we know remarkably little about the actual treatment of female defendants in late antique criminal judicial procedures, there is some evidence that it may have differed from that of men, both during trial and in terms of penalties. For example, classical Roman writers expressed

[10] J. Hillner, *Prison, Punishment and Penance in Late Antiquity* (Cambridge: Cambridge University Press, 2015).

qualms about holding female defendants in public prisons,[11] and we know that in late antiquity some women were held under house arrest awaiting or during their trial.[12] To be sure, shielding from the nastiness of the prison was probably mostly aimed at elite women (and at the concern for their families' honour). It can be paralleled with the general custom throughout the Roman period to hold male defendants of senatorial rank not in the public prison, but under house arrest.[13]

When the governor of Palestine mistook the Roman noble woman Melania (the Elder) for a slave-girl and put her in prison for tending to a number of Egyptian monks who had been banished to this province after 373, she was immediately released, with much apology, when she revealed her status.[14] The story confirms the consensus at the time that prison was unsuitable to high-status women. It also suggests, however, that for lower-rank women in the Roman provinces, such as the slave Melania was suspected to be, ending up in a public prison was a likely prospect.

In the course of the Christian persecution in the third century, we hear about many common women arrested and held in the public prisons, who were at times also submitted to torture.[15] Depending on the disposition of the judge and the severity of the crime, among these Christians could also be higher-rank individuals, such as, famously, the young *matrona* Perpetua, arrested in Carthage in 203. Yet, despite the unusual harshness with which Perpetua was treated, she was given some concessions, such as the freedom of having her baby with her, which may have been on account of her social status.[16]

Status hence may have played a role in the imposition of prison custody on female defendants and the regulation of their prison conditions. Yet, a fourth-century law by Constantius II ordered public prisons to have separate compartments for women and men. This suggests that, even though some women were expected to be in prison, a general uneasiness on how to handle this situation prevailed.[17] During the religious conflicts of the late antique period many stories circulated about the arrest and

[11] J.-U. Krause, *Gefängnisse im Römischen Reich* (Stuttgart: Franz Steiner Verlag, 1996), 171–2, with references.

[12] Ammianus Marcellinus, *Res Gestae* 28.1.47, W. Seyfarth (ed.), *Ammiani Marcellini Rerum gestarum libri qui supersunt*, 2 vols. (Leipzig: Teubner, 1978).

[13] Hillner, *Prison*, 125–33.

[14] Palladius, *Historia Lausiaca* 46.3–4 [PG 34.991–1278].

[15] Krause, *Gefängnisse*, 174, with references. On torture, see also Jerome's story on the adulteress in Vercelli below.

[16] *Acts of Perpetua and Felicitas* 3. On the unusual harshness of the judge in question see J. Rives, 'The Piety of a Persecutor', *Journal of Early Christian Studies*, 4 (1996), 1–25.

[17] *Cod. Theod.* 9.3.3 (340).

imprisonment of a wide array of women, which were meant to underline the injustice of the 'persecutors' of the 'orthodox'.[18] In the sixth century Justinian even prohibited holding female defendants in the public prisons at all, ordering instead that they should be bailed, if the offence was minor, or guarded in monasteries if they had been accused of a major crime.[19] The association of women, whatever their rank, and the prison continued to be problematic well into this late period.

Gender differentiation may also have underpinned the pronouncement of penalties in the secular courts. Early imperial jurists' commentaries explained that judges should take account of defendants' gender (in addition to age, mental health and level of education) in imposing penalties.[20] Such an approach was mirrored, if not even more frequently voiced, in imperial constitutions from the fourth century on. For example, a law by Constantine from 319 explained that for the crime of counterfeiting judges should find penalties that took account of the gender and the social status of offenders. However, in a slightly later law, from perhaps 326, the same emperor prohibited penalties differentiated by gender for those who had assisted in another woman's abduction, although the emperor seems to have been mostly concerned that such female offenders getting off lightly were of servile status.[21] The fact that differentiated penalties had to be prohibited for certain crimes, which were presumably deemed particularly heinous, suggests that at least some judges were habitually meting them out. Later in the fourth century John Chrysostom claimed that the rate of executions was 1:10,000 between female and male convicts.[22]

Some penalties imposed on women might have been lighter than those envisaged for men, as implied by yet another imperial constitution dated to 397 that dealt with the sons and daughters of conspirators.[23] Under the

[18] See, for example, Palladius' account of wealthy women in the public prisons of Constantinople after John Chrysostom's deposition in 404 (Palladius, *Dialogus* 10, A. M. Malingrey (ed.), *Pallade de Hélénopolis, Dialogue sur le vie de Jean Chrysostome*, 2 vols., SC 341–342 (Paris: Éditions du Cerf, 1988).

[19] *Nov. Iust.* 134.9 (556).

[20] *Dig.* 22.6.9pr (Paulus), 23.2.57a (Marcianus), 25.4.2.1 (Iulianus), 48.10.15.5 (Callistratus), 48.13.7 (6) (Ulpian), 49.14.2.7 (Callistratus); *Pauli Sententiae* 2.19.5, S. Riccobono, J. Baviera, C. Ferrini, J. Furlani and V. Arangio-Ruiz (eds.), *Sententiarum receptarum libri quinque qui vulgo Iulio Paulo adhuc tribuuntur, Fontes iuris Romani anteiustiniani* 2 (Florence: Barbera, 1940), 317–417. See O. Robinson, *The Criminal Law of Ancient Rome* (London: Duckworth, 1995), 16–17.

[21] *Cod. Theod.* 9.21.1 (319); *Cod. Theod.* 9.24.1.5 (326?) = *Cod. Iust.* 9.13.1.4. See further J. Beaucamp, *Le statut de la femme à Byzance*, 2 vols. (Paris: De Boccard, 1990–2), Vol. 1, 87–92.

[22] John Chrysostom, *Hom. Eph.* 15.3 [PG 62.9–176].

[23] *Cod. Theod.* 9.14.3.2 (397).

Christian persecutions we know that women were sometimes exiled, where men were put to death.[24] Women condemned to the mines were relieved from heavy work and sentenced to serve on the other workers instead.[25] Pregnant women were not to be executed, although in this case the sentence was merely delayed.[26] None of this is to say, however, that women were always spared cruel punishment. Women serving mine workers almost certainly were expected also to provide sexual services.[27] Particularly from the context of Christian persecution we also know of spectacular displays of female convicts in the Roman arena that were also at times emphasising their gender, such as, in the case of Perpetua and her slave Felicity, through the nakedness of their female bodies that had just given birth (with milk still dripping from breasts) and their pairing with a wild cow.[28] From the late antique period no such spectacular scenes of women's executions are reported, and it should be noted that, where they are in the early Roman Empire, the fact that such executions involved women was often commented on. They may hence have been considered remarkable, particularly where they involved higher-rank women.[29] Yet, even women belonging to the top of the elite could still be put to death in the later empire, such as Serena, sister of Honorius, executed for treason by strangling in Rome in 408.[30] Strangling was a demeaning penalty, as it involved the executioner touching the convict's body. Penalties for women were therefore not always lighter (although they could be), but they could differ from those assigned to men, and often drew attention to women's bodies and sexuality.

When it came to differentiation of penalties between men and women there was hence more at stake than just leniency. Some legal texts talked about the 'weakness' (*infirmitas*) of the female sex as justification for a differential treatment of women.[31] Yet, it would again be wrong to see this

[24] Cyprian, *Ep.* 80.1, W. Hartel (ed.), *Cypriani Epistulae*, CSEL 3 (Vienna: C. Gerold, 1871).

[25] *Dig.* 48.19.8.8 (Ulpian).

[26] *Dig.* 48.19.3 (Ulpian); John Chrysostom, *Hom. Eph.* 15.3 [PG 62.9–176].

[27] O. Robinson, *Penal Policy and Penal Practice in Ancient Rome* (London: Routledge, 2007), 125.

[28] *Acts of Perpetua and Felicitas* 20. For further Christian women in the arena, see D. Kyle, *Spectacles of Death in Ancient Rome* (London: Psychology Press, 1998), 91 (with references). On the meaning of these forms of public punishment, see K. M. Coleman, 'Fatal Charades: Roman Executions Staged as Mythological Enactments', *Journal of Roman Studies*, 80 (1990), 44–73.

[29] See, e.g., Dio Cassius, *Roman History* 60.16.1, E. Cary (ed. and trans.), 9 vols., LCL 32, 37, 53, 66, 82–3, 175–7 (London: Heinemann, 1914–27).

[30] Olympiodorus, *Fragment* 6, R. Blockley (ed.), *Fragmentary Classicising Historians of the Later Roman Empire: Eunapius, Olympiodorus, Priscus and Malchus*, Vol. II (Liverpool: Cairns, 1983); Zos. 5.38. For another case see PLRE I Euchrotia, 289.

[31] *Cod. Theod.* 9.14.3.2 (397); *Dig.* 22.6.9pr (Paulus), 48.5.39(38).4 & 7 (Papinian).

as the result of indulgence or permissiveness. The pervasive ancient assumption was that women were not only physically weaker, but, since body and soul were connected, also had less moral stamina.[32] The 'weakness' of women hence also meant that they were unpredictable, and therefore dangerous.[33]

Female deviance was particularly dangerous because in the ancient and late antique world male honour, and by extension the honour of their families, depended on how the integrity of female behaviour was judged by families themselves and others. A man's moral fitness for public leadership was, among other factors, assessed by how well he controlled his womenfolk – a father his daughters, and a husband his wife. The inability to do so, exemplified in female offence brought to public attention, had the potential of profoundly upsetting the male-defined moral order on which society rested.[34] This concept is powerfully demonstrated by the case of Perpetua, who was implored by her father to recant her faith, as otherwise she 'would destroy us [himself, her brothers, her mother and her son]'.[35] It is therefore perhaps not surprising that some women, such as Perpetua, were punished in a way that humiliated them on the basis of their sex, as such reconstituting a 'natural' moral order.

Perpetua's 'crime' was, of course, her Christianity, or what one might call civil disobedience. The threat of female deviance was multiplied where the misbehaviour was of a sexual nature. Such misbehaviour pertained to reproduction, and upset not only present morality but also the (agnatic) integrity of the family. In the Roman world the continuity of social status was tied to the holding of property and since the acquisition of property was predominantly through inheritance, female behaviour that had the potential of producing an illegitimate family line had to be suppressed.[36]

What is remarkable, and as we shall see further below was potentially problematic for some families, is that the protection of families along these lines was considered a duty of the Roman state. This explains the more

[32] S. Dixon, 'Womanly Weakness', *Tijdschrift voor Rechtsgeschiedenis*, 52 (1984), 357; E. Hartmann, 'Das "schwache Geschlecht" im römischen Recht – Frauen und Rechtsprechung', in M. Reuter and R. Schiavone (eds.), *Gefährliches Pflaster, Kriminalität im römischen Reich* (Mainz: von Zabern, 2011), 269–79.

[33] Robinson, *Penal Policy*, 29.

[34] K. Cooper, 'Closely Watched Households: Visibility, Exposure and Private Power in the Roman Domus', *Past & Present*, 197 (2007), 3–33.

[35] *Acts of Perpetua and Felicitas* 5: *ne universos nos extermines.*

[36] On property and the transmission of Roman social status, see P. Garnsey and R. P. Saller, *The Roman Empire: Economy, Society and Culture*, 2nd edn. (Berkeley, CA: University of California Press, 2015).

systematic definition of undesirable female sexual acts as 'crimes', i.e. offences that could lead to a charge in the secular courts, which continued into the post-Roman kingdoms. These included adultery (a woman's extramarital sexual relationships), *stuprum* (sexual relationships of a woman – girl or widow – of marriageable status), or *raptus* (abduction of a woman for the purpose of marriage in defiance of already made arrangements, such as betrothal or, in the case of religious women, ascetic vows).[37] In all these acts, even abduction, the involved women were usually suspected as being complicit. Statutory penalties varied, but seem to have become more severe between the first and the sixth century AD, from exile to execution.[38] In the early empire, adulteresses may at times have been paraded wearing the prostitute's formal dress, the toga, in public, possibly as a complement to or instead of the statutory penalty of exile (*relegatio*).[39] In fact, some imperial judges – free to deviate from statutory penalties if 'within reason' – condemned adulteresses to work as prostitutes, segregating them from respectable society at the same time as controlling their bodies. This penalty, reported at first in the context of Christian persecutions, persisted into the late empire, when, according to the historian Socrates, Theodosius I (d. 395) abolished it.[40] While some of the stories circulating about the prostitution of Christian persecuted women may have been overblown and feeding the motif to each other, Socrates' witness, reported as one of a series of Theodosius' government acts, seems genuine.

Differentiated treatment of women in the public courts hence did not try to protect women, but the honour of their families. It is in this light that we need to see apparently contradicting calls for lenient sentences and for spectacularly degrading ones. Roman public criminal procedure was ruthlessly humiliating – from custody in prison up to the execution of sentences, and even beyond, for convicts who had suffered status-affecting

[37] Robinson, *Criminal Law*, 54–73; A. Arjava, *Women and Law in Late Antiquity* (Oxford: Clarendon Press, 1996), 193–229; J. Harries, *Law and Crime in the Roman World* (Cambridge: Cambridge University Press, 2007), 86–105; S. Wemple, *Women in Frankish Society: Marriage and the Cloister* (Philadelphia, PA: University of Pennsylvania Press, 1981), 41–3.

[38] Arjava, *Women*, 201.

[39] T. A. J. McGinn, *Prostitution, Sexuality and the Law in Ancient Rome* (Oxford: Oxford University Press, 1998), 166.

[40] On prostitution and Christian persecution: T. A. J. McGinn, *The Economy of Prostitution in the Roman World* (Ann Arbor, MI: University of Michigan Press, 2004), 237. Theodosius abolishes the penalty: Socrates, *Historia Ecclesiastica* 5.18, G. Hansen (ed.), *Sokrates, Kirchengeschichte*, GCS, Neue Folge, 1 (Berlin: Akademie Verlag, 1995).

punishments such as flogging or exile carried a lifelong stigma, *infamia*.[41] A woman's exposure to this would have meant a serious dishonour to her family, which was to be avoided if her offence was minor or she was still on trial. On the other hand, in the case of conviction for heinous female crime, the Roman state aimed at restoring the honour of the respective husband and family – and the integrity of society – by making visible the consequences of female sexual downfall. The treatment of female defendants was a complex business that needed to tread a careful path to ensure maximum protection of the honour and property of female punishment's male beneficiaries.

Judicial and Extrajudicial Redress of Female Crime

If late antique state authorities had to perform a difficult balance act when it came to the punishing of female offenders, this was even truer for their families themselves. The male honour culture that ruled Roman and post-Roman society meant that female behaviour reflected back on their male relatives, but also that visible state punishment of women had the potential of degrading their families, exposing their male relatives' ineptness. Public penalties such as death, banishment, or infamy also foreclosed less spectacular or more conciliatory solutions to the problem of female misbehaviour. In fact, the development of criminal procedures particularly around the crime of adultery shows that such considerations may have well occurred within some families. In 326 Constantine limited the right to bring an accusation for adultery to husbands in the first instance and a woman's agnate relatives (her *paterfamilias* and his other descendants).[42] As Roman criminal procedure relied on an accusatory system, from Constantine on a woman's relatives could hence choose not to charge her, while before, and since Augustus' *Lex Iulia de adulteriis* from 18 BC, every citizen would have had the right to bring an accusation, which of course had reduced the possibility of families keeping quiet about female misdemeanour considerably. This might have been the point of Augustus' legislation, intent on eradicating tolerance of lax female sexual morals among the senatorial elite.[43] Constantine's law may have responded to

[41] See S. Bond, 'Altering Infamy: Status, Violence and Civic Exclusion in Late Antiquity', *Classical Antiquity*, 33 (2014), 1–30.

[42] *Cod. Theod.* 9.7.2 (326).

[43] See S. Treggiari, *Roman Marriage. Iusti Coniuges from the Time of Cicero to the time of Ulpian* (Oxford: Clarendon Press, 1991), 264–77, 307–9.

long-term resistance to such state interference into innermost family business.[44]

To be sure, individual families, and individual men, likely handled female offences according to their own personal circumstances. Jerome told of a husband who had accused his wife and her lover in front of the provincial governor of Liguria in ca. 370, on his visit to the city of Vercelli. They were both tortured, but the woman refused to confess. Eventually, because her lover had confessed, she was condemned to be decapitated, but was miraculously saved as the attempts of a series of executioners failed to strike her neck properly. Whisked away by clerics (*clerici*) as if dead, she was hidden on a country estate among Christian virgins (*quibusdam virginibus secretiorem villulam*), until Jerome's friend Evagrius (later bishop of Antioch) obtained a pardon for her from the emperor.[45] Despite the rhetorical embellishment, meant to exemplify God's protection of the innocent, the specifics of names and places suggest that the incident was historical.[46] If so, it shows at the very least that some adulterous women certainly continued to be brought to court by their husbands even after Constantine's law. It also shows, however, the interference of Christian authorities in public criminal procedure and, intriguingly, given the later penalty of monastic confinement we will discuss below, the use of ascetic space to shield against the fatal consequences of such procedure. In Jerome's story, such protection was aimed at the innocent. Contemporary Christian leaders, such as Augustine, however, also strongly advised men against bringing adulterous women to court, even if guilty, as it would mean killing them (i.e. they could be sentenced to death).[47]

While some men seem to have chosen the route of public criminal procedure to deal with sexual female deviance, others preferred to take private vengeance against women. For husbands, however, this was illegal under Roman law, which granted the right to kill an adulterous woman only to a father, and only if she had been caught in the act, if the sexual act

[44] J. Evans Grubbs, *Law and Family in Late Antiquity: The Emperor Constantine's Marriage Legislation* (Oxford: Oxford University Press, 1995), 212.

[45] Jerome, *Ep.* 1, I. Hilberg (ed.), *Eusebii Hieronymi Epistulae*, Vol. 1, III, CSEL 54, 56 (Vienna: F. Tempsky, 1910, 1918). Jerome calls the woman *muliercula*, which implies she was from a low background, although the choice of execution (by sword) and the possibility of imperial pardon suggest that she was of higher standing.

[46] J. Harries, 'Constructing the Judge: Judicial Accountability in and the Culture of Criticism in Late Antiquity', in R. Miles (ed.), *Constructing Identities in Late Antiquity* (London: Routledge, 1999), 229.

[47] Augustine, *De adulterinis coniugiis* 2.14–17, J. Zycha (ed.), *Augustinus, Ad Pollentium de adulterinis coniugibus libri duo*, CSEL 41 (Vienna: F. Tempsky, 1900), 347–410.

had happened in his own house and if he also killed her lover, as such considerably narrowing down the parameters of such vengeance.[48] In the post-Roman world, also husbands (both Roman and 'Barbarian') gained the right to kill adulterous wives caught *in flagrante delicto* on the spot, without having to go through judicial procedure, perhaps testifying to a society where private redress of crime was more acceptable or more common.[49] It should be noted, however, that in both contexts non-legal texts usually describe a husband's violence as directed not against the woman, but her lover (which under some circumstances was legal also under Roman law), or at least as stopping short of killing.[50]

While these texts reveal the persistent desire of men to deal with domestic crime autonomously – and the state's more or less willingness to give in to these desires – it is impossible to say how often killings of women occurred in practice.[51] Even in the usually considered more openly vindictive post-Roman world, a law collected in the Visigothic Code (published 654) implies that a husband might have wanted to leave his options open on how to handle his wife's adultery. The law ordered that adulterers who had not been caught in the act should be brought to court (i.e. not killed extrajudicially), but, if they were found guilty, to be handed back to the husband, 'that it may pertain to his judgement what he wishes to do about them'.[52] This law may hence have envisaged a less lethal solution, but one that also protected male control of women. It certainly gave men a choice; a choice that another Visigothic law giving fathers the right to kill their adulterous daughters also expressed: 'If he wishes to keep (*reservare*) her, he has the power to do with her and the adulterer whatever he wishes'.[53]

48 *Dig.* 48.5.23.4 (Papinian), 48.5.24.4 (Ulpian), 48.5.33.pr (Macer).

49 Arjava, *Women*, 199. On female killing being possibly more common in the post-Roman world see J. F. Hatlen, 'Honour and Domestic Violence in the Late Roman West, c. 300–600 AD', unpublished PhD thesis, Norwegian University of Science and Technology, Trondheim (2014).

50 Lib. *Or.* 1.147, R. Foerster (ed.), *Libanii opera*, 12 vols. (Leipzig: Teubner, 1903–27); Jerome, *Ep.* 147.11, John Chrysostom, *Virg.* 52.3; Cassiodorus, *Variae* 1.37, T. Mommsen (ed.), MGH, AA, 12 (Berlin: Weidmann, 1894). On the legality of the killing of the lover, see *Pauli Sententiae* 2.26.7; *Nov. Iust.* 117.15 (542).

51 During late antiquity, we only hear about cases where adulterous wives were killed by male family members from Merovingian Gaul: Gregory of Tours, *Hist.* 5.32 (the reference here is ambiguous and may actually be to a judicial death penalty); 6.36; 8.19.

52 *Leges Visigothorum* 3.4.3: *ut quod de eis facere voluerit in eius proprio consistat arbitrio*, K. Zeumer (ed.), MGH, Leges, 1 (Hanover: Hahn, 1902).

53 *Leges Visigothorum* 3.4.5: *si certe reservare eam voluerit, faciendi de ea et de adultero quod voluerit habeat potestatem.*

Families looking for restorative, rather than retributive justice when it came to female misbehaviour undoubtedly existed in the late antique world. It is at this point that it is worth returning to Jerome's description, detailed above, of Church interference with public criminal procedure in the case of the adulterous woman in Vercelli. While in this instance, Church authorities intervened *against* the wishes of the woman's family, we also hear of cases where male family members approached a bishop to adjudicate domestic troubles in the first place.[54] This is particularly attested, as I have shown elsewhere, where the crime pertained to extra-marital relationships of unmarried girls.[55] Here, fathers were at times interested in a low-key solution to their problem, in order not to jeopardise their daughters' life prospects and chances of marriage. They could (and by secular law should) have brought these cases to the attention of a secular court, but some did not, because the overarching accusatory nature of criminal justice at the time allowed them to choose the judge that best suited their goal.[56] To be sure, the recorded families were usually clerical ones and may have naturally turned to their bishop for justice. However, their objectives did not necessarily set them apart from lay families. In fact, late antique laws were anxious about the prospect and frequency of parents reaching agreements with the abductors of their daughters, proposing harsh penalties for such actions.[57]

Abducted or sexually violated daughters were a different matter from adulterous wives, with a different impact on family dynamics, although it could be argued that forcing these women into marriage was also a way for families to restore control over their behaviour. In any case, they may have been in less danger of being killed by their male relatives.

The Roman jurists who had discussed the legitimacy of extrajudicial killing of an adulterous woman had conceded the right only to fathers. The reason was that, in their opinion, such killings would then happen less frequently, for a father would act out of love and spare his child, while a husband would be looking for vengeance; something that the law had to restrain.[58] Nonetheless, at least Christian writers expected husbands of

[54] See also K. Sessa, 'Ursa's Return: Captivity, Remarriage and the Domestic Authority of Roman Bishops in Fifth-Century Italy', *Journal of Early Christian Studies*, 19 (2011), 401–32.

[55] Hillner, *Prison*, 75–6, 296–7.

[56] On such 'forum shopping' see C. Humfress, 'Law in Practice', in P. Rousseau (ed.), *A Companion to Late Antiquity* (Oxford: Blackwell, 2009), 377–91.

[57] J. Evans Grubbs, 'Abduction Marriage in Antiquity: A Law of Constantine (CTh IX. 24. I) and Its Social Context', *Journal of Roman Studies*, 79 (1989), 65.

[58] Dig. 48.5.23.4 (Papinian): *quod plerumque pietas paterni nominis consilium pro liberis capit: ceterum mariti calor et impetus facile decernentis fuit refrenandus.*

adulterous women not to either kill their wives or bring them to the secular court, but to submit them to the pastoral care of Church leaders. Early Christian council canons abounded with prescriptions on penitential requirements for adulterous wives.[59] To be sure, the performance of penance could be at times as visibly humiliating as a secular penalty (in the Roman Church, for example, penitents had to stand in a separate space during mass), but there was much regional variation and ecclesiastical legislation was often surprisingly vague in spelling out what exactly penance entailed.[60] Yet, the prescriptions show that some adultery cases may not have been filed with secular courts, but with the Church. One such case, involving a cleric and an unnamed but apparently high-status woman, is recorded for late fifth-century Rome, under bishop Gelasius (d. 496). Even though Gelasius was sharply rebuked by members of the senatorial aristocracy for not punishing the cleric appropriately (no mention is made of what was to happen to the woman), it is clear that the accusers were content with letting the bishop, rather than a secular court (in Rome, of the urban prefect), handle the case.[61]

When it came to female sexual misconduct, late antique men had a menu of legal and practical options for handling the situation and securing redress. Perhaps contrary to how they would have treated male offenders (including the lovers of adulterous women), they at times chose extrajudicial redress that stopped short of killing women. Perhaps like the emperor Constantine in 326, their motive seems to have been to deflect shame from the family; in Constantine's case there may have also been the need to prevent damage to his sons' prospects to imperial succession through a public execution of his wife. As we will see now, such extrajudicial redress sometimes included the domestic confinement of women.

Female Domestic Seclusion in the Late Antique World

Men across the ancient Mediterranean held strong ideas that the natural environment for well-born women, both wives and daughters, was the

[59] Evans Grubbs, *Law and Family*, 222–5, who also gives council canon references.

[60] On the Roman church, see J. Gaudemet, *L'Eglise dans l'empire romain (IV–V siècle)* (Paris: Sirey, 1958).

[61] *Collectio Avellana*, ep. 100, O. Günther (ed.), *Epistulae imperatorum, pontificum, aliorum inde ab a. CCCLXVII usque ad a. DLIII datae Avellana quae dicitur collectio*, 2 vols., CSEL, 35 (Vienna: F. Tempsky, 1895–8). On the case see also G. Demacopoulos, *The Invention of Peter: Apostolic Discourse and Papal Authority in Late Antiquity* (Philadelphia, PA: University of Pennsylvania Press, 2013), 76–7.

shelter of their home. We find these ideas in many classical Greek, Roman, and Rabbinic texts, and they continued to be expressed in late antique writing, including from the post-Roman world.[62] Such calls for female segregation not only sought to shield women from men, but also to draw distinctions between women, to separate reputable from disreputable women. Female unrestrained liberty of movement was a hallmark of defilement, fit for prostitutes.[63]

Since this association of women and domestic seclusion existed as an ideal, punitive confinement was a logical step to reassert male control over women who had violated the rituals of domesticity. It was a way to put them back, as it were, in their natural place. This happened, for example, to Iusta Grata Honoria, Valentinian III's sister. In about 449, she was discovered of having a love affair with her estate steward, Eugenius. In response, Valentinian, who was not only the emperor but also Honoria's eldest agnatic relative, sent his sister to live away from the court.[64] Valentinian could have tried Honoria for *stuprum* and inflicted the death penalty on her, but, perhaps similar to Constantine in 326, chose a less conspicuous route to deal with her misbehaviour, but one that also ostensibly returned Honoria to a suitably sheltered life. This was particularly important, as Honoria probably had been dedicated to a life of Christian virginity in her youth (she was already 30 years old in 449).[65] Valentinian clearly thought that the family's honour would be restored, despite or perhaps because of the fact that Honoria was not submitted to customary criminal procedure. Eugenius, by contrast, was put to death, and his death advertised.[66] Strikingly, Honoria was spared death not just once, but twice: not content with her fate, she famously used her time away from court to correspond with the empire's enemy, the Hunnic king

[62] See G. Clark, *Women in Late Antiquity: Pagan and Christian Lifestyles* (Oxford: Oxford University Press, 1993), 94; L. Alberici and M. Harlow, 'Age and Innocence: Female Transitions to Adulthood in Late Antiquity', in A. Cohen and J. Rutter (eds.), *Constructions of Childhood in Ancient Greece and Italy* (Princeton, NJ: ASCSA, 2007), 201; V. Vuolanto, 'Elite Children, Socialization, and Agency in the Late Roman World', in J. Evans Grubbs and T. Parkin (eds.), *The Oxford Handbook of Childhood and Education in the Classical World* (Oxford: Oxford University Press, 2013), 594.

[63] McGinn, *Prostitution*, 334.

[64] Jordanes, *Getica* 224, T. Mommsen (ed.), *Iordanis Getica*, MGH, AA, 5.1 (Berlin: Weidmann, 1882); Priscus, *Fragment* 17, Blockley (ed.), *Fragmentary Classicising Historians*, Vol. II; Marcellinus Comes, *Chronicon*, s. a. 434, T. Mommsen (ed.), *Chronica Minora*, MGH, AA, 11 (Berlin: Weidmann, 1894); John of Antioch, *Fragment* 199.2, S. Mariev (ed.), *Ioannis Antiocheni fragmenta quae supersunt* (Berlin, New York: De Gruyter, 2008), reported that Honoria was also betrothed to a trusted courtier on the occasion, which was an additional measure to reassert control over her; see PLRE II Iusta Grata Honoria, 568.

[65] H. Sivan, *Galla Placidia: The Last Roman Empress* (Oxford: Oxford University Press, 2011), 153.

[66] As we can conclude from the fact that our sources (see n. 64) reported on it.

Attila. This time, Valentinian agreed that Honoria should live with their mother, Galla Placidia.[67]

Where wives perceived as troublesome were concerned, it is especially in Christian writing that we find endorsement of their confinement. This was at times presented to husbands as a superior alternative to wife-beating, of which Christian authors did not on the whole approve.[68] Indeed, Christian ecclesiastical councils legislated on this issue. The first council of Toledo, in 400, ordered male clerics to keep their sinful wives in the house and to impose 'salutary but not fatal' fasting on them, until their penance reverted them to the 'fear of God'.[69] This canon, originating from a council combating Priscillianism and much concerned with perceived female subversion may not reflect general practice of how Christian men treated or were supposed to treat their misbehaving wives. Yet, it demonstrates at least one possibility of how the performance of female penance, so often prescribed without further specifications by other ancient church councils, was envisaged. The Toledo canon is also remarkably similar to a prescription in another late antique religious text, whose origin lies at the other end of the Mediterranean over two hundred years later. The famous Surah 4.15 of the Qur'an suggested that wives whose sexual misconduct was proven should be placed into domestic confinement, either permanently or 'until Allah ordain for them some (other) way'.[70]

Despite such strong cross-cultural endorsements of domestic confinement of daughters and wives, the practice was, however, not uncontroversial. As Kate Wilkinson has shown recently, the calls for domestic seclusion in ancient literature were complex. While reputable women stayed at home, there was also a necessity for others to witness their virtues of domesticity, in order for them to maintain the right reputation. Domesticity was therefore never a matter of total seclusion or incarceration, but a matter of being seen as properly managing relations with the outside world and adhering to the rituals of gender segregation (through

[67] John of Antioch, *Fragment* 199.2.

[68] J. Hillner 'Family Violence: Punishment and Abuse in the Late Roman Household', in L. Brubaker and S. Tougher (eds.), *Approaches to the Byzantine Family* (Aldershot: Ashgate, 2013), 21–45.

[69] Council of Toledo I (400), can. 7: *ad ieiunia salutaria non mortifera cogentes . . . nisi forte ad timorem Dei acta poenitentia revertantur*, J. Vives (ed.), *Concilios visigóticos e hispano-romanos* (Barcelona, Madrid: Consejo Superior de Investigaciones Científicas, 1983).

[70] *The Holy Qur'an*, surah 4.15, A. Yusuf Ali (trans.) (Ware: Wordsworth Editions, 2000). This promulgation is usually seen as the original statement about adultery in the Qur'an, later superseded by a new revelation recorded as surah 24.4, which prescribed a hundred lashes for both the adulterous wife and her lover, see S. A. Spectorsky, *Women in Classical Islamic Law: A Survey of the Sources* (Leiden: Brill, 2010), 52.

the employment of chaperones on public outings or having strict times to receive visitors at home, for example).[71] Furthermore, late antique women, under Roman, but also some 'Barbarian' law, had civic rights and the legal right to own property, which inevitably included the possibility of contact with the outside world, particularly in the urbanised areas of the Mediterranean.[72] All this means that the expectation of women's seclusion was likely not matched by reality in the late antique world (and before), even though there may have been some regional variation.[73]

It is therefore perhaps not surprising that we also find voices that seem to decry the seclusion of women. In his treatise *On Virginity* John Chrysostom deplored the travails of the wife whose jealous husband kept her at home and surrounded her with slaves as guards meant to spy on her every word.[74] The key words John Chrysostom used here to describe the wife's domestic confinement were 'prison' (*phulakē*) and 'fetters' (*desmōtou*). These were powerful terms, because they drew a parallel to the public prisons, which, as we have seen, were generally seen as unsuitable for women of high rank. They also associated the treatment of freeborn wives with that of slaves for whom confinement and shackles were customary punishments; with individuals, hence, who were not in control of their own bodies.[75] Such rhetorical strategies show that in late antiquity the distinction between acceptable or even desired domestic seclusion and shocking imprisonment of women could be easily blurred. Even though John Chrysostom who, as we have seen above, elsewhere endorsed the practice, in *On Virginity* represented it as abusive behaviour, as here it suited his plea for virginity over marriage.

What seems to have been at stake in the case described by John, and in other texts where the injustice of female seclusion was claimed, was the surrounding of the woman in question with guards and other measures that would have limited her movement even *within* the house.[76] Here we

71 K. Wilkinson, *Women and Modesty in Late Antiquity* (Cambridge: Cambridge University Press, 2015), 59–74. On the expectation that *matronae* would be accompanied by a chaperone (*comes*) see Dig. 47.10.1.2 (Ulpian).

72 K. Cooper, *The Fall of the Roman Household* (Cambridge: Cambridge University Press, 2007) 111–12; Wemple, *Women*, 45–9.

73 On regional variation in gender segregation see L. Dossey, 'Wife Beating and Manliness in Late Antiquity', *Past & Present* 199 (2008), 3–40.

74 John Chrysostom, *Virg.* 52.5. See Jonathan Tallon's chapter in this volume for more on the theme of surveillance in John Chrysostom's sermons.

75 On the shackling of late antique slaves, see K. Harper, *Slavery in the Late Roman World,* AD *275–425* (Cambridge: Cambridge University Press, 2011), 231. See Chris L. De Wet's chapter in this volume for more on the punishment of slaves.

76 See Hillner, *Prison*, 161–3 for further references.

should remember a particular feature of late antique domestic architecture, and Roman architecture in general. Roman houses seem not to have had spaces segregated by gender. Instead, domestic space was used in a dynamic way and its function was determined by different individuals using the space at different times of the day.[77] Women may have been excluded from certain spaces on certain occasions and certain times. This might even have happened for punitive reasons. The bishops at Toledo in 400, as we have seen, advised excluding unruly wives from mealtimes and hence also from central domestic rooms dedicated to dining.[78] It was a different matter, however, to then also physically confine women to a specific space.

This could easily be defined as abuse, as a late antique hagiographical text, possibly from sixth-century Rome, shows. In the *Passion of Anastasia*, the pagan senator Publius brought a criminal charge of magic against his Christian wife Anastasia and then imprisoned her at home. Neither of them are probably historical characters. At the same time, the story has some elements that ring true. The author probably drew on knowledge about customary and honourable house arrest for Roman elite women on criminal trial which I have discussed above. It should also be noted that according to contemporary sixth-century Roman law, roughly at the time of the author's writing, a husband who brought a charge of adultery against his wife on suspicion was allowed to 'detain' (*detinere*) her, probably at home, while the matter was investigated. This suggests, again, that late antique husbands might have been afforded considerable involvement in public criminal procedure against their wives, including arranging their house arrest, and that our author knew about this.[79] At home, however, Publius imposed prison-like conditions on Anastasia: he shut her up in a windowless room without food and surrounded her with guards. It was hence not house arrest in line with legal and moral requirements, but a

[77] On the lack of gendered space in the (late) Roman household and the dynamic use of space see J. A. Hendon, 'The Engendered Household', in S. M. Nelson (ed.), *Women in Antiquity. Theoretical Approaches to Gender and Archaeology* (Lanham, MD; Plymouth: AltaMira Press, 2007), 141–68; for the discussion of Eastern Mediterranean evidence see E. M. Meyer, 'The Problems of Gendered Space in Syro-Palestinian Domestic Architecture: The Case of Roman-Period Galilee', in D. Balch and C. Osiek (eds.), *Early Christian Families in Context: An Interdisciplinary Dialogue* (Grand Rapids, MI: Eerdmans, 2003), 44–69; but see S. Ellis, *Roman Housing* (London: Duckworth, 2000), 178 on the possible existence of women's quarters in Greek houses.

[78] On late Roman dining spaces see Ellis, *Housing*, 171–4.

[79] *Cod. Iust.* 9.9.29. This law, included in the Code of Justinian (534), repeated the adultery law of Constantine (Cod. Theod. 9.7.2) but added this clause.

substitution of proper imprisonment, which helped the author to cast Publius in the role of both 'bad husband' and 'bad public official'.[80]

It is clear, then, that late antique domestic discipline at times included confinement of women, both in theory and in practice. Yet, particularly where the women were of high rank, such domestic confinement had to be carefully managed. The social requirement to advertise female domesticity appropriately and to respect women's legal independence meant that it was difficult to curtail women's freedom of circulation within and beyond the house completely. Shutting women up in separate rooms with guards was dangerously similar to the treatment of slaves or the public prison, and opened the way to an accusation of abuse. As we shall see now, the emergence of monastic confinement of wayward women may have, at least partly, served to address such anxieties around domestic custody.

Female Monastic Confinement

From the early sixth century on, lawgivers started to lay down monastic confinement as a statutory penalty for a number of well-defined crimes. This happened both in the Eastern Roman empire and in the post-Roman West, although it should be noted that in the former the penalty was introduced by a lay ruler, the emperor, while in the latter it was established in an ecclesiastical context, through bishops' synods.[81] What this means is that in the East the penalty could be more easily and comprehensively prescribed for clerical, ascetic and laypeople, including laywomen. The Western ecclesiastical legislation concerned mostly misbehaving ascetics and clergy, although the penalty came to be extended to female members of clerical families, such as the widows of clerics, and to female ascetics.

80 On the figure of the 'bad husband' in late antique hagiography see K. Cooper, 'Of Romance and *Mediocritas*: Re-reading the Martyr *Exemplum* in the *Passio Anastasiae*', in G. Barone (ed.), *Modelli di comportamento e modi di santità* (Turin: Rosenberg & Sellier, 1994), 107–23. See the chapters by James Corke-Webster, David Natal, and Thomas Dimambro in this volume for Christian hagiography as a 'narrative of resistance'.

81 The relevant texts for the sixth century are, in chronological order: Council of Agde (506) can. 50, C. Munier (ed.), *Concilia Galliae a. 314–506*, CCSL 148 (Turnhout: Brepols, 1963, repr. 2001); Council of Épaone (517) can. 22 and Council of Orléans III (538) can. 8, C. De Clercq (ed.), *Concilia Galliae a. 511–695*, CCSL 148a (Turnhout: Brepols, 1963); *Nov. Iust.* 117.13 (542), 131.14 (545), 123.10 (546), 123.11 (546), 123.20 (546), 123.30 (546), 123.43 (546), 127.4 (548), 134.10 (556), 134.11 (556), 134.12 (556); Council of Mâcon (585) can. 16, Council of Auxerre (561–605) can. 23, 26, and Council of Narbonne (589) can. 5, all De Clercq (ed.), *Concilia Galliae.* Relevant legal texts are also numerous for the seventh century and later, particularly in the Visigothic kingdom, see *Leges Visigothorum* 3.5.1, 3.5.3; 4.5.6 and 6.2.4; Council of Seville II, can. 3; Council of Toledo IV, can. 29; Council of Toledo VII, can. 3 and can. 5; Council of Toledo VIII, can. 6 and 7; Council of Toledo X, can. 5, all Vives (ed.), *Concilios visigóticos e hispano-romanos.*

Although the penalty was prescribed for both men and women, there are some crucial differences. Most importantly, for clerics, who made up the bulk of male offenders for whom the statutory penalty was proposed, forced monastic residence could be short-term. For male clerics, monastic confinement arguably served as a penitential process to prepare for return to the external world and to clerical office.[82]

By contrast, most of the women for whom the statutory penalty was prescribed were to stay in their monasteries permanently. The differential timing suggests that when it was imposed on women the purpose of the penalty differed as well. This becomes even more apparent when we consider the offences for which the penalty was prescribed. For clerics, the penalty was envisaged for a wide range of misconduct, including fraud, perjury, fornication, and gambling, which suggests that it came to be seen as the appropriate procedure to deal with misbehaviour in office generally. For women the range was narrower and exclusively pertained to sexual or marital misconduct, which links the penalty to late antique considerations of family honour described earlier in this chapter. Such female offences included the illicit filing for unilateral divorce, deaconesses' (an ancient clerical office open to women) cohabitation with men, remarriage of clerical widows, and adultery.[83]

In the case of adultery, a remarkable caveat was proposed in an imperial law of 556: an adulteress was first to be sent to a monastery for two years, after which her husband could decide whether he wanted to take her back. If he decided against, or died in the interim, she had to stay in the monastery for life, assuming the monastic habit. A related case is attested in the West in 559, when Pelagius, bishop of Rome, ordered an adulterous woman and her lover to be consigned to separate monasteries; her husband was consulted in the ruling, and was given the opportunity to take his wife back.[84] Like that of the illicit divorcee and the misbehaving deaconess, the property of the adulterous wife was then assigned in part to the monastic institution.

Justinian's law is strikingly similar to the Visigothic law discussed above, which remanded an adulterous woman to her husband for further decisions on her fate.[85] It is reasonable to assume, therefore, that Justinian's law reflects family practices described earlier in this article. Where it is

[82] Hillner, *Prison*, 298–306.

[83] *Nov. Iust.* 117.13 (542), 123.43 (546), 134.10 (556), 134.12 (556); Council of Mâcon (585) can. 16, De Clercq (ed.), *Concilia Galliae*.

[84] Pelagius *Ep.* 64. [85] See above n. 52.

distinctive is in its addition of monastic custody to the menu of options for husbands, either as a short-term option, perhaps designed to allow for completion of an unwanted pregnancy and the baby's weaning, or permanently. In either case, the family honour was preserved. The spiritually enhanced seclusion simultaneously emphasised the disciplining of female sexuality,[86] and shielded husbands against accusations of abuse of the type discussed in the previous section. In fact, ordering female defendants to be held in monasteries rather than prisons in another law already mentioned above, Justinian drew a stark distinction between the two institutions, highlighting the role of monasteries in the redress of female crime.[87] So the monastery here emerged as a new form of confinement which offered the benefits of other forms, while avoiding the problems posed by domestic confinement or imprisonment.

Similar concerns were at play in the ecclesiastical prohibition of remarriage of clerical widows, who were consigned to a monastery if they defied the norm. The prohibition also may have aimed to prevent the raising of children born into a clerical household (and presumably the heirs of their clerical fathers' property) by their mothers' new, non-clerical husbands – in other words, outside the control of the Church. While secular and ecclesiastical law may have tried to protect different institutions (lay families vs. the clerical establishment), they shared the view that these institutions at times benefitted from removing some women permanently from circulation in the outside world and on the marriage market.

When we turn our attention from legal norms to actual incidents reported in contemporary sources, we notice a similar pronounced differentiation between male and female monastic confinement in terms of length and purpose. Many of the men confined in monasteries were clerics who had been deposed and banished in the course of the religious controversies of the fifth and sixth centuries. Most of these were interned for religious coercion, in order to make them subscribe to the emperor's perspective of doctrine, and many were in fact released upon doing so.[88] Even though Justinian promulgated a law that prescribed permanent stay in a monastery for a deposed and dissident bishop, in actual practice Justinian and others made wider use of temporary confinement.[89] Clerics sent to monasteries for life, sometimes with direct reference to legal norms,

[86] On the emergence of and rationale behind enclosure of ascetic women in late antiquity: I. Stahlmann, *Der gefesselte Sexus. Weibliche Keuschheit und Askese im Westen des römischen Reiches* (Berlin: Akademie Verlag, 1997), 188–93.

[87] See above n. 19. [88] Hillner, *Prison*, 316–21. [89] *Nov. Iust.* 123.11 (546).

were more numerous where this followed an ecclesiastical dispute.[90] But again, decisions were not always obeyed. For example, Gregory of Tours failed in keeping the priest Riculf, who had plotted against him, in the monastery he had confined him to.[91]

Also where laymen are concerned, monastic walls seem to have been at least intermittently permeable. A number of sources record successful efforts to escape from forced monastic residence. Marcian, the son of former Western emperor Anthemius, who tried to usurp the throne of Zeno in 479, was made to reside in a monastery in Caesarea in Cappadocia, but managed to flee. A similar course of events occurred about one hundred years later in Merovingian Gaul. Merovech, son of king Chilperic, in 576 was suspected of treason against his father and sent to the monastery of Anille in Subdinnum (Le Mans), from which he also escaped. Both men were also forcibly ordained as priests. Presumably it was felt that this would control their movements, and their attempts to return to worldly power, more tightly.[92]

While cases of male monastic confinement apparently could arise from a variety of offences, ranging from religious dissidence over 'fornication' to fraud or treason, the majority of female cases again involve sexual or domestic misconduct, though there are a few instances of women who supported the 'heretical' side during religious conflict. Other cases include misbehaving nuns who were transferred to different monasteries to allow for stricter discipline; a slave woman who had formed an illicit relationship with a deacon; an adulteress who had married a tenant of the Roman Church; the widow of a subdeacon who had remarried; and a number of royal women, both in the Eastern Roman empire and in post-Roman Gaul.[93] Some of the female offences for which forced monastic

[90] Hillner, *Prison*, 293–8.

[91] Gregory of Tours *Hist.*, 5.49. For other cases see J. Hillner, 'Gregory the Great's "Prisons": Monastic Confinement in Early Byzantine Italy', *Journal of Early Christian Studies*, 19 (2011), 433–71.

[92] Marcian: Evagrius *Historia ecclesiastica* 2.26, A. Hübner (ed.), *Evagrius Scholasticus. Historia ecclesiastica*, Fontes Christiani 57 (Turnhout: Brepols, 2007); Merovech: Gregory of Tours *Hist.* 5.2.3, 14, 18. Merovech was not sent to the monastery for ascetic conversion, but to be trained as a priest.

[93] Heretical women: John of Ephesus, *Historia ecclesiastica* 3.2.12, E. W. Brooks (ed.), *Iohannis Ephesini historiae ecclesiasticae pars tertia*, Corpus Scriptorum Christianorum Orientalium, Scriptores Syri 3.3 (Louvain: L. Durbecq, 1935–6); nuns: Gregory, *Ep.* 1.42, 4.6, 5.4, P. Ewald and L. M. Hartmann (eds.), *Gregorii I Papae Registrum Epistolarum*, 2 vols., MGH, Epistolae, 1–2 (Berlin, 1893); female slave: Pelagius, *Ep.* 47; adulterous woman: Pelagius, *Ep.* 64; remarried clerical widow: Gregory, *Ep.* 4.34; royal women: John of Antioch, *Fragment* 234.2 (Verina) and 234.4 (Leontia); Gregory of Tours, Hist. 4.26 (Theodechild).

residence was imposed were recognised public crimes, such as adultery or unilateral divorce, that is, could have potentially led to a charge in a secular court; others, such as remarriage, were violations only of Church discipline. It is quite clear that in such cases the decision to make these women retire to monasteries followed similar considerations as those underpinning the legal norms detailed above: the protection of male honour or the honour of institutions.

It is therefore not surprising that the mobility afforded to men on whom monastic confinement was imposed seems have been less available to women forced to reside in monasteries. To be sure, we should not overestimate the impact of the late antique ideal of 'monastic enclosure' on reality; it was not only men who managed to leave their assigned monastery.[94] Yet, we have no record from this period of a case in which forced monastic residence of a woman was *intended* to be for a short term only, as happened for men. Furthermore, the most gruesome story about the curtailing of escape from a monastery in this period is told about a woman. In 567 Theodechild, widow of the Merovingian King Charibert, had offered herself in marriage to her husband's brother, King Guntram. But instead, Guntram seized her treasure and forced her to enter a monastery at Arles. When Theodechild tried to leave with the outside help of another suitor, the abbess had her flogged and 'shut up in a cell' for the rest of her life.[95] We struggle to find comparable harshness in treatment of men sent to monasteries in this period.[96]

Royal women such as Theodechild were potential carriers of dynastic legitimacy, and monastic confinement shut down their route to remarriage and hence undesired transmission of worldly power. Theodechild's treatment can therefore directly be compared to that of Valentinian III's transgressive sister Honoria more than a century earlier, discussed above, who was confined, in order to shield her family from defilation of lineage. Being a dowager queen or an unmarried princess was of course no offence per se. But the retirement to monasteries of dowager queens and other royal women nonetheless became increasingly common across the post-Roman west. In seventh-century Visigothic Spain it was even enshrined in

[94] See E. T. Dailey, 'Confinement and Exclusion in the Monasteries of Sixth-Century Gaul', *Early Medieval Europe*, 22 (2014), 305–14.

[95] Gregory of Tours, *Hist.* 4.26.

[96] The worst maltreatment of contemporary men confined in monasteries amounted to consumption of acid wine and being prevented from going to the baths: John of Ephesus, *Historia ecclesiastica* 3.1.15, 3.1.17, 3.2.2.

church council decisions.[97] The apparent ease with which removal of royal women to monasteries happened or was prescribed, even without taking recourse to criminal charges, as seems to have been required for men forced to reside at monasteries, is revealing about the advanced development of monastic infrastructure and the high prestige of such institutions at the end of antiquity. Yet, it is also revealing about male ability to control female agency and movement even where no rules had been broken, and this was hardly new.

Conclusion

Over twenty years ago, Judith Evans Grubbs speculated that instead of bringing a delinquent woman to court, many late antique families might have found it 'more efficient to try [her] in the privacy of the family circle ... to acquit her or to punish her, perhaps by death, perhaps by permanent confinement'.[98] This article has brought fresh evidence to support this statement, and has further attempted to understand the profile of female punitive confinement as a way to redress female misconduct – or potential for unwelcome agency – that avoided the inconvenience, visibility, and unpredictability of public justice while side-stepping the risk of criminal charges carried by extrajudicial killing. The reasons why families chose this route were varied, and even where confinement ostensibly benefitted a female offender by protecting her from death and offering shelter, it was not necessarily leniency that determined her fate. Rather, the motive seems to have been a concern for reputation, whether that of the family or, where women were attached to clerical households, of the Church. Yet we can see from the case of the emperor Constantine, with which we began this study, that this was not always successful. Ironically, or perhaps predictably, it may have been the concealment of the empress Fausta that set in motion the rumour mill concerning her death and her involvement in that of Crispus.

The rise of Christianity brought with it the emergence of new institutions, such as the bishop's court, that broadened the judicial options of families beyond the 'privacy of the family circle' and the public courts. The use of female confinement as a disciplinary measure, and the emergent

[97] Already Clotilde, widow of Clovis, had retired to a monastery in 511 (St Martin in Tours): Fredegar, *Chronicon* 3.17, B. Krusch (ed.), *Chronicarum quae dicuntur Fredegarii Scholastici libri quattuor cum continuationibus*, MGH, SRM, 2 (Hanover: Hahn, 1888). On Visigothic conciliar decisions, see Council of Saragossa, can. 4, Vives (ed.), *Concilios visigóticos e hispano-romanos*.

[98] Evans Grubbs, *Law and Family*, 214.

use of monastic space for this purpose, offers an illuminating instance of this wider phenomenon. The institution of forced monastic residence made it easier to manage female confinement, but also to circumvent the controversies surrounding it. Monasteries, like houses, could be used to conceal women, but because they were also highly regarded as penitential and holy spaces distinct from the outside impure world, they were far removed from any association with the degrading and defiling public or slave prison. Women's sexual virtue could thus be restored and the restoration advertised, to the benefit of their families.

Punitive confinement in a monastery therefore was a logical development of the tendency toward domestic confinement as a strategy aimed specifically at women. To be sure, forced residence in a monastery was also prescribed for high-ranking men in this period. It is this development that is perhaps more surprising, though it is surely a reflection of the prestige of monasteries and of monastic penance. But there were significant differences: not only was male confinement in monasteries usually short-term, it was, as I have argued elsewhere, also often challenged as unjust imprisonment,[99] to an extent that we rarely see happening with female monastic confinement.

This gender asymmetry was destined to reach far into the future. As Gwen Seabourne has recently shown in her excellent study *Imprisoning Medieval Women* (2011), gender differentiation continued into the later medieval period: although both men and women at times suffered extra-judicial imprisonment, it was consistently presented as a far more acceptable measure for women.[100] When we consider Michel Foucault's thesis of the 'birth of the prison' in the early nineteenth century, we should hence pause to reflect whether it was not just for men that punitive confinement was 'born' in that period. As the late antique evidence shows, for women the history of the prison developed along a different trajectory.[101]

99 Hillner, *Prison*, 335–41.

100 G. Seabourne, *Imprisoning Medieval Women: The Non-Judicial Confinement and Abduction of Women in England, c. 1170–1509* (Aldershot: Ashgate, 2011).

101 M. Foucault, *Surveiller et punir. Naissance de la prison* (Paris: Gallimard, 1975).

CHAPTER 2

Holy Beatings

Emmelia, Her Son Gregory of Nyssa, and the Forty Martyrs of Sebasteia

Vasiliki Limberis

Introduction

In his *Encomium in xl martyres ii*, Gregory of Nyssa relates a significant bit of biographical information that leaves his audience, both now and in the later fourth century, intrigued and slightly disturbed.[1] On the one hand, the passage is intriguing because it is quite revealing, though frustratingly short. Gregory wittingly exposes a life-changing episode during a time of great transition for him and his family at a personal level rarely seen by his audience. On the other hand, it is also hauntingly disturbing because it is violent. Gregory explicitly provokes both responses by assigning multiple meanings to the violence in the biographical episode. Yet one must remember that this violent incident, fundamentally entwined in his domestic situation, is itself imbedded in a panegyric to the Forty Martyrs that already glorifies the torturous suffering the forty soldiers endured for professing Christ. An analysis of the particular meanings of violence Gregory brings to bear on this incident is the subject of this paper.

The event can be summed up as follows. Sometime between the years 355 and 358, Emmelia, mother of Gregory of Nyssa, expressed her fervent piety to the Forty Martyrs of Sebasteia by building a magnificent shrine for them at Ibora, only one mile from the family's estate in Annesi in Pontus. She intentionally had the martyrium erected next to her family's crypt, where her husband Basil and her son Naucratius were already buried. Christians during the fourth century valued burial as close to the martyrs

[1] Gregory of Nyssa wrote two homilies in honour of the Forty Martyrs. The first one is divided into two parts and was delivered in 383 in Sebasteia. See discussion of dating in V. Limberis, *Architects of Piety, The Cappadocian Fathers and the Cult of the Martyrs* (Oxford: Oxford University Press, 2011), 23, 64. See *Encomium in xl martyres i* [PG 46.749–772]. For an English translation, see J. Leemans, 'First Homily on the Forty Martyrs of Sebaste Ia and Ib', in J. Leemans, W. Mayer, P. Allen and B. Dehandschutter (eds.), '*Let Us Die That We May Live*': *Greek Homilies on Christian Martyrs from Asia Minor, Palestine, and Syria* (London: Routledge, 2003), 93–107. For the second homily see Gregory of Nyssa, *Encomium in xl martyres ii* [PG 46.772–788].

as possible for two reasons. They believed that they would not only partake in the martyr's holiness; but, more importantly, at the second coming they were firmly convinced that they would be first to rise from the dead along with the martyrs.[2] Those Christians who were richest and had an ecclesiastical connection had the greatest advantage, since they had the means and privilege to be buried near martyr shrines. Such was the case with Gregory of Nyssa's family. The feast day of the martyrs was always celebrated with a *panegyris*, a liturgical festival for the martyrs. As 9 March approached that year, the feast day of the Forty Martyrs, Emmelia informed her young son, Gregory, that he must attend the solemn rituals of the inaugural *panegyris* and witness the deposition of the relics. Eventually Gregory grudgingly obliged and made the journey to Ibora for the important event. Unable to endure the long service, the distracted young Gregory sneaked into a copse of the garden of the martyrium where the vigil was in progress and soon nodded off. But sleep brought him no escape. The Forty Martyrs visited him in an extraordinary 'waking' dream. They scolded him for his laziness and clubbed him with long sticks. When he awoke, he was profoundly distressed and immediately returned to the shrine to join in the prayers, begging the martyrs for their forgiveness. The violent incident had such a tremendous effect on him that not long afterwards Gregory changed his life. Within several years he was baptized.[3] About twenty-five years later, in one of his two homilies on the Forty Martyrs, Gregory relates the astounding details of the vision and, more significantly, the role the Forty Martyrs assumed in his family dynamics when they violently intervened in his life that extraordinary day.

When readers coalesce the bits and pieces of family biography from Gregory's *Life of Macrina* with this incident, they realize that they have been made privy to a time of change, tension, upheaval, and finally resolution in his family's life. The recent deaths of his father and his brother, along with the move of the family to Annesi, understandably would have caused friction in the family dynamics, and, specifically in this case, between adolescent Gregory and his mother Emmelia. Examples of these quotidian familial interchanges, though utterly normal and acknowledged in everyday life, are most rare in Patristic literature. This is not to say in the least that Emmelia should be characterized as constantly bossy and

[2] Gregory of Nyssa, *Encomium in xl martyres ii* [PG 46.776.16].

[3] Gregory of Nyssa, *Encomium in xl martyres ii* [PG 46.784.56–785.30]. See also discussion in Elias Moutsoulas, *ΓΡΗΓΟΡΙΟΣ ΝΥΣΣΗΣ, Βίος, Συγράμματα, Διδασκαλία* (Athens: Eptalophos A.B.E.E., 1997), 26.

overbearing, any more than that Gregory was persistently wilful and utterly self-centred. Rather what the episode does show is a unique glimpse of the family's life during a vulnerable time when there is actual conflict between mother and son, surprising violence at the *panegyris*, and finally the innovative resolution of the violence confirmed in Gregory's life. Such personal, even candid, revelations are uncharacteristic in the highly stylized literature of the Cappadocian Fathers. Nevertheless the fissures of the story expose Gregory's 'personal truth', as he gives theological purpose and dignified meaning to his experience of disruption and violence, from the hindsight of twenty-five years.

This article examines the violent episode from three perspectives. First is the discussion of what 'acceptable' violence is within the household of an elite Cappadocian family in the fourth century. What status and what gender can legitimately mete out corporeal punishment, and in turn receive it? These questions frame the examination of the tension and resolution between Emmelia and Gregory, as mother and son. Next, what valence Gregory gives this particular traumatic event in his life is explored especially with regard to its meaning in the larger context of his familial history. Both were extremely important to Gregory and inextricably bound to the Forty Martyrs. The article ends with an analysis of the startling ways Gregory employs the beating in the sermon, both to reify his family as kin to the martyrs, and to assiduously promote imitation of the martyrs among the faithful. The particular consequences of family violence upon Gregory as an elite Cappadocian Christian thus unfold.

The Law and Corrective Violence in the Household in Fourth Century Cappadocia

Research on violence in late antiquity confirms what contemporary theorists of criminal justice stress: like all forms of crime, violence occurs in a social relationship. Then as now 'violence is rarely random, it inevitably involves particular social meanings and occurs in particular hierarchies of power. Moreover the impact of violence is predicated on the relationship within which it occurs, between victim and offender.'[4] Late Roman society, so defined by family, offers ample evidence of family members

[4] J. Young, 'Risk of Crime and Fear of Crime: A Realist Critique of Survey-Based Assumptions', in M. Maguire and J. Pointing (eds.), *Victims of Crime: A New Deal?* (Milton Keynes: Open University Press, 1988), 164–76, at 174, as quoted in J. Mooney, *Gender, Violence and the Social Order* (New York, NY: St Martin's Press, 2000), 30.

engaged in power struggles that often included violence. Throughout this paper 'violence' is defined as 'physical force' that threatens the physical safety and bodily integrity of a person (in the family) and intensifies and changes the meanings of threats and humiliation.[5] As such violence can be categorized as either punitive or corrective. In the case of Gregory and his clash with the Forty Martyrs, the violence is a little of both, and, in his experience, definitely within the family.

When Gregory experienced his beating by the Forty Martyrs, his mother Emmelia was a widow. What this meant legally for Emmelia, Gregory, and his siblings in the mid fourth century is not explicitly addressed in any of the Cappadocians' texts, but we can piece together a reasonable context of their situation from legal texts of the period. When Emmelia was married to her husband Basil sometime in the 320s, in terms of Roman law and current social practice, the marriage was probably *sine manu*. This meant that she was not under her husband's power, since that form of marriage had fallen out of favour after Augustus.[6] In other words, Emmelia's father would have retained *patria potestas* over her until he died. At her father's death she would have become independent, *sui iuris*, and it is likely that she inherited extensive wealth in her own right, from maternal and paternal inheritance.[7] When her husband died in 345, the extent of Emmelia's legal control over her family and all of his vast property holdings is not completely clear. We do know that she paid taxes to three different governors after his death, indicating significant wealth.[8] As *materfamilias* she would have inherited complete control over whatever her husband left *specifically* to her, with the rest of the inheritance left to their children. Gregory specifically states, 'Later, when their property was divided nine ways in accordance with the number of children, the share of each had been so bountifully increased that the children lived more prosperously than their parents.'[9] Her husband's will could have stipulated that she have usufruct over the children's property until they would come of age. There was one significant aspect to Roman law that mitigated a

[5] Mooney, *Gender*, 143.

[6] J. Evans Grubbs, *Women and the Law in the Roman Empire* (New York, NY: Routledge, 2002), 21.

[7] Evans Grubbs, *Women*, 21.

[8] Gregory of Nyssa, *Life of Saint Macrina*, V. Woods Callahan, *Saint Gregory of Nyssa: Ascetical Works*, FOTC 58 (Washington, DC: Catholic University Press, 1967), 167.

[9] Gregory of Nyssa, *Life of Saint Macrina*, Woods Callahan, *Saint Gregory of Nyssa: Ascetical Works*, 177.

widowed mother's full power: she had no power over her children's property.[10] Though the law recognized that 'a woman had to be accorded the same honours and dignities as her husband', Emmelia's power as a widow over both her children and the family's property was curtailed, conferred as it were by default – death.[11] In late antiquity Roman law did not 'recognize any maternal power which would have resembled *patria potestas*'.[12] Yet within the confines of the family home, both parents were due proper respect, correct deportment, and the *pietas* of their children; and both parents had an active role in their upbringing.[13] Thus at her husband's death Emmelia would have assumed many responsibilities of the *paterfamilias*, especially if she had usufruct over the property of her underage children.

What did this mean for Emmelia and Gregory? Legitimate Roman children were under their father's *potestas* until he died. In order to protect a child's future property and inheritance from the father's will, a guardian was supposed to be chosen for the child by the mother.[14] A *tutor* served for children who were under the age of puberty (12 or 14), and a *curator minorum* guarded the interests of a child between the ages of puberty and 25, the legal age of maturity.[15] Though children would continue to live with their widowed mother, as she saw to their care, education, and upbringing, the guardian served to protect the child's fiduciary interests. 'Under classical law, a woman could not serve as guardian, even of her own children, though papyrological evidence shows that in the Greek east many mothers did exercise the functions of guardian over her children.'[16]

There is no evidence that Emmelia did or did not appoint guardians for her children when their father died, though her entire brood would have been in need of guardians. At the death of their father, Macrina would have been around 16 or 17, Basil 14 or 15, Naucratius 12 or 13. The youngest son, Peter, would have been a toddler, around 2 years old. Though we know there were four other nameless daughters (possibly one was named 'Theosebeia'), and then Gregory, we do not know their

[10] A. Arjava, *Women and Law in Late Antiquity* (Oxford: Clarendon Press, 1996), 89.

[11] Arjava, *Women*, 85, 89. Many legal scholars of late antiquity argue that the laws simply codify what was in practice long before.

[12] Arjava, *Women*, 84. [13] Arjava, *Women*, 84. [14] *Cod. Iust.* 6.56.3.

[15] Evans Grubbs, *Women*, 236–40.

[16] Evans Grubbs, *Women*, 220; although the evidence is from Egypt, Evans Grubbs also cites evidence, as customary precedent, from Asia Minor (second and third centuries BCE) that widowed mothers served as their children's guardians, see 254–5.

birth order. Gregory could have been born any year between 335 and 341.[17] But given the trajectory of his career, it is likely that he was born between 335 and 338. So when his father died he was somewhere between 7 and 10 years old.

Thinking about whether Emmelia appointed guardians is important in this context for several reasons. Even though guardians only protected the children's financial interests and did not play a central role in the family, such interests would loom large in this family if there were no guardians. Quite often in the fourth century mothers neglected to appoint tutors and guardians.[18] And the children's father could have avoided guardians by stipulating either that his wife should have usufruct over the children's property until majority, or that his property be given to his wife on condition she give it to the children when they come of age.[19] If Emmelia was one of the women who did not appoint guardians, or if her husband evaded the laws of guardianship through his will, she would have had an inordinate amount of responsibility, in addition to raising her children and running the household. It is not unreasonable to assume that Emmelia did serve as her children's guardian. Evidence from all over the empire, but especially the east, shows a significant number of mothers who served as guardians for their children.[20] In fact by the end of the fourth century the law seems to have caught up with custom in the eastern part of the empire, including the rescript of 390, stating that widowed mothers 25 years and older who had taken a vow never to remarry could act as guardians of their children.[21]

In either case, whether she possessed guardianship or not Emmelia would have had the potential for more family troubles arising from either situation. Contemporaneous examples demonstrate how. In Antioch, Libanius reports that his mother refused to appoint a guardian for her children when she was widowed, 'fearing the wickedness of guardians', and her overriding concern for her own shame, were she forced to go to court

[17] Limberis, *Architects*, 112–3, for a different interpretation of Theosebeia's identity, see A. M. Silvas, *Gregory of Nyssa: The Letters* (Leiden: Brill, 2006), 1–58.

[18] Arjava, *Women*, 90.

[19] Arjava, *Women*, 90.

[20] Arjava, *Women*, 91 points out that there is a lack of manuscript evidence for the legislation from the fourth century.

[21] J. Evans Grubbs, *Law and Family in Late Antiquity: The Emperor Constantine's Marriage Legislation* (Oxford: Clarendon Press, 1995), 332; *Cod. Theod.* 3.17.4 (390) as cited in C. Pharr, *The Theodosian Code and Novels and the Sirmondian Constitutions: A Translation with Commentary, Glossary, and Bibliography* (Princeton, NJ: Princeton University Press, 1952), 78 and Evans Grubbs, *Women*, 247.

against them.[22] Gregory of Nyssa would voice this same visceral antipathy for the demeaning altercations that took place in the law courts several years later in his treatise, *On Virginity*.[23] Family conflicts between widowed mothers and their children most often had to do with squabbles over money and property. The legal records give evidence for the cases in which conflicts grew to such an extent that they could not be settled within the household.[24] These family conflicts exposed in the courts all had to do with money and the lack of the child's proper *pietas* towards the widowed mother.

This is *not* to claim that Emmelia suffered any of these legal conflicts. There is no evidence of this. But it *is* to say that guardianship would have added an excessive burden in addition to her widowhood and her children. In such circumstances, family tensions, outbursts of violent speech, and even violent actions could occur for all sorts of reasons. And conversely, even without guardianship, Emmelia's life as a widow would have had moments of heightened family tension; and one time is evident in this episode of Gregory's life. The legal cases add evidence that custom and law roundly prohibited a minor child's contumaciousness towards his/her parents.[25] After the death of the husband 'widows had to shoulder the responsibility [of raising children] alone. Yet the extent of *materna potestas* is uncertain.'[26] How was a widow to deal with a stubborn, contrary son who was a minor in the mid fourth century?

In late Roman households the father had the right to beat their slaves and their children. But rarely did legitimate children receive corporal punishment as slaves did. To live in fear of being physically struck was the overriding characteristic of the status of slave. Roman society from even Republican times considered corporal punishment of all sorts fit for slaves but not for free people, since it was violation of the person's space and honour, the 'grossest form of invasion and hence a deep

[22] Libanius, *Oration* 1.4, A. F. Norman (ed.), *Libanius' Autobiography (Oration 1)* (London: Oxford University Press, for the University of Hull, 1965). See also the other examples cited in Evans Grubbs, *Law*, 332–3.

[23] Gregory of Nyssa, *On Virginity* 3, Woods Callahan, *Saint Gregory of Nyssa: Ascetical Works*, 20.

[24] Arjava, *Women*, 85; J. Evans Grubbs, 'Parent–Child Conflict in the Roman Family: The Evidence of the Code of Justinian', in M. George (ed.), *The Roman Family in the Empire, Rome, Italy, and Beyond* (Oxford: Oxford University Press, 2005), 93–128, at 97.

[25] *Cod. Iust.* 8.46.4 (293), as cited in Evans Grubbs, 'Parent–Child Conflict', 98; *Cod. Theod.* 8.13.4 (358), 8.14.1 (367), as cited in Pharr, *The Theodosian Code*, 215–6.

[26] Arjava, *Women*, 85.

humiliation'.[27] Thus for late Romans beatings inflicted the worst insult, both social and psychological.

In the household it appears that corporal punishment meted out to slaves was different from the type that children received, though in theory both slaves and children were subordinate to the father and subject to corporeal punishment. The distinction lay in this fact: slaves were humiliated, while children were disciplined. Physically punishing a child was considered one of the chief characteristics of *patria potestas*, and as such continued to be 'recognized as a fact of life' throughout the Empire in late antiquity.[28] A father had to guarantee that his property and his children's inheritance would survive him intact and that his children, especially his sons, would grow up to be responsible citizens, squandering neither honour nor goods. Evidence from Augustine shows that he thought the practice of thrashing sons was quite common and necessary.[29] Lactantius could not understand how children could be raised without a father's complete power over his children.[30] And in Libanius' experience as a famous professor of rhetoric teaching rich young men, he yearned for a return to the days when fathers taught their unruly sons through corporeal punishment, instead of overly indulging them.[31] In Libanius' opinion, if fathers would physically discipline their sons, he would have much less trouble with rowdy, disrespectful boys in his classroom.

Physical punishment was viewed as a 'natural' right of fathers over their minor children – those children who were not yet 25 years old or who had not been emancipated beforehand. Legally, though, a man who was over 25 and whose father was still living was under *patria potestas* unless his father had emancipated him. And legally, in such a situation, his father could hit him until he, the father, died or until the son was emancipated. Since she was under the power of her living father and not under her husband's power, a married daughter could also be struck by her father. Yet after sons and daughters attained the age of 25, even remaining under

[27] R. P. Saller, 'Corporal Punishment, Authority, and Obedience in the Roman Household', in B. Rawson (ed.), *Marriage, Divorce, and Children in Ancient Rome* (Oxford: Clarendon Press, 1991), 144–65, at 151–2.

[28] A. Arjava, 'Paternal Power in Late Antiquity', *Journal of Roman Studies* 88 (1998), 147–65, at 161.

[29] Augustine, *Commentary on John* 7.3 in J. Rettig, *Tractates on the Gospel of John 1–10*, FOTC 78 (Washington, DC: Catholic University Press, 1988), 160–1.

[30] Lactantius, *Institutes* 4.3.15 in M. F. McDonald, *The Divine Institutes, Books, I–VII*, FOTC 49 (Washington, DC: Catholic University Press, 1964), 230.

[31] Libanius, *Oration*, 62.24–25, R. Foerster (ed.), *Libanii opera*, 4 vols. (Leipzig: Teubner, 1903–8), Vol. IV, 342–83.

patria potestas, it is difficult to imagine that fathers exercised their right to beat their adult children.[32]

Roman law does not stipulate that a matron could physically punish her children, though she could hit slaves, and she probably administered physical discipline to her small children.[33] Yet in the case of slaves, it was more typical for her to get another person to inflict the actual flogging. In the case of older children, she would refer the matter of punishment to her husband. At her husband's death, she did not inherit her husband's power to beat adolescents or adult children. Widowed mothers still had powerful means to exercise their power over her children through coercion, wheedling, and most often through withholding money and inheritance. Incidences of hostility and strife between mothers and adolescent sons were common in late antiquity.[34]

In addition to their deportment, in late antiquity Christian mothers had the added responsibility of religious education for all the children. In pagan households, by contrast, the responsibility to teach the children religious duties was divided according to gender: fathers taught their sons gender-specific rites and mothers taught daughters. Though Christian fathers continued to oversee their sons' education in the world, mothers in Christian households were charged with insuring everyone's salvation for eternity. Wealthy or influential mothers would try to get a deceased child buried close to a martyr's shrine, for the benefit of salvation and rising first at the resurrection. Most important, because of this added responsibility Christian mothers could be blamed for their children's spiritual and religious failings. In light of this it is quite understandable why Christian parents insisted that the obligations between parent and children be reciprocal.[35]

Such was the wider legal and social context of Gregory and his mother Emmelia in the mid 350s. It is possible that Emmelia was serving as Gregory's guardian by that time. Their relationship was informed by Roman expectations of respect and obedience to his mother on Gregory's part, and on Emmelia's part protection, education, and spiritual guidance for her son, reinforced by law and custom. With this in mind, we can now

[32] *Cod. Theod.* 2.17.1 (324), as cited in Pharr, *The Theodosian Code*, 52. This rescript ruled that young people who wanted to govern their own property could apply to the Emperor for their independence; young women could do so at age 18, and young men at age 20.

[33] Saller, 'Corporal Punishment', 162.

[34] G. Nathan, *The Family in Late Antiquity: The Rise of Christianity and the Endurance of Tradition* (London; New York, NY: Routledge, 2000), 34–5.

[35] Nathan, *Family*, 142.

turn to the examination of the situation at Ibora, when, among other things, misunderstanding and tension abounded between mother and son.

Family Circumstances Surrounding Gregory's Traumatic Event

Given their family circumstances and the nature of public liturgies, there is little doubt that for Emmelia and her entire family the dedication of the martyrium to the Forty Martyrs was a momentous occasion fraught with strong personal emotions and unavoidable social concerns about the *panegyris*. Emmelia had been a widow for over ten years; and, compounding her grief, she had lost her precious son Naucratius recently in a fishing accident.[36] Several years before his death, Naucratius, like his older sister Macrina, had given up the promising life of an elite Cappadocian landowner for the ascetic life. His older brother Basil had left to study in Constantinople and then in Athens. At the time young Gregory was at school in nearby Caesarea.

In 356–357 Basil had just returned from Athens a short time when Naucratius' tragic death occurred. With Emmelia so utterly grief-stricken and unable to cope with day-to-day affairs, Macrina began to support the family immensely, assuming the responsibility of running the household and raising little Peter. Sometime during 355–358, however, Emmelia felt well enough to oversee the construction of a beautiful martyrium in honour of the Forty Martyrs of Sebasteia. Such munificence publicized her eminent social status in connection with her devotion to the Forty Martyrs, helped spread their cult to new centres in the area and, significantly, ensured her family a certain place at the resurrection of the dead, since they were buried so close to the martyrs.[37]

Family conflicts most often erupt when special holidays and life-cycle occasions occur. This is especially true at the celebration of birthdays, weddings, and funerals, since these occasions 'involve reassignments of family roles and material dispositions'.[38] And certainly the dedication of the martyrium qualified as such an occasion. Along with a host of other religious and social aims, the initial *panegyris* was a public performance announcing for eternity the changes in roles of the members of

[36] Gregory of Nazianzus, *Epigrams* 156–8, in W. R. Paton, *The Greek Anthology, Books* VII–VIII, LCL 68 (Cambridge, MA: Harvard University Press, 2000), 468–9.

[37] Gregory of Nyssa, *Life of Saint Macrina*, Woods Callahan, *Saint Gregory of Nyssa: Ascetical Works*, 187.

[38] S. Dixon, 'Conflict in the Roman Family', in B. Rawson and P. Weaver (eds.), *The Roman Family in Italy: Status, Sentiment, Space* (Oxford: Clarendon Press, 1997), 149–68, at 151.

the great Cappadocian family, through the efficient distillation of liturgical ceremony.

Apparently at first the occasion was too much for Gregory to bear; he simply did not want to renegotiate these family roles in public at this grand, liturgical occasion in honour of the Forty Martyrs. The beautiful martyrium in Ibora, built by his mother's beneficence, was a public acknowledgement that his father and his brother Naucratius were now with the martyrs, and thus eventually would all the rest of his family be for eternity. As a young student, travelling back and forth from school in Caesarea, Gregory had experienced a short period of life in the world, separated for a while as he was from the intense changes and monastic rigours of family life at the estate in Annesi. But now at this inaugural *panegyris* dedicating the martyrium, he was confronted with the considerable changes his family had endured during the past ten years. At this point in Gregory's young life, he was coping to a different extent than his family was with their overwhelming Christian piety and extensive commitment to the ascetic life, all of which was about to be displayed at the inaugural festival.

It is clear from the text that Gregory initially had no desire to attend the *panegyris*. Even though Gregory recounts his memories two and a half decades later, time and his rhetorical style still do not hide his youthful apprehension and disquiet over the event at Ibora. His own recalcitrance could have stemmed from a combination of ambivalence, youthfulness, and sheer wilfulness. Though he softens his intractability by making excuses for his youth and his busy schedule, his own needs and desires emerge as his foremost concern, as he judges the events surrounding the new shrine in light of the impact they would have on him.[39] Such reactions fit the profile of an adolescent around the age of 19, and they make Gregory's text all the more gripping for his honesty.

Though he accepts full responsibility for not wanting to attend the *panegyris*, he nevertheless highlights Emmelia's role now as the *materfamilias*. Her extraordinary influence demonstrated both through her liturgical munificence in building the beautiful martyrium to the Forty Martyrs and also, most tellingly, by her requirement that he attend the *panegyris* was a public proclamation that the family had come through all their changes intact, with powerful social influence and solid commitment to

[39] 'πόῤῥω τε διάγοντα, καὶ ἔτι νέον ὄντα, κἀν τοῖς λαϊκοῖς ἀριθμούμενον. Οἷα δὲ φιλεῖ γίνεσθαι ἐπὶ πράγμασι κατεπείγουσιν, ἄσχολος ὢν', Gregory of Nyssa, *Encomium in xl martyres ii* [PG 46.784.56–785.35; here PG 46.785.1–5].

the Christian faith. It is useful here to remember that Gregory's religious upbringing was Emmelia's responsibility as a Christian *matrona*. Were her son Gregory to fail, Emmelia would be blamed, as his mother.

Gregory's recounting of the event that day is embedded in a sermon to the Forty Martyrs of Sebasteia, saints exceedingly popular in the regions of Cappadocia and Pontus, and indeed in all of Asia Minor. Though his digression into the powerful episode is brief, it is full of pathos, awe, and piety both for his mother and for the Forty Martyrs. Gregory starts by commending his mother's efforts at establishing the martyrium at Ibora, describing her as the 'assembler and the arranger of the festival for God'. Yet he does not equivocate on her instructions to him: she ordered him to be present for the festival.[40] He has no desire to go and responds to her request with a series of excuses to evade her insistence.

Gregory captures his voice as a young adolescent when he comments on his behaviour. Even with twenty-five years of hindsight, he still begins by begging off, justifying his conduct in several ways. Yet he expresses his own embarrassment at the mediocre initiative and lazy attitude he had as an adolescent. His first excuse is that he was away 'at some distance', probably at school in Caesarea. Second, he tells us he was young at the time, blaming his actions and inability to comprehend the gravity of the occasion on the folly of youth. When he confesses that he was still a layperson, he implies that he did not have sufficient commitment to Christianity to heed his mother's directive. Finally, he adds that he felt pressed upon by 'being busy', though in retrospect he labels himself 'senseless', we might even say in this context, 'stupid', as he 'sluggishly' responded to her command to attend the festival.[41] In sum, his admission to these lame excuses belies the retrospective composure he attempts to bring to the text. The intensity of the feelings he had experienced in the interaction with his mother many years before surface in the text as embarrassment, anxiety, and dissemblance. He is also setting up the reader for the possibility of a violent encounter since he is acknowledging that he is in need of correction

[40] 'αὕτη γὰρ ἦν ἡ κοσμοῦσα τὴν ἑορτήν, ἡ δὲ ἥκειν με πρὸς τὴν μετουσίαν τῶν δρομένων ἐκέλευσε . . .' I choose to translate κελεύω as 'order' here for the following reasons. Emmelia is not only the *materfamilias*, with all the responsibilities that the role requires, she is also the patron of the martyrium and 'the leader and organizer' (συνάγουσα καὶ κοσμοῦσα) of the festival. In light of these duties, it is reasonable that Emmelia ordered Gregory to attend. It does not mean that Emmelia was overbearing or that Gregory was hostile to her because of her authority. In fact, it means that she was within her rights to do so as widow and head of the household, which he clearly acknowledges when he states that he was 'slow to attend', Gregory of Nyssa, *Encomium in xl martyres ii* [PG 46.785.1–6].

[41] Gregory of Nyssa, *Encomium in xl martyres ii* [PG 46.785.1–6].

and on the brink of a new way of life. Whatever corrective altercation should come his way will be justified. It is through domestic violence that his new identity as a baptized Christian will take place.[42] How this is interpreted as 'domestic' violence will be explained shortly.

Some of the pressure he describes must have come from Emmelia. His writing is skilfully evasive in this section, as he switches the subject back and forth between himself and Emmelia, though he clearly accepts the blame for negative feelings and reactions to their rather argumentative interaction. If Emmelia had spent a considerable amount of money and time building the martyrium and organizing the *panegyris*, it is quite reasonable that she should react with some frustration and anger at Gregory's stubborn refusal to attend. Such dynamics come out when he says that he 'blamed her a little' when she refused to move the *panegyris* to a later date at his suggestion – a certain sign of the self-centredness of the adolescent Gregory![43] Nevertheless Emmelia proceeded to take Gregory in hand; she reorganized his priorities post-haste, compelling him to attend the inauguration festival of the martyrium to the Forty Martyrs she had commissioned.

Yet his recalcitrance did not cease once he reached Ibora. His actions there betray his lingering defiance against his mother's wishes. The audience hears Gregory's truthful voice of youth as he recounts the disagreement with his mother and then *merges* it with the violent experience he has at the *panegyris* at Ibora. Together these two incidences exemplify '"intimate violence", which may be particularly traumatic and mind-altering, given that the victim's [Gregory's] place of refuge and safety now provoked anxiety'.[44] When he arrived at the celebration, though he acknowledges that people were singing psalms in the vigil in the garden, distracted, bored, and tired he avoids the liturgical celebration and finds a shelter where he falls asleep.

He then recounts the vivid, violent waking vision he had in a dream, certainly understandable after his mother compelled him to attend the festival. The content of the dream certainly corroborates the contention that his being forced to attend the festival was 'mind-altering'. The Forty Martyrs appear at the gate of the garden of the martyrium complex, as if guarding it. As Gregory approaches the gate in the dream, they all arise at

[42] See Jamie Wood's chapter in this volume.

[43] 'βαρύτερον ὁ ἀνόητος ἐδεξάμην τὴν κλῆσιν, ὑπομεμψάμενος τῇ μητρὶ, ὅτι μὴ ἐις ἄλλον καιρὸν ὑπερέθετο τὴν πανήγυριν, ἀλλά με πολλῶν ἀποκινήσασα φροντίδων, μεθείλκυσε ταύτῃ, καὶ πρὸ μιᾶς τῆς συνόδου'. Gregory of Nyssa, *Encomium in xl martyres ii* [PG 46.785.6–9].

[44] S. Herzberger, *Violence within the Family* (Boulder, CO: Westview Press, 1996), 48.

once to protect it. Wielding their clubs, they attack Gregory in a furious rush. All except one of the Forty Martyrs beat him.[45]

When he awakens, he is overwhelmed by a sense of shame. Sorrowfully, he gradually realizes the mistakes he has made with regard to his mother's request. Even more, he perceives that the vision of the Forty Martyrs has delivered a message for him. Gregory responds with mournful wails, regretting his folly. As he approaches the reliquary of the Forty Martyrs, he pours out bitter tears of remorse in order that 'God might hold me in good favour and the holy soldiers might be gladdened by the forgiven misdemeanour'.[46] The vision of the Forty Martyrs reveals Gregory's belief in 'immanent justice'.[47] With the gift of retrospection, Gregory's remorsefulness characterizes him as the 'bad child'.[48] He both attributes responsibility for the beating he received to his own behaviour and is also completely convinced that the Forty Martyrs – and his mother – are completely justified.[49]

Following his description of the violent episode, Gregory adds one more layer of interpretive veneer to the mother–son interaction that redoubles what he wants us to know about his disagreement with Emmelia. What does he say she actually did to him? Since Gregory was in late adolescence, as we have discussed, it is unlikely that either parent would have hit him. And according to his text, she did not. Yet Gregory's desultory behaviour certainly would have provoked his mother to thrash him. Emmelia's displeasure at her son's grumbling equivocation comes through in these stalwart actions: she commanded him, refused to change the date of the festival, redirected his priorities, and dragged him off to the festival at Ibora.[50] It is in the dream where Gregory experiences the violent blows. Gregory counts on the foundation of these cultural cues, as he deftly adds the Forty Martyrs to the number of his familial intimates.

[45] 'πλῆθος ὤφθη στρατιωτῶν προσκαθήμενον τῇ εἰσόδῳ, ἀθρόον δὲ οἱ πάντες διαναστάντες, ῥάβδους ἐπανατεινόμενοι, καὶ ἀπειλητικῶς ἐφορμῶντες, οὐ συνεχώρουν τὴν εἴσοδον; ἔλαβον δ' ἂν καὶ πληγὰς, εἰ μή με εἷς, ὧς εδόκουν, φιλανθρωπότερος ἐξῃτήσατο', Gregory of Nyssa, *Encomium in xl martyres ii* [PG 46.785.15–21].

[46] Gregory of Nyssa, *Encomium in xl martyres ii* [PG 46.784.56–785.25].

[47] Herzberger, *Violence*, 50.

[48] "Ως δέ με ὁ ὕπνος ἀφῆκε, καὶ ἦλθον εἰς ἀναλογισμὸν τῆς ἐπὶ τῇ κλήσει πλημμελείας, ᾐσθόμην μὲν εἰς τί ἔφερεν ἡ τῶν στρατιωτῶν ἐπίφοβος ὀπτασία. πολλοῖς δὲ θρήνοις ὠδυρόμην τὴν ἐμαυτοῦ ματαιότητα'. Gregory of Nyssa, *Encomium in xl martyres ii* [PG 46.785.20–25].

[49] Gregory of Nyssa, *Encomium in xl martyres ii* [PG 46.785.20–25].

[50] Gregory of Nyssa, *Encomium in xl martyres ii* [PG 46.785.3–8], referring to Emmelia's strong stance: 'ἐκελεύσε; ὅτι μή εἰς ἄλλον καιρὸν ὑπερέθετο τήν πανήγυριν; ἀποκινήσασα φροντίδων; μεθείλκυσε ταύτῃ'.

In his sophisticated rhetorical style, he delicately skims over the story of the Maccabean mother, further justifying the entire event with Scriptural authority. In such a way he elegantly reinforces not only the similarities between the Forty Martyrs and the Maccabean Martyrs, he also fuses the Maccabean mother's virtue with Emmelia's, and glorifies the violence. Gregory explains that the Maccabean mother did not blame the tyrant Antiochus, but because of her 'extraordinary love for God considered all the tortures against her sons a benefaction'.[51] Gregory omits the gruesome details of the exceptional tortures the Maccabees endured. Rather what he stresses is the mother's fearless instruction to her boys: 'Accept death, so that in God's mercy I may get you back again along with your brothers.'[52] Though she does not inflict the tortures, her urgent instruction requires that her sons die for God through violent torture.

By briefly alluding to the Maccabean mother, Gregory further justifies Emmelia's purposeful command. Each mother is responsible for the religious conduct of her children; and in Gregory's view, such a responsibility can include beatings – though not by her own hand – if the situation warrants. And in his case it did. The Maccabean mother lends Biblical authority to Emmelia's role.[53] Both are widowed, and both have authority to subject their sons to whatever may be required for the glory of God, including violence. Though neither mother strikes her son, each of them may well have: such is part of the rhetorical rationale for introducing the Maccabean mother. Each mother unleashes a stream of instruction and action to correct her sons' behaviour. Each mothers' persistence is so ardent, so focused, and so intent that it paves the way for the physical violence inflicted on their respective sons for God's purpose. According to Gregory's rhetorical schema, both the Maccabean mother and Emmelia work in tandem with those who actually beat their sons.

What is more, the violent beating channelled through his mother's authority reorients Gregory. Not only is it necessary and justified, it is the means by which he commits himself wholly – like his family – to Christianity. Through the beating Gregory leaves his ambivalence and his

[51] Gregory of Nyssa, *Encomium in xl martyres ii* [PG 46.785.38–44].

[52] 2 Macc 7:29. See also 4 Macc 8:12–14; 14:11–12; 16:16–24.

[53] Interestingly, Gregory does not mention in this sermon the mother of one of the Forty Martyrs. One of the Forty did not die as soon as the others did, and the executioner spared him from being put on the cart with the other thirty-nine bodies. The mother railed against the executioner, urged her son on to martyrdom, and lifted him onto the cart. Gregory gives the full account in his other sermon on the Forty Martyrs. It would have been exceedingly interesting for him to have included her in this one. There would have been three mothers urging their sons.

independent ways of thinking and 'internalises the core beliefs and practices of the community'.[54]

Emmelia cannot be separated from the beating the Forty Martyrs gave Gregory. The actions of Emmelia and the Forty Martyrs are part of a continuum of one event. She is rhetorically instrumental in the beating, if not actually, since she had no legal authority to do so. When the Forty Martyrs clubbed Gregory, they honoured Emmelia as a devoted Christian mother. They also reinforced her authority in her pedagogical role as Christian teacher responsible for her son's salvation. And finally they worked for her as eternal family members. In fact, in terms of custom of the late antique family, the Forty Martyrs were providing the paternal correction that he needed so badly and that he lost long before. And cleverly, through this 'paternal correction' the Forty Martyrs take on familial intimacy. In this way the Forty Martyrs were much more effective than his father ever would have been.

Preaching the Beating: Violence and Meaning for the Faithful

Claiming the saints as spiritual kin was not new for Gregory of Nyssa. Indeed kinship with the martyrs was integral to their family *mythos*. Creating quasi-consanguineous relationships to certain martyrs distinguished their family from the masses of other Christians and gave them special advantages in the Church. Both Gregory and his brother Basil laid special claim to the great saint of Pontus, Gregory Thaumaturgus, as their 'spiritual great grandfather'.[55] They diligently preserved – and promulgated – the family lore that, as a child, their grandmother Macrina had learned Christian teachings from the Wonderworker himself.

There was one most outstanding spiritual ancestor in their family, the powerful and famous Saint Thecla of Iconium. In *Life of St Macrina*, Gregory's magnificent memorial to his sister Macrina, he discloses the secret of her birth. When Emmelia was in labour with her first child, she had a vision of a celestial figure who repeated three times that she should name her baby girl 'Thecla'. Though Emmelia wanted to comply in gratitude to St Thecla, the baby was named Macrina, after her grandmother. Nevertheless, Emmelia let the family know that Thecla, one of the

[54] See the Introduction to this volume by Kate Cooper and Jamie Wood.

[55] Basil of Caesarea, *Letters* 204, 207 [NPNF 8, 244, 248]; Gregory of Nyssa, *The Life of Gregory the Wonderworker* 14, 15 in M. Slusser, *St Gregory Thaumaturgus, Life and Works*, FOTC 98 (Washington, DC: Catholic University of America Press, 1998), 83–4; Limberis, *Architects*, 132–5.

greatest saints of Asia Minor, had established an intimate, familial connection to Macrina from the time of her birth. And 'Thecla' was the secret name of her daughter, as the saint had instructed.[56] As in the panegyric to the Forty Martyrs, Gregory's exploration of Saint Thecla's relationship to his sister 'allows us to see the process whereby Christian authors struggled with Christianity's relationship to the family unit'.[57]

What is even more significant, Thecla *qua* spiritual godmother of Macrina reveals that Gregory invested in the kinship with the martyrs two more theological 'patterns' which he uses to explain the dynamics of his very devout family. First, it is the saints, Thecla and the Forty Martyrs, who resolve family conflict. Like Gregory's conflict with Emmelia, Macrina herself experienced the tension of defying her parents' wishes at the death of her fiancé. But the *Life of Macrina* is concerned to present a unified picture of Gregory's family.[58] Macrina eventually convinces her mother and father that a life of perpetual virginity is her true desire, after they 'kept foisting eligible bachelors' on her, suggesting a 'turbulent reality' in the household.[59] Gregory assures his reader that the family squabbles were temporary, because Emmelia knew that Macrina's momentous decision was sanctioned by Saint Thecla herself, who gave Macrina her true identity.

Second, Gregory's 'saintly relatives', Thecla and the Forty Martyrs, resolve the family troubles by presenting themselves in a dream, or incubation. Widespread was the belief that when the martyr visited in a dream, especially at a *panegyris*, it proved the piety of the believer. Even more, it was an almost certain guarantee of an ensuing miracle, one of the chief sources of medical remedy in the fourth century.

Most people actively sought such a holy visitation in incubation. It is telling that Gregory precedes his own incubation with a miracle he witnessed at the shrine of the Forty Martyrs at Ibora. A lame soldier comes to the *panegyris* to implore the martyrs to cure his foot. He is quite fortunate to have the Forty Martyrs visit him in a dream and discuss the extent of his disability. In the morning the soldier finds his foot completely cured. The soldier's own elation and thankfulness spills over in Gregory's report and contextualizes his own incubation, soon to follow in the encomium, as a miracle.[60]

56 Gregory of Nyssa, *On Virginity* in Woods Callahan, (trans.), *Ascetical Works*, 164.
57 See James Corke-Webster's chapter in this volume.
58 See James Corke-Webster's chapter in this volume.
59 See James Corke-Webster's chapter in this volume.
60 H. Delehaye, *Les légendes hagiographiques* (Brussels: Société des Bollandistes, 1927), 145; Gregory of Nyssa, *Encomium in xl martyres ii* [PG 46.784.56–785.30].

With the Forty Martyrs, Thecla, and Gregory Thaumaturgus, Gregory established his family's connection to the martyrs that perpetuated an ancestry of sanctity, demonstrably direct and intimate. But unlike his accounts of the family's relationship to the Thaumaturgus and Thecla, the Forty Martyrs demonstrate their familial authority in an act of corrective punishment directed at him alone. Though Gregory's account is a highly sophisticated, well-crafted rhetorical narrative, it is also simultaneously a 'narrative of adolescence, providing the most poignant description of [his] attempt to account for violence'.[61] His remembrance of that time in his young life, so emotionally tense, rarefies the violence because it stems from his location in the family, the very foundation of his 'affiliations and sense of belongingness'.[62]

Gregory deems the violent beating as fully deserved. Moreover, the beating serves as proof that the Forty Martyrs were part of his family, on earth and in eternity, since he contextualizes the beating so seamlessly within the confines of family interactions. Their violent, familial intervention obliged him to change his life, which is further justification for the beating. Gregory not only accepts the corrective beating, he glorifies it as saintly violence. For him the beating is an honour, since the Forty Martyrs are saints and since they possess the privilege of familial intimacy.

By designating the Forty Martyrs as kin, Gregory's parenetic feats are twofold. First, the faithful know that martyr piety brings about salvation. Friendship with the martyrs is available to everyone, exemplified by random, through frequent miracles that come about at the festivals of the martyrs to those who are fervently devoted. But Gregory's second accomplishment is exclusionary. Though the faithful are urgently beckoned by the power of martyr piety, Gregory's claims on the Forty Martyrs carefully delineate his family from the wider Christian populace. The faithful would have no doubt that the Forty Martyrs acted as family intimates with their violent intervention in Gregory's own life. Through the narrative Gregory has appropriated the Forty Martyrs as relatives. The faithful can only admire such celestial kinship from afar. What is more, such special kinship between the martyrs and Gregory's family is demonstrably materialized for them in the beautiful martyrium. Only a great Christian matron of Emmelia's wealth and status could build a shrine to the martyrs adjacent to her family's crypt. In the faithful's hearing, the

[61] I. Arias, 'Complexities of Family Violence and the Need for Belongingness', in R. C. A. Klein (ed.), *Multidisciplinary Perspectives on Family Violence* (New York, NY: Routledge, 1998), 212–19, at 216.

[62] Arias, 'Complexities', 216.

Forty Martyrs were indeed imbricated in the great family. Thus Gregory succeeds in elevating his family's privilege through the martyr narrative, excluding ordinary Christians from such intimate, immediate access to the saints.

Conclusion

This essay began by remarking that the traumatic episode of the Forty Martyrs' thrashing of Gregory of Nyssa is both intriguing and disturbing because it is short and violent. Indeed this is also a useful way to conclude. Gregory's inclusion of this personal vignette in the longer panegyric to the Forty Martyrs would have captivated his credulous audience with a brief glance into the family dynamics of one of the most powerful families of Cappadocia in the fourth century. He counts on its brevity and biographical intimacy to spellbind them. Once he has the audience's attention, he assumes their knowledge of societal custom and law regarding family life to 'fill in' the code of proper behaviour between a widowed matron and her adolescent son. That context is one of hierarchical power and as such it presupposes that violence is completely within the bounds of late Roman family life, especially when the son's deportment challenged his mother's authority. As such the violence is both corrective and transformative. Though the conflict between Emmelia and Gregory is not over money or property, it is over something even more valuable to the family: their status as Christians. Although the violence may be disturbing to a contemporary reader, it is not so for Gregory or his fourth-century audience. A helpful way to sum up the multiple positive meanings Gregory gives to the beating he received from the Forty Martyrs is to remember the paramount characteristic of Christian rhetoric of late antiquity. Above all, Gregory's treatise is 'agonistic'.[63] Like other bishops of his time, Gregory 'was out to convince someone of something'. In this particular case involving the Forty Martyrs, Gregory succeeds at producing a single positive reading of violence, smoothing over all the potential hermeneutical differences depending on context and life situation. Gregory unflaggingly reiterates the positive construal he gives to violence in the following different ways. He deserves the beating from Emmelia and Forty Martyrs.

[63] M. M. Mitchell, 'Christian Martyrdom and the Dialect of the Holy Scriptures: The Literal, the Allegorical, the Martyrological', in R. S. Boustan, A. P. Jassen and C. J. Roetzel (eds.), *Violence, Scripture, and Textual Practice in Early Judaism and Christianity* (Leiden: Brill, 2010), 174–203, at 182.

Their violent intervention brings him sorrow over his disobedience to his mother and his inattentiveness to Christianity. In fact it acts as the foundational event that brought him to baptism a few years later. Violence is what likens Emmelia to the mother of the Maccabees. By extension the connection between Emmelia and the Maccabean mother gives a Biblical patina to his own family. And above all, violence enables Gregory to claim a kinship with the Forty Martyrs: as 'family' they can beat him, thus rarefying his family's position and authority over the ordinary faithful forever.

CHAPTER 3

Power, Faith, and Reciprocity in a Slave Society

Domestic Relationships in the Preaching of John Chrysostom

Jonathan Tallon

> A son, should he see his father living to a great age, is depressed [βαρύνεται].[1]

Preaching in Antioch and Constantinople in the last decades of the fourth century, the ascetic John Chrysostom (349–407) was known for telling it like it is, always willing to cast his listeners in an unflattering light – even the imperial family – if by doing so he could challenge them to reach a state of clear-eyed self-irony. Still, for all his mocking honesty, Chrysostom was no revolutionary. However incisive his critique of the power structures of civil society, self-knowledge, rather than social upheaval, was the end toward which his critique was aimed. This is nowhere truer than in his preaching on domestic relationships.

One of the most interesting aspects of Chrysostom's social preaching was his persistent interest in structuring human relationships according to the nature of faith itself. Yet this aspect of his preaching has not been adequately understood. While modern theological debate tends to understand 'faith' in a narrow cognitive sense, as the belief that something is true, or that God exists,[2] in the preaching of late antiquity 'faith' – *fides* in Latin or πίστις in Greek – tended to be framed in a relational rather than a cognitive sense. Concepts such as allegiance and fidelity or trust and obedience come far closer to capturing the essence of *fides* and πίστις than does the anachronistic modern concept of 'belief'.[3]

This contribution examines how preaching about πίστις served as an arena for evaluating power relationships in Chrysostom's preaching, with

[1] *Hom. Col.* 1 [PG 62.303]. Chrysostom compares varieties of human love with the greater love of the Spirit.

[2] Most online comments on 'religious' articles seem to assume this understanding, whether for or against Christianity.

[3] See T. Morgan, *Roman Faith and Christian Faith:* Pistis *and* Fides *in the Early Roman Empire and Early Churches* (Oxford: Oxford University Press, 2015), who argues for the importance of recognising the full semantic range of πίστις.

special attention to the domestic sphere. Chrysostom's emphasis on relations of faithful obedience within the household served to encourage his congregations in their faithful obedience toward God. At the same time, attention to the relationship between an individual and God cast a searching light on the reciprocal yet unequal relationships between husband and wife, father and son, and master and slave.

Sources

Chrysostom's preaching has attracted enormous interest in recent decades, both because of the great quantity of surviving material and because of its witness to social and religious identity, patterns of ancient churchgoing, and the role of the bishop.[4] Yet much remains to be done in assessing the interaction between the social and theological aspects of Chrysostom's preaching. Within the limited scholarship on Chrysostom's preaching on πίστις, there has been little interest in placing his theological reflection within the social and economic context of his time.[5]

While Chrysostom used many metaphors drawn from everyday life in his preaching on the Christian's relationship with God, it is his use of the domestic relationships within the household that is the focus here.

[4] See for example I. Sandwell, *Religious Identity in Late Antiquity: Greeks, Jews and Christians in Antioch* (Cambridge: Cambridge University Press, 2007); W. Mayer, 'John Chrysostom as Bishop: The View from Antioch', *Journal of Ecclesiastical History*, 55 (2004), 455–66; P. Allen and B. Neil (eds.), *Crisis Management in Late Antiquity (410–590 CE): A Survey of the Evidence from Episcopal Letters*, Supplements to Vigiliae Christianae 121 (Leiden: Brill, 2013); W. Mayer, 'Who Came to Hear John Chrysostom Preach? Recovering a Late Fourth-Century Preacher's Audience', *Ephemerides Theologicae Lovanienses*, 76 (2000), 73–87; J. L. Maxwell, *Christianization and Communication in Late Antiquity: John Chrysostom and His Congregation in Antioch* (Cambridge: Cambridge University Press, 2006); A. M. Hartney, *John Chrysostom and the Transformation of the City* (London: Duckworth, 2004); B. Leyerle, *Theatrical Shows and Ascetic Lives: John Chrysostom's Attack on Spiritual Marriage* (Berkeley, CA: University of California Press, 2001); M. M. Mitchell, *The Heavenly Trumpet: John Chrysostom and the Art of Pauline Interpretation* (London: Westminster John Knox Press, 2002); W. Mayer, 'Poverty and Generosity toward the Poor in the Time of John Chrysostom', in S. R. Holman (ed.) *Wealth and Poverty in Early Church and Society* (Grand Rapids, MI: Baker Academic, 2008), 140–58; R. L. Wilken, *John Chrysostom and the Jews: Rhetoric and Reality in the Late 4th Century* (Eugene, OR: Wipf and Stock, 2004).

[5] Studies include A. Kenny, 'Was St John Chrysostom a Semi-Pelagian?', *The Irish Theological Quarterly* 27 (1960), 16–29; M. F. Wiles, *The Divine Apostle: The Interpretation of St Paul's Epistles in the Early Church* (Cambridge: Cambridge University Press, 1967); D. Trakatellis, *Being Transformed: Chrysostom's Exegesis of the Epistle to the Romans* (Brookline, MA: Holy Cross Orthodox Press, 1992); P. E. Papageorgiou, 'A Theological Analysis of Selected Themes in the Homilies of St John Chrysostom on the Epistle of St Paul to the Romans', unpublished PhD dissertation, Catholic University of America (1995); R. Brändle, '"Gott wird nicht allein durch richtige Dogmen, sondern auch durch einen guten Lebenswandel verherrlicht." Zur Verhältnisbestimmung von Glaube und Werken bei Johannes Chrysostomus', *Theologische Zeitschrift*, 55 (1999), 121–36.

The household, οἶκος or *domus*, was a central institution in the Roman social order.[6] While *familia* denoted the dependents – whether slave or free – of a Roman *paterfamilias*,[7] *domus* was a wide-ranging term that could cover the physical premises belonging to the landowner,[8] but also the humans within the household constellation – including the wife, who was not under the *potestas* of her husband, as well as slaves, children, and others.[9] For the highest elite, the *domus* was effectively a family firm, covering all the economically active possessions and properties of both husband and wife.[10]

The *domus* was also the stage upon which the householder (*dominus* or *domina*) portrayed him- or herself to the public gaze, 'a testing ground for a man's ability to sustain relationships of reciprocity with dependants and allies'.[11] Each type of relationship in the household – between husband and wife, father and son, master and slave - involved asymmetrical reciprocity; a failure to elicit loyal obedience from subordinates could affect the fragile honour of the householder.[12] Although Chrysostom was by no means naïve regarding the potential for abuse in asymmetrical power relations, in the cases under discussion, I will argue, he put forward the view that asymmetrical power relations here on earth could – and should – make visible a crucial aspect of the divine relation to humanity.

6 K. Cooper, *The Virgin and the Bride: Idealized Womanhood in Late Antiquity* (Cambridge, MA: Harvard University Press, 1996), 14: 'The *domus*, along with its aspects of family and dynasty, was the primary unit of cultural identity, political significance, and economic production.'

7 Richard P. Saller, '*Familia*, *Domus*, and the Roman Conception of the Family', *Phoenix* 38 (1984), 336–55; Kate Cooper, 'Approaching the Holy Household', *Journal of Early Christian Studies*, 15 (2007), 131–42.

8 For the relationship between *domus* and 'family home', see J. Hillner, 'Domus, Family, and Inheritance: The Senatorial Family House in Late Antique Rome', *Journal of Roman Studies* 93 (2003), 129–45.

9 Saller, '*Familia*, *Domus*, and the Roman Conception of the Family', 342.

10 See, e.g., work on the Apion estates: J. Banaji, *Agrarian Change in Late Antiquity: Gold, Labour, and Aristocratic Dominance* (Oxford: Oxford University Press, 2001); P. Sarris, *Economy and Society in the Age of Justinian* (Cambridge: Cambridge University Press, 2006); R. Mazza, *L'archivio degli Apioni. Terra, lavoro e proprietà senatoria nell'Egitto tardoantico* (Bari: Munera, 2001).

11 K. Cooper, 'Closely Watched Households: Visibility, Exposure and Private Power in the Roman *Domus*', *Past & Present* 197 (2007), 3–33, at 7. Chrysostom uses this as leverage, for example, in discouraging drunkenness, *Hom. Rom.* 13 [PG 60.521].

12 I focus here on the male householder. Females could also be in positions of authority and power. For discussion of Chrysostom's critique of female slave-owners, see J. A. Schroeder, 'John Chrysostom's Critique of Spousal Violence', *Journal of Early Christian Studies*, 12 (2004), 413–42 at 422, 423.

Husband and Wife in Chrysostom's Preaching

In the fourth century, elite wives remained legally under the power of their fathers, which meant that they had some independence in their dealings with their husbands, especially if they came to the marriage with wealth. Through her conduct in the household, a wife played a significant role in establishing her husband's status, and as a supporting character in her husband's social performance she could reasonably be expected to make or break his success. Perhaps for this reason, Roman-period inscriptions emphasise faithfulness (πιστις or *fides*) among the virtues for married women, alongside marriage to one husband, piety, industriousness, harmony, and respectful obedience (*obsequium*).[13] An Athenian epitaph illustrates the importance of faithfulness,[14] and the sentiment is repeated in numerous inscriptions.[15]

When Chrysostom spoke of husbands and wives, it was often in the context of a divine marriage metaphor, with connotations of obedience and self-control (faithfulness in action), and also trust (faithfulness in belief).[16] Affirming traditional Roman marriage virtues, Chrysostom emphasised, especially in his preaching on Ephesians 5:21–33, that wives should be subject to husbands, abetting the public display of a harmonious marriage and household.[17] Other passages laud chastity, industriousness,

[13] See G. Williams, 'Some Aspects of Roman Marriage Ceremonies and Ideals', *Journal of Roman Studies* 48 (1958), 16–29; S. Treggiari, *Roman Marriage: Iusti Coniuges from the Time of Cicero to the Time of Ulpian* (Oxford: Clarendon Press, 1991). J. Evans Grubbs shows that these ideals persist into late antiquity, *Law and Family in Late Antiquity: The Emperor Constantine's Marriage Legislation* (Oxford: Oxford University Press, 1995). See also Cooper, *The Virgin and the Bride*, 17. For the close semantic overlap between *fides* and πίστις see Morgan, *Roman Faith and Christian Faith*, 7.

[14] Donald W. Bradeen (ed.), *The Athenian Agora. Volume 17* (Princeton, NJ: The American School of Classical Studies at Athens, 1974), no. 112, found at Athens, undated: 'Pōlla, faithful wife of Izmēnios Diradiōtos' (Πῶλλα Πιστη Ἰζμηνίου Διραδιώτου γυνή).

[15] Johannes Kirchner (ed.), *Inscriptiones Graecae II et III: Inscriptiones Atticae Euclidis anno posteriores*, second edition, 3 parts (Berlin: de Gruyter, 1913–40), part 3.1, no. 3850; part 3.2, nos. 8172, 8802. Otto Kern (ed.), *Inscriptiones Graecae, IX, 2. Inscriptiones Thessaliae* (Berlin: de Gruyter, 1908), no. 448. H. Engelmann and R. Merkelbach (eds.), *Die Inschriften von Erythrai und Klazomenai*, 2 vols. (Bonn: R. Habelt, 1972), no. 152. R. Heberdey, *Tituli Asiae Minoris, III. Tituli Pisidiae linguis Graeca et Latina conscripti, I. Tituli Termessi et agri Termessensis* (Vienna: Imperial Academy of Sciences, 1941), no. 819. H. Dessau (ed.), *Inscriptiones Latinae Selectae* (Berlin: Weidmann, 1906), Vol. II, part 2.

[16] A well-known scriptural metaphor, for example: Eph. 5:21–23; Rev. 21:9; Hosea.

[17] *Hom. Eph.* 20 [PG 62.136]. 'Harmony' would have had special resonances in Antioch, where a church was dedicated to *Homonoia-Concordia* by Constantine after reuniting the empire. E. H. Kantorowicz, 'On the Golden Marriage Belt and the Marriage Rings of the Dumbarton Oaks Collection', *Dumbarton Oaks Papers*, 14 (1960), 14, shows the continuing importance of harmony as a marital virtue during the Christianisation of the empire.

and affection – the same marital virtues that had been traditional in Roman culture for hundreds of years.[18] When Chrysostom uses πίστις and its derivatives in the context of marriage, it is also in its traditional marital sense of sexual fidelity.

As bishop of Constantinople, in 402 and returning from several months' absence from the capital,[19] he praises his congregation, telling them they are like a sensible wife, so that he can be 'confident of your good intent, your love, your faithfulness, your goodwill [τῇ γνώμῃ, τῇ ἀγάπῃ, τῇ πίστει, τῇ εὐνοίᾳ], because I know that my wife is a woman who strives to be sensible [σωφρονοῦσαν]'.[20]

Chrysostom regularly makes use of marriage as a metaphor for the Christian's relationship with Christ, and places πίστις within this context, as the following examples demonstrate. In particular, the dowry the bride brings Christ is regularly described as πίστις or obedience, with Chrysostom sometimes switching between the two in the same sermon.

In the example that follows, Chrysostom is preaching on Romans 8:24: 'For we are saved by hope':

> So what saved you? Only hoping in God, and trusting him [καὶ πιστεῦσαι αὐτῷ] about what he has promised and given, and you have nothing more to bring ... So don't say to me, yet again hope, yet again what we can expect, yet again faith [πάλιν πίστις]. For in the beginning you were saved like this, and you brought only this dowry to the bridegroom [καὶ ταύτην τὴν προῖκα εἰσήνεγκας τῷ νυμφίῳ μόνον].[21]

Chrysostom uses here the way that πίστις can be situated in the marriage relationship to good effect, comparing it to the bride's dowry. Marriage, trust, and faithfulness are intertwined in seeking to transform the Christian's relationship with God.

It is in preparation for baptism that foundations of faith are addressed and patterns laid down for thought and behaviour. It is striking that Chrysostom reaches for the marriage metaphor directly from the start of his baptismal instructions:

[18] See, for example, *Hom. Gen.* [PG 54.443]. See also John Chrysostom, *Quales ducendae sint uxores (= De laude Maximi)* [PG 51:230–31].

[19] See J. N. D. Kelly, *Golden Mouth: The Story of John Chrysostom – Ascetic, Preacher, Bishop* (London: Duckworth, 1995), 181–3.

[20] John Chrysostom, *De regressu* 3, Antoine Wenger (ed.), Revue des études byzantines 19 (Paris: Institut Français d'Études Byzantines, 1961), translation adapted from Wendy Mayer and Pauline Allen, *John Chrysostom* (London: Routledge, 2000), 99.

[21] *Hom. Rom.* 14 [PG 60.532].

> This is a time for joy and gladness of the spirit. Behold, the days of our longing and love, the days of your spiritual marriage [τῶν πνευματικῶν γάμων], are close at hand. To call what takes place today a marriage would be no blunder . . .[22]

Chrysostom expands on the metaphor, inviting his hearers to identify themselves as a prospective bride, and outlines the wealth and kindness of Christ the bridegroom.[23] Continuing the metaphor, he explores the nature of the dowry contract:[24]

> What, then, is the dowry contract [τὰ προικῷα γραμματεῖα] in this marriage? Nothing but the obedience [ἡ ὑπακοὴ] and the agreement which will be made [αἱ συνθῆκαι αἱ μέλλουσαι] with the Bridegroom.[25]

Here the dowry brought by the bride is obedience; the 'agreement' is a reference to the declaration made during the baptism service, renouncing Satan and entering into Christ's service.[26] The metaphor implies that the Christian will forsake everything else, and be faithful and obedient to Christ. Marriage and πιστις-related language are combined in other baptismal homilies. Chrysostom can declare 'listen, faithful ones [οἱ πιστοί], to what kind of bridegroom [νυμφίῳ] you are coming' to encourage modest behaviour.[27] In a separate homily, the connection is made more explicitly. Chrysostom begins with an extended metaphor of the bridegroom and bride:

> Do you want to learn what she [the bride] is called? She is called faithful and holy [βούλει καὶ τὸ ὄνομα αὐτῆς μαθεῖν; πιστὴ καλεῖται καὶ ἁγία]. The bridegroom is called faithful and a saint.[28]

Later in the homily, the preacher again compares the declaration with the dowry that the bride brings, seeing it also as a contract with the bridegroom.

[22] *Illum. catech.* 1.1, Antoine Wenger (ed.), SC 50 (Éditions du Cerf, 1958), 108; P. W. Harkins (trans.), *St John Chrysostom: Baptismal Instructions*, ACW 31 (New York: Paulist Press, 1963), 23.

[23] *Illum. catech.* 1.15.

[24] For the background to the arrangement of marriages and dowries, see Evans Grubbs, '"Pagan" and "Christian" Marriage', 365.

[25] *Illum. catech.* 1.16, Harkins (trans.), *St John Chrysostom: Baptismal Instructions*, 29.

[26] See, e.g., *Illum. catech.* 2.17–21, which uses the same imagery in a separate series of baptismal instructions, John Chrysostom, *Catechesis ultima ad baptizandos*, A. Papadopoulos-Kerameus (ed.), *Varia Graeca sacra* (St Petersburg: Kirschbaum, 1909), 173.

[27] John Chrysostom, *Catechesis de juramento*, Papadopoulos-Kerameus (ed.), *Varia Graeca sacra*, 164.

[28] John Chrysostom, *Catechesis ultima ad baptizandos*, Papadopoulos-Kerameus (ed.), *Varia Graeca sacra*, 169.

The dowry metaphor is repeated in another homily, *Homilia de capto Eutropio.*[29] Chrysostom addresses the dowry that the bride is to bring:

> What does the bride contribute [εἰσφέρει]? Let us see. What then will you bring, so that you won't be without a dowry [ἄπροικος]? 'What do I have' she says, 'to bring from altars, from the steam of sacrifices, from demons? What do I have to bring?' What? Your will and faithfulness [Γνώμην καὶ πίστιν].[30]

Chrysostom continues by arguing that the bride is to abandon her parents (by implication, pagan gods) and be united to Christ her lover. The πίστις that the bride will bring means abandoning other gods and being faithful to Christ. Again, Chrysostom proceeds to link this to obedience, using them as synonyms.[31]

Declaring that the Church (and the individual Christian) was the bride of Christ encouraged congregations to be loyal to their bishop at the same time as reinforcing the importance of a wife's faithfulness, obedience, and respect in a context where wives had legal and financial opportunities for freedom from their husband's control. Faithfulness to husband, bishop, and God were intertwined.

Father and Son in Chrysostom's Preaching

Chrysostom treats the father–son relationship differently from the husband–wife, in part because of the different balance of power, but also because of his theological agenda. A wife had some freedom of manoeuvre in her relationship with her husband; she could divorce him and walk away with her own wealth, though any offspring would remain within the father's *familia.* Nonetheless, her children owed her *reverentia* and *obsequium*, just as they did their father.[32]

Expectations for sons were different to those for wives. Legally, father–son relationships were governed by *patria potestas.*[33] Socially, a faithful son

[29] John Chrysostom, *Homilia de capto Eutropio* [PG 52.395–414]. For dating, see A. Cameron, 'A Misidentified Homily of Chrysostom', *Nottingham Medieval Studies*, 32 (1988), 34–48. The homily is also discussed by Kelly, *Golden Mouth*, 153–6.

[30] John Chrysostom, *Homilia de capto Eutropio* [PG 52.412].

[31] Compare two different episodes in John Chrysostom, *Homilia de capto Eutropio* 16, 17 [PG 52.412, 414].

[32] See R. P. Saller, 'Symbols of Gender and Status Hierarchies in the Roman Household', in S. R. Joshel and S. Murnaghan (eds.), *Women and Slaves in Greco-Roman Culture: Differential Equations* (London: Routledge, 2001), 86.

[33] The possible origins of *patria potestas* are discussed by J. A. Crook, 'Patria Potestas', *Classical Quarterly*, 17 (1967), 113–22.

exhibiting πίστις was expected to show *pietas* and *obsequium* to his father; the father was expected to show *pietas* to and exercise *auctoritas* over his son.[34] A son could obtain independence from the father either through emancipation or, in a more limited sense, through the grant of a *peculium*. Alternatively, he could attach himself to the imperial civil service, which would remove him from the father's immediate control, ensure the avoidance of future curial and tax duties, and (as a notionally military office) furnish a legally independent wage, the *peculium castrense*.[35] In the fourth century an ambitious young man might well do better to move from his provincial hometown and join the imperial civil service than to remain and, as a town councillor, stand liable for tax demands.[36] The authority of the now-distant father would of course be considerably weakened. Nonetheless, the threat of disinheritance remained considerable, as can be seen in the experience of Gregory of Nazianzus, forced to return to his father or face disinheritance,[37] as well as Libanius, in his orations, bemoaning the fact that fathers failed to use this threat frequently enough.[38]

The father–son relationship was further destabilised by the rising popularity of Christianity, which offered a potential resource for justifying rebellion against parents by preaching moral independence and asceticism.[39] Whilst Christianity offered some reassurance that obedience was still required, sometimes this was redirected to a spiritual father such as a bishop.[40]

Given the designation of Jesus as the Son of God, it might be assumed that Jesus' faithfulness to God (and vice versa) would be used as a model

[34] See G. Nathan, *The Family in Late Antiquity: The Rise of Christianity and the Endurance of Tradition* (London; New York, NY: Routledge, 2000), 143–4. An overview of *patria potestas* in late antiquity is given by A. Arjava, 'Paternal Power in Late Antiquity', *Journal of Roman Studies*, 88 (1998), 147–65.

[35] See Arjava, 'Paternal Power', 149–50.

[36] Achieving senatorial status (*honorati*) through the imperial civil service gave exemption from tax on returning home. For opportunities to accumulate wealth in the imperial civil service, see C. Kelly, *Ruling the Later Roman Empire*, Revealing Antiquity 15 (Cambridge, MA: Harvard University Press, 2004). For the changing fourth-century economy, see Banaji, *Agrarian Change*.

[37] Gregory of Nazianzus, *De vita sua* 500–15, C. Jungck (ed.), *Gregor von Nazianz. De vita sua* (Heidelberg: Winter, 1974). See J. A. McGuckin, *St Gregory of Nazianzus: An Intellectual Biography* (New York, NY: St Vladimir's Seminary Press, 2001), 15.

[38] Libanius is complaining about student behaviour, a perennial problem for educators. Libanius, *Orationes*, 62.24, R. Foerster (ed.), *Libanii opera*, 12 vols. (Leipzig: Teubner, 1903–27), 342–83. See Jamie Wood's chapter in this volume for more on Libanius' problems with his pupils.

[39] Numerous Christian texts suggest to young men that they listen to conscience above their father, K. Cooper, *The Fall of the Roman Household*, (Cambridge: Cambridge University Press, 2007), 28.

[40] Alluded to in Cooper, 'Closely Watched Households'.

for Christians to follow. But Chrysostom and others generally avoid doing this.[41] One of the few occasions where Chrysostom does is in his handling of Heb. 3:1–2:

> What does 'being faithful [Πιστὸν ὄντα] to the one who made him' mean? It means this: being caring, guarding those belonging to him, and not letting them be blown away.[42]

Chrysostom is therefore occasionally prepared to attribute qualities like obedience or faithfulness to Christ (with the proviso that they refer to the incarnate nature), but this is infrequent in his preaching, and qualified when it appears.[43]

Chrysostom does make use of the metaphor of God as heavenly father and Christians as his children, however. When he does this, in addition to the inheritance and honour, it can also be used to emphasise obedience. This can be seen in Chrysostom's preaching on Romans 4:17, when he describes Abraham as the father of all who have faith:

> For what does he say? '... in the presence of God in whom he trusted [Κατέναντι οὗ ἐπίστευσε Θεοῦ]'. He means something like this. Just as God is not God of just a part, but father of everyone [ἀλλὰ πάντων πατὴρ], so also is [Abraham]. And again, just as God is father not according to a natural relationship [οὐ κατὰ τὴν φυσικὴν συγγένειαν], but according to the affinity of faith [κατ' οἰκείωσιν πίστεως], so also is he. For obedience makes him father of us all [ἡ γὰρ ὑπακοὴ ποιεῖ πατέρα πάντων ἡμῶν].[44]

The relationship that human beings can claim to both God and Abraham is not through physical descent, but through faith (πίστεως). Chrysostom links this with obedience, and with the father–children relationship. He is content to make the link between πίστις, obedience, and sonship, so long as it steers clear of the relationship between Christ and God the Father.[45]

But along with other pro-Nicenes of the period, Chrysostom made only limited use of the analogy of human father–son relationships in speaking of the relationship between God the Father and Son.[46] Where the analogy

41 See, for example, how Heb. 3:1–2 is handled in Athanasius, *Orationes Contra Arianos* 2, K. Metzler and K. Savvidis (eds.), *Athanasius: Werke*, Band I. Die dogmatischen Schriften, Erster Teil, 2. Lieferung (Berlin: de Gruyter, 1998). See also I. G. Wallis, *The Faith of Jesus Christ in Early Christian Traditions* (Cambridge: Cambridge University Press, 1995), 200–9.

42 *Hom. Heb.* 5 [PG 63.50]. 43 See also *Hom. Heb.* 8 [PG 63.69].

44 *Hom. Rom.* 8 [PG 60.460].

45 Cf. his willingness to praise biblical characters for their obedience to their fathers, e.g., Joseph, *Hom. Gen.* 61 [PG 54:525].

46 This links to the New Testament *pistis Christou* controversy, reignited by the landmark study by R. B. Hays, *The Faith of Jesus Christ: The Narrative Substructure of Galatians 3:1–4:11*, new edn.

was used, it was kept to the sphere of honour and inheritance, and kept apart from issues of faithfulness, loyalty, or obedience, lest these imply a diminution in the honour or equality of God the Son.[47] His reluctance to ascribe πίστις to Christ as a son limits the metaphor's power.

Master and Slave in Chrysostom's Preaching

We now turn to the master–slave relationship. Chrysostom's preaching interventions in and use of the master–slave dynamic are part of a varied pattern of responses of preachers within early Christianity. Kimberley Flint-Hamilton traces some of these response.[48] She identifies three facets: that slaves should accept their lot in life; uncritical acceptance of slave stereotypes; and (occasionally) arguments against slavery. All three facets can be found in Chrysostom.

Flint-Hamilton notes that even in early documents such as the Didache slaves are urged to be obedient to their earthly masters as being an image of God.[49] She argues that when the master was present, slaves were 'to consider themselves in the physical presence of God. When they look at the master, they are to think of God.'[50] Chris de Wet, in this volume, highlights what he terms a doulological discourse, as boundaries between the social reality and the metaphor blur, leading to a justification for punitive violence against slaves.

Flint-Hamilton argues that Chrysostom offers both negative stereotypes and a more radical trajectory. The particular example of negative stereotyping she gives is misleading, but sheds light on Chrysostom's attitudes and approach.[51] Preaching on 1 Tim. 6:1–2, Chrysostom argues that masters are faithful [πιστοί], giving more to slaves than vice versa, and that slaves ought to honour their masters. This leads him to compare the service human masters give to God – the ultimate faithful master – with

(Grand Rapids, MI: Eerdmans, 2002). For lack of interest in using the Father–Son analogy, see Nathan, *The Family in Late Antiquity*, 146.

47 Intriguingly, McGuckin, *St Gregory of Nazianzus*, 19, 281 argues that the doctrine of the equality of the Son with the Father, as articulated in Gregory of Nazianzus' conception of his relationship with his own father, undermined the notion of *patria potestas*.

48 K. Flint-Hamilton, 'Images of Slavery in the Early Church: Hatred Disguised as Love?', *Journal of Hate Studies*, 2 (2003), 27–45. P. Garnsey, *Ideas of Slavery from Aristotle to Augustine* (Cambridge: Cambridge University Press, 1996) also traces antique attitudes to slavery, arguing that the Aristotle's theory of natural slavery provided ideological backing for owners, and cautions against assuming that Stoics were against this theory.

49 *The Didache* 4:11, M. W. Holmes (ed.), *The Apostolic Fathers* (Grand Rapids, MI: Baker Academic, 2007).

50 Flint-Hamilton, 'Images of Slavery', 30.

51 Flint-Hamilton, 'Images of Slavery', 41.

the service the slaves offer, to the detriment of the masters. Sweeping aside any objections about devious household slaves [μὴ γάρ μοι τοὺς μοχθηροὺς εἴπῃς τῶν οἰκετῶν], Chrysostom showcases both his knowledge of the stereotype and (in this case) his rejection of it.[52]

Flint-Hamilton finds a more positive trajectory in a homily of Chrysostom's on 1 Corinthians. Here, Chrysostom argues that slavery was established as a result of sin, that Christ has ended this period of history, and that masters need no slaves. Chrysostom will allow them at most a couple; the remaining slaves should be taught trades and freed.[53] This does come close to condemning slavery. But although a concern for slave welfare is evident, along with a theology suggesting that slavery should end, in practice the concern is for the masters avoiding what de Wet terms 'social gluttony'.[54] Even if the call for masters to train up slaves in a trade prior to manumission is progressive, de Wet reminds us that Chrysostom does not consistently encourage slaves to seek freedom.[55]

Chrysostom's attitudes are also revealed in his preaching on Philemon. Commenting on Phlm. 2 – 'to the church in your household' – Chrysostom argues that Paul writes this to include both slaves and master in an acceptable way:

> Because the name 'church' does not leave the masters [τοὺς δεσπότας] irritated, if they are counted with the household slaves [οἰκέταις]. For the church does not know of a distinction between master and slave, but distinguishes one person from another by good actions or sins. So when in church, don't be irritated when your slave [δοῦλος] is greeted with you.[56]

This demonstrates both Chrysostom's radical side – all are equal in church – but also his conservative side: the behaviour is specific to church, and there is no hint that society should change.

Chrysostom's views are also shown in his preaching on Tit. 2:9–10. Chrysostom first argues that it condemns those seeking to separate slaves from masters, affirming traditional property rights.[57] Having argued that

52 *Hom. 1 Tim.* 16 [PG 62.589–90]. 53 *Hom. 1 Cor.* 40 [PG 61.353–54].

54 C. de Wet, 'John Chrysostom on Slavery', *Studia Historiae Ecclesiasticae*, 34 (2008), 1–13.

55 *Hom. 1 Cor.* 19 [PG 61.156], where he comments on 1 Cor. 7:21, explaining why the verse should not be interpreted as meaning slaves should seek freedom.

56 *Hom. Phlm.* 1 [PG 62:705], citing Gal. 3.28 as support.

57 Driven by concern for the reputation of the church; some might have encouraged slaves to flee to the desert to become monks. See Socrates, *Historia ecclesiastica* 2.43, P. Maraval and P. Périchon (eds.), *Socrate de Constantinople, Histoire ecclésiastique*, SC 477, 493, 505–6 (Paris: Éditions du Cerf, 2004–7).

slaves who serve their masters well witness to the gospel, he appears to descend into stereotyping:

> For even among themselves, and everywhere, this is conceded: how the race of slaves [τὸ τῶν δούλων γενος] is reckless, hard to change, stubborn, not very much suited to teaching in virtue . . .[58]

However, he lays the blame for this not on the nature of the slaves themselves but on the negligent upbringing from their masters, who he claims only worry about slave morality when they are directly affected by bad behaviour. Because of this, good slaves are rare – and because they are rare they make good witnesses. Thus Chrysostom protects the institution of slavery in practice, and uses the tropes of the lazy and loyal slave to encourage better supervision from masters and better service from slaves. As Garnsey points out, 'There was no need to bring force into play against slaves, if they could be persuaded that virtue was of greater value than legal status and was within their grasp.'[59]

The loyalty of slaves was thus a virtue to be encouraged. Chrysostom repeatedly uses πίστις and related words to make his point. For example, preaching against wealth, Chrysostom compares it to a faithless slave:

> For nothing is so faithless [ἄπιστον] as wealth, which I have often said, and never stop saying, for it is a senseless runaway slave, a house-slave with no loyalty [ὅτι δραπέτης ἐστὶν ἀγνώμων, οἰκέτης πίστιν οὐκ ἔχων] . . .[60]

On the positive side, he quotes Matthew 24:45 ('Who then is the faithful and wise slave [Τίς ἄρα ὁ πιστὸς δοῦλος καὶ φρόνιμος]?') in a number of different contexts, exploiting the image of the faithful slave.[61]

The same easy use of the metaphor in connection with faith can be found in Chrysostom's preaching on Romans 1:5, and the 'obedience of faith' [ὑπακοὴν πίστεως]. Chrysostom links this to a household metaphor including slave and master:

> Notice the politeness of the household slave [οἰκέτου]. He wants nothing to be of himself, but everything to belong to the Master [τοῦ Δεσπότου].[62]

This is part of a repeated pattern where Chrysostom uses the slave–master relationship as a metaphor for the Christian's relationship with God.[63]

58 *Hom. Tit.* 4 [PG 62.685]. 59 Garnsey, *Ideas of Slavery*, 67. 60 *Stat.* 2 [PG 49.39].

61 For example, *Sacr.* 2, A.-M. Malingrey (ed.), SC 272 (Paris: Éditions du Cerf, 1980). See also *Hom. Matt.* 77 [PG 58.705], *Hom. Philip.* 13 [PG 62.280] and *De Mutatione Nominum* [PG 51:124].

62 *Hom. Rom.* 1 [PG 60.398].

63 Note also Chrysostom's regular use of ὁ Δεσπότης for Christ (over sixty times in this way in his homilies on Romans).

Because it is so easy to move between slave–master relationships and Christian–God relationships, injunctions to obey God faithfully without question also imply that masters on earth should receive the same treatment.

The preaching raised some challenges for masters. First, there is the challenge to do without most of their slaves; with fewer slaves comes the implication of potentially losing status in the eyes of others.[64] Secondly, there is the challenge to be a good, faithful master who cares properly for his slaves. This challenge is proposed both directly and implicitly through the picture of God as master of all.

Ultimately, the motif of the successful slave–master relationship took into account the possibility of failure, whether in the form of a negative relationship, or the slave's running away altogether. Moses Finley describes the concern as 'almost an obsession in the sources', with chains, collars, notices of rewards, the involvement of the authorities, and paid slave-catchers as examples of this obsession.[65] In his reading of Paul's Letter to Philemon, for example, Chrysostom can assume that Onesimus is a runaway slave.[66]

The slave could also exercise limited power within the household itself. The actions of the slaves reflected on the householder; the power lay in their ability to help polish the owner's reputation or tarnish it through 'incompetence' or lack of respect. Bradley notes that 'the frequency with which servile idleness is referred to must be taken as a firm indication of its prevalence'.[67]

In part, the tension over whether a slave would accept his or her role was resolved by ascribing a fictive kinship between slave and master after baptism. For the slave, this might have produced mixed emotions. A person with no honour was now equal to his or her master. Yet daily life would remain mostly unchanged. There is a challenging tension between the spiritual and legal status of the slave.

In his homilies on Philemon, Chrysostom emphasises the equality of honour (ἰσοτιμία) that Onesimus is given through Paul claiming him as

[64] Chrysostom saw the slave entourage as being a form of conspicuous consumption. See, e.g., his comments on the rich surrounding themselves with herds of slaves [ἀνδραπόδων ἀγέλας] to impress others: *Hom. Jo.* 28 [PG 59.166].

[65] M. I. Finley, *Ancient Slavery and Modern Ideology* (Harmondsworth: Penguin, 1980), 111–13. See also S. Llewelyn, 'P. Harris I 62 and the Pursuit of Fugitive Slaves', *Zeitschrift für Papyrologie und Epigraphik*, 118 (1997), 245–50.

[66] *Hom. Phlm.*, Argumentum [PG 62.701].

[67] K. R. Bradley, *Slaves and Masters in the Roman Empire* (Oxford: Oxford University Press, 1984), 32. See also K. Hopkins, 'Novel Evidence for Roman Slavery', *Past & Present*, 138 (1993), 3–27.

his son. As de Wet notes, Chrysostom sees Paul as deliberately giving Onesimus honour through this fictive kinship.[68] Chrysostom also emphasises that Paul asks Philemon to receive Onesimus back as a brother, again stressing the equality of honour. Chrysostom then addresses the masters, pointing out that masters and slaves are brothers in the eyes of God: 'Look how he is honouring us. He calls our slaves his own brothers, and friends and fellow-heirs.'[69] However, the lesson for masters is limited: the fictive kinship should encourage them to treat their slaves better, to be more forgiving.

The same tensions are visible when Chrysostom addresses female owners and their slaves, commenting on Eph. 4:31. He first advises female owners to avoid shameful anger and shouting. He allows that slaves sometimes need to be beaten (though not too harshly).[70] He also agrees that his congregation might truthfully argue that slaves are difficult to deal with, but points out alternatives to physical punishment in order to correct (ῥυθμισαι) them. Here he introduces the idea of kinship:

> She has become your sister, so far as faith is concerned [ἀδελφή σου γέγονεν, ἄν ᾖ πιστή].[71]

Chrysostom here reinforces the negative stereotypes, allows for beatings, and yet also tries to temper the relationship between slaves and owners as spiritual siblings.[72]

We can now see how fictive kinships for slaves led to only a slight adjustment in the status quo. Slaves were required to obey their masters, and expected to show faithfulness and loyalty (πίστις). The preaching of Chrysostom encouraged masters to see slaves as their kin, at least within the church building. Within the household, though, the move wasn't to treat slaves as brothers and sisters, but as sons and daughters, even if only in certain regards. This move was relatively painless for masters to make. Children, like slaves, were part of the *familia* and under the *patria potestas* of the master. Children, like slaves, were expected to show πίστις –

[68] *Hom. Phlm.* 2 [PG 62.710]. Chris de Wet, 'Honour Discourse in John Chrysostom's Exegesis of the Letter to Philemon', in D. Francis Tolmie (ed.), *Philemon in Perspective: Interpreting a Pauline Letter* (Berlin: de Gruyter, 2010), 317–31. Recently, U. Roth, 'Paul, Philemon, and Onesimus', *Zeitschrift für die Neutestamentliche Wissenschaft und die Kunde der älteren Kirche*, 105 (2014), 102–30, argued that Paul was co-owner of Onesimus, maintaining simultaneously Onesimus' slavery in the flesh with brotherhood in the Lord.

[69] *Hom. Phlm.* 2 [PG 62.711]. [70] *Hom. Eph.* 15 [PG 62.109].

[71] *Hom. Eph.* 15 [PG 62.109].

[72] See also *Hom. Eph.* 22 [PG 62.155]. Chrysostom acknowledges the paradox of the slave being a brother in God's eyes yet called to obey their human master.

obedience and loyalty – to the *paterfamilias*. The main change required of owners was to treat slaves better, not only with *aequitas* but also with *pietas* and *iustitia*. Angry owners were urged to find different ways to correct (ῥυθμισαι) their slaves – the same term that Chrysostom also uses in discussing how to bring up sons.[73] However, owners were not expected to treat slaves like sons in other, important respects. While the analogy from Son of God to Christian was limited to honour and inheritance, the analogy for slaves becoming fictive family members missed out these elements entirely. In this sense, fictive kinship remained precisely that: fiction. Chrysostom never pressed the potentially challenging part of such analogies. Chrysostom's main revolution is a quiet encouragement for masters not to treat their slaves quite so badly. In the changing world of the late fourth century, with the power dynamics of traditional relationships changing, this was a relatively comforting message for the elite.

Conclusion

Given its social importance, the household naturally figures largely in Chrysostom's preaching. In this volume, Blake Leyerle shows that Chrysostom's makes strategic use of fear in preaching, while Chris de Wet demonstrates how he justifies the punishment of slaves for curative purposes. Here, I suggest that πίστις was an additional tool for social control.

Regulating the Christian household was a delicate task. The elite male *paterfamilias* might be concerned about a wife who could leave him, taking her wealth; a son who might be out of his control through work in the imperial civil service (and perhaps morbidly waiting for an inheritance); a slave might be a would-be runaway. Christianity exacerbated these concerns by producing an ideology which could justify transferring obedience from husband, father, or master to the heavenly groom, father and Lord of all, combined with a message of equality and freedom for all in Christ. To reach an elite congregation required neither denying the ultimate authority of God, nor frightening the horses too much. This delicate negotiation informs how Chrysostom uses household analogies in his preaching, and the role of πίστις within this.

With regard to husband and wife, Chrysostom can adopt the conventional Roman view of marriage; the analogy of heavenly groom and bride works well. Here, πίστις plays its traditional role as a reciprocal term: the wife is faithful to the husband in heart, mind, and body, just as the

[73] See, for example, *Inan.* 245, 276, 349.

Christians must be faithful to God (for example, by not worshipping other gods, joining heretical sects, or questioning the bishop). Similarly, the husband is faithful towards his wife, reliably looking after her. Through this rhetoric, Chrysostom reinforces not only the relationship with God, but also the authority of the bishop as the Church's – and God's – representative. Yet the reinforcement works the other way as well. The duty of the wife to be faithful to, to respect, and to obey her husband is reinforced. The rhetoric buttresses the position of the elite husband; not to be faithful and obedient to your husband is not to be faithful to God.

With regard to father and son, Chrysostom neglected the seemingly obvious analogy of πίστις, faithfulness from son to father, reflecting that between God the Son and God the Father. The fear of giving ammunition to those attacking the divinity of the Son ensured that the focus of the analogy centred on honour and inheritance, two aspects in which slaves, as spiritual 'sons', did not share. There is still an expectation of obedience, seen when Christians are treated as spiritual children of God, which in turn leads to a similar dynamic to that of husband and wife: the spiritual and physical aspects mutually reinforce the requirement of obedience, whether to God or to a human father. However, the rejection of the analogy using Christ as son limits the power of this reinforcement: an elite *paterfamilias* would still face the economic and social tensions straining his relationship with his son; the son might still focus on the divine Son's equality of honour and power with the heavenly Father, and the supremacy of God over family, to go his own way.

With regard to master and slave, things become more complex. The relationship in antiquity was characterised by mutual suspicion and fear. Nevertheless, tropes of good masters and good slaves existed, and Chrysostom leverages these in his analogy of God as heavenly master and Christians as his earthly slaves. The ideal slave was loyal and obedient; the ideal master considered the well-being of his slaves. Here too πίστις acted as a reciprocal term for the relationship, indicating that the Christian ought to be completely loyal, obedient to and unquestioning of the heavenly master, even as God in return showed his care. However, the contrast between spiritual freedom in Christ and real-life subjection remained as a source of unresolved tension. Here, Chrysostom played it relatively safe, reassuring owners that slaves should not be freed against the owners' will. His exhortations to do with fewer slaves – not any – had more to do with social gluttony than the rights or wrongs of slaveholding. The church as a whole seems to have dealt with this potentially revolutionary issue through fictive kinship: already part of the *familia*, slaves became part of the family. Masters hearing this message could hope that their slaves would get the message about loyalty and faithfulness to them; slaves might hope that their masters might treat them a little more kindly.

This examination of the link in Chrysostom's preaching between πίστις and the household context demonstrates a number of key points. First, πίστις evokes a reciprocal relationship. Failure to recognise this will mean failure to recognise what Chrysostom and his congregations understood by the allusions to πίστις in his preaching. Secondly, the common understanding of πίστις in everyday domestic contexts illuminates how Chrysostom envisaged the relationship of the Christian and God. Thirdly, attention to πίστις enables us to see how Chrysostom sought to adjust – or to defend – the power balance within the small worlds of late antique households.

How radical was Chrysostom's preaching? A potentially revolutionary and transformative message was re-cast into comparatively safe exhortations to live more generously within the existing structures of society, instead of challenging structures already under pressure from elsewhere. Within this context, πίστις played a role that was simultaneously utopian and conservative, calling on listeners to dedicate themselves to the tireless pursuit of virtues whose fulfilment is only rarely achieved.

CHAPTER 4

A Predator and a Gentleman

Augustine, Autobiography, and the Ethics of Christian Marriage

Kate Cooper

Among the Christian writers of late antiquity, the restless fourth-century bishop Augustine of Hippo stands out as one who captured the imagination of later generations. A master at using storytelling to engage an audience, Augustine was not above weaving together narration of his own past failures and uncertainties with the hypothetical scenarios characteristic of legal reasoning to involve his readers in moral reflection. Nowhere is this technique of engagement more visible than in the *Confessions*. Indeed, it will be argued here, Augustine's retelling of one of the more disturbing episodes of his youth may hold the key to understanding one of his most influential contributions to pastoral theology, his idiosyncratic and original theology of Christian marriage.

It is well known that Augustine saw Christian marriage as something other than what he knew it to be in Roman law, a revocable agreement that the children born to a designated woman should be recognised as the heirs of a specific man. His view was that marriage should be something different and revolutionary: a permanent and otherworldly union of hearts. Marriage bound the two partners into a *fida societas* – a bond with an eternal dimension, firmly rooted in the Christian idea of the afterlife.[1] To reconceive marriage in this way involved a far-reaching paradigm shift.

Previous Christian writers had attempted to steer the faithful away from divorce, thinking of the apostle Paul's promise that the end of the world was near.[2] But they had certainly not seen divorce as something impossible to achieve; they lived in a world where marriage was by definition reversible. Since the time of Constantine, restrictions on divorce had begun to be imposed if one of the partners wished to remain married, but consensual

[1] The phrase *fida societas* is Augustine's. *Letter* 262, 5, to Ecdicia (CSEL 57, 625): *et laudaretur deus in operibus vestris, quorum esset tam fida societas, ut a vobis communiter teneretur non solum summa castitas verum etiam gloriosa paupertas.*

[2] In other words, the faithful should not bother to revise their existing plans for life on Earth (1 Corinthians 7:20).

divorce remained freely available. As late as 536 CE, a Novel of the Emperor Justinian emphasised the reversibility of marriage. The fact rested on a fundamental principle: 'of those things that occur among human beings, whatever is bound can be unbound'.[3]

Yet in the Latin West Augustine's imaginative leap made possible a new way of thinking that ran counter to the Roman legal tradition. Building on the foundation laid by Augustine, Justinian's contemporary Fulgentius of Ruspe argued that the marriage partnership involved nothing less than an irrevocably binding vow – one that yoked the partners indivisibly for all eternity.[4] This principle would come to govern marriage ethics in the Latin churches up to the Reformation.

Yet influential though it was, Augustine's vision of marriage as irreversible may not have been the most profound of his innovations. What I aim to demonstrate here is that Augustine quietly engineered a reframing of the very nature of the marriage partnership. By doing so he challenged a long-standing consensus, shared by pagans and Christians, regarding the place of marriage within the sexual experience of the male Roman citizen.

Marriage had always been a sexually asymmetrical institution. A wife owed fidelity to a sole sexual partner while a husband had access to multiple (free and enslaved) partners even if he could only marry one wife. In his moral treatise *On the Good of Marriage*, Augustine would challenge this way of thinking, proposing instead a symmetrical pairing between a man and one woman. A wife, he argued, should be a unique partner to whom the husband owed a duty of equal and opposite fidelity (*fides*). This, he argued, was the divinely ordained frame for male sexual experience. While he drew on earlier Christian tradition, his way of framing the problem was all his own, owing less to tradition than to an evocative emotional logic.

In this Augustine made use of an unprecedented tool – his own story. One of the most disturbing aspects of *On the Good of Marriage* is the resonance between its arguments and the autobiographical narrative of the *Confessions*. Central here is the painful narrative of his early sexual liaison with a low-status woman – the mother of his son, Adeodatus – and of the liaison's brutal ending when Augustine was presented with the chance to marry into a wealthy senatorial family.

[3] The reference is to Justinian's Novel 22 of 536. See discussion in P. L. Reynolds, *Marriage in the Western Church: The Christianization of Marriage during the Patristic and Early Medieval Periods* (Leiden, 1994), 63, citing J. Noonan, 'Marital Affection', *Studia Gratiana*, 12 (1967), 479–509.

[4] For an orienting overview of Augustine's influence, see K. Cooper, 'Marriage, Law, and Christian Rhetoric in Vandal Africa', in S. T. Stevens and J. P. Conant, *North Africa under Byzantium and Early Islam* (Washington, DC: Dumbarton Oaks, 2016), 237–49.

The young Augustine's willingness to cast aside the mother of his son can only seem callous to the modern reader. Indeed, part of the emotional pull of the *Confessions* is our sense that as he looks back at his earlier self, the older man must be unhappy with what he discovers. But although the young Augustine's insensitivity is deeply disturbing, the evidence suggests that it was not unusual. A sense that low-status women were somehow disposable was shared by the majority of his male contemporaries, pagan and Christian alike.

It was the older Augustine, with his sharper sense of moral accountability, who was the outlier. Reading the *Confessions* alongside *On the Good of Marriage* sheds light, it will be suggested here, not only on the nature of Augustine's own relation to the mother of his son, but also on his evolving understanding of Christian sexual ethics, and his changing understanding of marriage itself.

The *Confessions* and *On the Good of Marriage* have traditionally been dated to the same period, the years directly after Augustine's consecration as a bishop, although in fact the date of both texts is uncertain.[5] Yet they do not need to have been written at the same time for the connections between them to be important.

Robert Markus argued some years ago that while Augustine claimed he had written *On the Good of Marriage* as a response to the monk Jovinian, who had defended the institution of marriage, it was in fact an attempt to temper the effect of Jerome of Stridon's *Against Jovinian*, written in 393,[6] which painted the married pillars of established society as hypocrites, cutting them down to size by well-observed satire. Augustine, too, trains the unsparing eye of satire on the sexual habits of Roman men, but his irony has a different flavour. Above all, it is his own failings that interest him.

Reconceiving the Roman Sexual Landscape in Late Antiquity: Sexual Symmetry or Asymmetry?

A sea change has taken place in Roman-period scholarship with respect to sexual ethics, thanks to a growing awareness that our view of the evidence

[5] In *Retractationes* 2.22 Augustine mentions having written *On the Good of Marriage* as a response to the Roman monk Jovinian, who argued in the 390s that marriage and virginity had equal value in the sight of God. The traditional dating of the *Confessions* to this period has been challenged by Pierre-Marie Hombert, *Nouvelles recherches de chronologie Augustinienne* (Paris: Collection des études augustiniennes, 2000), 9–23. Neither text can be firmly dated.

[6] R. A. Markus, *The End of Ancient Christianity* (Cambridge: Cambridge University Press, 1990), 45–6. Chapter Four of the same volume, 'Augustine: A Defence of Christian Mediocrity', 45–62, offers an indispensable overview of Augustine's social thought.

for the ancient world has been filtered to accommodate unexamined assumptions. This is nowhere more true than with respect to the notion that marriage involves an intrinsically symmetrical pairing between a single male and a single female, or its corollary, that when multiple partners distort the symmetry of the couple, this is necessarily a violation of norms.

The one-man-one-woman norm is perhaps the most deeply engrained of the hidden paradigms we have inherited. In fact, monogamy itself – the sexual system which prescribes that a man will marry only one woman, even if he has other non-marital sexual partners – was not widespread in the ancient world.[7] Greeks and Romans shared a monogamous view of marriage,[8] but subject peoples within the Roman Empire carried forward their own norms and legal traditions, some of which were polygamous. For example, the Rabbis carried forward the Hebrew tradition of polygamy well into the Middle Ages.

It is also important to recognise that neither the Roman nor the Hebrew legal tradition expected that marriage encompassed the scope of a man's sexual reach, only the scope of his accountability. Marriage was a contract whose principal aim was to bring order to questions of inheritance. Its purpose was to provide a secure answer to a single question: which woman's children could claim rights as a man's heirs?

If a single word can clarify our understanding of sexual asymmetry, the word is slavery. Control over enslaved bodies stands as one of the privileges of powerful men.[9] In Rome, as Thomas McGinn has noted, 'slaves were sexually available and completely subject to the will of their owners'.[10] This simple fact shaped the balance of sexual expectation. Even if its form of marriage is monogamous, a slave society is by definition polygynous.

Over the past generation, major studies have reframed our understanding of how slavery impacted the Mediterranean household in the Roman

[7] W. Scheidel, 'Sex and Empire: A Darwinian Perspective', in I. Morris and W. Scheidel, *The Dynamics of Ancient Empires: State Power from Assyria to Byzantium* (Oxford: Oxford University Press, 2009), 255–324, cited in K. Harper, *Slavery in the Late Roman World, AD 275–425* (Cambridge: Cambridge University Press, 2011), 285.

[8] Roman-period literature celebrated mutually faithful sexual partnerships; see, for example, D. Konstan, *Sexual Symmetry: Love in the Ancient Novel and Related Genres* (Princeton, NJ: Princeton University Press, 1994), Chapter One, 'The Greek Novel: Sexual Symmetry', 14–59.

[9] Sexual exploitation was not limited to female slaves, but relations between men and low-status women are the focus of this essay.

[10] T. A. J. McGinn, *Prostitution, Sexuality, and the Law in Ancient Rome* (New York, NY and Oxford: Oxford University Press, 1998), 196. Perhaps unsurprisingly, sexual access to male slaves by female owners was not condoned; see J. Evans Grubbs, '"Marriage More Shameful than Adultery": Slave-Mistress Relationships, "Mixed Marriages", and Late Roman Law', *Phoenix*, 47 (1993), 125–54, for discussion.

period. One of the more recent, Kyle Harper's *Slavery in the Late Roman World,* AD *275–425*, draws on the work of Orlando Patterson to explain the centrality of sexual exploitation in Augustine's world. 'There is a tendency, derived from older, moralizing traditions', Harper notes, '. . . to think of the sexual exploitation of slaves as a sort of subjective failure, the indiscretion of the master, the outcome of individual choice: in short, a sin.'[11] But this sexual use is not an aberration resulting from individual moral failure. Although some slave societies adopt a moralising pose toward sexual exploitation, it is virtually always understood as a legitimate exercise of the master's right over his property.[12] To quote Harper again, 'Sex was simply a domestic service. Legally, the master had no inhibition to the sexual abuse of his slaves. Sexual access was part of his proprietary interest.'[13]

This meant that while sex for pleasure and sex for procreation could sometimes overlap, they belonged to different categories. From the early Republic, the Romans had seen marriage as a necessary tool for supplying the state with a stream of well-established citizens, and men of property with legitimate heirs. Although the faithfulness of a wife was greatly valued even if the marriage was childless,[14] the aim of the union was fundamentally reproductive.

The connection between marriage and the production of heirs was so central as to be a commonplace. In her landmark study of Roman marriage, Susan Treggiari tells the story of Carvilius Ruga, a consul of the third century BCE who reluctantly divorced his barren wife for the sake of the Republic.

> We are told that it was part of the censor's job to enquire of each man who presented himself at the census whether he was married. That the question took the form 'Have you a wife for the purpose of breeding children?' is suggested by the story that Carvilius Ruga (c. 230 BC) could not in

11 Harper, *Slavery*, 283–4.

12 On this point, Harper cites Orlando Patterson: 'The use of slaves as sexual objects is one of the most persistent, cross-cultural features of slave systems' (Harper, *Slavery*, 284, citing O. Patterson, *Slavery and Social Death: A Comparative Study* (Cambridge, MA: Harvard University Press, 1982), 260–1. See also Patterson, 'Slavery, Gender, and Work in the Pre-Modern World and Early Greece: A Cross-Cultural Analysis', in E. Dal Lago and C. Katsari (eds.), *Slave Systems: Ancient and Modern* (Cambridge: Cambridge University Press, 2008), 32–69, and K. Ali, 'Concubinage and Consent', *International Journal of Middle East Studies*, 49 (2017), 148–52.

13 Harper, *Slavery*, 295. M. J. Perry has noted that Roman literature's stereotype of female slaves is as objects of lust: idem, *Gender, Manumission, and the Roman Freedwoman* (Cambridge: Cambridge University Press, 2013), 13–17.

14 M. Lightman and W. Zeisel, 'Univira: An Example of Continuity and Change in Roman Society', *Church History*, 46 (1977), 19–32.

conscience take the oath that he had a wife to bear him children, since he knew her to be sterile.[15]

The defining characteristic of *iustum matrimonium* was the mutual pact that the female partner's offspring would be recognised by the male partner as his heirs. This was referred to by the jurists as *affectio maritalis*, a 'marital attitude'.[16] Roman monogamy was not based on the view that men are naturally monogamous; it was based on the view that society is best served by imposing limits on a man's accountability to his biological offspring.[17]

In other words, what distinguished sex within marriage from other kinds of sex was its distinctive capacity to convey legal rights and obligations. The principal aim of laws and norms around marriage was to provide clarity about which biological children could claim filial rights. *Reproductively* – where the production of recognised heirs was concerned – the marriage relationship was central for men, as it was for women. But *sexually*, from a male perspective marriage was only a single element within a larger mosaic of possibilities.

It was not unusual for men to progress through different types of sexual union at different points in the life-cycle; since the focus of marriage was on the transmission of property within the context of *patria potestas*, so it was relevant only to men at a specific life stage. In youth or old age a man might prefer not to beget heirs; for example, a widower with grown children might take a concubine rather than a second wife to avoid creating confusion in his estate. For married women, by contrast, sexual infidelity was a crime.

The emotional cost to women of this asymmetry was sometimes commented on, in comic descriptions of the household or in the rare surviving advice to wives, which consistently encourages them to meet infidelity with forbearance.[18] (Augustine reports in the *Confessions* that his mother gave advice to her friends along these lines.) But in the world where

15 S. Treggiari, *Roman Marriage: Iusti Coniuges from the Time of Cicero to the Time of Ulpian* (Oxford: Clarendon Press, 1991), 58, citing Servius Sulpicius, *De Dotibus* (as excerpted in Aulus Gellius, *Attic Nights*, 4.3.2).

16 Treggiari, *Roman Marriage*, 54.

17 Harper offers a characterisation of this regime from the husband's point of view: 'For men, however, sex was not even normatively confined to marriage. Marriage was a patrimonial alliance, a relation with the explicit purpose of creating an heir. A wife was the woman with whom a man tried to create heirs. But this did not monopolize his use of sex' (Harper, *Slavery*, 288).

18 See, for example, L. Dossey, 'Wife Beating and Manliness in Late Antiquity', *Past and Present*, 199 (2008), 3–40, and J. A. Schroeder, 'John Chrysostom's Critique of Spousal Violence', *Journal of Early Christian Studies*, 12 (2004), 413–42.

Augustine came of age, a man's sexual pursuit of women other than his wife was not judged as 'infidelity'. It was taken as a given.

Roman-period Jews and Christians drew on Biblical norms in their thinking about extramarital unions, but not in order to condemn them. The rich documentation of late Roman (and non-Roman) Jewish households in Rabbinic literature has allowed Catherine Hezser to document the routine sexual use of slaves by masters in late ancient Judaism, a practice that is largely in line with the era of the biblical patriarchs. Alongside the multiple partners sanctioned within polygamy, it was taken as a matter of course that male heads of household had access to additional sexual relationships with enslaved or other low-status women.[19]

Another valuable study, Jennifer Glancy's *Slavery in Early Christianity* has shown that the early Christians did not translate the apostle Paul's statement that 'there is neither ... slave nor free, for you are all one in Christ Jesus' (Galatians 3:28) into a challenge to power relations as modern readers might instinctively expect.[20] So although evidence for the Christian household is poor by comparison to Rabbinic Judaism, there is little reason to imagine that Christian slave-owners did not exploit their slaves sexually in the same way that is documented for their pagan and Jewish counterparts. Indeed, Augustine's own sermons suggest that they did.[21]

It is tempting to see the 'one man, one woman' principle in the story of Adam and Eve. Yet this is not how the ancients read the story. In the writings of the earlier Church Fathers, the disastrous consequences of Eve's curiosity were given as a reason for women's subordination to men, but her partnership with Adam was not seen as implying that the Creator intended humanity to be monogamous. Indeed, the Genesis narrative moves smoothly from the symmetrical pairing of Adam and Eve to the multiple wives and concubines of Abraham and the patriarchs.[22]

[19] C. Hezser, *Jewish Slavery in Antiquity* (Oxford: Oxford University Press, 2005), Chapter 7, 'Master–Slave Relationships', 149–78, and Chapter 8, 'Prostitutes and Concubines', 179–201.

[20] J. A. Glancy, 'Slavery and the Rise of Christianity', in K. Bradley and P. Cartledge, *The Cambridge World History of Slavery, Volume I: The Ancient Mediterranean World* (Cambridge: Cambridge University Press, 2011), 456–81, with J. A. Glancy, *Slavery in Early Christianity* (New York, NY and Oxford: Oxford University Press, 2002).

[21] Augustine, *Sermon* 224 (*PL* 38, 1095) characterises the indignant response of a slave-holder who has been advised to contain his lust: *'Ancilla mea concubina mea est, numquid ad uxorem alienam vado? Numquid ad mertricem publicam vado? An non licet mihi in domo mea facere quod volo?'*

[22] While Augustine reads Genesis as belonging to the polygamous stage of marital development (*On the Good of Marriage* 33), later writers would derive from Adam and Eve the idea of a mutually exclusive pairing. See C. J. Reid, *Power over the Body, Equality in the Family: Rights and Domestic Relations in Medieval Canon Law* (Grand Rapids, MI: Eerdmans Publishing, 2004), 89–91, on the

Yet although earlier Church Fathers did not see Genesis as a source for monogamy, Augustine attempts to claim it in *On the Good of Marriage* for precisely this purpose. His tactic is not to project monogamy onto Adam and Eve; instead, he suggests that the Creator intended marriage to be organised differently at different periods of history. He suggests that the Hebrew patriarchs had rightly taken multiple wives at a time when the human population needed to multiply, while for later generations the need for children was less urgent. Marriage remained a social good, 'not only for the procreation of children, but also because of . . . the companionship between the two sexes'.[23] While Augustine was not the only fourth-century Christian to explore new ways of framing the male–female relation, he was the first to theorise a Christian understanding of marriage as a stable and symmetrical pairing and to introduce mutual fidelity as one of its principal aims.

In the late empire, then, a freeborn citizen male – whether pagan or Christian – could expect to have socially and legally sanctioned access to three main types of sexual union. Children born in the first two types of union joined the biological father's *familia* (or of his *paterfamilias*, if he was not himself a *paterfamilias*), while children of relationships in the third class did not.

(1) If he was married, a man could of course sleep with his own wife. Children born to her joined his *familia* as legally recognised heirs (*filii iusti*).[24] Indeed, the intent to beget heirs was the feature distinguishing marriage from other sexual unions with citizen women. (Note that in the type of marriage common in the later Roman empire, the wife herself did not join her husband's *familia*; she remained under the *potestas* of her father.)[25]

(2) If he owned a slave, a man could sleep with her (or him). Slaves were understood to have no honour, so nothing was owed them, and there were no laws or widely held norms restricting how many slaves a man

fifteenth-century legal writer Juan Lopez's use of natural law reasoning to assert that the marriage of Adam and Eve should be read as indicating an implicit monogamous norm.

[23] *On the Good of Marriage* 3: *Quod mihi non uidetur propter solam filiorum procreationem, sed propter ipsam etiam naturalem in diuerso sexu societatem* (ed. & tr. P.G. Walsh [Oxford: Clarendon Press, 2001]), 2.

[24] If the husband was not legally independent (*sui iuris*), the children would join the *familia* of his own *paterfamilias*.

[25] For a review of theories on the decline of *manus* marriage, see S. E. Looper-Friedman, 'The Decline of Manus-Marriage in Rome', in *Tijdschrift voor Rechtsgeschiedenis*, 55 (1987), 281–96.

could sexually exploit.[26] Procreation was not the aim of these unions, although births brought economic benefit to the father, since the children inherited their mother's enslaved status and became his property. (In other words, they joined his *familia*, but as slaves – not as what a modern reader would think of as family members.) Numerous Roman inscriptions record affection for *vernae* (home-born slaves), but a master's enslaved children had no claim to special treatment. A father-owner's unofficial affection, if he chose to bestow it, was entirely at his discretion.

(3) A man could also sleep with prostitutes (who might be slave or free) or other women of low status not belonging to his *familia*. He bore no legal relationship to any resulting children. Unions of this last type conveyed no right or claim on the biological father by the mother or her children. Children from these unions were understood as a by-product, not as an intended result of the union, and they were legally classed as fatherless. They had no *paterfamilias* unless the mother was a slave, in which case they belonged to her owner.[27] It is also worth noting that the sex did not have to be consensual. Neither law nor custom sanctioned a man who forced sex upon low-status women.

Spanning the second and third categories is a relationship type that held special importance to Augustine's ethical thinking. This was *concubinatus*, an established sexual relationship between a citizen man and a low-status woman who could be either enslaved or free. (If free, the woman would often be a freedwoman of the male partner's *familia*.) The arrangement conveyed no rights on the female partner or her children, and the children bore no legal relationship to their father, though he was free to make gifts or bequests to the children if he wished.[28]

[26] On the Roman slave as a person who is 'legally dead' and 'a person without honour', see Patterson, 'Slavery, Gender, and Work', 35.

[27] Having no legal father, *spurii* were legally independent (*sui iuris*), but did have some kinship rights in relation to their mothers; for discussion, see J. Evans Grubbs, 'Making the Private Public: Illegitimacy and Incest in Roman Law', in C. Ando and J. Rüpke (eds.), *Public and Private in Ancient Mediterranean Law and Religion* (Berlin: Walter de Gruyter, 2015), 115–42. On the position of extramarital children in the period before Constantine, M. Nowak, 'The Fatherless and Family Structure in Roman Egypt', in D. F. Leão and G. Thür (eds.). *Symposion 2015: Vorträge zur griechischen und hellenistischen Rechtsgeschichte (Coimbra, 1.– 4. September 2015)* (Akten der Gesellschaft für griechische und hellenistische Rechtsgeschichte, no. 25, Wien: Österreichische Akademie der Wissenschaften, 2016), 99–114.

[28] Since *indignitas* prohibited testamentary bequests between partners in *stuprum* or *adulterium*, a concubine might have to prove in court that she was a person of low status if a bequest was left to her or her children. McGinn considers a complex case discussed by the third-century jurist Papinian

The term *concubinatus* is often used as if it referred to a legal institution, but the rights attached to it existed in a grey area, and the term for the female partner, *concubina*, was sometimes used of incidental sexual partners.[29] The focus of law and custom was on bringing order to the status of a man's offspring rather than to his sex life.

The different types of sexual union available to freeborn citizen men could for the most part be enjoyed concurrently; only established *concubinatus* and marriage were viewed as mutually incompatible. (By definition a woman was not a respectable concubine if her partner also had a wife.)[30] Some philosophical writers frowned on simultaneous access by men to numerous sexual partners, but generally, it was the female partner, the wife or *concubina*, who was expected to be faithful.[31]

For men, the consensus was that only *stuprum* – the violation of a respectable person's sexual honour – was out of bounds. If the female partner to an incidental liaison was of high status, the male partner was liable to an accusation of *stuprum*. According to McGinn, Augustus' *Lex Iulia de adulteriis coercendis* of 18 or 17 BCE established penalties for *stuprum* as well as adultery, and seems to have identified only slaves, noncitizens, procuresses, and prostitutes as 'safe' objects of extramarital sex.[32] But in practice a circular definition seems to have been in play. The jurists recognised *stuprum* only where the victim was understood to be respectable, and respectability was a luxury which the poor could not afford. Reviewing the somewhat ambiguous reasoning of the Roman jurists on *stuprum*, Susan Treggiari concludes: 'any free woman who becomes a concubine . . . at once becomes a woman with whom a man cannot commit fornication [*stuprum*] . . . if this is right, the men with *concubinae* and the *concubinae* themselves would always escape the law on *stuprum*'.[33]

involving the illegitimate daughter of a freeborn woman and a senator (McGinn, 'Concubinage and the Lex Iulia', 354–8).

29 An example is the imaginary exchange between Augustine and a married slave-owner cited above at n. 21; the slave-owner characterises his slave as a *concubina* even though he is married and thus not able to keep a proper concubine (*PL* 38, 1095).

30 Constantine's decree that a man cannot not have an established concubine if he is married is preserved at *CJ* 5.26.1 (AD 326); for comparable views from the earlier jurists see T. A. J. McGinn, 'Concubinage and the Lex Iulia', *Transactions of the American Philological Association*, 121 (1991), 335–75, at 336 n. 8.

31 A. Rousselle, *Porneia: On Desire and the Body in Antiquity* (tr. Felicia Pheasant, Oxford: Basil Blackwell, 1988).

32 S. Treggiari, 'Concubinae', *Proceedings of the British School at Rome*, 49 (1981), 59–81 (here, 76); see also McGinn, 'Concubinage and the Lex Iulia', 342.

33 McGinn, 'Concubinage and the Lex Iulia', 349–50. For an exploration of *stuprum* rooted in Republican sources but taking into consideration the evidence of the second- and third-century CE jurists, E. Fantham, '*Stuprum*: Public Attitudes and Penalties for Sexual Offences in Republican

If a master wanted to claim a slave as an exclusive sexual partner, however, it was advisable to free her. As a slave, she was exposed to forced sex with other men, but as a freedwoman, the claim to exclusivity established by her partner would give her at least some protection. It was seen as acceptable to force another man's slave to engage in sexual relations, but not to damage the master's property by harming the slave physically. (The crime in this instance was against the owner, not the slave.)

Adultery was prohibited, but applied only to cases where the female partner was married; it was understood as a crime against her husband, who had a right to expect that any children born to his wife were his own. In this case, as in the case of a slave partner, the guiding principle was to avoid encroaching on the rights of another *paterfamilias*.[34]

The social anthropologist Laura Betzig has characterised the Roman Empire as a polygynous society, in which men's predatory sexual behaviour served as a tool for establishing status.[35] Possession of a high-born wife or a rare and beautiful slave was a symbol of a man's dominance. This was also true of incidental sexual partners, whether consensual or victims of exploitation and sexual violence.[36]

The aspects of this sexual economy that did not directly involve high-status men are comparatively less well documented, but papyri and funerary inscriptions allow a glimpse into the lives of other social groups. From the early Empire, we have Sara Phang's remarkable study of the private lives of Roman soldiers. Even during the age when soldiers were barred from marriage during their period of service, non-marital relationships could endure for decades, producing offspring and deeply felt emotional bonds. Yet these men also illustrate the darker end of the asymmetrical sexual economy: predatory sexual behaviour by soldiers was widespread, and sexual violation of civilian women was an expected component of military occupation.[37] The threat of an occupying army was the extreme version of the intimidation effected by sexual exploitation and

Rome', *Echos du monde classique: Classical Views*, 35 (1991), 267–91, with clarification (at 271) that a charge of *stuprum* could only be levied if the object of penetration (who could be male or female) was of respectable citizen status.

34 Legally, a female slave-owner's rights would also be protected in this way.

35 L. Betzig, 'Roman Polygyny', *Ethology and Sociobiology*, 13 (1992), 309–49.

36 Betzig, 'Roman Polygyny', 322.

37 S. E. Phang, *The Marriage of Roman Soldiers (13 BC–AD 235): Law and Family in the Imperial Army* (Leiden: Brill, 2001), 230: 'soldiers, as "*the* instrument of violent force wielded by the central power structure of the empire", occupied a position of power relative to the provincials that may have promoted asymmetrical sexual relationships, namely various forms of sexual exploitation (slave ownership, prostitution) and rape'.

sexual violence as mechanisms of male status assertion. We know from Augustine's letters that these fears were felt acutely during the conflicts that seized Africa at the end of the fourth century and the beginning of the fifth.[38]

Wives and Concubines: Augustine's Moral Logic

Where did marriage fit into this landscape for a Christian writer? In the fourth century, Christian writers and preachers were beginning to address the hypocrisy of the double standard in sexual ethics. In his *Divine Institutes*, for example, Lactantius argued that while 'in public law the rule applies only to the woman who has another man ... God's law joins two people together in matrimony (into one body, that is) on equal terms'.[39] John Chrysostom took things further, exploring in his sermons the distress men caused to their wives by their philandering.[40]

Augustine's own contribution was ambitious. Not only did he aim to offer a firm theological basis for the idea of fair play between the sexes, his intent was to reconsider the nature of marriage itself. Here is how he develops the idea that each partner should be accountable to the other in the same way in *On the Good of Marriage*:

> they owe equal fidelity to each other ... betrayal of this fidelity is called adultery, when through the prompting of one's own lust, or through acceding to the lust of another, sexual intercourse takes place with another man or woman contrary to the marriage-pact.[41]

This is a radical departure from the Roman legal definition of adultery which dismisses the marital status of the male partner as insignificant.

[38] On Augustine's response to soldier rape in the Sack of Rome, see M. Webb, '"On Lucretia Who Slew Herself": Rape and Consolation in Augustine's *De ciuitate dei*', *Augustinian Studies*, 44 (2013), 37–58. A complex fifth-century Syriac narrative touching on the subject is discussed in T. Dimambro, 'Women on the Edge: Violence, "Othering" and the Limits of Imperial Power in *Euphemia and the Goth*', in this volume.

[39] Lactantius, *Divine Institutes*, 6.23 (ed. & tr. A. Bowen and P. Garnsey [Liverpool: Liverpool University Press, 2003], 381). Philosophical writers had previously addressed the double standard – one thinks of Musonius Rufus' *On Sexual Indulgence* (ed. C. E. Lutz, 'Musonius Rufus, the Roman Socrates', *Yale Classical Studies*, 10 (1947), 3–147, at 87–9, with discussion in Treggiari, *Roman Marriage*, 221–2 – but these criticisms had never entered the mainstream.

[40] Harper offers a close reading of John Chrysostom's sermon on 1 Corinthians 7, *To Avoid Fornication, Let Every Man Have His Own Wife*, exploring his 'personal crusade' against male sexual predators. Chrysostom's emphasis is on the distress a man's sexual infidelity causes to his wife, rather than to the extramarital partners, but Harper rightly notes that the most likely partners would have been slaves who could not withhold consent (Harper, *Slavery*, 281–3).

[41] *On the Good of Marriage* 4.4 (Walsh 2001, 9).

Augustine steers definitively away from framing adultery as a crime that turns on the rights of a married woman's husband, instead framing the problem as one of mutual fidelity – *fides* – the sacred bond which united humans to one another and to god.

In distinguishing between marriage and concubinage Augustine will again diverge from the long-established legal principle that marriage is defined by the father's intent to produce heirs. This was by no means a matter of ignorance. We will see below that in the *Confessions* he explicitly considers 'what a gap there is between the sanctioned scope of marriage, a bond contracted for the purpose of having children, and a deal arising from lustful infatuation, from which progeny is born *against* the parents' fervent wishes' (4.2.2). It is no accident that the passage references the criterion of intent to produce children, which is referenced in Latin marriage documents and imperial rescripts,[42] and which we saw in the story of Carvilius Ruga above. Augustine was clearly aware of the importance of this aspect of marital intent to Roman law.

So Augustine's departure from the long-accepted terms of the Roman legal tradition is surprising. In framing the question of what 'can be called a marriage', he begins from the starting point not of begetting heirs, but of lust.

> It is customary to ask whether it can be called a marriage when a man and a woman, neither he anyone else's husband, nor she anyone else's wife, are joined to one another not for the sake of having children, but – because of their incontinence – for the sake of sexual intercourse alone, with the agreement that he will not do it with another woman, nor she with another man. And perhaps indeed this can without absurdity be called a marriage (*potest quidem fortasse non absurde hoc appellari connubium*), if they stayed by their decision up to the death of one of them, and they did not avoid having children, even though they were not joined for that purpose.[43]

Augustine's principal concern here seems to be to understand whether lust can give way to a more ethically motivated kind of bond. Even in the

[42] J. Evans Grubbs, 'Marrying and Its Documentation in Later Roman Law', in P. L. Reynolds and J. Witte, Jr (eds.), *To Have and to Hold: Marrying and Its Documentation in Western Christendom, 400–1600* (Cambridge: Cambridge University Press, 2007), 86.

[43] *On the Good of Marriage* 5.5: *Solet etiam quaeri, cum masculus et femina, nec ille maritus nec illa uxor alterius, sibimet non filiorum procreandorum, sed propter incontinentiam solius concubitus causa copulantur ea fide media, ut nec ille cum altera nec illa cum altero id faciat, utrum nuptiae sint vocandae. Et potest quidem fortasse non absurde hoc appellari connubium, si usque ad mortem alteriuse eorum id inter eos placuerit et prolis generationem, quamvis non ea causa coniuncti sint, non tamen vitaverint, ut vel nolint sibi nasci filios* (Walsh 2001, 10).

absence of marital intent, he suggests, a marital ethos may evolve between a couple as the result of shared experience.

It is here that he takes the unprecedented step of blurring the distinction between concubinage and marriage. That human beings can establish a bond on one basis and suddenly find themselves crossing an invisible line arriving at another is an important pastoral insight, and it is one that pulls against the legal and moral tradition Augustine inherited. In *On the Good of Marriage*, Augustine takes the definitional fluidity of the Roman law of marriage and pushes it to its most extreme limit.

We know from Augustine's other writings, such as his Letter 262 to the *matrona* Ecdicia, that he had questioned the equation of marriage to reproduction from the other side. In an established marriage, he argued, the lack of desire to produce children should not be seen as the moral equivalent of divorce. Ecdicia's letter offered him the opportunity to think this out in detail. Moved by ascetic enthusiasm, she had taken a vow of continence without consulting her husband; the husband in retaliation had taken up with another woman. Augustine's reply to Ecdicia reminds her that her choice to embrace the ascetic life did not in itself dissolve her marriage, and her first priority should be reconciliation with her husband.[44] In other words, at the same time as his definition of concubinage was drifting toward involving a quasi-marital element, Augustine's definition of marriage was drifting away from the intent to produce children. Indeed, it is in the letter to Ecdicia that he coins the phrase *fida societas* to emphasise the importance of mutual fidelity (*fides*) within marriage.

Augustine's account of how he himself had reckoned with the problem of sexual partnership can help us to make sense of this shift. His experience of concubinage involved two successive arrangements with two different women: the first a long relationship with the mother of Adeodatus, and afterward, a briefer and less deeply felt arrangement with a second partner.

In the *Confessions*, Augustine describes the first and more important relationship in a way that reflects both shame and yearning.

> In those years I had one woman – not that I acquired carnal knowledge of her in what's called a lawful union, but rather, my roving heat, with no good sense to its name, had tracked her down. But there was only one woman, and I stayed loyal to her bed.[45]

[44] *non enim quia pariter temperabatis a conmixtione carnali, ideo tuus maritus esse destiterat* (*Letter* 262.4 [CSEL 57, 624]).

[45] *Confessions* 4.2.2: *in illis annis unam habebam non eo quod legitimum vocatur coniugio cognitam, sed quam indagaverat vagus ardor inops prudentiae, sed unam tamen, ei quoque servans tori fidem* (ed. O'Donnell, i, 33; tr. Ruden, 77).

The attempt here is both to underline the distinction between lawful marriage and the yoke of lust and at the same time somehow to undermine the same distinction.

> With her I learnt by direct experience how wide a difference there is between the partnership of marriage entered into for the sake of having a family, and the mutual consent of those whose love is a matter of physical sex, where children are born against the parents' will, although, once they are born, they compel their parents to love them.[46]

With this reference to his son Adeodatus, Augustine calls attention to the power of human emotions to erode the boundaries within which they are meant to be contained.

Returning to *On the Good of Marriage*, there is a moral ambiguity in the hypothetical case where a couple remain together in a sexually exclusive relationship for life, even if its basis is 'not for the sake of having children, but ... for the sake of sexual intercourse alone'.[47] That Augustine has some inkling of how self-serving an open-ended scenario could be from the male partner's perspective is made clear by what follows. He next describes a second scenario, in which a male partner explicitly imposes the time limit on the union:

> For if a man take a woman to himself on a temporary basis (*si aliquam sibi vir ad tempus adhibuerit*), until such a time as he find another one to marry who is an equal, worthy either of his rank or means, in his very spirit he is an adulterer, not in relationship with her whom he wishes to find, but with her with whom he sleeps in such a way that his relations with her are non-marital.[48]

The fluidity here has become quite remarkable. Indeed, the unstable line between marital intent and the quasi-marital *fides* of mutually committed concubinage has been abandoned altogether. Adultery is now no longer defined by the strict criterion of the male partner's stated intent. Instead, it is defined by the state of his heart.

On this reading, Augustine's second scenario is understood as a contrasting and clarifying counterpart to the first. The relationship between

[46] *Confessions* 4.2.2: *in qua sane experirer exemplo meo quid distaret inter coniugalis placiti modum, quod foederatum esset generandi gratia, et pactum libidinosi amoris, ubi proles etiam contra votum nascitur, quamvis iam nata cogat se diligi* (ed. O'Donnell, i, 33; tr. Ruden, 77).

[47] *On the Good of Marriage* 5.5 (cited above at n. 43).

[48] *On the Good of Marriage* 5.5: *Etenim si aliquam sibi vir ad tempus adhibuerit, donec aliam dignam vel honoribus vel facultatibus suis inveniat, quam comparem ducat, ipso animo adulter est, nec cum illa, quam cupit invenire, sed cum ista, cum qua sic cubat, ut cum ea non habeat maritale consortium* (Walsh 2001, 10–11).

the two can be summarised thus: if a man does not wish for children but intends to live faithfully with his concubine until death (despite the arrival of any children), it can be seen as a kind of marriage, but if he intends to leave her (and eventually does so), it should be seen as a kind of adultery, because the union is intrinsically marriage-like, and yet even while he is still with the concubine, he is already mentally betraying her with a future wife.

If we apply this reasoning to Augustine's own situation described in the *Confessions*, he seems to be saying that if he had always intended to remain with the mother of his son faithfully until death, their union might reasonably have been called a marriage even without any intent to produce heirs. However, if he knew the arrangement to be temporary, his conduct was the moral equivalent of adultery. At the same time, by knowingly assenting to a relationship on that basis, she had effectively condoned what amounted to adultery against herself.[49]

Yet Augustine also knew that these provisional relationships could drift into permanence. The *Code of Justinian* preserves rescripts from the third and fourth centuries showing that citizens who could not produce a written marriage contract worried about whether the status of their heirs was secure. In theory, the answer was yes. But the reality was sometimes more complicated.[50] We know that at least some men of property took up concubines for the sake of pleasure and later sought – retrospectively – to confer rights of heirship on the resulting children. Our source is a lost law of Constantine preserved in a fifth-century constitution, which shows that the first Christian emperor tried to close the loophole that made it possible, though the attempt to close it was not entirely successful.[51] So both Augustine and the mother of his son may have been lulled into complacency by an ambiguity in the terms of their partnership.

Augustine mentions that as young men he and his childhood friend Alypius frequently debated whether they should avoid marrying so they could dedicate themselves to the philosophical life. Alypius, whose experience of sex had evidently been limited to prostitutes, made the case against marriage, while Augustine took up the defence. In doing so, he

[49] *On the Good of Marriage* 5.5: *Unde et ipsa hoc sciens ac volens, impudice utique miscetur ei, cum quo non habet foedus uxorium* (Walsh 2001, 10).

[50] Evans Grubbs, 'Marrying and Its Documentation in Later Roman Law', 43–94.

[51] A fifth-century constitution of the emperor Zeno (474–91) cites a law of Constantine, now lost: see J. Evans Grubbs, *Law and Family in Late Antiquity: The Emperor Constantine's Marriage Legislation* (Oxford: Oxford University Press, 1995), 298, with discussion in K. Cooper, *The Fall of the Roman Household* (Cambridge: Cambridge University Press, 2007), 156–7.

brought forward his own domestic situation – 'the delights of my established relationship with a woman' – as evidence. Eventually Alypius conceded, Augustine tells us: 'if the respectable name of marriage were added to this relationship, he shouldn't find anything amazing in the reasons for my inability to disdain this way of life. He himself began to long for marriage.'[52] The happiness of Augustine's domestic arrangements, which both men clearly saw as at least superficially marriage-like, was persuasive.

And yet – Augustine's was not a real marriage. The importance of this fact was in how it left the door open to the call of ambition. Augustine clearly understood the difference between his existing domestic arrangement and a 'proper' marriage as involving not only respectability, but also – more importantly – money. He gives a vivid description of his youthful stream of consciousness on the topic:

> And just think how much progress there's already been toward an appointment to some high public office. What more is there to wish for in this world? Plenty of powerful friends are backing us; provided that we pour our effort – a lot of effort – into one thing, we could even be granted a lower-ranking governorship. A wife has to be acquired – one with a certain amount of money, so that the expenses of office-holding aren't too burdensome . . .[53]

A governorship, he knew, could give him entry into the senatorial class, with far-reaching opportunities for himself, and innumerable benefits to his family.

And so a suitable bride was found, whose fortune could fund Augustine's political career. The mother of his son was sent away.

> Meanwhile, the number of my sins was growing. The woman I'd been accustomed to sleeping with was torn from my side, because she was supposed to be an obstacle to my marriage. My heart, which had fused with hers, was mutilated by the wound, and I limped along trailing blood. She went back to Africa, vowing to you that she would never know another man (*vovens tibi alium se virum nescituram*).[54]

[52] *Confessions* 6.12.22: *delectationes consuetudinis meae, ad quas si accessisset honestum nomen matrimonii, non eum mirari oportere cur ego illam vitam nequirem spernere, coeperat et ipse desiderare coniugium* (O'Donnell, i, 69-70; tr. Ruden, 161).

[53] *Confessions* 6.11.19: *ecce iam quantum est ut impetretur aliquis honor. et quid amplius in his desiderandum? suppetit amicorum maiorum copia: ut nihil aliud et multum festinemus, vel praesidatus dari potest. et ducenda uxor cum aliqua pecunia, ne sumptum nostrum gravet, et ille erit modus cupiditatis* (ed. O'Donnell, i, 69; tr. Ruden, 159, slightly emended).

[54] *Confessions* 6.15.25: *Interea mea peccata multiplicabantur, et avulsa a latere meo tamquam impedimento coniugii cum qua cubare solitus eram, cor, ubi adhaerebat, concisum et vulneratum*

Augustine's description of the pain is brief but fierce. Later, he would renounce his marriage and, with it, the glittering political career that his fiancée had been meant to support – but this was all in the future. And getting married involved an ordeal of waiting. On account of his fiancée's extreme youth – she was ten – the marriage could not take place for nearly two years, until she came of age.

What happened next was unremarkable, at least within the cultural frame of Augustine's upbringing. Seemingly without much thought, he replaced the departed concubine with a new woman, to serve on a temporary basis until he could marry.

> I was no lover of marriage but instead a slave to my lust, so I secured another woman – but not a wife, to be sure. It was as if I wanted my soul's disease to be maintained unimpaired, or maybe even augmented ... But that wound of mine made by hacking off the woman I'd had before wasn't healing; on the contrary, after excruciating inflammation and pain came putrefaction and a growing numbness and hopelessness.[55]

The gesture of disclosure here is disquieting. Augustine's intent is certainly to expose the thoughtlessness of his younger self.

This was Augustine's situation in the summer of 386, when he had to make a final choice between marrying his heiress and renouncing her money. Although he had sent his concubine back to Africa in 385, at the time of his betrothal, marriage to her may not yet been out of the question. To be sure, she had left vowing never to know another man (*vovens tibi alium se virum nescituram*, *Conf.* 6.15.25), but there is no evidence (aside from the ambiguous evidence of the vow itself) to suggest that she had joined a religious community.

The outcome of Augustine's struggle is no secret. He renounced his dream of senatorial advancement and abandoned his betrothal. There is no evidence that he tried to return to the mother of his son; instead, his choice opened the way to an unexpected future.

We should not lose hold of the fact that the younger self whom Augustine remembers in the *Confessions* was not in any obvious way a saint in the making. He may not have been intentionally cruel, but – Augustine is very clear about this – he was remarkably self-involved. So the

mihi erat et trahebat sanguinem. et illa in Africam redierat, vovens tibi alium se virum nescituram (ed. O'Donnell, i, 71; tr. Ruden, 164).

[55] *Confessions* 6.15.25: *quia non amator coniugii sed libidinis servus eram, procuravi aliam, non utique coniugem, quo tamquam sustentaretur et perduceretur vel integer vel auctior morbus animae meae ... nec sanabatur vulnus illud meum quod prioris praecisione factum erat, sed post fervorem doloremque acerrimum putrescebat, et quasi frigidius sed desperatius dolebat* (ed. O'Donnell, i, 71; tr. Ruden, 165).

reflection of the younger Augustine in the later man's writings is not always a flattering one.

Augustine's faithlessness toward his first concubine should not be forgotten when we read his assessment in *On the Good of Marriage* of a union that both parties know is temporary. Especially involving is his discussion of the moral accountability of the female partner:

> if the woman knows and approves the situation, she is clearly in an immoral relationship with the man with whom she does not have the compact of a wife. However, should she maintain sexual fidelity with him, and after he takes a wife she gives no thought to marriage herself and steels herself to refrain utterly from sexual intercourse, I should not perhaps readily presume to call her an adulterer. But would anyone claim that she does not sin when she knows that she is having intercourse with one not her husband? Yet if for her part all that she seeks from that intercourse is children, and she undergoes unwillingly such sexual activity as is not aimed at procreation, she is to be ranked higher than many matrons.[56]

Augustine's attempt to think out the situation from the woman's point of view captures a sense that her own motivations and concerns might not be the same as those of her partner, and – more importantly – that she might be forced by circumstances to accept terms not of her own choosing.

The discussion accords reasonably well with what we know of the mother of Adeodatus. A number of details suggest that she may have been a freedwoman of Augustine or one of his parents. To begin with, he kept the boy with him in Milan when the liaison ended and the boy's mother was sent back to Africa. It would have been unusual for a natural father to retain custody if the boy were not somehow one of his dependants, since a father bore no responsibility for children born out of wedlock. In any case, custom encouraged freeborn youths who were not yet ready to marry to take a concubine from among the slaves or trusted former slaves of his family.

Another indication is her vow, mentioned above, that she would not take up with a new man once she was sent back to Africa. While some readers have taken this as a sign that she intended to pursue the monastic life, the vow can also be taken as evidence that she felt she could expect her sexual integrity to be respected. This probably means she was not a slave, since a slave could not reasonably expect to control how her body was used. It may also support the possibility that she was a freedwoman of Augustine's family, since her chance of having her sexual intentions

[56] *On the Good of Marriage* 5.5 (tr. Walsh 2001, 13 [emended for clarity]).

respected would have been far greater if she were living among her former lover's dependants. A final point of evidence suggesting that the mother of Adeodatus was not (or no longer) enslaved is Augustine's assertion at 4.2.2 that their relationship was not entered into for the sake of begetting children. The assertion would have been superfluous – and perhaps even nonsensical – had she not been free.

Thus a likely profile for Augustine's relationship with his son's mother can be summarised as follows:

(1) As a Roman provincial of curial status, Augustine established a relationship in his late teens (perhaps shortly after his father's death in 372, when he was around 17 or 18) with a slave or freedwoman belonging to a member of his family. The relationship was established without marital intent, but there was technically no impediment to marrying her at a later date. The only complication would arise if he were raised to senatorial status (senators were barred from marrying freedwomen), but Augustine was only likely to gain an appointment conferring senatorial status if he had a rich wife whose dowry could support a political career.

(2) Years later, in late 384, Augustine gained a position in Milan with a level of access to the imperial court of a type he could not previously have expected to achieve, though it may have been an aspiration. As a result, it became clear that marrying 'up' (the 'wife with some money' mentioned at *Confessions* 6.11.19) would allow him to gain a political appointment carrying senatorial status (the governorship mentioned in the same passage).

(3) In 385 and 386, the option of marrying the concubine was still technically on the table – even if she was a freedwoman as we suggest. Neither continuing in the relationship nor converting it into a marriage was compatible with Augustine's political ambitions, since either would bar marriage to a woman able to fund them.

Before settling on this reading of Augustine's situation, we should take into account an ingenious essay by Danuta Shanzer which argues for a very different reading of the same sources. On Shanzer's view, the first, idealised scenario describing a lifelong relationship in *On the Good of Marriage* reflects Augustine's relationship to his first concubine. (Shanzer refers to her as 'Anonyma 1' and to the second concubine as 'Anonyma 2'.)

Shanzer sees Anonyma 1 as a person of culture, though not necessarily one of high social status, since cohabitation with a high-status woman would have opened Augustine to the charge of *stuprum*.[57] 'The following is a somewhat risky argument,' she suggests, 'but one might deduce Anonyma 1's literacy and education, though not necessarily her status, from the tempting shopping-list for an *uxor* presented by Ratio to Augustine in the *Soliloquies*.'[58] In other words, Augustine remembered the woman who captured his heart as a model of the ideal wife.

Instead of considering the possibility (argued for here) that Anonyma 1 was a person of low status who aspired to respectability, Shanzer's main aim seems to be to argue against the view that Anonyma 1 came from one of the professions (such as an actress or prostitute) classed as infamous.

> Anonyma 1's orthodoxy, her fidelity to Augustine, and her eventual choice of chastity and perhaps even the monastic life do not suggest a woman of ill repute – unless Augustine's was an even more colourful romance than we imagined or he intimated. Furthermore the *Confessions*' audience would have included some people who knew Augustine well, e.g. Alypius. If his had been a liaison with a legally unmarriageable woman, and this would have included one of servile status, one wonders how intimates would have heard all his attempts to equate the relationship with a marriage, or to say that it was a 'quasi-marriage'.[59]

Shanzer here draws an important connection between Augustine's assertion that 'perhaps this can without absurdity be called a marriage' (*On the Good of Marriage* 5.5) to Alypius' admiration of Augustine's relationship at *Confessions* 6.12.22 (which suggests that in the relationship lacked only the *honestum nomen matrimonii*).

As a result, Shanzer sees the first, idealised union in *On the Good of Marriage* as a description of Augustine's relationship to his first concubine. It follows that when Augustine speaks of a man who plans eventually to leave his concubine for a socially appropriate marriage, he is thinking of his relationship with Anonyma 2 in 385–86 (after Anonyma 1 had left for Africa).

[57] Citing Rousselle, Shanzer argues: '"Concubines were essentially women who could not marry *or whom men did not wish to marry*." The latter alternative must be kept in mind, and is, I shall argue, the correct one'; D. Shanzer, '*Avulsa a latere meo*: Augustine's Spare Rib – Confessions 6.15.25', *Journal of Roman Studies*, 92 (2002), 157–76, at 166.

[58] Shanzer, 'Avulsa', 165, citing Augustine, *Soliloquia* 1.17.4: *Ratio: Quid uxor? Nonne te delectat interdum pulchra, pudica, morigera, litterata, vel quae abs te facile possit erudiri, afferens dotis tantum, quoniam contemnis divitias, quantum earn prorsus nihilo faciat onerosam otio tuo, praesertim si speres certusque sis nihil ex ea te molestiae esse passurum?*

[59] Shanzer, 'Avulsa', 165.

> The second instance is the man *(si ... vir)* who takes a concubine temporarily *(ad tempus)* until he can find a wife worthy of his rank and means. This, one might suggest, describes his second concubinage. While it is possible that Augustine all along intended to supplant his first concubine with a wife, such an intention cannot be proved from his writings. The *Confessions,* instead, suggests that the search started only later on at Monica's instigation, after the improvement of his prospects in Milan.[60]

The reasoning seems to be that if Augustine did not have a firm plan to abandon his first concubine from the outset, he would have remembered his good intentions rather than the fact that he had failed to fulfil them. In other words, Shanzer thinks it likely that as a young man Augustine did not expect to marry a bride whose family was socially acceptable to his own (and that he did not anticipate that he might become involved in dowry-hunting). This assumption is difficult to defend in light of one of Augustine's own sermons. After declaring that married men are not allowed concubines, he adds, 'and if you do not have wives, you are not allowed to have concubines of the kind you afterward send away so you can marry wives'.[61] In other words, whether the young Augustine actively expected to set his first concubine aside or simply (and self-interestedly) failed to think ahead to the future, the older Augustine would be inclined to hold him accountable.

An important difference between our reading and Shanzer's is a different way of assessing the class imbalance between Augustine and his sexual partners. Shanzer aims to distance Anonyma 1 from the salacious profile associated with the infamous professions, but fails to consider the increasingly well-established evidence that many low-status Roman women sought a modest respectability through established non-marital unions. Funerary inscriptions show that this was sometimes with men of similarly low status and sometimes with the slave-owning class (indeed, in some cases the woman had belonged to her partner as a slave prior to being manumitted).[62] If, as we suggest, the mother of Adeodatus was part of the

60 Shanzer, 'Avulsa', 163.

61 *Sermon* 392.2 (*PL* 39: 1710): *Et si non habetis uxores, non licet vobis habere concubinas, quas postea dimittatis, ut ducatis uxores.*

62 The essential studies are B. Rawson, 'Roman Concubinage and Other *de facto* Marriages', *Transactions of the American Philological Society,* 104 (1974), 279–305, and Treggiari, 'Concubinae', with, more recently, M. Tramunto, *Concubini e concubine nell'Italia romana: Le iscrizioni* (Fabriano: Fabriano edizioni, 2009). I am very grateful to Tatjana Sandon of the University of Edinburgh for sharing an unpublished paper on this subject: T. Sandon and L. Scalco, 'More Than Mistresses, Less Than Wives: The Role of Roman *concubinae* in Light of Their Funerary Monuments' (forthcoming).

respectability-seeking (rather than the infamy-embracing) category of low-status women, Augustine's statement that Alypius saw the relationship as marriage-like[63] would indeed have been appropriate to a relationship with a woman whom he did not intend to marry.

There is one last difficulty with Shanzer's reading. This is the phrase 'until such time as he may find another one to marry' (*donec . . . inveniat),* which is central to Augustine's darker scenario of concubinage. Shanzer's suggestion that it refers to Augustine's relationship with Anonyma 2 (the second concubine) seems clumsy, since the phrase indicates that the future wife has not yet been identified. Augustine tells us, however, that the second relationship was only embarked upon once he had already become engaged to his future wife. In other words, when Augustine speaks of the man who 'take(s) a woman to himself on a temporary basis, until such a time as he find another one to marry who is an equal', it is almost certainly of his relationship with the mother of his son that he is thinking. Augustine knew that it was on account of his own faithlessness that the relationship did not live up to the idealised picture of which he says 'perhaps indeed this can without absurdity be called a marriage'.[64]

The class difference makes the young Augustine's actions especially poignant. Whether intentionally or through banal, self-interested thoughtlessness, he had let himself drift toward marrying for money at the same time as the woman he loved was steeling herself against an uncertain future. On this reading, the older Augustine makes deft use of empathy and moral indignation in *On the Good of Marriage* to persuade the reader of the double standard's cruelty. By referencing his own experience and indeed his own failings, he is able to defuse the moral one-upmanship of pastoral exhortation, reassuring the men he most needs to reach that his own failings are at least as disturbing as their own. 'In his very spirit he is an adulterer': the man Augustine is condemning here is his younger self.

Augustine's reasoning can be summarised as follows. Just as a married man can violate the marriage bed (his own) even with an unmarried woman, so an unmarried man (such as Augustine's own younger self) commits a kind of spiritual adultery when he sleeps with a woman whom he intends later to abandon. Yet the adultery is not toward his future bride – but rather toward his soon-to-be-abandoned partner.

[63] Aside from the fact that it did not have the 'respectable name' of marriage (*honestum nomen matrimonii*): *Confessions* 6.12.22 (O'Donnell, i, 69; tr. Ruden, 161).

[64] *On the Good of Marriage* 5.5: *potest quidem fortasse non absurde hoc appellari connubium.*

The thinking here is noticeably out of line with the older view of Roman marriage. To begin with, the idea that a married man is liable to a charge of adultery on the basis of his own married state was eccentric, even if it built on an emerging Christian moral tradition. Further, the idea that a man could be held responsible for treating someone who was not his wife as if she were would have been viewed by Augustine's contemporaries as an absurdity, since the presence or absence of intent to recognise a woman as a wife was the criterion defining whether the union was a marriage or in fact something else.

Conclusion: Christians, Marriage, and the Evolving Role of Bishops

In his *Paradoxe sur le Comédien*, Denis Diderot tells the story of a humiliating put-down at a dinner party. Only after leaving the upstairs dining-room and going downstairs into the street, he says, did he think of an adequate reply to the slight. Ever the *philosophe*, he draws the moral: after a humiliation, a man is temporarily defenceless. 'He loses his head – and it is only at the bottom of the stairs that he finds it again.' The space between the incident and the delayed flash of insight is a space of ambiguous vulnerability. If the afterthought is one of self-condemnation rather than self-exoneration, the episode takes on even greater interest. The spectacle of a sinner wrestling with his own failings is intoxicating to witness.

It has been argued here that wrestling of this kind was central to Augustine's pastoral exploration of the problem of Christian marriage, and that the narrative interest of his delayed insight into his own regrettable behaviour made his pastoral musings all the more fascinating. It may further be suggested that his attempt to reconcile personal experience with pastoral reflection contributed to the profound influence his writings on marital ethics exerted on later generations.

The full significance of Augustine's effort to establish an ethics relevant to both marital and non-marital relationships lies also in his effort to consider the difference between male and female experience. By acknowledging the fact that the male and female partners in the same union might be responding to differing pressures and motivations, Augustine introduced a dimension of masculine self-irony to the ambiguity of marital intent as defined by the jurists.

While Augustine's intervention was distinctive, he was not the first bishop to engage with the fact that under Roman law it was not always entirely clear who was married and who was not.[65] Already in the second century at least some bishops had begun to serve as informal guarantors of Christian unions by offering a blessing.[66] The ritual had no formal status in public law, but it could help to cement a social fact in the memory of the community. If there was ever a dispute – for example, if a Christian died intestate and there was a contest between self-designated heirs – the blessing could be called up in memory to shed light on the deceased's family arrangements. In other words, the blessing's earthly value lay not in the power of the bishop, but in the witness of the community. It also had the pleasing side effect of adding an important element to the bishop's place in the life-cycle of Christian families.[67]

Yet fourth- and fifth-century Christian writers give evidence that old habits did not die easily.[68] For example, in the 450s Rusticus of Narbonne wrote to Pope Leo to ask whether the daughter of one of his priests could marry a man who already had children by a slave concubine. The concern seems to have been that the marriage would thus count as a second marriage, but Leo replied that the relationship presented no impediment and could be dissolved without legal action since it was not actually a marriage.[69] Another fifth-century letter, from Sidonius Apollinaris to his episcopal colleague Ambrosius, praises a young man for setting aside a slave concubine in order to marry a girl of noble family and character. Instead of criticising the young man's infidelity, he celebrates his willingness to be steered by his bride toward 'good morals'.[70]

In other words, change came slowly to Roman households, and efforts to bring order to the polyamorous leanings of the men within them met with uneven success. It was probably a matter of centuries – reaching well

[65] Evans Grubbs, 'Marrying and Its Documentation in Later Roman Law', 48 and 85–8.

[66] D. G. Hunter, 'Marrying and the *Tabulae Nuptiales* in Roman North Africa from Tertullian to Augustine', in Reynolds and Witte, *To Have and to Hold*, 95–113.

[67] As Hunter has noted, some Christian sources stressed the role of the bishop. Already in the early third century Tertullian of Carthage's treatise *On Monogamy*, written ca. 213 during his Montanist period, plays up the bishop's role in creating the union. 'Tertullian deliberately employed technical terms drawn from Roman marriage customs. For example, when he spoke of "that marriage which the church arranges" (*quod ecclesia conciliat*), Tertullian was referring to the role of the *conciliator* in arranging the match' (Hunter, 'Marrying and the *Tabulae Nuptiales*', 99). Augustine's *Sermon* 332 (*PL* 38:1463) suggests that he saw it as common for a bishop to be present and to sign the marriage contract.

[68] 'In the fourth-century redaction of the *Apostolic Constitutions*, a Christian who had a concubine should "cease the relationship if she is a slave and marry someone legally, or if the woman is free, marry her according to law"' (Harper, *Slavery*, 317).

[69] Leo, *Letter* 167 (PL 54, 1204–5). See Reynolds, *Marriage in the Western Church*, 39 and 163–4, with Evans Grubbs, *Law and Family*, 309–16, and Arjava, *Women and Law*, 209.

[70] Sidonius, *Letter* 9.6 (*PL* 58, 620–1); for discussion, see Evans Grubbs, *Law and Family*, 315–16.

beyond the scope of this essay – before Christian laymen began to take seriously the proposition that asymmetrical sexual relations should be seen as a regrettable weakness rather than a demonstration of strength.

What we are left with, then, is a small but pivotal episode in a wider transformation. Augustine's incipient awareness that the male and female sexual partners faced different pressures and circumstances can be recognised as a departure. Where women of low status were concerned, to be sure, Augustine was never fully able to see into the blind spots shared by elite men of his day. But he had learned from experience that the asymmetry of Roman sexual relations had a cost.

PART II

'Slaves, be subject to your masters'
Discipline and Moral Autonomy in a Slave Society

Part II considers how Christian authors addressed the issue of slavery. In the late Roman world, slavery functioned as a fundamental socio-economic framework around which contemporaries organised their lives, conceptually and practically.[1] Just as Jonathan Tallon's chapter in Part I shows how slavery within the household found acceptance, albeit sometimes grudgingly, in the writings of John Chrysostom, so the following chapters demonstrate how slavery was woven into the fabric of Christian society in later antiquity. Christian writers and preachers used metaphors of slavery in order to communicate with their audiences, while slaves were ever-present, if not always recorded, in Christian communities.

Slavery was as deeply embedded in monasteries as it was elsewhere in late Roman society, though distinctive pressures were placed on the slave–master relationship in monastic households. Lillian Larsen concludes that the ascetic ideal coloured, but did not suspend, traditional slave–master relationships, a point very similar to that argued by Jonathan Tallon in his chapter on Chrysostom's references to slavery in his preaching. Maria Chiara Giorda traces the presence of child slaves in late antique Egyptian monasteries, demonstrating how deeply integrated they were in the social and economic life of the community. This correspondingly reinforced the power of the metaphor of slavery in monastic education.

Indeed, as Chris de Wet argues in the first chapter of Part II, the idea of the slave's humiliation before his master is a central conceptual tool of monastic thought in late antiquity. Rather than challenging a social hierarchy which demanded the slave's humiliation, writers such as

[1] K. Harper, *Slavery in the Late Roman World,* AD *275–425* (Cambridge: Cambridge University Press, 2011); C. L. de Wet, *The Unbound God: Slavery and the Formation of Early Christian Thought* (London: Routledge, 2017).

Chrysostom, Theodoret, and others made creative use of extreme status inequality in order to lend urgency to the spirituality of self-renunciation that was central to ascetic practice. In all three cases, then, we see a dynamic and sometimes disturbing relationship between the metaphor of enslavement, the project of ascetic self-reinvention, and the social reality of slavery itself.

CHAPTER 5

Modelling Msarrqūtā

Humiliation, Christian Monasticism, and the Ascetic Life of Slavery in Late Antique Syria and Mesopotamia

Chris L. de Wet

When Worlds Collide

Slavery was one of the most elaborate and pervasive institutions of power in the ancient world.[1] The institution of slavery represents what this volume's approach would label a 'big' world of power relations – a macrocosm. Despite its notoriety even among some authors of late antiquity,[2] slavery was not an underground phenomenon. It was legislated and regulated by the Roman state, and even taxed in some instances.[3] Up to late antiquity, the channels of supply and demand of slaves were open and functioned like a well-oiled machine. Jennifer Glancy understands slavery as a habitus in ancient society – it was ordinary and shaped the very ephemeral rhythms of daily life.[4] The beginning of an individual's self-fashioning was the recognition that one was either enslaved, freed, or freeborn, and one's behaviour had to match one's status. Children's identity was constructed by the very rules of engagement between slave

[1] In this study I refer to slavery generally, which includes what we might call 'metaphorical' or symbolic slavery, and physical institutional slavery. It will become evident to the reader that these distinctions are not really helpful, since differences between them, in the sources, are cursory at best. When I refer to proper legally enslaved persons, I use the term 'institutional slavery'.

[2] There are what we might call contained and inchoate critiques of slavery among some authors of late antiquity; see J. A. Glancy, 'Slavery in *Acts of Thomas*', *Journal of Early Christian History*, 2 (2012), 3–21; I. Ramelli, 'Gregory of Nyssa's Position in Late Antique Debates on Slavery and Poverty, and the Role of Asceticism', *Journal of Late Antiquity*, 5 (2012), 87–118; I. Ramelli, *Social Justice and the Legitimacy of Slavery: The Role of Philosophical Asceticism from Ancient Judaism to Late Antiquity* (Oxford: Oxford University Press, 2016).

[3] Prostitution, which was essentially inseparable from slavery, was taxed; T. A. J. McGinn, *Prostitution, Sexuality, and the Law in Ancient Rome* (Oxford: Oxford University Press, 1998), 254–5; see also K. Harper, *Slavery in the Late Roman World, AD 275–425* (Cambridge: Cambridge University Press, 2011), 98.

[4] J. A. Glancy, 'Christian Slavery in Late Antiquity', in R. Hörmann and G. Mackenthun (eds.), *Human Bondage in the Cultural Contact Zone: Transdisciplinary Perspectives on Slavery and Its Discourses* (Münster: Waxmann, 2010), 63–80.

and free, even from the age of infancy.[5] In other words, the fundamental structure and structuring principle – as Bourdieu describes the notion of habitus –[6] that produced the individual subject and regulated social interactions and social reproduction in Roman antiquity, was slavery.

If we look more closely at slavery in later Roman antiquity, the picture that emerges is somewhat consistent with past centuries of Roman rule. Upon reading Kyle Harper's fundamental analysis of slavery in later Roman antiquity, we may be initially surprised to find that one of the first items on Harper's agenda is to show that slavery was still active in the late ancient Roman world.[7] Anyone who has read the treatises and homilies of authors like Augustine, Ammianus Marcellinus, John Chrysostom, or Libanius may simply assume that there were slaves in the world of these men owing to the copious references to slaves and slavery in their works. Nevertheless, Harper's work has allowed scholarship to survey the depths of slavery in late antiquity with confidence. One of the lacunae in Harper's otherwise sterling work is that the contexts of Christian Syria and Mesopotamia, and the Syriac literature in general, receive much less attention compared to Greek and Latin sources.[8] Yet, when surveying the Syriac sources, the prevalence of slavery is once again confirmed even in those of later periods contemporaneous with the rise of early Islam.

In this contribution I aim to address the lacuna of analysis of slavery in the sources from late antique Syria and also Mesopotamia.[9] In line with the broader vision of this volume, I hope to show how the macrocosm of slavery, along with its violent measures of discipline and punishment, was assimilated into and reproduced by Christian ascetic culture of late antique Syria, both in urban and rural spaces. I will thus begin by investigating the nature of slaveholding practices in the cities and outlying villages of the region. Thereafter, I will ask how the type of slavery that was characteristic of Syria may have affected the ascetic practices of monks, who lived on the fringes of the cities and villages. This is where the big world of slavery meets the small worlds of lone monks and monastic communities. Syrian

5 W. M. Bloomer, 'Schooling in Persona: Imagination and Subordination in Roman Education', *Classical Antiquity*, 16 (1997), 57–78.

6 P. Bourdieu, *The Logic of Practice*, R. Nice (trans.) (Cambridge: Polity, 1990), 52.

7 Harper, *Slavery in the Late Roman World*, 11–16.

8 Harper gives ample attention to the Greek sources of Roman Syria, and Ephrem the Syrian receives some attention in the analysis.

9 For a far more extensive analysis of slavery in Syrian Christian theological thought, although with a different focus from this study, see C. L. de Wet, *The Captive Monk: Slavery and Asceticism in Early Syrian Christianity*, Routledge Studies in the Early Christian World (London: Routledge, forthcoming).

Christian monasticism has been shown to have its own distinct character in its early stages, before organized (Pachomian) monasticism was popularized.[10] To what extent did practices of institutional slavery influence Syrian ascetic self-understanding and self-fashioning? Were the disciplinary and even punitive impetuses of institutional slavery transferred onto ascetic discipline, and if so, how were these impetuses transformed, and what could the strategies of this assimilation have been?[11] In this regard, I am especially interested in determining whether the aspect of monastic shame or humiliation, in Syriac known as *msarrqūtā*, had any relation to slavery. If the humiliation that characterized slavery did in fact play a role in Syrian monastic self-fashioning, then there would be two important implications. First, it means that a distinct discursive relationship existed between ascetic self-fashioning and practices of institutional slaveholding, and that these two practices influenced and shaped one another – and in effect, mutually supported the continued existence of one another. That is, if ascetic practice became increasingly doulological,[12] and socially admirable according to some, it could mean that mirroring practices related to institutional slaveholding would be regarded in a similar, positive way. Second, it means that we need to envision ascetic practice as a doulological expression – by this I mean that the ascetic practices that essentially defined Christian monasticism mirror slavery, and that asceticism could be understood, along with numerous other categories (like the contest, or *agōn*, or the soldiery of Christ), as an expression of slavery.

The initial focus of the study will be on the late fourth and early fifth century; however, in order to understand the ascetic afterlife of slavery in Christian Syria and Mesopotamia I will also explore the nature and ascetic

[10] A. Vööbus, *History of Asceticism in the Syrian Orient*, 3 vols., Corpus Scriptorum Christianorum Orientalium 184 (Louvain: Secrétariat du Corpus SCO, 1958), Vol. 1; S. P. Brock, 'Early Syrian Asceticism', *Numen*, 20 (1973), 1–19.

[11] In my theorization of discipline and punishment I am especially reliant on the frameworks and concepts developed by Michel Foucault; see esp. *Discipline and Punish: The Birth of the Prison*, A. Sheridan (trans.) (New York, NY: Vintage, 1977); *On the Punitive Society: Lectures at the Collège De France, 1972–1973*, A. I. Davidson (ed.) and G. Burchell (trans.) (New York, NY: Palgrave Macmillan, 2015).

[12] 'Doulology' and its derivatives refer to the discourse of slavery; more specifically, when slavery as a constitution of knowledge, a language, and a social practice is enunciated and used to produce and reproduce meanings and behaviours in various related contexts; more detail may be found in C. L. de Wet, *Preaching Bondage: John Chrysostom and the Discourse of Slavery in Early Christianity* (Oakland, CA: University of California Press, 2015), 1–44, 282; C. L. de Wet, *The Unbound God: Slavery and the Formation of Early Christian Thought*, (London: Routledge, 2018), 1–39.

function of slavery in some later sources of the sixth and even seventh centuries.[13] This exploration into later times – gauging the potency of discourses and practices of slavery, as it were – in turn will make us aware of just how powerful, pervasive, and persistent doulological discourse and discursive shifts were in late antiquity.

Institutional Slavery in Urban and Rural Syria and Mesopotamia: The Witness of John Chrysostom

An investigation into the nature of slaveholding in urban and rural contexts is necessary to better understand how the social institution might have influenced and shaped Syrian Christian ascetic self-expression. In this regard, the homilies and treatises of John Chrysostom, perhaps more than anyone else, provide us with extensive insight into the social world of urban Christian Syria; they also give us a startling glimpse into the realities of slaveholding within the borders of Antioch. Exceeded only by Augustine, Chrysostom is one of the authors who has left us with one of the largest literary corpora of late antiquity. Chrysostom did not write a specific treatise on slavery (*douleia*), but he refers to the oppressive institution countless times throughout his works.

From these references, it becomes clear that slavery was deeply entrenched in the social fabric of Antiochene society. Chrysostom often refers to the buying and selling of slaves in his homilies, showing that his audience was familiar with it – most in his audience probably owned their own slaves. The inhabitants of Antioch fully exploited slave labour to their own benefit, and if Chrysostom's comments are accurate, many of the city's well-off citizens had numerous slaves. Chrysostom speaks of elite women entering Antioch's market place with litters of slaves.[14] For Chrysostom, this attested to the vanity of the city's elite. He was so perturbed by the

[13] Late antique Syria was a highly bilingual society, with Greek and Syriac dominating the literary landscape. I will therefore refer to both Greek and Syriac sources to characterize the relationship between slavery and asceticism in this context; see also D. G. K. Taylor, 'Bilingualism and Diglossia in Late Antique Syria and Mesopotamia', in J. N. Adams, M. Janse and S. Swain (eds.), *Bilingualism in Ancient Society: Language Contact and the Written Text* (Oxford: Oxford University Press, 2002), 298–331.

[14] Such a spectacle would have been common, both in Antioch and Constantinople; see *Hom. Heb.* 28.4 [Field 7.320–21], *Hom. Jo.* 80.3 [PG 59.436.21–41], *Hom. Rom.* 18[17].4, 21[20].2 [Field 1.303, 353]; see more generally, L. Lavan, 'The Agorai of Antioch and Constantinople as Seen by John Chrysostom', *Bulletin of the Institute of Classical Studies*, 50.S91 (2007), 157–67. Note: for Chrysostom's homilies on the Pauline epistles and Hebrews, I use the editions of F. Field, *Ioannis Chrysostomi interpretatio omnium epistularum Paulinarum*, 7 vols. (Oxford: J. H. Parker, 1854–62), abbreviated with 'Field' followed by the volume and page number.

high numbers of slaves owned by some – although, at times, he does seem to exaggerate the numbers –[15] that he beseeches his audience: 'One master only needs to employ one slave; or rather two or three masters one slave.' But in order not to be too harsh, he adds: 'We will allow you to keep a second slave. But if you collect many, you no longer do it for the sake of benevolence, but to indulge yourself.'[16] No doubt, even the allowance of only two slaves, not mention having one shared between different masters, would have been considered radical and an extreme ascetic rigorism to Chrysostom's audience. A minority may have followed the advice,[17] but others probably shrugged it off as something appropriate only for monks. The inhabitants of Antioch liked their slaves, and often increased their ranks with new slaves.

During his time in Antioch, Chrysostom wrote his now famous treatise *On the Priesthood*, in which he details the sale of a slave. 'Those who want to purchase a slave, show him to the physician, and request sureties for the sale, and information about him from their neighbours,' Chrysostom explains, 'and after all this they still do not confirm the venture without asking for a period of time to scrutinize the slave.'[18] This transaction could have happened at the slave market or, more informally, between two masters – many of the slave transactions of late antiquity were of such an informal and ordinary nature.[19] In one of his instructions to catechumens, Chrysostom even uses the slave transaction as a metaphor to describe salvation – how Christ also buys his slaves, even if they are wicked and wretched.[20] Christ is, in his own way, a slaveholder in Chrysostom's thought. What becomes evident from these statements is that buyers of slaves were particularly paranoid that they may buy a 'dud'; their fears may be confirmed by a study undertaken by J. Albert Harrill on the techniques

[15] In *Hom. Matt.* 63.4 [PG 58.608.31] Chrysostom says that some households in Antioch own one or two thousand slaves, which may be hyperbolic, although such a number is not impossible, especially among illustrious households.

[16] *Hom. 1 Cor.* 40.6 [Field 2.515–16]. Chrysostom seems to feel quite strongly about this principle, as he also repeats it to his Constantinopolitan audience some years later in *Hom. Heb.* 28.4 [Field 7.320].

[17] Not necessarily to the benefit of slaves. I have shown that urging people to own fewer slaves (which is, of course, very different from abolishing slavery altogether) would have made circumstances for the remaining slaves much worse, since they would probably have had to focus on performing very basic tasks such as sewerage management; see my discussion of strategic and tactical slaveholding: de Wet, *Preaching Bondage*, 105–13.

[18] *Sacr.* 4.2.17–20 [SC 272.240].

[19] K. R. Bradley, 'On the Roman Slave Supply and Slavebreeding', in M. I. Finley (ed.), *Classical Slavery* (London: Routledge, 1987), 53–81; Harper, *Slavery in the Late Roman World*, 42–74.

[20] *Illum. catech.* 2.5 [PG 49.239.17–20].

employed by slave-traders, those mistrusted yet necessary social jackals, to make slaves appear younger, stronger, and healthier.[21] This meant that of all bodies in ancient society, the body of the slave was subject to the most intense scrutiny.

The number of gazes to which the slave body was subject is astonishing to say the least – hence the notion of *dokimasia*, that is, scrutiny or examination. Being mostly naked when traded (and there is no evidence to suggest that ordinary Christian slaveholders were not ashamed of naked slaves during transactions), slave bodies were subject to the medical gaze, to check for health deficiencies; also to the logistical gaze, to ensure that the slave body is suited for the work the slave would have to perform, be it physical or intellectual. And, of course, the sexual gaze was never absent – one of the 'duties' of slaves was to be sexually available to the master, and attractive slaves could fetch a high price at the market. Related to this is the reproductive gaze – despite the high costs of feeding, clothing, and housing slaves, slaveholding could be profitable if slaves produced offspring, so fertility was highly appraised. There is also what we may call the domestic gaze, to see whether the slave fits in with the motions of the household, and performs his or her tasks to the satisfaction of the supervisor, who may have been another slave or the wife of the household. Chrysostom himself says: 'A new slave is not entrusted with anything in a house until he has given proof of his character, having undergone many trials.'[22] We find therefore a society practically obsessed with the slave body, and the slave body becomes the tablet on which society's corporeal ideals are written. Chrysostom also added another gaze, that of the divine or the 'sleepless Eye' – God never sleeps and always watches – which became a virtual panopticon that constantly monitored slaves, in turn aiming to intensify internal self-examination.[23] In short, slaves were always under some form of surveillance and scrutiny; this scopic economy of disciplinary gazes never subsides.

The slave body also becomes a point of negotiation between different perspectives of corporeal ideals. When Chrysostom educates fathers on

[21] J. A. Harrill, 'The Vice of Slave Dealers in Greco-Roman Society: The Use of a Topos in 1 Timothy 1:10', *Journal of Biblical Literature*, 118 (1999), 97–122.

[22] *Hom. 1 Tim.* 11.1 [Field 6.85].

[23] This is based on statements in the New Testament household codes found in Ephesians 6:5–9 and Colossians 3:22–24, in which God is depicted as the ever-watchful Master of all. For more on this, see de Wet, *Preaching Bondage*, 210–14. On the dynamics of domestic surveillance in late antiquity, see K. Cooper, 'Closely Watched Households: Visibility, Exposure and Private Power in the Roman Domus', *Past & Present*, 197 (2007), 3–33.

how to educate their sons, he does so by contrasting the subjectivity of the freeborn son with that of the slave. Slaves and children were, socially, considered in very similar terms,[24] so it was the task of parents (and their surrogates, like pedagogues and nurses, who were, ironically, mostly slaves themselves) to bring up their free children in such a way as to contrast the subjectivity of the slave. In this regard, the slave body becomes a training ground for virtue, a pedagogical space in itself, where the elite freeborn male may learn the habitus of Roman freedom.[25] A father, and his surrogates (like the pedagogue), may then use the body of a slave as a pedagogical tool, a disciplinary site in itself, to fashion the masculinity of the *filiusfamilias*, teaching him proper control of the passions and how to deal with emotions like anger, lust, and pity.[26]

But slaves were not merely apparatuses to teach freeborn persons virtue. In late ancient Christian thought the slave body became subject to an ascetic experiment in virtue that transformed the façade of slaveholding in antiquity. The Christian households of Syrian Antioch were one among many social 'laboratories' in which this experiment took place. Chrysostom firmly believed that slaves were capable of virtue, if they were schooled in the correct techniques of virtue, and disciplined and punished for the advancement of virtue:

> And if you want to hear the principles regarding slaves, listen to what I said about children up to now. Teach them to be pious, and everything else will follow from necessity. But now, when someone is going to the theatre, or going off to the bath, he drags all his slaves behind him; but when he goes to church, not for a moment; nor does he admonish them to attend and listen. Now how will your slave listen, when you, his master, are busy with other things? First of all make it clear what God wants him to do, to be kind towards his fellow slaves, and to take virtue very seriously.[27]

Virtue therefore had to be a concern for slaves and free, and the fact that the slave body is capable of virtue meant that it could be deployed in a strategic manner in Chrysostom's moral philosophy. He often castigates the free, telling them that slaves behave themselves better; he also denigrates Greek philosophers, saying that Christian slaves outshine these philosophers in virtue and philosophy.[28]

[24] R. P. Saller, 'The Hierarchical Household in Roman Society: A Study of Domestic Slavery', in M. L. Bush (ed.), *Serfdom and Slavery: Studies in Legal Bondage* (London: Routledge, 1996), 112–29.

[25] *Inan.* 71 [SC 188.172].

[26] De Wet, *Preaching Bondage*, 158–62.

[27] *Hom. Eph.* 22.2 [Field 4.334–35].

[28] *Hom. Tit.* 4.1 [Field 6.297–98].

But how were slaves taught virtue in these urban domestic contexts? On the one hand, slaves were trained in Christian virtue in some ways that were the same, or at least similar, to that of the free. Particularly, slaves were included in household religious rituals such as scripture reading and teaching, singing of psalms, and prayer. We also know that slaves at times accompanied their masters to church, or at least, Chrysostom expected masters to bring their slaves to church, and have them baptized.[29] But, on the other hand, Chrysostom still subscribes to the ancient stereotype that, if they are not strictly controlled, slaves are prone to vice and degeneracy. This is not because of nature, but rather due to problems of upbringing, Chrysostom believes.[30] The other issue here is that slavery, both in Chrysostom and in most other early Christian authors, was directly related to sin – although being enslaved or even owning slaves is not seen as a sin, the institution that is slavery Chrysostom sees as a consequence of sin that is actually put in place by God to minimize the damaging effects of sin, similar to the purpose of marriage and imperial government.[31]

The problem now is that the slave body became subject to techniques of discipline and punishment that could be very extreme. 'Thus, to discipline and punish ignorant slaves is a great accolade, and not a perchance commendation,' Chrysostom says, 'when one can drive out wickedness using domestic violence against those who are the most evil.'[32] Chrysostom uses the terms discipline (*paideuō*) and punish (*sōphronizō*) explicitly. With regards to punishment, *sōphronizō* refers to teaching the slave self-control and modesty (*sōphrosynē*); these were also the defining features of Christian ascetic subjectivity.[33] Chrysostom expected slaves to exhibit *sōphrosynē*, and at times, violent measures were undertaken. In a newly discovered fragment of Chrysostom's homilies *Against the Jews*, preached in Antioch in the late 380s, we read:

> And when a noble and free man has an incontinent slave woman, who lures in all the bystanders for licentious purposes, he does not allow her to go out into the street, or to be seen in the alley, or to burst into the marketplace; rather, he confines her to the house, and binding her with fetters, he commands her to stay inside permanently, so that the restriction of the place and the constraint of the chains will be her starting point for modesty [*sōphrosynēs*].[34]

[29] *Hom. Eph.* 8.2 [Field 4.185]. [30] *Hom. Tit.* 4.1 [Field 6.298].

[31] *Serm. Gen.* 4.1.21–31 [SC 433.220–21]. [32] *Hab. eun. spir.* 3.7 [PG 51.287.4–8].

[33] De Wet, *Preaching Bondage*, 221.

[34] *Adv. Jud.* 2.124ra, W. Pradels, R. Brändle and M. Heimgartner (eds.), 'Das bisher vermisste Textstück in Johannes Chrysostomus, *Adversus Judaeos*, Oratio 2', *Zeitschrift für antikes Christentum*, 5 (2001), 36.

Here Chrysostom shows that one way to teach modesty is by chaining and confinement.[35] The chaining and confinement of the body makes it docile and open to receive virtue. There are numerous instances in which Chrysostom refers to the chaining of slaves, especially runaways, as a form of discipline and punishment.[36] But this is not all. Slaves were also taught discipline by means of food deprivation. 'Thus the workman has often sworn that he will not allow his apprentice to eat or drink, not before he has finished all his assigned tasks. And so also the pedagogue has often acted towards a youth,' Chrysostom explains in a homily preached during the tense time when the Antiochene imperial statues were destroyed, 'and a mistress towards her female slave; and when the evening has overtaken them, and the work has remained unfinished, it is necessary that those who have not completed their task should perish with hunger.'[37] We also hear of slaves eating only the most basic types of food, like dry bread, and sleeping only on straw – [38] perhaps not too different from what one might find in the monastic lifestyle.

The whipping of slaves was a common sight in Antioch,[39] and a practice that Chrysostom does not wholly condemn.[40] Chrysostom does, however, recommend violent discipline and punishment only in moderation – excessive violence he condemns, which means that it was probably a common feature of slavery in Antioch.[41] The regulation of sexuality was also an important aspect of slaveholding. Chrysostom is vocally against any form of sexual abuse of slaves.[42] Another way of disciplining a licentious slave girl (in addition to chains, confinement, and scourging) was this: 'Yoke her to a husband, remove the opportunities for her to commit fornication.'[43] Chrysostom approved of forced marriage of slaves if it was in the interest of virtue. But most of all, Chrysostom believed that slaves could also live a life of continence and virginity.[44] Slaves are taught virtue through the deprivation and humiliation of the body and this humiliation, at times, turned violent.

[35] See also J. Hillner, *Prison, Punishment and Penance in Late Antiquity* (Cambridge: Cambridge University Press, 2015), 163–72.

[36] *Hom. 1 Cor.* 40.6 [Field 2.515]; *Stat.* 9.3 [PG 49.108.7–12]; *Virg.* 41.2.15–29 [SC 125.236–38].

[37] *Stat.* 14.4 [PG 49.145.11–15].

[38] *Hom.1 Cor.*19.6 [Field 2.224]; *Hom.1 Tim.*16.2 [Field 6.144].

[39] *Hom. Matt.* 42.3 [PG 57.455.7–10]; *Hom. Eph.* 15.2 [Field 4.258–59]; *Hom. Phlm.* 2.2 [Field 6.344].

[40] Again, he states that a licentious slave girl and a wicked conscience should be ripped apart with the scourge; *Hom. Matt.* 42.3 [PG 57.455.8–10].

[41] De Wet, *Preaching Bondage*, 170–220.

[42] *Propt. fornic.* 4 [PG 51.213.48–214.5, 214.18–20].

[43] *Hom. Eph.* 15.2 [Field 4.259–60].

[44] *Hom. Col.* 12.2 [Field 5.307]; *Hom. Eph.* 20.6 [Field 4.313].

What was the nature of slavery in rural contexts in late antique Syria and Mesopotamia? Once we move outside the confines of Syrian urban centres like Antioch, an intriguing picture emerges. Slavery, and the threat of enslavement, was a constant feature of the desert regions of rural Syria and Mesopotamia – this is a point that has been convincingly demonstrated by Noel Lenski.[45] These regions were, in the first place, a stage for an epic conflict between Rome and Persia, and what Lenski has shown is that both empires supported, to their own benefit, the capturing and enslavement of their enemy's inhabitants.[46] Most of all, in this regard, we must note the activity of so-called Saracens, who were specialists in capturing and enslaving those who dared to venture the desert roads. Lenski's focus is particularly on the Saracens, and he notes that their pastoral lifestyle made them ideal for cultivating slavery. And the slave markets of Rome, like those in Antioch, Persia, and also Ḥimyar – all sedentary kingdoms – benefitted from the activities of the Saracens. Many captives were enslaved.[47] Christian monks were often among the victims of Saracen raids, as Jerome's famous *Life of Malchus* accounts.[48] So in the first place, we can say that the threat of enslavement by Saracens was an important aspect of rural slavery in late antique Syria and Mesopotamia. Other groups, like the Isaurians, added to this threat.

Yet slavery may have been more 'organic' and intrinsic in this area simply owing to the political geography and levels of social stratification, which were different from the urban centres. This is because of the nature of labour exploitation in the area which, interestingly, resembles quite vividly the situation of Roman land-bound peasants, or *coloni*.[49] The *coloni*, according to later Roman legislation, were practically bound to the land they inhabited as if they were slaves, and the landowners could

[45] N. Lenski, 'Captivity and Slavery among the Saracens in Late Antiquity', *Antiquité Tardive*, 19 (2011), 237–66; see also W. D. Ward, *Mirage of the Saracen: Christians and Nomads in the Sinai Peninsula in Late Antiquity*, TCH 54 (Oakland: University of California Press, 2014).

[46] Lenski, 'Slavery and Captivity', 248; see also B. Dignas and E. Winter, *Rome and Persia in Late Antiquity: Neighbours and Rivals* (Cambridge: Cambridge University Press, 2007), 123–32, 260–62.

[47] Dignas and Winter, *Rome and Persia*, 124–25; Lenski, 'Slavery and Captivity', 256 allows for the possibility of human sacrifice among the Saracens.

[48] For the text and translation, see C. Gray, *Jerome: Vita Malchi*, Oxford Classical Monographs (Oxford: Oxford University Press, 2015).

[49] From sources like Libanius and John Chrysostom, it seems apparent that there were *coloni* (Greek: *geōrgoi*) just outside Antioch; see J. Banaji, *Agrarian Change in Late Antiquity: Gold, Labour, and Aristocratic Dominance* (Oxford: Oxford University Press, 2001), 203–6. However, the presence of *coloni*, in the technical sense, in the broader regions of Syria and Mesopotamia is difficult to determine. I am not arguing here for the presence of *coloni* throughout Syria and Mesopotamia, but rather pointing out the possible similarities between *coloni* and various classes of peasant labourers (who may or may not have been land-bound like *coloni*) in rural Syria and Mesopotamia.

even command these peasants as such.[50] In rural Syria, as Richard Payne notes, the basic unit of labour was the dependent labourer who came from the outlying villages (*qrīte*) – these villagers were often violently and forcefully exploited, like *coloni*, by the landholders.[51] What is most interesting is that such a villager, in the Syriac sources, is often called an *ᶜabdā*, which is also the Syriac word for slave. *Coloni* were similarly called *servi*. In the Sasanian context, the Middle Persian terms *bandag* (subordinate, servant) and *anšahrīg* (slave) occur. Payne notes that the latter term, *anšahrīg*, was mostly used to refer to persons *not* bound to a specific land (which differs somewhat from the situation of *coloni*), and could often refer to Christian deportees.[52] For the *ᶜabde* of rural Syria, the difference between slave and free, which appeared very pronounced in an urban context like Antioch, was perhaps not so apparent.

In conclusion, distinctions between slave and free were probably clearer in urban contexts (despite some exceptions, especially with regard to displaced foreigners) than in rural contexts. It may be that just being outside of urban centres brought individuals, especially non-elites, closer to the realities of slavery and exploitation. This could happen by being kidnapped, or by simply trying to make a living in the villages of the outlying regions as a labourer. Slavery, however, was characteristic of both urban and rural landscapes. The similarities are even more telling. The techniques of discipline and punishment were probably not very different in urban and rural contexts. Whipping, chaining, and confinement were present in both instances. The characteristic of the disciplining of the slave body was humiliation – the body had to be broken down to a point where it can be refashioned with the aim of obedience and compliance, and in Chrysostom's vision, *sōphrosynē*. This is all part of an almost obsessive preoccupation with the virtue of the slave body, fully deployed in the Christian ascetic experiment. But most of all, in both contexts, we note clearly that one's status as enslaved was not seen as an impediment to Christian virtue and discipline, and that slaves could even lead a monastic life characterized by virginity and modesty, without having to be manumitted. Slavery and chastity could be mutually inclusive in the Christian moral *imaginaire* of late antiquity.

[50] See *Codex Justinianus* 52.1.393, cited in A. H. M Jones, *The Later Roman Empire, 284–602: A Social Economic and Administrative Survey*, 2 vols. (Oxford: Basil Blackwell, 1964), Vol. II, 796–801, 1328.

[51] R. E. Payne, *A State of Mixture: Christians, Zoroastrians, and Iranian Political Culture in Late Antiquity* (Oakland, CA: University of California Press, 2015), 137–38.

[52] Payne, *State of Mixture*, 73, 138.

Modelling Msarrqūtā: Slavery and Syrian Asceticism

But if slavery was, on the one hand, so common and unproblematic if practised within the confines of Christian virtue, and on the other, so widespread as a threat to those living in the desert areas, and practically embedded in the political geography of the area, how did Syrian Christian asceticism respond to and develop in relation to slavery? The centrality of shame and humiliation in early Christian monastic thought has been elucidated by Virginia Burrus. 'A plunge into the abyss of abjection was necessarily undertaken by those who aspired to transcendence,' writes Burrus. 'In imitation of Christ, holy men and women of late antiquity engaged in elaborate rituals of self-humiliation through which they might hope to escape the unbearable weight of selfhood registered in the relentless drag of bodily existence'[53] – and what could be more humiliating than enslavement? Shame and humiliation serve as crucial components in early Christian conceptualizations of salvation. Christ had, after all, set the example for all. In the apostle Paul's Epistle to the Philippians 2:6–8, probably part of one of the earliest Christian hymns, we read that Christ,

> who, though he was in the form of God, did not count equality with God something to be held on to, so emptied himself, by taking the form of a slave and being born in the likeness of humanity. And being found in human form, he humbled himself further by becoming obedient to death, even death on a cross.

This text was to become one of the most influential texts in early Christian theological debates. With regard to its context in earliest Christianity, Sheila Briggs rightly notes that the hymn is ambiguous; it 'does not challenge the interests or beliefs of slave-masters. Yet there is an irreducible tension in the idea of a God who becomes a slave.'[54] But for the Christian monks of late antique Syria, there was nothing ambiguous about the text – for these individuals, Christ set one example, namely that of humiliation. When Christ assumes flesh, he assumes the subjectivity of the slave, and it was by his embrace of shame and humiliation that he was exalted.

This association with the humiliation of slavery is perhaps nowhere as evident as in the late fourth- or early fifth-century work known as the Syriac *Book of Steps* (or *Liber graduum*). This work is presented as a

[53] V. Burrus, *Saving Shame: Martyrs, Saints, and Other Abject Subjects*, Divinations: Rereading Late Ancient Religion (Philadelphia, PA: University of Pennsylvania Press, 2008), 81.

[54] S. Briggs, 'Can an Enslaved God Liberate? Hermeneutical Reflections on Philippians 2:6–11', *Semeia*, 47 (1989), 149.

collection of thirty *mēmre*, or homilies, that was probably written in the region of upper Mesopotamia – almost in the centre of the Roman–Persian conflict zone.[55] Slavery would have been a very real and present phenomenon to the communities to whom the *Book of Steps* is addressed. In the moral theology of the work, two main groups are highlighted, namely the Upright and the Perfect. The groups known as the Perfect are ascetics who have totally renounced the world and its pleasures; they have taken an oath of celibacy and practise the most rigorous ascetic regime. Although the work has been associated with so-called Messalianism in the past, this view has proven to be problematic.[56] The work is one product of the diverse monastic milieux that characterized late antique Syria and Mesopotamia. However, perfection in the *Book of Steps* is attained through practices of shame, and ascension is achieved by means of humiliation.

Mēmrā 29 in the *Book of Steps* specifically covers the issue of the discipline of the body, and upon reading, the influence of doulology – the discourse of slavery (*ᶜabdūtā*) – becomes apparent:

> 'I will subdue my body and subordinate [it],' says Paul, 'lest while I preach to others, I myself will be rejected' [1 Cor. 9:27]. I will make my body a slave and discipline it and I will not allow it to clothe, put on shoes, feed, and refresh itself according to its own will. And I will not allow it to be honoured whenever it wishes, not even to sleep with honour, but I will subdue it with hunger, thirst, and nakedness, vigil, weariness, asceticism, and emaciation, and with much fasting and prayer, with supplication and loud crying, with many bitter tears, and with lowliness, endurance, and patience. I will subdue myself in order to honour everyone as a slave and in order to stand before and greet everyone before me, bowing [my] head before everyone. I will make my body run on foot like a slave in order to reconcile with its enemies, while not offending them, and to bow its head before whoever is less than it, just as our Lord bowed his head . . . I will make my body wash the feet of its enemies and greet its murderers . . . I will lead [my body] wherever it does not wish [cf. John 21:18]: to its despisers and those who are angry against it. Just as our Lord went to teach his crucifiers and despisers, I will make it visit as the slave of everyone, the slave of slaves, just as our Lord visited the evil and insolent ones who held him in

[55] G. Greatrex, 'The Romano-Persian Frontier and the Context of the *Book of Steps*', in K. S. Heal and R. A. Kitchen (eds.), *Breaking the Mind: New Studies in the Syriac 'Book of Steps'*, CUA Studies in Early Christianity (Washington, DC: Catholic University of America Press, 2014), 9–31.

[56] R. A. Kitchen and M. F. G. Parmentier (trans.), *The Book of Steps: The Syriac* Liber Graduum, Cistercian Studies 196 (Kalamazoo, MI: Cistercian Publications, 2004), xviii–xxi; on 'Messalianism' more generally, see C. Stewart, *'Working the Earth of the Heart': The Messalian Controversy in History, Texts, and Language to* AD *431*, Oxford Theological Monographs (Oxford: Clarendon Press, 1991).

> contempt . . . On account of this [being received as children of God], Paul wrote to us, 'Examine your bodies and then eat the body of the Lord and drink his blood. For whoever does not chastise his body should examine and subordinate it until he subdues it and it is obedient to him, and then he may eat the body of our Lord and drink his blood. He will eat and drink to his condemnation' [1 Cor. 11:27–29]. Because you do not restrict your bodies from food and nor make supplication to our Lord that he set you free, there are many sickly and ill people among you, and many who sleep and many who are drunken, greedy, and unrestrained, because they do not examine themselves and subdue their bodies.[57]

For the author of the *Book of Steps*, ascetic discipline is envisioned in stark doulological terms. Basing the argument on Paul's words in 1 Corinthians 9:24–27, the practices of humiliation that will bring forth perfection entail the enslavement of the body and its passions. In the Greek, Paul utilizes the term *doulagōgō*, which literally means, 'I subdue/treat [the body] as a slave' – the Syriac equivalent in the *Book of Steps* is *mšaᶜbed*, related to the Syriac word for slave, *ᶜabdā*. The technologies of discipline prescribed by the author include regulations and deprivations related to food, clothing, sleeping arrangements, and shelter – these are all strategies employed in institutional slaveholding to discipline slaves. Depriving slaves of food becomes the analogue for fasting, while vigils and prayer resemble strategies to break the body of the slave through inadequate sleeping arrangements and begging for the necessities. Basic actions of slaves are repeated in this section, such as foot washing, greeting, running on foot, and avoiding eye contact (that is, the bowing of the head). The monastic habitus envisioned for the Perfect by the author of the *Book of Steps* is practically identical to the habitus of institutional slaves.

The point of cohesion between the big world of institutional slavery and the small world of asceticism of the *Book of Steps* is humiliation. In the *Book of Steps* ascetic renunciation is described in the term *msarrqūtā*. Sebastian Brock, in his insightful analysis of the concept of *msarrqūtā* in Syriac literature, marks the *Book of Steps* as one of the first to use the term – the paᶜel of the root *s-r-q* – in this grammatical construction.[58] The term is related to the notion of emptying, the key facet of Philippians 2:7, and is

[57] *Lib. grad.* 29.1 [PS 3.808–13]; translation modified from Kitchen and Parmentier: I have translated *ᶜabdā* as 'slave' and not 'servant' as in the translation of Kitchen and Parmentier.

[58] See *Lib. grad.* 1.2, 12.1, 21.9, 29.12 [PS 3.13–15, 3.285–88, 3.608–9, 3.843–44]; S. P. Brock, 'Radical Renunciation: The Ideal of *Msarrqûtâ*', in R. Darling Young and M. J. Blanchard (eds.), *To Train His Soul in Books: Syrian Asceticism in Early Christianity*, CUA Studies in Early Christianity (Washington, DC: Catholic University of America Press, 2011), 122–33; R. A. Kitchen, 'Disturbed Sinners: In Pursuit of Sanctity in the *Book of Steps*', in K. S. Heal and R. A. Kitchen (eds.), *Breaking*

derived from the Syriac translation of the Greek *heauton ekenōsen*, 'he emptied himself.'[59] Christ's humiliation, experienced in the form of the slave, gave the monks of Syria and Mesopotamia a model to imitate. Perfection could not be attained outside of *msarrqūtā*.[60] *Msarrqūtā* brings freedom, releasing the mind from impure thoughts and evil spirits.[61] Through these doulological practices of renunciation, the monk becomes a stranger (Greek: *xenos*; Syriac: *ᶜaksnāyā*)[62] – but the estrangement sought by monks also has its correlate in the social estrangement experienced by slaves.[63] Both the slave and the monk are in society, but not part of society. Their social exclusion and alienation are the characteristic features of their identity in relation to the community.

Finally, and perhaps most importantly, the principle of examination is also present in the *Book of Steps*, and the obsession with what we may now call the doulological body – the body enslaved either by ascetic practice or formal institution – remains an object of obsession and target of various gazes. And while it is reasonable to expect that monks surveilled one another, the examination that defined the slave body is now turned inward – the slave of God must examine himself, not only in body, but also in soul. Without examination, according to the *Book of Steps*, both the individual and the community are in danger. The lack of proper surveillance, discipline, and punishment results in illness and vice overtaking the individual and social body. As with institutional slavery, the examination and surveillance of the ascetic-doulological body becomes a measure of security and a technology for establishing group cohesion and also exclusion. Only the perfect body, one that has passed all the standards of examination, may eat the body and drink the blood of the Lord – thus, become one body with the body of Christ, the heavenly Master. Chrysostom also intensified self-examination among both Christian slaves and ascetics with his frequent references to God's 'sleepless Eye' that always watches.[64] The principle of *msarrqūtā* is paradoxical at heart – the more the body is enslaved, the more free the subject becomes; the more the body

the Mind: New Studies in the Syriac 'Book of Steps', CUA Studies in Early Christianity (Washington, DC: Catholic University of America Press, 2014), 205–20.

59 Brock, 'Radical Renunciation', 123–5.

60 *Lib. grad.* 13.5, 15.11 [PS 3.316, 3.361–65].

61 *Lib. grad.* 6.2, 7.8-9 [PS 3.141–44, 3.164].

62 *Lib. grad.* 13.5 [PS 3.316]; see also Kitchen and Parmentier, *Book of Steps*, xliii.

63 On slavery and alienation, see esp. O. Patterson, *Slavery and Social Death: A Comparative Study* (Cambridge, MA: Harvard University Press, 1982), 35–76.

64 *Hom. Col.* 10.1 [Field 5.277].

is humiliated, the greater will its glory be.[65] Constant and intensive self-examination lies at the heart of this unbroken chain of humiliation. Institutional slaves in early Christianity, from the earliest times, were exhorted to endure suffering and humiliation willingly – like Christ – because they will be rewarded and exalted in heaven.[66] Like the monk, the slave who suffers unjustly does not retaliate, but in a willing and disciplined way becomes a model of humiliation. Chrysostom explains:

> For the one who suffers wrong in abundance claims an act for himself that he did not initiate, by allowing himself to be beaten on the other cheek as well, and not simply by enduring the first blow. For this last act may perhaps resemble cowardice, but it is in fact a mark of a high philosophy. In this way you will show that it was for the sake of wisdom that you also endured the first blow. And so in the case at hand, show here too that you bear slavery also willingly.[67]

The similarities between Chrysostom and the *Book of Steps* are apparent. We see here, again, the principle of exaltation through humiliation and suffering.[68] Syrian asceticism is therefore characteristically doulological, and we find many other instances in which practices of this doulological asceticism become manifest.

The monks of Syria and Mesopotamia were famous – and, at times, infamous – for wearing heavy chains over their bodies and collars around their necks. This symbol of *msarrqūtā* had its own model to imitate, namely the apostle Paul, who writes: 'I am in chains for Christ. And because of my chains, most of the brothers have become confident in the Lord and bold to fearlessly proclaim the gospel.' These words are said in Philippians 1:13–14, just before the Christological hymn that was the basis for the principle of humiliation. Paul mentions his chains repeatedly in his Epistle to Philemon.[69] For Chrysostom, the chains of Paul had a rich symbolic life.[70] Margaret Mitchell writes: 'Paul's chains constitute an example of the devotion and endurance of a slave, which Chrysostom

[65] Interestingly enough, Andrew Crislip has pointed out a similar dynamic with regards to illness in Christian monastic thought. Illness becomes a means of cultivating psychic health. Like slavery, illness, in Crislip's view, becomes an ascetic practice, A. Crislip, *Thorns in the Flesh: Illness and Sanctity in Late Ancient Christianity*, Divinations: Rereading Late Ancient Religion (Philadelphia, PA: University of Pennsylvania Press, 2012), 81–108.

[66] In the New Testament, see esp. 1 Peter 2:18–25; see also C. L. de Wet, 'The Discourse of the Suffering Slave in 1 Peter', *Ekklesiastikos Pharos*, 95 (2013), 15–24.

[67] *Hom. Eph.* 22.1 [Field 4.332].

[68] For the importance of suffering in early Christian identity formation, see J. Perkins, *The Suffering Self: Pain and Narrative Representation in the Early Christian Era* (London: Routledge, 1995).

[69] See Philemon 10, 13.

[70] See for instance *Laud.* 6.8 [SC 300.274].

presumably thought particularly appropriate to the epistolary occasion and rhetorical situation of this letter [Philemon].'[71] It is very likely that the chains and collars of monks even had some apotropaic value – if not for the monk, then certainly for those who followed the monk. Among the many relics that filled late antique churches were, supposedly, Paul's actual chains. Chrysostom desired to see these chains, which were likely housed at a Pauline shrine in Philippi,[72] 'at which the devils feared and trembled'.[73]

In such chains and collars, the value of *msarrqūtā* enters the material realm and, paradoxically, chains became a sign of great honour among monks.[74] Fettering and collaring were also common techniques used to restrain slaves in late antiquity, particularly with the rise of Christianity.[75] According to Theodoret, James of Cyrrhestica had highly personalized chains. Apparently, James had a 'great load of iron that bound his waist and his neck; and other chains, two in front and two behind, extending obliquely from the circle round his neck to the circle below, and forming the shape of the letter X, connected the two circles to each other, both in front and behind; and beneath his clothing his arms bore other bonds of this kind round his elbows'.[76] Theodoret lists Symeon the Stylite as another monk who wore heavy chains.[77] Gender was no disqualifier either; Theodoret speaks of women wearing chains and collars that were so heavy that the restraints permanently damaged their bodily posture.[78] According to one Roman source, new slaves were at times forced to stand chained, without sitting down, for long periods of time – an act of humiliation that was definitive of the master's power over the slaves.[79] In that regard,

[71] M. M. Mitchell, *The Heavenly Trumpet: John Chrysostom and the Art of Pauline Interpretation* (London: Westminster John Knox Press, 2002), 177.

[72] E. Dassmann, 'Archeological Traces of Early Christian Veneration', in W. S. Babcock (ed.), *Paul and the Legacies of Paul* (Dallas, TX: Southern Methodist University Press, 1990), 288–95; Mitchell, *Heavenly Trumpet*, 180.

[73] *Hom. Eph.* 8.2 [Field 4.177].

[74] S. A. Harvey, *Asceticism and Society in Crisis: John of Ephesus and The Lives of the Eastern Saints* (Berkeley, CA: University of California Press, 1990), 19–20.

[75] Since tattooing was frowned upon; see also D. L. Thurmond, 'Some Roman Slave Collars in CIL', *Athenaeum*, 82 (1994), 459–78.

[76] Theodoret, *Historia monachorum*, 21.8, P. Canivet and A. Leroy-Molinghen, (eds.), *Théodoret de Cyr: Histoire des moines de Syrie*, SC 257 (Paris: Éditions du Cerf, 1977, 1979), 80–1.

[77] Theodoret, *Hist. mon.* 26.10 [SC 257.178–81].

[78] Theodoret, *Hist. mon.* 29.4–5 [SC 257.234–37]; see also Harvey, *Asceticism and Society*, 114; T. Urbainczyk, *Theodoret of Cyrrhus: The Bishop and the Holy Man* (Ann Arbor, MI: University of Michigan Press, 2002), 108.

[79] We read about this in one of Plautus' plays, aptly named, *The Captives*; see R. Stewart, *Plautus and Roman Slavery* (Malden, MA: Wiley-Blackwell, 2012), 56.

Theodoret relates the story of Eusebius of Teleda, who also wore paining fetters but never sat down. Eusebius only kneeled or stood, as a sign of reverence to his heavenly Master.[80]

Eusebius of Teleda's tale is worth closer inspection. Apparently, as Theodoret explains, Eusebius was gazing at ploughmen working on a farm, and for a moment he delighted in the spectacle of human labour he was witnessing. Some monks, including those of the *Book of Steps*, were extremely opposed to manual labour, seeing it as the result of Adam's disobedience.[81] In an act of self-punishment, Eusebius 'made a rule that his eyes were never to look at that plain nor feast upon the beauty of the heavens or the choir of the stars'. Eusebius confined himself and 'in addition to this resolve, [that] some duress should compel him to this, he bound his waist with an iron belt and attached a very heavy collar to his neck and then used a further chain to connect the belt to the collar, so that bent down in this way he would be forced uninterruptedly to stoop to the ground. Such was the penalty he imposed on himself for looking at those farm-workers.'[82]

Eusebius punishes himself like a disobedient slave, humiliating his body. The presence of chains and collars tells us that the habitus of slavery that the monks idealized was highly physical – they were not only expected to have an attitude of humility, but their very bodily posture and gait had to speak of subjection and humiliation, just like real institutional slaves. The physical deportment of a honourable freeborn man would be very different from a slave.[83] But this new doulological habitus also represented the new standards of masculinity founded in the desert sands of late antique Syria and Mesopotamia. Being a slave of God, both in body and mind, became the epitome of manliness in this period and region. If the body is disciplined as a slave of God, it will not become a slave of the passions and sin.

The only practice of slavery of which I could not find an equivalent in sources is that of self-flagellation. Whipping, as we have seen, was a very common form of punishment for slaves. John Howe shows that Peter Damian (1007–72) is one of the earliest sources for self-flagellation in Christian monasticism, and dismisses unsubstantiated claims of self-flagellation in earlier periods, and in Syria specifically.[84] Why did this

[80] Theodoret, *Hist. rel.* 4.12 [SC 234.318–23]. [81] *Lib. grad.* 21.20 [PS 3.632].

[82] Theodoret, *Hist. rel.* 4.6 [SC 234.302–5].

[83] M. W. Gleason, *Making Men: Sophists and Self-Presentation in Ancient Rome* (Princeton, NJ: Princeton University Press, 1995), 55–81.

[84] See Peter Damian's letter *In Praise of Flagellation* [PL 145.679–686c]; J. Howe, 'Voluntary Ascetic Flagellation: From Local to Learned Traditions', *Haskins Society Journal: Studies in Medieval History*,

one fundamental practice of slavery not find resonance in Syrian ascetic practice? The answer may lie in the religious environment of late antique Syria. Practices of self-flagellation, but also castration, another practice that characterized slavery, were common features in other, non-Christian religions of the region, which was probably the reason why these two practices never became entrenched in Syrian ascetic self-expression.[85] Some centuries later we do have evidence of self-flagellation among Shi'ite adherents of early Islam, but as Reza Aslan notes, there were major differences between Shi'ite self-flagellation and medieval Christian self-flagellation.[86] Of course, just because the sources do not attest to self-flagellation among Christian monks in Syria does not mean it did not occur, at least minimally, in some instances. It is quite plausible that some monks may have done it, but exactly because of the controversial nature of the practice, the sources choose to remain silent.

But not all Christian authors of late antiquity praised the Syrian monks for these physical practices of doulological asceticism and self-humiliation. Not all considered such practices admirable or masculine – some were quite offended by these monks. Epiphanius of Salamis forbade monks to wear slave collars publicly, relegating it to the heretical.[87] For Epiphanius, physical restraints like chains and collars were a direct assault on the divine gift of free will, since they force the monk to submit to God.[88] Epiphanius further refers to initiates of the cult of Cronos who also put heavy iron collars around their necks.[89] This may explain why practices like chaining

24 (2012), 41–62; see also G. Flood, *The Ascetic Self: Subjectivity, Memory and Tradition* (Cambridge: Cambridge University Press, 2004), 187–9.

85 H. J. W. Drijvers, 'The Persistence of Pagan Cults and Practices in Christian Syria', in H. J. W. Drijvers (ed.), *East of Antioch*, Collected Studies 198 (London: Variorum Reprints, 1984), 35–43.

86 R. Aslan, *No God But God: The Origins, Evolution and Future of Islam* (New York, NY: Random House, 2008), 180.

87 Epiphanius of Salamis, *On Faith*, 13.8, 23.6, K. Holl and J. Dummer (eds.), *Epiphanius: Panarion haer. 65–80. De fide*, GCS 37 (Berlin: De Gruyter, 1985), 512–14, 524; see also T. S. Berzon, *Classifying Christians: Ethnography, Heresiology, and the Limits of Knowledge in Late Antiquity* (Oakland, CA: University of California Press, 2016), 91–5.

88 Epiphanius of Salamis, *Panarion*, 48.13.4, K. Holl and J. Dummer (eds.), *Epiphanius*, GCS 31 (Berlin: De Gruyter, 1980), 238.

89 Epiphanius of Salamis, *On Faith*, 11.2, Holl and Dummer (eds.), *Epiphanius*, 511; there is literary evidence for the cult of Cronos in Egypt from the first to the fifth century CE. Slaves may have had a special place in the cult and its festivals (depending on the relation to the Saturnalia); for an early analysis within Greece, see L. R. Farnell, *The Cults of the Greek States*, 5 vols. (Cambridge: Cambridge University Press, 1896), Vol. 1, 23–34; see also the brief but helpful discussion in D. Frankfurter, *Religion in Roman Egypt: Assimilation and Resistance* (Princeton, NJ: Princeton University Press, 1998), 117.

and collaring were practically outlawed in Egypt.[90] It may have been for the same reasons that self-flagellation and castration are absent in Syria – they were practices that were practised by non-Christian religious groups. Unlike, Epiphanius, Chrysostom is more accepting of doulological ascetic practices performed by monks:

> Do you not see those who are in the mountains? They renounce both houses, and wives, and children, and all esteem, and shut themselves away from the world, clothing themselves in sackcloth, strewing ashes beneath them; they wear collars hung around their necks, and have enclosed themselves in a small cell. Nor do they stop here, but exert themselves with fasting and constant hunger.[91]

Some monks may have physically resembled slaves. Chrysostom gives us better insight into this. In one of his homilies on the Beatitudes in the Gospel of Matthew, specifically the one that delimits the blessedness of the 'poor in spirit' (Matt. 5:3) – that is, the humble – Chrysostom writes: 'So that even though you are a slave, a beggar, in poverty, a stranger and unlearned, there is nothing to hinder you from being blessed, if you emulate this virtue [of humility].'[92] In a different homily, Chrysostom states that slaves and beggars could resemble one another, and that both are deserving of mercy – if they believe in God, of course.[93] Monks are expected to renounce any kinship ties and any claims to inheritance, again, similar to slaves. Jamie Wood's insightful comparison of institutions of 'violent training' in this volume agrees: 'In the monastery, however, violence was used to force initiates to break free of former family bonds and to remake themselves in new contexts.' This species of violence is exactly what is found in slaveholding contexts. Natal alienation, as Orlando Patterson describes it,[94] was common to the enslaved and monastic experience.

Furthermore, Chrysostom describes the men in the furnace from Daniel 3 thus: 'For captives as they were, and slaves, and youths, and strangers and stripped of all resources of their own'.[95] If one reads this in the context of Daniel Caner's work on so-called wandering, begging monks, the similarities are again striking.[96] Both monks and slaves were considered strangers,

[90] Slavery did have its own unique discursive life in Egyptian monasticism, as the chapters by Lillian I. Larsen and Maria Chiara Giorda in this volume demonstrate.

[91] *Hom. Eph.* 13.3 [Field 4.241]. [92] *Hom. Matt.* 15.2 [PG 57.225.31–34].

[93] *Hom. Jo.* 60.4 [PG 59.333.8–10]. [94] Patterson, *Slavery and Social Death*, 21–3.

[95] *Hom. Matt.* 4.10 [PG 57.51.51–53].

[96] D. F. Caner, *Wandering, Begging Monks: Spiritual Authority and the Promotion of Monasticism in Late Antiquity*, TCH 33 (Berkeley, CA: University of California Press, 2002).

and could find themselves begging because of poverty or neglect. In the context of rural Syria, where the distinctions between slaves and free (but non-elite and impoverished) were already opaque at best, the monks probably looked very similar to the poor and exploited *ᶜabde* of the Syrian villages. This may also be the reason why the villagers approached the monks as patrons and guardians, as Peter Brown has shown.[97] The monks were part of them, the villagers could relate to them, and they all stood in stark contrast to the oppressive and wealthy elite landowners of fourth- and fifth-century Syria and Mesopotamia.

Slavery as Ascetic Practice at the Dawn of Islam

By the time John of Ephesus wrote his *Life of the Eastern Saints*, in the sixth century, the expression 'slave of Christ' (*ᶜabdā damšīḥā*) had practically become a technical term that referred to a revered monk.[98] Practices of doulological asceticism continued in this period, and John often tells of monks wearing chains and other restraints. The monk Zacharias kept a stone in his mouth and had a coil around his wrist, which he calls 'the irons of my service'.[99] According to John, the chains of another monk, Harfat, nearly killed him. For Harfat, the bonds had a clear disciplinary and punitive dimension – they reminded the monk of the slavery of sin, and helped the monk to avoid sin.[100]

Doulological asceticism, moreover, seemed to have had an influence on the martyrology of these later centuries. For instance, in the late sixth- or early seventh-century Syriac *Life of Febronia*, we read of a female Christian martyr, supposedly living during the persecution of Diocletian. When her monastic community is raided by the Romans, the courageous Febronia remains, and when she appears before the Roman tribunal, the author describes her in the following terms: 'They brought her in, with her hands tied and the heavy iron collar around her neck.' Febronia

97 P. Brown, 'The Rise and Function of the Holy Man in Late Antiquity', *Journal of Roman Studies*, 61 (1971), 80–101.

98 See, for instance, John of Ephesus, *Vit.* 27 [PO 18.555–58]. In some later hagiographic material, when an individual becomes a monk, they 'lose' their name and take on the title 'Slave of Christ'; see for instance the so-called *History of the 'Slave of Christ'*, in A. M. Butts and S. Gross (eds), *The History of the 'Slave of Christ': From Jewish Child to Christian Martyr*, Persian Martyr Acts in Syriac: Text and Translation 6 (Kalamazoo, MI: Gorgias, 2016); and the Arabic *Martyrdom of ᶜAbd al-Masīḥ*, in M. Swanson, 'The Martyrdom of ᶜAbd-al-Masīḥ, Superior of Mount Sinai (Qays al-Ghassānī)', in D. Thomas (ed.), *Syrian Christians under Islam: The First Thousand Years* (Leiden: Brill, 2001), 107–30. For a fuller discussion of the meaning of the appellation 'slave of Christ' in early Christianity, see de Wet, *Unbound God*, 9–39.

99 John of Ephesus, *Vit.* 19 [PO 17.270–72].

100 John of Ephesus, *Vit.* 11 (PO 17.160–66).

resembles the fettered monks of the Syrian countryside. What is even more interesting is this:

> Lysimachos addressed her, 'Tell me, young girl, what are you, slave or freeborn?' Febronia replied, 'Slave.' 'Whose slave are you, then?' asked Lysimachos. 'Christ's,' said Febronia.[101]

Not only does she look like a monk and a slave, but she also confesses that she is not free, but a slave of Christ. In the *Life of Febronia*, any distinctions between what we may call 'spiritual' or 'metaphorical' slavery and actual institutional slavery disappear. When Febronia calls herself a slave of Christ, she is established as an ascetic par excellence. This means that doulological asceticism was so influential that it even shaped the historical consciousness of later authors who reinvented the past with the colours of their present.

But in the sources we find something even more curious. In several primary sources covering the regions of Syria, Mesopotamia, Sinai, and the Arab regions, we have accounts of monks actually being institutionally enslaved, usually after being captured by marauders. The first account that comes to mind, of course, is Jerome's *Life of Malchus.* Jerome recounts the story of Malchus and his unnamed female companion, who are both kidnapped by Saracens and enslaved – they later escape, miraculously, and live to tell the tale.[102] Despite exhibiting its own narrative embellishments, I agree with Lenski that the basic historical data of the text – notably the events surrounding the kidnapping and enslavement of Malchus – are plausible. In the fifth-century *Narrations* of Pseudo-Nilus we also read of a man, aptly called Theodoulus (meaning 'slave of God' in Greek), and his father, who are kidnapped by Saracens while on journey to Mount Sinai – they wanted to become monks, and the tale of Theodoulus becomes one in which the worthiness of Theodoulus for the monastic life is tested in the furnace of enslavement.[103] This literary *topos* of the captive and enslaved monk may be building on a much earlier tradition found in the apocryphal *Acts of Thomas*, a work that was extremely influential in the making of Syrian Christian asceticism, with a long, complicated, and developed manuscript history in both Greek and Syriac in later centuries.

[101] *Life of Febronia*, 21, P. Bedjan (ed.), *Acta martyrum et sanctorum*, Vol. v (Leipzig: Otto Harrassowitz, 1895), 593; S. P. Brock and S. A. Harvey (trans.), *Holy Women of the Syrian Orient*, TCH 13 (Berkeley, CA: University of California Press, 1998), 164.

[102] Gray, *Jerome: Vita Malchi.*

[103] Pseudo-Nilus, *Narrations*, 4–5, F. Conca (ed.), *Nilus Ancyranus: Narratio*, Bibliotheca Teubneriana (Leipzig: Teubner, 1983), in D. F. Caner (ed. and trans.), *History and Hagiography from the Late Antique Sinai*, TTH 53 (Liverpool University Press, 2010), 128–34.

In the *Acts of Thomas*, the protagonist, Judas Thomas, is sold into actual slavery by Christ as a way to compel him to obedience and undertake a missionary journey to India. Some of the later manuscripts of the *Acts of Thomas*, like the tenth-century Syriac manuscript in the British Library,[104] were probably adapted to be used in the debates not only with Gnostic groups and Manichaeans, as the argument stands,[105] but also in debates with early Muslim thinkers about the nature of human free will.[106]

Could it be that we have found more than we bargained for? Along with slavery becoming a chief formative discourse in the expression and practice of Syrian Christian monasticism, could it be that some of these monks actually willingly sought out institutional slavery as mode of *askēsis*? In her work on the missionary activities of the early Syriac churches, Jeanne-Nicole Mellon Saint-Laurent does note, though only in a passing footnote, the presence of the 'holy man qua slave motif'.[107] And we also know that slaves could become monks despite their status as enslaved.[108] The first objection to such a hypothesis might be that enslavement held sexual risks for monks – they could be forced into marriages and compelled to sexual intercourse in order to produce offspring. This is a valid point, and exactly what happened in the case of Malchus (who was not wilfully enslaved, but rather enslaved as a type of punishment and as a means to return to God and his monastery). The fear of physical harm and death would also no doubt be a deterrent to some. But the opportunity to die a martyr may have been a prospect that some of these monks welcomed. Malchus himself attempts suicide after being forced into marriage, but is dissuaded by his new unnamed 'wife'.

It is also very significant that Theodoret addresses this very fear in his *History of the Monks of Syria*. Apparently, the Devil taunted James of Cyrrhestica with the fear of Isaurians attacking from the east:

> He [James] related too how, at the time when those wicked brigands coming from Isauria burnt and plundered most of the east, he was terrified at the thought, not of being killed – he was not so in love with the body – but of enslavement and captivity and witnessing impiety and lawlessness. The Devil, perceiving this fear – for he often heard him express it to his

104 A. F. J. Klijn, *The Acts of Thomas: Introduction, Text, and Commentary*, Supplements to Novum Testamentum 108 (Leiden: Brill, 2003), 1–2; W. Wright, *Apocryphal Acts of the Apostles* (Amsterdam: Philo Press, 1968).

105 Klijn, *Acts of Thomas*, 100–2.

106 De Wet, *Unbound God.*

107 J.-N. Mellon Saint-Laurent, *Missionary Stories and the Formation of the Syriac Churches*, TCH 55 (Oakland, CA: University of California Press, 2015), 22.

108 See numerous instances of slaves participating in monasticism in John of Ephesus, *Vit.* 21, 31, 44, 56 [PO 17.289–90, 18.581, 18.665, 19.198].

> friends – imitated by night the wailing of women. 'I thought I could hear,' he continued, 'the enemy arriving and setting fire to the villages. I at once parted the hair on my head, drawing some on the left and some on the right down my shoulders to my chest, and made my neck ready to be severed by the sword, so that receiving the blow immediately, I might be spared the sight I deprecated. When day came and some people arrived, after spending the whole night like this, all the time expecting an assault, I asked what they had heard of the Isaurians. They replied that during these days they had heard nothing of them. That (he concluded) was how I discovered that this too was a diabolical illusion.'[109]

James does not fear death, but captivity, enslavement, and the impieties associated with it. But the story implies that it is a diabolical fear that should, in fact, be conquered. The threat of captivity and enslavement was a very real possibility, and spiritual and psychological strategies to cope with this threat would have been common. There is also the thought that, if the monk remains faithful, God will guard the chastity of the monk, as he did with Judas Thomas. The very fact that ascetic practice was so doulological may have even served as a *praeparatio* for the likelihood of being institutionally enslaved by Saracens or Isaurians.

Some monks, in imitation of the legendary enslaved apostle Judas Thomas, may have sought enslavement as test of their calling, to prove their worthiness to themselves and their peers – possibly even as an initiation or a rite of passage – and at the same time, to use it as a missionary strategy.[110] There is certainly literary evidence for this. In addition to the narratives of Jerome's Malchus and Pseudo-Nilus' Theodoulus, in narratives accounting for the spread of Christianity into Arabia, we read of several enslaved monks doing missionary work. While discussing the spread of Christianity in the Najrān, the early Muslim author Ibn Ishāq, in his *Life of the Messenger of God*, recounts the journeys of the enslaved Faymiyūn and Ṣāliḥ, who spread the Christian message, confronted a palm-tree god, and all the while, were protected by God in their enslavement.[111] Similarly, and after being warned of the likelihood of enslavement by their friends, Paul of Qenṭos and John of Edessa still departed on a pilgrimage journey, without fear of enslavement. They are then indeed kidnapped and taken to Ḥimyar, where they continue their missionary work.[112]

[109] Theodoret, *Hist. rel.* 21.27 [SC 257.110–13].

[110] Saint-Laurent, *Missionary Stories*, 22–4.

[111] *Sīr. ras. All.* 20–22, in A. Guillaume (trans.), *The Life of Muhammad: A Translation of Ibn Ishaq's Sirat Rasul Allah* (Oxford: Oxford University Press, 2002), 14–16.

[112] See H. Arneson et al. (trans.), *The History of the Great Deeds of Bishop Paul of Qentos and Priest John of Edessa*, Texts from Christian Late Antiquity 29 (Piscataway, NJ: Gorgias, 2010). Lenski, 'Slavery and Captivity', 260–1, rightly identifies some possible intertextual influence between the narratives of Pseudo-Nilus, Faymiyūn and Ṣāliḥ, and Paul of Qenṭos and John of Edessa.

Conclusion

In conclusion, we have found that slavery was characteristic of the urban and rural landscapes of late antique Syria and Mesopotamia. But the institution of slavery did not leave Christian ascetic culture untouched. In the analysis of monastic literature, from John Chrysostom and Theodoret to the *Book of Steps* and John of Ephesus, and beyond, it has been shown that slavery fundamentally shaped Syrian ascetic teaching and practice, and that it is possible to even speak of doulological asceticism. Central to this ascetic expression was the value of humiliation, or *msarrqūtā*, which enabled slavery to gain a firm grip on the self-fashioning of the monks – this was affected through various scriptural traditions like those of Philippians 2:6–11 and in imitation of models like Jesus, Paul, and Judas Thomas. Monks may have even physically looked like slaves. The implication is that, along with other discourses like the contest and spiritual soldiery, the discourse of slavery, which was just as violent as these other discourses traditionally associated with martyrdom and asceticism, must be included in future analyses of the relationship between asceticism, monasticism, and late antique society and culture. The social obsession with the slave body is now mirrored in the anxieties of the ascetic body – both were subject to intense and almost constant examination and surveillance.

Socially, the strategy of doulological asceticism would bind the monks closely to the non-elite inhabitants, especially those of the impoverished villages outlying urban areas, which adds insight and support to Peter Brown's initial reading of the holy man in this region. Despite the transcendence and other-worldliness of the monks, who acted as patrons to the poor in these villages, these holy men – or holy slaves of God – embodied a habitus that was not too foreign to the villagers. There was room for association; the monk would be considered as 'one of them.' Thus we see the confidence of impoverished villagers approaching the monks for aid.

Thus, in addition to the above social strategy, the doulological asceticism that characterized Syrian Christian monasticism most likely served a psychological purpose. With the real threat of being captured and enslaved by one of the many bands of brigands, like the Saracens or Isaurians, the practice of asceticism *as* slavery may have prepared monks for the inevitable. The violence inflicted wilfully on the self prepared such an individual for the possibility of involuntary and external violence. Some monks may have even consciously embraced slavery as a way to validate their calling, test their obedience, and provide them with an opportunity for evangelization – or martyrdom. The distinctions between 'spiritual' and real slavery now fully evaporate – slavery becomes a form of asceticism that, paradoxically, brings freedom. What is especially telling is that Maria Chiara Giorda's contribution to this volume highlights a similar dynamic, broadly speaking, taking place in the monasteries of late antique Egypt, in which some children and even adults who were admitted into the monastery had to take up servant roles similar to slaves. We thus mark a notable moment in what we might label the history of power relations, violence, and oppression. The sources attest to an eclipse, a full discursive alignment between the violent macrocosm of institutional slavery and the self-disciplinary microcosm of monasticism; and in the monk who actively pursues enslavement, there is even an assimilation of these worlds, in which the micro- becomes absorbed into the macrocosm. What we must finally realize is that this discursive colonization of asceticism by institutional slavery would have embedded and ramified the oppressive institution in the late antique and early medieval east for centuries. Also in this volume, Lillian Larsen comes to a similar conclusion: that monastic ideals and ideologies reinscribed the hierarchies of slavery. The humiliation of asceticism would feed off and into the further humiliation and violation of millions of victims of institutional slavery in the ages that followed.

CHAPTER 6

Constructing Complexity
Slavery in the Small Worlds of Early Monasticism

Lillian I. Larsen

In her groundbreaking study, *Slavery in Early Christianity*, Jennifer Glancy observes that while scholars of early Christianity have historically relied on constructing 'a seamless picture of ancient life that disguises the jagged edges of the documentation', it is in fact a harsher reality that best reflects the contours of embodied experience.[1] Because 'any description of slavery in antiquity is the product of multiple scholarly decisions', it remains a question 'whether one can discern links among miscellaneous sources to tell a connected story'.[2] Glancy observes that while surviving texts are 'laced with images and metaphors borrowed from the rhetorical domain of chattel slavery', their allusions 'are almost always cryptic'.[3] If they promise 'windows into the lives of real people', any evidence they provide is fragmentary.[4] She premises that it is only by recognizing that the 'attitudes of slaveholders remained constant', and 'conditions in which slaves lived and worked persisted from generation to generation', that one can document the presence of slaves in ancient sources.[5] The task of listening for voices that echo in silence, of discerning bodies that remain invisible, is one of reading around the edges and between the lines.

J. Albert Harrill's textually focused study of *Slaves in the New Testament* also emphasizes the scholarly gap separating interpretive refractions from

An early layer of this research was presented in the 'Meals in the Greco-Roman World' seminar at the 2008 SBL Annual Meeting. These preliminary results are published in Lillian I. Larsen, 'Early Christian Meals and Slavery', in D. Smith and H. Taussig (eds.), *Meals in the Early Christian World: Social Formation, Experimentation, and Conflict at the Table* (New York, NY: Palgrave Macmillan, 2012), 191–204 (my thanks to the SBL Meals group for their questions and comments). Intrigued by the unexpected richness and complexity of the monastic sources, I elected to expand this core content in contributing to 'The Violence in Small Worlds' symposium, organized by Kate Cooper and Jamie Wood, at Oxford in the summer of 2011. My thanks to Kate Cooper, Jamie Wood, and those who attended this meeting for their collegial commendations and useful feedback.

[1] J. A. Glancy, *Slavery in Early Christianity* (Minneapolis, MN: Fortress Press, 2006), 3.
[2] Glancy, *Slavery in Early Christianity*, 3.
[3] Glancy, *Slavery in Early Christianity*, 4–5.
[4] Glancy, *Slavery in Early Christianity*, 5.
[5] Glancy, *Slavery in Early Christianity*, 3.

harsh, historical antecedents.[6] Extending exploration introduced in his *Manumission of Slaves in Early Christianity*, Harrill identifies the conceptual disconnect presented by the 'surprisingly little [substantive] discussion of [slaves] by ancient authors', and the 'significance of slaves in ancient daily life'.[7] As he catalogues the ubiquitous presence of slaves in early Christian narrative material,[8] Harrill documents the degree to which slaves served as 'a natural referent for . . . Christians . . . accustomed as Romans to use such language for self-definition and the construction of religious community'.[9] He suggests that here, as elsewhere, Christian moral hierarchies were perpetuated 'through the retelling of . . . stories . . . [that made common] use of slaves and masters as literary figures'.[10]

Kyle Harper's more recent consideration of *Slavery in the Late Roman World* shifts the focus to a slightly later period. Yet, like Glancy and Harrill, Harper stresses the conceptual dissonance that divides scholarly description from late-ancient lived experience.[11] In particular, Harper examines assumptions that attach Christianization of the Roman Empire to a 'thesis of amelioration'. Emphasizing the optimism implicit in scholarly valuation of the influence exerted by Paul's assertion that in Christ Jesus 'there is neither Jew nor Greek, male nor female, slave nor free' (Gal. 3:28), Harper underscores the ways in which interpretive predisposition has effectively effaced harsher realities.[12]

Reaffirming the persistent practice premised by Glancy and Harrill, Harper's careful analyses provide essential context for examining a late-Roman world, where to be a slave-owner remained a 'manifest symbol of honour',[13] and even less than elite family structures assume the implicit presence of slaves.[14] Simultaneously, that 'monasticism' is notably absent from Harper's exhaustive index, in some sense registers the challenges implicit in identifying cracks and fissures in what remains an

[6] J. A. Harrill, *The Manumission of Slaves in Early Christianity*, Hermeneutische Untersuchungen zur Theologie 32 (Tübingen: Mohr Siebeck, 1998).

[7] Harrill, *Manumission of Slaves*, 18.

[8] J. A. Harrill, *Slaves in the New Testament: Literary, Social, and Moral Dimensions* (Minneapolis, MN: Fortress Press, 2005); see Chris L. de Wet's chapter in this volume for additional discussion of Harrill's work.

[9] Harrill, *Slaves in the New Testament*, 3.

[10] Harrill, *Slaves in the New Testament*, 3.

[11] Kyle Harper, *Slavery in the Late Roman World, AD 275–425* (Cambridge: Cambridge University Press, 2011), 210.

[12] Cf. Harper, *Slavery in the Late Roman World*, 33–4.

[13] Harper, *Slavery in the Late Roman World*, 29.

[14] Cf. Harper, *Slavery in the Late Roman World*, 144–62. C. L. De Wet, 'John Chrysostom's Advice to Slaveholders', *Studia Patristica* 67 (2013), 359–66 argues that late-ancient terms of 'servile responsibility' may have grown more onerous.

essentially seamless landscape. Harper's study itself attests the 'lingering distortions introduced by a paradigm that managed to hold the field . . . for at least a century'.[15]

Slavery in Jewish/Christian Asceticism

As the present chapter seeks to trouble a trajectory where hagiography has long been read as history, it makes no claim to be exhaustive. Instead, building on the seminal research that grounds each of these prior studies, it re-examines a range of sources long used to support an ascetic 'premise of amelioration', then applies emergent insight to less familiar literary, material, and regulatory landscapes. In extending Glancy, Harrill, and Harper's foundational work, it offers preliminary answers to a simple question: 'If one chooses an alternate starting point, what comes out differently that might be of interest?'[16]

Philo (20 BCE–50 CE, Alexandria)

A conventional starting point for exploring the question of slavery in emergent ascetic settings remains Philo's first century account of the *Vita contemplativa*. As Philo traces the contours of idealized communal practice among the semi-monastic *Therapeutae*, the absence of slaves is a point of particular emphasis:

> . . . they do not have slaves to wait upon them as they consider that the ownership of servants is entirely against nature. For nature has borne all men to be free, but the wrongful and covetous acts of some who pursued that source of evil, inequality, having imposed their yoke and invested the stronger with power over the weaker. In this sacred banquet there is . . . no slave, but the services are rendered by free men who perform their tasks as attendants not under compulsion nor yet waiting for orders, but with deliberate goodwill anticipating eagerly and zealously the demands that may be made. For it is not just any free men who are appointed for these offices but young members of the association chosen with all for their special merit who as becomes their good character and nobility are pressing on to reach the summit of virtue. They give their services gladly and proudly like sons to their real fathers and mothers, judging them to be

[15] Harper, *Slavery in the Late Roman World*, 210.

[16] This eloquent query was coined by K. King, 'Mackinations on Myth and Origins', in E. A. Castelli and H. Taussig (eds.), *Re-imagining Christian Origins: A Colloquium Honoring Burton L. Mack* (Valley Forge, PA: Trinity Press International, 1996), 165.

> the [common] parents of them all . . ., in a closer affinity than that of blood, since to the right minded there is no closer tie than [virtue]. And they come in to do their service ungirt and with tunics [let] down, that in their appearance there may be no shadow of anything to suggest the slave . . . [i]n this banquet . . .[17]

There is little question that Philo's prose is structured in conversation with the traditional roles accorded Graeco-Roman household slaves.[18] His account likewise echoes broader discussions of slavery encountered in Stoic sources and teaching.[19] Whether Philo's idealized community ever existed, or registered real resistance to wider norms, is less certain. As depicted, however, the exceptional character of a 'world without slaves' is implicit.

Generations of Paul (~30–120 CE, Asia Minor)

In more explicitly Christian discussions of slavery, the canonical letters attributed to Paul have proved alternately foundational. In contrast to Philo's idealized characterization of the *Therapeutae*, the ascetic refractions included in the Pauline corpus suggest a concrete historical setting and belie a more textured landscape. While critical scholars argue that only seven of the thirteen letters that bear Paul's signature can be securely attached to the 'Apostle' himself, tracing a trajectory that spans three generations, and sixty years, Paul's own instructions, and the emendations introduced by subsequent pseudonymers, remain central reference points in both late-ancient discussion, and subsequent scholarly refraction of a 'Christian' response to slaveholding.

The seven letters most securely ascribed to Paul span roughly a decade (49–60 CE). This 'undisputed' correspondence includes: one letter to the Thessalonians, two letters to the Corinthians, individual letters to the Philippians, Galatians, and Romans, as well as a single anomalous missive to the householder, Philemon (about his slave, Onesimus).

[17] *Vita contemplativa* in *Philo* (trans. by F. H. Colson; 10 vols; LCL; Cambridge: Harvard University Press, 1941, 1995), 9.70–72. Philo's description finds interesting echo in the richly detailed monastic meal codes of the sixth century *Regula magistri*; Cf. Larsen, 'Early Christian Meals and Slavery', 200–1; L. I. Larsen, 'Monastic Meals: Resisting a Reclining Culture?', in Smith and Taussig (eds.), *Meals in the Early Christian World*, 253–5.

[18] See discussions in S. Marks and H. Taussig (eds.), *Meals in Early Judaism: Social Formation at Table* (Minneapolis, MN: Fortress Press, 2014).

[19] Glancy notes the degree to which 'the rhetoric of slavery haunts the [Stoic] claim that the only real bondage is . . . servility of will, of mind, or of spirit', *Slavery in Early Christianity*, 30; In discussing the *Manumission of Slaves* in Early Christian communities, Harrill also explores the ways in which a *topos* of slavery proved integral to Stoic teaching, *Manumission of Slaves*, 11–30.

Two subsequent generations of letters are widely viewed as pseudonymously penned by followers of Paul. Written in Paul's name and claiming his authority, one trio of letters is provenanced to the decades immediately following Paul's death (70–90 CE);[20] a second, to the late first, early second century (90–120 CE).[21] Both individually and generationally, these letters attest the ubiquitous and unremarkable presence of slaves in ancient society. More than half address interactions between masters and slaves. In defining practice, however, respective tiers remain chronologically distinct.

Within the documents most securely linked to Paul, the concrete valence of articulated directive remains opaque. To the Galatians Paul writes: 'there is neither Jew nor Greek ... slave nor free ... male nor female; for ... all [are] one in Christ Jesus' (Gal 3:28 [RSV]). To the Corinthians, his nomenclature is linguistically more ambiguous. Even today, a secure translation of Paul's message to slaves in this community (I Cor. 7:21–24), remains elusive.[22] Similarly, while Paul's letter to Philemon takes as its central focus the plight of a runaway slave, some scholars read Paul's petition as an overt appeal for clemency and manumission, others maintain the opposite.

Subsequent reworkings iteratively clarify residual traces of implicit ambiguity. Even the first layer of redaction registers subtle but significant shifts. While Paul's letter to the Galatians asserts that 'there is neither Jew nor Greek ... slave nor free ... for ... all [are] one in Christ Jesus' (Gal. 3:28 [RSV]), the pseudonymous letters to Colossae and Ephesus introduce a caveat. Clarifying that in the *new nature* there will be neither 'Greek [nor] Jew, circumcised [nor] uncircumcised, barbarian, Scythian, slave, [nor] free' (Col. 3:11 [RSV]), in the present state, slaves are enjoined to

> obey in everything those who are your earthly masters, not with eye-service, as menpleasers, but in singleness of heart, fearing the Lord. Whatever your task, work heartily as serving the Lord and not men, knowing that from the Lord you will receive the inheritance as your reward; you are serving the Lord Christ. (Col. 3:22–24 [RSV]; cf. Eph. 6:5–8)

20 This small corpus includes 2 Thessalonians, alongside Ephesians and Colossians.

21 This later trio of 'Pastoral' letters includes 1, 2 Timothy and Titus.

22 For example, the RSV and the NRSV imbue their respective translations of Paul's address with contrasting emphases. The RSV translates Paul's counsel as encouraging enslaved members of the Corinthian community to avail themselves of the chance 'to gain [their] freedom' if the opportunity should arise. The NRSV, in turn, translates Paul's directive as enjoining slaves to endure with patience their subject state (I Cor. 7:21); Harrill's detailed discussion of the passage usefully catalogues attendant interpretive debate, *Manumission of Slaves*, 68–126.

Each missive additionally instructs masters to treat 'slaves justly and fairly' (Col. 4:1; cf. Eph. 6:9). Whether slave or free, all are encouraged to be 'subject to one another in fear of Christ' (Eph. 5:21).[23]

A subsequent trio of 'pastoral' letters (90–120 CE) expands these linguistic adjustments, assigning slave-masters greater privilege, and delineating the duties of slaves in closer detail. For example, in the first of two letters to 'Timothy', 'all who are under the yoke of slavery' are enjoined to

> regard their masters as worthy of all honour, so that the name of God and the teaching may not be defamed. Those who have believing masters must not be disrespectful on the ground that they are [brothers and sisters]; rather they must serve all the better, since those who benefit by their service are believers and beloved. (1 Tim. 6:1–2 [RSV])

An attendant letter addressed to 'Titus', instructs

> slaves to be submissive to their masters and to give satisfaction in every respect; they are not to [contradict], nor to pilfer, but to show entire and true fidelity, so that in everything they may adorn the doctrine of God our Saviour. (Titus 2: 9–10 [RSV])

As the lines between Christian masters and slaves are rendered patent, any traces of residual ambiguity are here effectively effaced.

Slavery in Late Antiquity

Tracking the full trajectory of Pauline interpretation lies beyond the purview of this relatively brief essay. However, as one encounters 'the Apostle' in fourth-century threads of reception history, the implicit weight assigned to authoritative tradition is clear.[24] If the Stoic ideals characteristic of Philo's communal constructs remain active in principle, it is material

[23] The reminder of ultimate accountability to a heavenly 'master' ironically relies on the nomenclature of slavery in ostensibly softening starker mandates. In his chapter in this volume, Chris L. de Wet names this the 'Christic panopticon'. He suggests that rendering Christ a divine slaveholder makes slaves and slaveholders alike subject to 'a never-ending cycle of surveillance'.

[24] Late ancient ascetics found a similar range of models readily available in early Christian narrative traditions; cf. Harrill, *Slaves in the New Testament*. For example, Mark's gospel (10:42–45) uses the language of slavery as a metaphor for the appropriate demeanour of an ideal disciple. Within the narrative frame of the Last Supper, the Gospel of John (15:15–16) depicts Jesus addressing his own disciples as slaves. In the Apocalypse to John, the 'slaves' of God are depicted waiting at the foot of God's throne, with '*his* name ... on their foreheads' (Rev. 22:3–4) [RSV]. Softening this stark language, both the RSV and the NRSV routinely translate δοῦλος as 'servant' rather than 'slave'.

selected from the Pauline/deutero-Pauline corpus that finds explicit echo.[25] Simultaneously, like their first- and early second-century counterparts, late-ancient redaction reflects ideological investments in important ways. Which texts are cited, when and by whom, is arguably not incidental.[26]

John Chrysostom (347–407 CE, Antioch)

Kyle Harper has appropriately named John Chrysostom 'one of the great sources for the historian of everyday life in late antiquity'.[27] As his fourth-century sermons address a Christian audience comprised of both masters and slaves, Chrysostom derivatively depicts the settings where emergent monasticism found its form. Weaving varied layers of tradition into a skilfully threaded fabric imbued with 'the Apostle's' authoritative voice, Chrysostom's homilies refract a world where biblical precedent served to reinforce a social system in which 'the foundations of slavery ... were never seriously challenged'.[28] In a newly 'Christianized' Empire 'energetically committed to the project of ruling a slave society',[29] his vivid prose affirms the 'steady state mentality'[30] that made slavery a central element of the late-ancient economy. In the fourth century as in the first, a 'world without slaves' remains anomalous.

Citing 'Paul's' first letter to Timothy, Chrysostom urges slaves 'that have believing masters' not to despise them 'because they are brethren', but to count themselves fortunate to be 'worthy of so great a benefit, as to have ... masters ... [as] brethren'. Mandating full submission, not only because master and slave share familial status in the Christian community, but because masters 'pay [slaves] the larger service', Chrysostom premises

[25] See Chris L. de Wet's chapter in this volume for more detailed elucidation of Stoic echoes in Paul's discussions of slavery.

[26] E. A. Clark, *Reading Renunciation: Asceticism and Scripture in Early Christianity* (Princeton, NJ: Princeton University Press, 1999), documents the agility with which late ancient authors reworked biblical content. The fluidity of such strategic deployment of authoritative text is particularly patent in homiletic material that addresses slavery.

[27] Harper, *Slavery in the Late Roman World*, 205.

[28] Susanna Elm, '*Virgins of God': The Making of Asceticism in Late Antiquity* (Oxford: Clarendon Press, 1994), underscores the multivalent character of emergent interpretive trajectories. While Elm follows earlier scholarship in asserting that late antiquity brought a 'gradual amelioration of the lot of individual slaves', she likewise observes that 'the Church relied increasingly on its own slaves, which contributed to the preservation of barriers between slaves and masters' (86–7).

[29] Harper, *Slavery in the Late Roman World*, 27.

[30] K. R. Bradley, 'The Problem of Slavery in Classical Antiquity', *Classical Philology*, 92 (1997), 273–82.

that by virtue of 'furnish[ing] the money to purchase ... sufficient food and clothing; and bestow[ing] much care upon [their slaves] in other respects', masters 'contribute greater benefits to their servants, than servants to their masters'. Since owners 'suffer much toil and trouble for [a slave's] repose', they ought to receive 'much honour' in return.[31]

Viewed generously, Chrysostom premises a mutually beneficial contract between masters and slaves. Subsequent portions of this sermon, however, bring the harsh edges of lived experience into sharp focus. Turning his attention to the position of wealthy landowners relative to God, Chrysostom's detailed address offers a sobering summary of life as a fourth-century slave:

> Beloved ... [l]et us ... serve our Master, as our servants serve us ... They have only food and lodging; but we, possessing much and expecting more, insult our Benefactor with our luxury ... They receive many insults from fear of us, and endure them in silence with the patience of philosophers. Justly or unjustly they are exposed to our violence, and they do not resist, but entreat us, though often they have done nothing wrong. They are content ... to receive no more and often less than they need; with straw for their bed, and only bread for their food, they do not complain or murmur at their hard living, but through fear of us are restrained from impatience ... [S]ay not they are under necessity, when [you] too are under a necessity in the fear of hell ... [Why do you] not render to God as much honour, as [you] receive ... from [your] servants.[32]

In conclusion, Chrysostom enjoins his listening householders to render service to God 'with as much zeal as [slaves] do their master'.[33]

Chrysostom's reliance on the pseudonymous portions of Paul's attributed corpus is not unexpected. However, in melding Paul's early injunctions with the detailed directives of later writers, his parsing is adept. For example, a homily addressing Paul's letter to Philemon addresses the tensive status of individuals who while named equal in the sight of God, remained fully subject to the unmitigated authority of their Christian masters.[34] Urging slaves to give little heed to their servile status but rather attend to Paul's 'best counsel', Chrysostom repackages a portion of Paul's

[31] *Hom. 1 Tim.* 16.2 (PG 62.588.38–589.11; trans. *NPNF*[1] 13, 465).

[32] *Hom. 1 Tim.* 16.2 (PG 62.589.54–590.20; trans. *NPNF*[1] 13, 466).

[33] *Hom. 1 Tim.* 16. 2 (PG 62.590.42–43; trans. *NPNF*[1] 13.466). The residual presuppositions that ground Chrysostom's homiletic exposition of Titus 2:10 are similarly resonant; cf. *Hom. Tit.* 4.3 (PG 62.685.4ff).

[34] Cf. C. L. de Wet, 'Honour Discourse in John Chrysostom's Exegesis of the Letter to Philemon', in D. Francis Tolmie (ed.) *Philemon in Perspective: Interpreting a Pauline Letter* (Berlin: De Gruyter, 2010), 317–32.

first letter to the Corinthians in a manner that effaces its implicit ambiguity: '[Are you] called, being a servant? Care not for it: but if even [you] . . . be made free, use it rather . . . to abide in slavery'.[35]

The same homily simultaneously includes a surprising series of warnings that suggest a competing range of 'ascetic' priorities. The first cautions against heeding those who have 'reduced [many] to the necessity of blasphemy . . . [by] saying Christianity has been introduced into life for the subversion of everything'. A second remonstrates against 'masters having their servants taken from them . . . [as] a matter of violence'.[36] Refracting interpretive perspective that appears to assign alternate valence (and weight) to primary strains of proto-Christian precedent, elsewhere Chrysostom attributes these positions to a group of individuals who 'under the pretense of continence [likewise] separate . . . wives from their husbands'.[37]

Slavery in Monastic Asceticism

In scholarly examination of slavery in early monasticism – as in broader address of slavery in Constantine's newly Christianized Roman Empire – the ascetic ideals encountered in the early writings of Paul (and Philo) have often informed interpretive habits that equate relatively slim slices of hagiography with representative history. In developing more nuanced reading strategies, engaging a broader range of literary, material, and regulatory landscapes affords essential context that can potentially expand familiar models in richly textured ways.

Monastic literary sources like the *Vita Macrina*, alongside select portions of the *Historia Lausiaca* and the *Apophthegmata Patrum*, have long been used to categorically define late-antique ascetic *loci* as havens for manumitted slaves. However, closer examination of these same literary landscapes complexifies established constructs. If 'everyday' details are assigned a measure of historical weight, seemingly singular habits which rhetorically render fictional depictions 'plausible' may as readily register persistent patterns of practice.[38]

[35] Chrysostom, *Hom. Phil.* Prologue (PG 62.704.8–13; trans. *NPNF*[1]) 13, 546; cf. I Cor. 7:21; see further discussion in n. 22, above.

[36] *Hom. Phil.* Prologue (PG 62.704.19–23; *NPNF*[1] 13, 546).

[37] *Hom. Tit.* 4.3 (PG 62.684.60–685.2; trans. *NPNF*[1] 13, 533).

[38] L. I. Larsen, 'The *Apophthegmata Patrum*: Rustic Rumination or Rhetorical Recitation', *Meddelanden från Collegium Patristicum Lundense*, 22 (2008), 21–31; cf. Ronald Hock and Edward O'Neil, *The Chreia in Ancient Rhetoric* (Atlanta: Society of Biblical Literature, 1985).

Gregory of Nyssa, Vita Macrinae *(329–389/90 CE, Cappadocia)*

Gregory of Nyssa's account of the ascetic practice undertaken by his sister Macrina is easily among the most detailed – and familiar – descriptions of household commerce between masters and slaves. While Gregory elsewhere articulates overt condemnation of slavery,[39] the refractions included in this fourth-century *Vita* suggest a more nuanced stance. Like Philo, Gregory draws on Stoic sensibilities in picturing Macrina's wealthy household as a locus where slavery has, in some sense, gone 'out of vogue.' As reported:

> [Macrina] persuaded her mother to give up their accustomed way of life ... and the services she had previously been accustomed to receive from her maids ... [putting] herself on an equal footing with the many in spirit ... to share a common life ... [by] making [her maids] sisters and equals instead of slaves and servants ... [and] turning away from all she was accustomed to ... so as to share with them one table, bed, and all the needs of life, with every difference of rank eliminated ... In them no anger, envy, hate, arrogance, nor any such thing was seen ... Their only care was for divine realities, and there was constant prayer and the unceasing singing of hymns, extended equally throughout the entire day and night so that this was both work, and respite from work, for them.[40]

As familiarity has softened this text's jagged edges, it is easy to overlook the fact that Macrina's progression from less permeable to more permeable social boundaries leaves troubling questions of agency unaddressed. Within this domestic reconfiguration, Macrina's exemplary humility effectively serves as a patent register of the gap that divides masters and slaves.

Absent any explicit register of social critique, Macrina's practice is implicitly framed in conversation with established norms of slavery. At once, dismantling and instantiating institutionalized hierarchies, the presence of slaves at the table inversely marks Macrina's elite ascetic, and social, status. If one eschews idealized interpretations, it is arguable that enforced 'table fellowship' simply imposes an alternate type of servitude upon individuals who remain, nonetheless, subordinate.

[39] See discussion in Jonathan Tallon's chapter in this volume; cf. Gregory of Nyssa, *Hom. Eccl.* 4 (PG 44.664 ff).

[40] Gregory of Nyssa, *Vita Macrina* 7–11, P. Maraval (ed.), *Grégoire de Nysse. Vie de sainte Macrine*, SC 178 (Paris: Éditions du Cerf, 1971); V. W. Callahan (trans.), *Saint Gregory of Nyssa: Ascetical Works*, FOTC 58 (Washington, DC: Catholic University Press, 1967); cf. Elm, *Virgins of God*, 78–105.

Palladius (368–431 CE), Historia Lausiaca

Like the *Vita Macrinae*, a number of the vignettes included in Palladius' *Historia Lausiaca* have served as routine reference points in discussions of slavery in monastic settings. Of these, the story of Melania the Younger, a wealthy householder, is among the most familiar.

In Palladius' recounting of his protagonist's embrace of the 'ascetic life', her personal austerities are enumerated in close detail. As reported, Melania

> ate every other day . . . and arranged to do some of the manual work of her slave women, whom she made her associates in her ascetic practices . . . dwelling in the country, sometimes in Sicily, again in Campania, with fifteen eunuchs and sixty maidens, both freewomen and slaves.[41]

Readers are told that this young householder also 'set free eight thousand slaves who desired freedom'. However, when she attempted to manumit the rest, they 'did not want this . . . choosing rather to serve her brother, to whom they were sold for three pieces of money'.[42]

Palladius' *History* is introduced as a record of lifestyles and praxis of male and female ascetics he has seen or 'heard about', or with whom he lived in 'the Egyptian desert and Libya, in the Thebaid and Syene'.[43] Interspersed with familiar accounts, like that of Melania the Younger, the *History* also includes encounters with elite figures, in more complex guises. For example, Palladius reports that when the desert monks Isidore, Pisimius, Adelphius, Paphnutius, Pambo, and Ammonius were banished to Palestine,[44] 'they were not allowed servants'. Instead, the wealthy Melania (mother of Melania the Younger) 'wore a slave's hood [in order] to bring them what they needed at evening'.[45]

As interesting are slave referents that attach to ascetic figures of less elite station. Palladius describes the 'Christian maiden' Potamiaena as 'a slave of someone or other during the time of Maximian', who was handed over to the prefect of Alexandria to be tortured after 'her master was unable to seduce her'.[46] The Galatian priest Philoromus, 'a most ascetic and patient man . . . was born of a mother who was a household slave and a father who

41 Palladius, *Historia Lausiaca* (hereafter: *Hist. Laus.*) 61, G. J. M. Bartelink (ed.), *Palladio. La storia Lausiaca* (Verona: Fondazione Lorenzo Valla, 1974), R. T. Meyer (trans.), *The Lausiac History*, Ancient Christian Writers 34 (Mahwah, NJ: Paulist Press, 1964).

42 *Hist. Laus.* 61.5.

43 *Hist. Laus.* Prologue 2.

44 Elsewhere identified as the 'tall brothers'.

45 *Hist. Laus.* 46.3.

46 *Hist. Laus.* 3.1–2.

was a freedman'.[47] The Cappadocian Sisinnius, disciple of Elpidius, is named 'a slave by birth, but free by faith'.[48]

In traditional interpretive discussion, this wider range of ascetics is rarely referenced. Likewise, while the relative status of these subjects is left unstated, that Palladius' survey of monastic settings includes both elite householders and less privileged counterparts affirms a recurring pattern.

Apophthegmata Patrum *(fifth to seventh centuries)*

Like the *Historia Lausiaca*, refractions woven into extant collections of the *Apophthegmata Patrum* register protagonists of both elite and pedestrian lineage.[49] Echoing familiar detail, a vignette recounting the pre-monastic life of Abba Arsenius defines his ascetic praxis relative to a world where he was 'surrounded by thousands of slaves (χίλιοι δοῦλοι) with golden girdles, all wearing collars of gold and garments of silk'.[50] A subsequent description of Arsenius' desert existence reduces this coterie to more ascetic proportions:

> A Father went to see Abba Arsenius. When he knocked at the door the old man opened it, thinking that it was his servant. But when he saw that it was someone else he fell on his face to the ground. The other said to him, 'Get up, Father, so that I may greet you.' But the old man replied, 'I shall not get up till you have gone,' and in spite of much pleading he did not get up until the other had gone away.[51]

While tradition has uniformly framed the attendants that share the cells of illustrious 'desert fathers' as self-designated protégés, reading this *apophthegm* in light of broader source material suggests a more complex

[47] *Hist. Laus.* 45.1. [48] *Hist. Laus.* 49.1.

[49] C. Faraggiana di Sarzana, '*Apophthegmata Patrum*: Some Crucial Points of their Textual Transmission', *Studia Patristica*, 29 (1997), 455–67, offers a summary of the *AP*'s complicated history. While many of the narratives included in extant collections are ostensibly set in the Egyptian desert, their provenance remains a matter of wide debate.

[50] Arsenius 36, *Apophthegmata Patrum*, Collectio Alphabetika (hereafter *Apoph. Patr.* Coll. Alpha.), J. B. Cotelier (ed.), in *Ecclesiae Graecae Monumenta* 1 (Paris, 1677); Reprinted in PG 65.101.39–104.12; B. Ward (trans.), *The Sayings of the Desert Fathers: The Alphabetical Collection* (rev. edn) (Kalamazoo, MI: Cistercian Publications, 1984). Glancy, *Slavery in Early Christianity*, 88, notes that Constantine deemed slave collars a more humane alternative to the branded tattoos that had previously served to mark possession; cf. D. L. Thurmond, 'Some Roman Slave Collars in CIL', *Athenaeum*, 82 (1994), 63–73; W. Westermann, *Slave Systems of Greco-Roman Antiquity* (Philadelphia, PA: American Philosophical Society, 1955), 118, 154–5.

[51] Arsenius 37, *Apoph. Patr.* Coll. Alph. (PG 65.104.13–19); Ward (trans.).

literary landscape.[52] As represented, upon retreating to the desert, Arsenius may not have left '[all] his servants behind'.[53]

Elsewhere, narrative detail incorporates the essential nomenclature of slavery into the structures which define mundane depictions of monastic life. For example, an *apophthegm* attributed to Abba Joseph of Pelusia describes

> a brother who was good, ascetic, and handsome. He came to church for the synaxis dressed in a little old *mafort* darned all over. Once when I saw him coming to the synaxis I said to him, 'Brother, do you not see the brothers, looking like angels for the synaxis in church? How can you always come here in that garb?' He said to me, 'Forgive me, abba, but I have nothing else.' So I took him in to my cell and gave him a tunic and whatever else he needed. After that he wore them like the other brethren and was like an angel to look at. Now once it was necessary for the Fathers to send ten brethren to the emperor about something or other and he was chosen as one of the group to go. When he heard this, he made a prostration before his Father saying, 'In the Lord's name, excuse me, for I am the slave of a great man down there and if he recognizes me, he will deprive me of my habit and force me to serve him again.' The brothers were convinced and left him behind. But later, they learned from someone who had known him well when he was in the world that he had been head of the administration and that he had spoken as he did as a ruse, so that no-one should know this or bother him about it. So great, amongst the Fathers, was their concern to flee from glory and the peace of this world![54]

Another *apophthegm* reports that the monk, Abba Mius

> [who] had been a slave and ... had become a true reader of hearts ... went [every year] to Alexandria, taking his wages to his masters. They went to meet him with great respect, but the old man put water into a basin and brought it to wash his masters' feet. They said to him, 'No, Father, do not overwhelm us.' But he said to them, 'I acknowledge that I am your slave and I acknowledge that you have left me free to serve God; I wash your feet, and you accept my wages, which are here.' They argued, not wishing to receive them, so he said to them, 'If you refuse to accept them, I shall remain here and serve you.' Since they revered him, they allowed him to do what he wanted; then they saw him off, giving him many provisions and

[52] Larsen, 'Rustic Rumination', 21–31.

[53] See Chrysostom's critique of retaining large numbers of slaves. See also Jonathan Tallon's chapter in this volume, which offers suggestive support for reading Arsenius' limited coterie as a narrative marker of ascetic self-denial.

[54] Cronius 5, *Apoph. Patr.* Coll. Alph. (PG 65.249.11–38); Ward (trans.).

> money so that he could give alms for them. For this reason he became famous and beloved in Scetis.[55]

Offering, at once, tensive confluence and stark counterpoint to broader refractions of late-antique life, as household constructs are reformulated and/or dissolved, less familiar landscapes relativize the exaggerated dimensions of larger than life literary constructs. As an integral element in literary landscapes defined by established cultural norms, whether manumitted, sold at discount rates, named ascetic associates, or tagged as narrative markers, the presence of slaves remains routine.

Monastic Material Landscapes

Relative to recurrent discussion of elite figures who 'humbly' assume the duties of a slave, more mundane monastic links to actual slavery have elicited little interest among scholars. Similarly, material referents have often served simply to provide detailed context for the literary landscapes that define a well-integrated web of emergent monastic life. Nonetheless, even cursory survey of a limited range of material remains suggests more complex affiliations. While there is little that challenges the rearticulated guidelines refracted in more familiar source material, the physical affinities that link emergent landscapes are difficult to ignore.

For example, in assessing Egyptian monastic settlements excavated at Esna, Roger Bagnall emphasizes the mundane delineations that separate the 'ideal' and the 'real'. Here, finds have revealed underground atrium-style houses, with floor plans not unlike those that characterize the homes of prosperous Mediterranean families. Balancing 'pervasive attempts of the literary sources to describe a self-denying way of life for ascetics in the desert', Bagnall premises that such material *loci* suggest that at least some monks lived 'lives of self-mortification in a setting designed to remind them of wealth, not poverty'. He observes that living quarters 'give the impression of being modelled after upper-class houses in towns, rather than . . . the habitations of the poor'. Cells range from simple to relatively elaborate, 'with rooms, a court, a well, and other amenities'. A number of habitations include 'cool rooms for the storage of dry bread, movable doors, and even glass in some windows'.[56]

[55] Mius 2, *Apoph. Patr.* Coll. Alph. (PG 65.301.30–47); Ward (trans.)

[56] R. Bagnall, *Egypt in Late Antiquity* (Princeton, NJ: Princeton University Press, 1993), 296–7.

In considering the parameters of a slave's physical position within such domestic settings, like Bagnall, Andrew Wallace-Hadrill defines his analysis of household and communal norms relative to excavated structural remains. He particularly calls attention to the patterns of proximate, daily interaction that marked relationships between ancient masters and their slaves. Arguing that the absence of discrete sleeping quarters for domestic slaves indicates that slaves generally lived within the master's house, he suggests that slaves had little choice but to remain fully immersed in the mundane rhythms of daily life. Such fluid patterns of interaction offer rich perspective when considering the details which define 'household' dynamics across a spectrum of monastic literary landscapes.[57]

More particular intersections emerge in a corpus of late-ancient correspondence encountered among the material remains that derive from the Monastery of Epiphanius at Thebes. Again, elucidating tensive links between the ideal and the real, the appellations preserved on a sizeable collection of ostraca register nomenclature used to designate communal roles of 'father', 'brother', 'son', and 'mother'.[58] More jarring is the repeated delegation of duties to individuals identified simply as 'this man of mine'.[59]

Monastic Legal Landscapes

Both literary and material landscapes affirm Glancy's premise that it is often only by recognizing that the 'attitudes of slaveholders remained constant', and 'conditions in which slaves lived and worked persisted from generation to generation', that one can document the presence of slaves in ancient settings.[60] Similarly, the degree to which monastic sources remain 'laced with images and metaphors borrowed from the rhetorical domain of chattel slavery' is difficult to ignore.[61] In listening for monastic voices that echo in silence, discerning bodies that remain invisible, it is a spectrum of legal landscapes that render silence audible and hazy shadows visible.

Complementing refrains encountered in oft-cited literary sources, manumission codes introduced under Constantine are relatively familiar.

[57] A. Wallace-Hadrill, 'The Social Structure of the Roman-House', *PBSR*, 56 [1988], 78–81.

[58] Cf. L. I. Larsen, 'Redefining Solitude: Monastic Registers of Fictive (and Factual) Family', *Forum*, 3rd Series, 9/1 (2020), 77–102.

[59] H. E. Winlock and W. E. Crum, *The Monastery of Epiphanius at Thebes*, 2 vols. (New York, NY: Metropolitan Museum of Art, 1926), Vol. I, 180–3; Vol. II, 33–109, 179–283, nos. 103–518; see, e.g., Vol. II, 74, 228 no. 283; cf. Larsen, 'Early Christian Meals and Slavery'.

[60] Glancy, *Slavery in Early Christianity*, 3.

[61] Glancy, *Slavery in Early Christianity*, 4–5.

Legislation stipulated that slaves might be manumitted in one of two ways: *manumissio in ecclesia* or *manumissio inter amicos*. As summarized by Susanna Elm, '*Manumissio in ecclesia* ... authorized Christian congregations to free their own slaves.'[62] This took place through a formalized procedure that 'involved a declaration in the presence of the bishop or his representative and the entire congregation'.[63] A slave thus freed 'became a full citizen and *persona sui iuris*'.[64] In turn, *manumissio inter amicos* was less complicated and less far-reaching. Here, 'a [master/mistress] simply declared a slave to be [his/her] friend'. This might be expressed 'by letter (*per epistulam*) or by inviting [him/her] to dine at the same table (*per mensam*)'. Elm notes that, while this resulted in a slave becoming 'latinized ... *manumissio inter amicos* did not result in full citizenship'.[65] As a result, 'former slaves ... continued to be of a lesser rank than their former masters, not merely in social, but also in legal terms'.[66]

Tradition has depicted such monastically restructured settings as nodes within amicable neighbourhood networks. However, once again, less familiar injunctions preserve a register of more tensive threads of negotiation. For example, as the regulatory codes established by Basil of Caesarea (330–379) take up the question of 'bound slaves who flee to religious communities for refuge',[67] Basil adds monastic texture to Chrysostom's invective against those who separate slaves from their masters (and wives from their husbands). Drawing support from Paul's letter to Philemon he counsels that slaves be returned to their masters, because 'although [Paul] had begotten Onesimus through the Gospel, [he] sent him back to Philemon'. Turning to the deutero-Pauline corpus, Basil additionally

[62] Elm, *Virgins of God*, notes that guidelines are outlined in two edicts, issued between 316 and 323.

[63] Elm, *Virgins of God*, 85–6. [64] Elm, *Virgins of God*, 85.

[65] Elm, *Virgins of God*, 85–6; given the tenor of extant literary description, Elm posits that manumission in Macrina's household took the latter form.

[66] Elm, *Virgins of God*, 85–6. Westermann, *Slave Systems of Greco-Roman Antiquity*, 154–5, observes that 'manumission *in ecclesia* seems to have spread slowly during Constantine's reign'. Sources indicate neither 'widespread use ... by the Church or even a deep interest in it'. Westermann also calls attention to the relative nature of the 'freedom' extended to Christian slaves. Challenging notions that the legal dispensation 'to manumit *in ecclesia*' registered Christian rejection of institutionalized slavery, he suggests that 'quite the opposite seems to be true'. An absence of evidence for 'any noteworthy increase in the volume of manumissions' rather attests Christianity's continued embrace of institutional slavery 'with all of its mundane formulas and practices'.

[67] Basil, *Regulae fusius tractatae* (hereafter *Reg Fus*) 11 (PG 31.948.4–34); English translations by M. M. Wagner, *Saint Basil: Ascetical Works* (New York, NY: Fathers of the Church, 1950); cf. A. M. Silvas, *The Asketikon of St Basil the Great* (Oxford: Oxford University Press, 2005).

affirms 'that the yoke of slavery, borne in a manner pleasing to the Lord [will] render [the runaway] worthy of the kingdom of heaven'.[68]

Basil offers less clear-cut parameters for runaway slaves who serve 'a wicked master'. In situations where a slaveholder 'gives unlawful commands and forces [a] slave to transgress the command of the true Master ... Jesus Christ', he suggests that attempts be made first to reconcile the slave 'to bearing the sufferings that afflict him/[her] by reason of his/[her] obeying God rather than men'. However, if resolution proves impossible, he enjoins that the slave be afforded refuge, and the community 'accept in a manner pleasing to God [any] trials encountered ... on his/[her] behalf'.[69]

In striking ways, the *Synodical Letter* of the Council of Gangra (variously dated between 325 and 381), can be read as addressing what may be identified as just such a monastic scenario. Marking a counterpoint to conduct refracted in the writings of Basil (and Chrysostom), this legislation anathematizes 'any one [who] shall teach a slave, under pretext of piety, to despise his master and to run away from his service, and not to serve his own master with good-will and all honour'.[70] Still more explicit is condemnation of ascetic communities that encourage 'slaves [to leave] ... their masters, and ... [act] insolently towards their masters'.[71]

Some decades hence, the Canons of the Council of Chalcedon of 451 affirm enduring tension (and practice), threatening with excommunication any individual who receives a slave 'into any monastery to become a monk against the will of his/[her] master'.[72] Elsewhere, one encounters legislation that allowed slaves to take monastic vows, but only with their master's consent. As a monk, the slave bore designation of a freedperson.

[68] Basil, *Reg. Fus.* 11 (PG 31.948.12–14); Wagner (trans.); Cf. Col. 3.22–24. Per the Stoic principles espoused by Philo's *Therapeutae*, elsewhere Basil affirms that in most cases, slavery constitutes a deviation from an individual's 'natural state'. Simultaneously, he posits that sometimes slavery is appropriate so that the 'worst can be educated; according to the wise and mysterious providence that bad children were condemned to serve the wiser and better ones'. Basil, *Homilia in Psalmum*, 32 (PG 29.336); Cf. *De Spiritu Sancto*, 20.

[69] Basil, *Reg. Fus.* 11 (PG 31.948.33); Wagner (trans.). H. C. Lea, 'The Early Church and Slavery', in *Studies in Church History* (Philadelphia, PA: Henry C. Lea and Sons, 1883), 536, observes that Basil's caveat is not unique: legal codes legislated under Antoninus Pius mandated that 'when a slave was exposed to intolerable oppression, the magistrates on appeal could oblige the master to sell him/[her] on reasonable terms'; Cf. Justinian, *Inst.* 1.8.2.

[70] *Canons of the Council of Gangra* 3 (PL 67.56; trans. *NPNF*² 14.93).

[71] *Synodical Letter of the Council of Gangra* (PL 67.56; trans. *NPNF*² 14.91); discussion in Glancy, *Slavery in Early Christianity*, 90.

[72] *Canons of the Council of Chalcedon (451)* 4 (PL 67.90; trans. *NPNF*² 14.270); discussion in Glancy, *Slavery in Early Christianity*, 90.

If, however, this individual abandoned monastic life, the slave-owner's proprietary claims were reinstated.[73]

Conclusion

While this sample of literary, material, and legal landscapes represents only a fraction of the evidence that must inform more substantive treatment of 'slavery in early monasticism', with striking persistency emergent patterns appear iteratively consistent. Challenging idealized pictures of monastic life, both common refrains and recurrent counter-voices return the reader's gaze to less noted details in the sources. The complementary contours (and jagged edges) of literary, material, and legal landscapes introduce complex questions with few straightforward answers.

In the most familiar literary landscapes, the circumstances of actual slaves rarely surface. Instead, narratives like the *Life of Macrina* and Palladius' recounting of the austerities embraced by respective Melanias focus squarely on the illustrious ascetic, for whom assuming the duties of a slave functions as an alternate register of 'elite' status. Non-elite intersections with slavery appear decidedly less fluid. In turn, the relative place accorded 'real' slaves within ascetic communities remains an open question. With patent precision, however, the same duties ascribed to slaves in the first century appear to be understood as the particular domain of slaves in the sixth.[74] Equally enduring are the roles implicit to the discursive rhetoric of slavery – even when the institution itself is ostensibly absent.[75]

[73] Cf. Lea, *Studies in Church History*, 523–76.

[74] The sixth century *Regula Magistri* (*Reg.Mag.*) records what is perhaps the logical outcome of performative ambiguity. Here the duties that attend meal service have become an idealized venue for 'practicing humility' (*Reg. Mag.* 18.8; A. DeVogue (ed.), *La Règle du Maître*, SC 105 (Paris: Éditions du Cerf, 1964); L. Eberle (trans.), *The Rule of the Master*, CS 6 (Kalamazoo, MI: Cistercian Publications, 1977). Dissolving the lines between slave and free, the 'disciplines' and duties associated with slavery are framed as routinized aspects of monastic life. In rotation, the 'brothers' who comprise the Master's community 'serve in the kitchen for periods of seven days' (*Reg. Mag.* 18.1; SC 105; Eberle [trans.]). In the week during which 'these brothers serve at the community meals . . . [t]hey [also] take care of the monastery's household affairs' (*Reg. Mag.* 19.19; SC 105; Eberle [trans]). 'They take off the shoes of all the brothers . . . and also repair them . . . [D]uring the same week they clean the monastery, wash the rest places, chop the wood, bring water for the face. They pour the water on the hands of the brothers as they go in for Communion. They wash the table napkins, bath towels, face towels and the brothers' soiled laundry during the time not devoted to cooking. Every day they ignite and extinguish the monastery's lamps trimmed by the cellarer' *(Reg. Mag.* 18–19; SC 105; Eberle [trans.]).

[75] Cf. Larsen, 'Early Christian Meals and Slavery'; see Larsen, 'Resisting a Reclining Culture', for more detailed discussion of a longer trajectory of this practice.

Material finds affirm these continuities. Adding particular dimensionality to the rhythms of elite and less-elite life captured in the *Vita Macrina*, the *Historia Lausiaca*, and the *Apophthegmata Patrum* – corroborated in the homilies of John Chrysostom – even cursory survey of physical structures, household configurations, and extant artefacts renders recurrent literary motifs more emphatic.

That dominant registers of elite privilege remain normative in monastic sources (and scholarship) is hardly surprising.[76] However, that iterative reification fails to drown out a recurrent and surprisingly tensive countervoice is interesting. As late-ancient legislative codes intersect with rarely referenced literary refrains, they respectively suggest that a monastic response to slavery was not uniform, nor was it a simple or settled question. Legislation aimed at regulating monastic response to slaves seeking asylum, alongside iterative enactments that restrict monastic absorption of runaway slaves, imbues dominant depictions of emergent monastic life with disruptive dimensionality.[77]

Adding real world resonance to Basil's discussion of 'bound slaves who flee to religious communities for refuge',[78] in early research Johannes Leipoldt observes that under Shenoute's leadership the White Monastery may have afforded asylum to runaway slaves.[79] More recently, Lois Farag has argued that Egyptian desert communities appear to have provided 'safe spaces' for women forced into prostitution and slavery as a result of family debt.[80] Complexifying the benevolent egalitarianism tradition has assigned elite monastic households – and the harsh hierarchical austerity attributed to less mainstream counterparts – such inversion invites investigation that moves beyond hagiographic hyperbole and introduces a register that refracts a spectrum of practice.

Less monolithic monastic landscapes, defined by competing ideals, trigger a host of questions. What dimensions delineate the cracks and fissures in a non-'seamless' reconstruction of monastic investment? What

76 In a seminal essay, V. Wimbush, 'Interpreting Resistance, Resisting Interpretation', *Semeia*, 79 (1997), 1–10, at 1, premises that 'all interpretive efforts, their methods and approaches, illuminate some things, cast shadows over others ... [they] foreground some things, render into the background certain others'.

77 Each likewise introduces suggestive texture into long-running, often highly spiritualized debates about the causes of (and sources of) burgeoning monastic populations in late antiquity.

78 Basil, *Reg. Fus.* 11 (PG 31.948.4); Wagner (trans).

79 As cited in Westermann, *Slave Systems of Greco-Roman Antiquity*, 155.

80 L. Farag, 'Heroines not Penitents: Saints of Sex Slavery in the *Apophthegmata Patrum* in Roman Law Context', *Studia Patristica*, 64 (2013), 21–32.

real, perhaps less than spiritual, motivations made monastic existence attractive?[81] Were monastic vows, for some, a stepping stone to a better life? Were they, for others, simply an alternate form of bondage?[82] Once accepted into a monastic 'family', what was the slave's experience?[83] What roles might the guise of 'humility' in fact disguise? Were slaves accorded equal status? As importantly, was their 'vulnerable position' exploited?[84] Seeking answers to these emergent questions invites embracing the positionality of a disenfranchised slave, rather than that of his or her elite owner. Derivatively, it introduces a monastic landscape where both the idealized and jagged edges of lived experience are tempered by the unpredictable messiness of human hunger for survival and agency.

81 L. I. Larsen, 'Redrawing the Interpretive Map: Monastic Education as Civic Formation', *Coptica*, 12 (2013), 1–34; cf. Lea, *Studies in Church History*, 566–7.
82 See Maria Chiara Giorda's chapter in this volume.
83 Cf. C. Schroeder, 'Children in Early Egyptian Monasticism', in C. Horn and R. R. Phenix (eds.), *Children in Late Antique Christianity* (Tübingen: Mohr Siebeck, 2009), 317–38.
84 Cf. Glancy, *Slavery in Early Christianity*, 90.

CHAPTER 7

Disciplining the Slaves of God

Monastic Children in Egypt at the End of Antiquity

Maria Chiara Giorda

The fact that laypeople lived in late antique monasteries and were employed in various roles is well known.[1] Among the more interesting inhabitants of the monasteries of Byzantine Egypt are, no doubt, the children.[2] As has been highlighted in the important work of Caroline Schroeder, many questions about children, youth, and family dynamics in Egyptian monasticism remain unanswered.[3] Many normative sources for monasticism in late antique Egypt say that children were forbidden from residing in monasteries: they should not even be allowed to stay for a short period of time, to receive an education, to work, or to attend liturgies.[4] However, other sources reveal that children were often present in monastic communities throughout the late Roman and Byzantine period:

> Despite frequent prohibitions and dire warnings of the consequences, it seems clear that the tradition of accepting quite young children did not

[1] An interesting category is the one represented by the *pistoi*, the faithful to the monastery; the most complete study concerning monastic *pistoi* was proposed by E. Wipszycka, *Moines et communautés monastiques en Egypte (IVe–VIIIe siècles)* (Warsaw: Taubenschlag Foundation, 2009), 381–3.

[2] I analysed this topic extensively in three of my previous works that were used in writing the current chapter: M. C. Giorda, *"Il regno di Dio in terra": I monasteri come fondazioni private (Egitto V–VII secolo)* (Roma: Edizioni di Storia e Letteratura, 2011), esp. chapter 5.4; M. C. Giorda, 'I bambini nei monasteri dell'Egitto bizantino (V–VIII secolo)', *Iuris Antiqui Historia, an International Journal of Ancient Law*, 4 (2012), 93–104; and M. C. Giorda, 'Children in Monastic Families in Egypt at the End of Antiquity', in C. Laes and V. Vuolanto (eds.), *Children and Everyday Life in the Roman and the Late Antique World* (Oxford; New York, NY: Routledge: 2017) 232–46.

[3] I am greatly indebted to the works of Caroline T. Schroeder: *Monastic Bodies: Discipline and Salvation in Shenoute of Atripe. Divinations: Rereading Late Ancient Religion* (Philadelphia, PA: University of Pennsylvania Press, 2007); 'Children and Egyptian Monasticism', in C. Horn and R. R. Phenix (eds.), *Children in Late Antiquity* (Tübingen: Mohr Siebeck, 2009), 317–38; 'Queer Eye for the Ascetic Guy? Homoeroticism, Children, and the Making of Monks in Late Antique Egypt', *Journal of the American Academy of Religion*, 77 (2009), 333–47; 'Child Sacrifice in Egyptian Monastic Culture: From Familial Renunciation to Jephthah's Lost Daughter', *Journal of Early Christian Studies*, 20 (2012), 269–302.

[4] R. Greenfield, 'Children in Byzantine Monasteries: Innocent Hearts or Vessels in the Harbor of the Devil', in A. Papaconstantinou and A. M. Talbot (eds.), *Becoming Byzantine: Children and Childhood in Byzantium* (Cambridge, MA: Harvard University Press, 2009), 253–82, esp. 259.

> completely evaporate in the later Byzantine period . . . children of all ages thus appear regularly within the fabric of Byzantine monastic life, albeit usually in small numbers and under carefully controlled circumstances.[5]

How can we reconcile the constant prohibitions with the ongoing presence of children in monasteries for such a long period of time? The prohibition might be due to the immaturity of a child, who is either suggestible or unprepared for choosing a monastic life. Another possible reason, consistently referred to in various rulings concerned with monastic life, is that the physical immaturity of children meant that they were not ready for the physical dangers of the ascetic life.

A wide range of evidence thus suggests that children grew up, were educated, and became adults within monastic communities; while some were accompanied by their parents, others were left alone.[6] The reason for their presence in the monastery is often unclear. The absence of a strong family group, difficult social or economic circumstances, and physical or mental illness could all be responsible for the arrival of a child as a welcome or unwelcome guest at a monastery. Abandonment of, and trade in, children are phenomena that are not yet fully understood. Opposed by the Church and forbidden by both ecclesiastical[7] and imperial[8] law, both

[5] Greenfield, 'Children', 259.

[6] For studies dedicated to the subject of childhood and asceticism, see V. Vuolanto, *Children and Asceticism in Late Antiquity. Continuity, Family Dynamics and the Rise of Christianity* (Farnham: Ashgate, 2015); A. Pudsey, 'Children in Late Roman Egypt: Family and Everyday Life in Monastic Contexts', in C. Laes, K. Mustakallio and V. Vuolanto (eds.), *Children and Family in Late Antiquity: Life, Death and Interaction* (Leuven: Peeters, 2015), 215–24. See also L. Larsen and S. Rubenson (eds.), *Monastic Education in Late Antiquity: The Transformation of Classical Paideia* (Cambridge: Cambridge University Press, 2018).

[7] Canon 12 of Council of Elvira (306) used the word *lenocinium* to describe those parents who sold their children: '*Mater vel parens vel quaelibet fidelis, si lenocinium exercuerit, eo quod alienum vendiderit corpus vel potius suum, placuit eam nec in finem accipere communionem.*' See also: Council of Vaison (442), can. 9–10; Council of Arles (443 or 452), can. 51; Council of Agde (506), can. 24. See Ch. J. Hefele (ed.), *Histoire des conciles d'après les documents originaux*, Vols. 1.1, 2.1 and 2.2 (Paris: Letouzey et Ané, 1907, 1908).

[8] In 294, Diocletian and Maximian outlawed the selling and abandoning of children: '*Liberos a parentibus neque venditionis neque donationis titulo neque pignoris iure aut quolibet alio modo, nec sub praetextu ignorantiae accipientis in alium transferi posse manifesti iuris est*', *Cod. Iust.* 4.43.1. The legal status of the abandoned children and the sale of newborn infants were subject of laws made by Christian emperors: *Cod. Theod.* 9.271 (322); *Cod. Theod.* 5.5.10.1, 11.27.2, *Cod. Iust.* 8.51[52].2 (329); *Cod. Theod.* 5.9.2 (412); *Cod. Iust.* 8.51[52].3 (529); *Nov. Iust.* 153 (541). See also: *Sirmondian Constitutions* 5 (419), in T. Mommsen and P. M. Meyer (eds.), *Theodosiani Libri* XVI *Cum Constitutionibus Simodianis et Leges Novellae ad Theodosianum pertinentes* (Berolini: Apud Weidmannos, 1905). See also J. C. Tate, 'Christianity and the Legal Status of Abandoned Children in the Later Roman Empire', *Journal of Law and Religion*, 24 (2008/9), 123–41.

practices persisted throughout our period.[9] For many children, life with the monks offered safety and an improved standard of living.

But there are a number of cases which suggest that conditions did not always improve for children in monasteries. As we will see, violence and insecurity were not always kept at bay by entry into the monastery.[10] For example, in some cases, children who entered did so as the human property of other members of the monastic community, as slaves. From a juridical point of view, these children had been donated to the monastery in perpetual servitude.[11] Once they had become adults, they were not free and became subject to even more violent forms of authority.[12] As Lillian Larsen demonstrates elsewhere in this volume, ascetic ideals of community in monastic households did not suspend the distinct pressures that underpinned slave–master relationships elsewhere in society, a similar observation to that which is made in Jonathan Tallon's essay on John Chrysostom's preaching on slavery.[13] Christian theories and practices in relation to monastic slavery were by no means inimical to the existing social order.

Although the focus here is on Byzantine Egypt, reference is also made to relevant examples from other eastern and western contexts. Such an approach underlines the continuity between the different cultural and geographical environments, especially in relation to monastic rules. It is clear that the metaphor of slavery persisted across time and space in monastic education. Obedience, dependence, loyalty, and reciprocal obligation were keywords in the everyday life of monasteries, articulating and reinforcing small-world hierarchies. Symbolic and psychological submission functioned, alongside corporal punishment, as mechanisms of social control and were pivotal in the formation of children both as child subjects of the monastic community *and* as potential future monastic subjects themselves (i.e. as monks).[14]

9 A fundamental study is J. Eastburn Boswell, *The Kindness of Strangers: Abandonment of Children in Western Europe from Late Antiquity to the Renaissance* (London: Lane, 1988).

10 I refer to the multiple levels of violence suggested by Kate Cooper and Jamie Wood in the introduction of this volume. Violence – in these socialisation processes – operates simultaneously at different levels: cognitive, emotional, and disciplinary.

11 P. KRU 78, 34; 82, 20; 92, 14; 93, 14. References to papyri have been taken from http://papyri.info/docs/checklist (accessed 23 July 2018). Slavery registers a recurring refrain across monastic textual traditions, on the levels of language and practice. For more on servitude/slavery in ancient monasticism, see Lillian I. Larsen's chapter in this volume. See also J. A. Glancy, *Slavery in Early Christianity* (Oxford: Oxford University Press, 2002).

12 See C. Leyser, *Authority and Asceticism from Augustine to Gregory the Great* (Oxford: Oxford University Press, 2000) and the examples from Basil in Jamie Wood's chapter in this volume.

13 See Lillian I. Larsen's chapter in this volume.

14 See the Introduction by Kate Cooper and Jamie Wood, as well as Wood's chapter in this volume.

The Monastery as Refuge: Children Whose Survival Depended on Monks

An important issue that must be addressed at the outset of this study is how children were defined in this period, especially in monasteries. Here it is important to carefully assess the lexical ambiguity found in the Egyptian literature and documents: included among the generic terms are παῖς (pais), παιδίον (paidíon), and τέκνον (téknon). These terms do not always refer to infants and children, but also to servants and disciples, as well as to sons (biological and spiritual).[15] We shall see that the same difficulties are present when interpreting recurring polysemantic terms in Coptic texts. Generally speaking, the term παῖς does not apply beyond the age of 16, but it can also refer to much younger children, those whom we would classify today as pre-schoolers. Philo of Alexandria (25 BCE–C. 50 CE), in *De opificio mundi (XXV–XXVII)*, separates the ages of man according to the number seven. According to Philo, when we talk about children, we are referring to 'people' ranging in age from 7 to 14.[16] The criteria used by Philo are useful in giving an idea of accepted age divisions.[17]

Limitations supposedly controlled the age at which one could choose to become a monk.[18] We must also remember the position held by Basil of Caesarea in the second half of the fourth century and taken up by other

[15] The term *pais* appears six times in the *Apophthegmata Patrum*, while the term *paidion* appears forty times. Cf. Giorda, *"Il Regno di Dio in terra"*, 148, n. 85.

[16] See *Philo in Ten Volumes (and Two Supplementary Volumes)*, Vol. 1, translated by F. H. Colson and G. H. Whitaker (Cambridge, MA: Harvard University Press, 1981), 83–7. See also L. Walt, *Paolo e le età della vita*: https://letterepaoline.net/2008/10/03/le-eta-della-vita/ (accessed 15 June 2020).

[17] The issue of separation has been called into question by G. Prinzing, 'Observations on the Legal Status of Children and the Stages of Childhood in Byzantium', in Papaconstantinou and Talbot (eds.), *Becoming Byzantine: Children and Childhood in Byzantium*, 15–34 at 17 and 19, who believes that both *pais* and *teknon* were not in fact technical terms, but rather generic terms used to indicate young age (the equivalent of 'child' in English). See also Giorda, *"Il Regno di Dio in terra"*, 148, n. 85.

[18] Age restrictions were not the same for all monasteries: Basil suggests that girls should not choose the monastic life before reaching the age of reason (once they become responsible for their own decisions), meaning around 16 or 17 years of age. Cf. Canon 18 of Basil (Ep. 199 to Amphiloch, PG 32.715–9); *Regulae fusius tractatae*, 15 (PG 31.952–7); see also the critical edition A. M. Silvas, *The Rule of St Basil in Latin and English: A Revised Critical Edition* (Collegeville, MN: Glazier Book-Liturgical Press, 2013), 89–92 (Question 7). Canon 40 of the Council in Trullo (691) forbids the taking of vows from children under 10 years of age; these differences reflect variations in the positions and presence of children in monasteries. P P Joannou, *Discipline générale antique (IVe–IXe s.), I.1: Les canons des conciles oecuméniques* (IIe–IXe) (Grottaferrata-Roma: Tipografia Italo-Orientale "S. Nilo", 1962), 175–7. See also R. Greenfield, 'Children in Byzantine Monasteries', 258. We must differentiate between entering a monastery and the choice – made official through ceremony – of becoming a monk. In Egypt, for example, in the *Sinaxarium Arabe-Jacobite* we read of an eight-year period (PO 3.431) and of an informal path whose length might have varied according to the candidates (PO 3.284; 3.443; 11.684).

monks and clergymen:[19] it was up to the interested person to make the choice of virginity and the monastic life and not a decision to be taken either lightly or on their behalf.[20] Younger people were supposedly more susceptible outside influence through persuasion, or psychological and even physical violence. It may also be that the focus on age was intended to avoid the violent imposition of the ascetic life on children who were too young to make an informed decision for themselves. Hence, a 12- or 13-year-old boy was considered more mature and free to choose than a 7- or 8-year-old boy.[21]

Regardless of the severe prohibitions from church and state authorities, in late antiquity, parents continued to abandon their children to the care of monasteries for a variety of reasons and, in particular, because the monastery could take care of them during unfavourable social and economic times. There were a number of terms for transferring *potestas* over a child, including *oblatio*,[22] *expositio*, and sale.[23] Abandonment is the key semantic concept here, even if the parents were dead, because a person or institution – in this case the monastery – took over the role of the child's *familia*.

19 Besides Basil (n. 17 above), see Augustine, *Ep.* 262.8, A. Goldbacher (ed.), *S. Aureli Augustini Hipponiensis Episcopi, Epistulae, Pars IV*, CSEL 57 (Vienna: Tempsky, 1911), 8, and Leo the Great, *Ep.* 167.14.15 (PL 54.593–1218)

20 Regarding the West, Benedict's rule aimed to prohibit children donated to the monastery from going back to the world, *Regula Benedicti* 59 (PL 66.839–840): 'May every way be shut, and may the child harbour no illusion which may deceive him and lead him – God forbid! – to his ruin, as we have learned by experience.' Canon 17 of Council of Aachen (817) specified that the child must confirm the decision made by others in his stead: see G. Archetti, 'Ildemaro a Brescia e la pedagogia monastica nel commento alla Regola', *Brixia Sacra*, 3 (2006), 125–6, nn. 44–45. The Council of Aachen also established that without the consent of his parents a boy or a girl could not receive the monastic tonsure ('Sans le consentement de ses parents, aucun fils ne peut recevoir la tonsure, ni aucune fille le voile'), Hefele (ed.), *Histoire des conciles*, Vol. 4.1 (Paris: Letouzey et Ané, 1911), 28–9.

21 On this topic, see M. Aletti and C. Alberico, 'Tra brainwashing e libera scelta. Per una lettura psicologica dell'affiliazione ai Nuovi Movimenti Religiosi', in M. Aletti and G. Rossi (eds.), *Ricerca di sé e trascendenza* (Turin: Centro Scientifico Editore, 1999), 35–48; D. G. Bromley and J. G. Melton (eds.), *Cults, Religions, Violence* (Cambridge: Cambridge University Press, 2002); D. Kelemen and E. Rosset, 'The Human Function Compunction: Teleological Explanation in Adults', *Cognition*, 111 (2001), 138–43. D. Kelemen and R. Rottman, 'Is There Such a Thing as a Christian Child? Evidence of Religious Beliefs in Early Childhood', in P. McNamara and W. Wildman (eds.), *Science and the World's Religions: Origins and Destinies* (Santa Barbara, CA: Praeger Press, 2012).

22 Concerning the *oblatio puerorum*, see A. Steinwenter, 'Kinderschenkungen an koptische Klöster', *Zeitschrift der Savigny-Stiftung für Rechtsgeschichte*, 42, Kanonistische Abteilung, 11 (1921), 175–207. See also T. Sebastian Richter, 'What's in a Story? Cultural Narratology and Coptic Child Donation Documents', *Journal of Juristic Papyrology*, 35 (2005), 237–64, at 246 n. 26.

23 For the finer points of child sale, see Sebastian Richter, 'What's in a Story?', 249; V. Vuolanto, 'Selling a Freeborn Child: Rhetoric and Social Realities in the Late Roman World', *Ancient Society*, 33 (2003), 169-207; Pudsey, 'Children in Late Roman Egypt', 218.

Economic, social and religious factors contributed to the practice of abandonment, and it is only with great difficulty that we may be able to establish in detail the original context and causes of such behaviour.[24]

It is clear, however, that child abandonment was a strategic practice employed by families as an alternative to abortion, contraception, or infanticide. In certain cases, the practice continued to be accepted from the fourth to the seventh century as an alternative to infanticide. Children were often oblates, donated to the monastery by their parents, after which monks would care for and raise them. This phenomenon was of a long-term nature, occurring throughout late antiquity and well into the Middle Ages, and had a broad geographic range occurring across both East and West.[25] For example, according to Basil of Caesarea (fourth century), the monks were responsible for judging the attitude of those who entered the monastic life from the youngest age. They must accept all orphans who showed up at the monastery, while those that still have their parents (if accompanied to the monastery by them) must be accepted in the presence of a number of witnesses.[26]

There were a number of different circumstances under which children were donated to Egyptian monasteries.[27] Some children were donated to the monastery by their parents in order to overcome a negative socio-economic situation, as can be read in the Life of Matthew the Poor, who lived in the latter half of the fifth century:

[24] M. de Jong, *In Samuel's Image: Child Oblation in the Early Medieval West* (Leiden: Brill, 1996), 1–6, for a summary of issues relating to the origins of oblation. See also Joseph H. Lynch, 'Monastic Recruitment in the Eleventh and Twelfth Centuries: Some Social and Economic Considerations', *American Benedictine Review*, 26 (1975), 425–47.

[25] In the longer term, it is worth noting that there were a great many *pueri nutriti* in Carolingian monasteries.

[26] Basil, *Regulae fusius tractatae*, 15.1 (PG 31.952). L. Cremaschi (ed.), *Basilio di Cesarea, Le regole* (Bose: Qiqajon, 1993). In Benedict's *Regula* (sixth-century Italy), children are also accepted into the cloister and participate in an evocative ceremony of oblation (cf. *Regula Benedicti*, 59, PL 66.839–40), where both nobles and paupers may leave their children to a monastery, after an agreement by the candidates or their family, declaring their loyalty and obedience to the rules of monastic life and renouncing possession of family assets. The rule attests a practice of *oblatio* that spread further during the course of the Middle Ages, until the eleventh century. G. Peters, 'Offering Sons to God in the Monastery: Child Oblation, Monastic Benevolence, and the Cistercian Order in the Middle Ages', *Cistercian Studies Quarterly*, 38 (2003), 288–9, 291.

[27] A more ancient source which speaks of children offered to the monastery is Theodoret of Cyrus, *Historia monachorum*, 3, R. M. Price (trans.), *A History of the Monks of Syria*, Cistercian Studies 88 (Collegeville, MN: Cistercian Publications, 1985). See also Theodor Nissen, 'Unbekannte Erzählungen aus dem Pratum Spirituale', *Byzantinische Zeitschrift*, 38 (1938), 351–76; A. Papaconstantinou, 'Child or Monk? An Unpublished Story Attributed to John Moschos in MS Coislin 257', *Bulletin of the American Society of Papyrologists*, 45 (2008), 171–84; see also *P. Vat. Copt. Doresse* 7 from the monastery of Wadi Sarga, discussed above.

> A woman knelt before the feet of my father apa Matthew, begging him: 'My holy Father, remember me in your prayers so that God may give me a son; if the Lord accepts to be moved by me, the fruit he will give me, after I have weaned him, I shall bring and donate to your holiness; if it is a boy, I shall donate him to the monastery under your holiness, if it is a girl I shall donate her to the convent of the virgins, so that she may become a nun. So, whatever the Lord may give me thanks to your holy prayers will be a promise to the Lord for every day of its life.' Our father apa Matthew blessed the woman saying: 'May the Lord God, who can do everything, who granted Anna's wish and gave her Samuel who became a prophet to all of Israel, grant you your wish, and may he grant your request into the hands of God, without further delay; and you, also, keep your word, so that it may be a promise to God.'[28]

In this as in many other cases, the scriptural model is Samuel.[29] The child's father calls a slave merchant whose offer establishes that his son is worth ten gold coins. The father therefore offers twelve to apa Matthew to get his son back, but Matthew does not want to negotiate because now the child belongs to the monastery. This tentative exchange seems to have been enough to fracture the agreement with God, and, following three days of sickness, the child dies.

A similar story is contained in *Victor's Praise*, written by Celestine of Rome, a text which was copied in Edfou, not far from Djème in Middle Egypt, and dates from the late eighth century.[30] A childless couple goes to pray at Victor's sanctuary and promises to donate their hoped-for child to the saint's *martyrion* until the end of his days. When the child reaches the age of five, his parents change their mind and, after consulting a slave merchant to establish the value of their son at forty gold coins, they take the money to the *martyrion* instead of the child. The younger Victor dies a few days later, but revives thanks to the martyr's power after his parents have vowed themselves and their son into slavery to the martyr: the fact of belonging to/being a slave brings the child back to life.

Another case is that of Moses in the *Life of Moses the Archimandrite*, an example of abandonment/education and training in the monastery by

[28] *Vie de Matthieu le pauvre*, E. Amélineau (ed.), *Monuments pour servir à l'histoire de l'Égypte chrétienne*, Mémoires de la Mission d'Archéologie Française, 4, 2 (Paris, E. Leroux, 1888–95), 720.

[29] Samuel spending his childhood in the temple is the model for all these stories: I Sam. 1–3.

[30] E. A. Wallis Budge (ed.), *Coptic Martyrdoms in the Dialect of Upper Egypt* (London: British Museum, 1914), 52–6, 305–9. See also A. Papaconstantinou, 'ΘΕΙΑ ΟΙΚΟΝΟΜΙΑ. Les actes thébains de donation d'enfants ou la gestion monastique de la pénurie', *Mélanges Gilbert Dagron, Travaux et Mémoires*, 14 (Paris: Amis du Centre d'Histoire et Civilisation de Byzance, 2002), 520.

acting as a servant for the community and then becoming a monk. The reading of Moses' life and deeds in church moved a couple that already had children. The woman promised that if she were to give birth again she would call her offspring Moses, would raise him in the grace of God and when he turned five would then presumably fulfil other promise(s), of which we have no specific details. At this point, the story breaks off due to the fragmentary state of the manuscript. It begins again when Moses is five and is taken to a church as a gift and offered on the altar (*thysiasterion*) and given to the presbyter, so that he can become his spiritual son.[31] Later on, following a vision, Moses becomes a monk and founds a monastery.

A group of twenty-six Coptic documents published by Walter Crum (P. KRU 78–103)[32] and dating to the eighth century (734–785) can shed further light on the issue of children entering monasteries as slaves.[33] Arietta Papaconstantinou – who has studied all these texts very carefully – noticed that these signed legal documents are mostly written by fathers (six are by both parents, four are by widowed mothers) and addressed to the people in charge of Phoibammon monastery in the west Thebaid, sealing a pact concerning the exchange of a small child between the family – usually led by the *paterfamilias* – and the monastery. The texts are very similar in terms of style and content: the father writes the document to the *dikaion* (the administrative core) of the monastery of Phoibammon to testify that the donation of his child after an illness to the monastery is an indestructible act. The child will be a servant of the monastery, where s/he will be cured. The father says that in the future should his child no longer be a servant of the monastery, he will have to donate everything he earns to

[31] *Vie de Moïse*, in Amélineau (ed.), *Monuments*, 682–3.

[32] W. E. Crum, G. Steindorff and A. A. Schiller, *Koptische Rechtsurkunden des achten Jahrhunderts aus Djeme* (Leipzig: Zentralantiquariat der Deutschen Demokratischen Republik, 1912).

[33] See the following writings: L. S. B. Mac Coull, 'Child Donations and Child Saints in Coptic Egypt', *East European Quarterly*, 13 (1979), 409–15; E. Wipszycka, 'Donation of Children', *Coptic Encyclopaedia* (New York, NY: MacMillan, 1993), Vol. III, 918–19; S. Schaten, 'Koptische Kinderschenkungsurkunde', *Bulletin de la Société Archéologie Chrétienne*, 35 (1996), 129–42; A. Biedenkopf-Zienher, *Koptische Schenkungsurkunden aus der Thebais. Formeln und Topoi der Urkunden, Aussagen der Urkunden, Indices*, Göttinger Orientforschungen IV Reihe: "Ägypten" 41 (Wiesbaden: Harrassowitz, 2001); A. Papaconstantinou, 'ΘΕΙΑ ΟΙΚΟΝΟΜΙΑ', 511–26; A. Papaconstantinou, 'Notes sur les actes de donation d'enfants au monastère thébain de Saint Phoibammon', *Journal of Juristic Papyrology*, 32 (2002), 83–105; T. S. Richter, *Rechtssemantik und forensische Rhetorik: Untersuchungen zu Wortschatz, Stil und Grammatik der Sprache koptischer Rechtsurkunden* (Leipzig: H. Wodtke und K. Stegbauer, 2002). See also the connection between the practice of donating children to monasteries and the Hierodule services in Egypt, H. J. Thissen, 'Kinderschenkungsurkunden. Zur Hierodulie im christlichen Ägypten', *Enchoria*, 14 (1986), 117–28, quoted by S. Richter, 'What's in a Story?', 248–9.

the monastery. All texts in this archive follow this model in terms of style and content.[34]

All of these donations of children demonstrate how monasteries could help families (and their children) to overcome difficult socio-economic conditions. Both the family and the monastery benefit from this arrangement. The child has an increased chance of survival and the family has one less mouth to feed, while the monastery receives a new member into the community. The donation of children thus helped to build the monastic community.[35] At the same time as the parents guaranteed that their child would forever be in physical proximity to and at the service of the monastery, there is an exchange of physical and spiritual health that benefits both parties – *aeterna gratia et aeterna salus*.

Children in Monasteries: Rules Governing an Uneasy Presence

Egyptian monks in late antiquity took care of orphans, children born into poor families, children born with deformities, kidnapped children, and especially abandoned children. There are also cases in which children broke away from their families deliberately. Young boys and girls decided to become ascetics, virgins, or monks against the wishes of their parents, asserting their autonomy, sometimes violently, from traditional family dynamics and social expectations.[36]

In monasteries children received food and shelter, but they also learned to read and write. It is difficult to establish the extent to which the training of slave children differed, if at all, from the disciplinary regime experienced by those child oblates. In both cases, children were expected to conform to a culture which valued obedience, often to the extreme. The distinction between discipline for the sake of salvation and discipline as an expression of power relations often seems to have been difficult to maintain in practice.

[34] Papaconstantinou, 'ΘΕΙΑ ΟΙΚΟΝΟΜΙΑ', 515–26; See also Richter, 'What's in a Story?', 240, 243 n. 18: the texts proceed according to the style of purchase or sale documents.

[35] Shared practice, knowledge, and experience, interactions between leaders and followers, and relationships between individual and communal identities are the core of the constructions of communities of practice: E. Wenger, *Communities of Practice: Learning, Meaning, and Identity* (Cambridge: Cambridge University Press 1998); see also the Introduction to this volume by Kate Cooper and Jamie Wood.

[36] V. Vuolanto, 'Choosing Ascetism: Children and Parents, Vows and Conflicts', in Horn and Phenix (eds.), *Children in Late Antiquity*, 255–91.

It is clear, however, that some monastic children in Egypt were educated in both classical and Christian literature.[37] Monasteries served an educational function and, as explored by Jamie Wood elsewhere in this volume, the learning process that they experienced was similar to that which took place in 'secular' schools. Learning within the monastic curriculum, including experiencing various forms of discipline, was a process of moving towards full participation to the monastic community, of integrating individual and community identities. Processes of education therefore played a pivotal role in reproducing the monastic order.[38]

Caroline Schroeder has suggested that aside from the well-defined educational programme laid down for the monasteries founded by Pachomius and his followers,[39] children appear to have had few clearly delineated responsibilities in Egyptian monasteries. So, although we know that, as teenagers, children had already begun to learn occupations and to undertake tasks that were essential to the everyday monastic routine, such as taking care of the lamps on the altar and distributing supplies for weaving, many details of their everyday lives in monasteries remain shrouded in mystery.

Among the evidence for the training of children in monasteries is a document from the monastery of Wadi Sarga (early seventh-century Egypt)[40] that refers to the donation of a child.[41] In the monastery of Epiphanius there are several letters containing salutations addressed to children,[42] while other documents refer to children living in the monastery. There is also the case of a child who is learning the Holy Scriptures.[43] There is a 'children's cell' in the apa Jeremiah monastery in Saqqara, the

[37] On this topic, see: R. Cribiore, *Writing, Teachers, and Students in Graeco-Roman Egypt* (Atlanta, GA: Scholars Press, 1996); R. Cribiore, *Gymnastics of the Mind: Greek Education in Hellenistic and Roman Egypt* (Princeton, NJ: Princeton University Press, 2001). See also C. Kotsifou, 'Papyrogical Perspectives on Orphans in the World of Late Ancient Christianity', in Horn and Phenix (eds.), *Children in Late Antiquity*, 339–73. L. I. Larsen, 'On Learning a New Alphabet: The Sayings of the Desert Fathers and the Monostichs of Menander', *Studia Patristica*, 55 (2013), 59–77; Pudsey, 'Children in Late Roman Egypt', 215–24, esp. 222, 229 focusing on the monastery of Epiphanius.

[38] P. Bourdieu: *Distinction: A Social Critique of the Judgement of Taste* (Cambridge, MA: Harvard University Press, 1984); P. Bourdieu, *The State Nobility: Elite Schools in the Field of Power*, translated by L. C. Clough (Stanford, CA: Stanford University Press, 1996).

[39] Schroeder, 'Children and Egyptian Monasticism', 317-38, esp. 322-323; 328-330.

[40] WS 99 where an Apa Enoch writes: 'Be kind and allow the children.' See also CO 15: this is a prayer or a homily of a head father for a child of the monastery.

[41] This is the *P. Vat. Copt; Doresse* 7 papyrus. G. Schenke, 'Kinderschenkungen an das Kloster des apa Thomas', *Journal of Juristic Papyrology*, 37 (2007), 177–83.

[42] P. Mon. Epiph. 318, 337, 448, 477. Pudsey, 'Children in Late Roman Egypt', 226–32.

[43] P. Mon. Epiph. 140, for the child who is educated in the holy texts, following the instructions of a monk. Other examples of children can be found in P. Mon. Epiph. 546, 179, 209, 326; P. Mon. Epiph. 697, where there is a (spiritual?) son of a man who also has another son.

ancient necropolis of Memphis, referred to in inscriptions published in 1912 by Thompson. A space intended for children appears to be depicted on those inscriptions which can be dated to the middle of the seventh century (numbers 314 and 315).[44] These inscriptions tell us that the students had to follow strict rules and a timetable.[45]

The *Apophthegmata Patrum* also mention several cases of children living among the monks and later becoming monks themselves, while they refer to others as being employed elsewhere in monastic communities.[46] A few children visited the monasteries, often taken by parents who were looking for aid from a monk or nun, although sometimes they went to the monasteries by themselves to try to secure a blessing or spiritual comfort, or to speed recovery from an illness.[47] There are many examples of children seeking blessings. One such example is Theodoret of Cyrus who tells us that, as a child, he had been taken to Peter each week for a blessing.[48]

In the desert the categories of 'young' and 'elder' do not correspond with actual age, since a *geron* or *abba* is not necessarily the person who is oldest, but rather he who has acquired most experience and has progressed furthest in the ascetic life.[49] Among the children mentioned in the *Apophthegmata*, there is Zacharius, who, thanks to his obedience and innocence, was able to surpass his father Carion in humility and silence. The history of Zacharius is a history of strong choices, of a hard flight from

44 Cf. Schroeder, 'Children and Egyptian Monasticism', 332–7.

45 For these sources, see Schroeder, 'Children and Egyptian Monasticism', 33.

46 See Schroeder, 'Queer Eye for the Ascetic Guy?', 335.

47 In the *Apophthegmata* we read of certain cases of children brought by their parents because of an illness and then healed by the monks; e.g. *Alph.Macarius* 15; *Alph.Poemen* 7; *Alph.Sisoes* 18. The abbreviation *Alph.* refers to the alphabetical collection of *Apophthegmata Patrum* (PG 65.71–440); L. Regnault, *Les sentences des Pères du désert, collection alphabétique* (Sablé sur Sarthe: Abbaye de Solesmes, 1970). The abbreviation N refers to the Anonymous collection: L. Regnault, *Les sentences des Pères du désert, série des anonymes* (Bégrolles-en-Mauges: Abbaye de Bellefontaine, 1985).

48 Theodoret, *Hist. mon.*, 9.4. The sources include several cases of children who frequent monasteries, including a miracle-like episode connected to the arrival of a young nephew of a monk to his uncle's monastery. See *Life of Lazaros of Mt Galesion* 155, Richard P. H. Greenfield (trans.), *The Life of Lazaros of Mt Galesion: An Eleventh-Century Pillar Saint*, Byzantine Saints' Lives in Translation 3 (Washington, DC: Dumbarton Oaks Research Library and Collection, 2000); and also R. Greenfield, 'Children in Byzantine Monasteries', 279, n. 74.

49 One such example is Macarius of Egypt, who, owing to his spiritual progress, was called the 'young-old man' at the age of 30. Cf. Palladius, *Historia Lausiaca* 17.2 (PG 34.1043). See also the English version: *Palladius: The Lausiac History*, translated by R. T. Meyer, ACW 34 (Majwah, NJ: Paulist Press, 1965), 54–5. On monastic terminology and monastic authority, see Wipszycka, *Moines et communautés monastiques*, 292–31; C. Rapp, *Holy Bishops in Late Antiquity: The Nature of Christian Leadership in an Age of Transition* (Berkeley, CA: University of California Press, 2005), 16–7, 56–60.

the world, whose conclusion is very violent, since his body is transformed physically. Zacharius goes with his father from Scete to the Thebaid, and then returns from the Thebaid to Scete, where the child, of his own accord, dips himself in a natron pond from which he emerges disfigured.[50] Zacharius lives for about fifty years in the desert with other famous elderly monks, imbued with the richness of the Spirit and an exemplary obedience and innocence. Zacharius is an example of *paidaiogeron* (the 'old'/'expert' child) who overturns the traditional order and hierarchy by his ascetic achievements.[51]

Yet biological relationships can also assist in the reproduction of monastic communities and the development of ascetic subjectivities. Zacharius' example is one of a number of cases of children who followed one of their parents in choosing an ascetic lifestyle from a tender age and decided to adopt an ascetic lifestyle in a monastery.[52] It is impossible to establish how much pressure was placed on such children to follow the parental vocation, although we can imagine that the mixture of powerful spiritual model and traditional parental authority would have had a strong psychological influence. In such cases, the father's choice influenced the son even if, not long afterwards, the son became a true 'desert-father', acting as a model even for his biological father.

The collection of Pachomian rules is another useful source for children's presence in monasteries. Young monks or novices (often called 'little ones', stressing that they were different from 'older' monks) were clearly thought to be present by the authors of the rules, although we are given no precise indication of their age. There were also some children (*pueri*) in the monastery. Number 7 of the *Praecepta atque Judicia* is a good example:

> If a brother is found laughing or happily playing with children (*pueri*)[53] and entertaining friendships with the youths (*aetatis infirmae*), he will be

[50] *Alph.Carion*, 2 (PG 65.229–31).

[51] The *puer–senex* topos is present in monastic literature (the scriptural basis is Luke 2:39–52), B. Chevallier Caseau, 'Childhood in Byzantine Saints' Lives', in Horn and Phenix (eds.), *Children in Late Antiquity*, 127–66.

[52] De Jong, *In Samuel's Image*, 23, comments on children in the monasteries mentioned by Cassian and Sulpicius Severus: 'They may as well have been sons who entered the community together with their fathers or orphans who found a safe haven within monastic precincts.'

[53] In the Latin version of Jerome, *Praecepta atque judicia S. P. N. Pachomii*, 166 (PL 23.82), the child is *puer*, while the youths are those of an infirm age, *aetas infirma*. The term *puer* referred to youths between 7 and 14 years of age, according to the *Regula Benedicti*, 30, 37 and Isidore of Seville, *Etymologies* 20.2, W. M. Lindsay (ed.), *Isidorus, Etymologiarum libri xx* (Oxford: Clarendon, 1911), 11.2 (*De aetatibus hominum*). Concerning the division of ages, see also Seneca, *Epistula* 49, translated by R. M. Gummere, *Seneca: Epistles, Volume 1: Epistles 1–65*, LCL 75 (Cambridge, MA: Harvard University Press, 1917), 324–30.

> warned for three times to refrain from this sort of familiarity and be reminded of the love and fear of God. If he does not cease this practice, may he be corrected as he deserves by means of severe punishments.[54]

The monks were thus disciplined if they did not maintain appropriate standards of behaviour in relation to the children in the monastery. If children did not obey, they too could be corrected by means of severe corporal punishment. The infliction of violence on the body was thought to be an effective tool for the education of children, helping to create (or enforce) a sense of participation and order within the community.[55]

Although the literary sources do not refer often or in much detail to the different types of corporal punishment, the fragments of Shenoute's canons (IV c.) suggest that a very harsh system of discipline was in operation. This kind of attitude towards punishment was probably widespread in Egypt due to the successful diffusion of the Pachomian and Shenoutian rules. The penalties meted out in Egyptian monasteries are reprehensible by contemporary standards, but it is important to stress the social function of punishment within the authoritarian system established by Shenoute in particular (everything in its place; everything under control) and its deep connection to the theological aim of dismissing and annihilating the monastic body.[56] Physical punishments signal the violence to which male and female ascetics could be submitted in Egyptian monasteries in an effort to integrate them forcibly into the community, reproducing the institutional identity of the monastery at the same time as promoting the annihilation of the individual.

Institutional Perspectives: Children and the Reproduction of the Monastic Community

Moreover, it is necessary to take into consideration the perspective of the monastery as an institution. By accepting children, regardless of their psychological and physical condition, the monastery was performing an act of charity at the same time as it was making an investment in the

[54] Jerome, *Praecepta atque judicia S. P. N. Pachomii*, 166 (PL 23.82): '*Si deprehensus fuerit aliquis e fratribus libenter cum pueris ridere et ludere, et habere amicitias aetatis infirmae, tertio commonebitur, ut recedat ab eorum necessitudine, et memor sit honestatis et timoris Dei; si non cessaverit, corripietur, ut dignus est, correptione severissima.*'

[55] The key point of reference on the importance of bodily discipline and physical punishment in the reproduction of the social order is Michel Foucault; see the introduction to this volume by Kate Cooper and Jamie Wood for more on this topic.

[56] See Schroeder, *Monastic Bodies: Discipline and Salvation in Shenoute of Atripe*, 17–18.

individual that had been accepted.[57] There were therefore other reasons beyond the purely spiritual or charitable for monasteries to accept children. Greater manpower might increase the economic power of the monastery and it is likely that at least some parents made financial or other donations when they pledged their child to the institution.[58] As we have already seen, some youths later took on important roles as novices and monks within monasteries. In Shenoute's canon number 9, we read that

> Those who are assigned with supervising the children and who do not take care of them, since they play around and have fun with them, and make practical jokes, must be removed from that task and must never again receive it. The same goes for the women which have been assigned to take care of the girls. If the children, once grown up, have passed our judgement, we shall do with them as is written; if they do not obey and do not learn to be mean of heart, we shall remove them from these premises.[59]

Accepting children into the monastery was clearly an act of social and institutional reproduction as well as one of charity.

Although children were often educated within monastic schools, it was normal practice for monasteries to maintain and raise the children that they took in as subjects/objects of the institution itself: not all of them became monks and freed themselves from their condition as servants/slaves of the monastery. It is certain that the monastic community had responsibility for deciding the future of such children who were, in effect, reshaped by their new (monastic) family. Monks became strict 'parents' to the children who were socialised into a new identity: they were raised in the monastic way of life and in turn gave their lives to the monastery.[60]

Among the problems which arose from living together with children, we must take into account promiscuity and sexual temptation.[61] In male-only

[57] Peters, 'Offering Sons to God in the Monastery', 293.

[58] Peters, 'Offering Sons to God in the Monastery', 295. For a summary of various economic, social and religious explanations, see Papaconstantinou, 'ΘΕΙΑ OIKONOMIA', 511, 516. In my opinion, the donation of children to monasteries, motivated by economic issues, should not be limited to the eighth century, but also to earlier and later periods. The particularly harsh period under Arab rule clearly played a major role, but the increase in abandonments/donations to monasteries should not be attributed solely to the relative tightening of fiscal conditions. Cf. Giorda, 'I bambini nei monasteri dell'Egitto bizantino', 101, n. 2.

[59] J. Leipoldt, *Sinuthii archimandritae vita et opera omnia* (Paris: Imprimerie Nationale 1913), 105–6.

[60] See Jamie Wood's chapter elsewhere in this volume for more on the subject of monastic formation.

[61] See also the proverb attributed to Isaac (*presbytero Celliorum*) concerning the ruin of Scete caused by the children: *Nolite huc pueros adducer. In Sceti enim quator ecclesiae propter pueros ad solitudinem sunt redactae, Alph.Isaac* 5 (PG 65.226). See C. Laes, 'Kinship and Friendship in the *Apophthegmata Patrum*', in C. Krötzl and K. Mustakallio (eds.), *De Amicitia: Friendship and Social Networks in Antiquity and the Middle Ages* (Rome: Institutum Romanum Finlandiae, 2010), 115–34.

and female-only ascetic communities in which adults and children (with no necessary biological bonds) were thrown together in conditions of semi-isolation, it was inevitable that there would be instances of sexual relations and promiscuity, even if such actions were often condemned and prohibited by the sources.[62] Schroeder notes that

> Shenoute's rules contain very specific prohibitions against kissing children, touching children, and unsupervised activity with children (such as anointing or bathing them). They also forbid children from engaging in potentially erotic activities with each other (such as shaving or pulling a thorn from another boy's foot).[63]

Although monastic literature places particular – and often negative – attention on sexuality and sexual temptation, sexual activity and even pederasty seem to have been regular features of life in late antique Egyptian monasteries. In other words, even if monastic rule makers were strict in their attitudes towards sex and abstention, there were many cases of transgression of the rules and a relatively high possibility that children would be exposed to sexual abuse.

Another problem posed by the presence of children in the monastery was the risk of interrupting and disturbing the concentration and silence of the monks.[64] For example, there are parts of the rules attributed to Pachomius in which children murmur, joke, and make noises, thereby disturbing the older monks.[65] Basil also states:

> The apostle said: Fathers, you must not exasperate your children, but raise them in the Lord's education and discipline (Eph. 6:4). If those who take the children to the community do so for this reason, and if those who

62 For the discourse with Greek philosophers about the sexual abuse of children, see *Vita Antonii* 74.3, in *Athanasius of Alexandria, The Life of Anthony: The Coptic Life and the Greek Life*, translated by T. Vivian and A. N. Athanassakis, Cistercian Studies 202 (Kalamazoo, MI: Cistercian Publications, 2003). For a good approach to the use and the development of *paidophthoria* during the first centuries of Christian period, see J. W. Martens, '"Do Not Sexually Abuse Children": The Language of Early Christian Sexual Ethics', in Horn and Phenix (eds.), *Children in Late Antiquity*, 227–54; P. Rousseau, 'Blood Relationships among Early Eastern Ascetics', *Journal of Theological Studies*, 23 (1972), 135–44 on sexual temptations of children in monastic communities.

63 Schroeder, 'Children and Egyptian Monasticism', 341.

64 In monastic literature, even demons can take on the look of children to tempt the monks, disturbing their tranquillity. The anonymous apophthegmata (e.g. N 338) say that children disturb the monks' peace. R. Greenfield, 'Children in Byzantine Monasteries', 260–1, 269–71: the desire of the parents to exploit their children's monastic vocation may have served as a deterrent for accepting children in the monasteries.

65 E.g., *Praecepta atque Iudicia* 13 and *Praecepta et Instituta* 18 attributed to Pachomius. See A. Boon (ed.), *Pachomiana latina. Règle et épîtres de St Pachôme, épître de St. Théodore et "Liber" de St Orsiesius. Texte latin de St Jérôme*, Bibliothèque de la Revue d'Histoire ecclésiastique 7 (Leuven: Universiteitbibliothek, 1932).

> welcome them are certain to have the means of raising them in the Lord's education and discipline, then may they observe what was ordered by the Lord: *Let the children come unto me and do not forbid them, for the kingdom of heaven is of those who are like them* (Matt. 19:14). However, if these intentions and hopes are not present I believe that this is neither appreciated by God, nor opportune or convenient for yourselves.[66]

Transgression of the rules of silence and calm resulted in stringent punishment for the transgressors. Children and adults were subject to corporal punishments.[67]

The entry of children into the monastery went some way towards ensuring the continuity of the community over time. The sometimes harsh treatment that children experienced both prepared them for the rigours of a monastic lifestyle and prevented them from disrupting the vocation of the monks and the mission of the monastery itself.

Children, Not Only *in* But Also *of* the Monasteries: Strategies of Autonomy and Belonging

Egyptian sources regarding the donation of children to monasteries refer to their relationship with and their services at the monastery, both as children and once they had become adults. Although Egyptian monastic writers and leaders were interested in welcoming children into their institutions, entrance into the monastery did not result in full acceptance into the monastic life. This meant that children who had been raised and educated in the monastery did not have to join the community as adults.[68] The fact that these children did not become monks was not necessarily due to their unsuitability as candidates (due to illness, disability or having received diabolical visions, for example).[69] It is important to take into consideration

[66] Basilius, *Regulae brevius tractatae*, 292 (PG 31.1287), W. K. L. Clarke (trans.), *The Shorter Rules of St Basil* (London: S.P.C.K., 1925); A. Silvas, *The Asketikon of St Basil the Great* (Oxford University Press, 2005). See also Jamie Wood's chapter in this volume for an analysis of the training regime laid down in the ascetic writings of Basil of Caesarea.

[67] M. C. Giorda, 'De la direction spirituelle aux règles monastiques. Péchés, pénitence et punitions dans le monachisme pachômien (ive–ve siècles)', *Collectanea Christiana Orientalia*, 6 (2009), 95–113.

[68] The conflict between parent and monastery, concerning the destiny of a child donated or sent for education, remains significant: whether he became a monk or not, the monastery claimed rights of property on that child. For a perspective on the conflict among the parties involved, see Papaconstantinou, 'Child or Monk?' Moreover, *Nov. Iust.* 23.41 of Justinian forbade parents from taking children who chose a monastic life away from the monastery (*Interdicimus autem parentibus filios suos monachicam vitam eligentes ex venerabilibus monasteriis abstrahere*).

[69] Richter, 'What's in a Story?', 260–1.

the complex network of relationships that underpinned monastic life in the social, religious, and economic spheres.

In this regard, a vital piece of information is that, whatever their occupation, the children *belonged* to the monastery: 'No one else may be the child's lord, outside the monastery, for all the days of his life.'[70] The children were the monastery's servants/slaves and in many papyri we find explicit statements to this effect:

> The child will stay in the monastery for all days of his life;
> He will work in the monastery as an ancient slave (*assayoun*);[71]
> He is submitted (*upotagē*) to the monastery;
> He must serve and work for the monastery (a Coptic word – *sayon; schmschal* – is used to underline this condition, and these are the same terms used to refer to a servant or a slave).[72]

In the light of these expressions, it is highly significant that in both of the stories discussed above (Matthew and Victor) the children are appraised by merchants as if they were slaves. This suggests that the parents handed over the right to dispose of their sons to the monastery just as any other proprietary right over an asset could be passed to the monastic institution ('everyone can do as he pleases with what is in his possession'). In such cases, it seems that the children were donated to the monastery in perpetual servitude.[73]

It is also important to note the close association in these contexts of the child with the concept of *pais* (a slave). Something more exact is meant than a general etymological analogy between slave and child. The suggestion is that their social positions are essentially similar and it is hardly surprising therefore that children came to act as servants within the monastic environment.[74] The monastery takes authority over the child in terms which derive directly from the semantic range of the teacher–disciple and lord–servant/slave relationship. For instance, we find the terms *upotagē nomē*, *exousia*, and *despoteia*, which refer to relationships of

[70] P. KRU 81,26.
[71] The Coptic term (in Greek, '*palaios*'): a 'slave' in antiquity, the status of which was well defined legally, Papaconstantinou, 'Notes sur les actes de donation d'enfants', 93 n. 50; 92-93.
[72] P. KRU 98, 7; 82, 16; 97, 19; 81, 27. As Lillian I. Larsen notes in her chapter in this volume, whether manumitted, sold, named as ascetic associates or tagged as narrative markers, slaves remain integral to an inextricable web of service within the monastery. Concrete and verbal codes dictated the roles accorded masters and slaves are firmly inscribed in monasticism. Papaconstantinou, 'Notes sur les actes de donation d'enfants', 92.
[73] P. KRU 78, 34; 82, 20; 92, 14; 93, 14. Papaconstantinou, 'ΘΕΙΑ OIKONOMIA', 525.
[74] M. Golden, '*Pais*, "child" and "slave"', *L'Antiquité Classique*, 54 (1985), 91–104.

authority and subservience.[75] The children (or their parents) offer to the monastery the services of their bodies and in return, the monastery shall be their teacher and shall supervise the work that each of them will perform with their hands. In the documents surveyed above, the parents are not selling their children in exchange for money but rather in exchange for a favour granted by God (healing, for example).[76]

The formulas used in these acts of donation, which refer to the purchase and the management of the children, are taken directly from the language used to transfer property.[77] The monastery is responsible for their nutrition and care, and for ensuring that they have adequate clothing.[78] In fact, once they have learned to perform certain duties, the children are meant to take care of jobs that have been done previously by the monastery's adult servants (i.e taking water from the wells, maintaining the altar lamps, giving bread to pilgrims, cleaning the monastery's cells, and taking the animals out to pasture).[79] They have to perform all of the tasks that need to be done to ensure that the monastery functions effectively, ensuring that the institution reproduces itself over time.[80] Their status is the same as that of those servants who have been bought for money: donated children are the servants of the monastery in the same way as the 'ancient slaves'.[81] Many contracts emphasise the monastery's ownership of the child's body, a defining element of the slave condition. If someone wants to take the child from the monastery, he must pay a price of between thirty and thirty-six golden pieces, a price which takes into account the fact that the child should belong to the monastery for his entire life.[82]

An enduring relationship of dependence is thereby created and maintained between children (now adults) and monasteries. Although there were some cases in which children, having grown up, lived, and worked outside the monastery, get married and have children of their own,[83] even in these

[75] P. KRU 78, 25; 79, 59; 91, 27; 97, 20; 78, 26. Papaconstantinou, 'Notes sur les actes de donation d'enfants', 92–3.

[76] See Papaconstantinou, 'Notes sur les actes de donation d'enfants', 92–102, on the status of children as oblates.

[77] Steinwenter, 'Kinderschenkungen an koptische Klöster', 185, n. 9.

[78] P. KRU 87, 90, 103.

[79] See Richter, 'What's in a Story?', 244 n. 21, which lists the tasks assigned to the children (P.KRU 93, 32–33; 93, 34; 92, 14; 79, 47; 80, 38; 93, 32); Papaconstantinou, 'Notes sur les actes de donation d'enfants', 101–2; and Id., 'ΘΕΙΑ ΟΙΚΟΝΟΜΙΑ', 517–18.

[80] P. KRU 80, 39; 95, 18; 101, 7; 87, 19.

[81] P. KRU 98, 7.

[82] *Cod. Iust.* 7.7.1 (*De servo communi manumisso*). For prices in this period, see C. Morrisson and J. C. Cheynet, 'Prices and Wages in the Byzantine World', in A. Laiou (ed.), *The Economic History of Byzantium from the Seventh through the Fifteenth Century* (Washington, DC: Dumbarton Oaks Press, 2002), 847.

[83] P. KRU 89, 42; 96, 79. Papaconstantinou, 'Notes sur les actes de donation d'enfants', 102–4.

cases they had to pay a tax to the monastery, the so-called *demosion*.[84] By taking on the practical roles within the monastic community, because of their status as slaves and/or servants, such individuals ensured the institutional reproduction of the monastery over time.

Conclusion

The Egyptian monastic family of late antiquity lived an autonomous and collective life that in many ways conformed to patterns of family life elsewhere in Egypt. Yet there was one arena in which it was not self-sufficient: the ability to maintain and regenerate itself over time. This problem was solved, at least partially, if free children could become servants in the monastery and could contribute both to the growth of the numbers of monks and nuns within the community and to the economic life of the monastery as servants. Monasteries helped children to survive extreme situations such abandonment, kidnap, illness, and poor or socially dysfunctional families, as well as providing opportunities for children to receive training and education. They also provided families and their children with the opportunity to attain salvation through monastic intercessions, prayers, and liturgies.

Economic motives must therefore have been an important reason for abandoning or donating children. Furthermore, this was no one-way street: the economic imperative would have been taken into account by both the parents and the monastery. The family had one less mouth to feed but also one less pair of hands to rely on. The monastery took on the responsibility of feeding, educating, and providing security for the child, but could draw on their labour within the monastic workforce. In other words, there was one less child for the biological family to worry about and one more servant for the monastic family to make use of.

From the perspective of the monastic *familia*, children were not only *filii*, but in certain cases also *famuli* of the monastery, which was able to exercise legal and economic control over them. They were an object to be exchanged between families and monasteries in a process of mutual exchange and reciprocal advantage. And yet a complex picture emerges from this context, from both an economic and spiritual point of view. While the presence of these children doubtless aided the monastery

[84] P. KRU 81, 21; 92, 19; 99, 13. Papaconstantinou, 'Notes sur les actes de donation d'enfants', 102. See also Richter, 'What's in a Story?', 245, nn. 23–4.

economically, we should not forget that there were spiritual as well as material aspects to their presence. As both authority figure and owner of its servants, the monastery both cost them their freedom and guaranteed their safety, in the process cultivating them as subjects of the monastic life and agents within a specific monastic community.[85]

[85] A Coptic document makes this clear in the following formula: 'To the attention of the *dikaion* of the monastery of apa Phoibammon of Mount Djème and the *oeconomus*, since they shall take care of the "divine economy" of the monastery, for their safety, I have established this act of donation' (P. KRU 78, 70–6. Papaconstantinou, 'ΘΕΙΑ ΟΙΚΟΝΟΜΙΑ', 521–6).

PART III

Knowledge, Power, and Symbolic Violence
The Aesthetics of Control in Christian Pedagogy

The studies in Part III explore how the Christian preachers and writers of late antiquity used a wide range of pedagogical and literary techniques to evoke empathetic responses in their audiences. Deployed effectively, such techniques could prove pivotal in cultivating both empathy and an imaginative apparatus for thinking about the relationship between individuals and the community to which they belonged, at the same time establishing the authority of the teacher within their particular small worlds, from classroom to monastery and beyond. Yet, making a success of this intermediary position was not easy and, as we shall see, such victories were often hard won in the face of interference from superiors, competition from peers, and the recalcitrance of audiences.

Preachers and teachers seem to have been particularly adept at manipulating their audience's emotions as a means of promoting learning about their relationship with the broader group. For example, Blake Leyerle's exploration of the uses of fear in John Chrysostom's preaching shows how emotional agitation could be harnessed as a tool to enhance complicity between preacher and audience, while Jamie Wood stresses how fear was a powerful driver towards learning and social conformity in the classroom of Libanius and the monasteries of Basil the Great's rules. These emblematic Christian and pagan orators of the later fourth century thus stand within the same tradition, making strategic use of fear in pedagogic contexts in order to educate their audiences. Aaron Johnson's essay on 'textual violence' in Eusebius explores the bishop of Caesarea's aesthetic of violent correction and its enhancement of the authority of the interpreter, while Blossom Stefaniw examines the imaginative framing of the ascetic life as an athletic and military subculture through the metaphor of wrestling with the Devil.

Melissa Markauskas delves into the practical challenges of teaching at the turn of the fourth century. The chapter maps the hierarchies and tensions within the catechetical organisation of Carthage in the time of

Augustine, suggesting that the shared experience of violence may form a powerful bond even where resources – and individuals – are stretched to the limit. Clergy responsible for catechetical instruction within the crowded religious marketplace of the late Roman city faced strikingly similar challenges to Libanius, their contemporary, in Antioch: a variegated and sometimes disinterested or even hostile audience; a high level of competition; and a structurally vulnerable position within a hierarchical system. In response to such challenges, those entrusted with instruction drew on a variety of resources and devised a range of strategies. As Wood's chapter demonstrates, one strategy was the use of physical discipline to bring people into line, while another was the use of violent narratives to engage the audience. In this regard, Christian and non-Christian teachers faced similar challenges and experimented with a similar range of potential solutions.

CHAPTER 8

John Chrysostom and the Strategic Use of Fear

Blake Leyerle

Acts of violence can be motivated by reasons ranging from the hotly impulsive to the coolly considered. Prominent among the latter is an appreciation for the effectiveness of fear as a means of social control. Once durably inscribed, fear no longer depends upon repeated acts of aggression; it can be triggered by even the prospect of pain.[1] In this sense, fear not only depends upon actual violence but can also replace it. The purpose of these imagined severities, Foucault argued about a much later historical period, was not only obviously pedagogic – to teach a lesson – but also undeniably creative – to produce disciplined, 'docile' bodies. A similarly complex dynamic, I argue, is apparent in the preaching of John Chrysostom, who had a very high estimation of the strategic utility of fear.

Chrysostom spoke often of this emotion, both in the wake of actual situations of violence, such as the Riot of the Statues, when the populace as a whole quaked in fear, and also in the course of his regular preaching, when he deliberately evoked terror in his listeners by imaginatively conjuring punitive scenarios. In his fierce discourses against Judaizing Christians, for example, he argues for the superiority of churches over synagogues precisely on the grounds that the former are 'truly frightening and filled with fear . . . In [them] we hear countless sayings on eternal punishments, on rivers of fire, on the venomous worm, on bonds that cannot be broken, on exterior darkness.'[2] Nor is this high estimation of fear confined to polemics. In a homily on Second Thessalonians, he declares that 'Nothing

For a more extended argument with respect to Chrysostom's understanding of fear, see my forthcoming book, *The Narrative Shape of Emotion in the Preaching of John Chrysostom* (Oakland, CA: University of California Press, 2020). All translations are my own, unless otherwise attributed.

[1] 'It is not pain itself that frightens, but those things – or even signs of those things – that portend pain', D. Konstan, *The Emotions of the Ancient Greeks: Studies in Aristotle and Classical Literature* (Toronto: University of Toronto Press, 2007), 130–1.

[2] *Adv. Jud.* 1.4.1 [PG 48.848], P. W. Harkins (trans.), *Saint John Chrysostom, Discourses against Judaizing Christians* (Washington, DC: Catholic University of America Press, 1977), 14 (slightly amended).

is more profitable than talking about hell.'[3] And early in his cycle on Lazarus, he openly wishes that he could 'always and continually speak about hell'.[4] Such unalloyed enthusiasm is rather hard to take. On first reading, it suggests little more than a strongly repressive disciplinary agenda. But fear, as both Aristotle and Foucault have noted, is a complex emotion and Chrysostom was, among other things, a very astute observer of human nature.

His praise of fear, I will argue, springs from an appreciation not only for its positive contribution – its ability to overcome indifference and spur ethical action – but above all, for its capacity to promote a deliberative state in which values can be reassessed and temporal frames clarified. To make this argument, I intend to draw primarily on his advice to parents on how to raise their children and his series of homilies delivered in response to the Riot of the Statues. By examining his rhetoric in these two quite separate contexts, we can gain a clear sense of John's understanding of the emotion as well as the techniques he favoured for mitigating and exacerbating fear.

The Bridle of Fear

The repressive force of fear emerges strongly from Chrysostom's comments on child rearing.[5] Because children are timorous by nature, parents can effectively restrain bad behaviour by mobilizing fear.[6] Mothers, he suggests, can silence crying children by threatening to throw them into the jaws of wolves, and fathers can constrain wayward sons by threatening to

[3] Οὐδὲν οὕτω χρήσιμον, ὡς τὸ περὶ γεέννης διαλέγεσθαι, *Hom. 2 Thess.* 2.3 [PG 62.477].

[4] *Hom. Laz.* 2.3 [PG 48. 985], Catharine P. Roth (trans.), *St John Chrysostom: On Wealth and Poverty* (Crestwood, NY: St Vladimir's Seminary Press, 1984), 44.

[5] Had Cain been afraid of God, he would not have murdered his brother; nor would Joseph's brothers have planned to take their brother to a lonely place and kill him, *Hom. 2 Cor.* 5.3 [PG 61.432].

[6] Children can be easily moulded, since they are 'still trembling and fearful and afraid (ἔτι τρέμοντα καὶ φοβούμενον καὶ δεδοικότα) in look and speech and everything else', *Inan.* 19 [SC 188.104]. Borrowing from Plato the analogy of the soul to a city, Chrysostom notes that the first task is 'to draw up laws for this city and its citizens, laws that inspire fear and are strong, and to uphold them', *Inan.* 26 [SC 188.112]. Others in childlike positions of dependency, such as women and slaves, should also be constrained by fear. For slaves, see C. L. de Wet, *Preaching Bondage: John Chrysostom and the Discourse of Slavery in Early Christianity* (Oakland, CA: University of California Press, 2015), esp. 134–5, 146–9, 203–6. Chrysostom's understanding of the position of women is complex: he endorses their subordination, E. A. Clark, 'Sexual Politics in the Writings of John Chrysostom', *Anglican Theological Review*, 59 (1977), 3–20; but is categorically opposed to spousal violence, J. A. Schroeder 'John Chrysostom's Critique of Spousal Violence', *Journal of Early Christian Studies*, 12 (2004), 413–42; Leslie Dossey, 'Wife Beating and Manliness in Late Antiquity', *Past & Present*, 199 (2008), esp. 7–11.

disinherit them.[7] Such threats were preferable to actual violence. For if a boy is often beaten, Chrysostom reasons, he will become inured to the pain and learn to 'despise it'.[8] Instead, he should live constantly in the expectation of punishment. In this way, his fear remains unquenched, 'like a raging fire drawing thorny brushwood from every side or like a sharp and searching pick digging to the very depths'.[9] A lively sense of dread also characterized the older child's experience of school or apprenticeship. Chrysostom acknowledges that masters, teachers, and pedagogues routinely used threats to ensure compliance. Indeed, the propensity to keep order through violence was so well known that Artemidorus considered it self-evident that dreams of learning the alphabet portended fear as well as drudgery.[10] This use of fear seems both powerful and straightforward.

Of interest, however, is the way in which Chrysostom recommends a programme of biblical story telling as a means of internalizing this fear. The story with which he begins is that of Cain and Abel and, in his retelling, he dwells on the best ways by which parents can convey Cain's fear. For example, they might say:

> 'the murderer lived for many years suffering miserably and continuously, with fear and trembling as his companions, and endured ten thousand afflictions and was punished every day'. Describe his punishment with intensity and do not simply say that 'he heard God say: "Groaning and trembling you shall be on the earth."' For a young child does not yet know what this means. But say, 'Just as when you are standing before your teacher full of anxiety over whether you are about to be beaten, you tremble and are afraid, even so did that man live continuously, because he had offended God.'

Parents should underscore the story's message by asking their children pointed questions, such as, 'Do you see how evil it is to envy a brother? Do

7 *Adv. Jud.* 3.1 [PG 48.848]; *Inan.* 71 [SC 188.172]; *Stat.* 7.3, 19.4 [PG 49.94, 197]. Parents can manipulate their children by getting slaves 'to enact fearful things', *Hom. Matt.* 11.6 [PG 57.191]. Plato, *Crito* 46c, *Phaedo* 77d–e, *Respublica* 1.330e, *Theaetetus* 166a, 168d, also notes that children are naturally timorous and can be threatened with monsters and wolves to make them behave.

8 *Inan.* 30 [SC 188.120].

9 *Inan.* 30 [SC 188.120], M. L. W. Laistner (trans.), *Christianity and Pagan Culture in the Later Roman Empire* (Ithaca, NY: Cornell University Press, 1951), 100. Chrysostom also underscores the superior potency of threats, rather than actual physical punishment, in his advice on managing slaves: fear, unlike blows, causes 'perpetual agitation', *Hom. acta apost.* 12.4 [PG 60.104]; de Wet, *Preaching Bondage*, esp. 203–6. Because of the good effect of fear, fathers set tutors over their children and lawgivers place magistrates over cities, *Stat.* 15.1, 13.4 [PG 49.153, 141].

10 Artemidorus, *Oneirocritica.* 1.53. Fear of teachers was common, *Stat.* 17.1 [PG 49.172]; *Inan.* 39.552–54 [SC 188.136]; *Hom. Col.* 4.3 [PG 62.329]. A certain amount of pain was thought to be educative, *Hom. acta apost.* 42.4 [PG 60.302]. Masters, teachers, and pedagogues often threatened their apprentices, students, or charges, *Stat.* 14.1 [PG 49.145]. *Inan.* 39 [SC 188.136].

you see how evil it is to think to hide anything from God? For he sees everything, even the things done in secret.'[11] It is this last moral that Chrysostom emphasizes, promising parents that if they only 'sow the seed of this teaching in the child, he will have no need of a pedagogue, because this fear that comes from God, this total fear, has instead taken possession of the boy and shakes his soul'.[12] The inculcation of scriptural stories is thus inseparable from the inscription of the truth of justice: 'in the penalty', Foucault observed, 'one will read the laws themselves'.[13]

The inhibitory force of frightening tales becomes even clearer when John addresses the difficult task of checking emergent sexual desire. 'How shall we tie down this wild beast?' he asks, 'What shall we contrive? How shall we place a bridle on it? I know of none, save only the restraint of hell (γεέννης).'[14] Adolescence was thus the time for 'more fearful stories'. But boys even as young as eight or ten could profitably hear about the devastating flood, the annihilation of Sodom, and the selling of Joseph into slavery.[15] The purpose of telling these stories was not that children should acquire a mastery of scripture, but rather that scripture should master them.[16] The effect of this mastery is a durable state of fear, as Chrysostom overtly notes: 'if a story so seizes their soul that it is thought worthy of belief – indeed true – will it not take possession of the children and fill them with great fear?'[17] The choice of verbs here is telling; for in a

[11] *Inan.* 40 [SC 188.138]. As W. I. Miller, *The Mystery of Courage* (Cambridge, MA: Harvard University Press, 2000), 137–42, at 137 notes, 'Being looked at is threatening.'

[12] *Inan.* 40 [SC 188.138]. From their earliest youth, children should learn that 'there is a Judgement and that there is a punishment; let it be drummed into their minds'. This fear will produce good effects: they will become orderly and obedient 'like a well-broken horse', *Hom. 2 Thess.* 2.4 [PG 62.478].

[13] M. Foucault, *Discipline and Punish: The Birth of the Prison*, A. Sheridan (trans.) (New York, NY: Vintage, 1979), 110.

[14] *Inan.* 52, 76 [SC 188.150, 178].

[15] These 'fortify his hearing' (Τούτοις περίφραττε αὐτοῦ τὴν ἀκοὴν) and 'offer sufficient protection' (ἱκανὰ πρὸς φυλακὴν), *Inan.* 52, 58, 61 [SC 188.150–52, 156, 158–60]. For Chrysostom's view of amulets, see my, '"Keep Me, Lord, as the Apple of Your Eyes": An Early Christian Child's Amulet', *Journal of Early Christian History*, 3 (2013), 73–93.

[16] Still less is it to provide children with a way to explore danger in a secure setting or to offer them a vicarious thrill, as a modern analysis of frightening fiction for children has suggested, A. Piese, '"Something Under the Bed Is Drooling": The Mediation of Fear through the Rhetoric of Fantasy in Literature for Children', in K. Hebblethwaite and E. McCarthy (eds.), *Fear: Essays on the Meaning and Experience of Fear* (Dublin: Four Courts Press, 2007), 145–57.

[17] *Inan.* 44 [SC 188.142]. 'Even as God rules the world with the fear of hell and the promise of his kingdom, so too must we rule our children', *Inan.* 67 [SC 188.166]; the same advice holds good for adults: 'Let us consider the blessings of the kingdom and the miseries of hell and thus regulate and school ourselves (οὕτως ἑαυτοὺς ῥυθμίζωμεν καὶ παιδαγωγῶμεν)', *Hom. 2 Thess.* 3 [PG 62.476].

slave-owning society, as I have argued elsewhere, 'seize' and 'possess', coupled with fear, are not only strong, but actually graphic expressions.[18]

It is again in terms of the story of Cain that Chrysostom describes the tense situation in Antioch, in the spring of 387. In response to a new tax levy, rioting had broken out, in which statues of Theodosius and his family had been toppled and dragged through the dust.[19] In recounting the situation, John has recourse to the Platonic simile of a runaway horse: the populace, which had previously been 'well-ordered and gentle, like an obedient and well-tamed horse', had suddenly bolted and caused unspeakable damage.[20] Clearly, a strong restraining hand was needed. And this fear had provided: in dread of the emperor's reaction and state-sponsored violence, the whole populace was 'enduring the penalty of Cain'.[21] The result, Chrysostom exults, was improved self-control: no one had been seen drunk, or singing lascivious songs, or giving way to unseasonable laughter or impure words.[22]

The benefits of fear, however, transcend simple restraint. Fear is adaptive in that it urges action.[23] Melissa Markauskas' analysis of Augustine's strategies for rousing discouraged catechists shows that he appreciated the motivational force of fear.[24] Chrysostom signals his interest in this energizing effect when he comments early in his homilies on the Statues, 'I do not fear the anger of the Emperor as much as I fear your indifference.'[25] An appreciation for the stimulating force of fear also informs his pedagogical advice.

[18] Κατέχει τὴν ψυχὴν ... κατάσχῃ καὶ πολλοῦ φόβου ἐμπλήσῃ. See B. Leyerle, 'Appealing to Children', *Journal of Early Christian Studies*, 5 (1997), 243–70.

[19] *Stat.* 5.3, 15.1 [PG 49.73, 154–55]. For the sequence of events, see F. Van de Paverd, *St John Chrysostom, The Homilies on the Statues: An Introduction* (Rome: Pontificium Institutum Studiorum Orientalium, 1991), 19–160. Chrysostom preached his *Homilies on the Statues* in the second year of his priesthood.

[20] *Stat.* 2.1 [PG 49.34].

[21] Even 'in the midst of sleep, starting up through constant agony of mind' and during the day, 'jumping at our own shadows and trembling at every sound', *Stat.* 2.2, 6.1, 11.1, 13.1 [PG 49.35, 83, 120, 135–37]. An awareness of sin 'makes the sinner a timid being that trembles at any sound', *Stat.* 8.2 [PG 49.99].

[22] *Stat.* 6.1 [PG 49.82]. Fear is a powerful inhibitory force: it is 'nothing less than a wall, and a defence and an impregnable tower', *Stat.* 15.2 [PG 49.156].

[23] Both these aspects are neatly summed up in a passage from Chrysostom's fifteenth homily on the Statues: as in a house where an armed guard stands watch, so none of the servile passions will easily attack us 'while fear possesses our mind', *Stat.* 15.1 [PG 49.154]. Miller's reflections on 'critical distance' are of interest: 'Well-known animal studies show that within a critical distance, that distance within the kill range of the predator, the prey responds to threat by fighting; if still within flight distance it flees if the predator decides to attack', *Mystery of Courage*, 86, citing Plutarch, *Apophthegmata laconica, Agesilaus* 9.

[24] See Melissa Markauskas' chapter in this volume.

[25] *Stat.* 3.7 [PG 49.57].

Fear as a Goad

Chrysostom has observed that fathers sometimes deliberately increased their children's fear of their teachers not to restrain potentially bad behaviour but to promote diligence.[26] For fear, as Jamie Wood has shown, was widely understood to be 'a particularly useful aid to learning'.[27] Chrysostom returns often to this bracing quality of fear in his homilies on the Statues, insisting that terror of imperial reprisal has stimulated virtue.[28] As proof, he cites the fact that, whereas his listeners had previously ignored his exhortations to keep away from the theatre and racecourse, they have now taken the initiative in shutting up the orchestra.[29] Nothing, the preacher concludes, causes virtue to increase like 'a perpetual state of dread'. Thus God 'threatens like a teacher', and frequently sends fearful trials 'to arouse us when we are dozing, or falling down, and to stir us up and make us more religious'.[30]

The stimulating quality of fear made it useful in changing habitual behaviours,[31] but it was an even more crucial ally in overcoming a kind of moral slackness or torpor that Chrysostom called ῥαθυμία.[32] In his eyes, this failing was the cause of the calamitous riot – not only because none of the citizens had roused themselves to restrain the violence of the rioters, but also because their indolence had provoked divine correction.[33] The danger of indifference is a recurrent theme in Chrysostom's preaching. Indeed, it seems to have been for him, as Robert Hill has suggested, 'the universal cause of human failing'.[34] This was the fault of which the first

26 Some fathers would hand over their children with the explicit instructions, 'Don't spare them', *Hom. Matt.* 55.1–3 [PG 58.542–43]; but they might also take the teacher aside and ask him privately not to be too harsh, *Hom. Matt.* 35.4 [PG 57.411]; despite a reputation for severity, it was not unheard of for a tutor to intercede with a father on a child's behalf, *Hom. Col.* 4.3 [PG 62.330].

27 See Jamie Wood's chapter in this volume.

28 'The city is now in all respects, like the pattern of a modest and virtuous woman, decorous, free and well-behaved', *Stat.* 6.1 17.2 [PG 49.82, 178]. Threats are usually more effective than promises in impelling people to virtue, *Stat.* 7.2 [PG 49.94].

29 *Stat.* 15.1 [PG 49.153].

30 *Stat.* 16.5, 14.1 [PG 49.168, 144]; God lets the devil loose on humanity, to stir people from their negligence, *Hom. Gen.* 23.6 [PG 53.205].

31 'Where there is fear, habit (συνήθεια) is easily broken, even if it is deeply engrained', *Stat.* 14.6 [PG 49.152]; *Hom. 2 Cor.* 7.7 [PG 61.452].

32 Noted also by Xenophon, *Memorabilia* 3.5.5–6. In classical thought, however, this stimulating function was more often attributed to anger. See F. Leduc, 'Gérer l'agressitivé et la colère d'après l'oeuvre de Saint Jean Chrysostome', *Proche-Orient Chrétien*, 38 (1988), 31–63.

33 Chrysostom repeatedly identifies *rhathumia* as the cause of the Riot of the Statues; see, e.g., *Stat.* 2.4, 3.7 [PG 49.38, 57].

34 R. C. Hill, *John Chrysostom, Homilies on Genesis 18–45*, FOTC 82 (Washington, DC: Catholic University of America Press, 1990), 430, n. 31.

couple was guilty: for despite having heard the command of God and the threatened consequences, they paid no attention and ate the fruit.[35]

The danger of indifference was also the main message in the destruction of Sodom. For Chrysostom, the focus of that story lies less on the unruly actions of the citizens than on the contrasting reactions of Lot and his wife. Whereas Lot acted admirably with eager hospitality, inviting in the angelic visitors and heeding their warning to flee without a backward glance, his wife responded culpably with slack indifference. Despite the explicit injunction of the angels, she looked back 'and accordingly paid the penalty for her indifference'.[36] The pillar of salt and its surrounding region thus function as witnesses: they confess the truth of divine punishment. In this respect, they have a kind of universal hortatory value. Chrysostom thus urges his listeners to visit the devastated region. Looking at the blasted landscape, they will understand that such calamity could happen to them and feel terror.[37] This fear will, in turn, fuel moral renovation.[38]

But not everyone witnessing the sufferings of others feels afraid. For the process of identifying things as frightening involves a sophisticated calculus.[39] One is not afraid of everyone, but only of those who occupy a position of superior power. Nor do people tend to feel frightened if they possess great strength, connections, or wealth, since these instil confidence. As Aristotle explains, 'Those who either are, or seem to be, highly prosperous do not think they are likely to suffer anything; wherefore they are insolent, contemptuous, and rash, and what makes them such is wealth, strength, a number of friends, power.'[40] This is precisely the mindset that Chrysostom attributes to Dives in the Lukan parable of Lazarus. As we meet him in Chrysostom's retelling, the rich man confidently voices his sense of security:

[35] 'It was not the tree that caused the harm, but slothful will (ῥᾴθυμος) and contempt displayed for God's command', *Hom. Gen.* 16.6 [PG 53.134], R. C. Hill (trans.), *St John Chrysostom. Homilies on Genesis 1–17*, FOTC 74 (Washington, DC: Catholic University of America Press, 1986), 220–1; see also *Hom. Gen.* 17.1 [PG 53.134].

[36] *Hom. Gen.* 43.6 [PG 54.405]; see also *Hom. Gen.*, 42.5, 44.1 [PG 54.392, 407]. For Lot's admirable reaction, see *Hom. Gen.*, 43.5 [PG 53.403–04]. See also B. Leyerle, 'Lot's Wife on the Border', *Harvard Theological Review*, 107 (2014), 59–80, esp. 62–3.

[37] Like Antioch, the Cities of the Plain were well endowed. 'What could be more illustrious', Chrysostom asks, 'than the cities of Sodom? For the houses and buildings were splendid and so were their walls; and the country was rich and fertile', *Stat.* 17.2 [PG 49.177].

[38] Where there is fear, 'there is zeal in almsgiving, and intensity of prayer, and warm and continuous tears and groans full of compunction', *Stat.* 15.1 [PG 49.154].

[39] Konstan, *Emotions*, 132–3.

[40] Aristotle, *Rhetorica* [hereafter: *Rhet.*]. 2.5.14 1383a, J. H. Freese (trans.), *Aristotle, The Art of Rhetoric*, LCL 193 (Cambridge, MA: Harvard University Press, 1926, 2000), 207. 'Confidence is the contrary of fear', *Rhet.* 2.5.16.

> Why do I need piety and virtue? Everything flows to me as though from a fountain, I enjoy great abundance and great honour and glory. I anticipate nothing unexpected (οὐδὲν ὑπομένω τῶν ἀδοκήτων). Why should I seek virtue? This poor man, although living in righteousness and piety, suffers horribly.[41]

The rich man's assumption of invulnerability, based on wealth, status, power, and connections, insulates him from fear. He does not think that the sufferings of the poor man will ever befall him. Nor is he exceptional.[42] 'Even now', Chrysostom adds, 'many people express these thoughts.'[43] In order to evoke their compassion, Chrysostom must first prompt fear.[44]

He does so by labouring the evanescence of worldly security and thus the proximity of danger. He shows how all the goods in which the rich man trusted vanished in a moment. None of it ever had any more reality than a stage performance, from which he was 'led away naked and alone'.[45] The preacher's message is clear: when the rich man saw the suffering of Lazarus, he should have assessed his own situation, realized that he too was vulnerable to the nine different kinds of suffering endured by Lazarus, and carefully enumerated by John, and felt afraid.[46] This fear would, in turn, have led him to feel compassion for Lazarus. Simply hearing the story of the rich man's punishment presents the same opportunity for Chrysostom's congregation that seeing Lazarus offered the rich man: the poor man's suffering 'becomes a means of salvation, by making them more diligent out of fear of what happened to him'.[47]

41 *Hom. Laz.* 2.4 [PG 48.987].

42 *Hom. Laz.* 2.3 [PG 48.986], Roth (trans.), *St John Chrysostom: On Wealth and Poverty* 45. As Aristotle comments: those who think themselves supremely fortunate are incapable of pity. 'For if they think that all good things are theirs, it is clear that they think that they cannot possibly suffer evil', *Rhet.* 2.7.3–4, 1385b, Freese (trans.), *Aristotle, The Art of Rhetoric*, 225. Aristotle also notes that those 'who consider themselves utterly ruined' are also incapable of pity. See M. C. Nussbaum, *Upheavals of Thought* (Cambridge: Cambridge University Press, 2001), 342–3.

43 Ταῦτα δὴ πολλοὶ καὶ νῦν πολλάκις λέγουσιν, *Laz* 2.4 [PG 48.987].

44 The pain of pity and the pain of fear are closely allied. 'In a word, all things are to be feared which, when they happen, or are on the point of happening, to others, excite compassion', *Rhet.* 2.5.12 1382b, Freese (trans.), *Aristotle, The Art of Rhetoric*, 205. To feel pity, however, 'one has to recognize a resemblance with the sufferer, but at the same time not find oneself in precisely the same circumstances', Konstan, *Emotions*, 201–2. See also Nussbaum's extended reflection on compassion, *Upheavals of Thought*, esp. 301–27.

45 *Hom. Laz.* 2.3 [PG 48.986].

46 The nine different sufferings correspond to many of the distressing things enumerated by Aristotle as likely to prompt pity, *Rhet.* 2.8.9–11.

47 *Hom. Laz.* 3.8 [PG 48.1003], Roth (trans.), *St John Chrysostom: On Wealth and Poverty*, 73. From it we learn that no one can escape punishment: whoever lives in great comfort and plenty now, will suffer later. This was indeed the message Chrysostom derived from the terror that fell upon the city after the riot, *Stat.* 2.4 [PG 49.38].

This ability of fear to spread from person to person represents another dimension of its stimulating nature. Thucydides was an early witness to fear's contagious quality. Watching a battle, he observed how the Greek hoplites slowly moved in an arc to the right. In his words: 'This is because fear makes every man want to do his best to find protection for his unarmed side in the shield of the man next to him on the right, thinking that the more closely shields are locked together, the safer he will be.'[48] This 'bunching', as it is called, is one of the most primal responses to fear. It is apparent not only among humans, but also among herbivores and even fish. To catch fear, as William Ian Miller notes, one does not need to know the underlying facts; it is enough to notice another's fear.[49] Shared cognitive belief can enhance this phenomenon.

Chrysostom shows a vivid awareness of this effect, noting how people, in the aftermath of the Riot of the Statues, sought comfort in the proximity of others. They thronged to church and turned fervently to prayer.[50] No other means had proved so effective in generating group solidarity.[51]

But fear does more than strengthen corporate identity and encourage ethical action. As Aristotle notes, it is in the very nature of fear to encourage deliberation.[52] Much of Chrysostom's enthusiasm for the emotion springs directly from his interest in prompting his listeners to assess their situation and re-examine their values.

Fear as a Deliberative State

Although experienced viscerally, fear depends, like all emotions, on a complex cognitive process.[53] It involves, first, a careful assessment of the nature of the threat. For not all evils are feared, according to Aristotle, but

[48] Thucydides, *Historiae* 5.71, Miller (trans.), *Mystery of Courage*, 131.

[49] Miller, *Mystery of Courage*, 92–105; 214–15: ancient warfare made use of this instinct. Part of the effectiveness of the Roman legion derived from the close press of bodies, which also provided comfort. Bunching now poses a problem for military strategists, since it is no longer adaptive under the conditions of modern warfare.

[50] 'The forum is indeed empty, but the church is filled', *Stat.* 4.1 [PG 49.59]; see also *Stat.* 6.1, 15.1 [PG 49.82, 154]. For fear promoting prayer (and curses), see Miller, *Courage*, 215–16.

[51] Although Peter Brown focuses on Chrysostom's teachings on sexuality and poverty, his summary of John's programme as preaching 'a brotherhood of bodies at risk' is germane, *The Body and Society: Men, Women, and Sexual Renunciation in Early Christianity* (New York, NY: Columbia University Press, 1988), 305–22, at 316.

[52] *Rhet.* 2.5, 1382a5.

[53] This claim is supported by neurological analysis, which suggests that perception and evaluation of objects are processed separately, J. E. LeDoux, *The Emotional Brain: The Mysterious Underpinnings of Emotional Life* (New York, NY: Simon and Schuster, 1996), 69, 284.

only those that have 'size'.[54] No one goes around fearing that their coffee cup will break or in lively dread that someone will take their paper clip, as Martha Nussbaum observes.[55] And even apparently serious evils cease to be frightening if they are discovered to be relatively or wholly harmless. As an example, Chrysostom cites the rhetorical commonplace of a person recoiling from a snake glimpsed on a road, until he perceives that it is only a piece of rope.[56] In a similar fashion, parents can calm their children's fears by showing and allowing them to touch an apparently threatening object, such as a mask or skein of wool.[57] A second factor influencing fear is proximity. For no evil is feared if it seems remote. Thus while all people know that they will die, no one is actively afraid of death unless it seems near at hand.[58] It is this careful assessment of size and proximity that prompts Aristotle to observe that 'fear makes people deliberative'.[59]

Chrysostom is vitally interested in both aspects of this deliberation. Because fear depends upon a vivid sense of the future, he can adjust his listeners' temporal framework by deliberately arousing the emotion. And because fear arises only from the prospect of serious loss, the emotion provides a clear index of his listeners' values. It is only because they place a high premium on wealth, honour, and life, that their diminishment seems fearful.[60] By confronting the emotion, he can address and modify these beliefs. This process of cognitive restructuring, if it operates at a deep

[54] They must involve 'great pain or destruction', *Rhet.* 2.5, 1382a.

[55] M. C. Nussbaum, *The Therapy of Desire: Theory and Practice in Hellenistic Ethics* (Princeton, NJ: Princeton University Press, 1994), 370.

[56] Chrysostom uses this example several times; see, for example, *Exp. Ps.* 9.1 [PG 55.122]; *Illum. catech.* 2.1 [PG 49.233]; *Hom. Matt.* 20.4 [PG 57.292]; *Hom. Eph.* 12.3 [PG 62.92]. It was an example drawn from the schools; see Sextus Empiricus, *Pyrrhoniae hypotyposes*1.33.

[57] Children are innately timorous; even a skein of wool can cause alarm, *Hom. Col.* 4.4 [PG 62.330]; *Inan.* 20.290–92 [SC 188.104–06]. Slaves often show frightening masks to children to raise a laugh, *Adv. Jud.* 1.3 [PG 48.848]; *Hom. Matt.* 28.3 [PG 57.353]; *Ex. Ps.* 9.11, 114–115.1 [PG 55.139, 316]; *Hom. 1 Thess.* 5.4 [PG 62.428]; *Hom. Tit.* 2.4 [PG 62.675]. See also Dio Chrysostom, *Libycus mythos* (*Or.* 5) 17, *De Gloria i* (*Or.* 66) 20; Epictetus, *Diatribai* (*Dissertationes*) 2.1.15, 3.22.106; Strabo, *Geographica* 1.2.8. Chrysostom notes that fear can be allayed by showing a child an object, *Hom. Col.* 4.4 [PG 62.330].

[58] Cephalus in Plato's *Republic* expresses a similar view, *Respublica* 330d.

[59] *Rhet.* 2.5, 1382a5; Konstan, *Emotions*, 134–49.

[60] Chrysostom is thus quite certain that telling a young man that his beautiful financée will not marry him if he lives a life of sloth will cause him 'to reflect deeply (πολλὴν ποιήσεται τὴν φροντίδα)', precisely because the threat endangers what he most values, *Inan.* 82 [SC 188.188]. He appears to paraphrase Aristotle when he writes, 'the expectation of good does not comfort us as much as the fear of pain causes us distress. After all, only when good things are expected with confidence do they produce pleasure, but if unhappiness is merely suspected, it immediately confounds and disturbs the soul', *Virg.* 57.1 [SC 125.308], trans. Sally Shore, *John Chrysostom: On Virginity; Against Remarriage* (New York, NY: Edwin Mellen, 1983), 91.

enough level, will allay their fear. This is what Chrysostom means when he asserts that fear 'comes from choice, not nature'.[61]

The dread that oppressed the people of Antioch after the Riot of 387 was, above all, terror of imminent death: that in retaliation for the insult to himself and his family, the Emperor would order the destruction of the city and the annihilation of all its inhabitants. To this fear, Chrysostom speaks directly. Like any good philosopher, he first attacks the belief that death is an evil, presenting it instead as a release from tumult and a swift transportation to a peaceful haven. Death, he further observes, is wholly natural: it comes to everyone.[62]

> It is a journey for a season, a sleep longer than usual. So, if you fear death, be afraid of sleep too! If you grieve for those who are dying, grieve also for those who are eating and drinking – for this is as natural as that! Let not natural things sadden you.[63]

To those who retort that they are not afraid of dying *per se*, but rather of dying unjustly and shamefully, Chrysostom responds somewhat acerbically that surely they would prefer to be put to death unjustly rather than justly. And he points to the example of the martyrs.[64] Taken together, these arguments insist that death, even violent death, is not an evil and thus should not be feared.

The fear initially felt by Christians in Antioch also revealed the high value that they placed on material goods. For when the imperial letter first arrived levying the new tax, people were afraid of financial loss. After the riot, this threat no longer had size. In dread of losing their lives, people no longer cared about their possessions, and no longer feared their loss.[65] Along similar lines, Chrysostom suggests that the reason people are now afraid of death is that they do not fear hell. For if people were truly seized by 'dread of future punishment', they would scorn those who fear

[61] *Exp. Ps.* 9.1 [PG 55.122], Robert C. Hill (trans.), *St John Chrysostom: Commentary on the Psalms* (Brookline, MA: Holy Cross Orthodox Press, 1998), 179. Aristotle observes: 'the kind of courage that comes from a spirited temper seems to be the most natural and becomes true courage when choice and purpose are added to it', *Ethica Nicomachea* 3.8, 1117a3, M. Ostwald (trans.), *Aristotle, Nicomachean Ethics*, Library of Liberal Arts (Indianapolis, IN: Bobbs-Merrill, 1962), 74.

[62] *Stat.* 5.2–3 [PG 49.70–72].

[63] *Stat.* 5.3 [PG 49.73–74]. Logically, we should grieve no more for those who die than for those who are born, *Stat.* 6.4 [PG 49.86]; see also *Stat.* 7.1 [PG 49.92].

[64] *Stat.* 5.2, 5.3 [PG 49.71, 72].

[65] *Stat.* 5.3, 6.5 [PG 49.73, 87]. 'When you see anything good and great in the present life, think of the kingdom, and you will consider it as nothing. When you see anything frightening, think of hell, and you will laugh at it', *Hom. 2 Thess.* 2.3 [PG 62.476].

death, even as they laugh at children who are afraid of masks, but do not fear fire.[66]

Chrysostom's argument here benefits from the confluence of two separable philosophical strands: the Stoic conviction that virtue is a person's only truly durable possession, and the Christian belief that all losses sustained by the righteous will be made good in heaven. It is this latter point that Chrysostom labours in a series of pointed questions:

> What is there that anyone can do, by which he can cause a noble-minded man to grieve? Take away his riches? He has wealth laid up in heaven. Exile him from his country? He will set forth to that city above . . . Destroy his body? Yet he shall rise again.[67]

Only sin threatens real and significant loss and thus, it alone should be feared.[68]

All of Chrysostom's arguments reveal his robust belief in the essentially rational structure of fear: his conviction that if he can show his listeners that a threatened loss, which initially aroused fear, is in fact neither serious nor painful, their fear will subside. For the argument to work, his congregation must agree with his assessment of size: they must share his beliefs, of which an essential component is a vivid belief in the afterlife.

An awareness of the immediacy of a threat is essential to Aristotle's definition of fear, as we have already noted.[69] It is this aspect of fear, I would suggest – its ability to make people acutely aware of the proximity of the future – that Chrysostom most values. He believed that the terror in which people lived immediately after the riot was beneficial, not only because it constrained bad behaviour, spurred correct behaviour, or even fostered corporate bonding, but above all because it reinforced belief in an

66 *Stat.* 5.3 [PG 49.73]; *Exp. Ps.* 10.11 [PG 55.139]. 67 *Stat.* 5.4 [PG 49.74].

68 *Stat.* 5.2 [PG 49.70]. At the conclusion of his treatise on child-rearing, Chrysostom links fear of God to contempt for 'wealth or worldly reputation or power or death or the present life on earth', *Inan.* 86–87 [SC 188.192], Laistner (trans.), *Christianity and Pagan Culture* 121. As Anne-Marie Malingrey, *Jean Chrysostome: Sur le sacerdoce*, SC 272 (Paris: Éditions du Cerf, 1980), 193, n. 3, comments, 'La crainte de Dieu joue un rôle important dans la spiritualité de Jean Chrysostome. C'est un thème qui mériterait une étude détaillée dans son oeuvre si vaste.'

69 Like hope, fear is future directed. Aristotle, *Ethica Nicomachea* 3.6, 1115a10. Fear, indeed, depends upon a certain amount of hope: 'for it is a necessary incentive to fear that there should remain some hope of being saved from the cause of their distress', *Rhet.* 2.5, 1383a, Freese (trans.), *Aristotle, The Art of Rhetoric*, 207. David Pears, 'Courage as Mean', in A. O. Rorty (ed.), *Essays on Aristotle's Ethics* (Berkeley, CA: University of California Press, 1980), 174–5.

imminent judgement. He thus seizes the opportunity to draw explicit and concrete parallels between imperial and divine judicial procedures.[70]

Like the emperor, God interposes an interval between transgression and punishment designed to produce fear and amendment.[71] Only fools would misread this delay and, supposing that they had escaped punishment, 'make light' of their offence.[72] And just as legislators prefer to select a few malefactors for spectacular punishment rather than punishing all the guilty, 'so Christ uses the experiences of one or two notorious sinners as a warning to all'.[73] This was the role of Cain, who became, in effect, a 'living edict' and a 'walking monument'.[74] The ruins of Sodom also functioned in this way. In his homilies on Genesis, John characterizes the region as a 'a land screaming aloud, so to speak, and revealing the traces of punishment, even after such a number of years, as though inflicted yesterday or the day before – so vivid are the signs of God's wrath'.[75] The value of these traces derives from their status not only as a 'memorial of past wrath' but also, and far more importantly, as a 'prediction of future punishment'.[76] The site is a 'strong lesson' for spectators because it conjures the future in immediate and tangible ways.

Again and again Chrysostom labours the terrors of hell.[77] Preaching on the Gospel of Matthew, he dilates in concrete terms upon the violence and suffering of that place:

[70] As C. Kelly, *Ruling the Later Roman Empire*, Revealing Antiquity 15 (Cambridge, MA: Harvard University Press, 2004), 232–45 has observed, early Christian images of God's Judgement were modelled on contemporary Roman judicial practice.

[71] The benefits of this political strategy were multiple: it secured not only law and order, but also a reputation for clemency, with a minimal deployment of force.

[72] 'If you sin, beloved, and are not punished, do not grow presumptuous, but be more alarmed precisely for this reason, knowing that it is an easy matter with God to recompense when he pleases', *Stat.* 3.7 [PG 49.58].

[73] *Virg.* 23 [SC 125.168]. Doctors do the same: when preparing to remove stones or amputate gangrenous limbs, they bring the patient into the middle of the marketplace 'not out of a wish to make a display of human misadventures, but for everyone to take great care of their own health', *Vidi Dom.* 5.2 [SC 277.132], R. C. Hill (trans.), *St John Chrysostom, Old Testament Homilies, Vol. II, Homilies on Isaiah and Jeremiah* (Brookline, MA: Holy Cross Orthodox Press, 2003), 98–99. Masters behave in the same fashion: 'by beating one slave, they make the rest behave better out of fear', *Hom. Laz.* 3.7 [PG 48.1003].

[74] Νόμον ἔμψυχον ... στήλην περιερχομένην, *Vidi Dom.* 4.6 [SC 277.128]; see also *Hom. Gen.* 19.5 (PG 53.165); *Adv. Jud.* 8.2 [PG 48.930].

[75] Chrysostom, *Hom. Gen.* 42.5 [PG 54.392], Hill (trans.), *John Chrysostom, Homilies on Genesis 18–45*, 430. As a place bearing 'the traces of calamity', it makes a 'deeper impression upon the mind' than a report, *Stat.* 19.2 [PG 49.191]. For the same reason, Hadrian left the bare foundation of the Jerusalem temple standing to remind the Jews of their defeat, *Adv. Jud.* 5.11 [PG 48.900].

[76] Ὀργῆς ὑπομνήματα ὄντα, τῆς μελλούσης κολάσεως προμηνύματα, *Perf. carit.* 7 [PG 56.288].

[77] *Adv. Jud.* 1.4 [PG 48.848].

> Just as those who work in the mines are delivered over to certain cruel men, and see none of their household (οὐδένα τῶν οἰκείων), but only those who are set over them, so will it be then – or rather not so, but even far more terrible. For here it is possible to go and petition the emperor, and free the condemned person: but there, it is no longer possible, for he does not permit it. But they continue being broiled, suffering a kind of anguish that cannot be described. For if no words can describe the excruciating pain of those who are burned here, that of those suffering there is far worse. For here, everything is over in a brief moment of time, but in that place there is burning, but that which is burnt is not consumed.[78]

John acknowledges that his words frighten and pain his listeners; but precisely for this reason, they bring great benefit. They drive home the reality – and proximity – of divine judgement. The anguish of those condemned to the mines makes the imagined sufferings palpable of those condemned in the afterlife; it gives them size and makes them seem close.[79] The force of Chrysostom's argument is increased by its circularity: as belief in imminent judgement prompts real fear, so fear makes the idea of imminent judgement real.[80]

Ideally, this temporal horizon would be reinscribed each day. Again, fear is the central mechanism of this process. In his instructions to those seeking baptism, Chrysostom urges:

> Let each one leave the church to take up his daily tasks, one hastening to work with his hands, another hurrying to his military post, and still another to his post in the government. However, let each one approach his daily task with fear and anguish, and spend his working hours in the knowledge that at evening he should return here to the church, render an account to the Master of his whole day, and beg forgiveness for his falls.[81]

One becomes Christian by feeling fear: fear not of death, nor of the loss of material possessions, but of divine judgement. To live in this dread constitutes a kind of proof that one has internalized a set of values, in which the only evil that has 'size' is sin, and a keen sense of the proximity of judgement.

Such constant remembrance would, no doubt, sharpen a sense of religious identity, even as Gregory had used claims concerning the violent

[78] *Hom. Matt.* 43.4 [PG 57.462].

[79] Compare Foucault, *Discipline and Punish*, 113–14 on the creation of 'the punitive city'.

[80] F. Leduc, 'L'eschatologie: une préoccupation centrale de saint Jean Chrysostome', *Proche-Orient Chrétien* 19 (1969), 109–34 rightly points to the importance of eschatology for Chrysostom.

[81] *Illum. catech.* 8.18 [SC 50.257], Paul Harkins (trans.), *St John Chrysostom, Baptismal Instructions*, ACW 31 (New York, NY: Newman Press, 1963), 127.

intervention of the martyrs to delineate his family from the wider Christian populace.[82] The preacher may also have aimed to foster intergroup solidarity: for the manipulation of fear, as Jamie Wood has argued, can be a powerful tool in the formation of groups, 'priming individuals to accept authority, to act . . . on command and to believe in the moral superiority of their group'.[83] Shared cognitive belief can enhance the phenomenon of 'bunching', which, as we have seen, is one of the most immediate reactions to fear. Indeed, to have this effect, fear need not be acute, but can resemble something closer to awe.

Conclusion

In the end, it is not hard to appreciate the strategic utility of fear for John Chrysostom. He understood fear as a powerful ally in the formation of ethical selves. By fear of violence, people were restrained from doing what he believed they should not, and goaded out of listlessness into doing what he believed they should. A central task for parents, as for preachers, was thus the durable inscription of scriptural stories of punishment upon the minds of their charges. The contagious aspect of fear, moreover, was useful in breaking down the sense of invulnerability fostered by social superiority and in reinforcing group identity. But perhaps most importantly, fear encouraged a deliberative state in which the preacher could effectively question the value of material goods and insist on the proximity of future reality. Fear has thus not only a repressive, but also an undeniably creative– even imaginative – aspect.[84] It is easy then to understand why Chrysostom spoke so warmly about fear and overtly wished that he could always talk about hell.

[82] See Vasiliki Limberis' chapter in this volume. Whether or not Chrysostom intended this result is debated. I. Sandwell, *Religious Identity in Late Antiquity: Greeks, Jews and Christians in Antioch* (Cambridge: Cambridge University Press, 2007) asserts this forcefully. J. H. W. G. Liebeschuetz, *Ambrose and John Chrysostom: Clerics Between Desert and Empire* (Oxford: Oxford University Press, 2011), esp. 190–94 objects.

[83] See Jamie Wood's chapter in this volume.

[84] Compare Foucault, *Discipline and Punish*; M. Foucault, 'The Subject and Power', *Critical Inquiry*, 8 (1982), 777–95.

CHAPTER 9

The Fear of Belonging
The Violent Training of Elite Males in the Late Fourth Century

Jamie Wood

Since Edward Gibbon, scholars have argued about the role that Christian social and moral values and practices played in the decline and fall of the Roman Empire. Gibbon saw the flight of elite Roman youths from the legions into the monasteries as a clear sign of the decay that left the Empire unable to withstand internal dissension and external aggression.[1] John Matthews, on the other hand, argued that it was an increasing privatisation of power and concentration of resources within the hands of the super-elite that reduced the ability of the state to respond to and recover from crises within and threats without. Aristocratic power increased at the expense of that of the Emperor, in the West at least.

According to Matthews, an important stage in this process was the development of an empire-wide bureaucracy of service (*militia*) during the late third and fourth centuries, followed by its gradual takeover by the senatorial aristocracy who started to monopolise offices that would previously have been held by equestrians.[2] Matthews' young Roman men were thus socialised to chase office and status within the imperial system, while Gibbon's were taught to pray rather than to guard the frontiers.

Research over the past two decades has suggested that this division between Christian and senatorial values does not take full account of the complex interaction of religion, society and politics in the late Roman Empire and that the success of Christianity in the century after the conversion of Constantine lay in the ability of its proponents to mould

I would like to express my gratitude to the participants in the workshop at Oxford in 2011 for their comments on my paper there, as well as on subsequent drafts. Additional thanks must go to Kate Cooper, Philippa Hoskin (Lincoln), and Caroline Musgrove (Cambridge) for their helpful comments on this chapter; all remaining errors are, of course, my own.

1 W. H. C. Frend, 'Edward Gibbon (1737–1794) and Early Christianity', *Journal of Ecclesiastical History*, 4 (1994), 661–72; J. Bremmer, *The Rise of Christianity through the Eyes of Gibbon, Harnack, and Rodney Stark*, 2nd edn. (Groningen: Barkhuis, 2010); J. G. A. Pocock, *Barbarism and Religion*, 6 vols. (Cambridge: Cambridge University Press, 1999–2015).

2 J. Matthews, *Western Aristocracies and Imperial Court AD 364–425* (Oxford: Clarendon Press, 1975).

the religion to the pre-existing practices and values of the elite.[3] This chapter unpicks one of the key methods by which Christianity was mapped onto existing Roman social framework: education. It explores the role of violent training practices in the social and moral formation of elite young men in traditional civic education and in the socialisation practices of Christian ascetic communities. The argument is that Christian educational practices in ascetic contexts map almost seamlessly onto those used for training members of the urban elite, young men who would traditionally go on to leadership roles within their local communities and possibly take up positions within the imperial bureaucracy. Conceptions of how young men were trained to be members and leaders of communities may have reflected the growing allegiance of the elite to the new Christian faith, but such allegiance was based firmly in long-established traditions of elite training within rhetorical schools. The success of the early impresarios of Christian monasticism thus lay as much in their ability to deploy long-established training methods to form Christian subjectivities and communities as it did in their ability to promote 'flight' from the Roman 'world'.

Since the work of Pierre Bourdieu, social scientists have acknowledged that social elites manipulate education and training processes to establish and maintain boundaries and hierarchies and therefore their own pre-eminence. Bourdieu argued that, although modern educational systems are often predicated on claims that they promote social mobility, they actually reproduce the pre-existing order and reinforce inequalities.[4] Education and the discourses that surround it thus function as forms of 'symbolic violence'.[5] Scholars of late antiquity have used Bourdieu's ideas to demonstrate that elites went to considerable lengths to maintain communal cohesion and identity in a changing social, political and religious landscape.[6] The aim of this essay is to examine more fully *how* they did so.

[3] K. Cooper, 'Insinuations of Womanly Influence: An Aspect of the Christianization of the Roman Aristocracy', *Journal of Roman Studies*, 82 (1992), 150–64; K. Cooper, *The Fall of the Roman Household* (Cambridge: Cambridge University Press, 2007); M. R. Salzman, *The Making of a Christian Aristocracy: Social and Religious Change in the Western Roman Empire* (Cambridge, MA, Harvard University Press, 2002).

[4] P. Bourdieu, *Distinction: A Social Critique of the Judgement of Taste* (Cambridge, MA, Harvard University Press, 1984); P. Bourdieu, *The State Nobility: Elite Schools in the Field of Power*, L. C. Clough (trans.) (Stanford, CA: Stanford University Press, 1996).

[5] On the idea of 'symbolic violence', see G. Lakomski, 'On Agency and Structure: Pierre Bourdieu and Jean-Claude Passeron's Theory of Symbolic Violence', *Curriculum Inquiry*, 14 (1984), 151–63.

[6] E.g. W. Pohl, 'Introduction: Strategies of Distinction', in W. Pohl and H. Reimitz (eds.), *Strategies of Distinction: The Construction of Ethnic Communities, 300–800*, The Transformation of the Roman World 2 (Leiden: Brill, 1998), 1–16 examines the early medieval West, while I. Sandwell, *Religious Identity in Late Antiquity: Greek, Jews and Christians in Antioch* (Cambridge: Cambridge University

According to Bourdieu, a key element of the economy of symbolic violence that operates within modern educational systems is the system of competitive examinations. Competition also played an essential role in the educational institutions of late antiquity. Teachers competed for pupils, while pupils were set against one another constantly.[7] We shall see how Libanius, a fourth-century teacher of rhetoric from Antioch, reacted strongly against any criticisms of his pedagogic approach, no doubt because of the high-stakes rivalry between the teachers of Antioch. He also encouraged competitions between his pupils. Teresa Morgan has argued persuasively that the competitive nature of education in the Roman world played an essential role in defining and maintaining elite dominance over subordinates. Competition in education, alongside wealth, personality and social connections, functioned as a gate-keeping mechanism modifying and usually slowing or preventing social mobility.[8]

Basil Bernstein, a contemporary of Bourdieu, also analysed how education reproduces social formations, a process he termed 'cultural reproduction'. The key insight of Bernstein's work was that 'process' plays a role equally significant to 'content' in cultural reproduction. Bernstein suggested that the social structures in which information is communicated to the learner are as significant as its actual content: for successful socialisation to occur, the message and medium must work in tandem. For Bernstein, like Bourdieu, modern educational systems function to reinforce the status quo and reproduce the existing social order.[9] The alignment between process and content can be observed in the ways in which violence was deployed pedagogically in the schools of late antiquity. Students were often beaten, both to maintain order and to discipline them into learning, while violent narratives, from the adventures of Aeneas to accounts of the sufferings of the Christian martyrs, played an equally

Press, 2007), compares the efforts of John Chrysostom and Libanius to create and maintain religious identities in late-fourth-century Antioch.

7 Authors who wrote about the training of Roman soldiers, too, thought that recruits should be trained through competitive means, especially through combat simulation; P. Rance, '*Simulacra Pugnae*: The Literary and Historical Tradition of Mock Battles in the Roman and Early Byzantine Army', *Greek, Roman, and Byzantine Studies*, 41 (2000), 223–75.

8 T. Morgan, 'Assessment in Roman Education', *Assessment in Education: Principles, Policy & Practice*, 8 (2001), 20.

9 B. Bernstein, *Class, Code and Control, Vol. III: Towards a Theory of Educational Transmissions* (London: Routledge, 1975); B. Bernstein, *Class, Code and Control, Vol. IV: The Structuring of Pedagogic Discourse* (London: Routledge, 1990); B. Bernstein, *Pedagogy, Symbolic Control and Identity: Theory, Research, Critique* (London: Taylor and Francis, 1996).

important role in teaching.[10] Even the content of grammatical instruction had violent undertones:

> in the fourth-century *Canons* of the famous grammarian Theodosius – a collection of rules about the declensions of nouns and adjectives and conjugations of verbs – the verb adopted as the model is *typtein* ('to beat').[11]

In the schools of late antiquity, students thus experienced and reflected on physical and imaginative violence throughout their studies. We shall see in what follows that instructors in the late Roman world were well aware of the dynamic relationship between process and content in promoting cultural reproduction, and that they sought actively to exploit its potential in instructional contexts.

Studies of 'education' in the Roman world traditionally stress the formal literary training of elites, and in recent decades much valuable work has been done on the role of sub-elites such as grammarians in the education of Roman youths.[12] Rather than examining elite literary education or the social position of the teacher, this chapter focuses on processes that can be considered 'educational' in a broader sense, encompassing learning activities that were intended to develop an individual's skills, knowledge and dispositions beyond the rather narrowly defined literary canon of Latin and Greek *paideia*. The focus will be on the role of both explicit and implicit violence in this wider pedagogy, analysing how writers of the mid-to-late fourth century thought that young men could be trained in all-male environments such as schools and monasteries.

The chapter examines concepts of violent 'training' in the works of two writers who were contemporaries: Libanius, a pagan teacher of rhetoric from Antioch, and Basil of Caesarea, who became a bishop in Cappadocia and wrote extensively on asceticism. Both were active in the mid-to-late fourth century, and both provide detailed – though rhetorically inflected and highly idealised – descriptions of the procedures that were used to

10 R. A. Kaster, 'Controlling Reason: Declamation in Rhetorical Education at Rome', in Y. L. Too (ed.), *Education in Greek and Roman Antiquity* (Leiden: Brill, 2001), 317–37; C. M. Chin, *Grammar and Christianity in the Late Roman World* (Philadelphia, PA: University of Pennsylvania Press, 2008), 111–18.

11 R. Cribiore, *Gymnastics of the Mind: Greek Education in Hellenistic and Roman Egypt* (Princeton, NJ: Princeton University Press, 2001), 69; the same verb is also conjugated in many surviving school exercises.

12 H. I. Marrou, *A History of Education in Antiquity*, G. Lamb (trans.) (London, Sheed and Ward, 1956); S. F. Bonner, *Education in Ancient Rome: From the Elder Cato to the Younger Pliny* (London, Methuen, 1977); see R. A. Kaster, *Guardians of Language: The Grammarian and Society in Late Antiquity* (Berkeley, CA: University of California Press, 1988) for the classic study; Chin, *Grammar and Christianity* studies the relationship between Christianity and grammatical instruction.

train individuals to take on specialised functions within late Roman society. While Libanius trained his pupils to act as heads of families and as lawyers representing their cities within the imperial system, Basil encouraged his readers as ascetics living in monastic communities. Violence figures prominently in both authors' visions of education. For example, both draw frequent analogies with athletic competition and warfare.[13] The chapter argues that, far from being in tension, there was a high degree of alignment between late Roman educational practices and those that were deployed in Christian ascetic communities. Libanius and Basil saw violence of different forms as essential to the formation of individuals within their respective communities. This congruence can be witnessed on a number of levels: the alignment of violent process and violent content; the cultivation of feelings of fear in trainees; and a recognition that violent practices were especially effective means of forging individuals into members of communities.

Violence was pivotal to the practical process of education in classrooms and other sites of instruction, serving a disciplinary function, to bring young men into line. Violence was applied by figures of authority such as teachers, fathers, pedagogues (slaves with a special responsibility for supervising the education of their master's children) and superiors within monasteries, as well as by other members of the community. Violence also formed an essential element of the content of students' education in schools and monasteries. They were encouraged to read violent stories in Basil's monastery, received lectures about their own violent actions in Libanius' school, and in both contexts were expected to reflect on what they had read and heard. Violent texts were envisaged as providing young men with the moral and intellectual resources and dispositions to help them manage the transition to adult life.

Fear can be a powerful tool in the cultivation of masculine identities and the formation of all-male groups, in the modern and the ancient world.[14]

[13] M. Gaddis, *There Is No Crime for Those Who Have Christ: Religious Violence in the Christian Roman Empire* (Berkeley, CA: University of California Press, 2005), 24 and n. 79 (for bibliography); see also the chapter by Blossom Stefaniw in this volume.

[14] A. Errante, 'Where in the World Do Children Learn 'Bloody Revenge'? Cults of Terror and Counter-Terror and Their Implications for Child Socialisation', *Globalisation, Societies and Education*, 1 (2003), 146–7; J. T. Gibson, 'Training People to Inflict Pain: State Terror and Social Learning', *Journal of Humanistic Psychology*, 31 (1991), 78–81; A. T. Chappell and L. Lanza-Kaduce, 'Police Academy Socialization: Understanding the Lessons Learned in a Paramilitary-Bureaucratic Organization', *Journal of Contemporary Ethnography*, 39 (2010), 203–5; J. E. Mathieu, 'A Causal Model of Organization Commitment in a Military Training Environment', *Journal of Vocational Behaviour*, 32 (1988), 331.

The need to rely on and watch over one another creates a climate of competition and surveillance in which all members of the community are implicated. Fear, including anxiety about surveillance by authority figures and peers, was considered an essential motivation to learning in monastery and school.[15] Youths in Basil's monastery were supposed to be examined from an early age. In order 'to avoid being caught frequently dwelling on forbidden subjects, a boy will avoid wrong thoughts and keep recalling his mind from them, fearing the shame entailed by the scoldings he will receive' (τὴν ἐκ τῶν ἐλέγχων αἰσχύνην φοβούμενος).[16] Libanius also thought that students should be afraid of their teachers and that this would help to maintain order in the classroom. Research in biology has demonstrated that humans consistently seek to attain positive social recognition. Triggering a fear of being watched when acting dishonestly or in one's own self-interest is sufficient to encourage an individual to behave in a more socially acceptable manner and act more cooperatively.[17] Fear thus plays an important role in socialisation because such processes are meant to create individuals who can deal with stress in their adult lives, and it is clear that Libanius and Basil saw the pedagogic potential in manipulating such emotions.

In the fourth-century sources that are the focus of this chapter, violent training was viewed as serving a developmental function. Physical and psychological violence and intimidation forced individuals to dissociate themselves from previous social relationships and cognitive assumptions, breaking old affective ties and making new ones to their peers and the group to which all now belonged. Discipline, surveillance and the strategic use of fear also encouraged integration into new social contexts – the shared experience of violent training served to bond individuals more strongly into the new social context as an elite adult male in civic society or as a monk. Violent training thus functioned to break individuals free from established ways of thinking and practising and to reintegrate them into a new state of being within a radically altered social context. However, violent educational experiences did far more that increase commitment to

[15] Elsewhere in this volume, Blake Leyerle explores the use of fear in the preaching of John Chrysostom, a former pupil of Libanius who seems to have reproduced his master's rhetorical practices.

[16] Basil, *The Longer Rules* 15, W. K. L. Clarke (ed.), *The Ascetic Works of Saint Basil* (London: S.P.C.K, 1925), 145–228.

[17] M. Bateson, D. Nettle, and G. Roberts, 'Cues of Being Watched Enhance Cooperation in a Real World Setting', *Biology Letters*, 2 (2006), 412–14; K. J. Haley and D. M. T. Fessler, 'Nobody's Watching? Subtle Cues Affect Generosity in an Anonymous Game', *Evolution of Human Behaviour*, 26 (2005), 245–56. I would like to thank Abigail Dorr (University of Lincoln) for bringing these references to my attention.

the community; they turned boys into men who were equipped to protect the groups to which they belonged – families, cities, monasteries – from outside threats. It is clear, for example, that Libanius wanted his students to learn about the appropriate and inappropriate use of force so that later in life they would be better able to maintain order within their household and to protect their family and community.

Violent Process and Violent Content in Libanius' Classroom in Late Roman Antioch

The following section analyses the educational writings of Libanius, an orator and teacher of rhetoric who was active in Antioch in the second half of the fourth century.[18] While it would be anachronistic to describe Libanius as working within an educational 'system' as a modern audience might understand the term, he did work within a long-established civic tradition of rhetorical schooling.[19] The purpose of the competitive structures of education in the city was to prepare young men to function effectively as heads of their families, as advocates for their city within the imperial system and, for a minority, as functionaries within the late Roman bureaucracy.[20] Letters that report on the progress of his students and commend his former charges to potential employers are of particular relevance to understanding Libanius' thoughts about the role of violence in education, as are orations defending his school from criticism or outlining his pedagogic methods.[21]

In both letters and orations, Libanius used violent language when describing the process of teaching rhetoric. The outcomes of rhetorical education, too, had connotations of violence. Libanius often likened the prestige that advanced educational institutions reflected on a city such as Antioch to the military triumphs of former ages.[22] Both source groups reveal that Libanius conceived of rhetorical education as underpinned by

[18] Key recent studies on Libanius, which cite classic bibliography, include: L. van Hoof (ed.) *Libanius: A Critical Introduction* (Cambridge: Cambridge University Press, 2014); R. Cribiore, *Libanius the Sophist: Rhetoric, Reality, and Religion in the Fourth Century* (Ithaca, NY: Cornell University Press, 2013); R. Cribiore, *The School of Libanius in Late Antique Antioch* (Princeton, NJ: Princeton University Press, 2007).

[19] For Libanius and the tradition of rhetorical education at Antioch and the east of the Roman Empire more generally, see Cribiore, *The School of Libanius*, 13–82.

[20] Cribiore, *The School of Libanius*, 197–228 examines the destinations of Libanius' students.

[21] For an introduction to the orations, see P.-L. Malosse, 'Libanius' *Orations*', in van Hoof (ed.), *Libanius*, 81–106. For an introduction to Libanius' letters, see B. Cabouret, 'Libanius' *Letters*', in van Hoof (ed.), *Libanius*, 144–59.

[22] Libanius, *Epistulae* [hereafter: Libanius, *Ep.*] 140.2, R. Foerster (ed.), *Libanii opera*, 12 vols. (Leipzig: Teubner, 1903–27), Vols. X–XI (for letters). Translations of the letters derive (with

reflection on, and experience of, violence in both content and process. It produced young men who had not only been disciplined through the considered application of chastisement by their tutors and so understood the limits of violent action, but who also would not be afraid to act violently when it was necessary in their future roles as father, advocate and governor.

Libanius' penchant for using violent imagery when describing rhetorical education was, at face value, not matched by an enthusiasm for imposing physical punishments on his students. In *Oration* 62, which was directed against the critics of his pedagogic approach, Libanius suggested that harsh words could have a similar disciplinary effect to physical chastisement: 'I know how to denounce boys who are disorderly, but I also know how to praise those who keep within the rules.'[23] Yet Libanius' inability or unwillingness to use physical force to impose order on his students meant that some of them were unable to restrain their own violent tendencies. For example, critics blamed Libanius' failure to impose discipline severely enough when a group of them abused a pedagogue:

> they put the blame on me and on my leniency. 'If only he knew how to administer a proper thrashing (πικρῶς κολάζειν),' they say, 'this misbehaviour would not happen.' However, I would prefer my students well-disciplined (εὔτακτος) as a result of argument than as a result of the lash, and because of respect rather than because of a beating (μετὰ μαστίγων καὶ διὰ τὸ αἰδεῖσθαι μᾶλλον ἢ διὰ τὸ πλήττεσθαι).[24]

Elsewhere in his writings on his educational system, however, there are clues that physical chastisement was in fact sometimes used in Libanius' classroom. In the autobiographical *Oration* 1, delivered in 386, after explaining how the Emperor Theodosius I (d. 395) had imposed discipline by sentences of exile and flogging, Libanius says that he dealt with a breakdown of order by waiting to see if they recognised that they had acted badly before 'some compulsion was applied' (προσεγένετό τι τὸ τὴν ἀνάγκην).[25] Although he did not specify what kind of compulsion was

occasional slight modifications) from Cribiore, *The School of Libanius*, 233–321 (with concordance at 329–30).

[23] Libanius, *Ep.* 62.2; see also Libanius, *Ep.* 65 and Libanius, *Orationes* [hereafter: Libanius, *Or.*] 62.6, Foerster (ed.), *Libanii opera*, Vol. IV, 342–83. Translations of orations 3, 31, 58 and 62 are taken (with occasional modifications) from A. F. Norman, *Antioch as a Centre of Hellenic Culture as Observed by Libanius*, Translated Texts for Historians 34 (Liverpool: Liverpool University Press, 2000).

[24] Libanius, *Or.* 58.38, Foerster (ed.), *Libanii opera*, Vol. IV, 175–200.

[25] Libanius, *Or.* 1.241–242, A. F. Norman (ed. and trans.), *Libanius' Autobiography (Oration 1)* (London: Oxford University Press, for the University of Hull, 1965), 126–7. Trouble in the schools

applied, the reference to Theodosius' use of physical punishment to impose order suggests that force was applied occasionally to restore discipline among Libanius' students.

Further clues to the key role that physical punishment sometimes played in Libanius' school can be gleaned from the references that he makes to cooperation between teachers, parents and pedagogues. According to Libanius, teachers were not solely responsible for the education of young people or for the use of violence to bring them into line when they proved unwilling to learn or misbehaved. Indeed, in *Oration* 62 he criticises those parents who failed to discipline their sons, overturning the hierarchy and undermining the overall educational regime: the fathers have changed positions with their sons 'so that the sons wear angry looks and the parents cower before them' (ὥστε οἱ μὲν ὀργίλον βλέπουσιν, οἱ δὲ ὑποπτήσσουσι).[26]

Although the *paterfamilias* had ultimate responsibility for disciplining his children and directing their moral formation, this role devolved onto the pedagogue when they were supervising the child in school.[27] Pedagogues were thus permitted to use physical means to discipline students and to encourage them to learn. This might explain why Libanius was reluctant to impose punishments directly: pedagogues, acting *in loco parentis*, were responsible for disciplining students in his classroom.[28] It is thus hardly surprising that in Libanius' school pedagogues played an active role in maintaining discipline and encouraging their charges to learn:

> Bitter has turned sweet for Daduchius, and he now loves the hard work he used to avoid. It might also have been a god who urged him, but visibly it was the excellent Florentius [= his pedagogue], who checked everything carefully, grew angry when something was neglected, and urged him to improve the situation, saying that the boy would avoid blame if he became

is to be identified with persistent indiscipline (cf. Libanius, *Or.* 3) and the desertions of registered pupils from one teacher to another (Libanius, *Or.* 43); cf. Libanius, *Or.* 36.13.

[26] Libanius, *Or.* 62.24.

[27] Morgan, 'Assessment in Roman Education', 16: the absence of formal assessment in education was made up, or its place taken principally by, two other practices. One was a good deal of informal interest and interference by parents, other relatives and family friends. For the role of the *paterfamilias* in the formation and disciplining of children, see R. P. Saller, '*Patria Potestas* and the Stereotype of the Roman Family', *Continuity and Change*, 1 (1986), 7–22; R. P. Saller, 'Corporal Punishment, Authority, and Obedience in the Roman Household', in B. Rawson (ed.), *Marriage, Divorce and Children in Ancient Rome* (Oxford: Clarendon Press, 1991), 144–65.

[28] For paternal responsibility for correcting and punishing his son to instil discipline and improve the son's character, see Libanius, *Ep.* 60, 346, 472 and 600.1. See also Norman, *Libanius' Autobiography*, xxiii.

> a good student instead of a bad one. Daduchius promised and did not lie, but now he is one of those who get annoyed when we are on holiday.[29]

There were, however, rules governing the application of force in the classroom. Pedagogues could only inflict corporal punishment on their own charges, and students were not permitted to act violently towards the pedagogues of other children.[30]

The infliction of physical violence within Libanius' classroom was not solely a punitive measure; it was carefully calibrated to maintain order and to establish an optimal learning environment.[31] Libanius considered that the 'pedagogues' lashes' (ἱμάντας παιδαγωγῶν) could aid learning when they were applied appropriately.[32] In particular, the repeated infliction of pain was thought to aid memory and therefore practical performance:

> In fact, the learning that he himself imparts to the boy is preserved for him by the attendant, and the method of such preservation is for the attendants to apply pressure, shout at them, produce the cane and wield the strap, drive the lesson into their memories by tasks to this end, some painful, some, as a result of practice, troublesome no more.[33]

> καὶ τὰ παρ' αὐτοῦ δὲ τοῦδε διδόμενα τῷ παιδὶ τῷ παιδαγωγῷ φυλάττεται. δι' ὧν γὰρ ἂν ἡ φυλακὴ γένοιτο, τῶν παιδαγωγῶν ἐστιν ἐπικειμένων, κεκραγότων, ῥάβδον δεικνύντων, σκύτος σειόντων, εἰς μνήμην τὸ ληφθὲν ἀγόντων τοῖς περὶ αὐτὸ πόνοις τοῖς μὲν ἀνιαροῖς, τοῖς δ' ὑπὸ τῆς μελέτης οὐκ ἔτι λυποῦσιν.

This was not an unusual attitude in late antiquity. Numerous commentators suggested that physical pain improved memory. Discipline and learning were thus inextricably linked for Libanius and teachers like him.

Fear, the Maintenance of the Pedagogic Order and the Formation of the Elite Male Subject

As we have already seen in the case of the negative example of fathers cowering before their sons due to a lack of discipline within the family,

[29] Libanius, *Ep.* 1164.1. See also Libanius, *Or.* 34.29–30 for a pedagogue who does not cooperate with Libanius and criticises his pedagogic methods. Libanius, *Ep.* 44.5, Cribiore (trans.), *The School*, 316: 'So the pedagogue would urge on the laziest student, but the love for rhetoric would suffice this lad for a pedagogue'; Libanius, *Ep.* 300.3, Cribiore (trans.), *The School*, 277: 'And the greatest thing of all is that, with your mother gone and your father not there, you put yourself under the supervision of a desire for excellence as if it were a pedagogue.'

[30] Libanius, *Or.* 58.35.

[31] Libanius, *Ep.* 139.2, Cribiore (trans.), *The School*, 234: 'his pedagogue's role is not insignificant: he threatens, urges, rouses the boy, works hard with him'.

[32] Libanius, *Ep.* 911.2.

[33] Libanius, *Or.* 58.9.

violence in educational settings also helped to reproduce – and its lack to subvert – the social order. In *Oration* 58, for example, Libanius reflected on a case in which his students had acted harshly towards a pedagogue. These delinquents had inflicted an excessive and humiliating punishment – known as 'carpeting' (τάπης), which involved forcibly wrapping the victim in a carpet and violently shaking him – on a pedagogue who had spoken against one of the Latin teachers in Antioch. Libanius' main complaint was that his students had failed to consider the immorality of their actions: 'you should have told this fine teacher, "We will do what we ought, if you tell us, but not everything. We shall not do anything wrong."'[34]

Doing wrong, even when following the orders of an authority figure, had the potential to overturn the social hierarchy: 'We shall not beat (πατάσσω) our parents, nor yet overthrow altars, when people tell us to, nor yet kill any enemies of theirs.'[35] Libanius aimed to dissociate himself from the extreme actions of these students and to ensure that they understood that there were more appropriate ways of enforcing order. *Oration* 58 was thus an opportunity for Libanius simultaneously to defend his educational approach and to teach his students and the rest of the audience about the proper use of physical force.

Physical force had to be applied in a measured manner and by the proper authorities and because Libanius' students had used excessive force in an inappropriate context, and had no legitimate basis for their behaviour, they had, in effect, undermined their own teacher. They had degraded *all* pedagogues of Antioch; all pedagogues feared a similar fate.[36]

> Worst of all for a pedagogue, the fear he exercised upon his charges will be removed. If he finds them idling their time away, he will find them staring him out and bringing the carpet forward.[37]
>
> ὅ τε μέγιστον ἐν παιδαγωγῷ, φόβος ὁ κατὰ τῶν ἀγομένων ἀναιρεθήσεται. ἣν γὰρ ἅπτηται βλακευόντων, ἀντιβλέποντάς τε ἕξει καὶ προφέροντας τὸν τάπητα·

In overturning the proper pedagogic hierarchy, they had undermined the pedagogues' ability to inspire fear and therefore maintain order inside and outside of the classroom. To Libanius' mind, therefore, fear maintained order in educational settings. When teachers, pedagogues and parents were no longer able to rely on its motivational effects, learning suffered.[38]

[34] Libanius, *Or.* 58.30. [35] Libanius, *Or.* 58.30. [36] Libanius, *Or.* 58.6.
[37] Libanius, *Or.* 58.37; see also Libanius, *Or.* 58.20.
[38] This is underlined further in Blake Leyerle's chapter in this volume on the ways in which John Chrysostom sought to manipulate fearful emotions when preaching.

Limiting Individual Violence and Producing and Protecting the Community

Pedagogic violence within rhetorical education prepared students to endure hardships, to act responsibly and to cultivate the priceless virtue of self-command. Teaching with and about violence was intended to enable elite individuals to understand the limits of violent action and its potential consequences because they would have to function in social and professional situations later in life that would require them to control their own impulses and those of others, for example as lawyers, judges or governors.[39] They experienced stress and fear while being trained and at the same time learned how to manipulate such feelings in, and potentially to inflict violence on, others because 'a political career usually required the infliction of violence'.[40] Some of the parents of Libanius' students did not understand the point that violence could have negative consequences and should be constrained. He thus had to lecture them in order to correct their faults and show that his school was not dysfunctional.

In *Oration* 3, Libanius confronts his students for misbehaving during one of his speeches. He justifies his decision not to inflict punishment on the miscreants by stating that his schooling had trained him to endure harsh treatment rather than to retaliate with force: 'It is also a characteristic of mine to be reluctant to settle old scores, and I have been schooled to endure rather than to hit back' (φέρειν μᾶλλον ἢ κολάζειν πεπαιδευμένης).[41] The experience of physical punishment could instil patience and control in students (in Libanius at least). The actions of the students in punishing the pedagogue summarily through carpeting demonstrated that they had not understood what Libanius had taught them about the need to redress grievances through the proper channels and with appropriate force.[42] This was potentially strong evidence for the failure of Libanius' school. Critics could suggest that his disinclination to impose

[39] On the position of the governor in the later Roman Empire, which was often problematic in terms of their role in mediating relationships between the imperial 'centre' and the provinces, see D. Slootjes, *The Governor and His Subjects in the Later Roman Empire* (Leiden: Brill, 2006). On the complexities of the later Roman bureaucracy more generally, see C. Kelly, *Ruling the Later Roman Empire*, Revealing Antiquity 15 (Cambridge, MA: Harvard University Press, 2004).

[40] G. Clark, 'Women and Asceticism in Late Antiquity: The Refusal of Status and Gender', in V. L. Wimbush and Richard Valantasis (eds.), *Asceticism* (Oxford: Oxford University Press, 1998), 36–7.

[41] Libanius, *Or.* 3.34, Foerster (ed.), *Libanii opera*, Vol. III, 119–46.

[42] Libanius, *Or.* 58.15–18.

order through physical punishment had created a group of young men who had no idea about the appropriate use of violence to maintain order.

Libanius reports that certain parents were unwilling to discipline their sons for aggressive behaviour in class because they thought that such behaviour would serve them well in manhood:

> Some have already commended their sons when they were bent upon illicit intercourse, and admired them when they fill the schoolroom with fighting and disorder (πληγῶν καὶ ταραχῶν ἐμπλήσαντα τὸ διδασκαλεῖον ἐθαύμασε), and declare that that conduct, which ought to make them choke with anger, will make him cock of the roost when he becomes a man.[43]

The students who carried out the carpeting of the pedagogue were clearly not the only ones who did not learn the lesson about proper ways of resolving disputes.

On other occasions, Libanius seems to have been more successful in containing the violent inclinations of his students. When writing to Acacius, the father of one of his students, in 359, Libanius stresses that he has had some success in this matter:

> when you were thinking of sending him to us, you added to the other praises that he would be of the greatest use when it came to fists. But although he confirmed everything else, in this he proved you wrong, since he values peace more than the weak students do. Therefore it is up to you either to punish him for this or to admire this, too (τῶν ἀσθενῶν μᾶλλον τὴν ἡσυχίαν τιμήσας. σὸν τοίνυν ἢ δίκην τούτου λαβεῖν ἢ καὶ τοῦτο θαυμάσαι).[44]

Under Libanius' guidance, the son of Acacius had overcome his youthful tendency to resort to fisticuffs to solve problems. According to Libanius, students like this would be better placed to benefit their communities in the courts of law during their adult lives because they had learned to manage their own violent inclinations through accepting the discipline of their parents, teachers and pedagogues. Experiencing violence during their rhetorical education was thus intended to teach students about self-control, a characteristic that would enable them to manage subordinates later in life: 'Peregrinus is dedicating himself to law, piling weapon on weapon' (νόμων ὅπλον ἐφ' ὅπλῳ κτώμενος) 'and from this he has hopes of wealth, offices, and other power' (πλούτου καὶ ἀρχῶν καὶ τῆς ἄλλης ἰσχύος).[45]

[43] Libanius, *Or.* 62.25. [44] Libanius, *Ep.* 60.2. [45] Libanius, *Ep.* 1539.1.

There were collective as well as individual benefits to rhetorical education. In *Oration* 31, 'To the Antiochenes for the Teachers', Libanius argued that the system of rhetorical education has raised Antioch to its illustrious and prosperous position because it enabled the city 'to overcome the irrational impulses of governors by dint of rational argument'.[46] Oratory offered the potential for protection, or at least for the mitigation of excess, within what could be an exploitative bureaucracy. Libanius moves on to make an extended comparison between the glory of military victory and rhetoric:

> If peoples who win power from arms and victory in battle ignore any decline in the manufacture of arms, they would injure themselves as regards what they have won and they would encompass their own destruction: similarly, those who have made the greatest contribution to the art of eloquence would be held to blame if they did not maintain the profession of rhetoric.[47]

Rhetorical education was designed to prepare its students to perform in the service of their families, their cities, and the empire and Antioch's security was assured within the imperial system by the protection of the rhetoricians and their students.[48]

The educational programme outlined in Libanius' letters about his students and orations about his school thus demonstrate the central place that violence occupied in the education of civic elites in the later Roman Empire. Students were taught to take on elite roles in a violent social world through experiencing violence directly and reflecting on it repeatedly during their formative years. In order to teach his students how to operate in adult roles as *paterfamilias*, advocate or governor, Libanius, and the parents and pedagogues with whom he cooperated, integrated violence into both the process and content by which youths were taught. Old identities had to be broken down and new ones cultivated. Physical violence and fear encouraged students to leave the habits of youth behind and to prepare for leadership roles in which they would have to use violence and instil fear in others.

Libanius, a pagan entrusted with training the social and political elite, criticised the takeover and destruction of temples by Christian monks in the late fourth century and the general hostility of hardline Christian

[46] Libanius, *Or.* 31.7, Foerster (ed.), *Libanii opera*, Vol. III, 119–46. [47] Libanius, *Or.* 31.7.

[48] This is analogous to the protection that the martyrs of Edessa and their representatives offered to their city in the face of the depredations of imperial troops, as examined in Thomas Dimambro's chapter in this volume.

ascetics to pagans and heretics. Libanius thought that the actions of the monks were highly disruptive and potentially destructive of the social order that he had worked so hard to maintain through his teaching.[49] This attitude was not shared by all members of Libanius' class, as demonstrated by the tolerance – and in some cases overt support – of prominent members of the imperial government for the monks.[50] One of Libanius' most prominent Christian contemporaries, Bishop Basil of Caesarea (d. 379), turned out to be a vigorous proponent of asceticism, if not of its more extreme practitioners.[51]

Violent Process and Content in Ascetic Training in the Communities of Basil the Great

In both East and West, ascetics and monastic founders, including Pachomius and Martin of Tours, were former soldiers. Bishops and ascetic writers such as Basil and Augustine of Hippo – who talks in the first book of the *Confessions* about the punishments he suffered at school – had received extensive rhetorical training at the hands of teachers like Libanius.[52] It is thus hardly surprising that early monastic writings splice military metaphors and training practices with those derived from elite educational institutions.

Basil, whose family came from the region of Pontus and who was bishop of the important see of Caesarea in the 370s, was one of the three bishops of the Greek Church who came to be known collectively as the Cappadocian Fathers.[53] Highly educated and a writer in polished Greek, he became embroiled in Christological controversies during his episcopate and a large proportion of his surviving works deal with the burning theological questions of the day. Another strand within Basil's writings, and well integrated with his pastoral and polemical writings according to Philip

[49] For example, Libanius, *Or.* 30.8; Cooper, 'Insinuations of Womanly Influence', 161.

[50] On the praetorian prefect Cynegius, see N. McLynn, 'Genere Hispanus: Theodosius, Spain and Nicene Orthodoxy', in K. Bowes and M. Kulikowski (eds.), *Hispania in Late Antiquity: Current Perspectives* (Leiden: Brill, 2005), 77–120.

[51] For biography of Basil, see P. Rousseau, *Basil of Caesarea* (Berkeley, CA: University of California Press, 1998).

[52] Augustine, *Confessiones* 1.9.14–15, L. Verheijen (ed.), *Sancti Augustini, Confessionum Libri XIII*, CCSL 27 (Turnhout: Brepols, 1981), 8–9. On corporal punishment in schools more generally, see W. M. Bloomer, 'Corporal Punishment in the Ancient School', in W. M. Bloomer (ed.), *A Companion to Ancient Education* (London: Wiley-Blackwell, 2015), 184–98.

[53] On the Cappadocian Fathers, see R. Van Dam, *Families and Friends in Late Roman Cappadocia* (Philadelphia, PA: University of Pennsylvania Press, 2003).

Rousseau, deals with the issue of ascetic practice.[54] As outlined by Vasiliki Limberis and James Corke-Webster elsewhere in this volume, Basil's asceticism was rooted in a family tradition that developed over time from household-based practices to more organised communities.

Basil is remembered as the founder of coenobitic monasticism and, although he was not the first to write a monastic rule and was influenced by earlier practitioners of the ascetic communal life such as Eustathius of Sebaste, his rules, written in the 360s and 370s, have a distinctive emphasis on the spiritual value of living in community.[55] Indeed, the focus of these writings is less on laying down exact guidelines about the organisation of communal life than on giving moral advice on how to live a Christian life in a community. It is hard to pin down the exact dates of the different 'rules', but his first was the small *Asketikon*, which was written in the early 360s and focuses on the moderation necessary for communal living, possibly based on observation of some of the excesses of the followers of Eustathius. He probably wrote the part of the *Asketikon* known as the *Longer Rules* in the second half of the 360s. These rules, which might more properly be described as spiritual essays, propose a message of ascetic renunciation for the entire Christian community, although they were certainly addressed to the members of the male and female communities founded by Basil.[56] Another element of Basil's *Asketikon* is the *Shorter Rules*, which are a series of 313 responses of Basil to specific questions posed by members of his communities. Like other ascetic guidebooks, Basil's rules advertise the separation of the Christian ascetic group from the 'world' occupied by the elite males of the type produced by Libanius, although he envisaged that the communities would be located either in towns or close to them so that their members could be of use to church and society.[57] The following section will demonstrate how, in order to achieve his socially responsible form of asceticism, Basil laid down rules for the induction and training of new entrants into the community that were strikingly similar to those of Libanius.

The main objective of Libanius, and other practitioners of traditional civic education, was to form individuals who were capable of taking on

[54] On Basil's ascetic project see Rousseau, *Basil of Caesarea*, 190–232.

[55] On Eustathius and his influence on Basil and his family see C. A. Frazee, 'Anatolian Asceticism in the Fourth Century: Eustathius of Sebastea and Basil of Caesarea', *Catholic Historical Review*, 66 (1980), 18–25.

[56] See Frazee, 'Anatolian Asceticism', 25–30.

[57] Frazee, 'Anatolian Asceticism', 29–30. On Basil's monastic project in general, see Rousseau, *Basil of Caesarea*, 190–232.

leadership roles within the community.[58] Basil, on the other hand, emphasised the formation of new entrants (both young and older people) as members of the community rather than as individuals. Formal instruction by a specially appointed monk, including instruction in reading and writing, rote learning of scripture, and offering reward and praise in return for good performance, played a large role in Basil's ascetic project.[59] Although Basil's objectives differed somewhat from those of Libanius, he still had to consider the training of individuals if he was to realise his ideal ascetic community. He developed a regime in which individuals were trained to think constantly about their effect on others and how others affected them. Thus he encouraged the monks to think about setting an example, speaking (and listening to) edificatory words and readings at appropriate times, continually practising desirable habits, unlearning undesirable habits, singing Psalms and preaching the word of God.[60]

Basil's ascetic school had much in common with other late Roman educational institutions in both the process and content of schooling, and here too, violence played a key role. Violence was ever-present in both the process of learning and in the stories on which new monks were meant to reflect in Basil's communities. For example, the ascetics were encouraged to reflect on the combative actions of earlier Christian martyrs as examples worthy of emulation: 'remembering how the Saints contended even unto death on behalf of godliness, we may be incited to a like zeal' (καὶ τοῦ εἰς ὑπόμνησιν ἐλθόντας τῆς τῶν ἁγίων ὑπὲρ εὐσεβείας μέχρι θανάτου ἐνστάσεως πρὸς τὸν ζῆλον τὸν ὅμοιον προτραπῆναι).[61] As well as thinking about the violent victories of Christian history, the children from the 'world' who attended monastic schools were supposed to be nurtured through 'the chastening and admonition of the Lord' (ἀλλ' ἐκτρέφετε αὐτὰ ἐν παιδείᾳ καὶ νουθεσίᾳ Κυρίου).[62] This intersection of violent process and violent content enabled Basil, like Libanius, to construct a training programme that prepared monks to function effectively in their social world. We can see the vital role that violence played in the reproduction of Basil's monastic community even more clearly if we explore some of the methods that were used to discipline the monks.

58 Morgan, 'Assessment in Roman Education', 14–15, for the individual focus of elite education in the Roman Empire.

59 Basil, *The Longer Rules* 15, 95–6, 164.

60 Basil, *The Morals* 70.1.3–7, Clarke (ed.), *The Ascetic Works*, 101–31; Basil, *Another Ascetic Discourse* 325E, Clarke (ed.), *The Ascetic Works*, 141–4; Basil, *The Longer Rules* 13 (on silence, which aids the forgetting of bad habits), 15, 180.

61 Basil, *The Longer Rules* 40.

62 Basil, *The Shorter Rules* 292, Clarke (ed.), *The Ascetic Works*, 229–351.

In his ascetic writings, Basil developed a carefully calibrated and textually grounded system of correction and punishment. This disciplinary system is presented and justified as an aid to ascetic training, driving lessons into the minds of learners and punishing mistakes. Rebukes were to be based on scripture, and further layers of textual authority are added by the repetition of this disciplinary regime across Basil's ascetic corpus.[63]

In Basil's imagined ascetic community, correction is carried out through a variety of means. Sometimes words are enough, but on other occasions misbehaving monks might be compelled to carry out certain actions in order to remedy their faults because the cause of a sin can best be purged by practising the exact opposite treatment.[64] For example, vainglory is cured by humility, idle speech by silence, excessive sleep by 'watchings with prayer', bodily idleness by labours, unseemly eating by deprivations of food, and murmuring by separation.[65] If necessary, discipline was intensified in order to cure sins. Although Basil recognised that there might be a distinction to be drawn between minor and more serious sins, in the end he rejected the possibility of pardoning those who were guilty of the former because 'He that spareth the rod, hateth his son; but he that loveth him, chastiseth him diligently' (Prov. 13:24) and 'long-suffering and mercy should be joined with severity' (Χρὴ γὰρ τὴν μακροθυμίαν καὶ τὴν εὐσπλαγχνίαν ἐπιφέρεσθαι τῇ ἀποτομίᾳ).[66] Correction thus functioned to bring individuals and the community as a whole back to the right path.

As well as correction, punishment was central to the ways in which Basil imagined that his ascetic communities would function. He states repeatedly that the punishment must be in proportion to the sin that has been committed and, as in Libanius' classroom, there is a clear hierarchy within the monastic educational system. The Superior takes on a central role in disciplinary procedures, 'avenging' (ἐκδίκησις) every sin that is committed and acting as a sounding board for the entire community.[67] Every member should lay bare the secrets of his heart to the Superior:

> For in this way what is praiseworthy is strengthened, to what is wrong is adjudged the appropriate penalty (τῆς προσηκούσης θεραπείας), and from such co-operation in discipline (ἔκ τε τῆς τοιαύτης συνασκήσεως) we shall win perfection through gradual additions of goodness.[68]

[63] Basil, *The Morals* 26.1. [64] Basil, *The Shorter Rules* 289. [65] Basil, *The Longer Rules* 51.
[66] Basil, *The Shorter Rules* 4, 293.
[67] Basil, *The Longer Rules* 50; see also Basil, *The Shorter Rules* 82, 106.
[68] Basil, *The Longer Rules* 26.

The Superior should first act with patience towards those who hesitate to obey the Lord's commands, and should then correct them 'sharply before all the brethren and apply methods of healing by every method of exhortation' (ἐμβριθέστερον ἐλέγχειν ἐπὶ πάσης τῆς ἀδελφότητος, καὶ μετὰ πάσης παρακλήσεως προσάγειν αὐτῷ τὰς ἰατρείας).[69] Only if such measures fail should he act like a doctor and cut the miscreant away from the communal body.[70] The aim was to secure every member of the community by ensuring that every individual behaved correctly.

Delegation and cooperation were important aspects of the monastic system of schooling, as they were in Libanius' school in which pedagogues and parents played pivotal roles. Punishments were to be determined by a monk with special responsibility for overseeing discipline or, within the monastic school, by teachers.[71] The 'superintendant of the common discipline' (τὸν ἔφορον τῆς κοινῆς εὐταξίας) is responsible for punishing sins that suggest 'moral perversion' (τῆς τοῦ ἤθους διαστροφῆς) because 'it is not every man's duty to rebuke' (ἐπιτιμάω), 'but only the duty of him to whom the Superior himself has entrusted it after full examination' (δοκιμασίας πλείονος).[72] Common surveillance could thus rehabilitate miscreants but it was the job of specific individuals within the monastery actually to inflict punishment, as seems to have been the role of pedagogues in the classroom of Libanius.

Basil also included advice on how individuals should respond to such treatment. For example, those who are angry with their correctors draw the community away from their 'spiritual contest' (τοὺς ἀγωνιζομένους).[73] The recipient of punishment should therefore think about it in the following terms: 'though the method of treatment is bitter and painful (πικρὸς καὶ ἐπώδυνος), yet he must be fully convinced of both the love and the experience of him who inflicts the punishment (ἐπιτιμία) and must desire to be healed' (κἂν πικρὸς καὶ ἐπώδυνος ᾖ ὁ τρόπος τῆς θεραπείας, ἐν πληροφορίᾳ τῆς τε ἀγάπης καὶ τῆς ἐμπειρίας τοῦ ἐπιτιμῶντος, καὶ ἐν ἐπιθυμίᾳ τῆς ἰάσεως).[74] Discipline, whether physical or otherwise, was thought to impact positively on the moral and intellectual formation of those who endured it and to improve their ability to think about, and interact with, others, including those who had inflicted the punishment.

[69] Basil, *The Longer Rules* 28. [70] Basil, *The Longer Rules* 28.

[71] Basil, *An Ascetic Discourse* 322D, Clarke (ed.), *The Ascetic Works*, 133–9; Basil, *The Longer Rules* 15.

[72] Basil, *The Longer Rules* 53. [73] Basil, *The Shorter Rules* 159.

[74] Basil, *The Shorter Rules* 158; cf. Basil, *The Longer Rules* 52.

Fear, Shame, and the Formation of the Ascetic Subject

We saw above how Libanius thought that fear, like discipline, could be a useful weapon in the armoury of those who were entrusted with the education of the young men of Antioch. Pedagogues were less effective when students were no longer afraid of them. Basil was of a similar opinion: he judged a number of ostensibly negative (to the modern mind at least) emotions to have a positive impact on ascetic formation. For example, children in the monastic school should be examined regularly on their thoughts in order to cultivate feelings of shame.[75] If they felt shame, they were more likely to remember the lessons that they had been taught and the discipline that they had received.

Testing and surveillance were used to correct inappropriate conduct. All potential members of Basil's community were to be examined before entry and underwent a process of probation prior full acceptance. Teachers examined children in the monastic schools regularly, and even the Superior was to be examined before, and observed after, taking up his position.[76] Life within the ascetic community 'should have witnesses, so as to be free from evil suspicion' (μάρτυρον γὰρ εἶναι προσήκει τὸν τοιοῦτον βίον, ὡς ἂν ἐκτὸς εἶναι πονηρᾶς ὑποψίας).[77] To live outside the monastery was thus judged negatively because the lack of witnesses opened the ascetics up to suspicion.

Fear was seen to be a desirable outcome of the surveillance culture that Basil proposed, because it kept monks in line after their initial training and reduced the risk of others falling into sin due to the fear (φόβος) that will have been instilled into them.[78] A similar point is made elsewhere: admonishment and rebuke are to be used on 'despisers' (καταφρονητής) and 'unbelievers' (ἄπιστος) until they can be persuaded to fear God as a righteous judge or to believe that God really exists and be terrified.[79] Fear was desirable within the monastic community for two reasons. First, fear encouraged ascetics to learn (or believe) the right kinds of things. Second, fear was a sign that the monks had understood that they were constantly

[75] Basil, *The Longer Rules* 15.

[76] Basil, *The Longer Rules* 10, 15, 27; Basil, *An Ascetic Discourse* 320E–321A.

[77] Basil, *An Ascetic Discourse* 320C; cf. Basil, *The Longer Rules* 7 and Basil, *The Shorter Rules* 178.

[78] Basil, *The Morals* 70.2; see also: Basil, *Another Ascetic Discourse* 326C: those who are entrusted with the discipline of convents should be treated with gravity, fear and respect.

[79] Basil, *The Shorter Rules* 81.

being watched by one another. Fear was emotional proof that Basil's culture of ascetic surveillance had been internalised by his ascetics.[80]

Ascetic pedagogies of surveillance and fear in late antiquity – of which Basil's is by no means the only example – were designed to create obedient people who were subservient to the needs of the group.[81] Very similar strategies of examination, harassment and even brutalisation are used by modern military and paramilitary organisations to train recruits to break existing social bonds with family and friends, to disregard former belief structures and to follow orders.[82] Such training is necessary if recruits are to be relied on in stressful situations. Basil was firmly of the opinion that his ascetics were under attack from various human and diabolical forces. His training methods therefore used fear to simulate wartime conditions and to cultivate subjectivities that would enable his monks to fight and overcome their enemies.[83]

Training Individual Ascetics and the Formation of the Monastic Community

Given that the ascetic vocation involved an explicit effort to overcome the body's sexual needs and impulses, as well as the separation of the individual from their prior affective bonds to friends and family, one of the main challenges facing monastic communities was to ensure their reproduction over time. Elsewhere in this volume, Maria Chiara Giorda helps to explain one means by which this was achieved: through carefully managing the entry of slaves into the monastery to support its economic existence and often to boost the number of monks. Another way in which the monastic community was sustained was through the articulation of a clear sense of mission, often framed defensively as protecting the community against outside threats of a physical and a supernatural nature. Libanius often described rhetoric as a form of wrestling, and Basil too defined his

80 Preachers and those who gave them advice, such as Augustine, also thought that fear (of God) was an appropriate motivating factor for those seeking Christian instruction. The chapter by Melissa Markauskas in this volume deals with Augustine's advice to those entrusted with catechesis, while Blake Leyerle's contribution explores the issue of fear in John Chrysostom's preaching.

81 J. Hillner, 'Monastic Imprisonment in Justinian's Novels', *Journal of Early Christian Studies*, 15 (2007), 205–37, for monastic surveillance; K. Cooper, 'Closely Watched Households: Visibility, Exposure and Private Power in the Roman *Domus*', *Past & Present*, 197 (2007), 3–33, for the 'surveillance culture' of the late Roman household.

82 Chappell and Lanza-Kaduce, 'Police Academy Socialization'; Mathieu, 'A Causal Model', 321–35.

83 See Blossom Stefaniw's chapter in this volume for more on rhetorical descriptions of Egyptian monks as soldiers.

educational system conflictually. Like the ascetic writers explored by Blossom Stefaniw elsewhere in this volume, Basil often described the ascetic life in highly militarised terms. Ascetics are soldiers in God's army, fight against His enemies and defend His community:

> But since He wishes thee to become good through dangers and has desired His army to contend with the opposing army, therefore thou must shrink from no toil in equipping thyself . . .[84]

> ἐπὰν δὲ καὶ διὰ κινδύνων ἀγαθὸν θέλῃ σε γενέσθαι, καὶ τὸ στράτευμα τὸ ἑαυτοῦ θελήσῃ συμ βαλεῖν τῷ στρατεύματι τῷ ὑπεναντίῳ, ἐνταῦθα σὺ πρὸς πάντα πόνον ἀήττητος ἔσο τῇ παρασκευῇ . . .

The rewards for enrolment in this army are great because the ascetic warrior acts as representative and protector of the broader social group, which both recognises and celebrates their achievements:

> great shall be thy glory even upon earth, and thou shalt be precious among thy friends, who have found thee a champion and helper and good ambassador. They shall provide for thee as a good soldier. They shall honour thee as a noble hero.[85]

The power of the ascetic comes not from bodily strength, but from their training in continence which is betokened 'by emaciation of body and paleness, which is the bloom of continence, showing that he is truly an athlete of Christ's commandments' (ἀθλητὴς . . . τῶν ἐντολῶν τοῦ Χριστοῦ) and can thus overcome his enemy 'in the contests of religion' (ἐν τοῖς τῆς εὐσεβείας ἄθλοις).[86]

As with the young men of the social elite who attended Libanius' school and learned lessons that would enable them to protect their families and their cities from the excesses of the imperial system, individual monks went through a violent training process so that they were able to defend their community from outside threats. Although training took place at an individual level within the monastery, Basil's main aim was to promote group cohesion and defence through violent disciplinary methods. Basil, like Libanius, judged that discipline and punishment aided 'positive' learning. However, a vital outcome of violent training in both city and monastery was the cultivation of feelings of fear. Fear had two important

84 Basil, *Preliminary Sketch of the Ascetic Life* 200C, Clarke (ed.), *The Ascetic Works*, 55–9.

85 Basil, *Preliminary Sketch of the Ascetic Life* 201B–C; Basil, *Preliminary Sketch of the Ascetic Life* 201C–D makes clear that women can also be part of this army. See also Basil, *Renunciation of the World* 204C, Clarke (ed.), *The Ascetic Works*, 60–71.

86 Basil, *The Longer Rules* 17.

theoretical effects for Basil. First, because they were afraid of being under surveillance, monks would modify their behaviour to become 'better' members of the community. They would conform to the behaviour that Basil deemed ideal. Second, fear created a militant mentality at both the individual and the group level, thereby better enabling the monastery to resist outside threats.

Conclusion

The later Roman Empire was a militarised society both culturally and in the sense that the taxation and bureaucratic systems were concerned above all with supporting the army.[87] If the aim of training is to produce individuals who are capable of operating successfully in a social context, then the ubiquity of violence in the late Roman pedagogical imagination should hardly surprise us. The imaginative framework of the texts we have surveyed was as militarised as the society from which it emerged.

The focus of this chapter has been on the discourses of two highly trained rhetorical operators. More work still needs to be done to understand the extent to which such pedagogic theories were put into practice. Yet it is clear that the rhetoric of violent training articulated by Libanius and Basil was essentially concerned with extracting individuals from old identities and resocialising them in new contexts: from youth to adulthood in the case of Libanius, from civilian to monk in the case of Basil. Trainee rhetors and monks were to be forced from one state of being into another, reconstituting themselves on the other side of identity thresholds. If successful, they became fully fledged members of a new group.

Religious difference may explain some of the variation between the processes that were proposed by Libanius and Basil, for the former was a pagan and the latter a Christian. But difference may also be explained by the focus of training, whether individual or collective, or by genre constraints. Basil's ascetic writings encouraged cooperation in order to form the group, whereas Libanius aimed to mould individuals through competition.[88] The ascetic works are prescriptive and normative, whereas Libanius' orations and letters provide us with a much more personalised – though rhetorically polished and probably highly idealised – vision of education. Yet both Libanius and Basil thought that education should be

[87] A. Cameron, *The Later Roman Empire, AD 284–430* (Cambridge, MA: Harvard University Press, 1993), 33–5, 145–6.

[88] Morgan, 'Assessment in Roman Education', 15–20 for competition in Roman education.

a cooperative enterprise. Libanius worked with the fathers of the youths he was teaching. In his classroom, violence reinforced parental authority through the pedagogue and the teacher with the aim of reproducing traditional elite values. The individual was thus to be cultivated as a functioning member of society, respecting the hierarchy within the school and in society more broadly. In the monastery, however, violence was used to force initiates to break free of former family bonds and to remake themselves in new contexts. Despite the seeming divergence in approaches and attitudes towards violence, Basil – and John Chrysostom, one of Libanius' former pupils who also took on a leadership role within the Christian community, examined in this volume by Blake Leyerle – were well able to harness aspects of the traditional civic education to promote an idealised Christian community.[89] Despite these important distinctions between the texts and the contexts in which they were written (and perhaps used), our two late-fourth-century authors share the view that violence in training contexts can be used to encourage learning and socialisation.

Teachers sought to socialise pupils by exploiting the relationship between process and content in instructional situations. Violence was used to reinforce the authority of the master, to break students away from old ways of being and to encourage adherence to new practices and beliefs, which might often entail developing the ability to act in a violent manner. Corrective learning and, at its extreme, physical punishment were absolutely vital to the monks' formation *as monks* in Basil's ascetic imagination, just as correction was necessary to make young members of the elite in Libanius' school. This is not to deny that learning also happened through 'positive' personal and social experiences, reading, listening and reflecting individually and as a community on violent stories. But it also occurred through a more violent process of learning *what not to do* and *what not to be*. This was often accompanied by verbal admonition, physical punishment, and social exclusion, surveillance and humiliation.

Teachers in elite schools and monasteries, or at least those who wrote about them, thought that the manipulation of fearful emotional responses was a particularly effective pedagogic tool. In these two contexts, as elsewhere, what would nowadays be known as 'peer pressure' was seen to have positive benefits, both controlling the student body and promoting learning. Surveillance, by teachers, pedagogues and fellow students served a similar purpose.

[89] See the contributions on John Chrysostom by Chris L. de Wet, Blake Leyerle and Jonathon Tallon elsewhere in this volume.

The considered deployment of violence in educational contexts served to mediate the interrelationship between the individual trainee and the community of practice that they aspired to join.[90] The objective of violent training was to enable the individuals concerned to secure and protect the community from outside threats. After they had been trained, Basil's novices should have prepared their minds and bodies for fighting the spiritual enemy in battle, just like the monks who read about the demons that Saint Antony had battled in the desert of Egypt.[91] Libanius' aim was to enable his young charges to protect their cities and their families from rival elites and the excesses of the imperial government. Other contributions to this volume explore the promotion of divine sponsors and protectors for individual families and cities within the late empire.[92] Military training, too, was envisaged as developing troops who both respected the hierarchy, and were able to protect the empire from its enemies.[93]

The forms of training that were proposed by Christian writers such as Basil were not opposed to traditional Roman forms of elite education such as those practiced by Libanius. The rhetoric of Christian training that had developed by the late fourth century was so effective precisely because it drew on existing forms of civic formation. Violence – in terms of both process and content – was inflicted on elite young men during training in order to prepare them to assert their dominance over outsiders and inferiors, to defend their social group – family, monastery or empire – and, by the end of the century, to protect and propagate their faith. The cultivation of an empire-wide militia and the growth of Christian ascetic infrastructure during the fourth century were thus complementary developments that depended on violent training practices both to break and remake individuals and groups. The 'muscular Christianity' of the late fourth century faced aggressively outwards against demons, heretics and barbarians, but such a stance depended on the systematic application of violence inwards on young members of the Christian elite and their subordinates.[94]

90 See the Introduction to this volume by Kate Cooper and Jamie Wood for more on communities of practice.

91 See Blossom Stefaniw's contribution to this volume.

92 See the chapters by Vasiliki Limberis, James Corke-Webster, David Natal and Thomas Dimambro elsewhere in this volume.

93 Y. Le Bohec, *The Roman Imperial Army* (London: B. T. Batsford, 1994), 105–19.

94 On the concept of 'muscular Christianity', which has been explored by scholars of Victorian religion and masculinity, see the chapters in D. E. Hall (ed.), *Muscular Christianity: Embodying the Victorian Age* (Cambridge: Cambridge University Press, 2006) and N. Watson, S. Weir, and S. Friend, 'The Development of Muscular Christianity in Victorian Britain and Beyond', *Journal of Religion & Society*, 7 (2005), 1–21.

CHAPTER 10

Words at War
Textual Violence in Eusebius of Caesarea

Aaron P. Johnson

Written words take hold of (or are held by) violence in manifold ways. In the first place, they may be the causes or products of violent acts or practices (the use of slaves as amanuenses; or the appropriation of books from an executed person's private holdings, e.g., the libraries of Longinus[1] or George of Cappadocia;[2] or the anathemas of councils, prohibitions in legal declarations,[3] or cataloguing and codification of heretical groups). The (often tacit) purposes may be the leisure, aggrandisement, or legitimising of those in power and their activities. Second, texts may narrate violent acts performed by or upon bodies. The purposes for such narrative description may be to legitimise such acts; to enact a cathartic process (to relieve social or psychological tension, or as therapeutic resolution of the readers' violent memories or tendencies); to strengthen sharp identity claims and embolden social action based on a particularly constructed understanding of relations between self and others (whether collective or individual);[4] to constrain the behaviour of the reader through fear;[5] or to provide a catalyst for the perpetration of violence for a particular cause or against a particular people. Third, they may adopt violent language in

This paper has benefited from multiple conversations with participants of the workshop on violence held on 8 August 2011 at Worcester College, Oxford, and the Seminar on Late Antiquity, University of Tennessee at Knoxville, on 30 November 2011 (where Tina Shepardson was, as always, an ideal host and source of encouragement and advice).

[1] See P. Kalligas, 'Traces of Longinus' Library in Eusebius' *Praeparatio Evangelica*', *CQ*, 51 (2001), 584–98.

[2] See Julian, *Ep.* 107, J. Bidez and F. Cumont (eds.), *Imp. Caesaris Flavii Claudii Iuliani. Epistulae Leges Poemata Fragmenta Varia* (Paris: Les Belles Lettres, 1922); on George's own literary works, see now M. Del Cogliano, 'The Literary Corpus of George of Laodicea', *Vigiliae Christianae*, 65 (2011), 150–69.

[3] We might identify this mode of textual violence as a form of textual 'punitive violence', on which, see the discussion of Chris L. de Wet in this volume.

[4] For possibly similar purposes, though a different set of literary effects, see Vasiliki Limberis' contribution to this volume.

[5] See Blake Leyerle's and Jamie Wood's chapters in this volume.

describing some event, people, or idea of an otherwise non-violent nature.[6] The purposes for such violent language may be apologetic (truth will 'conquer' its enemies), polemical (the atheists 'war against the gods' like the mythical Giants in the Gigantomachy), or intertextual (to connect one's own written words to an authoritative literary piece and establish oneself within a literary tradition, e.g., allusions to Homer's battle narratives).[7]

Finally, in a manner loosely related to the first and third modes of textual violence, texts may identify the positions, ideas, or ways of life adopted by others in such a way as to control, restrict, or harm them. In other words, a text can seek to 'violate' another's self-ascribed identity. Representational choices come into play here in ways that might otherwise be missed in the analysis of violence in texts that limits itself to overt descriptions: verbatim quotation, abbreviation of varying degrees, and paraphrase of an opponent's writings or ideas provide the second text (the one quoting, abbreviating, or paraphrasing) with varying degrees of latitude in rendering the position invalid, indefensible, and generally foolish, and so more easily rejected.[8] Such a mode of textual violence opens up a range of possibilities for violating any merits of a position that are held by its adherents. Critical debate might seek to avoid the performance of textual violence and aim for a 'fair' use of its sources, though the temptation to do so seems to have been strong.

The following discussion investigates a particular literary example from the early fourth century, Eusebius of Caesarea's *Praeparatio Evangelica*, in order to draw out the interplay of violence and text, as well as to problematise our determinations of that interplay. Eusebius makes a striking author to think through the issues of texts and violence, and textual violence, in late antiquity. With respect to texts, he composed several thousand pages of still extant works, while his care and use of the library at Caesarea is well known (though we still do not know whether that

[6] Whether the situation is truly non-violent by nature is disputable and depends at the very least upon one's definition of violence.

[7] In both the apologetic and polemical contexts, a perception of threat will usually be communicated and along with the communication of threat could belong recommendations for responding to (ameliorating, suppressing, eradicating) the threat; on 'Bedrohungskommunikation', see M. Becker, *Porphyrios, 'Contra Christianos'. Neue Sammlung der Fragmente, Testimonien und Dubia mit Einleitung, Übersetzung und Anmerkungen* (Berlin: De Gruyter, 2015), 32–41, esp. 38.

[8] On Eusebius' use of quotation, see variously, S. Inowlocki, *Eusebius and the Jewish Authors* (Leiden: Brill, 2006); A. P. Johnson, 'Introduction', in A. P. Johnson and J. Schott (eds.), *Eusebius of Caesarea: Tradition and Innovations*, Hellenic Studies 60 (Washington, DC: Center for Hellenic Studies, Trustees for Harvard University, 2013), 3–10.

library was personal, ecclesiastical, or scholastic).[9] With respect to violence, Eusebius witnessed many acts of brutality in the Great Persecution and, even if not a 'court theologian', spoke in laudatory terms of emperors whose reigns were deeply marked by violence of a military, civil, and personal nature.[10] Both in his *Ecclesiastical History* and the *Life of Constantine* he narrated imperial violence – whether on the battlefield, in the court against Christians (as in the case of the persecuting emperors), or at pagan temples (as in the case of Constantine) – so as to provide religious legitimation or delegitimation of a reign and express his own distinctive historiographical vision. In his writings of philosophical and theological polemic (such as the *Praeparatio Evangelica* and his later *Contra Marcellum*), Eusebius' extensive use of quotation from his opponents' own texts is frequently viewed as the forceful seizure of their words, taken out of context, and misleadingly pieced together to form a sort of 'straw man' rather than a faithful representation of their views.[11]

From Voltaire to Athanassiadi,[12] the bishop of Caesarea has been castigated as a promoter of religious intolerance and hence morally implicated in the later history of violent acts, attitudes, and ideas performed and produced by Christians. Consideration of the four modes of relationship of violence and literature in the *Praeparatio* will allow for a proper evaluation of this assessment of Eusebius' role in the larger history of violence. Inquiry into other works of Eusebius would fill out and complicate the picture; but the *Praeparatio* belonged to an educational context (see below), and thus discussion of it can fruitfully join the other discussions in this volume of violence in educational contexts to widen as well as complicate our picture of education and violence in late antiquity. The *Praeparatio* is, in any case, particularly acute in its presentation of textual violence and (it is hoped)

[9] On the extant corpus, see L. Perrone, 'Eusebius of Caesarea as a Christian Writer', in A. Raban and K. Holum (eds.), *Caesarea Maritima: A Retrospective After Two Millenia* (Leiden: Brill, 1996), 515–30; on the library at Caesarea, see A. Carriker, *The Library of Eusebius of Caesarea* (Leiden: Brill, 2003).

[10] For caution or criticism of the misleading description of Eusebius as a court theologian, see M. J. Hollerich, 'Religion and Politics in the Writings of Eusebius: Reassessing the First "Court Theologian"', *Church History*, 59 (1990), 309–25; A. P. Johnson, *Ethnicity and Argument in Eusebius'* Praeparatio Evangelica (Oxford: Oxford University Press, 2006), 186–97; A. P. Johnson, *Eusebius* (London: I. B. Tauris, 2014), 85–112, 143–69.

[11] On the *Contra Marcellum*'s [hereafter: *c.Marc.*] use of quotation, see Johnson, 'Introduction', 9–10. I do not include reference to the *Contra Hierocles*, since I agree with Thomas Hägg's argument that Eusebius is not the author of that work; see A. P. Johnson, 'The Author of the *Against Hierocles*: A Response to Borzì and Jones', *Journal of Theological Studies*, 64 (2013), 574–94.

[12] See S. Morlet, 'L'Antiquité tardive fut-elle une période d'obscurantisme? À propos d'un ouvrage recent [P. Athanassiadi, *Vers la pensée unique, la montée de l'intolerance dans l'Antiquité tardive* (Paris, 2010)]', *Adamantius*, 16 (2010): 413–21; see Athanassiadi, *Vers la pensée unique*, 65–70, 71–9.

might prove sufficient for prompting an appreciation of the possibilities of expression within other works, genres, and authors.

The fifteen-book apologetic treatise was written between AD 313 and 325, and thus seems to be one of the first works he composed as bishop of Caesarea.[13] It forms a 'diptych' with its sister work, the *Demonstratio Evangelica*, which followed it.[14] The widespread assumption that both works were aimed at Porphyry's notorious *Against the Christians* has only recently been put to question in a serious manner.[15] It seems more likely that Eusebius constructed his master apologetic argument according to his own conceptions and as an improvement on the previous apologetic tradition.[16] The *Praeparatio* dealt with the common pagan accusation that Christians had wrongly rejected the traditions of their (Greek) forefathers for a new and irrational faith. Approximately 71 per cent of its fifteen books consists of the quotation of other, mostly pagan, philosophical works (a point that will concern us below).[17] The *Demonstratio* turned to address the issue of the accusation that Christians claimed to adopt the Jewish writings but yet rejected the legal demands and other teachings of those writings.[18]

While both works offered a defence (*apologia*) against external criticisms the target audience was explicitly identified as those who had recently converted to Christianity. In fact, the *Praeparatio* was to be a 'primer and introduction (*stoicheiōseōs kai eisagōgēs*)' for recent converts.[19] The genre of *eisagōgē* texts, especially those produced in philosophical schools, bore the purpose of introducing students to the texts or doctrines deemed foundational for a given school.[20] The *Praeparatio*'s massive bulk of quotations is

[13] See J. Sirinelli and E. des Places, *Eusèbe de Césarée. La Préparation Évangélique*, SC 206.1 (Paris: Éditions du Cerf, 1974), 8–14.

[14] I adopt the term 'diptych' from Sebastien Morlet, *La* Démonstration Évangélique *d'Eusèbe de Césarée: Étude sur l'apologétique chrétienne à l'époque de Constantin* (Turnhout: Brepols, 2010), 50, passim.

[15] See A. P. Johnson, 'Rethinking the Authenticity of Porphyry, *c.Christ.* fr. 1', *Studia Patristica*, 46 (2010), 53–8; Sebastien Morlet, 'La *Démonstration évangélique* d'Eusèbe de Césarée contient-elle des fragments du *Contra Christianos* de Porphyre? À propos du fr. 73 Harnack', *Studia Patristica*, 46 (2010), 59–64. See now, Becker, *Porphyrios, 'Contra Christianos'.*

[16] See Johnson, *Ethnicity and Argument*; Johnson, *Eusebius*, 26–46; Morlet, *La* Démonstration Évangélique *d'Eusèbe de Césarée.*

[17] For the percentage, see J.-R. Laurin, *Orientations maîtresses des apologistes chrétiens de 270 à 361*, Analecta Gregoriana 61 (Rome: Université Grégorienne, 1954), 358.

[18] See Morlet, *La* Démonstration Évangélique *d'Eusèbe de Césarée.*

[19] Eusebius, *Praeparatio Evangelica* [hereafter: *PE*] 1.1.12; for discussion, see A. P. Johnson, 'Eusebius' *Praeparatio Evangelica* as Literary Experiment', in S. Johnson, ed., *Greek Literature in Late Antiquity: Dynamism, Didacticism, Classicism* (Aldershot: Ashgate, 2006), 67-89.

[20] See A. P. Johnson, 'Eusebius the Educator: The Context of the *General Elementary Introduction*', in C. Zamagni and S. Inowlocki (eds.), *Reconsidering Eusebius* (Leiden: Brill, 2011), 99–118; more

thus only partly an apologetic display of erudition (against the accusation that Christians were ignorant and resorted to faith alone), as is frequently noted in modern discussions.[21] More significantly the quotations, preceded and followed by Eusebius' comments on how to evaluate or contextualise them, exhibit the instructional practices typical of the isagogic textual tradition. Eusebius artfully contrived a defensive argument through the pedagogical process of teaching students how to read the texts of Greek philosophers and historians against themselves. Quotations of often several pages were introduced by remarks on what to look for in the material about to be given; then, concluding remarks would offer a recapitulation of the importance of the passage for his argument.

A noticeable feature of this procedure for the careful reader is the amount of quoted material apparently unnecessary for the point Eusebius sought to make. Certainly, an ostensible reason for the seemingly superfluous material is the erudite display of Christian knowledge about the whole range of Greek intellectual inquiry (especially historical and philosophical). Quotational excesses were a powerful means of self-authorisation. Eusebius' proud claim was that Christians (and in particular, Eusebius himself) knew the Greek traditions as well as, if not better than, the Greeks themselves. Such Christians could hardly be guilty of the accusation of blind faith – theirs was a well-schooled pursuit of reason (*logos*). As will become clearer below, Eusebius' quotation of sources marked a response 'from below' to the dominant culture. In fact, the *Praeparatio* provides a fascinating snapshot of a particular moment in the series of uneven shifts of the lower or marginal elements in the Mediterranean world transfiguring themselves into higher or more central cultural locations.[22]

Violent Historical Contexts

The single most important indication of the date of the *Praeparatio*'s composition is also a brief narrative segment recalling the purge of

generally, J. Mansfeld, *Prolegomena: Questions to Be Settled before the Study of an Author, or a Text* (Leiden: Brill, 1994).

21 'The most powerful argument of his entire apology', Laurin, *Orientations maîtresses des apologistes chrétiens*, 365; 'a deliberate, even ostentatious, parade of erudition', T. D. Barnes, *Constantine and Eusebius* (Cambridge, MA: Harvard University Press, 1981), 178; a 'profligate display of erudition', E. Gallagher, 'Piety and Polity: Eusebius' Defense of the Gospel', in J. Neusner, E. S. Frerichs and A. J. Levine (eds.), *Religious Writings and Religious Systems* (Atlanta, GA: Scholars Press, 1989), 154.

22 See the Introduction to this volume by Kate Cooper and Jamie Wood.

politically suspicious individuals by Licinius following the defeat of Maximinus Daia (313 AD).[23] At *Praeparatio* 4.2.10–11, Eusebius confirms his claim that the oracles that were delivered at various prophetic sites across the Mediterranean world were motivated either by human fraud or daemonic deception by invoking the recent episode of the trial of Theotecnus.[24] This priest of an oracular shrine of Zeus at Antioch and a supporter of Maximinus was tried and found guilty by Licinius' court.[25] Eusebius reports:

> Many of the most highly inspired even of their chief hierophants, theologians and prophets, who were celebrated for this kind of theosophy, not only in former times but also recently in our own day, under cruel tortures before the Roman courts declared that the whole delusion was produced by human frauds, and confessed that it was all an artfully contrived imposture; and they had the whole character of the system and the methods of their evil practices registered in the words uttered by them in public records.[26]

Eusebius next tells us that the guilty persons were members of three groups: philosophers, magistrates of Antioch 'who prided themselves in their outrages against us' during the persecution, and a philosopher-priest from Miletus.[27] We unfortunately know nothing more about the anonymous philosopher-priest;[28] but the episode at Antioch is taken up in greater detail in Eusebius' *Ecclesiastical History*. There we discover that Theotecnus had received support from Maximinus to establish a cult to Zeus Philios and in turn produced forged oracles encouraging the emperor to persecute the Christians. Along with other supporters and relatives of Maximinus, Theotecnus was duly executed later for his support of the emperor and manipulation of the divine voice when Licinius took control of the East.[29]

From these details a chain linking texts and acts of violence is formed: first a situation of imperial privilege results in the foundation of a

[23] Sirinelli and Des Places, *Eusèbe de Césarée*, 8–14; K. Mras, *Eusebius Werke VIII. Die Praeparatio Evangelica* (Berlin: Akademie Verlag, 1954), 1.LIV–LV.

[24] For the context of Eusebius' treatment of oracles, see Johnson, *Ethnicity and Argument*, 156–70; R. Stoneman, *The Ancient Oracles: Making the Gods Speak* (New Haven, CT: Yale University Press, 2011), 205–9.

[25] See Laurin, *Orientations maîtresses des apologistes chrétiens*, 84–8; J. Sirinelli, *Les vues historiques d'Eusèbe de Césarée*, 439–45.

[26] *PE* 4.2.10; E. H. Gifford (trans.), *Preparation for the Gospel*, 2 vols. (Grand Rapids, MI: Baker Book House, 1981).

[27] *PE* 4.2.11.

[28] See O. Zink and E. Des Places, *Eusèbe de Césarée. La Préparation Évangélique, Livres IV–V, 1–17*, SC 262 (Paris: Éditions du Cerf, 1979), 94 n. 4.

[29] See Eusebius, *Historia Ecclesiastica* [hereafter: *HE*] 9.3, 11.

priesthood; then, the new institution produces texts causative (both in intention and result) of violence (against Christians); next, the imperial powers of Licinius and Maximinus clashed, producing acts of violence 'inscribed' through torture and execution on the bodies of the vanquished, as well as written in the official records of the legal proceedings; relative, if uncertain, peace then prompted the composition of the *Praeparatio* (and *Ecclesiastical History*), which narrated the violence in terms both of Christian flourishing in spite of persecution and of confirmation of the accuracy of apologetic claims against oracles. The precise relationship between the violent deaths of the persecutors and their friends and the writing of an apologetic treatise must remain rather loose, however, since apologetic writings seem to be produced at varied times of persecution, pressure, peace, or privilege (as exhibited by the different circumstances behind the writings of I Peter, which calls for an *apologia* in time of persecution, at I Pet. 3:15; Justin Martyr; Origen; and, after Eusebius, Theodoret and Cyril of Alexandria).

At the outset, I had suggested that the use of slaves in the writing of texts (especially as shorthand note-takers) might be considered a potential context of violence. Unfortunately, we have little information on whether Eusebius used writing assistants at all in the composition of the *Praeparatio*, let alone the social status of such assistants and the systemic forms of power, restraint, and order (legitimised violence) undergirding that social status. It does seem likely that, with a text which was built upon the massive incorporation of quoted materials, Eusebius would have required the assistance of students or slaves in order to produce the *Praeparatio*.[30]

Indeed, the *Praeparatio* was itself a student-oriented text. As already noted, Eusebius declared that the work was not only to be a defence of the faith (*apologia*), but also an 'introduction'. Yet, we have no indication whether Eusebius employed students as readers and copiers of the texts quoted or the comments given (as we do for other teachers, such as Plotinus).[31] We furthermore have no indication of whether violence was

[30] Alternatively, K. Mras, *Eusebius Werke*, 1.LVIII supposes Eusebius' deacons served as notaries for the composition of the *Praeparatio*; cf. the possibilities of a 'team' of copyists who participated in the composition of the *HE* mentioned by M. Cassin, M. Debié, and M.-Y. Perrin, 'La question des editions de l'*Histoire ecclésiastique* et le livre x', in S. Morlet and L. Perrone (eds.), *Eusèbe de Césarée. Histoire ecclésiastique. Commentaire, Tome 1: Études d'introduction* (Paris: Les Belles Lettres, 2012), 187, 202.

[31] See Porphyry, *Vita Plotini* 14; for discussion, see A. P. Johnson, *Religion and Identity in Porphyry of Tyre* (Cambridge: Cambridge University Press, 2013), 152–5; R. Lamberton, 'The Neoplatonists and Their Books', in M. Finkelberg and G. G. Stroumsa (eds.), *Homer, the Bible, and Beyond* (Leiden: Brill, 2003), 195–212.

ever used on lazy or recalcitrant students (as we find in the sources for other schools).[32] In neither the production nor the reception of the *Praeparatio* do we have any hint of teacher–student violence. It might be suggested that a teacher's dominating control over a student's reading or interpretation involves violence. A teacher's containment of student reading so as to ensure a single right reading of quoted texts, which presumed and enforced a doctrine of a single original meaning, might readily be designated a form of violence. But, without further precision about the nature or degree of that control (for instance, the teacher could be caught between varying holders of power such as wealthy patrons or already highly educated students),[33] we should be wary of using such an open-ended and nearly vacuous sense of the term 'violence' (or even the sometimes more appropriate 'coercion') – especially in the case of an *eisagōgē* from an age that had not yet fallen under the modern individualist 'flight from authority' and for which a student's study under a master might be deemed a liberating or empowering apprenticeship. In addition, as will be seen at the conclusion of this paper, a different account of Eusebius' quotational practices may be more appropriate. The only firmly identifiable violent event behind the composition of the *Praeparatio* is that of the downfall of Theotecnus, even while a context of school violence remains a possibility.

Narrative Description of Violence

Eusebius' recollection of the trial of Theotecnus not only alerts us to the violent context behind the text of the *Praeparatio* but also stands as a brief narrative description of that violence. Though exceptionally brief in its description, the assumption exhibited in the narrative posits a strong relationship between violence ('under cruel tortures before the Roman courts') and oral speech (they 'declared' and 'confessed' the delusion and deception of their fake oracles), which is quickly transformed into written texts ('registered … in public records'). Other narratives of violence frequently occur in passages of pagan authors quoted by Eusebius. Quotations from Philo of Byblos recount the violent family relationships among the most ancient members of the Phoenician dynasty (1.10); passages of Diodorus Siculus narrate the violent deeds performed by

[32] Cf. Augustine, *Confessiones* 1; see also Jamie Wood's chapter in this volume.

[33] For the pressures from both above and below (i.e., from bishops or patrons and from recent converts, heretics, or outsiders) on those responsible for the performance of catechetical teaching, as well as their own attempts to pressure or coerce others, see Melissa Markauskas' discussion in this volume.

(and to) Heracles and other mythical-historical figures (2.2); the violent binding of the gods by humans with the requisite ritual knowledge, or the ordaining of human sacrifice or incitement to war by bloodthirsty daemons, was recorded by oracles related in the works of Porphyry and others (5.8–10, 19, 27); and so on.

Admittedly, there is little narration of violence beyond these instances, which derive from his sources rather than from Eusebius himself. Even though the reading (and rewriting) of texts involved the reader in a mimetic connection to the voice(s) of the text, Eusebius' repeated reminders that the quotations contained in the *Praeparatio* are not his own words but those of the opposition would seem to detract from that mimetic power to a substantial degree. Yet, the fact that the pages are filled with violence would have maintained a powerful emotive and rhetorical effect. It should not surprise that the *Ecclesiastical History* provides us with the sort of narration of violence we are looking for – it is, after all, a work dedicated to describing the historical consequences of the Jews' rejection of Christ and the memorialisation of martyrs (i.e., two groups who suffered the violence of Roman imperial might, but with two entirely different valences for Eusebius; the Jews deserved the destruction of their temple and homeland, while the martyrs were able to exhibit the philosophic truth of Christianity through their endurance of torture and death).[34]

Because the *Praeparatio* does not share these aims, but instead claims to defend the rightness of the Christian rejection of their ancestral customs, the narratives of violence identified in its quoted sources function to highlight that apologetic concern. The Christians rejected traditional cultic practices because they were instigated by wicked daemons (as proven, for instance, by the violence of human sacrifices). If the oracles were not the utterances of daemons but of wicked humans, the reminder of episodes of judicial violence against those humans proved their wickedness. Christians were right to leave behind the ways of their forefathers since the narratives of Heracles and others only exhibited a base and violent moral character.

Violent Language

The *Praeparatio* is of greater interest for its use of violent language (indeed, this was my initial reason for choosing this work to explore the relationship of literature and violence). Two modes of violent language

[34] Eusebius does, however, grant that the persecution was originally prompted by God's desire to discipline the Church, *HE* 8.1.

are identifiable: (1) the adoption of metaphors of violence in designating otherwise strictly textual practices, on the one hand and (2) the description of philosophical or scholastic disagreement in martial terms, on the other. The first may initially appear to be of less interest, though as should become clear it is worthy of consideration. It centres (1a) on Eusebius' precise practices of quoting his material and (1b) upon his account of the reading practices of pagan allegorists.

Violent Metaphors: Cutting

While he frequently quotes his sources with a high degree of accuracy and avoidance of any editorial intrusion into the original wording of those sources (insofar as textual critics have been able to determine when we have independent attestation of the source text, e.g., especially Plato),[35] there are several instances in the *Praeparatio* where Eusebius claims to be abbreviating his source. We may readily trace the degree of abbreviation in quotations of works that survive independently of Eusebius (especially Diodorus Siculus);[36] for the present discussion, what is significant is the terminology regularly used: *epitemnein* or *epitomē* and their cognates. The source texts were 'cut up' in order to excise those elements deemed worthy of inclusion in the *Praeparatio.* For instance, following several pages of abbreviated quotations from Diodorus, interspersed with comments from Eusebius noting the location of the materials quoted, he concludes: 'let us usefully epitomise so much' (*PE* 2.2.63). Elsewhere, in a manner frustrating for those attempting to reconstruct the thought of otherwise fragmentary works of the great anti-Christian Porphyry, Eusebius, our only source for the *On Images*, admits to have 'necessarily epitomised Porphyry's *On Images*' (*PE* 3.11.17; cf. 3.13.3).[37] Lengthy quotations from Alexander of

[35] See the series of relevant studies contained in E. DesPlaces, *Études Platoniciennes. 1929–1979* (Leiden: Brill, 1981); also, Inowlocki, *Eusebius and the Jewish Authors*, 87–8; cf. A. P. Johnson, '*Porphyry in Fragments: Reception of an Anti-Christian Text in Late Antiquity by Ariane Magny* (review)', *Journal of Late Antiquity*, 8 (2015), 231–3. The best argument for the possibility that Eusebius made slight emendations to a quoted text in order to support his own argument is by J. Mansfeld and D. T. Runia, *Aëtiana: The Method and Intellectual Context of a Doxographer* (Leiden: Brill, 1997), 1.130–141; but even here the evidence for tampering is limited.

[36] G. Bounoure, 'Eusèbe citateur de Diodore', *Revue des Études Grecques*, 95 (1982), 433–9.

[37] See A. P. Johnson, 'The Implications of a Minimalist Approach to Porphyry's Fragments', in I. Männlein-Robert (ed.), *Die Christen als Bedrohung: Text, Kontext, und Wirkung von Porphyrios'* Contra Christianos (Stuttgart: Franz Steiner Verlag, 2016), 41–58.

Aphrodisias conclude: 'these things have been epitomised out of a great many' (*PE* 6.9.32).[38]

It may at first be objected that such language was, by Eusebius' time, nothing more than a 'dead metaphor'.[39] The objection is appropriate (especially given the fact that Eusebius used 'epitome' in a positive sense in the *Ecclesiastical History* and there epitomised authors whom he greatly favoured);[40] but two observations should be made. First, another metaphor, that of the text as a body, seems to have been quite 'alive' in the third and fourth centuries.[41] The combination of the metaphors of textual cutting and textual bodies may have maintained a sort of symbiotic invigoration from each other within the conceptual world of the writer and reader. To epitomise was to cut into the body of a text in a way suitable to one's own rhetorical or polemical ends, thus violating the integrity of that body.

Second, an issue often related to violence in modern discussion is that of tolerance or openness to the voices of others. Even if *epitomē* was a dead metaphor and no longer carried visceral depth for readers, the act of manipulating quoted texts within a polemical quoting text is nonetheless worth examination with respect to the degree to which an author sought to silence, distort, or muffle the voices of other parties.[42] While I cannot offer an in-depth examination of the precise elements cut out of Eusebius' quotations here (and indeed, such an examination would show a remarkable attempt to remain faithful to the content of the epitomised text), the very fact of his doing so should remain a salutary consideration for our present concerns of the nature of textual violence (and violation of texts).

38 Cf. *Praeparatio Evangelica* (hereafter *PE*) 8.14.72: 'I epitomised these things from Philo); 8.5.11: 'let these things be epitomised by us from the aforementioned writing'. Elsewhere, Eusebius claims to quote from sources that have themselves been epitomising their sources: *PE* 8.6.10: 'saying these things Philo epitomised the *politeia* laid down by the Mosaic Law'; 3.2.7: 'Manetho spoke more broadly, but Diodorus presents it more concisely [*epitetmēmenōs*]'.

39 According to G. Lakoff and M. Johnson, *Metaphors We Live By* (Chicago, IL: University of Chicago Press, 2003), metaphors are never 'dead,' they only become more taken for granted and natural, and hence are all the more powerful.

40 In addition, authors in late antiquity sometimes made epitomes of their own works (e.g., Lactantius' *Epitome of the Divine Institutes*), thus exhibiting a positive valence of the term and its practice (although see the preface of Lactantius' *Epitome* for the difficulties and even authorial pain felt in such a practice).

41 A. van den Hoek, 'The Concept of *sōma tōn graphōn* in Alexandrian Theology', *Studia Patristica*, 19 (1989), 250–4. Cf. Eusebius, *c.Marc.*1.4.29.63: Marcellus mutilates the whole body of (the other bishops') thought.

42 Cf. Johnson, *Religion and Identity in Porphyry of Tyre*, 224–43.

It should not, however, be forgotten that in the case of the *Praeparatio* the number of verbatim quotations greatly outnumbers the instances of epitomisation. We shall return to this point later.

Eusebius was not alone in using the language of force for an interpretation he sought to delegitimise. Such a polemical tactic is seen notably in Porphyry of Tyre. Thus, Eusebius was adopting and adapting not only the sources of his rivals but their techniques of engagement as well.

Violent Metaphors: Forcing

In his treatment of philosophers who practiced allegorical interpretation of the Greek myths, Eusebius accuses them of interpretive violence. Here the metaphor adopted is that of 'overpowering by force' (*biazein* and cognates, especially in deponent form; the word is often used to denote 'rape' in classical literature).[43] The allegorists reduce 'forcibly (*bebiasmenōs*) and untruly ... the myths concerning the gods to allegories and physical interpretations and theories' (*PE* 1.9.25). Though Eusebius himself frequently adopted allegorical (or tropological) interpretations of Scriptural passages, the pagan allegorists were attacked as introducing 'a forced (*bebiasmenon*) and untrue embellishment of their myths' (*PE* 2.6.18); their allegories are 'strange and not beneficial, or rather, forced (*bebiasmenas*) and incoherent' (*PE* 2.7.9).[44] They can offer only 'a forced and deceptive physiology' (*PE* 3.3.21).[45] Such language represents the interpretive activity of the allegorists as something forceful and unnatural, perpetrated against the passive body of the texts they interpret, violating their simple or natural meaning.[46]

43 Liddell–Scott –Jones, *Greek–English Lexicon*, s.v. II.

44 On Eusebius' use of allegory, see Morlet, *La* Démonstration évangélique *d'Eusèbe de Césarée*, 497–506; C. Zamagni, 'Eusebius' Exegesis between Alexandria and Antiochia: Being a Scholar in Caesarea – A Test Case from Questions to Stephanos I', in S. Inowlocki and C. Zamagni (eds.), *Reconsidering Eusebius* (Leiden: Brill, 2011), 151–76.

45 See also, e.g., *PE* 1.10.55; 2.praef.3; 4.1.6; 11.6.23. It is unfortunate that Mras' index offers only two references. Cf. Eusebius, *Propheticae Eclogae* 1.12 [PG 22.1065C]; 3.8 [PG 22.1133C]; 3.46 [PG 22.1180A].

46 On the other hand, Eusebius' own interpretations are meant to appear reasonable, natural, and effortless. Cf. the characterisation of his interpretation as unambiguous (*anamphilektōs*) at *Propheticae Eclogae.* 1.12 [PG 22.1068C]. For an illuminating discussion of the manipulation of literal and allegorical in martyr literature, see M. M. Mitchell, 'Christian Martyrdom and the Dialect of the Holy Scriptures: The Literal, the Allegorical, the Martyrological', in R. S. Boustan, A. P. Jassen and C. J. Roetzel (eds.), *Violence, Scripture, and Textual Practice in Early Judaism and Christianity* (Leiden: Brill, 2010), 174–203.

Logomachia: Words at War

Beyond Eusebius' adoption of violent metaphors to designate textual practices of abbreviated quotation and allegorical interpretation, a second mode of violent language occurs in his employment of martial language to describe the disagreements of philosophers.[47] The language is primarily drawn from battle combat, but some instances denote boxing or wrestling, and sometimes both are combined. Eusebius may have been prompted by earlier uses of similar language in his sources, especially the Neopythagorean philosopher Numenius, who quoted lines of Homer depicting battle scenes to represent the discord of the successors of Plato in the Academy against each other and against Plato himself.[48] Numenius also used the language of civil war (*stasis* and its cognates) and more vividly drew upon violent episodes from myth: Plato was 'more wretched than any Pentheus' having his philosophy torn 'limb from limb', or again, the philosopher Arcesilaus 'cut himself and was cut by himself like a hydra' when he argued on both sides of an issue.[49] Likewise, Plato's *Sophist* had been quoted as describing the sophists as engaged in a great Gigantomachy.[50]

In his own use of battle imagery, however, Eusebius is not entirely dependent on sources such as these. He had begun to adopt such language before quoting these passages, and his language is sufficiently distinctive. For instance, he describes the successors of Plato as engaged in a 'war of words' (*logomachia*) and as 'noble boxers striking each other ambitiously'; he would present them, he claims, 'as if on a stage for spectators to see'.[51] More than his sources, Eusebius makes quite explicit the richness of such imagery for a textual engagement and its importance for the pursuit of truth. All the Greek philosophers 'came from all sides, kicking up dust against their neighbours, making war and wrestling in the most manly fashion; as with hand and tongue, or rather with pen and ink, they fortify themselves in war with each other, all but striking and being struck by spears and the full battle array of words'.[52] The right words, however, could even withstand the brute physical strength of the Empire: 'The ordinances of laws, plots of enemies, or oft-sharpened swords of enemies have not proven greater in power than the virtue of the words we

[47] The language of verbal violence was at least as old as Herodotus (*Historiae* 8.64) and as recent as Roland Barthes, *Criticism and Truth* (Minneapolis, MN: University of Minnesota Press, 1987), 30.

[48] See R. Lamberton, *Homer the Theologian* (Berkeley, CA: University of California Press, 1986), 55–9.

[49] *PE* 14.5.8 and 14.6.3 respectively.

[50] *PE* 14.4.9.

[51] *PE* 14.2.1.

[52] *PE* 14.2.3; cf. *HE* 8.1.7.

[Christians] pursue.'[53] The pen was like a sword and was, if expressive of the words of divine truth, even mightier than the sword. Surely, in this way, the *Praeparatio* marks a striking instance of the Christian deployment of educational resources to resist both Roman (military) and Helleno-centric (cultural) imperialism.[54]

Eusebius did not limit such language to the mere enrichment of his representation of philosophical or religious disagreement; it is, rather, formative of his conception of the apologetic task. Indeed, it is this very notion of scholastic dispute as a war (*logomachia*) that informed his understanding of the importance of his quotational methodology. He, too, was engaged in war against his pagan philosophical opponents; but importantly, his text was not the weapon wielded against the foe. Rather, in a brilliant extension of earlier apologetic uses of quotation (from Isocrates to Origen), the *Praeparatio* itself formed the field (or stage or stadium)[55] for the exchange of blows and casting of textual missiles.[56] He and his readers could watch on as the enemy defeated themselves 'with their own missiles.'[57] Its pages contain the numerous contingent (not to say ad hoc) deployments of texts from Eusebius' library as part of a *tactics* of intellectual, cultural, textual engagement. By pitting text against text (whether quoted verbatim, epitomised, or paraphrased), he was able to stand as spectator of the violent conflict between the texts that would, he frequently assured his reader, mark the truth and rightness of the Christian rejection of such *logomachia*, and would result in the triumph of Christian truth over its foes.

Quotation as 'Poaching': Complicating the Analysis of Textual Violence

Recalling the uncertainties for Christians of the Licinian regime, I have used the word 'tactics' above in a deliberate evocation of Michel de Certeau's distinction between strategy and tactics in his remarkable work *The Practice of Everyday Life*. There he identifies 'poaching' as a form of tactics by 'common' people or the subjugated (those colonised by the otherwise numbing effects of capitalist and colonialist processes of control)

[53] *PE* 14.3.5. [54] On which see the Introduction to this volume by Kate Cooper and Jamie Wood.

[55] *PE* 14.2.1 and 14.2.4 respectively.

[56] Cf. Isocrates *Antidosis*, passim; Josephus, *Contra Apionem*. 1.13,14,15; Clement of Alexandria, *Protrepticus*. 2.39.1 and *Stromateis* 6.4.3; Tatian, *Oratio* 31; Lactantius, *Divinae Institutiones*. 1.5; 5.4, 15; Ps.-Justin, *Cohortatio* 9.2.

[57] *PE* 14.2.6.

against the strategies of the powerful (containment, ordering, panopticism).[58] Reading – like walking or working in a factory line or office cubicle – could never discursively or spatially produce docile, fully ordered subjects; always present is the potential for ruses or practices of 'poaching', i.e., the use, misuse, or reuse of texts at the whim of the reader.[59] Authors and texts cannot control the eyes (and bodies) of readers even when they might seek to do so within familial spaces and educational contexts. Just as walking can avoid the grid-like network of ordered streets by taking oblique or circuitous routes, pauses, and retracings,[60] so reading remains open to the oblique movements, selectivity, skimmings or rereadings of the reader; the marginal notation, underlining, crossing out of words or sentences; dog-earing, forward or backward thumbing of pages; the bodily gestures, vocal exclamations, or fidgeting accompanying the movement of the eyes; the performance of reading in distinct physical places (behind the lectern, at the back of the classroom, beside the teacher or child or lover, on the toilet, on a park bench, in a cell); as well as the subsequent decisions to quote, paraphrase, or allude to the text in graffiti, homilies, poems, textbooks, or apologetic treatises.[61]

While many of these possibilities need to be altered when considering ancient readers (i.e., the physical rolling and unrolling of a scroll, or the marginal comment 'You're Arianising',[62] as well as the limitations of ancient literacy, both in terms of functional and elite literary capacities), they do raise the question of where precisely Eusebius should be located within the dynamics of ancient power relations, as both a reader of the texts of a dominant cultural tradition and a writer of texts for what would become a dominant cultural (and religious) tradition. Jeremy Schott recently suggested that we should understand the early apologists as 'mimic men' working within and against the imperial discourses of knowledge and

[58] M. de Certeau, *The Practice of Everyday Life*, S. Rendall (trans.) (Berkeley, CA: University of California Press, 1984), 34–42 (on tactics); 165–76 (on poaching).

[59] On walking, see de Certeau, *The Practice of Everyday Life*, 91–110.

[60] De Certeau, *The Practice of Everyday Life*, 97–102.

[61] De Certeau, *The Practice of Everyday Life*, 169: 'To read is to wander'; 174: 'readers are travelers, they move across lands belonging to someone else, like nomads poaching their way across fields they did not write, despoiling the wealth of Egypt to enjoy it themselves'.

[62] For just such a scholion in a manuscript of Eusebius' *Ecclesiastical Theology*, see E. Klostermann, *Eusebius Werke IV. Gegen Marcell, Über die kirchliche Theologie*, Griechischen Christlichen Schriftsteller 14 (Leipzig: J. C. Hinrichs'sche Buchhandlung, 1906), XIX; again, 'he openly Arianises', is written in the margins of ms. 1 (= Codex Marc. 341), fol. 105v of *PE* 7.12.1 (see Mras, *Eusebius Werke*, 2.431).

philosophic truth.[63] In other words, these Christians imitated the educational, cultural, and literary practices of the dominant elite while maintaining and developing a contrary identity for themselves. One might add that they also imitated broader aesthetic shifts that were even being performed by the emperor himself. In the same way that Constantine promoted a 'cumulative aesthetic' (most notably in the Arch of Constantine at Rome, which formed a composite of materials from earlier monumental art), Eusebius' accumulation of quoted material within a new literary monument conveyed the aesthetic shift of emphasis through the *Praeparatio*.[64] The view from de Certeau's work in our present discussion fills out this picture: by participating in the cumulative aesthetic Eusebius' reading and quotation of texts from the dominant literary and intellectual traditions exhibited a tactical manoeuvre of poaching, thus showing that subjects of Roman imperial Hellenism were not always docile or easily ordered, but developed interpretive ruses to produce new literary products and new identities.

There is a sort of violence to these tactics (as shown in the foregoing examination) but the tactics of quotational poaching demonstrates that textual violence may vary greatly as to its degree or place or directionality within relations of power. The relationship of violence and text within Eusebius' *Praeparatio* undercuts, therefore, any shallow (and to my mind, misleading) characterisation of Eusebius as a promoter of Christian imperial violence. Instead, the production of a text using so many of the words of its rivals opened up a textual space for hearing those rivals, which were preserved for the eyes of Christian students, in their own voices. With the presence of epitome and selective quotation of sources, one's initial response to the *Praeparatio* is probably to suspect the apologist of a form of textual ventriloquism, forcing texts to speak in a manner and for purposes contrary to their original intent (under the assumption that we can identify such a thing as authorial intent).[65] Nonetheless, a comparison

[63] J. Schott, *Christianity, Empire and the Making of Religion in Late Antiquity* (Philadelphia, PA: University of Pennsylvania Press, 2008); see also A. Jacobs, *Remains of the Jews: The Holy Land and Christian Empire in Late Antiquity* (Stanford, CA: Stanford University Press, 2004), 198; cf. L. Nasrallah, *Christian Responses to Roman Art and Architecture* (Cambridge: Cambridge University Press, 2010), 122.

[64] On the 'cumulative aesthetic' and Constantine's arch, see J. Elsner, 'From the Culture of Spolia to the Cult of Relics: The Arch of Constantine and the Genesis of Late Antique Forms', *Papers of the British School at Rome*, 68 (2000), 149–84; J. Elsner, 'Late Antique Art: The Problem of the Concept and the Cumulative Aesthetic', in S. Swain and M. Edwards (eds.), *Approaching Late Antiquity* (Oxford: Oxford University Press, 2004), 271–309; Johnson, 'Introduction', 3–10.

[65] As in the influential remarks of R. Barthes, 'Death of the Author', in S. Head (ed. and trans.), *Image-Music-Text* (New York, NY: Hill & Wang, 1977); de Certeau, on the other hand, gives a

with earlier authors who use paraphrase or quotation of sources highlights a remarkable feature of Eusebius' quotational method.

Eusebius' method is unlike that of Plutarch, on the one hand, who paraphrases Egyptian stories from within his own Hellenocentric position of cultural dominance and so stifles the 'native' voices who were the source of those stories,[66] and also unlike that of Clement of Alexandria, on the other hand, who quotes Greek poets and philosophers with great frequency but in short, restrictive quotations, thus allowing their voices only to say as much as would confirm his point and no more.[67] The *Praeparatio*, in marked distinction from these earlier thinkers (both of whom appear in its pages), prefers verbatim quotation to paraphrase or epitome, and prefers larger block quotations of its sources over short, single-sentence 'sound bites' from the earlier texts. Quotations of several pages, often accompanied by little or no commentary from the apologist, overwhelmingly mark out an approach that seriously weakens the possibility of a strong containment of meanings or forceful violation of the integrity of the earlier text. These quotations prevent the muffling of the voices quoted and restrict (though not entirely) the severe distortion of their points of view – Eusebius' often polemical comments before and after the quotations notwithstanding.

It would certainly go too far to claim Eusebius was a promoter and practitioner of tolerance (a term that remains uncomfortably anachronistic and ill-defined to my mind); but his apologetic work maintains a consistent practice of allowing the traditions of his opponents to speak in their own voices, even while being brought into a conversation they had not envisioned. The effect is polyphonic,[68] and necessarily remains open to the possibility of his readers succumbing to the siren songs of the sources that

more precise agency or intentionality to readers. Eusebius' *Praeparatio* is certainly a 'tissue of quotations' in a more blatant and obvious way than Barthes was considering. As a writer (*scriptor*) who rewrites what he reads, i.e., poaches, Eusebius performs a (non-originary) intentionality. It is this mode of agency, of the reader who writes, that Barthes leaves underexplored and that de Certeau fruitfully opens up.

66 For discussion of Plutarch's method of paraphrase and its importance for cultural centrism, see Johnson, *Religion and Identity in Porphyry of Tyre*, 226–31.

67 This statement simplifies Clement's quotational method (though it is more fitting for his use of Greek prose authors), which deserves analysis in its own right. My own impression is that Clement seems to allow much greater room for lengthier quotations in his quotation of Gnostic 'heretical' sources.

68 Cf. de Certeau, *The Practice of Everyday Life*, 162: 'Even philosophy … has labored to hear these voices again and thus to create an auditory space … The literary text [becomes] a plural body … a "stage for voices"' (albeit with reference to postmodern philosophy).

echo within the *Praeparatio*.[69] Unlike Odysseus, Eusebius refuses to put wax in his readers' ears and instead allows them to hear the tempting rills of Plato, Porphyry, Dionysius of Halicarnassus, and many others, not just for a brief moment but for what amounts to hours of reading. This is scarcely the method of 'intolerance', which would have preferred paraphrase to quotation. In spite of the fact that Eusebius composed the *Praeparatio* after years of brutal persecution driven by daemons and their 'friends' (some of whom were the very authors he quoted),[70] he chose to perform the task of apologetics within the confines of an *eisagōgē*. Even here he could have opted for techniques of paraphrase rather than quotation. His adoption of a method based on lengthy quotations – even while his commentary focused in on the primary point as he saw it – allowed the reader to discover broader contexts, different directions, or richer nuances within the quoted texts.

Later works, such as the final portions of the *Ecclesiastical History*, the *Life of Constantine*, or the *Against Marcellus* may mark a transition from tactic to strategy in their use of quotation,[71] and they certainly represent different rhetorical aims and historical/political contexts than the earlier *Praeparatio*, but they too might be profitably understood as forms of poaching (e.g., Eusebius' inclusion of and commentary on Constantine's letters for his own self-authorising purposes;[72] his narrative exaggeration of what may have been rather limited instances of imperial violence against pagan temples;[73] the narration of Constantine's military exploits within a biblical typological frame of reference;[74] and so on). I do not intend to solve the problem that these later works raise, only to pose them against the backdrop of the ways in which textual violence occurs in a work deemed by many to be the culmination of the Christian apologetic tradition and of pagan–Christian polemic. It is hoped that some or all of the modes of interplay between texts and violence (the violent contexts of composition, the narration of violence, the use of violent metaphors and

[69] For a different use of the Siren metaphor, see Eusebius, *Laus Constantini* 1.1.

[70] Especially Porphyry; *PE* 4.6.2; 5.1.9; 6.praef.3. For Eusebius' demonology, see H. Johannessen, *The Demonic in the Political Thought of Eusebius of Caesarea* (Oxford: Oxford University Press, 2016).

[71] On quotation in the *HE*, see Johnson, *Eusebius*, 93–6; for quotation in the *c.Marc.*, see Johnson, 'Introduction', 9–10.

[72] See Johnson, *Eusebius*, 162–5.

[73] On this tendentious issue, see Scott Bradbury, 'Constantine and the Problem of Anti-Pagan Legislation in the Fourth Century', *Classical Philology*, 89 (1994), 120–39.

[74] See M. S. Williams, *Authorised Lives in Early Christian Biography: Between Eusebius and Augustine* (Cambridge: Cambridge University Press, 2008), 25–57.

language, and the various modes of violating another's identity and voice) might serve as a useful model for inquiry into other texts by both pagans and Christians in late antiquity.

At the same time, these modes of interaction never stand outside of dynamic relations of power as either tactic or strategy. Whether conducted by members of the governing and cultured elite or the subjects of imperial culture, the employment of quotation, epitomisation, and paraphrase must, therefore, become a necessary object of investigation if we are to gain any meaningful appreciation of violence in late antique texts. Such textual modes of identifying and representing others (in compilation, quotation, codification, and so on) were not *necessarily* accelerators of violence (though they certainly could be); they could, rather, bear the effects (whether intended or not) of deferring or decelerating violence.[75] In spite of pressures toward conformity or singularity of thought (Athanassiadi's *monodoxia*),[76] which is a feature expressed differently but pervasively in any age or political context and is hardly unique to late antiquity, many literary manifestations of the cumulative aesthetic created polyphonic spaces, which might resist or divert the powerful tendencies to bring about the 'end of dialogue'.[77]

[75] Cf. J. Dawes, *The Language of War: Literature and Culture in the US from the Civil War through World War II* (Cambridge, MA: Harvard University Press, 2002), 23.

[76] Athanassiadi, *Vers la pensée unique*, esp. 14.

[77] Cf. the relevant essays in S. Goldhill (ed.), *The End of Dialogue in Antiquity* (Cambridge: Cambridge University Press, 2008); A. Cameron, *Dialoguing in Late Antiquity*, Hellenic Studies Series 65 (Cambridge, MA: Harvard University Press, 2014).

CHAPTER 11

Of Sojourners and Soldiers

Demonic Violence in the Letters of Antony and the Life of Antony

Blossom Stefaniw

At some point around AD 335,[1] the ascetic leader known to posterity as Antony the Great wrote to a religious community at Arsinoë in upper Egypt. In his letter, Antony provides his readers with his most detailed account of 'how the secret contrivances and manifold crafts of the Devil work and how they might be known'.[2] Only a few decades later, around AD 360, the Bishop Athanasius of Alexandria produced the *Life of Antony*, creating a textual world in which Antony, having withstood a series of diabolical assaults, comes forth from his seclusion to address his followers.[3] The character Antony dedicates a large segment of his speech to instruction on how to face up to demons, saying that 'at this time it is pressing and necessary for us to know their wiles against ourselves'.[4]

On the surface, Antony and Athanasius are doing the same thing, namely providing their followers with the information on the nature and behaviour of demons which is necessary for their religious practice. Each

[1] This dating follows the arguments of S. Rubenson, *The Letters of St Antony: Origenist Theology, Monastic Tradition and the Making of a Saint* (Lund: Lund University Press, 1990), 42–6, which places the earliest possible date of composition of the letters at the end of the 330s and suggests that they must have been written in Antony's old age.

[2] *Epistulae Antonii* [hereafter: *Ep. Ant.*] VI.23. English quotations are slightly modified from S. Rubenson (trans.), *The Letters of St Antony: Monasticism and the Making of a Saint*, Studies in Antiquity and Christianity (Minneapolis, MN: Fortress Press, 1995) (only this later edition of Rubenson's study includes a translation of the letters; there is no edition of the letters).

[3] There is continued debate about the authenticity of the *Life*. Some scholars have even reconsidered their position on this issue in the course of their careers. As a result of the difficulty of resolving this issue with certainty, I cannot commit to the view that the *Life* was certainly written by bishop Athanasius. The following interpretation of his polarising rhetoric may one day have to be reattributed to another, but equally pugnacious, name. For a summary of arguments against authenticity, see T. D. Barnes, 'Angel of Light or Mystic Initiate? The Problem of the Life of Antony', *Journal of Theological Studies*, 37 (1986), 353–68. For an argument in favour of authenticity, see D. Brakke, *Athanasius and the Politics of Asceticism*, Oxford Early Christian Studies (Oxford: Clarendon Press, 1995).

[4] *Vita Antoni* [hereafter: *VA*] 22 [PG 26.835–976]. English quotations from the *Life of Antony* are from R. C. Gregg (trans.), *Athanasius: The Life of Antony and the Letter to Marcellinus*, Classics of Western Spirituality (Mahwah, NJ: Paulist Press, 1980).

leader's act of instruction can be read as native and natural to an environment in which people commonly attributed adversity to diabolical agents; where there is widespread belief in demons, religious leaders must demonstrate their expertise in a field of experience which is of urgent concern to their followers. Without denying the validity of that way of explaining why fourth-century religious leaders offer demonological instruction, there may be a more refined way of reading these accounts of demonic violence. That is, we can read discussion of the nature, mode, and location of demons and the violence they work upon the ascetic as a medium for creating religious subjectivities in relation to a non-human adversary. Antony and Athanasius shape the subjectivity of their followers by cataloguing the sort of demonic violence to which a person can expect to be exposed and by providing appropriate means of defence for an ascetic to use when assaulted by demons. Athanasius and Antony supply their respective followers with significantly different maps for navigating this adversarial terrain. Comparing how each author orients his readers to demonic violence and examining the divergent subjectivities which are facilitated by each makes it possible to see what sort of differences lie below the surface of the respective demonologies. It also allows the larger religious significance of those differences to become apparent: Antony and Athanasius have diverging and partially incompatible notions of the human predicament and therefore also of the ethical urgencies to which a human being is subject.

The letters of Antony have traditionally been compared with the *Life of Antony* with a view to trying to identify which most closely reflects the historical Antony. This approach can entail treating the two texts as documentary evidence for what sort of doctrinal positions Antony held, or as more or less accurate pictures of fourth-century asceticism in Egypt.[5] Comparisons of this kind often struggle with the slippage which inevitably results from trying to line up a literary figure (Antony as the main character in the *Life*) with an authorial voice (Antony writing the letters). In order to navigate this discrepancy more securely, I will instead be comparing the discussion of demonic violence as it is set out by two authorial voices, that

[5] The prime example of this stance can be found in H. Dörries, *Die* Vita Antonii *als Geschichtsquelle*, (Göttingen: Vandenhoek & Ruprecht, 1949). A very grievous problem with this approach is the assumption that ascetic life in fourth-century Egypt was more or less homogenous, so that the differences we see in these two texts cannot both reflect the ideals and concerns of fourth-century Egyptian ascetics. Rather than adjudicating between them, the present essay argues that, even within the space of a few decades and in the same region, significantly divergent notions of ascetic subjectivity could and did co-exist.

of Athanasius in the *Life* and that of Antony in his letters. This provides a somewhat firmer footing because both authors are operating with a view to instructing others. Part of their shared pedagogical work is to define what demons are, what one should expect from them, how one can recognise their works, and what one should do to oppose them. In other words, we are comparing not only two authorial voices, but also two voices of religious leaders who are performing as suppliers of high-grade religious capital necessary to succeed in the ascetic life.

Most recently, David Brakke has compared the role of discourse about demons in these two texts along with several other monastic writings. While the discussion below does not contradict Brakke's findings, the focus of the current essay is different. Brakke discusses the *Letters* and the *Life* within a larger programme of explaining how discourse about demons functions to articulate 'the new religious identity of the Christian monk'.[6] While he discusses the *Letters* in part of the first chapter with a view to establishing their demonology's roots in Origenist and Valentinian thought, Brakke dedicates a whole chapter to the *Life*.[7] Here, the emphasis is reversed, with the interpretation of the *Letters* taking priority. This essay carries forward Brakke's study, proceeding from his understanding of demonology as a strong currency for forming ascetic identities, but works on a smaller scale. I seek to show substantial diversity in the use of discourse about demons even within a small chronological and geographical space, and to demonstrate how, even within that small space, demonological discourse could serve as a means of construing different, and partially incompatible, ascetic subjectivities.

The demons in the letters of Antony manipulate the thoughts, impulses, and emotions of the individual. Their work occurs inside the person and exploits the weakness of the human mind and body. For Athanasius, in contrast, demons function primarily in an external, corporeal, and physically violent mode. Athanasius locates the ascetic life in a large-scale conflict with demons that do not merely corrupt the monk's perceptions and emotions, as in the *Letters*, but also turn out in gangs and beat him senseless. This introduction of physicalised and externalised violence into the ascetic work of Antony moves the readers far away from the process of careful reflection and discernment of one's emotions and thoughts which the Antony of the *Letters* had encouraged as a defence against internally

[6] D. Brakke, *Demons and the Making of the Monk* (Cambridge, MA: Harvard University Press, 2006), 5.

[7] Brakke, *Demons*, 16–21 and 23–47 respectively.

located demons. This shift from a cognitive and therapeutic mode of resisting demonic violence to external, physical, and combative terms of engagement is one of several strategies that Athanasius is using to popularise and de-intellectualise asceticism.[8] Further, his new, more brutal demon serves to cultivate the sort of adversarial subjectivity conducive to disambiguated all-or-nothing religious conflict in which Athanasius himself specialised throughout his life.[9] The intensified and externalised violence of demonic opposition in the *Life of Antony* reflects a drive toward cultivating a more trenchant and unyielding religious subjectivity.[10]

What exactly does it mean to construe instruction on demons as a means of constructing specific subjectivities? What is a subjectivity? To put it in Foucauldian terms, 'the problem is to determine what the subject must be, to what condition he is subject, what status he must have, what position he must occupy in reality or in the imaginary, in order to become a legitimate subject of this or that type of knowledge'.[11] Athanasius and Antony can both be seen as working on just such a problem: who is the religiously ambitious subject under conditions of diabolical assault and violence? How should she think about herself and the violence she experiences? Both writers are providing knowledge of how a person can and should react to demonic violence, where violence is known to be a parameter of the religiously ambitious life.[12] To explain demonic violence is to explain who, or indeed what, the ascetic is, to orient her in a world in which there are demons who operate in a specific mode and to measure her legitimacy as a subject in relation to her ability to withstand the violence of demons. Demonological instruction gives the ascetic a way to imagine herself and the significance of the ascetic way of life she has undertaken.

[8] Cf. Brakke, *Asceticism*, for a full study of the political complexities of Athanasius' engagement with Egyptian asceticism.

[9] Athanasius' opposition to Arianism led to constant conflict throughout his episcopate. On an imperial level, he was brought to trial and sent into exile on numerous occasions. On a local level, Athanasius sustained controversies not only against the Arians, but also against the Melitians.

[10] It should be emphasised at the outset that the subjectivities which Antony and Athanasius seek to valorise and necessitate by means of demonological instruction are not polar opposites. Athanasius does not reject cognitive processes in the ascetic life, nor is Antony free of agonistic language in the instructions he gives in the *Letters*.

[11] This quotation, as well as the one following, are from Michel Foucault's pseudonymous self-definition in the *Dictionnaire des Philosophes* of 1984, which he contributed under the name Maurice Florence (M. Florence, 'Michel Foucault', in D. Huisman [ed.], *Dictionnaire des Philosophes* [Paris: Presses Universitaires des France, 1984], 942–4).

[12] For additional and expanded application of Foucauldian notions to early Christian discourses of violence, see Chris L. de Wet's chapter in this volume.

Subjectivity can also be defined as 'the way in which the subject experiences himself in a game of truth where he relates to himself'. This definition gives us a good grip for wrestling with the discourse of demonological instruction precisely because such instruction is serving to interpret and imagine the way that the religiously ambitious experience themselves when in pursuit of their goals. It also fits in with the use, by both authors, of cataloguing and surveying rhetoric. Such discursive strategies map out a topography of the truth about demons; they build the world in which the ascetic, literally, finds himself. Explanation of the motives, strategies, and habits of the demons give ascetics a way to understand what they are experiencing in their minds and bodies while striving for religious excellence.[13]

While demonological instruction is a good tool for cultivating subjectivity, the use of that tool in and of itself underdetermines what sort of subjectivity will be carved out. Demonological instruction in the *Life* and the *Letters* will be compared by first making a brief historical note on each author, then surveying the larger narrative framework of each text. Then explicit description of the demons and their activities will be examined, finally synthesising the position and obligations of the person in relation to demonic violence in order to identify the ascetic subjectivity valorised in each text. As we will see in the following comparison, a discourse of violence perpetrated by demons upon the person can be used to cultivate significantly differing subjectivities.

The Sojourner

Seven letters of Antony have been preserved in several diverging manuscript traditions, having been translated from the original Coptic into Greek, Latin, Arabic, Syriac, and Georgian.[14] Their authenticity is highly probable.[15] The date of composition lies towards the end of Antony's life.

[13] This approach aligns with the position outlined in the Introduction to this volume by Kate Cooper and Jamie Wood, according to which learning is a matter of assuming a new identity, often enough by means of violence, real or discursive.

[14] For a full account of the manuscript traditions and textual variations see Rubenson, *The Letters of St Antony*, 15–34.

[15] Arguments for authenticity include consistent attribution throughout a highly complex and diffuse manuscript tradition, reference to seven letters by Antony in Jerome's *De viris illustribus* of 392, quotations from the letters with consistent attribution by Shenoute and Besa, literal agreement between passages from the letters and sayings attributed to Antony in later anthologies, close affinities to the sermon in the *Vita Antonii*. Arguments against authenticity turn on methodological failures, the most severe of which is taking rhetorical ideals of early monks as uneducated and innocent of literary skill as reports on an actual state of affairs. On this view, if

The desire to consolidate his legacy before his death may have been the occasion for the composition of the letters. Communities of ascetics who respected Antony as an *abba* could elicit a summary of the teachings of Antony and continue to circulate the letters even after he had died. In fact, the manuscript tradition itself suggests that this is how the letters were used. All of the languages in which manuscripts are preserved correspond to religious communities which had established monasteries in Egypt and thereby gained direct access to collections of ascetic teachings in use there. This explanation for the composition of the letters is also consistent with their content that, unlike the protreptic letters of Iamblichus, for example, does not refer to any particular request for advice.[16] Antony's letters are removed from specific moral dilemmas and instead counsel the ascetic readers in terms of a generalised narrative of the religious life. We can, with some degree of certainty, take the addressees to have been communities of committed ascetics, because of the salutations at the beginning and end of many of the letters.[17]

Antony's Narrative Frame

In the letters, Antony's demonology is conceived of within a larger narrative framework which parses the spiritual life in terms of exile, sojourn, and homecoming. Antony frames the ascetic life within an account of original union, current alienation, and woundedness which will ultimately resolve into a state of healing connected with final homecoming. This story of the spiritual life, set out in most detail in Letter II, is repeated in slightly differing versions throughout the letters. The points most significant for framing religious subjectivity are the description of the human condition relative to divine provisions made through a sequence of dispensations and the location of the reader relative to the impending resolution of the narrative. The narrative of the spiritual life which pervades the corpus of the letters constitutes the imagined world

Antony was a monk, he was an illiterate Coptic peasant, thus he cannot have written letters representing an intellectualist strand in asceticism.

[16] Cf. Iamblichus of Chalcis, *The Letters*, J. M. Dillon and W. Polleichtner (trans.), Writings from the Greco-Roman World 19 (Atlanta, GA: Society of Biblical Literature, 2009).

[17] The salutations are generally directed at a group rather than an individual. The recipients are addressed in traditional familial terms as beloved children or brothers. At *Ep. Ant.* VI.1–2, Antony appears to be writing to a community which includes women: 'Antony greets all his dear brothers, who are at Arsinoë and its environs and those who are with you, in the Lord. All of you who have prepared yourselves to come to God, I greet you in the Lord, my beloved, the young and the old, men and women, Israelite children, saints in your spiritual essence.'

within which the ascetic is to understand herself as a subject. It is within this world that the demons function to disrupt the homeward progress of the ascetic exile.

Antony portrays the human being as wounded, vulnerable, childlike, and lost. In a loving accommodation of this condition, the divine makes provisions to comfort and protect the people, to guide them on the way home: 'In his irrevocable love the Creator of all desired to visit our afflictions and confusion.'[18] Provisions for the comfort and healing of the people are made in a sequence of dispensations, progressing through history: 'God did not visit his creatures only once, but since the beginning of the world, as soon as anyone has turned through the law of promise to the Creator of all, God embraces him in his benevolence, grace and Spirit.'[19] Each providential dispensation is mediated by a different class of such responsive individuals, first by the patriarchs, then by the prophets, and finally by the apostles. This sequence traces a qualitative progression; each category of mediators is more directly attached to the divine and closer to the final resolution of the human state of exile, i.e., coming home. Implicitly, Antony's readers are near the end of the narrative, and thus very close to achieving the final state of homecoming. This position on the brink of resolution intensifies the urgency of their struggle against the demons; if they fail to see their ascetic task through, they will forfeit not only their own work, but also that of all the patriarchs, prophets, and apostles who have gone before.

In Antony's narrative, each step in the journey towards reunion with God, from the call of Abraham through the gifts of the law and the spirit, is attached metaphorically to a phase of building a house, reinforcing the theme of humanity as existing in a condition of exile, in need of shelter:

> Moses built the house, yet did not finish it, but left and died. Then God by his Spirit raised up the council of the prophets, and they built upon the foundation laid by Moses, but could not complete it and likewise they left and died.[20]

The prophets continue the work already done by the lawgiver Moses. However, these workmen come to the conclusion that they will not be able to carry on. The task at which the lawgiver and the prophets have been toiling proves impossible. The people recognise their need and beg for help:

[18] *Ep. Ant.* II.9. [19] *Ep. Ant.* II.2. [20] *Ep. Ant.* II.11–12.

> Invested with the Spirit, they all saw that the wound was incurable and that none of the creatures was able to heal it, but only the Only-begotten, who is the very mind and image of the Father, who made every rational creature in the image of his image.[21]

The pivotal metaphor of woundedness and healing now finds its resolution. The saviour is portrayed as a great physician and the refrain from the book of Isaiah is recounted as the cry of the prophets upon their tragic insight. In this climactic moment, Antony shifts to a more immediate narrative focus:

> Knowing that the Saviour is a great physician, they all assembled and offered prayers for their members, that is for us, crying out and saying: Is there no balm in Gilead? Is there no physician there? Why then is not the health of the daughter of my people recovered? We would have healed her, but she is not healed: now therefore let us forsake her.[22]

The prophets find themselves helpless and, along with all the people, in need of aid and comfort. Antony quickly delivers the divine response to their plea: 'But God in his abundant love came to us and said through his saints, Son of man, make to thyself vessels of captivity.'[23] In articulating the coming of Christ as balm in Gilead, as the longed-for comfort for human woundedness and confusion, Antony marks the fulcrum of his narrative with an evocative conflation of biblical intertexts: 'our iniquities humbled him, and by his stripes we were healed'.[24] Divine compassion is as compellingly evoked as the desolate state of the people crying out. So far, demons are absent from the story. The only hindrance to human efforts at finding their way home is ontological rather than adversarial: the human condition as such, the greatness of the wound, is what thwarts their progress. This suggests a conflation of the work of demons and the state of woundedness which we must keep in mind.

This divine response to human need is the climax of the narrative, after which Antony telescopes back out to the epic perspective from which he began. The sequence of the lawgiver and prophets is carried forward and paralleled by a new set of collaborators with the divine, namely 'the servants of God'.[25] This category of people appears to be synonymous with the apostles. Because they have received the Spirit of adoption, Christ

[21] *Ep. Ant.* II.14. [22] *Ep. Ant.* II.15–17. [23] *Ep. Ant.* II.18.

[24] *Ep. Ant.* II.21. Antony conflates a phrase from Paul in Romans 8:32 and a longer passage from Isaiah 53:5.

[25] *Ep. Ant.* II.26.

says to them 'Henceforth I call you not servants, but brothers and friends' (John 15:15).[26] The servants of God:

> received the Spirit of adoption, and cried out saying, We have not received the Spirit of bondage again to fear; but we have received the Spirit of adoption, whereby we cry, Abba, Father. Now, therefore, O God, we know what Thou hast given us: that we are the children and heirs of God, and joint heirs with Christ.[27]

Within this narrative framework, Antony's readers are located in a dispensation following on the incarnation which allows for the attainment of the status of full adoption. They are on the cusp of the resolution of the state of alienation, very close to ending their sojourn.

The plot of this narrative is in essence an abstracted and fused reception of the stories of Abraham (leaving his father's house) and of Moses (going to the promised land). In order to pursue his desire to 'visit our afflictions and confusion', God 'raised up Moses, the Lawgiver, who gave us the written law and founded for us the house of truth, the spiritual Church, which creates unity, since it is God's will that we turn back to the first formation'.[28] The themes of provision, shelter, and restoration and return taken from the biblical stories mimic the movement from desolation to solace taken from Origenist cosmology. Thus Antony's narrative has both a cosmological and a historiographical aspect. Both of these three-point plots, of exile, sojourn, and homecoming on the one hand and union, fall, and restoration on the other, allow the reader to locate himself in the denouement towards the end of a metanarrative which is both biblical-historical and Origenist-eschatological. Again, the reader is positioned on the brink of success, where failure is most costly.

Antony plots out the religious life using metaphors of exile, struggling for shelter, desolation, woundedness, healing, adoption, and finally coming home to a state of perfect rest in attachment to a divine father.[29] The role of the person in this narrative frame fosters an identity of intimacy and election. The person has received extravagant provisions from a fatherly God and can be assured of the final restitution of a state of solace and comfort. There is no animosity in this narrative and the only danger

[26] *Ep. Ant.* II.27. [27] *Ep. Ant.* II.29–30, quoting Romans 8:15–17.

[28] *Ep. Ant.* II.10. Here the first person introduced is Moses and not Abraham, presumably because Antony is foregrounding a sequence of means of divine comfort which have been offered throughout history and, in this version, is approaching the narrative less in terms of models, patterns, and typologies. This shift in focus is consistent with Antony's double focus on the cosmological and on the historical.

[29] *Ep. Ant.* I.45.

involved arises from the human condition and not from external adversaries. It is an odyssey without anxiety. There is frailty, alienation, exile, and desolation, but there is no fear in this story. Antony's God is responsive and accommodating and there is no question that the provisions made to help people develop into a state of full sonship can ever be fundamentally disrupted or revoked. The person, in Antony, is indeed a sojourner, but she has a home.

Demonic Intrusion

While the interaction between God and humanity has grand scope and structures all of history to the end of time, human–demon contact occurs in a far more constricted theatre of engagement. Demonic activity in the letters of Antony is a work of claustrophobically concentrated violence, breaching the very membranes of the self. The aspects of Antony's demonology most important for construing the subject are the invisible and immaterial nature of the demons, their location inside the person, and their cognitively centred mode of engagement. It is only what happens on the battlefield of this internal microcosm that can sabotage the progress of the larger narrative.

In *Ep. Ant.* VI.55, Antony poses the rhetorical question

> who ever saw a demon fighting against us and preventing us from doing good, or opposing us, standing somewhere in the body, so that we should become afraid and flee from him? No, they are all hidden, and we reveal them by our deeds.

In this passage, Antony directly contradicts the notion that demons are analogous to a human adversary, capable of provoking a physical altercation (the very notion which Athanasius later commits to in his account of Antony's life). Antony's demons are immaterial and invisible and cannot be confronted man to man, so to speak. Their invisibility dictates the way they assault people as well as the way people can defend themselves.[30] Since Antony's demons do not have bodies of their own, they use human bodies and souls:

> And if you seek, you will not find their sins and iniquities revealed bodily, for they are not visible bodily. But you should know that we are their bodies and that our soul receives their wickedness ...

[30] The materiality which went along with the disruption of the primordial union also gives the demons a grip on humans: 'the power of the devil lies in the matter of this world'.

That means that the evil effects of demons can only be manifest in and through human beings and, more significantly for the question of subjectivity, that the body and soul of the person are permeable and receptive to diabolical invasion.

While the demons are immaterial, human materiality compromises the integrity of the intellect and allows for demonic invasion.[31] In Antony's world, persons are, most properly, intellects, and those intellects were pure and intact in the state of primordial union with God. Since falling, the human mind has prolapsed into a psyche and a body. As a result the mind has lost its state of unmoved rest and become vulnerable to disruption: '

> This I have said concerning the afflictions of the soul which have become mingled with what is natural to the body, in which the soul moves, so that it has become a guide to the evil spirits working in its members.[32]

The mutability arising from the fall into material allowed evil to penetrate the mind and alienate creatures from 'the nature of the spiritual essence'.[33] In *Ep. Ant.* VI.45, in fact, the body is defined as a container for strife: 'This our vessel in which we dwell is our destruction and a house full of war.' The fallen, embodied state as such makes the human being vulnerable to demonic attacks. Merely being a human being in this world allows the demons to gain purchase on one's mind and body. These are the conditions the person is subject to.

Because of Antony's conception of the person as most truly an intellect, his understanding of demonic violence is heavily weighted towards the cognitive. The cognitive focus of Antony's demonology has two branches. The intellect, because of its compromised state of embodiment, is a site of demonic violence, but the intellect can also serve as a defence against the demons when it is used correctly, that is, when it gains true knowledge of itself and of the spiritual world, including the demons. In *Ep. Ant.* VII.7, Antony describes demons as a force that interferes with the proper functioning of the mind. Failure to order and integrate the mind thus makes the person that much more vulnerable to attack: 'all who are not at peace draw battles upon themselves and are a judgement to themselves'.[34] The same principle as observed above is again at work here: any disruption of unity or integration opens a chink in one's psychic armour and gives the demons a way in.

If we construe asceticism as a means of defence against demonic violence, we can see how the system fits together: the human being is

[31] *Ep. Ant.* VI.51. [32] *Ep. Ant.* I.72. [33] *Ep. Ant.* VII.11. [34] *Ep. Ant.* III.14.

vulnerable because the embodied state compromises the integrity of the mind. Ascetic work, therefore, is not simply a matter of disciplining the body. It serves to mend the breach in the mind by making the material body less prone to the weaknesses of the material. Asceticism also patches up the emotions which, if destabilised, allow the demons to gain purchase on the individual. Asceticism is raising the drawbridge, pulling up the rope ladder, manning the ramparts, and sheltering the wounded.

Not only mental integrity, but also clear and correct knowledge are needed in order to re-establish and maintain the sovereignty of the intellect. Human ignorance of demons and their workings is one more side effect of having an embodied and irrational mind which Antony urges his followers to correct.[35] The importance given to accurate knowledge about demons makes sense if connected to Antony's ideal of self-knowledge as a cipher for the state of full integration and his conviction that only by means of self-knowledge can one know the true order of things. Demons are among the things one has correct and complete knowledge of when the mind is doing what it should. Failure to attain correct knowledge of demons means the person can be invaded and manipulated by them unawares. Thus the instruction on demons that Antony supplies in the letters constitutes the first line of self-defence for his followers. Learning about demons is part of a protective programme which must be undertaken in order to compensate weaknesses and vulnerability inherent in the embodied person. And here we can see why fighting against demons is invisible in the larger salvific narrative. Resistance against the demons is a silent and intimate strife, undertaken under the skin.

In *Ep. Ant.* VI, Antony offers a catalogue of demonic activities and describes their dispositions and motives. Both the particular things demons do and the secret, subtle, and seductive mode in which they operate again manifest their internal location and their focus on disrupting thoughts and perceptions.

> Truly, my children, they are jealous of us at all times with their evil counsel, their secret persecution, their subtle malice, their spirits of seduction, their fraudulent thoughts, their faithlessness which they sow in our hearts every day, their hardness of heart and their numbness, the many sufferings they bring upon us at every hour, the weariness which causes our hearts to be weary at all times, all their wrath, the mutual slander which they teach us, our self-justifications in our deeds, and the condemnations which they sow in our hearts so that we, when we are alone, condemn our fellows, though

[35] *Ep. Ant.* VI.23.

> they are not with us, the contempt they send into our hearts through pride so that we become hard-hearted and despise one another, becoming bitter against each other with hard words, and troubled every hour accusing each other and not ourselves, thinking that our struggle comes from our fellows, judging what is outside while the robbers are all inside our house, and furthermore with the disputes and divisions we have with each other until we have established our own words so that they seem justified in the face of the other, and they incite us to do things which we are unable to do (and whose time it is not), and make us weary of things we do and which are good for us. Therefore they make us laugh when it is time for weeping, and weep when it is time for laughter, simply turning us aside every time from the straight way. Through many other deceits they make us their slaves, but there is no time now to reveal all of them. But when they fill our hearts with all these and we feed on them and they become our food, then God is wroth with us.[36]

There are several remarkable features in this catalogue. The works of the demons all take place in the mind and the emotions, causing upset, confusion, and paranoia. Their effects on the mind weaken its grip on reality, so that perception of one's own and other's behaviour is skewed. The monk's ability to accurately assess the aptness of his own perceptions and respond appropriately is compromised; he believes others to be acting spitefully when they are not and he believes himself to be mature enough to take on more stringent ascetic exercises ('they incite us to do things we are unable to do and whose time it is not') which in fact are too advanced for him. The catalogue is consistent with the overall role of the demons as insidious and manipulative: they use 'secret persecution' and 'subtle malice'. It also emphasises the effects of the demons in community life, since they make people think about the supposed wrongdoings of their fellows, blaming others for their problems rather than realising that 'the robbers are all inside our house'. Here it becomes clear that the demons do not only disrupt the integrity and unity of the mind, but also attack the integrity of the community.[37]

In the demonology of the letters, violence occurs in an intrusive and insidious mode.[38] Demons perform their violence in the role of intimate

[36] *Ep. Ant.* VI.30–42.

[37] Brakke, *Demons*, 19 reads this passage in terms of the poles of unity and disunity around which he interprets the demonology of the *Letters* overall: 'Demons oppose the monk's quest for restored unity by promoting difference on two levels: through embodied vice they encourage a movement away from the invisible unity of spiritual essence and through interpersonal strife they incite division within the social unity of the Church.'

[38] See Brakke, *Demons*, 21, on the location of Antonine demons: 'Although they incite a movement toward false externality, they themselves are not forces external to the monk.'

vandals, operating under cover in the body, mind, and community, sabotaging the ascetic's efforts towards integration and unification. Compared to the thuggish demons of Athanasius, who we will meet in the following section, this sort of demon is subtle, cloying, and highly disturbing. Rather than terrorising humans by manifesting themselves physically, visibly, or materially, Antony's demons violate the mind internally, secretively, and invisibly. They are even able to cause evil thoughts in the person without that individual's knowledge or consent.[39] The work of these demons is violent in a very literal way, because it breaches the membranes of the person. In medical terms, the demons constitute an insult to the mind and indeed Antony's imagining of the work of demons draws consistently on metaphors of injury and illness.

Ascetic Subjectivity in Antony

In a world where vulnerability to demons is entailed by the human condition, articulating subjectivity is closely linked to explaining how people can attain healing for the wounds which allow the demons to penetrate. The location of the battle against demons is inside the body and the mind. Accordingly, resistance to demonic attacks must be mounted internally. Cultivating self-knowledge and doing the ascetic work prescribed for healing breaches in the integrity of the person are the defensive manoeuvres appropriate to demons which invade the boundaries of the self. Practicing asceticism corrects exactly the physical and mental instability which makes the person porous and vulnerable to demonic manipulation. For Antony, there is asceticism of the mind, performed through attaining self-knowledge and physical asceticism, which supports the healing of the mind by restoring order and stability to the body and emotions by means of fasts, vigils, and abstinence.[40] The tasks of attaining knowledge, exercising discernment, and striving for mental integration, which make up the asceticism of the mind, are all aimed at making the mind whole and intact, as it was originally.

Antony differentiates two compromising aspects of physicality which necessitate ascetic exercises. The ascetic is called upon to repair the

[39] The only modern concept approximating this notion of demons is the view of mental illness as something one 'has', something which causes distorted thoughts and actions but cannot be observed independently of a person, while the person is still spoken of as separate from the illness, so that the illness is an internal other.

[40] *Ep. Ant.* 1.62. The opposite is also true: people can 'fall in' with demons through gluttony and drunkenness.

embodied state as such, although Antony specifies that the vulnerability following from having a body is not culpable. The flesh still requires attention, however, because although its movements do not constitute diabolical attacks in and of themselves, they can be occasions for demonic incursion and therefore must be minimised and controlled. In addition, the ascetic must resist an additional set of 'movements of the body' which are directly caused by demons: 'The third movement comes from the evil spirits, tempting us out of envy and seeking to divert those who attempt to sanctify themselves.'[41] That is, the demons can provoke physical appetites towards sinful ends and corrupt the mental focus of the person by introducing the desire for pleasure. While fasts and vigils can mend the breach which allows demons to use the body for their own purposes, the mind can be shored up against invasive thoughts by adhering to 'the testimonies which the Spirit has given it'.[42] Failure to do so will open the person up to so much diabolical persecution that he will eventually, from sheer exhaustion, cry out for help, much in parallel to the cry for help from the assembly of the people which is such a key part of the historicised salvific narrative discussed above:

> But if the mind spurns the testimonies which the Spirit has given it, then evil spirits override the natural constitution of the body and stir up these movements until the soul grows weary and asks from where it can receive help and converts and adheres to the testimony of the Spirit and is healed.[43]

The physical subject is in a tenuous and paradoxical position. 'The natural constitution of the body', the non-culpable embodied state, requires a stalwart practice of discipline, control, and resistance to invasive attacks from the demons. On the other hand, in relation to divine provisions like the testimonies of the Spirit, the person is to express weariness and need, to collapse and surrender to a benevolent other. Here the proper relation to evil is hard, while the proper relation to the good is soft, but both relations follow from the weakness, need, and vulnerability of the human person. The individual must thus live in the throes of contradictory affect, maintaining a receptive stance towards divine mercy at the same time as cultivating a fortified front to repel demonic trespass.

Demons are an internal affront to the integrity of the mind and, accordingly, can be best resisted by integrating the mind. Since the demons are internal, (at least some) evil is internal and the person is at

[41] *Ep. Ant.* 1.41. The sophistication of this diagnostic taxonomy evokes the later, but far better known, system for discerning the work of demons developed by Evagrius Ponticus, e.g. in the *Antirrhetikos*.

[42] *Ep. Ant.* 1.43–4. [43] *Ep. Ant.* 1.43–4.

odds with herself, constantly required to examine her thoughts and motives and determine their source. This way of locating the demons and their effects constitutes an unstable subjectivity in which a person includes within herself both 'me' and 'not-me', while committed to a process of integration which eventually smothers the demonic 'not-me' and allows the mind, as rehabilitated through the aid of the Spirit, to have sole control of the person and her thoughts and actions. The ascetic subject is oriented towards the self-reflective work of developing the ability to discern which impulses and perceptions are caused by demons and which are proper to the progressively integrating self.

While Antony does use bellicose rhetoric, the war in his metaphors is internal and the person is not cast as a soldier. There is no exhortation to arm oneself against the demons, to fight against them, or to challenge them. The demons are never once credited with the ability to cause physical pain or bodily distress of any kind. In the same way, the person is never exhorted to take up any sort of directly confrontational stance or to do violence to the demons themselves. It is possible to fail to notice the work of demons upon oneself. Resistance to demons is affected by actions directed at the self, not actions directed at the demons. Antony's ascetic is cast not as a combatant but as a dogged and determined civilian, working away at mitigating the damage caused by the demons and at recovering and stabilising her resources in order to carry on with the task of reaching the safe haven of reunion with God. The role Antony thus gives to the human in relation to demons fits in with his larger framework of exile and return. Antony's ascetics live not as soldiers, but as sojourners, as refugees.

The Soldier

Translated into Latin soon after its composition in Greek by Athanasius of Alexandria, the *Life of Antony* quickly became immensely popular and represents a watershed in Christian literature. The *Life* set a standard for hagiography throughout and beyond the fourth and fifth centuries and moved readers as far afield as the young officials at Trier mentioned by Augustine of Hippo, who himself heard about the story in Milan.[44] At the time he wrote the *Life*, Athanasius was already a veteran of grave church-

[44] Augustine, *Confessiones* 8.6.14–15 [PL 32.659-868]: Pontitianus, an African, having spent time at the imperial court, tells Augustine about the *VA* and how he read it during his stay at Trier. On the *VA* as a model for later hagiography, see C. Tornau, 'Intertextuality in Early Latin Hagiography: Sulpicius Severus and the Vita Antonii', *Studia Patristica*, 35 (2001), 158–66.

political conflicts associated with the Arian controversy. He had been sent into exile numerous times and forcibly removed from the episcopate. With opponents as high up as the emperor himself, Athanasius' career saw him frequently struggling against all odds. Possessed of incredible tenacity, Athanasius deployed his pastoral, theological, and political talents in a many-fronted campaign to consolidate his position and his vision for Christianity in Egypt even in the face of constant adversity. His literary production, including the writing of the *Life*, was part of this campaign.[45]

Explicit discussion of demonology plays a much more prominent role in the *Life* than in the *Letters*. In addition, the narrative form of the *Life* allows Athanasius to include numerous confrontations between Antony and demons bent on sabotaging his ascetic quest. The use of narrative lets the demons appear as characters who move the plot along through their actions and in part governs the degree to which Athanasius' demons must be narratologically viable. That is, their function in a story which is intended to be popularly appealing encourages the portrayal of demons as external to the person, physical and thuggish. Antony in his letters, writing primarily to committed ascetics, can afford more subtle demons. While Antony provided demonological instruction through direct description, explanation, and cataloguing, Athanasius uses not only these media (primarily in the discourse given by Antony to his assembled followers in *VA* 16–43), but also narrative representation. By supplying examples of what the demons can do to a person, Athanasius teaches his readers what sort of actions they should undertake to defend themselves from demonic attacks. By portraying an ascetic hero who, despite his great gifts, must face intense combat for long years, Athanasius also gives his readers an impression of the scale and mode of demonic animosity.

The religious-political agenda within which Athanasius articulates his demonology reflects an agonistic orientation and a drive to give ordinary people a way to identify themselves as practitioners of right religion without also having to be intellectuals or philosophers. Both of these components play out in a programme of blurring the difference between ascetics and common churchgoers,[46] achieved in part by promoting an anti-intellectual form of asceticism which steers clear of valorising philosophical debate and increases the popular appeal of the ascetic as holy man, able to heal the sick and settle disputes. As a result, even when writing a biography of Antony, who in his letters demonstrates considerable intellectual sophistication, Athanasius cannot afford to foreground the

[45] Brakke, *Politics*, 207. [46] Brakke, *Politics*, 145.

intellectualist, introverted, and paradoxical ascetic subjectivity which Antony himself cultivated in his followers.

Athanasius' Narrative Frame

Two themes from within the narrative of the *Life of Antony* are of particular help in interpreting Athanasius' demonological instruction. These are the repeated motifs of combat and of colonisation.

The dominant metaphors in the *Life* are agonistic and recall the endurance of martyrs or soldiers, complete with God appearing as Antony's backer and ascetic training defined as training for combat.[47] Athanasius' Antony is directly confrontational in his interactions with the demons and also shows incredible perseverance and fortitude in fighting the demons. As soon as he sets out on his odyssey towards perfection, Antony is faced with a trenchant and incorrigible enemy. The first line of attack is emotional, producing distress through memories and feelings of concern about Antony's worldly responsibility towards his sister; then an assault on the level of sexual desire follows, along with efforts to tempt Antony with the desire for money (*VA* 3–7). Even though these temptations have to do with thoughts and emotions, Athanasius uses metaphors of a wrestling match or an ambush. Antony is already taking on the role of the heroic combatant, so much so that the devil 'saw his own weakness in the face of Antony's resolve and saw that he instead was being thrown for a fall by the sturdiness of this contestant' (*VA* 5).[48]

These first incidents establish a pattern which is repeated throughout the *Life*. The devil and his demons resort to increasingly desperate measures to take Antony down, but they are always bested by Antony's courage and resolve. Athanasius describes Antony, his model ascetic, as a fighter kitting up for confrontation when he moves further into demonic territory: 'Thus tightening his hold upon himself, Antony departed to the tombs' (*VA* 8). In the tombs, Satan brings along 'a multitude of demons' and subjects Antony to extensive physical attack and torture. Although Antony

[47] The agonistic metaphors so pervasive in the *VA* draw not only on the image of the soldier or the athlete, but also on that of the martyr. In *VA* 47, for example, Antony 'was daily a martyr in his conscience and a contender in the contests of the faith'. On metaphors of war, see Jamie Wood's and Aaron Johnson's chapters in this volume

[48] We noted above that in the *Letters* the demons remain invisible in the larger narrative framework because their arena is the inside the person. Brakke, *Demons*, 28, notes that in the *VA* the demons only appear in the narrative after Antony has subdued his desires. They are invisible as long as Antony is engaged with his inner world, because, in the *VA*, the arena proper to the demons is the outer world.

never gives up, he is eventually incapacitated and believed dead, so that his followers remove him from the tombs. In the night, he persuades a friend to carry him back into the tomb so he can continue to fight (*VA* 9). When Antony further encroaches on demonic territory and takes up residence in an abandoned fort, he is again assaulted (*VA* 13) and again withstands attack. In this early part of the story, Antony is the embodied performance of the courage which he later sets forth as the ascetic ideal in his discourse to his disciples.[49]

What is less prominent but equally revealing of the sort of world within which Athanasius wants his readers to imagine themselves is the theme of colonisation. Antony repeatedly encroaches on demonic territory, acting as vanguard to further monastic settlers. Antony's progress from the outskirts of his village into the inner desert is parsed in terms of laying claim to enemy territory through repeated acts of expulsion and invasion. Antony presses forward from the margins of his home village and gradually claims the desert for human occupation, specifically for settlement by orthodox ascetics.[50] Especially when he emerges from the abandoned fort, a metaphor of colonisation is deployed along with the rhetoric of heavenly citizenship (*VA* 14).[51] The demons fight back not by in turn encroaching on already settled land, but by attacking Antony's body. That is, Antony's body becomes the site of demonic violence because his body is the land he holds, it is where he has his spiritual stake.

In short, Antony enters into a turf war with the demons, and he wins. His victory is followed by the large-scale colonisation of the desert by monks, who are said to have made the desert a city (*VA* 14). The progress of Antony's heroically outmanned programme of encroachment into the demons' territory is the narrative framework onto which Athanasius' description of asceticism as combat with demons is pinned. It is a far cry, aesthetically and emotionally, from the narrative of healing and solace

49 Brakke notes that while the first section of the discourse (*VA* 22–7) closely reflects teachings from the *Letters*, when Athanasius shifts to expressing his own views (*VA* 28–43), there is a strong emphasis on the ideal of courage as the primary virtue that Christians and ascetics in particular should cultivate in order to withstand demons.

50 The progress of Antony into the desert is as follows. After he removes himself to the edge of his village and begins to discipline himself, the devil appears in *VA* 5 and tries to break his resolve by provoking thoughts of how difficult the path before him will be and raising doubts about the appropriateness of his decision. Antony resists through prayers and ascetic exercises. This early phase, which most resembles the work emphasised in the *Letters*, is quickly passed over, and Antony is then attacked physically when he moves forward to the tombs (*VA* 8–10) and then to the abandoned fortress (*VA* 12) and finally at the point that he goes into the inner desert (*VA* 51).

51 This is very much in line with Athanasius' programme of creating a Christian *politeia* as explicated in Brakke, *Politics*, esp. 266.

in the letters examined above. In contrast with Antony-in-the-letter's narrative in which the resolution of the state of exile takes place on a spiritual plane, outside of time and space, the Antony of the *Life* is staking a claim in this world.

The Demon Enemy

Unlike the demons in the letters, the demons in the *Life* are located outside Antony and, after he has stabilised his passions in the early part of the narrative, can only tempt him in the same mode as a human adversary campaigning to sabotage the resolution of a rival. Antony is constantly being confronted by gangs of demons or by the devil himself. Most of the actions of the demons consist of physical assault and terrorism. The aggression of the demons towards Antony is fiercely violent, but without content. It occurs most intensely whenever Antony makes another colonising step farther into the desert, which is the demons' territory. This pattern shifts the quality of violence from the insidious mode observed in the demons of the *Letters* to a physical, external, and openly confrontational mode.

Much unlike the more delicate and abstract demons in the letters, Athanasian demons operate in hooligan mode. They engage in malevolent acts of sabotage and tricksterism and can be compared to 'boorish youths or robbers', brawling and rioting and mugging travelling monks (*VA* 23–5). They do not invade the psyche as much as they play violent pranks and engage in fistfights with ascetics (*VA* 40). Athanasius' demons can have all manner of threatening bodies, appearing as women, black boys, or dragons (all in *VA* 6), or Satan himself can appear as a satyr.[52] This makes the demons unmistakably external, so that evil is squarely located outside the self.

Physicalising demonic violence also makes the demons far more worthwhile from the perspective of storytelling. An Antonine demon, which is an invisible movement of the intellect, is unsuited to a popularising agenda. An Athanasian demon that knocks on Antony's door, displaying

[52] Brakke, *Demons*, 34–5, explains the odd physical form of this demon as intended to evoke the Egyptian god Min, who was supposed to rule over the eastern desert. By brushing him off with such confidence, Antony thus asserts himself as victor over the demons of the desert. Should the reader fail to understand the significance of the allusion, the author provides an explanation at *VA* 53 where the demon responds to Antony's statement as follows: 'But the beast with his demons fled so quickly that it fell and died. The death of the beast was the fall of the demons, for they were eager to do everything to drive him out of the desert and were unable to do so.'

a grotesque half man, half beast appearance and then finds itself compelled to flee in chagrin is narratologically viable in ways that an immaterial impulse will never be. A demon of this kind also provides the ascetic with opportunities to respond with an appealing degree of grit and resolve: Antony's response to the sight of Satan coming to look for him is to say, 'I am a servant of Christ. If thou art sent against me, behold I am here' (*VA* 53). These are words of courage and fortitude as evocative as the Spartan general's *molon labe* at the Battle of Thermopylae, a rhetorical rallying point both harking back to the *christianus sum* of martyr trial and asserting itself in Athanasius' world as the benchmark of Christian manliness to which Athanasius' ascetic subject should orient himself.[53]

Ascetic Subjectivity in Athanasius

In the *Life*, Antony's primary ascetic work is construed not as a regime necessary for mental integration and healing, but as training, as building up the necessary toughness to make him able to face up to demonic assault (*VA* 7).[54] Since evil is external, the task of resistance is not integration and unity but rather domination. The person is a warrior who must fight against a recalcitrant adversary external to himself. From early on in the *Life*, Athanasius portrays Antony as endlessly tough. After the devil loses the first few fights with Antony, a chronic state of siege arises, a standoff with a lot of desperate manoeuvring and sniper fire, as when guerrillas try to take back occupied territory (*VA* 7).

In this story, it is Antony who is the occupying force – he is the true aggressor and has achieved domination of the land. Unlike the ascetics of the *Letters* who remain inside themselves, Athanasius' character ventures,

[53] These famous words are quoted in Plutarch, *Apophthegmata Laconica* 51.11, F. C. Babbitt, *Plutarch, Moralia, Volume III*, LCL 245 (Cambridge, MA: Harvard University Press, 1931) 242–424. Brakke, *Demons*, 26, draws a parallel to the self-assertion of the martyrs, identifying Antony as a new martyr. The commemoration of the words of Leonides as an act of defiant courage in the face of adversity (although the Spartans are enormously outnumbered by the Persians, who tell them to lay down their weapons, Leonides replies 'come and take them') was still in circulation in this period. See for example S. Pressfield, *The Warrior Ethos* (New York, NY: Black Irish Books, 2011), 54. The need for such courageous speech acts and their remembrance, both in Pressfield's modern discourse on the ethic of the soldier and the artist and in Athanasius' ancient discourse cultivating a soldierly ethic for Christians, arises out of the conviction that the primary enemy is fear. Hence the most important virtue is courage.

[54] This is not to suggest that Antony is not required to integrate his mind at all. The requisite condition of the intellect is close to the Stoic ideal. Rather than being helplessly overwhelmed by external impressions (especially evil or frightening impressions), the ascetic is supposed to exercise himself in discipline until he can remain unmoved in the face of fear and can consider rationally how to respond to the impressions that come upon him; cf. Brakke, *Demons*, 39–40.

physically, into demonic territory and calls the demons out. Later in his progress, Antony is able to remain oblivious to demonic attacks and not only is not afraid of them, but does not perceive them at all. When Antony has pressed on to occupy an abandoned fort, he is harassed by demons but remains unmoved, while the shouting and screaming of the demons is only heard by less hardened onlookers (*VA* 13). The sort of subjectivity which is being construed through Athanasius' narrative demonological instruction is tough, aggressive, tenacious, and indomitable. It is the subjectivity of the soldier determined to win. The goal of engagement with the demons is not healing, but victory.[55]

Conclusion: From Sojourner to Soldier

Demonological instruction serves to teach people about the nature, location, scope, and mode of the violence to be expected from their adversary and thereby orients them to themselves as subjects within a particular field of conflict and danger. The readers and heirs of Antony's letters are ascetic specialists, already committed to a life of religious striving. Such a context can allow the person to direct her attention inwards against an insidious and manipulative enemy. A vulnerable, therapeutic, and self-reflective subjectivity is not only affordable but desirable where matters of ethical urgency are those inherited from Neoplatonism and Origenism, namely a return to self-knowledge and full integration of the intellect, ultimately achieving a state of union with the divine. For Antony, the problem that the ascetic must solve is the fundamental weakness and lostness of the human condition. The appropriate solution to that problem is healing and mending breaches to the integrity of the self.

Athanasius, on the other hand, faces quite different problems. His ideal for ascetics, and for all Christians willing to strive for religious excellence, is adapted to a context of high-stakes conflict in which the subject must withstand assault even and especially when he is at a grievous disadvantage. For Athanasius, the fundamental human problem is fear, not brokenness.[56] Antony, who is both an exemplar for the religiously ambitious and a folk hero, models tenacity and grit. By physicalising the demons and making the mode of resistance against demons analogous to military or

[55] Brakke, *Demons*, 23, on why the demons of the *VA* are unsubtle and externalised: 'Its demonology was the creation of a bishop anxious to prevent a possible failure of Christian nerve just when the divine Christ appeared to have triumphed over the pagan gods.'

[56] See Brakke, *Demons*, 36, for discussion of Athanasius' diagnosis of the fear of death as the basic human predicament.

athletic training, Athanasius promotes a subjectivity in which the person sees himself as a soldier and his enemies as external and unambiguously other. These features are highly serviceable for motivating solidarity, courage, and resistance to real-life opponents, whereas the insidious demons of the letters both lack folk appeal and are unhelpful in cultivating other-directed rather than self-directed acts of resistance.

It is tempting to arrange these two ways of cultivating ascetic subjectivities through demonological instruction in a scheme of development, progression, or transition. On such a trajectory, Antony's monk would be a more refined and philosophical figure, whose mode of resistance to demonic attack is emotionally insightful and intellectually sophisticated. This sojourner-monk would then be seen as having been marginalised by the more adversarial ideology of Athanasius, who simplifies the monk's fight against evil, making it a matter involving far more brute force and aimed at vanquishing and dominating the demons. The new soldier-monk could be taken as superseding and replacing the sojourner-monk, whose introspective ways were less viable in the context of intense competition and controversy in the mid to late fourth century.

These two construals of the person in relation to demonic violence arise in the same region and only a few decades apart, so it would be cavalier indeed to differentiate them on a chronological trajectory. Apart from an aesthetic bias (which may well amount to a fallacy) towards interpreting differences in terms of narratives of organic development over time, there is no reason to assume that Antony's way of cultivating the self died out and was replaced by that promoted by Athanasius. Instead, the respective subjectivities cultivated in these texts should be differentiated according to their location in contexts with very different religious problems to be solved. At the same time that the *Life of Antony* was being written and circulated, followers of Antony were also circulating his letters and carrying on his teachings around Pispir, Arsinoë, and in the monastic settlements of Nitria and Sketis. In addition to that set of religious concerns, a Christian empire was beginning to bring with it new challenges. These included the need to win when faced with conflicts and controversies carried out publicly and at an imperial level. In addition, there was the need to provide everyone, including ordinary people, a way to identify themselves as legitimate and valuable practitioners of one right religion. That added set of religious problems to solve, and Athanasius' own struggle with those challenges, is what drives the promotion of an adversarial subjectivity. Thus, instead of looking for trajectories of development driven by supersession or organic development, it is more accurate to interpret different uses of demonological instruction as a tool for cultivating subjectivities in terms of diversity. Within the space of twenty or thirty years, in the same region and even within the focused context of asceticism attached to the figure of Antony, Christians were required to respond to different kinds of violence by becoming different kinds of people.

CHAPTER 12

Coercing the Catechists Augustine's *De Catechizandis Rudibus*

Melissa Markauskas

The term 'coercive conversion' is used to describe a religious authority forcing a shift in the religious allegiance of an individual or community. With certain Christian bishops allying themselves with the repressive violence of state power to pressure the conversions of non-Christians and 'heretical' Christians alike, North African Christianity has been seen as a significant case study for the phenomenon. This essay will re-evaluate the concept of 'coercive conversion' at the turn of the fifth century in Roman North Africa, focusing on the seldom-considered experience of catechist-deacons in this environment.

The writings of Augustine of Hippo are the key source for these occurrences, because Augustine's justification for 'coercive conversions' has been seen as precedent for later uses of judicial violence against those deemed religiously deviant. Little attention has been paid, however, to the organisational dynamics involved in cultivating a class of men who could exercise this coercion on the ground. Curiously enough, catechetical staff seem to have resisted the transition to a more coercive vision of confessional affiliation at least as actively as did those whom they instructed. The coercion of catechists, we will suggest, offers an illuminating angle from which to view the link between violence and religious identity in late Roman North Africa.

Augustine's apparent complicity in 'coercive conversions' has sat uncomfortably with scholars. In the 1960s, Peter Brown investigated Augustine's attitude towards coercive conversions.[1] Contrasting Augustine's early *De catechizandis rudibus*[2] with his later involvement in the forced

[1] P. Brown, 'St Augustine's Attitude to Religious Coercion', *Journal of Roman Studies*, 54 (1964), 107–16; P. Brown, *Augustine of Hippo: A Biography*, revised edition (London: Faber, 2000; originally published 1967), 236–40.

[2] Augustine, *De catechizandis rudibus*, J. B. Bauer (ed.) CCSL 46 (Turnhout: Brepols, 1969), 115–78, English translation by J. P. Christopher, *The First Catechetical Instruction* (London: Longman, 1952).

assimilation of Donatists to Augustine's Caecilianist position,[3] Brown argued that Augustine made increasing use of Caecilianism's imperial support as his optimism in less forceful methods waned.[4] However, the subsequent discovery of new Augustinian material has caused Brown and others to re-evaluate the authority available to Augustine, and hence, Augustine's ability to effect religious change in a coercive way.[5]

In 2005, James J. O'Donnell argued that it was the Donatists not Augustine's faction that enjoyed a demographic majority in North Africa at the start of Augustine's episcopate. Building on this, O'Donnell further argued that Augustine's alignment with a faction that was statistically fewer in North Africa would have had more impact on the question of his authority than the Caecilianist faction's affiliation with influential bishops overseas,[6] and thus, that Augustine's evocations of authority early in his episcopate should be recognised as claims to authority only.[7]

Recent studies of the conflict between the Caecilianist and Donatist factions have emphasised that when it came to 'coercive conversions' it was the religious identity of clergy that was primarily at stake.[8] It is true that the legal sanctions towards the Donatist church in the early decades of the 400s called for entire communities to renounce their affiliation with clergy seen to be 'Donatist'. However, in practice, most efforts focused on requiring previously Donatist-identified bishops and other clergy to switch their allegiance to the position ascribed by leading Caecilianist bishops including Augustine himself. This, too, suggests that it would be fruitful to

[3] Augustine did not describe his own position as 'Caecilianist' any more than Donatist bishops self-identified as 'Donatist'. Instead, both factions claimed universal identities like 'Catholic' and 'Christian.' I prefer 'Caecilianist' to 'Catholic' to describe Augustine's position, following B. D. Shaw, 'African Christianity: Disputes, Definitions, and "Donatists"', in M. R. Greenshields and T. Robinson (eds.), *Orthodoxy and Heresy in Religious Movements: Discipline and Dissent* (Lampeter: Edwin Mellen Press, 1992), 5–34. The so-called Donatist schism dates from a conflicted episcopal election in the early fourth century, with the North African Church dividing in support of two candidates, Donatus and Caecilian. In the same way that 'Donatist' invokes a faction who traced their episcopal lineage back to Donatus, Shaw's term invokes Augustine's affiliation with the party of Caecilian.

[4] Brown, *Augustine*, 314. [5] Brown, *Augustine*, 445–62.

[6] J. J. O'Donnell, *Augustine, Sinner and Saint: A New Biography* (New York, NY: Ecco, 2005), 209–19.

[7] O'Donnell, *Augustine*, 99. Although surveying many of Augustine's writings, O'Donnell does not explicitly mention *De Catechizandis Rudibus* in his analysis of the interplay between the rival episcopal factions and their congregations.

[8] On the legal developments, see E. Hermanowicz, *Possidius of Calama: A Study of the North African Episcopate in the Age of Augustine* (Oxford: Oxford University Press, 2008). On the violent enforcement of legal rulings and the violence such enforcement provoked in turn, see B. D. Shaw, *Sacred Violence: African Christians and Sectarian Hatred in the Age of Augustine* (Cambridge: Cambridge University Press, 2011).

reassess the concept of 'coercive conversions' in light of how Augustine sought to encourage lower Caecilianist clergy to promote the agendas of their superiors in seeking control of the North African religious landscape.

Written by Augustine at the request of Deogratias, a deacon of the Church at Carthage,[9] *De catechizandis rudibus* briefly describes how to offer a first introduction to Christianity. In addition to the focus on coercive conversions mentioned above, scholarly interest in this text has centred on Augustine's apparent interest in social divisions,[10] catechesis' role in the socialisation of contemporary converts to Christian norms,[11] and theoretical approaches to conversion, communication, and/or pedagogy.[12] Overall, these studies have focused on what this text can tell us about the relationship of bishop to prospective converts and what instruction a doctor of the Catholic Church like Augustine might offer to such people.

However, as noted above, Augustine did not address potential converts, but the deacons who would convert them. It is this unexplored relationship between bishop and subordinate clergy in this text that will be the topic of this chapter.[13] Rather than any potential violence experienced by converts in the course of their education as new Christians or the threats of imperial violence made use of by bishops, it is the violence that the

[9] Usually understood as a written request, but Augustine also notes discussing the topic with Deogratias in person. Augustine, *De catechizandis rudibus* 10.

[10] F. Edward Cranz, 'The Development of Augustine's Ideas on Society before the Donatist Controversy', *Harvard Theological Review*, 47 (1954), 308. However, see B. Stock, *Augustine the Reader: Meditation, Self-Knowledge, and the Ethics of Interpretation* (London: Belknap Press, 1996), 185, who rightly points out that Augustine distinguishes the composition of catechismal audiences, not society as a whole.

[11] F. Van der Meer, *Augustine the Bishop: The Life and Work of a Father of the Church*, B. Battershaw and G. R. Lamb (trans.) (London: Sheed and Ward, 1961), 453–67; W. Harmless, *Augustine and the Catechumenate* (Collegeville, MI: Liturgical Press, 1995); K. Cooper, 'Ventriloquism and the Miraculous: Conversion, Preaching, and the Martyr Exemplum in Late Antiquity', in K. Cooper and J. Gregory (eds.), *Signs, Wonders, Miracles: Representations of Divine Power in the Life of the Church*, Studies in Church History 41 (Woodbridge: Boydell & Brewer, 2005), 22–45.

[12] E.g. Stock, *Reader*; F. H. Russell, 'Augustine: Conversion by the Book', in James Muldoon (ed.), *Varieties of Religious Conversion in the Middle Ages* (Gainesville, FL: University Press of Florida, 1997), 13–30; E. Ferguson, 'Catechesis and Initiation', in A. Kreider (ed.), *The Origins of Christendom in the West* (Edinburgh: T & T Clark, 2001), 229–68. Modern pedagogical approaches developed from Augustine's works typically focus on his longer *De doctrina Christiana*, but for an approach centred on *De Catechizandis rudibus*, see R. Canning, 'Teaching and Learning: An Augustinian Perspective', *Australian E-journal of Theology*, 3 (2004), 1–10.

[13] Though catechismal manuals are rare, we have a far greater number of texts explicitly focusing on clerical discipline and organization. In this sense, *De catechizandis rudibus* could be compared with Ambrose's *De officiis ministrorum* or Pope Gregory I's *Regula pastoralis*. Augustine's efforts to reshape the experience of the catechist in this text parallels the process that Blossom Stefaniw identifies elsewhere in this volume in which Anthony and Athanasius seek to reshape the ascetic experience of their readers.

middlemen in this teaching process, the catechists as lower clergy, were threatened with that concerns us here.

In her critique of scholarship on this text, Catherine Chin noted that Augustine's stated reasons for writing are seldom examined: that 'early Christian catechesis, at least in Carthage, was boring'.[14] However, by focusing on the rhetorical function of this 'boredom', Chin does not consider the historical significance of the fact that catechesis might have actually been boring, or rather unpleasant and depressing, for Caecilianist catechists like Deogratias.

I propose to link the catechismal difficulties Augustine presents in *De catechizandis rudibus* with the climate of coercive conversion noted by Brown and O'Donnell among others. Foregrounding the treatise's purpose as teaching someone who will themselves teach others, the text complicates the traditional picture of Church and State acting against a grudging populace.[15] By appreciating the layering of instruction, from bishop to deacon, and from deacon to catechizand, we can see catechists themselves as recipients rather than agents of coercion. Concurring with O'Donnell's revision of Augustine's early authority, I would stress that *De catechizandis rudibus* shows how Caecilianist clergy in Donatist-majority North Africa found catechising to be difficult and depressing work. I will begin by sketching the religious tensions in North Africa and Augustine's position within them around the time of the text's composition,[16] and then discuss the difficulties the text expects catechists to find and the solutions Augustine offers to these problems. Finally, I will consider how Augustine's treatment of catechismal difficulties illuminates the bigger picture of Caecilianist bishops seeking to gain numbers, to better reflect and substantiate their claim to authority over the North African Church.

Becoming a Christian in Augustine's North Africa

Conversion and catechesis were intensely topical in Augustine's North Africa. The fourth century had seen the relationship between Church and

[14] C. Chin, 'Telling Boring Stories: Time, Narrative and Pedagogy in *De catechizandis rudibus*', *Augustinian Studies*, 37 (2006), 43.

[15] E.g., see Brown, 'Augustine's Attitude'.

[16] Usually dated to 399/400, L. J. van Der Lof, 'The Date of the *De catechizandis rudibus*', *Vigiliae Christianae*, 16 (1962), 198–204. However, see also P.-M. Hombert, *Nouvelles recherches de chronologie augustinienne* (Paris: Institut d'Études Augustiniennes, 2000), 41–4, who dates it to 403. For this paper, either date is acceptable, as religious tensions continued to escalate between these dates. See below for more on this topic.

State dramatically reoriented. Previously illegal and derided, Christianity became licit with Constantine's 313 Edict of Toleration and gained increasing Imperial patronage to end the century as the Empire's most socially acceptable religion. However, this change challenged the Church's self-identity, having previously distinguished herself in opposition to Caesar. In North Africa, the bishops split unevenly between the majority who maintained traditional resistance to Imperial interference with their religion ('Donatists'),[17] and those, including Augustine, who took their religious heading from overseas ('Caecilianists'). Non-Christian traditional beliefs and practices, philosophical schools, and Manichaeism were also present, and it may be understood that the majority of those identifying as Christian may not have appreciated the significance of the Caecilianist–Donatist binary as sharply as their bishops.

The effects of the increasing size of the overall Christian population further complicated this conflict, where both sides sought to claim the identity of the one, true Church. Now legal, Christianity attracted comparatively greater numbers of converts who were comparatively less fervent, not to mention that becoming a Christian no longer automatically meant orienting to particularly 'Christian' social norms, as wider society had in effect become 'Christian'.[18] Larger communities of Christians had led to reduced opportunities for most to participate in regular worship. The minimum length of catechumenate apprenticeships was shortened, and yet the time an average Christian might spend as a catechumen lengthened.[19] Indeed, Eric Rebillard has recently reminded us how little it might mean for someone to call himself or herself a catechumen.[20] Comparing the floor space of churches with the population of their towns, Ramsey MacMullen has noted that only a minority would be able to fit.[21] The increasing size of congregations does not appear to have been met by increasing numbers of preaching clergy, though there were some

[17] M. A. Tilley, 'Sustaining Donatist Self-Identity: From the Church of the Martyrs to the Collecta of the Desert', *Journal of Early Christian Studies*, 5 (1997), 21–35. On the schism's earlier history, W. H. C. Frend, *The Donatist Church: A Movement of Protest in Roman North Africa* (Oxford: Clarendon Press, 1952), is classic.

[18] On the growth rate of the early Christian Church, see R. Stark, *The Rise of Christianity: A Sociologist Reconsidered History* (Princeton, NJ: Princeton University Press, 1996).

[19] A. Kreider, 'Changing Patterns of Conversion in the West', in A. Kreider (ed.), *The Origins of Christendom in the West* (Edinburgh: T&T Clark, 2001), 3–46.

[20] E. Rebillard, 'Religious Sociology: Being Christian', in M. Vessey (ed.), *A Companion to Augustine* (Malden, MA: Wiley-Blackwell, 2012), 40–54.

[21] R. MacMullen, 'The Preacher's Audience (AD 350-400)', *Journal of Theological Studies*, n.s., 40 (1989), 503–11.

relaxations of customary restrictions on the right to preach.[22] For Augustine's Caecilianists, a large part of the struggle to convince this growing body of Christians to 'reform' was finding ways to communicate their agenda, to persuade converts of the necessity of identifying not only as 'Christians' but as identifying the Caecilianist faction specifically as the 'Catholic', universal option.

At the turn of the fifth century, Caecilianist–Donatist tensions were the most bitter. It was a conflict fought in the cities and towns, on the large estates, and in the Roman courts. Traditional accounts emphasise the violence of the Donatist faction, particularly a sub-group labelled the 'circumcellions', but it has been increasingly acknowledged this image is a product of few sources surviving independent of Augustine's substantial corpus and that the Caecilianist faction was also active in violent attempts to dominate the religious landscape of North Africa.[23] Brent D. Shaw's recent study has also highlighted that such violence though frequently bloody was neither random nor chaotic, but instead appears to have been strategically focused upon clergy who were seen to be directly involved in the conflict, either because they had personally switched from one faction to the other or because they were seen to be encouraging such other clerics to switch in this way.[24] This interfactional violence is an important backdrop to the experience of Caecilianist catechists in this period. Competition for converts was deadly serious, but its violence played out most often in conflict between the ranks of the clergy rather than between the clergy and the laity.

De catechizandis rudibus is a work of Augustine's early episcopate, and thus provides us with a window onto a less secure, less authoritative Augustine who nonetheless sought to advocate specifically Caecilianist Christianity. Having already completed several written works, he had recently gained significant celebrity with his *Confessions* (397–401), dated shortly before or concurrent with *De catechizandis rudibus*. The *Confessions* would become Augustine's first bestseller, but it was a lengthy literary text when the majority of those Augustine might seek to influence could not or did not read. However, Augustine was also capable of using an oral platform to publicise the themes found in his formal literary works to a

[22] Augustine was permitted to preach while a priest, though this was traditionally the preserve of bishops. Possidius, *Vita Augustini* 5, A. A. R. Bastiaensen (ed.), *Vita dei santi* III (Milan: Fondazione Lorenzo Valla, 1975), 130–240.

[23] O'Donnell, *Augustine*, 215–21. See also Shaw, *Sacred Violence*, esp. 348–408 and 698–718.

[24] Shaw, *Sacred Violence*, esp. 694–708.

relatively broader audience.[25] In his earlier civil career, Augustine had been a rhetor, a professional speaker, and a teacher of rhetoric. As a bishop, Augustine was expected to preach regularly to his community. This oral–textual relationship is useful when evaluating the reception of Augustine's writings during his own lifetime. As a text, *De catechizandis rudibus* would have an influential future in the Medieval West,[26] but its immediate reception would come via oral dissemination.[27] Furthermore, unlike the *Confessions*, *De catechizandis rudibus* speaks directly to the tense business of oral preaching, and, crucially, that of teaching others how to preach.

Augustine preached for participation in a particular 'Christianity,' one that did not have the weight of numbers to recommend it. Though increasingly unafraid to address the Donatists directly, particularly whenever one of their clergy had already embarrassed or offended, Augustine also employed the more subtle rhetoric of subsuming their beliefs and practices within 'paganism'. O'Donnell has argued that Augustine frequently covertly attacks Donatism under the label of 'paganism', noting that several practices Augustine criticises as explicitly pagan, for example, graveside vigils and festivities, were accepted in the Donatist tradition.[28] 'Paganising' Donatist practices in this way allowed Augustine more freedom to criticise, but also served to obscure how relatively few the Caecilianists were.[29] By recasting the majority of his opponents as pagan or pagan-influenced, Augustine moved them to the fringes of the Church and set his own faction at the centre.

The focus on catechesis in *De catechizandis rudibus* serves a similar function. Heretics are rarely mentioned in the text, and the Donatist faction is never named. And yet *De catechizandis rudibus* is deeply

[25] Brown, *Augustine*, 454–5, has tentatively connected Augustine's 397 sermons in Carthage and the writing of the *Confessions*. However, Augustine preached in Latin, not Punic or Libyc, excluding those segments of the population as potential listeners. P. Brown, 'Christianity and Local Culture in Late Roman Africa', *Journal of Roman Studies*, 58 (1968), 85–95. See above for MacMullen's comments on the limits of a preacher's audience.

[26] It is most notably echoed in Martin of Braga's *De correctione rusticorum*, through which Augustine's treatise would become the 'grandfather' text for Frankish exhortations on similar themes. J.-P. Belche, 'Die Bekehrung zum Christentum nach Augustins Büchlein *De catechizandis rudibus*', *Augustiniana*, 29 (1979), 247–79; Y. Hen, 'Martin of Braga's *De correctione rusticorum* and Its Uses in Frankish Gaul', in E. Cohen and M. de Jong (eds.), *Medieval Transformations: Texts, Power and Gifts in Context* (Leiden: Brill, 2001), 35–50.

[27] Although Augustine provided example sermons in *De catechizandis rudibus*, he hoped to inspire extempore preaching from Deogratias rather than a scripted performance. See below for more on this topic.

[28] O'Donnell, *Augustine*, 251–2.

[29] However, when discussing heretics, Augustine suggests, tellingly, at *De catechizandis rudibus*, 14, that the catechist warn the enquirer 'not to be stirred by their numbers'.

concerned with a specific subtype of preaching activity, catechesis, which was intended to realign individuals to one specific religious option and to valorise the importance of such a change. As in Augustine's general preaching, *De catechizandis rudibus* is concerned not merely with encouraging listeners away from 'paganism' to Christianity, but encouraging them to care deeply about which particular kind of Christianity they signed up to.

How to Manage Customer Expectations

Unpicking Augustine's explicit motives for writing *De catechizandis rudibus* illuminates the depressing experience of Caecilianist catechists in Roman North Africa. Despite a reputation for 'great ability in catechising',[30] Deogratias, the de facto catechiser of Carthage's Caecilianist church had become disaffected with his teaching and had requested some advice on the topic from Augustine. Deogratias' explicit request appears to have been two questions of rhetoric: where to begin and end the *narratio* of salvation history and whether to conclude with an *exhortatio* or a simple listing of the Decalogue.[31] However, Augustine also recalls hearing Deogratias often complain that:

> Because [he] talked for too long and with too little enthusiasm, it has befallen [him] to become commonplace and wearisome even to [himself], not to mention him to whom [Deogratias was] trying to instruct by [his] discourse, and the others who were present as listeners.[32]

According to Augustine, this is the more pressing problem.

> It is no hard task to give directions in regard to those truths which are instilled as articles of faith ... but our chief concern is what means we should adopt to ensure the catechiser enjoys his work; for the more he is able to do so, the more agreeable he will prove.[33]

Further on, Augustine reiterates that he sees Deogratias' main problem coming 'not from lack of things to say ... nor yet from a lack of words themselves, but from weariness of mind'.[34] Chin has suggested that this 'weariness of mind' be characterised as emotionally neutral boredom, but in the tense North African marketplace of competing Christianities, I would suggest that the grief that comes from failing to enthuse an

[30] Augustine, *De catechizandis rudibus*, 1.
[31] Augustine, *De catechizandis rudibus*, 1.
[32] Augustine, *De catechizandis rudibus*, 1.
[33] Augustine, *De catechizandis rudibus*, 2.
[34] Augustine, *De catechizandis rudibus*, 10.

enquirer about Caecilianist Christianity is a more plausible explanation. 'If we do not succeed in this,' Augustine empathises, 'we are sore grieved and are crippled and broken in the course of the instruction as though we were expending out labour fruitlessly.'[35] According to Augustine, Deogratias did not need his questions of rhetoric answered so much as he needed cheering up, though Augustine resolved to do both.[36] Consequently, Augustine gives advice about the performance of the salvation narrative[37] and the *exhortatio*,[38] but concludes with a discussion of the six main causes of dejection amongst catechists.[39] Overall, he emphasises that catechists should be cheerful, despite the ways catechesis challenged them.

De catechizandis rudibus suggests catechists faced two kinds of difficulty: those provoked by problematic enquirers, and those caused by their own negative attitude. Augustine's account of the varied motives that brought people to Christianity is perhaps the most frequently quoted passage of *De catechizandis rudibus*. Fear of God is presented as the ideal motivation,[40] but the catechist might also receive someone who comes 'in the hope of deriving some benefit from men whom he thinks he could not otherwise please, or to escape some injury at the hands of men whose displeasure or enmity he dreads'.[41] The 'injury' that a convert may seek to avoid suggests a form of coerced conversion involving violence, or at least a threat of violence, but is worth noting that Augustine positioned this threat outside of the conversation he creates with Deogratias in this text. He neither advocates nor discourages such potential violence: it is 'at the hand of men' other than the clergy. At this early point in Augustine's episcopate, violence can play a coercive role in conversion, but such violence does not appear to have been available to the catechists yet.

Augustine's discussion of the motives of converts for seeking catechesis focuses on the psychological impact that a variety of motives might have on the catechist. Although the individual will surely lie to conceal motives they know to be incorrect, they may also openly profess the wrong motivation.[42] In the first case, Augustine urges the catechist not to be dejected when recognising the lie, nor should they reveal that they are even

35 Augustine, *De catechizandis rudibus*, 10. 36 Augustine, *De catechizandis rudibus*, 2.

37 Augustine, *De catechizandis rudibus*, 3–6 and 8–9. 38 Augustine, *De catechizandis rudibus*, 7.

39 Augustine, *De catechizandis rudibus*, 10–14.

40 Augustine also implies that fear of God is what should ultimately inspire catechists in their work. See the discussion of Augustine, *De catechizandis rudibus*, 14, below. For more on fear as a motivational tool for preachers and teachers, see the chapters by Blake Leyerle and Jamie Wood elsewhere in this volume.

41 Augustine, *De catechizandis rudibus*, 5. 42 Augustine, *De catechizandis rudibus*, 5.

aware of it; instead, they should take the opportunity to build on the pretence and hope for its reality. In the latter case, the catechist should briefly, but impressively, communicate what the right motivation is, hopefully without causing the convert to simply conceal their improper motives in future. Finally, even if the enquirer has felt the fear of God, they may have done so in a dream, and have to be drawn from that perilous path of inspiration to the stability of Scripture.[43] After raising these negative possibilities, it is striking to note that Augustine chooses for his model sermon a man who, on being asked why he would like to become a Christian, answers exactly as he should.[44] In a teaching text aiming to encourage a positive outlook towards catechesis, it makes sense for Augustine to focus in the end on the most positive option.

The well- or semi-educated enquirer posed other problems for the catechist. Those who had studied the liberal arts were likely to have investigated Christianity before deciding to become a catechumen. Augustine stresses that they should not be given the exact same sermon as the uneducated, but that the catechist should pass over all points lightly, lest the educated enquirer feel condescended to, going into greater depth where necessary.[45] Implicit in this advice is the idea that enquirers with some education may talk back to their catechists, question, or dispute the instruction that was given to them based on information they had already accessed elsewhere.

Their libraries should be investigated, Augustine urges. The catechist must then sift 'Catholic' from 'heretical' writers known to the enquirer, and even among those writers who had died 'Catholic', whether the individual books were 'good' or 'bad', and whether the enquirer had understood the 'good' books correctly.[46] This process might allow the catechist to take back their authority as a teacher, as the arbitrator of Christian knowledge. This in turn implies that a catechist's authority had to be negotiated rather than being taken for granted.

Another point implicit in Augustine's advice about the well-educated is that, as book owners, they were likely to be wealthy and thus powerful and used to getting their own way. Augustine suggests that educated enquirers were also to be given more privacy than the unlearned, to be treated 'in a discreet conference'. This not only minimised the potential for public embarrassment of the catechist, but also accorded the wealthy enquirer

[43] Augustine, *De catechizandis rudibus*, 6.
[44] Augustine, *De catechizandis rudibus*, 16.
[45] Augustine, *De catechizandis rudibus*, 8.
[46] Augustine, *De catechizandis rudibus*, 8.

certain privileges of rank.[47] Educating those of greater social and/or economic status thus seems to have been an uncomfortable proposition for catechists.

The semi-educated 'who come from the ordinary schools of grammar and rhetoric', Augustine notes, are even more likely to humiliate the catechist; he recommends that the catechist should focus on teaching them the Christian virtue of humility.[48] They should also be warned that God receives the feeling rather than the form of the prayer, so that 'they will not smile contemptuously if they happen to observe that some ministers of the church either fall into barbarisms or solecisms ... or do not understand and badly punctuate words which they are pronouncing'.[49] Though Augustine concludes that even these argumentative, scornful enquirers would respond favourably to a catechist's guidance, it is easy to see why Deogratias would find them dejecting.

How to Manage Employee Dissatisfaction

Following his discussion of the problems posed by different classes of enquirers, Augustine lists six possible causes that inhibit catechists: pessimism about adequately communicating any thought in language, or uncertainty concerning the effectiveness of ability of one's own extempore speaking; pessimism about the productivity of addressing those whose religious understanding is far below the catechist's, or to an (apparently) apathetic audience; distress at being interrupted during other work, or when the catechist's mind is troubled by something else.[50]

These causes are also suggestive of the particular difficulties faced by Caecilianist catechists. Advocating a minority position made it essential for catechists to be able to communicate the importance of choosing their position over another. The implication of Augustine's list of six causes for dejection among catechists is that enquirers rarely cared as much about such nuances as their catechists (or perhaps, only their bishops). The full breadth of Augustine's understanding of language and communication has been treated capably elsewhere,[51] but Augustine's solution to this particular problem of communication in *De catechizandis rudibus* is worth noting. Though he empathises with the catechist's desire to 'make' the enquirer comprehend Christian salvation, he reminds this reader that the

[47] Augustine, *De catechizandis rudibus*, 8.
[48] Augustine, *De catechizandis rudibus*, 9.
[49] Augustine, *De catechizandis rudibus*, 9.
[50] Augustine, *De catechizandis rudibus*, 10.
[51] See Stock, *Reader*.

true agent of that change is grace, and indeed, that it may not be for the catechist to know at the time of instruction whether grace has worked or not.[52] Thus, he argues, it is essential to catechise all, regardless of the apparent reception or result. Though Deogratias is noted as someone with a successful reputation at catechesis, the potential difficulties discussed by Augustine all suggest that what Caecilianist bishops needed to manage in their catechist-deacons was the demotivating effect of a lack of success. Augustine's solution was to reposition the 'goal' of catechesis, the measure of success, from 'converting' someone to the opportunity that it created for aiding the operation of divine grace.

Augustine also deals with the problems associated with extempore preaching. Augustine's insistence that by 'touching the bare rules for developing your discourse in catechising . . . I have already . . . sufficiently made good my promise' suggests that Deogratias may have asked for example sermons that Augustine would rather not offer.[53] The two sample sermons that he does offer follow his discussion of theory and are preceded with the warning that 'you would learn this better by watching us and listening to us when actually engaged in the work itself than by reading what we dictate'.[54] Rather than dispense with extempore preaching, Augustine instead offers suggestions about how to ameliorate the difficulties catechists experience with this activity.

Augustine begins with the problem of argumentative listeners. Defending the use of one's own words, Augustine allows that errors are possible, but unlikely to be noticed by any but the catechist themselves; if some error is noticed, the catechist should take this correction humbly. One possibility for such discipline would be for a catechist to be corrected by his own bishop or a fellow cleric who might oversee the session. This is less problematic than the alternative Augustine focuses on: those 'who, blinded by insane jealousy, rejoice that we have erred'.[55] This source of conflict between enquirer and catechist, and the humiliation of the catechist's position as an authority on 'correct' Christian knowledge, is a more significant issue. This is more than simply the contempt of the grammarians for plain spoken Latin mentioned two chapters earlier in the text.

Augustine also notes the circumstance of the catechist saying something grammatically correct, but 'which from its very novelty is harsh because it

[52] Augustine, *De catechizandis rudibus*, 2. [53] Augustine, *De catechizandis rudibus*, 10.

[54] Augustine, *De catechizandis rudibus*, 15. This view challenges Augustine's usual emphasis on teaching by books, although a more appropriate distinction might be between instructing teachers and pedagogy in more general contexts; see Russell, 'Conversion'.

[55] Augustine, *De catechizandis rudibus*, 11.

is contrary to the belief and practice of a long-standing error, offends and disturbs the listener'.[56] This could just as easily refer to long-standing non-Christian traditions as it could to Donatist Christianity, which was of greater longevity in North Africa than Augustine's own Caecilianist Christianity. In either case, the enquirer feels confident in their own religious knowledge, gained from other sources, to challenge the catechist. Augustine's discussion of this problem highlights who in this situation had easier recourse to force to compel their will: vulnerable to discipline from both their bishops and their enquirers, it was certainly not the catechists themselves.

Augustine's solution to such difficulties also highlights the vulnerable position of catechists. He urges that correction should be applied if the enquirer is receptive, but if they are not, Augustine reminds that it is for grace, not the catechist, to cure the listener.[57]

Again, it is worth noting that Caecilianist catechists do not appear to have had access to any kind of force to compel correction no matter how much they thought it was merited. Although Augustine himself courted religious controversies frequently, he explicitly recommends that catechists avoid such practice. In light of the catechist's concerns about being mocked or scorned for their skill of expression, it seems likely that the average Caecilianist catechist may not have been up to such debate.

Augustine concludes on the happier note that confidence in one's own words will cheer a catechist more than reliance on another's text.[58] Though extempore preaching resulted in some difficulties, it could be hoped that practice and improvement in their ability to deliver such instruction would ultimately uplift them. It would also prepare them better for the eventuality that not all controversy could be avoided, that catechists themselves might not be the only ones deciding what was discussed during catechesis.

Augustine then turns to the problem of apathetic listeners or catechists. He suggests that sympathy for one's audience should move a catechist to be pleased to find their audience untaught on subjects that the catechist takes for granted, as there is the opportunity to take pleasure in showing not only familiar things, but also divine ones to someone for whom they are new.[59] There is a possible connection to Augustine's comments on educated converts, who disdain to be instructed in matters that they have

[56] Augustine, *De catechizandis rudibus*, 11.

[57] Augustine also urges catechists to avoid discussing religious controversies during catechesis, Augustine, *De catechizandis rudibus*, 6 and 7.

[58] Augustine, *De catechizandis rudibus*, 11.

[59] Augustine, *De catechizandis rudibus*, 12.

already learnt, and aristocrats coerced into the clergy with no particular enthusiasm for pastoral duty.

The audience's apathy also creates an opportunity for the catechist, as the techniques for relieving its varied causes suggest ways to fruitfully tailor the catechesis. Physical tiredness is presented as the most significant constraint, as it may also cause the enquirer to leave before instruction is complete.[60] Augustine recommends offering seating or an abbreviated conclusion to the sermon,[61] something he had already recommended as standard operating practice when catechising the educated. However, the frequent indications throughout the treatise of the necessary brevity of catechesis, most notably the fact that the shorter of Augustine's example sermons would take only thirty minutes,[62] suggest that even the attentive catechist might have found it difficult to sustain their enquirer's interest. The overall impression is that the enquirer's level of interest could not be taken for granted, but that the catechist must strive to enhance this as much as possible.

Catechesis was not the office of an individual cleric, and a catechist might be forced to perform it at times that were not of his choosing. Augustine notes that clergy may be 'forced, either by the command of one we are unwilling to offend or by the unavoidable importunity of some persons, to catechise someone'.[63] Augustine does not elaborate whether this command comes from the bishop or one of the lay patrons that Augustine urged to guide their clients to salvation.[64] The effect on the catechist would be the same. Indeed, a catechist could be subject to multiple, competing demands. Augustine does not raise the possibility of a catechist asked to teach one thing by a wealthy patron, who might care less about the nuances of different Christian positions, but another by his bishop. Many writers have suggested that Deogratias was performing catechesis so frequently because the Bishop of Carthage, Aurelius, had a busy schedule, without considering what other demands there might have been on Deogratias' time.[65]

Augustine's answer to these unpleasant interruptions follows what should now appear as a common theme: the catechist should trust in God, choosing to apply himself to the work God has placed before him

60 Augustine, *De catechizandis rudibus*, 13. 61 Augustine, *De catechizandis rudibus*, 13.
62 Augustine, *De catechizandis rudibus*, 26–7. For the time estimate, see van der Meer, *Bishop*, 466.
63 Augustine, *De catechizandis rudibus*, 10.
64 R. MacMullen, *Christianizing the Roman Empire (AD 100–400)* (London: Yale University Press, 1984), 65.
65 E.g., van der Meer, *Bishop*, 453.

rather than pining after his own choice.[66] If the catechist has been interrupted not in the midst of work but by mental anguish, he should also thank God for offering up the cheering sight of someone wanting to become Christian. Aware of this statement's idealism, Augustine allows that the catechist is most likely to be upset because of 'another's defection', or because 'the proselyte may become a child of hell – as we see many such, from whom those very scandals that distress us arise',[67] but this should spur instead of slow down the catechist. If it is a personal sin that distresses the catechist, he should take heart that by catechising he is helping another to avoid sin.[68] Augustine's discussion is layered with sympathy and positive encouragement, but there was no acceptable excuse not to catechise. Though grace is the agency of salvation, and the catechist should not pin their hopes on visible results, any occasion on which the catechist neglects to catechise will be counted against them at the final reckoning. This threatens the catechist with violence that they can avoid, but only by doing as Augustine recommends. How much better, then, Augustine concludes, to make oneself cheerful and just do it.[69]

Selling Christianity in a Buyer's Market

When it comes to the question of coercive conversions, *De catechizandis rudibus* has been interpreted as evidence for the Church and State coercively converting the laity in parallel, but certain passages of the text problematise this reading. The oft-quoted passage in chapter five that describes how enquirers are compelled to enter the church by the whims of authority[70] has a less well-known counterpart in chapter ten, where it is the catechists themselves who are being compelled to participate in catechism.[71] If we imagine the catechists as deacons like Deogratias instead of bishops like Augustine, we can better appreciate the disciplinary demands to which catechists were also subject from their superiors.

Furthermore, there is also much to suggest that the secular, social forces of coercion in the passage from chapter five did not directly parallel the agenda of Augustine and his Caecilianists. Both of his model sermons speak of the 'earthly kings' who once persecuted Christians now being

[66] Augustine, *De catechizandis rudibus*, 14. [67] Augustine, *De catechizandis rudibus*, 14.

[68] Augustine, *De catechizandis rudibus*, 14. This passage may seek to counteract certain concerns about clerical ritual purity that were associated with Donatism.

[69] Augustine, *De catechizandis rudibus*, 14. [70] Augustine, *De catechizandis rudibus*, 5.

[71] Augustine, *De catechizandis rudibus*, 10.

Christian themselves,[72] and also contrast heresy with the unity of the true Church.[73] However, if, as appears likely, Augustine's main impetus for writing appears to be catechists who are dejected by the variety of their success rates, this suggests that these ideas afforded minimal practical authority to Caecilianist catechists themselves. While the laity may feel compelled to become Christian for 'carnal' reasons, these seem to be driven by local social contact rather than legislation from the imperial centre. Augustine suggests making these arguments to enquirers, but he does not present them to the catechists directly as a reason to be cheerful about catechesis. Instead, the catechists must be coerced, persuaded to reconsider that the true wellspring of their enthusiasm should be their love of God, not their visible catechismal success in making 'good' converts. As with converts, catechists are compelled from two directions, in this case, the laity who demand to be instructed, and the bishops who demand that the catechists carry out instruction. The very discomfort of the 'hinge' position in which Augustine's catechists found themselves implies that these demands did not always coincide.

While Augustine presents his example catechismal narratives as ending with the enquirer joining the Church that day,[74] he appears to be more informed by the optimism that he urges than the likelihood of success. Augustine lists several apparently common reasons why enquirers chose not to join the Church. Some were 'stirred by [the Donatists'] numbers'; others saw nothing unique in the behaviour of those calling themselves Christian.[75] Augustine's urging for brevity in response to enquiries is also a sign of a 'buyer's market' for catechismal instruction.[76] Augustine can only encourage catechists like Deogratias to adapt their instruction to appeal to potential catechumens; they could not rely on a 'captive' audience. He urged the catechist to stress that Caecilianism represented the only true position, a risky proposition when the Donatists would probably have made the exact same point.

Though Donatist congregations would be forced to assimilate into Caecilianist communities after 411, *De catechizandis rudibus* belongs firmly to an earlier period. The lure of Donatism is one of the catechist's concerns, but what looms much larger is the apathy of both potential

[72] 'We too are now building up and planting you . . . and this is being done throughout the whole world, with the permission of Christian kings', Augustine, *De catechizandis rudibus*, 21; see also 27. These are the text's only references to imperial 'support' for the Caecilians.

[73] Augustine, *De catechizandis rudibus*, 24 and 27.

[74] Augustine, *De catechizandis rudibus*, 20 and 26.

[75] Augustine, *De catechizandis rudibus*, 14.

[76] Augustine, *De catechizandis rudibus*, 13.

converts and the Christian congregations they might have considered joining. Either group depressed the catechists, who were understandably dejected when their teaching either did not result in new Christians or when it produced Christians whose behaviour was not Christian 'enough' for their own standards, especially when these 'bad' Christians appeared to cost them new recruits. Those who enter the Church for some 'carnal' or this-worldly benefit are repeatedly mentioned in the example sermons, in the *narratio* in order to warn the listening enquirer away from such motives,[77] and as the main negative example of the *exhortatio*.[78] Social relationships appear to have compelled the laity to become Christian, but with far fewer numbers at the beginning of Augustine's episcopate and hence far fewer avenues of social pressure at their disposal, Caecilianist Christianity must have been a harder sell.

Conclusion

The desire of some to 'coerce' the conversions of others was certainly a significant element of the tensions surrounding religious allegiance in turn-of-the-fifth-century Roman North Africa. The fact that Christianity had become the most socially acceptable religion in the Roman Empire did not at all predict which form of Christianity, which practices and beliefs, this growing Church would profess in any particular location. If they were to gain ascendancy, passionate minorities needed to find ways to rouse and recruit the increasing numbers of apathetic individuals who entered the Church. *De catechizandis rudibus* can be seen as Augustine's answer to this challenge. My analysis of the text develops O'Donnell's argument that Augustine's authority was based on the manipulation of rhetorical training early in his career, at least in so far as he could not at this stage rely on social or legal pressure to recruit what he deemed sufficient numbers to his own faction. Instead, he chose to write a book about how to recruit better, and he chose address it to a catechist, rather than a potential convert. Writing a book about Christian instruction that drew on his high levels of rhetorical training was a concrete strategy by which Augustine could begin gradually to make his authority felt more strongly by a broader constituency: the catechists of Caecilianist Africa.

[77] Augustine, *De catechizandis rudibus*, 16, 17, 19, 20, 23, and 26.

[78] Augustine, *De catechizandis rudibus*, 27. On how apathetic members depress the enthusiasm of religious groups, see Stark, *Rise of Christianity*, 163–90.

Without recourse to anything like an imperially enforced monopoly on 'correct' Christianity, Augustine produced in *De catechizandis rudibus* what can be seen a company manual on customer relations, urging employee motivation as the way to achieve greater sales targets. Caecilianist Christianity was their product, a boutique religious option being sold in a local market with buyers who had no pre-existing appreciation for overseas trends or imperial endorsement. There do appear to have been social pressures coercing the laity into becoming Christian, which meant no lack of enquirers visiting catechists, but also no certainty of uptake and, perhaps even more importantly, no certainty that enquirers would wish to become specifically Caecilianist Christians. When seeking to improve the recruitment rate, Augustine focused his persuasive efforts on the catechists themselves. He argues that catechists must aim for a wilfully cheerful disposition, but also warns that refusing to catechise is a sin. Though he does not expend much detail describing the penalties of such sins, he makes it clear that they would be severe.

It is striking that Augustine's solutions boil down to encouraging optimism in the catechists on the one hand and threatening divine punishment for non-compliance on the other. It is clear from this that neither Augustine, nor Deogratias as catechist, had access to any earthly force to compel compliance from their would-be converts at this time. It is equally clear that one area in which a bishop like Augustine did potentially have power was towards lower-ranked clergy like Deogratias and that this power was centred on Augustine's known rhetorical ability. This rhetorical ability brought Deogratias' request to Augustine and it is through his ability that Augustine seeks to further influence Deogratias and other catechists. Although we are by no means sure that the book was successful in drawing more lay people to the Caecilianist side, it may have been more effective in reinforcing Augustine's power as a bishop over subordinates within the catechetical system in Africa. So, although it may not have functioned effectively as a catechetical manual, as an inscription of Augustine's status as a rhetorical and catechetical heavyweight it was just as important in the longer term.

PART IV

Vulnerability and Power
Christian Heroines and the Small Worlds of Late Antiquity

Part IV explores what Conrad Leyser has called a 'rhetoric of vulnerability' among the Christian writers of late antiquity, who saw personal vulnerability as a claim, under certain circumstances, to enhanced moral authority.[1] The righteous suffering of martyrs[2] and the fragile autonomy of virgins[3] offered powerful new symbolic capital to the Christian imaginary.

James Corke-Webster's study, 'Reading Thecla in Fourth-Century Pontus', considers how the second-century tradition of the virgin heroine Thecla of Iconium could come to have new meaning for a community of dedicated ascetic women two centuries later. Steve Nolan argued some years ago that a Foucauldian approach to the *Acts of Thecla* could reveal the power of the narrative as a resource for both the dominant and the dissident;[4] Corke-Webster shows that the meanings of such a narrative were both flexible and responsive to the needs of varied communities of interpretation. Gregory provided the rhetorical resources to reconcile the seemingly inherent tensions between an emerging Christian ascetic practice that rejected marriage and the traditions of late Roman family life, in the process naturalising the celibate Christian household as a legitimate site of social reproduction.

In contrast, Thomas Dimambro and David Natal offer alternative case studies for the rhetorical uses of pathos for political ends. Indignation on behalf of the suffering righteous, Natal argues, was a powerful engine which a skilled writer like Ambrose knew how to harness. A virgin of his

[1] C. Leyser, *Authority and Asceticism from Augustine to Gregory the Great* (Oxford: Clarendon Press, 2000).

[2] K. Cooper, 'The Voice of the Victim: Gender, Representation, and Early Christian Martyrdom', *Bulletin of the John Rylands University Library*, 80 (1998), 147–57.

[3] K. Cooper, *The Virgin and the Bride: Idealized Womanhood in Late Antiquity* (Cambridge, MA: Harvard University Press, 1996).

[4] S. Nolan, 'Narrative as a Strategic Resource for Resistance: Reading the *Acts of Thecla* for Its Political Purposes', in G. J. Brooke and J.-D. Kaestli (eds), *Narrativity in Biblical and Related Texts* (Leuven: Peeters, 2000), 225–42.

own family had died as a martyr, he averred, and her purity shone as a beacon for the righteous of the Nicene faith in Milan. In the face of opposition, Ambrose adapted stories of Christian heroines within his own family to rally the Nicene community in Milan around his leadership.

Thomas Dimambro explores how the story of wronged women could lend pathos to the identity claims of a larger community on the other side of the Empire in fifth-century Syria. *Euphemia and the Goth* is, on one reading, an extended reflection on the limits and legitimacy of violent action at individual, family, and communal levels. The righteousness of the heroine is established through her suffering, the same righteous status later legitimating her own violent actions and those of her protectors against her former oppressor.[5] This family drama also operates, however, as an extended meditation on the city of Edessa's relationship with the late Roman state. Barbarian troops protected and often, it seems, exploited the city, and its inhabitants were in large measure dependent on the whims of the imperial governor for redress of grievances. Dimambro's analysis reveals that in the face of the inconsistency of the imperial system, local communities looked to local heroes and heroines for practical and supernatural support.

[5] Euphemia's reliance on the assistance of male relatives to secure redress for her grievances may be compared to the case of Aurelia Artemis, as discussed briefly in the Introduction to this volume.

CHAPTER 13

Reading Thecla in Fourth-Century Pontus

Violence, Virginity, and Female Autonomy in Gregory of Nyssa's *Life of Macrina*

James Corke-Webster

> Then while she [Eugenia] with a spirit of chastity resisted this and other marriage proposals, the letters of the blessed Apostle Paul and the account of the virgin Thecla came into her hands, and reading them secretly she began to weep every day, and although she spent her time under the most pagan of parents, she began to be a Christian in her mind. And while every day she was turning over and over in her mind by what means she might become familiar with Christian teaching, she asked of her parents that she might rush from the city for a visit to their country house. And whiling away the journey, she read in her litter and turned what had happened to the virgin Thecla over and over in her mind.[1]

The *Passion of Eugenia*, one of the Roman martyr romances dated between the fourth and the sixth century, tells of Eugenia, the young and beautiful daughter of Philip, prefect of Egypt under Commodus (d. 192). It begins with the virginal heroine facing a society wedding. Having discovered Christian ascetic literature, she refuses her marriage, cuts her hair, dresses like a boy, and ventures out into the wider Mediterranean as a Christian, eventually becoming the abbot of a monastery. This dramatic change in her life's direction is a response to reading about the virgin Thecla. Thecla stood at the centre of one of late antiquity's most prominent martyr cults. At her legend's root was the *Acts of Paul and Thecla*, an anonymous Greek text now usually dated to the second century.[2] Preserved among the Apocryphal Acts

[1] Translations are my own. That of the *Passion of Eugenia* is based on the Latin text in Boninus Mombritius, *Sanctuarium seu vitae sanctorum*, II (Paris: Fontemoing, 1910), 391–7, under the title 'Passio Sanctorum Prothi et Hyacinthi Martyrum'. It is not broken into numbered sections. On the *Passio* see K. Cooper, 'The Bride of Christ, the "Male Woman," and the Female Reader in Late Antiquity', in J. Bennett and R. M. Karras (eds.), *The Oxford Handbook of Women and Gender in Medieval Europe* (Oxford: Oxford University Press, 2013), 529–44.

[2] On the *Acts of Paul and Thecla*, see, for example: D. R. MacDonald, *The Legend and the Apostle: The Battle for Paul in Story and Canon* (Philadelphia, PA: Westminster Press, 1983); V. Burrus, *Chastity as Autonomy: Women in the Stories of the Apocryphal Acts* (Lewiston, NY; Queenston: Edwin Mellon Press, 1987); S. Davies, *The Cult of Saint Thecla: A Tradition of Women's Piety in Late Antiquity* (Oxford: Oxford University Press, 2001), 6–35; S. Johnson, *The Life and Miracles of Thecla:*

of the Apostles, but echoing many features of Christian martyr literature, the *Acts* tell how Thecla, a young pagan woman from a prominent family in Iconium in Asia Minor, hears the apostle Paul's preaching and abandons her fiancé and family to follow him. For Eugenia, centuries later, reading Thecla's tale prompts her to follow her heroine's example.

This multi-layered anecdote introduces us to the Roman family, ancient marriage, and Christianity's impact upon them. It also exemplifies how Christian authors used interlinked narratives to think through such issues. While parent–child relationships in antiquity have received much scholarly attention in the last thirty years, questions remain about Christianity's impact on classic familial values. This article aims to illuminate this by focusing on its effect on young women's relationships with their parents, and the men that tried to understand, explain, and memorialise them.

Both the stories of Eugenia and Thecla provide evidence that Christian authors and their communities struggled with Christianity's impact on traditional family dynamics and marriage ties. In both, Christian heroines take stock of their relationship with pagan parents and the marriages those parents have engineered. In both, they leave home to pursue lives very different from those planned for them. Both texts are also anonymously authored and of uncertain date, the product of a lost literary process in which both protagonists and authors are obscure. A third text, however, Gregory of Nyssa's fourth-century *Life of Macrina*, reveals that literary process in situ. Moreover, Gregory's intimate portrait of his sister Macrina and mother Emmelia suggests a new solution to Christianity's historically troubled relationship with the Roman family.

Father Knows Best: Arranged Marriage and Parent–Child Complicity

The dynamic between Roman parents and children was the subject of a welcome boom in scholarship at the end of the twentieth century.[3] But

A Literary Study (Cambridge, MA: Harvard University Press, 2006); J. W. Barrier, *The Acts of Paul and Thecla: A Critical Introduction and Commentary* (Tübingen: Mohr Siebeck, 2009), and most recently R. I. Pervo, *The Acts of Paul: A New Translation with Introduction and Commentary* (Eugene, OR: Cascade Books, 2014). On Thecla's later cult see also G. Dagron, *Vie et miracles de Sainte Thècle*, Subsidia Hagiographica 62 (Brussels: Société des Bollandistes 1978); and more recently K. Cooper, 'A Saint in Exile: The Early Medieval Thecla at Rome and Meriamlik', *Hagiographica*, 2 (1995), 1–24.

[3] For example, B. Rawson (ed.), *The Family in Ancient Rome: New Perspectives* (London; New York, NY: Routledge, 1986 [repr. 1992]); B. Rawson (ed.), *Marriage, Divorce and Children in Ancient Rome* (Oxford: Clarendon Press, 1991 [repr. 2004]); B. Rawson and P. Weaver (eds.), *The Roman Family in Italy: Status, Sentiment, Space* (Oxford: Clarendon Press, 1997).

two areas remain underexplored. First, due to both the centrality of the father–son–slave triangle in Roman life and the nature of the ancient evidence, the equally fascinating bonds between parents and daughters remain frustratingly hard to access. Second, scholarly attention has focused on the Republic and early Empire, producing a broad consensus. But debate continues over the evolution of attitudes in late antiquity and Christianity's impact. This article attempts to address the latter via the former. Focusing on the evolving treatment of Roman daughters can, I suggest, produce new insight into Christianity's impact on the domestic sphere in late antiquity.

Traditionally, scholars thought the potential for parental coercion, including use of violence, was central to the Roman father's authority (*patria potestas*). Since the Roman *paterfamilias*, legal head of the family, had absolute power over his household, including that of life and death, the parent–child relationship was seen as hierarchical and domineering.[4] John Crook however pointed out that this view was largely drawn from legendary and legal material, and did not necessarily reflect everyday life.[5] Richard Saller's cumulative publications over the last thirty years have proposed a revised picture,[6] in which the Roman *pater*'s authority was grounded in reciprocal, affectionate relationships.[7] According to the

[4] See, for example, L. H. Morgan, *Ancient Society* (London: MacMillan, 1877); E. Sachers, 'Pater familias', in *Real-Encyclopädie der classischen Altertumswissenschaft*, 18 (Waldsee: Alfred Druckemüller Verlag, 1949), col. 2121–57; and the more sweeping P. Veyne, *A History of Private Life: From Pagan Rome to Byzantium* (Cambridge, MA: Belknap Press of Harvard University Press, 1987).

[5] J. A. Crook, 'Patria Potestas' *Classical Quarterly*, 17 (1967), 113–22.

[6] P. Veyne, 'La famille et l'amour sous le Haut-Empire romain', *Annales. Économies, Sociétés, Civilisations*, 33 (1978), 35–63, had argued earlier that Augustus' political emasculation of Roman men led to them reassessing their relationships with immediate kin, and produced a strengthening of those ties of affection that had been relatively insignificant during the Republic. Veyne, *A History of Private Life*, at e.g. 28, continued to assert the reality of the despotic father for the Republican period.

[7] This stemmed from analysis of funerary epigraphy which indicated no change in family relationships in the early Principate; see R. P. Saller and B. D. Shaw, 'Tombstones and Roman Family Relations in the Principate: Civilians, Soldiers and Slaves', *Journal of Roman Studies*, 74 (1984), 124–56. See subsequently R. P. Saller, '*Familia, Domus*, and the Roman Conception of the Family', *Phoenix*, 38 (1984), 336–55; R. P. Saller, '*Patria potestas* and the Stereotype of the Roman Family', *Continuity and Change*, 1 (1986), 7–22; R. P. Saller, 'Slavery and the Roman Family', *Slavery and Abolition*, 8 (1987), 65–87; R. P. Saller, '*Pietas*, Obligation, and Authority in the Roman Family', in P. Von Kneissl and V. Losemann (eds.), *Alte Geschichte und Wissenschaftsgeschichte: Festschrift fur Karl Christ zum 65. Geburstag* (Darmstadt: Wissenschaftliche Buchgesellschaft, 1988), 392–410; R. P. Saller, 'Corporal Punishment, Authority, and Obedience in the Roman Household', in Rawson (ed.), *Marriage, Divorce and Children*, 157–64; R. P. Saller, 'Roman Kinship: Structure and Sentiment', in Rawson and Weaver (eds.), *The Roman Family in Italy*, 7–34; R. P. Saller, 'Pater Familias, Mater Familias, and the Gendered Semantics of the Roman Household', *CP*, 94 (1999), 182–97; R. P. Saller, *Patriarchy, Property and Death in the Roman Family* (Cambridge: Cambridge University Press, 1994). Although most scholarship has followed Saller, see the useful methodological critique of D. B. Martin, 'The Construction of the Ancient Family: Methodological Considerations', *Journal of*

Roman ideal, the child was not simply a pawn at the parent's mercy but stood in a reciprocal relationship of respect and affection with them. This was as true of mothers as of fathers.

> *Pietas*, the Roman family virtue, was not merely filial obedience, but more broadly affectionate devotion among all family members. Most of the *exempla* repeated to illustrate this virtue had nothing to do with filial obedience, and many had nothing to do with fathers.[8]

Saller argues that Roman parents were bound to their children by 'mutual obligation and concern'.[9] This was what distinguished children from slaves, who were indeed the tools of their *dominus* or *domina*. Children were not to be coerced, since they were to become free agents themselves; they should instead be persuaded or corrected. Saller suggests that the symbolic divide between sons and slaves was often marked by symbolic violence, primarily whipping. Violence was appropriate for the servile but rarely for the free.

Such parent–child relationships impacted ancient marriage too. A Roman daughter was not to be merely a tool in her parents' social climbing. Although Roman elite marriage was always 'arranged', the law dictated that a daughter not be forced to marry; she had to give consent.[10] Ideologically, at least, parents did not so much impose marriages on their children as facilitate them to their mutual benefit. In practice, of course, consent might well be assumed unless vocally withheld, and withholding it might be considered improper.[11] And that the law forbade coercion did not mean it never occurred.[12] The affection and respect binding parent–child relationships were surely breached as often in

Roman Studies, 86 (1996), 40–60, which does not, however, invalidate Saller's conclusions about the reciprocal nature of parent–child ties.

8 Saller, *Patriarchy, Property and Death*, 131.

9 Saller, *Patriarchy, Property and Death*, 72–3. On daughters, see further J. E. Phillips, 'Roman Mothers and the Lives of Their Adult Daughters', *Helios*, 6 (1978), 69–80; J. P. Hallett, *Fathers and Daughters in Roman Society: Women and the Elite Family* (Princeton, NJ: Princeton University Press, 1984); and S. Dixon, *The Roman Mother* (London: Croom Helm, 1988). These studies are concerned for the most part with Latin evidence.

10 E.g., *Digest* 23.1.11 (Julian); see A. Watson et al. (ed.), *The Digest of Justinian*. Vol. II (Philadelphia, PA: University of Pennsylvania Press, 1985), 658. See further S. Treggiari, 'Consent to Roman Marriage: Some Aspects of Law and Reality', *Classical Views*, 26 (1982), 34–44; S. Treggiari, 'Digna Condicio: Betrothals in the Roman Upper Class', *Échoes du monde classique/ Classical Views*, New Series, 3 (1984), 419–51; S. Treggiari, 'Ideals and Practicalities in Matchmaking in Ancient Rome', in D. I. Kertzer and R. P. Saller (eds.), *The Family in Italy from Antiquity to the Present* (New Haven, CT: Yale University Press, 1993), 91–108; and S. Treggiari, *Roman Marriage: Iusti Coniuges from the Time of Cicero to the Time of Ulpian* (Oxford: Clarendon Press, 1991), 83–160.

11 *Digest* 23.1.12 (Ulpian); see Watson, *The Digest of Justinian*, 658.

12 Treggiari, *Roman Marriage*, 83.

antiquity as today.[13] But the ideal tells us how the Romans saw their family dynamics on their best day.

Marriage of young Roman women was not simply about status. Women were vulnerable not only physically but also socially. Though capable of citizenship and property possession, they were considered secure only when tied into wider family networks. A girl grew up under her father's protection before transferring to that of her husband. Puberty was a particularly concerning time, as a girl whose virginity had been compromised would not attract a suitable husband. Locking girls into marriage at young ages was done in part to ensure their long-term security.

Matters are less clear for late antiquity. Saller drew his evidence from the Republic and early Principate, but the 212 AD declaration of universal citizenship and Constantine's conversion a century later are only the two most prominent examples of deep-seated changes in social structure and cultural capital in the later period. The latter in particular marks Christianity's increasing influence, but the scale and pace of its impact on society continues to be debated.[14] Antti Arjava has demonstrated that legally *patria potestas* continued to have the force Saller ascribes to it.[15] And legal attitudes towards marriage changed so little that Judith Evans Grubbs can speak of 'the adoption of a pre-Christian marital ethos by late antique Christians'.[16] On paper, Christianity's impact on the family seems minimal.

But beyond the legal, matters are more ambiguous. In particular, the question of whether Saller's vision of the ideal parent–child relationship holds true for late antiquity remains unanswered.[17] The late antique

[13] J. Evans Grubbs, *Women and Law in the Roman Empire: A Sourcebook on Marriage, Divorce, and Widowhood* (London; New York, NY: Routledge, 2002), 197, gives rescript evidence of daughters' requests to magistrates to force their fathers to respect the law regarding consent, although, interestingly, these cases concern forced divorce not marriage.

[14] R. MacMullen, 'What Difference Did Christianity Make?', *Historia*, 35 (1986), 322–43, treats Christianity's impact on sexual norms and slavery but not parent–child relationships.

[15] A. Arjava, 'Paternal Power in Late Antiquity', *Journal of Roman Studies*, 88 (1998), 147–65, at 164.

[16] J. Evans Grubbs, *Law and Family in Late Antiquity: The Emperor Constantine's Marriage Legislation* (Oxford: Clarendon Press, 1995), 87; see also J. Evans Grubbs, '"Pagan" and "Christian" Marriage: The State of the Question', *Journal of Early Christian Studies*, 2 (1994), 361–412; A. Arjava, *Women and Law in Late Antiquity* (Oxford: Clarendon Press, 1996); and G. Nathan, *The Family in Late Antiquity: The Rise of Christianity and the Endurance of Tradition* (London; New York, NY: Routledge, 2000); for the alternate position see M. Kuefler, 'The Marriage Revolution in Late Antiquity: The Theodosian Code and Later Roman Marriage Law', *Journal of Family History*, 32 (2007), 343–70.

[17] For an overview of earlier scholarship on the family in Christian literature, see A. Jacobs and R. Krawiec, 'Fathers Know Best: Christian Families in the Age of Asceticism', *Journal of Early Christian Studies*, 11 (2003), 257–63.

evidence is simultaneously more abundant and predominantly Christian.[18] The *Acts of Paul and Thecla* is only one of many assorted martyr narratives and Apocryphal Acts from the second and third centuries in which conversion sparks explosive family altercations.[19] They prompt us to ask whether Christianity ushered in a new age of suspicion, whether its literature provided a new emotional space for contemplating resistance to family obligations, and whether it changed the ideal parent–child relationship more fundamentally.

There is little agreement here. Emiel Eyben argued for an essential continuity in father–son relations along Saller's lines.[20] Peter Garnsey acknowledged that the legal distinction between sons and slaves remained, and that while discipline for all family members became harsher, sons were still treated less violently than slaves. But he also suggested that Christian metaphorical use of servile and filial language blurred the distinctions. Slaves could be described as sons and sons as slaves.[21] The further question is whether this provided literary *Spielraum* for exploring more problematic dynamics? Did the equation of children with slaves increase their distance from their parents? And Garnsey focused exclusively on the father–son relationship, leaving us to wonder if Christianity also influenced parental interactions with daughters and their literary expression.

Much work on the late antique family has focused on the abundant writings of John Chrysostom.[22] Douglas O'Roark set out to show that late

[18] It includes narrative sources, liturgical material, and clerical correspondence. Augustine's generosity with personal information made him a source for the ancient family before the topic became fashionable. See, e.g., P. Brown, *Augustine of Hippo: A Biography*, revised edn. (London: Faber, 2000; orig. published 1967); B. D. Shaw, 'The Family in Late Antiquity: The Experience of Augustine', *Past & Present*, 115 (1987), 3–51, building on B. D. Shaw, 'Latin Funerary Epigraphy and Family Life in the Later Roman Empire', *Historia*, 33 (1984), 457–97.

[19] See K. R. Bradley, 'Sacrificing the Family: Christian Martyrs and Their Kin', *Ancient Narrative*, 3 (2003), 150–81, with supplements and corrections in J. N. Bremmer, 'The Social and Religious Capital of the Early Christians', *Hephaistos*, 24 (2006), 269–78. For discussion of Thecla and comparable female exemplars, see K. Cooper, *The Virgin and the Bride: Idealized Womanhood in Late Antiquity* (Cambridge, MA: Harvard University Press, 1996), 45–67, and K. Cooper, 'A Father, a Daughter, and a Procurator: Authority and Resistance in the Prison Memoir of Perpetua of Carthage', *Gender and History*, 23 (2011), 685–702. For a wide-ranging discussion of anti-familial themes in Christian literature, see E. A. Clark, 'Antifamilial Tendencies in Ancient Christianity', *Journal of the History of Sexuality*, 5 (1995), 356–80.

[20] E. Eyben, 'Fathers and Sons', in Rawson (ed.), *Marriage, Divorce and Children*, 114–43.

[21] P. Garnsey, 'Sons, Slaves – and Christians', in Rawson and Weaver (eds.), *The Roman Family in Italy*, 101–21.

[22] The problem is complicated by the growing divide between East and West. I have focused on eastern practice, since the texts here considered were authored and likely read in the east. For the west, see T. de Bruyn, 'Flogging a Son: The Emergence of the *pater flagellans* in Latin Christian Discourse', *Journal of Early Christian Studies* 7 (1999), 249–90, positing that through the third and

antique parents still maintained a close relationship with their children, something about which he felt Blake Leyerle – who addressed Chrysostom's remarks on children more generally – was overly hesitant.[23] But again there is no agreement about whether parent–child relationships retained their reciprocal, dutiful affection, though Leyerle did note a discomfort on Chrysostom's part regarding violence used against young children.[24]

In sum, scholars have effectively mapped parent–child relationships in the Republic and Principate as ideally marked by reciprocal affection, duty, and reason. Marriages were a matter of social contract, but not forced, and daughters were not without voice or agency. With the onset of late antiquity the evidence becomes harder to interpret, and there is no certainty over what difference Christianity made. Moreover, studies have mostly focused on the traditional father–son–slave triangle. Including later evidence for the relationship between parents – including mothers – and daughters allows, I suggest, fresh purchase on this question.[25]

Flying the Nest: Thecla, Eugenia, and the Spectre of Violence

The *Acts of Paul and Thecla* and the *Passion of Eugenia*, as literary texts, do not straightforwardly represent reality and are better read as the explorations of authors and communities wrestling with Christianity's relationship with the Roman family.[26] But they testify to very different attitudes within these few centuries. In the former, Thecla is promised to a wealthy

fourth centuries sons were increasingly whipped in practice, though for correction rather than coercion.

[23] D. O'Roark, 'Parenthood in Late Antiquity: The Evidence of Chrysostom', *Greek, Roman, and Byzantine Studies*, 40 (1999), 53–81; B. Leyerle, 'Appealing to Children', *Journal of Early Christian Studies*, 5 (1997), 243–70.

[24] Leyerle, 'Appealing to Children', 257; see too J. Schroeder, 'John Chrysostom's Critique of Spousal Violence', *Journal of Early Christian Studies*, 12 (2004), 413–42, at 420 n. 39, and the chapters by Chris de Wet and, especially, Jonathan Tallon elsewhere in this volume.

[25] S. A. Harvey, 'Sacred Bonding: Mothers and Daughters in Early Syriac Hagiography', *Journal of Early Christian Studies*, 4 (1996), 27–56, echoes my own conclusions, namely that that the study of ancient mother–daughter relationships reveals familial bonds sustained in ascetic contexts. She notes some parallels with the *Life of Macrina* in footnotes, e.g. n. 73 and n. 75.

[26] I assume, as does the majority of current scholarship, male authorship for the *Acts of Paul and Thecla*. The theses of MacDonald, *The Legend and the Apostle* (arguing for compilation in oral form by women) and Davies, *The Cult of Saint Thecla* (arguing for female authorship) have been largely abandoned in favour of positions that see female protagonists as literary tools for men to think with. See further K. Cooper, 'Insinuations of Womanly Influence: An Aspect of the Christianization of the Roman Aristocracy', *Journal of Roman Studies*, 82 (1992), 150–64.

and prominent young man called Thamyris.[27] But when Thecla hears the apostle Paul preaching on virginity, she loses interest in her fiancé, provoking both his and her mother Theocleia's wrath and anguish. Her resistance to attempts to force her into marriage brings her before the local authorities, where her mother eventually demands that the governor 'Burn this lawless girl; burn this girl who won't marry.'[28] When Thecla miraculously escapes, she leaves Icomium to follow Paul around the Mediterranean as a virgin and preacher. A straightforward reading sees here a paradigmatic statement of the common Christian view in this period that becoming a Christian and choosing virginity meant abandoning one's family.

By the fourth century, tales of Thecla were in wide circulation. Although Thecla herself was likely a figure of legend, she had become a model for female study and emulation, and her story a space for exploration of their concerns about marriage, virginity, and family.[29] Eugenia's life-changing decision is only the most dramatic example. But by invoking Thecla, the *Passion of Eugenia*'s author highlights both similarities and differences between these women's experiences. Like Thecla, Eugenia is a young, beautiful girl with an upcoming marriage to a prominent local man.

> His sixteen-year-old daughter, Eugenia, exceptionally fine in body but more so in mind, was esteemed as so polished in Greek and Roman speech and elite literature and as carrying herself with such dignity, that even philosophers admired her. When in time she was asked by her father if she would agree to become the wife of the son of the consul Aquilanus, she responded, 'A husband must be picked more for his integrity than his birth; he must be welcomed by us for his habits not his honours.'

The daughter of Alexandria's leading family, Eugenia was expected to accept the distinguished match arranged by her father, who is clearly trying to cement a high-status alliance. Eugenia, though, was having doubts even before her fateful encounter with Thecla on the page. Her father, fulfilling the Roman parenting ideal, had asked for her consent to the proposed match, which was not forthcoming. And when Eugenia's hesitation prompted her to ask her parents for a leave of absence, they agreed. She thus took her fateful carriage ride with her parents' blessing.

[27] *Acts of Paul and Thecla* 7, R. A. Lipsius and M. Bonnet (eds.), *Acta apostolorum apocrypha post Constantinum Tischendorf*, Vol. 1 (Leipzig: Mendelssohn, 1891 [repr. Hildesheim: Olms, 1972]), 235–72 (abbreviated to *Thecla* hereafter).

[28] *Thecla* 20.

[29] K. Cooper, 'The Virgin as Social Icon: Perspectives from Late Antiquity', in M. van Dijk and R. I. A. Nip (eds.), *Saints, Scholars, and Politicians: Gender as a Tool in Medieval Studies* (Turnhout: Brepols, 2005), 9–24, at 19.

Although Eugenia's eventual departure from home echoes Thecla's, the circumstances are very different. Her parents' interactions with her are a picture of cordiality. Eugenia's father, Philip, displays none of Theocleia's rage. When Eugenia embraces Christianity, there is no parental confrontation. She simply does not return home from their estate, and those left behind presume her dead and mourn her. Later in the story there is even a reconciliation, and Philip, his wife Claudia, and their household convert to Christianity. The *Passion of Eugenia* offers a more generous picture of Philip's and his wife's parenting than the *Acts of Paul and Thecla* does of Theocleia's.[30]

In both texts Christian authors judge Roman pagan parents' treatment of children. In so doing they are also negotiating the relationship between Christianity – a new phenomenon finding its place in Roman society – and the family – the key unit of that society, and intimately bound to its value system and process of social reproduction.[31] The *Acts of Paul and Thecla* at first glance reflects a deeply antagonistic view. It paints the Roman parent at their worst – violent, unreasonable, and uncaring of their child's welfare. The *Passion of Eugenia*, on the other hand, paints a parent not far from Saller's portrait. Nevertheless, though she does not clash with her parents, Eugenia still leaves. Both texts thus seem to conclude that the Christian virgin must abandon the family, though they disagree on the degree of violence with which the break must be made.[32]

Both these texts are the final stages of long literary processes of negotiation whereby real-life dramas were converted into community memory and institutional learning aids. We can get much closer to that literary process by considering another text where both author and protagonists are better known to us. Gregory of Nyssa's *Life of Macrina* explores these same issues from a more intimate perspective.[33] Gregory's text is a brother's biography of his sister, tracing her path through childhood, betrothal, and lifelong virginity. And it is also his attempt to think through and understand the complex dynamic between Macrina and their mother. What is more, like the *Passion of Eugenia*, it appeals to Thecla's example. But as the *Passion of Eugenia*'s generous picture of pagan parenting elicits a fresh valence from a text which

[30] See Cooper, 'The Virgin as Social Icon', 22–3.

[31] See the discussion in the Introduction to this volume by Kate Cooper and Jamie Wood.

[32] Cf. the simultaneous defence of virginity and attack on paternal authority in Ambrose's *On Virgins*, also referencing Thecla's example, discussed in David Natal's chapter in this volume.

[33] G. Luck, 'Notes on the *Vita Macrinae* by Gregory of Nyssa', in A. Spira (ed.), *The Biographical Works of Gregory of Nyssa. Proceedings of the Fifth International Colloquium on Gregory of Nyssa (Mainz, 6–10 September 1982)* (Philadelphia, PA: The Philadelphia Patristic Foundation, 1984), 21–33, at 22, thinks that this intimacy is distinctive of late antique hagiography.

seems to most readers to valorise violent departure, so Gregory's reference to Thecla pulls this multivalent intertext in a third direction. Closer exploration of the *Acts of Paul and Thecla* and Gregory's sensitive narration allows us to see first-hand a Christian author struggling with Christianity's relationship to the family unit, and feeling his way to a fresh solution.

Family Realities: Macrina, Emmelia, and the Pain of Compromise

The *Life of Macrina* was written by its eponymous heroine's brother after her death in 379.[34] Gregory was one of the Cappadocians, the great fourth-century theological triumvirate that also included his brother, Basil (the Great), and their friend, Gregory of Nazianzus. Nyssan and Basil were the two most famous sons of nine siblings, of whom Macrina was the eldest.[35] The *Life of Macrina* is unique: a letter apologising for being a book and a biography aspiring to be history.[36] As Momigliano notes, when Gregory wrote a comparable eulogy for his brother he chose a different genre: 'While Macrina is brought near by a biography, Basil is made distant by a panegyric.'[37] Gregory's decision to focus on family details reveals his desire to understand Macrina's role in their household, the ways that household had changed along with Macrina's relationship with her parents, and how that evolving household had in turn changed its inhabitants.[38]

[34] My numbering indicates the divisions of P. Maraval (ed.), *Grégoire de Nysse. Vie de sainte Macrine.* SC 178 (Paris: Éditions du Cerf, 1971), and in square brackets those of J. P. Migne, *Patrologiae Cursus Completus. Series Graeca* 46 (Paris: Migne, 1863), 960–1000.

[35] There is a debate over whether there were nine or ten children, since Gregory suggests the former at *Macrina* 5 [PG 46.966A] and the latter at *Macrina* 13 [PG 46.974A–B]. For discussion, bibliography, and a hypothesis favouring the former number, see Maraval, *Grégoire de Nysse*, 159 n. 3 and 186–7 n. 1.

[36] See, e.g., A. Momigliano, 'The Life of St Macrina by Gregory of Nyssa', in J. W. Eadie and J. Ober (eds.), *The Craft of the Ancient Historian: Essays in Honor of Chester G. Starr* (Lanham, MD: University Press of America, 1985), 443–58, at 445. On genre see further P. Maraval, 'La *Vie de Sainte Macrine* de Grégoire de Nysse: Continuité et nouveauté d'un genre littéraire', in G. Freyburger and L. Pernot (eds.), *Du héros païen au saint chrétien* (Paris: Études Augustiniennes, 1997), 133–8. On Gregory's literary enterprise as an act of thanksgiving inspired by Macrina herself, see D. Krueger, 'Writing and the Liturgy of Memory in Gregory of Nyssa's *Life of Macrina*', *Journal of Early Christian Studies*, 8 (2000), 483–510. For Gregory's appropriation of Macrina's voice, see E. A. Clark, 'Holy Women, Holy Words: Early Christian Women, Social History, and the "Linguistic Turn"', *Journal of Early Christian Studies*, 6 (1998), 413–30.

[37] Momigliano, 'The Life of St Macrina', 449, noting too at 450–1 that in further eulogies Gregory adopts still different genres (e.g. in his panegyric to Meletius of Antioch and his tributes to Pulcheria and her mother Aelia Flacilla).

[38] See, e.g., P. Rousseau, 'The Pious Household and the Virgin Chorus: Reflections on Gregory of Nyssa's *Life of Macrina*', *Journal of Early Christian Studies*, 13 (2005), 165–86, at 177; see too

That Gregory is also resolving his own issues is apparent in occasional glimpses the text gives of his own familial interactions.[39] When he visits Macrina on her deathbed, for example, it had been eight years since he had last seen her.[40] A letter of his indicates he may have known she was ill earlier; the opening of *On the Spirit and the Resurrection* suggests he found out only when he arrived.[41] The *Life of Macrina* prevaricates and claims he had a vision on the road hinting at her condition.[42] Either way, it is odd that he waited two years after Basil's death before returning home. And Rousseau suggests that when Gregory records Emmelia's dying blessings on Macrina and their brother Peter, 'his not having been there comes across as both a loss and a reproach'.[43] This literary family tribute was also in part a personal catharsis.[44]

At the text's centre is again Macrina's wish to remain, like Thecla and Eugenia, unmarried. She is described early on as 'a woman who lifted herself by philosophy to the utmost limit of human virtue'.[45] But her wishes too clash with those of her parents.[46] Her father Basil initially arranges a marriage with a promising young lawyer, asking for her permission.[47] But the young man in question dies before the marriage. Macrina's parents begin sourcing a replacement. But Macrina now refuses all comers, preferring lifelong virginity.[48]

In Gregory's description, as with Eugenia, this does not lead to parent–child conflict. In fact, Macrina explains her decision in terms of honouring them. She first 'called her father's decision a marriage, as if what had been only decided had actually taken place' and continues that it 'would be unnatural and unlawful not to accept the marriage sanctioned once for her by her father'. Her refusal stems from 'a resolve never to be parted from her own mother, not even for a moment'. Macrina's desire for virginity, far

R. Van Dam, *Families and Friends in Late Roman Cappadocia* (Philadelphia, PA: University of Pennsylvania Press, 2003), 112–13.

39 We might compare the personal revelations of his *Second Encomium on the Forty Martyrs*, discussed by Vasiliki Limberis in this volume.

40 *Macrina* 15 [PG 46.976A].

41 *Spirit and Resurrection* 19.10 and *Epistle* 19.10 [PG 46.1072–80 and 46.12–160, respectively].

42 *Macrina* 15 [PG 46.976A–B].

43 Rousseau, 'The Pious Household and the Virgin Chorus', 173.

44 See too D. Krueger, *Writing and Holiness: The Practice of Authorship in the Early Christian East* (Philadelphia, PA: University of Pennsylvania Press, 2004), 110–32, who considers the management of grief through storytelling as a liturgical act.

45 *Macrina* 1 [PG 46.960B–C].

46 Momigliano, 'The Life of St Macrina', 453, concludes from the absence of allegory that Gregory is careful that his portrait never strays far from everyday family life.

47 *Macrina* 4 [PG 46.964B–C]. 48 *Macrina* 5 [PG 46.964C–D].

from sparking conflict and departure, is here tied to respect for her parents and a desire to remain at home.[49]

Gregory also emphasises the harmonious dynamic between mother and daughter. He stresses Emmelia's nursing and unstinting education of her daughter,[50] recalling that their mother had often said that 'she had been pregnant with her other children for a set time, but Macrina she carried within her forever'.[51] Their relationship is mutually enforcing, 'For the mother cared for soul of the girl, and the girl cared for the body of the mother.'[52] When her sibling Naucratius died, Macrina becomes 'a support for maternal weakness'.[53] She then leads her mother to an increasing asceticism in which they progress together.[54] Even in death, Gregory notes, they were inseparable:

> For throughout the entirety of their life both begged God in unison that after death their bodies be intermingled and their shared existence while alive not be dissolved even in death.[55]

This harmonious picture is particularly striking given that the reality may have been less rosy. It seems possible – perhaps even likely – that mother and daughter had clashed. When Macrina reveals her chaste ambitions, her mother seems not to have supported her. After the death of the fiancé, Gregory tells how 'her parents often brought proposals of marriage to her'.[56] In response to the long line of suitors, Gregory gives us a calm, composed Macrina laying forth a logical case for chastity. Gregory notes, perhaps to pre-empt his readers' predictable scepticism, that 'her decision was steadfast beyond her years'. Even accepting Macrina's precociousness, we might still suspect that Gregory is skirting over a more turbulent reality. The very fact that her parents keep foisting eligible bachelors on her suggests they did not easily succumb to her desire for virginity.

Gregory's brief sketch of Emmelia's early life is pertinent here.[57] Emmelia was raised and orphaned in Pontus during the Great Persecution of 303–313 (her father was martyred; her mother's cause of death is unknown). Intriguingly, Emmelia 'clung especially to the pure and spotless

[49] She also refers to her fiancé as absent rather than dead, alluding to Penelope and her famed virtue, *Macrina* 5 [PG 46.964D]; for this and other Homeric parallels see G. Frank, 'Macrina's Scar: Homeric Allusion and Heroic Identity in Gregory of Nyssa's Life of Macrina', *Journal of Early Christian Studies*, 8 (2000), 511–30.

[50] *Macrina* 3 [PG 46.962C–D]. [51] *Macrina* 5 [PG 46.964D]. [52] *Macrina* 5 [PG 46.966A].

[53] *Macrina* 10 [PG 46.968D]. [54] *Macrina* 10 [PG 46.970B–C].

[55] *Macrina* 35 [PG 46.996B].

[56] *Macrina* 5 [PG 46.964C]; Van Dam, *Families and Friends*, 103, comments that this is surprising.

[57] For a fuller portrait of Emmelia see Van Dam, *Families and Friends*, 99–103.

manner of life, so as not willingly to have chosen marriage'.[58] Her wish was not fulfilled. Her beauty, and the seductive estate she had inherited, both unprotected by an older generation, rendered rapid marriage essential. Fearing the threat to her virginity, she married Basil (the Elder), a Christian respected for his legal skill.[59]

These faint cracks between the lines of the text suggest that Gregory is striving to present a unified familial picture. It may simply be that Gregory as a prominent public figure does not want to air his family's dirty laundry. But it may also be, I suggest, because of the opportunity afforded him to paint a powerful picture of the Christian family. The *Life of Macrina* is more than a memorial; it is a mission statement. It is no coincidence that its central dynamic is between mother and daughter, and that the prime cause of tension would seem to be the mother's lack of support for her daughter's virginal hopes. Emmelia's own desire for that lifestyle was dashed because fear of violence and wish for security made marriage her only option. Those same concerns might have sparked tensions with Macrina too. But in Gregory's text they do not. Gregory is here, I suggest, feeling his way to a fresh solution to Christianity's clash with Roman notions of female security.

The *Life of Macrina*'s appeal to Thecla is key here. Early in the narrative, when Emmelia is in labour, she has a dream presaging her daughter's birth.

> And when the time approached at which the child still in the womb needed to be released, she [Emmelia] fell into sleep and seemed to carry in her hands that which was still enfolded in her womb, and someone appeared more magnificent in appearance and form than a man, and addressed the girl she was holding by the name of Thecla; that Thecla held in great esteem among the virgins. And having done this three times he disappeared from her sight, and gave her an easy labour, so that she simultaneously awoke from sleep and saw her dream be reality.[60]

Throughout Gregory's text Macrina walks with Thecla's shade treading softly behind. This teasing invitation to read Macrina in light of her second-century predecessor deserves closer attention. Many have noted its presence, and that it was likely intended to be programmatic, since

[58] *Macrina* 2 [PG 46.962A]

[59] *Macrina* 2 [PG 46.962B]; E. Giannarelli, 'Macrina e sua madre: santità e paradosso', *Studia Patristica*, 20 (1989), 224–30, at 225–6, discusses this parallel as the basis of their later intimate relationship in Gregory's text.

[60] *Macrina* 2 [PG 46.962B].

Macrina like Thecla chooses virginity over a husband.[61] A number of studies have investigated it in more detail;[62] Rebecca Krawiec, for example, has noted that it is a name known only to her family.[63] But as we have seen with Eugenia, a reference to the multivalent Thecla need not be so simple. I suggest that it evokes here a rich landscape of sympathetic appreciation of the complexity of strained mother–daughter relationships, and even foreshadows a new conception of household which Gregory will make the pinnacle of his memorial.

Reading Thecla: The Many Roles of Emmelia

In the *Life of Macrina* we see Gregory turning his own complex family history into a personal memorial and a narrative of wider value.[64] As we have seen, if there were cracks in his family's relationships, Gregory has hidden them well. It therefore seems strange that he references a narrative famous for its antagonistic mother–daughter relationship.[65] But Thecla is not introduced in the same manner as in the *Passion of Eugenia*, when she inspires Eugenia to abandon her parents. Instead her name is revealed in a dream to Emmelia, Macrina's mother. This seems unlikely to be an allusion to violent mother–daughter discord. I suggest that Gregory found in the Thecla story a different cultural capital.

In fact Emmelia bears comparison with more than one character in the *Acts of Paul and Thecla*.[66] She had desired a life of virginity but eventually married from a desire for security. Basil was her Thamyris. She represents what Thecla might have been. And as a mother, she does not support her own daughter's desire for celibacy, paralleling Theocleia. But Emmelia does not easily fit the jilted, angry mother figure, and her relationship with

[61] See e.g. P. Wilson-Kastner, 'Macrina: Virgin and Teacher', *Andrews University Seminary Studies*, 17 (1979), 105–17, at 106–10; Cooper, *The Virgin and the Bride*, 70–1; P. M. Beagon, 'The Cappadocian Fathers, Women, and Ecclesiastical Politics,' *Vigiliae Christianae*, 49 (1995), 165–79, at 168, with further bibliography at 176, n. 15; Van Dam, *Families and Friends*, 104–5.

[62] R. Albrecht, *Das Leben der heiligen Makrina auf dem Hintergrund der Thekla-Traditionen* (Gottingen: Vandenhoeck & Ruprecht, 1986); E. Giannarelli, *La Tipologia femminile nella biografia e nell' autobiografia cristiana da* IV *secolo* (Rome: Istituto storico italiano per il Medio Evo, 1980); G. Luck, 'Notes on the *Vita Macrinae*'.

[63] R. Krawiec, '"From the Womb of the Church": Monastic Families', *Journal of Early Christian Studies*, 11 (2003), 283–307, at 298.

[64] Luck, 'Notes on the *Vita Macrinae*', 21, notes that Gregory of Nyssa, in contrast to Gregory of Nazianzus' comparable biography of his sister Gorgonia, makes no apology for the personal subject. Cf. Ambrose' rhetorical use of his female relatives in the third book of his *On Virgins*, discussed by David Natal in this volume.

[65] Noted by Van Dam, *Families and Friends*, 105, without resolution.

[66] *Thecla* 7.

Macrina, on Gregory's picture, never crumbles like that between Theocleia and Thecla. To understand the dynamics Gregory is teasing out we must return to the intertext.

The *Acts of Paul and Thecla*, though Thecla is its hero, does not treat her mother Theocleia entirely unsympathetically. Readers have largely condemned Theocleia as a caricature of the uncaring parent. But her portrayal is not so simplistic. The anonymous author affords her significant attention; in fact, he dedicates more time to explaining her traumatic experience of their rift than Thecla's. Theocleia even reappears at the text's climax when the reader might long have dismissed her.

The text gives us enough information to explain Theocleia's extreme reaction. Her concern is sparked by Thecla's neglect of her engagement, and that issue resurfaces before the governor.[67] And her initial response is to summon Thamyris. This would have indicated two things to the alert ancient reader. First, that it is Thamyris rather than a male relative summoned suggests that the betrothal is quite far advanced, an impression furthered by his affection towards Thecla and the raw emotion provoked by her rejection.[68] Similarly when Thecla disappears from home his reaction is more that of scared lover than scorned suitor.[69] This suggests that until Paul's arrival Thecla had been content with the marriage; she may even have chosen it. The author allows his readers to see how bizarre Thecla's behaviour seemed; she is described as 'one stricken' using a term, *paraplēx*, whose most common connotations were of madness.[70] Theocleia's lack of comprehension and emotional trauma are rendered more understandable.

Second, that Thamyris is Theocleia's first port of call makes glaringly apparent that she has no active male relatives. She is head of her own household.[71] An unmarried pair like Thecla and Theocleia would be vulnerable in antiquity's patriarchal and patronage-based society, where male public support was essential for social status and security. Its visibility meant that to be deficient in the ancient household produced acute public pressure. As Richard Saller summarises: 'In towns across the empire, the politically powerful advertised their position in the community by their

[67] *Thecla* 20–1. [68] *Thecla* 10. [69] *Thecla* 11.

[70] *Thecla* 10. J. N. Bremmer, 'Magic, Martyrdom and Women's Liberation in the Acts of Paul and Thecla', in J. N. Bremmer (ed.), *The Apocryphal Acts of Paul and Thecla* (Kampen: Pharos, 1996), 36–59, at 41–2, suggests that Thecla's state resembles the 'lovesickness' of the ancient Greek novels, and that references to 'binding' are intended to suggest erotic magic.

[71] See, e.g., Kate Cooper, *Band of Angels: The Forgotten World of Early Christian Women* (London: Atlantic Press, 2013), 191–224.

physical house, which daily provided the stage for assertion of power and influence.'[72] Such a weak household would have left Theocleia extremely exposed.[73]

Moreover, though silent throughout their early interactions, Thecla finally speaks to her mother at the text's end. Returning home she attempts a reconciliation, and her appeal is revealing: 'if you long for money, the Lord will give it to you through me. Or if you desire your child – look, I am here in front of you.'[74] This suggests that her mother was motivated by either maternal loss or finance. The latter may refer to the money available to the family if Thecla had married Thamyris, explicitly said to be the city's foremost citizen and extremely rich.[75] If Theocleia's social security was dependent on her daughter's match, her extreme reaction makes more sense. The breaking of an engagement, though not encouraged, was legally fairly insignificant in Roman society.[76] But it is easy to see its potential consequences in a self-policing local community. Read thus, Theocleia's public denunciation of her daughter becomes a vulnerable woman's desperate attempt to protect her future by publicly demonstrating her allegiance to the state.[77]

Further, we read more about the mother's worry than the daughter's dreams.[78] After Thamyris has reasoned fruitlessly with his fiancé, Theocleia appeals to her daughter.[79] When she too is unsuccessful, we read that 'they wept terribly; Thamyris missing a wife, Theocleia a child, and the maidservants a mistress. There was a great turmoil of mourning in the house.' Theocleia's violence towards her daughter is born not of callous disdain but of confusion, grief, and fear. She is wrestling to engineer safety and security for herself and her daughter in a world not kind to those without the men and means to support themselves. Thecla's actions would

[72] Saller, *Patriarchy, Property and Death*, 72; see further K. Cooper, 'Closely Watched Households: Visibility, Exposure, and Private Power in the Roman *Domus*', *Past & Present*, 197 (2007), 3–33.

[73] Noted also by MacDonald, *The Legend and the Apostle*, 50–1.

[74] *Thecla* 43.

[75] E.g. *Thecla* 11.

[76] Treggiari, 'Ideals and Practicalities', 94.

[77] Compare Cooper, 'A Father, a Daughter, and a Procurator', 685–702, on the last-gasp public attempts of Perpetua's father to get his daughter to sacrifice.

[78] One technique by which authors provoke sympathy for characters is by revealing their internal emotions and motivations. In what is observed in a text (*focalisation*), narratologists distinguish between the *perceptible* – actions and speech visible or audible to all in the sequence of events in a narrative – and the *non-perceptible* – dreams, thoughts, and feelings that are only visible if explicitly described. See, e.g., J. A. García Landa and S. O. Jaén (eds.), *Narratology: An Introduction* (London: Longman, 1996), particularly 116–25. *Non-perceptible* objects are focalised for both Theocleia and Thecla.

[79] *Thecla* 10.

not only have been incomprehensible; they would have seemed thoughtless, dangerous, and cruel.

This more sympathetic approach to Theocleia makes her a more natural reference point for Emmelia. As a girl Emmelia had shared the fear and desire for security that motivates Theocleia. And as a mother she faces similar problems. As Gregory emphasises, she has a 12-year-old daughter of dazzling beauty, permanently swamped by a 'great swarm of suitors'.[80] It was also around this time that Basil, Macrina's father and Emmelia's wife, died.[81] The exact timing is unclear, but Emmelia is clearly left alone with a vast estate around the time her daughter announces her ascetic intentions.[82] Gregory lists the stresses weighing upon her: 'she was the mother of four sons and five daughters, and paid [tax to] three governors because her property was spread between that number of districts'.[83] Read thus, we better understand her lack of support for her daughter's desire for virginity. Gregory may have understood the fear that lay behind both Theocleia's and his own mother's lack of encouragement of their virgin daughters.[84]

It is interesting too that Theocleia is not written off in the *Acts of Paul and Thecla*. Thecla returns home at the story's finale and encourages her mother to embrace Christianity, arguing that it will return to her both her daughter and worldly wealth. This sentiment expresses an awareness of Theocleia's concerns, and seeks to reassure her that with God she need be neither vulnerable nor lonely. Thecla wants a relationship with her mother, but with a Christian mother. The manuscript record is unclear on the result – some versions record that Theocleia rejects her daughter's overtures; others, the Coptic transmission in particular, leave it unresolved.[85] This text seems

80 *Macrina* 4 [PG 46.964A–B]. 81 *Macrina* 5 [PG 46.966B].

82 See, e.g., Van Dam, *Families and Friends*, 214–15 n. 16.

83 *Macrina* 5 [PG 46.966A–B]. As Van Dam, *Families and Friends*, 101, notes, Emmelia managed one of the wealthiest families in the region. But that does not mean that she 'had few practical worries', as Van Dam declares. As with Theocleia, she is now vulnerable because there is no male relative to ensure the estate's security. On the number of children see above, n. 35.

84 This turbulent period was also the context for Gregory's *Second Encomium on the Forty Martyrs* and its tensions between mother and son; see the chapter by Vasiliki Limberis elsewhere in this volume. See also Thomas Dimambro's chapter on the importance of the mother–daughter relationship when the *paterfamilias* is absent.

85 Only about two-thirds of the original 3,600 lines (according to Nicephorus' *Stichometry*) is preserved. The text is extant in forty-nine ninth- to sixteenth-century manuscripts, and in further versions translated into Coptic, Syriac, Latin, Armenian, Ethiopic, Slavic, and Arabic; see further P. Sellew, 'Paul, Acts of', in D. N. Freeman (ed.), *The Anchor Bible Dictionary* (New York, NY: Doubleday, 1992), Vol. v, 202, and K. Haines-Eitzen, 'Engendering Palimpsests: Gender, Asceticism, and the Transmission of the Acts of Paul and Thecla', in W. Klingshirn and L. Safran (eds.), *The Early Christian Book* (Washington, DC: Catholic University of America

to have been reaching for, or at least regretting the failing of, a reunion between mother and virgin daughter.[86] Such nuance would be an appropriate reference point for the *Life of Macrina*, since Emmelia and Macrina do prove able to collaborate, and in a remarkable fashion.

That collaboration deserves closer attention, since in it lies a further potential parallel revealing of Gregory's concerns. In the *Acts of Paul and Thecla*, Paul offers Thecla a means to live a virginal life. Her mother offers security in marriage instead. Thecla chooses the former, and her subsequent journeys around the Mediterranean are rife with exactly the threats to her chastity her mother had presumably dreaded.[87] Macrina also chooses virginity. But she does not need to leave Emmelia behind to achieve it, and it does not expose her to harm. She stays a virgin safely within the household.

This resonates with a later portion of the *Acts of Paul and Thecla* to which Gregory may have been subtly alluding. After Thecla has left Icomium she arrives at Antioch with Paul.[88] There a senior official, Alexander, who has fallen in love with Thecla and immediately been rebuffed, drags her for condemnation in the arena, where she miraculously survives repeated attempts to execute her.[89] Most interesting though are repeated references to a crowd of women who observe her sufferings, bemoan her fate, and continually appeal on her behalf.[90] Their ringleader is 'a certain rich queen called Tryphaena', a relative of the emperor and a widow.[91] When Thecla is condemned and asks for her chastity to be protected until her death, Tryphaena 'took her into her safe-keeping'.[92] That Tryphaena's household will preserve her virginity, and the constant presence of the sympathetic crowd of women, suggests that Tryphaena is head of an all-female household. The text makes reference to Tryphaena's 'handmaids', and later to her 'maidservants'.[93] After Thecla's arrival, this quickly becomes a house of Christian virgins.[94]

We have already seen how Emmelia parallels both Thecla, since Emmelia had once desired virginity, and Theocleia, understood both antagonistically

Press, 2005), 177–93, at 186. Haines-Eitzen's account of the manuscripts is based on the exhaustive study of M. Geerard, *Clavis Apocryphorum Novi Testamenti* (Turnhout: Brepols, 1992).

86 Noted by Bremmer, 'Magic, Martyrdom and Women's Liberation', 44.

87 E.g. *Thecla* 26.

88 *Thecla* 26.

89 *Thecla* 27.

90 *Thecla* 27–38. The prevalence of women in the *Acts of Paul and Thecla* is treated in detail by Davies, *The Cult of Saint Thecla*, 8–18.

91 *Thecla* 27 and 30. Tryphaena is likely based upon the queen of Pontus of the same name who ruled together with her son, King Polemon II, during the first century; see further MacDonald, *The Legend and the Apostle*, 20–1; Bremmer, 'Magic, Martyrdom and Women's Liberation', 52.

92 *Thecla* 27.

93 *Thecla* 36 and 39.

94 *Thecla* 30, 38, and 39.

and sympathetically. I suggest that she also parallels Tryphaena. In the *Acts of Paul and Thecla*, Thecla becomes a second daughter to Tryphaena, whose actual daughter Falconilla has died, and calls her 'my second child'.[95] Tryphaena takes Thecla home because Falconilla appears to her in a dream, saying 'Mother, you shall take Thecla the abandoned stranger in my place, so that she prays for me and I am transferred to the place of the righteous.'[96] Tryphaena meets her new daughter Thecla in a dream; Emmelia met her daughter, called Thecla, via the same medium.[97]

Tryphaena and her household can physically protect Thecla and her virginity.[98] When the disgruntled Alexander comes to Tryphaena's house to lead Thecla to execution, Tryphaena dismisses him.[99] When soldiers eventually take Thecla, Tryphaena goes with her, and the assembled women loudly denounce the judgement.[100] During her punishments, the beasts set loose on Thecla are confused and put to sleep by pungent herbs thrown by those same women.[101] The governor and Alexander only cease these abortive attacks when Tryphaena faints, leading the two men to fear repercussion from her imperial relatives.[102] And Tryphaena finally bequeaths her considerable means to Thecla, enabling her to support herself independently, thereby removing much of the risk inherent in her chastity.[103] Tryphaena severs the link between virginity and vulnerability.

The same is true of Emmelia. Like Tryphaena, Emmelia's changed attitude means she becomes a second mother to Macrina, her own Thecla. Though Emmelia initially fails to support her desire to remain a virgin she ultimately establishes together with her daughter a 'manor-turned-monastery' where women can remain virgins free from threats of violence.[104] Whether Gregory intended his audience to appreciate them or not – and it is not an unreasonable suggestion that highly literarily self-conscious educated Christians of the fourth century would – the evocative similarities between Emmelia and Tryphaena demand that we pay closer attention to Gregory's picture of the evolving relationship between Macrina and Emmelia, and the new model home they create together.

[95] *Thecla* 29. See MacDonald, *The Legend and the Apostle*, 51; A. Jensen, *Thekla – die Apostolin. Ein apokrypher Text neu entdeckt* (Freiburg; Basel; Vienna: Herder, 1995), 92; and M. Misset-van de Weg, 'A Wealthy Woman Named Tryphaena: Patroness of Thecla of Iconium', in Bremmer (ed.), *The Apocryphal Acts of Paul and Thecla*, 16–35, especially 32–4, who emphasises an early Christian mode of female patronage.

[96] *Thecla* 28.

[97] I note that after Eugenia is martyred later in the story, she too appears in a vision to her mother Claudia, who is eventually buried alongside her (although such post-mortem visions become common in early mediaeval female hagiographies).

[98] Misset-van de Weg, 'A Wealthy Woman Named Tryphaena', 29–30, notes the stress placed on this.

[99] *Thecla* 30. [100] *Thecla* 31–2. [101] *Thecla* 35. [102] *Thecla* 36. [103] *Thecla* 39.

[104] Krueger, 'Writing and the Liturgy of Memory', 484.

A Utopian Household: Gregory's Memorial and the Ascetic Female Home

This essay has used early Christian narratives revolving around mother–daughter relationships and arranged marriage to investigate the impact Christianity made on established Roman household values. In the three texts here treated we see three different models of the young Christian's relationship to their family. In the *Acts of Paul and Thecla* the author can see only a violent altercation between mother and daughter when the daughter embraces Christianity and abandons the secure marriage planned for her. Rejected by her mother, she leaves home. Even as he paints this clash, however, the author recognises the difficulties of the choice, and Thecla's eventual return indicates that the author neither desires nor advocates permanent estrangement. In the *Passion of Eugenia*, the author sees the same necessity to leave home and abandon marriage at the moment of conversion. But there is no confrontation with Eugenia's parents. And that text ends too in triumphant reunion when her parents convert to Christianity. Nevertheless, despite the different parental reactions, departure from the household remains necessary.

In the *Life of Macrina* Gregory presents a different picture. If there was conflict between Macrina and her parents, Gregory does not share it. Instead he works to portray Christian family unity.[105] As with the *Passion of Eugenia*'s author, Gregory does not revel in Christianity's potential for disruption. But more than that, for Macrina remaining a virgin does not even necessitate leaving home.[106] Instead, her relationship with her mother evolves and together they transform the household itself. Macrina and Emmelia's changing relationship and the growth of their new-look virginal household – perhaps foreshadowed via Thecla's dream appearance by a reference to the *Acts of Paul and Thecla*'s prototypical house of virgins – is the core of his literary enterprise.

As we have seen, Macrina resolves not to leave her mother, and becomes a staff in her old age, especially after her brother Naucratius' death.[107] Much attention has been paid to Macrina leading her mother into an ascetic lifestyle. She 'persuaded her mother to abandon her customary life and the vainer lifestyle and the service of attendants' as well as to 'add her own life to the lifestyle of the virgins, making equals and sisters of as many slaves and

[105] Rousseau, 'The Pious Household and the Virgin Chorus', 172.

[106] Cf. the widow and daughter's eventual security at home in *Euphemia and the Goth*, considered in Thomas Dimambro's chapter in this volume, although in the case of Euphemia the support of male relatives is needed.

[107] *Macrina* 9 [PG 46.970A].

domestics as she had with her'.[108] Thanks to Macrina's influence, 'the life of the virgin became her mother's guide towards this philosophic and immaterial lifestyle'.[109] Macrina thus certainly takes the lead. But Gregory makes clear that their evolving relationship is mutually supportive. We read:

> And as by her mother's training she cultivated for herself an unblemished life, watched and guided in everything by the maternal gaze, so at the same time she also provided her mother via her own life a great guide towards the same goal – I mean that relating to philosophy – drawing her bit by bit to the immaterial and simpler life.[110]

Like Tryphaena, Emmelia enables her daughter's virginity by providing a secure and financially strong environment. With men absent, Macrina and Emmelia radically adapt their household. Everything extraneous is set aside until their lives included 'only attention to divine affairs and incessant prayer and never-ending hymn-singing, stretching equally over the whole time, through the night and the entire day'.[111] Gregory describes their life as 'on the boundary between human and incorporeal nature'. Gregory paints a new vision of the Christian household, in which Christianity, virginity, security, and family are compatible.[112]

Interestingly, this household's impact extends beyond the women within its walls.[113] Its foundation was sparked by the absence of the senior male family members, Basil the Elder through death and his sons through education. But when the boys later return it does not revert to its patriarchal form. Instead, it changes them.[114] Basil returns from his rhetorical training steeped in classical wisdom. But it is his time at home with Macrina that makes him a great church leader. His stay in Antioch had made him 'strangely puffed up with pride in rhetoric'.[115] His return

[108] *Macrina* 7 [PG 46.966D] [109] *Macrina* 11 [PG 46.970C]. [110] *Macrina* 5 [PG 46.966B].

[111] *Macrina* 11 [PG 46.966D].

[112] On the familial nature of their ascetic community, see S. Elm, *Virgins of God: The Making of Asceticism in Late Antiquity* (Oxford: Oxford University Press, 1993), 78–105, charting its gradual institutionalisation; Van Dam, *Families and Friends*, 107; Krawiec, '"From the Womb of the Church"', and Rousseau, 'The Pious Household and the Virgin Chorus'.

[113] See, e.g., Elm, *Virgins of God*, 79 and 82–3, respectively noting that life in the new household was not solitary monastic confinement and refuting suggestions that Macrina's ascetic community simply echoed a male one Basil had established.

[114] Beagon, 'The Cappadocian Fathers, Women, and Ecclesiastical Politics', provides further examples of the historical importance of women to Cappadocian Christianity. This picture sits interestingly alongside the positive attitude to women expressed in the theology of Gregory and the other Cappadocians; see, e.g., V. Harrison, 'Male and Female in Cappadocian Theology', *Journal of Theological Studies*, 41 (1990), 441–71; and Wilson-Kastner, 'Macrina: Virgin and Teacher', 116–17.

[115] *Macrina* 6 [PG 46.966C].

home draws him 'to the goal of philosophy'.[116] He embraces asceticism and a 'virtuous life'. Gregory emphasises that Macrina was his teacher too.[117] This new utopian female household not only renders virginity possible for the women within its walls; it also creates the church's foremost bishops.[118]

Gregory's family biography was thus a space to reconsider the role of the household and parents, and Christianity's impact upon them. In both the *Acts of Paul and Thecla* and the *Passion of Eugenia* the traditional path of social reproduction via marriage is rejected, and the family and the household are left behind, though with differing degrees of violence. Gregory also rejects the necessity of marriage, but fights against the suspicion that Christian rejection of the security of marriage necessitated rejecting that of family too.[119] In the *Life of Macrina* Christian asceticism brings parent and child closer together.[120] Gregory sets out there, in the most intimate of settings, his belief that Christianity need not destroy the household and its inhabitants but can instead secure and transform it. This utopian celibate home is rooted in the traditional household and its relationships, but better equipped to house and cultivate a new means of social reproduction.

[116] The same term *scopon* was used for Macrina's guidance of Emmelia (*Macrina* 5 [966B]).

[117] Luck, 'Notes on the *Vita Macrinae*', 22.

[118] Gregory seems to be reacting here to the traditional modes and venues of social reproduction, considered in Jamie Wood's chapter in this volume, which also considers Basil's views on the matter. It is interesting, in the context of Macrina and Emmelia's vulnerability, to consider Basil's writings on the role of fear in ascetic development.

[119] D. Caner, 'Notions of "Strict Discipline" and Apostolic Tradition in Early Definitions of Orthodox Monasticism', in S. Elm, É. Rebillard and A. Romano (eds.), *Orthodoxie, christianisme, histoire* (Rome: École Française de Rome, 2000), 23–34, at 28, and Rousseau, 'Life of Macrina', 168, note Gregory's generally cooler attitude to asceticism.

[120] See Krawiec, '"From the Womb of the Church"', 291.

CHAPTER 14

Family Heroines

Female Vulnerability in the Writings of Ambrose of Milan

David Natal

Little is known of the family of Aurelius Ambrosius (d. 397), who was the provincial governor of the north Italian province of Aemilia-Liguria before becoming the bishop of Milan in 374. He never referred to his parents, who were briefly mentioned in Paulinus' *Vita Ambrosii*, a hagiographical account written in 412, and only alluded to three relatives: his brother Satyrus, his sister Marcellina, and their common ancestor Sotheris.[1] Ambrose described Satyrus in detail in two funeral speeches delivered after his brother's death in 379.[2] Much sketchier is the portrait of Marcellina; we only know that she was consecrated a virgin by Pope Liberius and lived as an ascetic in Rome.[3] The information about Sotheris is more limited still: Ambrose mentions that she had been martyred without providing any further details or information about the exact nature of their relationship.

Despite their incomplete profile, however, Sotheris and Marcellina play an important role in Ambrose's writings. Sotheris was mentioned in two treatises composed in different moments at which Ambrose was particularly vulnerable. She makes an appearance in the last paragraph of *On Virgins*, one of Ambrose's earliest treatises, published in 377, when he was trying to build his power as bishop over the divided Christian community of Milan.[4] Sotheris was again set as an example of faith and endurance in Ambrose's *Exhortation to Virginity*, a sermon preached in 394 in Florence, where he had fled from Milan in order to avoid contact with the usurper Eugenius (d. 394).[5] Marcellina was the dedicatee of *On Virgins* and was the addressee of three letters that recount what are usually considered as

[1] Paulinus, *Vita Ambrosii*, 3, A. Bastiaensen (ed.) (Milan: Mondadori, 1975), 51–124.

[2] Ambrose, *De excessu fratris*, O. Faller (ed.), *Sancti Ambrosii Opera*, CSEL 73 (Vienna: OeAW, 1955), 207–325.

[3] Ambrose, *De virginibus*, 3.1.1, Franco Gori (ed.), *Sancti Ambrosii Episcopi Mediolensis Opera*, 2 vols. (Milan: Biblioteca Ambrosiana, 1989), Vol. I, 99–241.

[4] Ambrose, *De virginibus*, 3.7.38–39.

[5] Ambrose, *Exhortatio virginitatis*, Gori (ed.), *Sancti Ambrosii*, Vol. II, 197–278.

some of Ambrose's most spectacular successes in conflicts with the emperors Valentinian II (d. 392) and Theodosius I (d. 395).[6]

The role of women in late antique Christian writings has attracted considerable scholarly attention over the last twenty years. Elizabeth Clark has explored how female characters became a polysemic discursive trope in Christian literature.[7] Kate Cooper has shown how insinuations of undue influence by women were used to delegitimise the political or religious authority of men, and how exposing female relatives to public scrutiny was crucial to the construction of political authority of late Roman aristocrats.[8] Recent historiography on Ambrose has also provided interesting insights into his treatises on virginity and widowhood. Neil McLynn has unpicked the political implications underlying Ambrose's moral rhetoric.[9] Similarly, Virginia Burrus and David Hunter have demonstrated how Ambrose's discourse on female virginity should be read in the light of struggles for power between men.[10]

This paper explores a less-studied aspect of the literary use to which Ambrose put his female relatives. I will argue that Ambrose displayed Sotheris and Marcellina symbolically at delicate moments during his episcopate, seeking to strengthen his legitimacy as bishop and to depoliticise his interventions in imperial politics. Ambrose presented Sotheris in order to construct a Christian family past that correlated with his current position as bishop of Milan, and to dignify the authority of former secular officials who, like him, had subsequently become religious leaders. In a similar fashion, Ambrose's letters to Marcellina provided him with an

[6] Ambrose, *Epistulae* [hereafter: Ambrose, *Ep.*] 76, O. Faller and M. Zelzer (eds.), *Sancti Ambrosi Opera, Epistulae et Acta*, CSEL 82.3 (Vienna: OeAW, 1982), 123–4; *Ep.* 77, CSEL 82.3, 135–40; Ambrose, *Epistulae extra collectionem* [hereafter: Ambrose, *Ep. extra coll.*] 1, Faller and Zelzer (eds.), *Sancti Ambrosi Opera, Epistulae et Acta*, 145–60.

[7] E. A. Clark, *Reading Renunciation: Asceticism and Scripture in Early Christianity* (Princeton, NJ: Princeton University Press, 1999), esp. 177–203; E. A. Clark, 'Ideology, History and the Constitution of "Woman" in Late Ancient Christianity', *Journal of Early Christian Studies*, 2 (1994), 155–84.

[8] Kate Cooper, *The Fall of the Roman Household* (Cambridge: Cambridge University Press, 2007), esp. 93–101; Kate Cooper, 'Closely Watched Households: Visibility, Exposure and Private Power in the Roman Domus', *Past & Present*, 197 (2007), 3–33; K. Cooper, 'Insinuations of Womanly Influence: An Aspect of the Christianization of the Roman Aristocracy', *Journal of Roman Studies*, 82 (1992), 150–64.

[9] N. B. McLynn, *Ambrose of Milan: Church and Court in a Christian Capital* (Berkeley, CA: University of California Press, 1994), 53–68.

[10] V. Burrus, 'Reading Agnes: The Rhetoric of Gender in Ambrose and Prudentius', *Journal of Early Christian Studies*, 3 (1995), 25–46; V. Burrus, '"Equipped for Victory": Ambrose and the Gendering of Orthodoxy', *Journal of Early Christian Studies*, 4 (1996), 461–75; D. G Hunter, 'The Virgin, the Bride, and the Church: Reading Psalm 45 in Ambrose, Jerome, and Augustine', *Church History*, 69 (2000), 281–303.

occasion for rewriting his episodes of conflict with emperors, downplaying the political and legal repercussions of events and instead presenting them as struggles for the moral well-being of the community.

Ambrose in Milan

The fact that Ambrose's writings are our main source of information about his life and episcopacy has deeply skewed our understanding of the true extent of his authority and intellectual reputation. Older scholarship tended to view Ambrose as a strong and influential bishop, who confronted aristocrats and emperors and was faithfully supported by his fellow bishops and the Milanese community. In the last three decades, however, revisionist energy has been directed against such a view. In their seminal monographs, Neil McLynn and Daniel Williams have convincingly argued that Ambrose's authority was much weaker than was previously thought and have fundamentally questioned the extent of the bishop's intellectual and spiritual prestige.[11]

Ambrose's weakness was especially evident in his first years as bishop. At that time, Milan was still much affected by doctrinal quarrels between Homoians and Nicenes, two Christian groups separated by their different theological conception of the Trinity. The controversy had started in 355, when the emperor Constantius II (d. 361) had summoned the Council of Milan in an attempt to put an end to the division between Arians, who contended that the Son of God was inferior to the Father, and Nicenes, who defended that both shared the same substance. Pressed by the emperor, the majority of the bishops at the council adopted an intermediate theological position, the so-called Homoian creed, which sustained that the Son was 'similar' to the Father. Far from putting an end to the debate, however, Constantius' measures spurred a new wave of religious conflict in the aftermath of the Council.

Three recalcitrant Nicene bishops, Dionysius of Milan, Eusebius of Vercelli, and Lucifer of Cagliari refused to subscribe to the Council of Milan's new Homoian formula in relation to the Trinity and were consequently condemned to exile. The banished bishops, however, continued to exert some influence over the north Italian Nicene communities that they represented, preserving a strong sense of Nicene communal belonging and a combative attitude to their opponents. During the following decades,

[11] McLynn, *Ambrose of Milan*, esp. 1–53; D. H. Williams, *Ambrose of Milan and the End of the Nicene–Arian Conflicts* (Oxford: Oxford University Press, 1995), 116–27.

local homiletic collections commemorated Eusebius as a martyr and a saint in Vercelli and the nearby parishes.[12] Similarly, the Nicene community of Milan celebrated the cult of the 'Innocents', remembering the execution of four Milanese Christians under Constantius, which later became an opportunity for manifesting disagreement with imperial policy.[13] These developments had traditionally been interpreted as an effort of Constantius II and those bishops who allied with him to impose the Homoian creed on the Nicene population of northern Italy. However, more recent research has suggested that the Homoian party was much stronger than the majority of Nicene sources are willing to admit.[14] In fact, many Homoian communities seem to have thrived between the 350s and the 370s, and did so not only in Milan, where imperial patronage was strongest, but also in other north Italian towns.

The presence of two partisan groups generated instability in the region and clearly affected the election of Ambrose as bishop in 374, when he was still the governor of the province Aemilia-Liguria. Our only source of information for this episode is the *Vita Ambrosii*. According to this text, after the death in 374 of Auxentius, the Homoian bishop of Milan, Ambrose went to the main basilica in order to prevent the outbreak of riots between Nicene and Homoians. Ambrose was then acclaimed bishop *laetitia cunctorum*, 'with the utmost grace and rejoicing among everyone'.[15]

Largely following this narrative, older historiography understood that Ambrose's special charisma and sanctity had persuaded the Homoians to accept his election, despite his clear Nicene affinities.[16] More recent scholarship, however, has suggested that Ambrose was equally far from meeting the expectations of both groups.[17] Although his connections with well-known Nicenes, such as Probus and the Pope Liberius, made obvious his position in relation to the Trinitarian controversy, Ambrose had very little in common with the banished bishops.[18] Unlike Eusebius and

[12] V. Zangara, 'Eusebio di Vercelli e Massimo di Torino. Tra storia e agiografia', in E. Dal Covolo, R. Uglione and G. M. Vian (eds.), *Eusebio di Vercelli e il suo tempo*, Biblioteca di scienze religiose 133 (Rome: Libreria Ateneo Salesiano, 1997), 257–322.

[13] H. I. Marrou, 'Ammien Marcelin et les "Innocents" de Milan', *Recherches de science religieuse*, 40 (1952), 179–90.

[14] R. Gryson, *Scolies ariennes sur le Concile d'Aquilée*, Sources Chrétiennes 267 (Paris: Éditions du Cerf, 1980), 81–5; Williams, *Ambrose of Milan*, 65–82.

[15] Paulinus, *Vita Ambrosii*, 9.3; McLynn, *Ambrose of Milan*, 51.

[16] F. H. Dudden, *The Life and Times of St Ambrose*, 2 vols. (Oxford: Clarendon Press, 1935), Vol. 1, 65; Y.-M. Duval, 'Ambroise, de son élection à sa consécration', in G. Lazzati (ed.), *Ambrosius episcopus: atti del Congresso Internazionale di Studi Ambrosiani* (Milan: Vita e Pensiero, 1976), 243–84.

[17] Williams, *Ambrose of Milan*, 112–16.

[18] Paulinus, *Vita Ambrosii*, 8.

Dionysius, he lacked the charismatic halo of those who had suffered exile for his creed. Quite the opposite, in his years as a barrister in Illyricum and as governor of the province Aemilia-Liguria in northern Italy, Ambrose had been in charge of implementing the emperor's religious policy. It is clear that in Milan he coexisted with the Homoian bishop Auxentius. Neither Ambrose nor his hagiographer mentioned any conflict with Auxentius, suggesting that they had an unproblematic relationship. In addition, Ambrose did not hide his aversion to diehard Nicenes; in his funeral oration for Satyrus, he explicitly attacked the followers of the exiled bishop Lucifer of Cagliari.[19]

Although Ambrose's theological neutrality can hardly have satisfied any of the contending Christian groups in Milan, he could rely on the support of powerful secular officials. The *Vita Ambrosii* relates how the prefect Probus had encouraged his election as bishop and the emperor Valentinian had gladly allowed it.[20] The involvement of important imperial agents may help to explain the irregularities in the process by which he was elected and confirmed in office: Ambrose was baptised by a priest on the same day that he was chosen as bishop, and was not then ordained in the presence of the required number of peers (three).[21] The episode did not pass unnoticed by Ambrose's enemies. In 381, Palladius, the Homoian bishop of Ratiaria in Illyricum, remarked that Ambrose owed more to his political connections than to his Christian credentials.[22] Palladius' bitterness is understandable because he had been expelled from his see at the Council of Aquileia (381), over which Ambrose had presided. It is likely that this kind of criticism was probably more frequent than our sources reflect and, as I shall explain later in this paper, Ambrose's anxiety about his past roles in the imperial administration and his lack of qualifications for holding high office within the church left a mark across his literary output. Throughout his episcopacy, Ambrose made great efforts to present himself as an ascetic devoted to the promotion of the Nicene faith and to defending his community. The anxiety that derived from the shakiness of Ambrose's original position was, however, especially evident during his first years in the episcopate.

[19] Ambrose, *De excessu fratris*, 1.47.

[20] Paulinus, *Vita Ambrosii*, 8; C. Corbellini, 'Sesto Petronio Probo e l'elezione episcopale di Ambrogio', *Rendiconti dell'Istituto Lombardo, Classe di Lettere, Scienze morali e storiche*, 109 (1975), 181–9; M. Sordi, 'I rapporti di Ambrogio con gli imperatori del suo tempo', in L. F. Pizzolato and M. Rizzi (eds.), *Nec timeo mori* (Milan: Vita e Pensiero, 1998), 107–19.

[21] McLynn, *Ambrose of Milan*, 44–52.

[22] Palladius, *Scholia Ariana*, 343v, 3–4; N. B. McLynn, 'The "Apology" of Palladius: Nature and Purpose', *Journal of Theological Studies*, 42 (1991), 52–76.

Building Legitimacy: Female Relatives in Ambrose's Early Episcopate

Conscious about his weak position, Ambrose played it safe after his episcopal election in 374; his first theological composition was only made at the request of the emperor in 378.[23] Around a year earlier, Ambrose had published his first three treatises, *On Virgins*, *On Widows*, and *On Virginity*, all of which focus on female asceticism. The longest and most elaborated of these writings is *On Virgins*, a collection of sermons reworked as a treatise in three books, which contains a passionate exhortation to sexual renunciation as well as Ambrose's first allusion to Sotheris and Marcellina.

Ambrose's interest in female asceticism was not coincidental. The topic did not require deep theological knowledge and meant that he could avoid mentioning the Trinitarian controversy, as both Nicenes and Arians promoted the ideal of renunciation.[24] By writing about asceticism, Ambrose presented himself as a moral and intellectual authority within his community. Ambrose did not reveal that he had borrowed much of the argument and content of the treatise from the earlier works of authoritative figures such as Cyprian and Athanasius. Jerome praised this act of 'plagiarism' with tongue firmly in cheek.[25] Despite his dependence on earlier Christian authors, *On Virgins* contains a number of original interventions in which Ambrose sought to justify his past as an imperial bureaucrat, and to define the two pillars of his legitimacy during the first few years of his episcopacy: his family's ascetic tradition and the Christian nature of his clerical authority, independent of his previous role as an imperial bureaucrat.

In *On Virgins*, Ambrose dignified the imperial service by offering an alternative reading of martyrdom. He consistently minimised the proactive role of imperial authorities in Christian persecutions and emphasised the involvement of male Roman citizens instead. This is especially perceptible in the first two books of the treatise, in which Ambrose focused on the cases of Thecla, Agnes, and an unnamed virgin from Antioch, young girls

[23] Ambrose composed his *De fide* between 378 and 380. An example of Ambrose's intellectual insecurity is *Ep.* 32 in which, fearing criticism, he asked Sabinus of Piacenza to review (*vellica*, literally to pluck) one of his writings, probably the *De fide*.

[24] McLynn, *Ambrose of Milan*, 60–8.

[25] Jerome, *Epistulae* 22, I. Hilberg (ed.), *S. Eusebii Hieronymi Opera Epistulae*, CSEL 54 (Vienna: OeAW, 1996 [1910]), 144; N. Adkin, 'Ambrose and Jerome: The Opening Shot', *Mnemosyne*, 46 (1993), 364–76; R. A. Layton, 'Plagiarism and Lay Patronage of Ascetic Scholarship: Jerome, Ambrose and Rufinus', *Journal of Early Christian Studies*, 10 (2002), 489–522.

who preferred to suffer a painful death rather than to lose their virginity. Ambrose presented martyrdom and virginity as two similar paths to Christian excellence and as the only ways of preserving female liberty and integrity: 'You have thus in one victim a double martyrdom, of modesty and of religion. She both remained a virgin and obtained martyrdom.'[26] Marriage, conversely, was despised and described as human trade: 'This is to buy a son-in-law, not to gain one who would sell a glance of their daughter to her parents.'[27] Ambrose's radicalism in relation to marriage, questioning one of the cornerstones of Roman family and society, has puzzled historians.[28] The extreme views of *On Virgins*, however, contrasted with the more moderate interpretation contained in a slightly later treatise, *De Paradiso*, in which male authority was considered essential to the instruction and correction of women.[29]

Nonetheless, undermining patriarchal authority fulfilled a purpose in *On Virgins*, allowing Ambrose to reinterpret martyrdom as the result of the actions of male authority figures within the community, but not the Roman government. Accordingly, the narration of Agnes' death does not contain any reference to imperial courtiers apart from the executioners. Ambrose described how the virgin had refused to marry, but omitted mentioning that a *iudex* had condemned her to be dragged to a brothel, an episode that was included in Prudentius' later account.[30] The downplaying of official involvement is also evident in Ambrose's description of the martyrdom of Thecla, who was 'condemned by her husband's rage'.[31] Thecla's defiance would ultimately led to her execution, but Ambrose did not mention the judge or any other imperial officers. A similar interpretation is placed on the story of the unnamed virgin of Antioch, for which Ambrose is the only source. He described how some 'wicked men' denounced the maiden, who was more concerned about 'those who plotted against her chastity' than the imperial authorities.[32]

[26] Ambrose, *De virginibus*, 1.2.9. [27] Ambrose, *De virginibus*, 1.7.33.

[28] Y.-M. Duval, 'L'originalité du "De virginibus" dans le mouvement ascetique occidental: Ambroise, Cyprien, Athanase', in Y.-M. Duval (ed.), *Ambroise de Milan: Dix études* (Paris: Études augustiniennes, 1974), 9–66; V. Burrus, *Begotten, Not Made: Conceiving Manhood in Late Antiquity* (Stanford, CA: Stanford University Press, 2000), 141–51; Hunter, 'The Virgin, the Bride', 281–303.

[29] Ambrose, *De Paradiso*, 10.46–48, C. Schenkl (ed.), *Ambrosius*, CSEL 32.1, (Vienna: OeAW, 1896), 265–336; Kate Cooper, *The Virgin and the Bride: Idealized Womanhood in Late Antiquity* (Cambridge, MA: Harvard University Press, 1996), 75–8.

[30] Ambrose, *De virginibus*, 1.2.5–19; 1.3.19–21; Prudentius, *Peristephanon* 14.15–20, H. J. Thomson (ed. and trans.) *Prudentius, Volume II*, LCL 398 (Cambridge, MA: Harvard University Press, 1949).

[31] Ambrose, *De virginibus*, 2.3.19. [32] Ambrose, *De virginibus*, 2.4.22–33.

In *On Virgins*, martyrdom was thus not presented as a conflict between the Christians and the empire, but between the ascetic and the family way of life. Ambrose's text describes two gendered forms of authority. The Church embodies a Christian authority and is presented as a nurturing mother who instructs her children in correct behaviour:

> In this way the holy Church, unspotted with intercourse, but fertile in bearing, is a virgin in chastity and a mother in offspring. She gave birth to us as a virgin, not filled by a man, but by the Spirit ... She feeds us as a virgin, not with the milk of the body, but with that of the Apostle, with which he fed the weak age of the arising people.[33]

In contrast, patriarchal authority is depicted as restrictive and oppressive: 'Parents speak against her ... they threaten to disinherit her ... You practice, virgin, by being urged. And the anxious pleas of your parents are your first battles.'[34] Earlier Christian literature had opposed the persuasiveness of clerics' unblemished behaviour to the hierarchical violence of imperial institutions.[35] Ambrose, however, went here a step further and implicitly blamed patriarchal society for persecuting and oppressing Christian ascetics.

Ambrose's idiosyncratic depiction of gender roles underpinned his argument about the nature of the relationship between patriarchy and asceticism. Many martyr writings depict a strident tension between the extreme vulnerability of delicate young girls and the repressive machinery of the Empire, represented through the fierce actions of male bureaucrats.[36] In *On Virgins*, however, this divergence is alleviated as officers turned into defenders of the unarmed maidens. An example is Ambrose's description of an Antiochene virgin who was saved by a soldier who at first had 'the aspect of a terrible warrior', but later dressed up as a virgin.[37] Ambrose followed a similar model for the description of Thecla's frustrated martyrdom. In the oldest version of this story, in the *Acts of Paul and Thecla*, probably composed at different stages during the second century, the virgin was condemned to death and thrown to the beasts. Once in the arena, a fierce lioness defended the virgin and was torn apart by a male

[33] Ambrose, *De virginibus*, 1.6.31. [34] Ambrose, *De virginibus*, 1.12.63.

[35] P. Brown, *Power and Persuasion in Late Antiquity: Towards a Christian Empire* (Madison, WI: University of Wisconsin Press, 1992), 118–30.

[36] L. L. Coon, *Sacred Fictions: Holy Women and Hagiography in Late Antiquity* (Philadelphia, PA: University of Pennsylvania Press, 1997), 28–38.

[37] Ambrose, *De virginibus*, 2.4.28–30.

bear.[38] Conversely, Ambrose emphasised the masculinity of the lion that defended the virgin:

> the beast reverenced his prey and, having forgotten his own nature, assumed the nature that men had rejected. By such a transfusion of nature, one could see men dressed in wildness, imposing cruelty on the beast, and the beast kissing the feet of the virgin, teaching them what was due from men.[39]

The metaphor of a male executioner protecting the virgin from the rest of the community was the perfect parallel to Ambrose's personal story as an imperial officer who had previously been entrusted with enforcing imperial legislation and had subsequently turned into a defender of the vulnerable of Milan.

This self-portrait emerges more clearly in the third book of *On Virgins*, in which Ambrose recalled his family's long Christian tradition. The section opens with Ambrose's account of Marcellina's consecration by Pope Liberius, and continues with a description of her especial ascetic virtues. Ambrose went on to mention the example of the virgin Pelagia, who was martyred in Antioch, and devoted the treatise's last paragraph to discuss the death of Sotheris, who is presented as a role model for Marcellina: 'But why do I use examples of distant people to you, sister, whom the inspiration of hereditary chastity has taught by descent from a martyred ancestor?'[40] Despite these references to his female relatives, Ambrose does not provide any further information about Marcellina and Sotheris, apart from some details relating to the latter's martyrdom. The main focus of this book is therefore Ambrose who, much like the repentant executioner in his martyr narratives, is implicitly presented as the protector of his consecrated sister and his martyred ancestor.

The particular depictions of Sotheris and Marcellina enabled Ambrose to foreground a distinctively Christian model of authority, which differed somewhat from traditional aristocratic rule. For the Roman nobility, family was not simply a domestic institution made up of a series of affective ties; it was politically significant too.[41] Roman aristocrats had long advertised their illustrious relatives in order to communicate the idea that the holding of public office was their natural place in society. Accordingly, male ancestors and their political achievements were frequently

[38] *Acts of Paul and Thecla*, 4.3–4, R. A. Lipsius (ed.), *Acta Apostolorum Apocrypha*, Vol. 1 (Leipzig: Mendelssohn, 1891 [repr. Hildesheim: Olms, 1972]), 235–72.

[39] Ambrose, *De virginibus*, 2.3.20; Burrus, *Begotten Not Made*, 140–51.

[40] Ambrose, *De virginibus*, 3.7.38.

[41] Cooper, 'Closely Watched Households', 9–10.

discussed in aristocratic sources from the Republic to late antiquity. An example is Symmachus, a pagan senator and Ambrose's contemporary, who included twelve letters to his father Lucius Aurelius Avienus, the prefect of Rome in 364 and 365, in his letter collection. Many of these letters emphasised the importance of patriarchal authority and the family patrimony, stressing aristocratic status and suggesting that Symmachus had been raised to take up office in the imperial bureaucracy.[42] On the contrary, Ambrose only made one reference to his ancestry, to Sotheris. He did not refer to his father who, according to Paulinus had been the prefect of Gaul. This has raised the suspicion of scholars, who have speculated that Ambrose's father had been executed due to his involvement in an unsuccessful coup against the emperor Constans (d. 350).[43] Silence over male ancestors generated a Christian family history that suited Ambrose's recently acquired episcopal dignity. This enabled Ambrose to downplay the role of his aristocratic pedigree and prior involvement in the imperial bureaucracy in his election. By using Sotheris and Marcellina as models of social and political behaviour, Ambrose emphatically rejected the imperial administration and embraced the Christian clergy.

Ambrose exploited the potential symbolic capital of his female relatives on other occasions. On the one hand, Sotheris was mentioned again in the sermon *Exhortation to Virginity*, preached almost twenty years after *On Virgins*. During the intervening period, Ambrose had become one of the most renowned bishops of the West: Gallic and Spanish clerics often appealed to him to sort out their differences, and emperors entrusted him their spiritual well-being.[44] Ambrose's position was markedly stronger in the mid-390s, yet he returned to his martyred ancestor in the *Exhortation to Virginity*. He delivered this sermon in Florence in 394 on the occasion of the consecration of a church that had been paid by the local *matrona* Iuliana, whose three daughters were consecrated virgins. Ambrose had left Milan on the eve of the invasion of the usurper Eugenius (d. 394), who had assumed the imperial power after the death of the emperor

[42] M. R. Salzman, 'Symmachus and His Father: Patriarchy and Patrimony in the Late Roman Senatorial Elite', in R. Lizzi Testa (ed.), *Le trasformazioni delle 'élites' in età tardoantica* (Rome: L'Erma di Bretschneider, 2006), 357–75; C. Sogno, *Q. Aurelius Symmachus: A Political Biography* (Ann Arbor, MI: University of Michigan Press, 2006), 23–4; M. R. Salzman, 'Reflections on Symmachus' idea of Tradition', *Historia*, 38 (1989), 348–64.

[43] S. Mazzarino, *Storia sociale del vescovo Ambrogio* (Rome: L'Erma di Bretschneider, 1989), 10–12.

[44] Ambrose, *De obitu Valentiniani*, Faller (ed.), *Ambrosius*, 327–67; Ambrose, *De obitu Theodosii*, Faller (ed.), *Ambrosius*, 369–401; *Acta Conc. Taur.* 6, C. Munier (ed.), *Concilia Galliae a. 314–506*, CCSL 148 (Turnhout: Brepols, 1963), 57–8.

Valentinian II in unclear circumstances in 392. It seems that in order to avoid becoming embroiled in the political conflict, Ambrose started a tour of the churches of Aemilia-Liguria, including Bologna and Florence. This strategy is also identifiable in Ambrose's letter to Eugenius, in which he avoids making any reference to the addressee's political legitimacy, and explains that he had absented himself from Milan out of fear of God, because the usurper had made concessions to the pagans.[45] In the *Exhortation to Virginity*, Ambrose presents Sotheris' martyrdom as an example of female independence and endurance that dignified Iuliana's position as the head of an ascetic family. In addition, as at the start of his episcopacy, Ambrose used Sotheris to emphasise his Christian past and to conceal his involvement in secular politics in a moment of political turmoil.

On the other hand, Ambrose made a number of allusions to Marcellina in the two funeral orations for their brother Satyrus, delivered in 378. Ambrose seized the opportunity to stress the family's Christian and aristocratic background in front of the Milanese flock; he alluded to the siblings' 'inheritance neither distributed nor diminished', and described Marcellina again as a pious virgin requiring the assistance of her two brothers.[46] Ambrose's portrait of his sister as a vulnerable domestic figure contrasts sharply with the topics that he discussed in his three letters to her, which contain accounts of some of his most remarkable interventions in imperial politics.

Exposed Domesticity and High Politics in Ambrose's Letters

Ambrose's letter collection is a complex composition. It was published in two stages.[47] A first batch of seventy-nine letters organised in ten books came out shortly before Ambrose's death. Most of the letters in the first nine books focus on issues of ecclesiastical discipline, such as pastoral care and theology, and were mostly addressed to north Italian clerics and citizens. Letters in book ten of the collection, in contrast, concentrate on issues of empire-wide concern and are addressed to key religious and

[45] Ambrose, *Ep. extra coll.* 10.1; M. R. Salzman, 'Ambrose and the Usurpation of Arbogastes and Eugenius: Reflections on Pagan–Christian Conflict Narratives', *Journal of Early Christian Studies*, 18 (2010), 191–223; McLynn, *Ambrose of Milan*, 330–40; J. Szidat, 'Die Usurpation des Eugenius', *Historia*, 28 (1979), 487–508.

[46] Ambrose, *De excessu Fratris*, 1.33–34; 1.59.

[47] M. Zelzer (ed.), *Sancti Ambrosi Opera, Epistulae et Acta*, Vol. II, CSEL 82.2 (Vienna: OeAW, 1990, pp. xx–xxviii; M. Zelzer, 'Plinius Christianus: Ambrosius als Epistolograph', *Studia Patristica*, 23 (1989), 203–8; H. Savon, 'Saint Ambroise a-t-il imité le recueil de lettres de Pline le Jeune?', *Revue des Études Augustiniennes*, 41 (1995), 3–17.

political actors such as the bishop Theophilus of Alexandria and the Emperors Valentinian II and Theodosius I. After Ambrose's death in 397, another seventeen letters were published, twelve of which were addressed to the aforementioned emperors and Gratian I (d. 383). This group, the so-called *Letters outside the Collection*, deals with some of the most controversial episodes of Ambrose's episcopate, such as the excommunication of Theodosius I, the Council of Aquileia, and his interactions with the usurper Eugenius.

Two of the letters to Marcellina, *Ep.* 76 and *Ep.* 77, appeared in book ten of the collection, while the other, the *Ep. extra coll.* 1, was included among the letters outside the collection. The first two are dated in 386 and focus on the so-called Conflict of the Basilicas, which brought Ambrose into conflict with the Homoian Empress Justina, the mother of Valentinian II.[48] The episode is only known through Ambrose's writings, meaning that it is difficult to develop a full understanding of the events, but the dispute seems to have been about the court's authority to implement its religious agenda without the obstruction of bishops.[49] The conflict started in 385 and escalated in December that year, when the court accused Ambrose of misusing ecclesiastical funds and causing public disturbances. In January 386, the court increased the pressure on Ambrose by issuing a law that imposed the death penalty for those who impeded Homoian ceremonies. Despite the threat, however, Ambrose refused to surrender a Milanese basilica to the Homoians, an act of disobedience that is revealed in *Ep.* 75 to Valentinian II. Imperial politics gave Ambrose some room for manoeuvre in his conflict with the Homoian court at Milan, which had to share power with two Nicene emperors, Maximus (d. 388) and Theodosius I. Nevertheless, Justina seems to have tried to expel Ambrose from his see and replace him with the Homoian bishop of Durostorum, Auxentius.

48 The chronology of the Conflict of the Basilicas and Ambrose's letters on the matter are debated, see J. H. W. G., Liebeschuetz, *Ambrose of Milan: Political Letters and Speeches* (Liverpool: Liverpool University Press, 2005), 130–5; T. D. Barnes, 'Ambrose and the Basilicas of Milan in 385 and 386: The Primary Documents and Their Implications', *Zeitschrift für antikes Christentum*, 4 (2000), 282–99; McLynn, *Ambrose of Milan*, 181–96; G. Nauroy, 'Le fouet et le miel. Le combat d'Ambroise en 386 contre l'arianisme milanaise', *Recherches Augustiniennes*, 23 (1988), 3–86.

49 C. M. Chin, 'The Bishop's Two Bodies: Ambrose and the Basilicas of Milan', *Church History: Studies in Christianity and Culture*, 79 (2010), 531–55; M. L. Colish, 'Why the Portiana? Reflections on the Milanese Basilica Crisis of 386', *Journal of Early Christian Studies*, 10 (2003), 361–72; D. H. Williams, 'Ambrose, Emperors and Homoians in Milan: The First Conflict over a Basilica', in M. R. Barnes and D. H. Williams (eds.), *Arianism after Arius: Essays on the Development of the Fourth Century Trinitarian Conflicts* (Edinburgh: T & T Clark, 1993), 127–46; A. D. Lenox-Conyngham, 'Juristic and Religious Aspects of the Basilica Conflict of AD 386', *Studia Patristica*, 18 (1985), 55–8.

It was at this moment that Ambrose composed his *Sermon against Auxentius*, preserved as *Ep.* 75a. A second round of the conflict occurred during Easter 386, when Ambrose thwarted the court's attempts to seize a church for the Homoians by resisting with his congregation inside one of the Milanese Basilicas. The court replied by besieging the Basilica with imperial soldiers over night, but withdrew the following morning. *Ep.* 76 to Marcellina was written after the court had lifted the siege.

Two months later, in summer 386, Ambrose discovered the relics of Gervasius and Protatius, two saints who soon became a symbol of his recent triumph over the court.[50] Ambrose's *Ep.* 77 to Marcellina explains the discovery and the ceremonies of relocation of the relics of Gervasius and Protasius in Milan and is the only contemporary source for this episode.

The other letter to Marcellina (*Ep. extra coll.* 1) narrates Ambrose's clash with Theodosius after a church of the Valentinian sect and a synagogue were burnt in Callinicum (Asia Minor) in late 388 or at the beginning of 389. Theodosius ordered the bishop of Callinicum to pay for the reconstruction of the synagogue and to put on trial the persons that caused the destruction. Ambrose protested, and Theodosius revoked his decision, which did not prevent Ambrose from later writing two different letters of reproach. In this instance it seems that the bishop had the upper hand. Theodosius had just arrived in Milan after his victory over Maximus in 388 and was trying to consolidate his power in the west. In this context, it was more important for the emperor to maintain the loyalty of the courtiers of the western imperial capital than to deal with a distant case of public disorder.[51] After Theodosius' withdrawal, Ambrose wrote two almost identical letters to the emperor: *Ep. extra coll.* 1a and an edited version of the former, *Ep.* 74, which reproduces almost verbatim the *Ep. extra coll.* 1a, except for the last paragraph, on which I shall comment later in this paper. Lastly, Ambrose wrote the *Ep. extra coll.* 1 to Marcellina, the only one that narrates the whole episode.

The three letters to Marcellina have three characteristics that differentiate them from the rest of the collection. First, Marcellina is the only woman and the only relative among Ambrose's addressees. Second, all three letters describe controversial episodes in which Ambrose justified

[50] Liebeschuetz, *Ambrose of Milan*, 204–14; J. San Bernardino, '*Sub imperio discordiae*: l'uomo che voleva essere Eliseo (giugno 386)', in L. F. Pizzolato and M. Rizzi, (eds.), *Nec timeo mori: atti del Congresso internazionale di studi ambrosiani* (Milan: Vita e pensiero, 1998), 709–36; McLynn, *Ambrose of Milan*, 209–19.

[51] Liebeschuetz, *Ambrose of Milan*, 95–123; McLynn, *Ambrose of Milan*, 298–314.

public disagreement with imperial policy. Third, these are the only letters that narrate past events. In all of the other letters, Ambrose intervened in ongoing affairs. Therefore these texts provide chronological accounts that explain and contextualise the Conflict of the Basilicas and the burning of the Synagogue of Callinicum, which were sketchily depicted in other letters, and constitute the only piece of contemporary evidence for the discovery of the relics of Gervasius and Protasius. These events would be extremely obscure without the letters to Marcellina, which seem to have offered Ambrose opportunities to craft particular accounts of past controversies in an attempt to determine how they were subsequently remembered.

There are three other cases in which additional letters seem to have been incorporated into Ambrose's collection in order to guide the readers' interpretation of specific episodes. One example is the records of the Council of Aquileia, held in 381, in which Ambrose is shown taking up a leading role during the proceedings and which accompanied his letter to the emperors announcing the decisions of the assembly.[52] Another case is the debate about the Altar of Victory, in which Ambrose conflicted with the pagan senator Symmachus. Ambrose included Symmachus' *Relatio* 3, asking the emperors to restore the Altar of Victory to the Senate House, within his letter collection, but bookends it with his own responses, refuting pagan arguments. This seems to have been intended to highlight Ambrose's rhetorical dexterity when confronting one of the most famous orators of his time.[53] Finally, Ambrose included a letter from Pope Siricius asking him to summon a provincial council to condemn the Roman monk Jovinian. This letter functioned as a *de facto* confirmation of the metropolitan status of Milan – and therefore of Ambrose.[54]

The letters to Marcellina also seem to have been intended to exaggerate Ambrose's authority. These texts display an unusually triumphalist tone that contrasts with that adopted in other letters dealing with the same episodes. For instance, *Ep.* 76 on the Conflict of the Basilicas presented the court's retreat as the result of the unconditional support of the Milanese Christians for their bishop: 'I was asked to restrain the people. I answered that it was in my power not to spur them up; but in God's hands to

[52] *Gesta Concilii Aquileiensis* 1–2, Faller and Zelzer (eds.), *Sancti Ambrosi Opera, Epistulae et Acta*, 126–40.

[53] Symmachus' *Relatio* 3 is preserved as *Ep.* 72a in Ambrose's letter collection.

[54] Siricius' letter is preserved as *Ep. extra coll.* 41a in Ambrose's letter collection.

appease them.'[55] On the contrary, Ambrose's two other writings on the matter, *Ep.* 75 and the *Sermon against Auxentius*, suggest that he was in a much weaker position, using legal arguments to defend himself from the charges: 'No one should consider me contumacious when I affirm what your [Valentinian II's] father of august memory not only replied verbally, but also sanctioned it in his laws, that ... clerics should judge about clerics.'[56]

Similarly, *Ep.* 77 contains an inflated description of the ceremonies of discovery and translation of the relics of Gervasius and Protasius. Ambrose briefly admitted that these relics raised some opposition in Milan:

> Those who usually do so are jealous of your fame; and because of their envious disposition they cannot endure your fame, they hate the cause of your fame, and go so far in their madness that they deny the merits of the martyrs, whose services even the evil spirits acknowledge.[57]

Most of the letter, however, is devoted to describing the enthusiasm of the Milanese:

> I addressed the people then as follows: When I considered the multitudinous and unheard number of you who are gathered together, and the gifts of divine grace which have shone in the holy martyrs, I must confess that I consider myself unworthy of this.[58]

The contrast between the victorious atmosphere of the letters to Marcellina and those sent to emperors is still more evident in the case of the synagogue of Callinicum. Ambrose's *Ep.* 74 to Theodosius shows him obsequiously requesting the revocation of the punishment of the bishop and the monks of Callinicum: 'I have gathered these matters in this sermon, Emperor, out of love and fondness for you.'[59] Ambrose showed more determination in the version that was published after his death, the last paragraph of which includes a threat to the emperor: 'I certainly have done all I could, while still being respectful, so you hear me in the palace, so it might not be necessary for you to hear me in church.'[60] The letter to Marcellina (*Ep. extra coll.* 1) describes the supposed meeting in the church between Ambrose and Theodosius: Ambrose interrupted the services to admonish the emperor, who recognised his mistake and agreed to revoke the punishment of the bishop and the monks of Callinicum. The letter closes with a boastful restatement of Ambrose's triumph: 'And so,

[55] Ambrose, *Ep.* 76.10. [56] Ambrose, *Ep.* 75.2. [57] Ambrose, *Ep.* 77.16.
[58] Ambrose, *Ep.* 77.2–3. [59] Ambrose, *Ep.* 74.25. [60] Ambrose, *Ep. extra coll.* 1a.33.

everything was done as I wished.'[61] His earlier letter to Theodosius, however, suggests that the emperor had by this point already pulled back.[62]

Apart from providing an inflated vision of the scale and success of his political interventions, Ambrose was able to exploit the fact that his sister Marcellina was the recipient of these letters. In the epistolary genre, the addressee is not a passive reader, but a key character that mediates the interpretation of the writing. Within Ambrose's collection, Marcellina was a unique actor and analysis of her presence can thus uncover potential new meanings and nuances.

Ancient letter collections were a form of public literature. Authors edited their contents before publication, in the process producing carefully tailored self-portraits.[63] Given its dialogical nature, however, the epistolary genre creates an illusion of private interaction between the author and the addressee, fostering a feeling of voyeurism among readers that influences the way the latter understand letters.[64] In so carefully crafting his 'private' letters to Marcellina, Ambrose sought to encourage his audience to lower their critical guard and to assume that he was sincerely describing to his sister real events that could not be explained openly in the official 'public' letters to the emperors. Privacy and sincerity were further emphasised by the use of a closer, less formulaic language and a blunter phrasing, perceptible in Ambrose's immodest insistence on his own success.

With Marcellina in the position of addressee, Ambrose was able to 'domesticate' the episodes he was describing, minimising their political implications. Instead they could be presented as Ambrose's honest efforts to defend the spiritual well-being of the community. As a consecrated virgin, Marcellina was the quintessential embodiment of femininity and domesticity, an outsider who was far from the arena of high politics in which Ambrose was involved. The bishop elaborated his message according to this rationale; these three letters make reference to fewer legal technicalities and contain more Christian language and imagery, helping him to emphasise the risks that he faced in opposing emperors and to mask just how opportunistic his interventions had actually been.

Ambrose further enhanced the sense of tension through the use of martyr imagery. A good example is the letters about the Conflict of the

[61] Ambrose, *Ep. extra coll.* 1.28. [62] Ambrose, *Ep.* 74.9.

[63] T. E. Jenkins, *Intercepted Letters: Epistolarity and Narrative in Greek and Roman Literature* (Lanham, MD: Lexington Books, 2006), 1–14.

[64] J. G. Altman, *Epistolarity: Approaches to a Form* (Columbus, OH: Ohio State University Press, 1982), esp. 57–9; 87–95.

Basilicas. In *Ep.* 75 Ambrose protested the harshness of the January 386 law that prescribed the death penalty for those who impeded Homoian cult: 'suddenly through many provinces it has been commanded, that whoever acts against the Emperor will be beheaded, that whoever does not surrender the temple of God will be immediately put to death.' Ambrose went a step further in *Ep.* 76 to Marcellina and presented the case not as a prosecution against those who opposed imperial law, but as a persecution against the Nicene community: 'many very heavy penalties were threatened against respectable men, if they did not surrender the basilica. Persecution erupted, and if they had opened the gates; they seemed likely to break into every kind of violence.'[65] The later letter included four classical elements of martyr narratives: the object of pity, embodied by the Nicene community; the vulnerable virgin; the oppressive empire; and the righteous ex-official who confronted the oppressive state – Ambrose himself. Ambrose presented events in a similar way in his letter about the synagogue of Callinicum, recounting how he had defied the emperor by recalling that 'the prophetic or priestly authority has to be straightforward, and to advise not so much what is pleasant as what is useful'.[66] However, it seems that in reality and unlike martyr narratives, Ambrose did not triumph by enduring torture and suffering death, but by a strategic combination of opposition and appeasement of imperial authority. Nor should we underestimate his ability to craft selectively accounts of past events to maximise his spiritual capital and authority as bishop. Much like *On Virgins*, therefore, the letters to Marcellina were exercises in self-legitimisation. Ambrose overstated the importance of his interventions in the imperial arena. In addition, addressing the letters to Marcellina bestowed greater credibility on Ambrose's account and allowed the bishop to reframe his interventions as martyr narratives, exaggerating the risks he had incurred and the magnitude of his triumph over the emperor.

Conclusion

Despite their apparent simplicity, Ambrose's references to his female relatives were the product of a carefully constructed process of rhetorical composition that built on Roman and Christian traditions. Ancient narratives on womanhood portrayed women as passive, nurturing, and fragile

[65] Ambrose, *Ep.* 76.7. [66] Ambrose, *Ep. extra coll.* 1.2.

individuals who needed male surveillance and protection.[67] Female bodies thus acquired important symbolic power and could be deployed rhetorically to convey ideas of (il)legitimate authority and (un)righteous violence. The motif of illegitimate violence against female bodies became central to Christian martyr literature, a large part of which presented defenceless women as recipients of excessively cruel male violence.[68] Centuries of production and consumption of such Christian narratives turned vulnerable women into objects with the potential to carry powerful emotional messages and evoke sentimental responses. After the great persecutions of the third century, martyr literature became a window from which Christian Romans could peer out into the sufferings of their predecessors. Such writings maintained their popularity at the end of the fourth century, when social change and political unrest heightened domestic insecurity and distrust towards imperial authorities. At this point in time, the symbol of imperilled women seems to have had particular potential to spark public fears about the despotic exercise of authority. Ambrose's allusions to his female relatives thus seem to have been designed to exploit such ambiguities and anxieties.

Marcellina and Sotheris were presented in Ambrose's writings in ways that fulfilled two main objectives. They were key to constructing Ambrose's identity and authority as a bishop. Marcellina and especially Sotheris helped Ambrose to overlook his past as an imperial officer and flaunt an illustrious family history without seeming incongruous with his present position as a bishop. In addition, by identifying himself with female ascetic relatives Ambrose's episcopal legitimacy was enhanced. Traditional attributes of feminine virginity, such as purity, decorum, and modesty, were a good fit for the public image and authority of the bishop. Female relatives symbolised affective ties and contrasted with the institutionally sanctioned violence of paternal and imperial authority.[69]

[67] K. Wilkinson, *Women and Modesty in Late Antiquity* (Cambridge: Cambridge University Press, 2015), 58–60; E. A. Clark, 'Holy Women, Holy Words: Early Christian Women, Social History, and the "Linguistic Turn"', *Journal of Early Christian Studies*, 6 (1998), 413–30; A. Arjava, *Women and Law in Late Antiquity* (Oxford: Clarendon Press, 1996), 230–55; G. Clark, *Women in Late Antiquity: Pagan and Christian Lifestyles* (Oxford: Clarendon Press, 1993), 94–118.

[68] K. Cooper, 'The Voice of the Victim: Gender, Representation, and Early Christian Martyrdom', *Bulletin of the John Rylands University Library*, 80 (1998), 147–57.

[69] On the importance of narratives about the familial past for reconstructing identity, see the classic works of S. Hall, 'Negotiating Caribbean Identities', *New Left Review*, 209 (1995), 3–14; J. L. Peacock and D. C. Holland, 'The Narrated Self: Life Stories in Process', *Ethos* 21 (1993), 367–83; R. L. Ochberg and G. C. Rosenwald, *Storied Lives: The Cultural Politics of Self-Understanding* (New Haven, CT: Yale University Press, 1992), 4–5.

Ambrose also used his female relatives to present very particular interpretations of his interventions in the arena of imperial politics. The letters to Marcellina offered Ambrose the opportunity to rewrite his controversial conflicts with the emperors, understating the motivating role of politics and exaggerating their spiritual and moral dimensions instead. Ambrose did this by minimising the legal and political terminology and by using a purportedly 'feminised' language, which built on Christian imagery and evoked a series of sentimental values. He reframed these accounts as martyr narratives, helping him to attribute negative moral characteristics to the groups with which he was disputing and defining himself as the protector of a threatened 'insider' community.[70] The trope of female vulnerability thus contributed to legitimating an individual bishop's resistance against the empire.

Ambrose's writings were not exceptional. A contemporary rise of sentimentalism and pity in political discourse reveals a change in public language and behaviour, exposing deep social transformations to view. Broader changes in family dynamics at the end of the fourth and into the fifth century led to the rise of a domestic ideology, which emphasised the confinement of women to the home, but also increased their potential social and political relevance. Exposing women's literary and moral achievements to public scrutiny became a way of displaying familial grandeur and negotiating male authority.[71] The case of Ambrose shows that the portrayal of female weakness, intended to evoke compassionate responses, enabled authors to put across alternative social and political messages. Deploying the trope of female vulnerability reinforced Ambrose's legitimacy and fuelled support for his agenda as bishop. For Ambrose, as for the Christian martyrs, vulnerability thus functioned as the seed of triumph.

70 H. A. Drake, 'Intolerance, Religious Violence, and Political Legitimacy in Late Antiquity', *Journal of the American Academy of Religion*, 79 (2011), 193–235.

71 Cooper, *The Fall of the Roman Household*, 93–7.

CHAPTER 15

Women on the Edge
Violence, 'Othering', and the Limits of Imperial Power in *Euphemia and the Goth*

Thomas Dimambro

Introduction

The anonymous fifth-century Syriac romance *Euphemia and the Goth* is almost unique in late Roman hagiography. A family drama in which Edessa's divine protectors, the Holy Martyrs, wreak vengeance on the enemies of a defenceless widow and her only daughter, the narrative guides the reader through a carefully constructed series of contrasts from the intimate relationship between mother and daughter to the political relationship between Edessa and the Roman Empire. These contrasts are a challenging and fascinating starting point from which to explore questions of gender, identity, violence, and power in the late Roman imagination from the standpoint of a Syriac text.

Like many Syriac works, *Euphemia* has been little discussed in modern English scholarship since its sole translation in 1913. The detailed analysis that has been conducted concentrates on proving the Syriac provenance of the text.[1] Scholarly opinion accepts a fifth-century date of composition for *Euphemia* due to the military events recounted in the text and its similarity to other fifth-century Syriac works.[2] As such, it provides a contemporary

[1] The Syrian text is edited and translated into English by F. C. Burkitt, *Euphemia and the Goth: With the Acts of Martyrdom of the Confessors of Edessa* (London: Williams and Norgate, 1913). Burkitt, *Euphemia*, 48–56, makes a clear and convincing argument that *Euphemia* was originally composed in Syriac. There are Greek versions of the text, but, given their later provenance, they are not considered here. Recent studies include S. A. Harvey, 'Sacred Bonding: Mothers and Daughters in Early Syriac Hagiography', *Journal of Early Christian Studies*, 4 (1996), 27–56; P. Wood, *'We Have No King but Christ': Christian Political Thought in Greater Syria on the Eve of the Arab Conquest (c. 400–585)* (Oxford: Oxford University Press, 2010).

[2] Wood, *'We Have No King but Christ'*, 96, considers a fifth-century date of composition 'likely' following Burkitt, *Euphemia*, 57–8. A. H. M Jones, *The Later Roman Empire, 284–602: A Social Economic and Administrative Survey*, 2 vols. (Oxford: Basil Blackwell, 1964), II, 632 n. 53, comments that 'the historical details in §4 are correct and the story rings true'. The arrival of the Huns in 396 is a key date in *Euphemia* and is also recorded in the Chronicle of Edessa, a sixth-century account of Edessan history, 'The Chronicle of Edessa', *Journal of Sacred Literature*, Series 4, 5 (1864), 28–45. For further evidence that *Euphemia* is a fifth-century composition, see n. 19.

and complementary viewpoint to the Greek and Latin texts considered in this volume. By this period Edessa had been part of the Roman Empire for over two centuries, the fifth century being regarded as the high point of its integration into the imperial system.[3] The Syriac-speaking part of the Roman Empire, of which it was the centre, had a distinct language, identity, and form of Christianity, but it also had much in common with the other areas of the Empire.[4] It is hardly surprising, therefore, that *Euphemia* engages with issues which confronted local communities throughout the late Roman Mediterranean, such as their reaction to barbarian immigrants and the fashioning of identity, within an increasingly disparate polity. It also engages with the position of women and the problem of how a female-led household could live successfully within a militarised society.

It will be argued that *Euphemia* serves at least two integrative functions. Firstly, the text's focus on the protection that the Martyrs of Edessa can offer to a humble widow and her daughter – even far from home – provides a model of protection and belonging within which female members of the community can find safety and security, albeit within a male-dominated framework. This is a community whose divine and earthly advocates will act to protect those who have been wronged. On a second and related level, the text situates Edessa within the Roman imperial system, indicating that whatever the excesses of certain (foreign) agents of imperial power, Roman law and government will protect its citizens and uphold the judgements of their divine sponsors, although notably doing so through the intercession of the Church. This positioning sits somewhat uncomfortably, but interestingly, alongside clear notions of Edessan identity promoted throughout.

Articulating and analysing contrasts will be the primary methodology employed to support the above arguments, doing so through a broadly structuralist reading of the text.[5] This will be augmented by focusing

[3] As argued by C. Shepardson, 'Syria, Syriac, Syrian: Negotiating East and West', P. Rousseau (ed.), *A Companion to Late Antiquity* (Oxford: Blackwell, 2009), 456.

[4] This 'interconnectedness' with other fields is seen as one of the key strengths of Syriac studies, L. van Rompay, 'Syriac Studies: The Challenges of the Coming Decade', *Hugoye: Journal of Syriac Studies*, 10 (2007), 35. For an overview of Syria in late antiquity that stresses the importance of Edessa as a centre of Syriac cultural production, the city's integration into the Roman Empire, and its distinctive position between the Roman and Persian worlds, see Philip Wood, 'Syriac and the "Syrians"', in S. Fitzgerald Johnson (ed.), *The Oxford Handbook of Late Antiquity* (Oxford: Oxford University Press, 2012), 170–94.

[5] For the application of structuralist readings of antique texts, see D. J. A. Clines, 'Reading Esther from Left to Right', in D. J. A. Clines, *On the Way to the Post-Modern: Old Testament Essays,*

discussion on the use of violence within the narrative, which aids with setting the contrasts. This method of analysis enables the portrayal of the position of women within Edessan society and of Edessan society within the Roman state to be revealed.

Synopsis

Euphemia is set in the year 396 in the city of Edessa and primarily concerns the relationship between Euphemia, the only child of the widow Sophia, and a Gothic soldier stationed in the city. The story purports to have been told to the author by the presbyter of the church in which the Martyrs' bodies reside. The Goth, who is anonymous throughout, is a soldier of the Roman army, sent to Edessa instead of existing allies (*foederati*) who would usually protect Edessa but whose loyalty is in question. While billeted at Sophia's house, the Goth pressures Sophia into giving him her daughter's hand in marriage. Initially the Goth remains in Edessa, but when the army leaves he announces that he intends to take Euphemia with him. Sophia protests but eventually gives in to his pressure, before making the Goth swear on the coffins of the Martyrs of Edessa that he will not harm Euphemia. It is the power of the Martyrs to protect against injustices of all kinds that the story explicitly and overtly advertises.

On arrival at his homeland, the Goth announces to Euphemia that he already has a wife (also unnamed). He reduces Euphemia to the rags of a slave, and her former husband warns her not to speak out about their marriage. This is an act of social rather than physical violence and is the Goth's sole violent act – surprisingly, he is perhaps the least violent major character in the narrative. His wife, on the other hand, is motivated by jealousy, and treats Euphemia abominably. She beats her frequently, this violence increasing when she discovers that Euphemia is pregnant. Eventually, she poisons and kills Euphemia's son, correctly assuming that he was fathered by the Goth. Yet Euphemia is no wallflower: she takes her revenge by using the same poison on her cruel mistress, calling on God to sanctify her actions: 'I shall see whether she made my son lick anything that he died: and if not, I shall know that it was by a death from God that my son died.'[6]

1967–1998, 2 vols., Journal for the Study of the Old Testament Supplement Series 292–3 (Sheffield: JSOT Press, 1998), Vol. 1, 3–22.

[6] *Euphemia*, 140.6–9.

After seven days of mourning Euphemia is subjected to the wrath of her mistress' family. There is no legal protection to be had: the judge is 'far from that place'.[7] The family members beat her and imprison her in a cave full of corpses, demonstrating their disregard for the dead. Euphemia calls on the Martyrs of Edessa for assistance and they turn the smell of the rotting corpses into spices and transport the poor girl to Edessa, where she awakes at their shrine. She is reunited with her mother, Sophia, and the city is astounded at her story and aghast at the actions of the Goth.

There is an opportunity for revenge, however, when the Goth returns to Edessa with the army, in order to repel Hunnic and Persian advances. Sophia's kin (male) hatch a plot and trick the Goth into admitting his crimes against Euphemia, recording all that he says in order to build a case against him. The kin then approach the bishop of Edessa, who intercedes for Sophia by informing the Roman governor of what has occurred between Euphemia and the Goth. The governor pronounces judgement upon the Goth; he is to be executed by the sword and his corpse burnt. However, in an act of defiance against the state, the bishop intercedes on the Goth's behalf, and after much persuasion his body is exempted from burning. The people then praise God and the power of the Martyrs of Edessa, who have heard the prayers of a lowly woman. It is a gripping tale that, with analysis, provides a rich insight into a contemporary view of Edessan society.

Syrian Identity and Roman Power in *Euphemia*

Founded by the Seleucids in the early third century BC, Edessa was ruled by an Arab dynasty from around 170 BC, when it functioned as the capital of the Kingdom of Osrhoene. This situation prevailed until AD 212, when the city was absorbed into the Roman Empire.[8] Its geographical location at the edge of the Empire meant it became a centre of trade and a city of strategic military importance. Given that Edessa's ruling powers varied over time and it was a late addition to the Roman Empire, it is

[7] This is stated twice, presumably for emphasis, at *Euphemia*, 140.20–21 and 141.11.

[8] The date Edessa became a *colonia* is discussed in F. Millar, *The Roman Near East: 31 BC–AD 337* (Cambridge, MA: Harvard University Press, 1993), 476. The most likely date for the city's accession into the empire is 212/13. The standard work for the history and culture of Edessa is still J. B. Segal, *Edessa, 'The Blessed City'* (Oxford: Clarendon Press, 1970). For the pre-Christian religion of the city, as well as a brief historical survey, see H. J. W. Drijvers, *Cults and Beliefs at Edessa* (Leiden: Brill 1980). For wider surveys of the imperial period in the Near East see Millar, *Roman Near East*, and M. Sartre, *The Middle East under Rome* (Cambridge, MA: Harvard University Press, 2005).

unsurprising that an indigenous and somewhat unique culture developed, albeit influenced by the all-consuming Graeco-Roman influence of the day.[9] In the city and the surrounding area, a form of proto-nation of Syriac speakers developed, known as the *Suryaya*.[10] The identity of this ephemeral group – which became articulated more fully when Syriac became a literary language from the third century onwards[11] – was built on the Syriac language, a shared history, and Christian religious practice. Edessa cultivated a tradition as one of the earliest centres of Christianity, which was bolstered by the famous correspondence between King Abgar V and Jesus of Nazareth described by Eusebius and elaborated in the Syriac *Doctrina Addai*, written around 400.[12] It was the city's status as an episcopal see that enabled the spread of Syriac throughout northern Mesopotamia and boosted its status as a centre of Syriac culture and learning.[13]

Euphemia reflects the deeply Christian nature of Edessa, celebrating the divine favour bestowed upon the city by its Martyrs: the text's focus on a relatively humble female-led household suggests an author who was seeking to promote a vision of Edessa that included all elements of society under the leadership of the church hierarchy and the protection of the Martyrs.[14] *Euphemia*'s eponymous heroine is presented as an exemplar of the virtues of Syriac Christianity: modesty (*nakpūta*),[15] virginity (*bṯūlā*), and oneness (*iḥidāyā*) or single-minded devotion to God.[16] The *Doctrina Addai* sought to accomplish a similar task by providing models for identity and behaviour for the Edessan priesthood and Church.[17]

Given this historical, linguistic, and religious identity, the modern reader would expect to find tensions in Syriac literature between promoting the *Suryaya* and avoiding potentially dangerous claims of independence

[9] Wood, 'Syriac and the "Syrians"', 170–94; J. F. Healey, 'The Edessan Milieu and the Birth of Syriac', *Hugoye: Journal of Syriac Studies*, 10 (2007), 32, argues that pre-Christian Edessa was Hellenized to a limited degree.

[10] Wood, *'We Have No King but Christ'*, 12–15.

[11] Wood, *'We Have No King but Christ'*, 12–15.

[12] Eusebius, *Historia ecclesiastica* i.13 and iii.1; Wood, 'Syriac and the "Syrians"', 175–7. It was also known in the Western Empire, for the Gallaecian nun Egeria visited the city for this reason on her pilgrimage around the holy sites of the East in the late fourth century, *Egeria's Travels*, trans. J. Wilkinson (London: SPCK, 1971), 17–19.

[13] Segal, *Edessa*, 117.

[14] See also Wood, *'We Have No King but Christ'*, who notes this alternative version of Edessan society within Euphemia.

[15] As noted by Harvey, 'Mothers and Daughters', 31–3.

[16] For a brief discussion of the latter two terms and further references see S. A. Harvey, *Asceticism and Society in Crisis: John of Ephesus and the Lives of the Eastern Saints* (Los Angeles, CA: University of California Press, 1990), 7.

[17] Wood, 'Syriac and the "Syrians"', 176–7.

from the Roman state. That this is exactly the case in *Euphemia* is demonstrated by the author's somewhat ambiguous attitude toward Roman power. The text stages a direct comparison of social relations in the civil society of the East Roman Empire to family relations in the land of the Goths, where domestic violence is used to achieve illegitimate ends. Wood has called attention to how the Roman Empire plays the role of political and military master in *Euphemia*, having no cultural impact upon Edessan society whatsoever.[18] Yet Rome's relationship with Edessa and Gothia is not simply one of master and slave; rather, there are various ways in which Roman power is limited, acting as a foil for the *Suryaya* identity and the power of the Church. Indeed, the very context of *Euphemia* demonstrates the limits of Roman power; attacks from the Huns, first independently and later with the assistance of the Persians, provide the need for a military presence in Edessa, and so the presence of our Gothic protagonist.

The threat the Huns and Persians pose cannot be dealt with by the *foederati*, as there is treachery amidst their ranks.[19] They can be distinguished from the regular Roman army, as the Goth is explicitly stated as being 'from that army of the Romans'[20] rather than the *foederati* even though the Goths often provided federate units to the imperial army in this period.[21] Instead, by choosing a member of the Imperial army, the author showed a further weakness in Roman power: not only that the Romans were forced to use foreign troops (*foederati*) to protect their own Empire, but that when they were unable to control them they had to call on yet more barbarian troops (the Goths) to defend Edessa.

This lack of control extends to the Goth who marries Euphemia. In *Euphemia*, this foreign element within the Roman army could only be brought to justice because of the patient actions of the Edessan community. Without this Edessan 'self-help', the Church there could not have acted as a conduit between people and state, and the Roman governor could not have functioned as the agent of legitimate Roman power in Edessa. As such, the very presence of the Goth in Edessa and his actions once there highlight the limits of Roman power in late fourth-century Syria.

[18] Wood, *'We Have No King but Christ'*, 98.

[19] *Euphemia*, 131.2–6. *Foederati* were troops allied to the Empire who fought under their own commanders. The use of *foederati* to mean 'allies' is a further indication *Euphemia* is an early fifth-century composition. Its usage changed in the late fifth century to mean any troops fighting under the command of the emperor, P. Heather, *The Goths* (Oxford: Blackwell, 1996), 153. For its usage in the time of Justinian see Segal, *Edessa*, 118.

[20] *Euphemia*, 131.7–8.

[21] Heather, *The Goths*, 155.

In the end, however, it is divine, not military power that ensures Euphemia's deliverance and the return of the Goth to Edessa. The will of God, not the Emperor, is responsible: 'by the Providence of God that was in this business the Goth came against his will to Edessa'.[22] The Emperor may have decided to send troops there, but divine power moved his hand and thus the crimes of the Goth could be judged.

The final scene further underlines the relationship between Edessa and the Roman Empire. Roman law is portrayed in *Euphemia* as one of the main and positive differences between Edessan society and Gothia. This law is presented as fair and just, ensuring protection for those who would otherwise be powerless. At the end of the story, when asked by the bishop if he would consider treating the remains of the Goth with leniency, the governor refuses for what appear to be pious reasons, fearing retribution from the Martyrs for having mercy upon such a wicked man.[23] Eventually, however, the governor accedes to the demands of the bishop and the people of Edessa and spares the Goth's body from burning. This final scene in the tale thus neatly encapsulates the negotiated nature of the relationship between the representatives of Roman imperial power and the representatives of the people of Edessa, namely their bishop and their Martyrs. Edessa is a part of the Roman order and the Edessans make use of Roman power for protection, but their identity is not subsumed by that of the Empire.[24]

Violence and Dislocation: Gothia and Edessa

The author uses the theme of distance within the narrative of *Euphemia* to contrast Edessan and Gothic societies. This theme allows the author to articulate and create contrasting attitudes to violence within Edessan and Gothic societies on three distinct levels: the individual, the kinship group, and the overall social system.

Distance is most obviously used by changing the physical location of characters. The author establishes shifts in identity and so reinforces the two overarching identities within the narrative: Edessan and Gothic. This is most apparent when the Goth takes Euphemia from Edessa to his homeland, a move which creates tensions at the individual level. The

[22] *Euphemia*, 146.15–23. [23] *Euphemia*, 152.23–153.4.

[24] Wood, 'Syriac and the "Syrians"', 188–9 argues that texts such as the *Doctrina Addai* served a similar purpose, 'placing Edessene history into a Roman imperial framework' but 'not subordinating themselves to the Roman world'.

geographical distance breaks the bond between mother and daughter. Indeed, this was the main reason why Sophia did not want the Goth to marry Euphemia, for she feared, quite rightly, that he would take her away. As Harvey has noted,[25] this demonstrates the strength of the mother–daughter bond in a household that was lacking a *paterfamilias*, a social context which is explored by James Corke-Webster in this volume.[26] This dislocation is further emphasised by the emotional reaction when mother and daughter are reunited: their minds 'were stirred with love and affection' and they embraced each other, weeping.[27]

The journey as identity change trope is common in ancient literature and the author of *Euphemia* deploys it effectively. As they near the end of their journey to Gothia, the Goth makes his true intentions known to Euphemia: he strips off the fine clothing and gold he has given her and reveals that he already has a wife. This is a key transitional moment in the text and marks Euphemia's change from a silent, passive daughter and bride to a woman who is active and her own agent in this land. This is the only point in the story where the Goth speaks directly to Euphemia, and the now enslaved woman speaks for the first time. Far from Edessa she is no longer subject to social convention and is willing to break the social code of female modesty and harangue the Goth for her plight. Her modesty (*nakputa*) in Edessa has gone, and tenacity appears that she is not allowed to express in her homeland; indeed, Euphemia speaks not a single word in her native city. In Gothia, however, the Edessan does speak and accuses the Goth of two things in the following order: taking her away from her homeland and taking away her freedom.[28] This order of accusation is replicated on the next two occasions on which her speech is reported, when she calls on God and the Martyrs of Edessa to save her.[29] The theme of being a stranger in a foreign land is common in Syriac Christianity.[30] Euphemia's distress derives from her separation from her mother and betrayal and maltreatment by her new husband, but also from the social dislocation that results from the physical movement.

By being torn away from Edessa, Euphemia is also torn away from civilisation. Although the Goth takes Euphemia close to a city, his resi-

[25] Harvey, 'Mothers and Daughters', 36–8.

[26] *Euphemia* can help shed further light on the nature of female relationships in the Late Antique period, complementing James Corke-Webster's chapter in this volume.

[27] *Euphemia*, 145.7–11. [28] *Euphemia*, 136.2–15. [29] *Euphemia*, 136.18–137.2; 137.16–19.

[30] S. P. Brock, 'Early Syrian Asceticism', *Numen*, 20 (1973), 9. Its repeated use here demonstrates that *Euphemia* was very much part of the Syriac literary style.

dence is outside the city and apparently some distance from it.[31] Physical distance is to be accompanied by cultural distance: the author makes a clear distinction between the Goth, his wife, and their family and the residents of the nearby city. This distinction is articulated fully when the author describes how the people of this city identify with Euphemia and were 'grieved'[32] when they saw her impending execution. Indeed, their sympathy is perceived as a threat, for the Goth's wife's kin roll a great stone across the entrance of the tomb in which they encase Euphemia, 'lest the people of the city should come and open [it] for her and let her out'.[33]

The social dislocation and distinction the author makes between the city and the countryside in Gothia is further enhanced by the change in access to, and attitudes toward, law. The author asserts this by twice stating that the 'judge was far from that place'[34] (i.e. the Goth's home). As a Roman soldier, the Goth presumably lives within imperial territory, although this does not mean that he would have been subject to Roman law: the Roman state granted Goths land within the Empire in 382, within which they were allowed to maintain their own laws.[35] Regardless of the exact location, the author makes clear that recourse to the law is impossible in Gothia, but accessible to all in Edessa.

Legitimising Violence

With the contrasts of distance so set, the author augments these by using a more discreet method to articulate identity: the distinction of legitimate and illegitimate violence. In the context of *Euphemia* what is legitimate and illegitimate violence can be defined as follows: that which is controlled and has the approval of the Roman state or God is legitimate, that which is gratuitous and has no authority from either state or deity is illegitimate. By making *Euphemia* a story of violence the author can articulate more fully the contrasts between Gothic and Edessan society to reinforce the Edessan identity and also the desirability of Roman rule.

The violence that requires legitimating in Gothia is Euphemia's murder of the Goth's wife. The most shocking violence is the murder of Euphemia's infant by the Goth's wife. The latter is the instigator of the ensuing

[31] In one instance, the Goth's wife sends Euphemia 'away to market, to a place a long way off', *Euphemia*, 139.8.

[32] *Euphemia*, 141.1. [33] *Euphemia*, 141.3–4. [34] *Euphemia*, 140.20–21 and 141.11.

[35] Heather, *The Goths*, 137. J. Barlow, 'Kinship, Identity and Fourth-Century Franks', *Historia*, 45 (1996), 230, makes an educated guess that the Goth was from the Trans-Danubian region, and the settlement in question somewhere in Thrace.

violence, subjecting Euphemia to punitive violence immediately on the heroine's arrival in Gothia.[36] She burdens her rival with physical work and beats her, increasingly so when she discovers that her slave is pregnant.[37] She resents Euphemia for her beauty, her relationship with the Goth, and because she has had a child by the Goth.[38] The Goth's wife is, not unreasonably, angry at her husband following the birth of Euphemia's child: the male infant was 'like his father [i.e. the Goth] exceedingly'.[39] This increases her hatred of the Edessan, leading this woman to pressure the Goth into granting her power over Euphemia. He breaks his sacred vow with the following words: 'Thou hast authority over her; everything thou dost wish to do, do, for she is thy slave.'[40] From the viewpoint of *Euphemia's* contemporary audience, nothing could be further from the truth. She is a freewoman, not a slave, so any violence against Euphemia by her new mistress is not only illegal in the context of Euphemia's Roman citizenship but transgresses a divinely ordained vow.[41] Subsequent events show, however, that even beyond the power of imperial law, divine justice can and will be dispensed by the Martyrs of Edessa to an Edessan who places her faith in their power.

The Gothic mistress' violence toward Euphemia then peaks, in what is the most shocking episode in the whole narrative: the Goth's wife administers a fatal poison to Euphemia's infant.[42] Here the author generates a disturbing contrast between the violent actions of the Gothic wife and the 'fair and comely'[43] Euphemia. But the heroine's revenge is equal and opposite: she uses the same poison to kill her mistress. Euphemia's action, or rather reaction, creates a paradox: how can a murderess be worthy of divine favour? The answer lies in faith: God and the Martyrs sanction her violence. Euphemia places her trust in God and accepts the murder of her son as a legitimate result of God's will, saying, when administering the poison to her mistress' wine, 'I shall see whether she made my son lick anything that he died: and if not, I shall know that it was by a death from

[36] *Euphemia*, 137.20–2. [37] *Euphemia*, 138.8–12.

[38] The child is said to be 'like her [the Goth's wife's] husband', *Euphemia*, 138.23. The couple have no children and were married prior to the Goth being sent to Edessa, giving her another reason to despise Euphemia.

[39] *Euphemia*, 138.22.

[40] *Euphemia*, 138.21–3. The fact that Euphemia is treated as a slave runs contrary to the prevailing view of barbarians, who were considered as natural slaves, Wood, *No King but Christ*, 21–5. This is a further way in which Gothia is contrasted with Edessa.

[41] For further discussion on the unacceptability of violence against women and non-slaves, see Vasiliki Limberis' chapter in this volume. For a detailed discussion on punitive violence within the Late Antique context, see Chris L. de Wet's chapter in this volume.

[42] *Euphemia*, 138.24–139.4. [43] *Euphemia*, 137.4–5.

God that my son died.'[44] With these words she claims that her action falls within the sphere of divine obedience. One thing can make violence the right course of action in a land where there is no law to protect the weak: the will of God.[45]

The same cannot be said of the gratuitous violence employed by the wife's kin. The author does not provide them with any religious affiliation, as with the Goth, so disallowing even the possibility that they could tacitly accept the will of God. Their violence is reactionary, instinctive, and extreme. When they realise that it was Euphemia who killed their kinswoman they beat her and imprison her in a tomb next to the wife's 'stinking corpse'[46] and intend to sleep outside in order to 'impale her on a stake and shoot at her with arrows'[47] the following morning. This intention is certainly the most violent in the story and is not legitimate in any way, as it has neither divine nor legal approval. The judge was, after all, 'far from that place'. Instead of having a legal hearing, the council of the Goths 'approved itself to their heart'[48] that she should be executed. This does not involve any sort of trial or consideration of evidence; rather it is simply an emotional reaction. Indeed, this decision is based upon the feelings of the council's 'heart'.[49] The behaviour of the Goths lacks any form of self-control, and along with the absence of law and rural location they are furnished with some of the prevailing trappings of barbarians.[50]

The contrast with the actions of Sophia's kin towards the Goth, when he later returns to Edessa, is stark. Their society operates under the purview of Roman law, a tool that can be used effectively to judge wrongdoers and mete out lawful punishments. The resulting violence, namely the execution of the Goth, is clearly legitimised. When Sophia's kin discover the Goth's crimes they do not approach him in a rash and violent manner, as do barbarians in Gothia, but with a well thought-out plan, conducted within the parameters of the law.[51] The Goth's subsequent confession is witnessed by Sophia's kin, who bind him in Sophia's house and record the affair in writing, subsequently delivering an affidavit

[44] *Euphemia*, 140.6–9.

[45] From a structuralist perspective, God is the sender and helper, while Euphemia is the subject of the object, which is ultimately deliverance, from her opponent, the Goth's wife. See Clines, 'Reading Esther from Left to Right', 5–6, for further discussion and application of this method in a Biblical context.

[46] *Euphemia*, 140.22.

[47] *Euphemia*, 141.10–11.

[48] *Euphemia*, 140.21.

[49] *Euphemia*, 140.21.

[50] Wood, *'We Have No King but Christ'*, 22–6.

[51] *Euphemia*, 147.9–151.3.

to the bishop.[52] This measured act of physical violence is a far cry from the beating and dragging to which the Goths subjected Euphemia. So whilst these actions are still violent, the way they are performed contrasts strongly with the behaviour of Goths in Gothia and emphasises the civility with which the Edessans conduct themselves. Further, the thought processes of the Edessans are clear and calculated and within the parameters of Roman law. Their actions result in the Roman governor playing the role of judge and executioner, with the Church also involved and working as the conduit between people and state. The Bishop, personalised as Eulogius, calls together the clergy who decide to deliver the affidavit to the Stratelates.[53] By including this step in the legal process, the author makes clear that any judgement that leads to violence will be legitimised by both state and church. The former is clearly the case, as the Goth's crime includes breaking the 'pure laws of the Romans',[54] a clear reference to the benefits of Roman rule and a statement which provides secular legitimacy to the impending execution.[55]

Family, Gender, and Power

It is by now obvious to the reader that women play pivotal roles in this rather gruesome tale. The story revolves around Euphemia, Sophia, and the Goth's wife, albeit with the Goth playing a crucial role. The women are also the most violent characters in the story. It is worth recalling that the Goth performs only one act that can potentially be viewed as violent, disrobing Euphemia, whereas both Euphemia and the Goth's wife commit premeditated murder. Understanding the role of women within the narrative, then, is key to understanding this portrayal of Edessan society and will be done in light of previous arguments regarding Edessan identity. Indeed, by using women as the main protagonists in this story, the author was able to demonstrate the role they could play in this version of Edessan society. Up to now the analysis has concentrated on what the ideal Edessa would look like; we now proceed to consider how it could operate and the part women should play within it.

52 *Euphemia*, 151.6–7 states that the bishop 'read what was written', suggesting that the affidavit had been taken down in writing.

53 *Euphemia*, 151.4–15. The Church is frequently depicted as conduit between people in contemporary literature, the apogee of which is the excommunication of Theodosius by Ambrose, Bishop of Milan, for which episode see David Natal's chapter in this volume.

54 *Euphemia*, 152.12.

55 Wood, *'We Have No King but Christ'*, 98.

Fully to appreciate the importance of the role of women in this story, what gives them presence and power or agency needs to be established. For without these characteristics, the three women would have little impact upon the male characters and would certainly be less memorable for the audience. The power the three women exert in *Euphemia* can broadly be placed into four categories: the power of voice, visual power, their power as part of a wider kin group, and the physical power of violence. These are used by the author to create three images of female agency: the first in Edessa prior to Euphemia's exit, the second in Gothia, and the third on Euphemia's return to her homeland. It is the latter that is the ideal, as will become clear. The above categories of power are useful tools for analysing how the author has created these, at times, quite subtle distinctions and will demonstrate the vision of female agency that has been created in this literary work.

In the Edessa presented before Euphemia's departure to Gothia, the female characters are presented as weak and with no recourse to protection. Sophia cannot control the Goth in any way and is 'overcome like a weak woman'[56] as his threats and pressure, always verbal, finally take their toll and Sophia agrees to her daughter marrying the Goth. She does not call upon her (male) kin, so cannot exert even the threat of physical violence or restraint upon the Goth, unlike when Euphemia returns from Edessa after her exile. This presents a skewed view of Edessa and perhaps a warning to female-only households acting independently of a wider male kin group.

This warning appears to extend to how a mother should control her daughter. The source of Euphemia's problem is that the Goth catches a glimpse of her and is instantly inflamed with desire. This is a clear demonstration of the visual power Euphemia could exert, and does not need to be complemented by any form of speech. Soon after this unfortunate visual revelation, Sophia realises the effect her daughter has had on the Goth and she hides her away so the unwelcome guest cannot see the reason for his infatuation. This is too late and the Goth does not desist, eventually getting his way. In this section of the story, his words have power, particularly when they are coupled with the potential religious legitimacy they gain when the Goth swears a vow on the bones of the Martyrs. The words of Sophia and the Goth are similar but opposite; Sophia's have no power, the Goth's have power, but both have serious consequences for each other. Sophia loses her daughter for a time, whilst the Goth eventually loses his life.

[56] *Euphemia*, 133.6–7.

The use of speech and effect of visual power in the opening scene demonstrate exactly what should not be done in Edessa and how female agency should not operate. The visual power of an attractive young woman should be concealed and only revealed when the time is right. The power of speech should not be underestimated and can be used by those who are untrustworthy to achieve ill-gotten ends. And females should not try to operate alone, without the help of their male kin and community; to do so spells disaster.

In Gothia female agency is turned upside down. Gone are silence and visual power, replaced with loud words and raw violence. As has been mentioned, Euphemia suddenly gains a voice at the key transitional moment of disrobing, when she ceases to exist as a freeborn Edessan and becomes a foreign slave. This Gothia appears to be a land in which the female voice has impact, for both Euphemia and the Goth's wife have strong voices which men both listen to and heed. The Martyrs respond to Euphemia's calls for aid and the Goth's wife uses words to pressure him into granting her power over Euphemia.[57] In this respect he is very like Sophia, but overcome like a weak man in a dystopia where men cannot resist the power of the female voice.

The Goth also cannot control female actions. One can assume that he would not want his son nor his beautiful Edessan bride killed, but he does nothing to prevent either instance of violence, nor does he react to them in any way. Indeed, the Goth conducts no actions whatsoever in his homeland. The child is presumably his only son, as no mention is made of other children and his Gothic wife is jealous of the child. As such, this newborn would have given an added dimension to the Goth's identity, as he would have been a father. The author does not allow this; he is not a father, no kin are mentioned so he has no son, and he is not really a husband either. He has no control over his Gothic wife, he cannot even stop her killing his own son, and he tricked Euphemia into marrying him, leaving him with no real role as a husband. This is the opposite of what a man should be in Edessa and indeed what the Goth could have been if he had stayed in Edessa; a father, a husband, and a son to Sophia.

The strength of his wife's kin is a further measure of the Goth's weakness. The Goth appears to live in his wife's home with her kin and be subject to their expectations.[58] He is forced to give up his possession (Euphemia) partly because of these expectations and even warns his slave against speaking out for fear that she will be killed by his wife and her

[57] *Euphemia*, 138.20–23. [58] Barlow, 'Kinship', 230.

kin.[59] That he requests this on her arrival and that this is the only time he speaks to Euphemia in the entire story gives it added emphasis. Further, it is her kin, and not the Goth, who react to his wife's death and hold the power of physical violence in this land. The Goth can neither influence nor be the bearer of the crude retribution that follows.

The female agency that is exhibited in Gothia creates a situation in which the Goth is almost entirely emasculated and his identity is diluted even further. This shell of a man clearly has little power in his own domestic household, unlike when he is first in Edessa and can easily take control of a female-only household which has no male support. In Gothia that is simply not possible, as the women are too strong. The emasculation that the author subjects him to works to reinforce the ability of females in Gothia to act as their own agents, in opposition to the ideal position of women in Edessa when Euphemia returns.

Euphemia's journey from Gothia to Edessa marks the final stage in this story and the realisation of what this author posits the ideal Edessa to be. When Euphemia arrives in her homeland, she opens her eyes and has a vision of one of the Martyrs, Mar Shmona. He disappears and she is left at their shrine, giving thanks to the power of the Lord that resides in bones of the Martyrs, significantly thanking them for taking her away from slavery and back to her homeland, thus giving her back the identity the Goth so cruelly stole. This is the longest piece of reported speech by Euphemia and, importantly, is the only utterance she makes at any time in Edessa. Aside from this she is completely silent in her home town, where her mother speaks for her instead. This is a far cry from the strength of her words in Gothia. This silence does not mean, however, that Euphemia is without power nor that speech itself has no power in Edessa. Rather, Euphemia's power lies in her visual appearance, something which her mother can now control in this new version of Edessa.

This power is realised when the Goth visits Sophia's house at the behest of her neighbour. She greets him and asks after her daughter, now hidden within the house. Unlike when the Goth was pressuring her into granting Euphemia's hand in marriage, his replies hold no traction and she can withstand his lies; she is no longer a 'weak woman'. Her reply to his lies is strong and Sophia castigates him for breaking the oath he made. She then reveals Euphemia, showing her daughter to the Goth at a time of her choosing. He is stunned into silence, to such an extent that 'like a dead

[59] *Euphemia*, 135.18–23.

man so he became'.[60] Here the visual power of Euphemia has overcome the verbal power of the Goth. Given that his power in Edessa rested on his words, if he is unable to speak then he is powerless.

This episode demonstrates how a female-only household could protect itself against a male intruder. However, Sophia is only able to reveal Euphemia to the Goth because of the intervention of her male kin. It is worth remembering that these two women are of the most vulnerable in society, being a widow and an only daughter,[61] and require the male assistance of their kin to protect them and to use the powers they have effectively. As well as the kin being male, a further change is that the domestic sphere has been made public, a change which is clearly for the better. Her home is now the setting for a public display of justice, in which the Goth is revealed as a liar and the entire scene recorded in a legal document, the affidavit. By harnessing her familial and community connections Sophia can create a document which can be used to harness the power of both Church and state, for it is this that is brought to the Bishop and the governor and against which the Goth is judged; 'Is it true what thou hast heard written in this affidavit?'[62] asks the governor, to which the Goth gives a positive reply. Here the written word holds the greatest power, something which was written and used by men, but could only be created by the actions of women and is ultimately used to protect them.[63]

In this idealised Edessa the position of two vulnerable women can be summarised as follows; they can exert power and live successfully as a female-only household, but only with the support of a male kin group and the male representatives of Church and state. Nevertheless, that a female-only household could live quite successfully within a male-dominated environment is a notable finding. The mother–daughter relationship is very strong here and the necessity for a *paterfamilias* is simply not there. The kin group can quite easily fill this role. The Goth as husband is not needed, a role which was not generally considered the ideal in Syriac literature of this period.[64] This version of how a female-only household could exist successfully within a male environment, notably without a

[60] *Euphemia*, 150.7–8. [61] Harvey, 'Mothers and Daughters', 37. [62] *Euphemia*, 152.6.

[63] For judicial proceedings brought by women against their husbands in late Roman Egypt, see Ilias N. Arnaoutoglou, 'Marital Disputes in Greco-Roman Egypt', *Journal of Juristic Papyri*, 25 (1994), 11–28. There are striking similarities between this story and the use that women in late Roman Egypt made of the Church as an intercessor in order to seek justice and respite from abusive marriages through divorce.

[64] See n. 72 below.

paterfamilias, is a step away from the prevailing view of the Late Antique household, where this figure was changing from the previously Roman military figure to a Christian father.[65] As such, the author of *Euphemia* presents a view of how a Late Antique female household could exist, and in so doing demonstrates the changes that had occurred since the arrival of Christianity.[66]

Aside from protection by the kin group, the author may be suggesting an alternative method of successful female-only living, namely, the Syriac phenomenon that was the *bnay/bnat qyama*, the 'Sons/daughters of the Covenant'.[67] These were a specifically Syrian group of lay brethren who dedicated their lives in service of the Church. They lived an ascetic lifestyle, committed to virginity, but were permitted to live within a wider secular community, such as a city, and in mixed groups. Ideas of 'oneness' with God, as well as virginity, were traits of the *bnat qyama*, and both are used to describe Euphemia. Indeed, the author may have wanted to restore Euphemia to some form of virginity by having her child and husband killed in the narrative.[68] There is certainly an element of reintegration into Edessan society, the transition allowed owing to the miracle the Martyrs perform in transporting her back to Edessa. On Euphemia's return there is a definite behavioural change to Euphemia and Sophia; both regain their modesty (*nakpūta*) and show increased devotion to God through constant prayer.[69] The potential for their new identity within the *bnat qyama* is marked by a new practice on their part. This devotion is clear on Euphemia's arrival in Edessa, for she praises the Martyrs in a short speech which

[65] As discussed in K. Cooper, 'Gender and the Fall of Rome', in P. Rousseau, (ed.), *A Companion to Late Antiquity* (Chichester: Wiley-Blackwell, 2009), 187–200.

[66] An overview of the changes in literary sources is discussed in James Corke-Webster's chapter in this volume, who also discusses the similar, albeit overtly ascetic, female-only household in Gregory of Nyssa's *Life of Macrina*.

[67] For a brief overview and attendant bibliography on the *bnat qyama* see S. A. Harvey, 'Revisiting the Daughters of the Covenant: Women's Choirs and Sacred Song in Ancient Syriac Christianity', *Hugoye: Journal of Syriac Studies*, 8 (2005), 125–49.

[68] Interestingly, there is no suggestion that Euphemia should seek an annulment, even though such a course of action would have been legally possible. Euphemia's consent, a legal requirement is not mentioned. Further, unilateral divorce may have been possible, even within the restrictive limits of the fourth century. For unilateral divorce to be possible, the accused had to have either prepared poisons, be a murderer, or disturbed tombs. The Goth, or at least his wife and kin, had transgressed each stipulation willingly. That Euphemia did not seek a divorce emphasises the horrific nature of the Goth's crimes in the view of the imagined audience.

[69] *Euphemia*, 146.10–14. They pray at the shrine of the Confessors 'in all modesty [*nakpūta*]'. Gregory of Nyssa's *Life of Macrina* also portrays a daughter who encourages greater devotion from her mother, for which see James Corke-Webster's chapter in this volume.

includes sections of psalms, and is indeed reminiscent of one.[70] Song played an important part in the *bnat qyama*, and singing psalms was one of their duties, as laid down in the fifth-century Rabbula Canons, which set out rules for the community.[71] It is certainly not stated that Euphemia is a part of the *bnat qyama*, but because of the events in the story she could now become part of it, perhaps the ideal position of such young women in Edessa. The ideal was certainly not the married life, which is little mentioned in other sources of the fourth and fifth century,[72] and had been so disastrous for Euphemia. This version of reintegration is hypothetical, yet the possibility is there and posits a notion of how women could live without men in their immediate domestic environment.

Conclusion

This essay has considered a little-known Syriac work in order to bring out its narrative richness in a way that allows it to become part of a wider discourse about identity, violence, and the role of women in the Late Antique eastern Empire. By employing a structuralist methodology, the story can be viewed as one of strong and highly developed contrasts, ultimately used by the author to articulate a view of an ideal Edessa. Through the use of distance, dichotomies of barbarian and civilised are set and reinforced with the complementary dichotomy of legitimate and illegitimate violence. This latter contrast also allows the primary benefit of Roman rule to be made clear, namely the rule of law which ensures justice for vulnerable female-only households against outsiders who attempt to disrupt them. Nevertheless, the reactive nature of the Roman state and the fact that it can be used by the Edessan people and coerced by the local church hierarchy sends a clear message: Edessa wishes to have Roman rule, but it can and will be used to the advantage of Edessans using the social structures in place.

The social structure of a lay female-only household described in *Euphemia* is distinct from the heavily ascetic female households found in contemporary Greek Christian writings. Further, given the apparent warning to such households that they should not act outside of male frameworks, seen in the anguish Sophia and Euphemia have to endure when

[70] *Euphemia*, 143.18–144.10. [71] Harvey, 'Revisiting', 1.

[72] S. J. Murray, 'The Characteristics of the Earliest Syriac Christianity', in R. W. Thomson, T. Matthews and N. G. Garsoian (eds.), *East of Byzantium: Syria and Armenia in the Formative Period* (Washington DC: Dumbarton Oaks, 1982), 6; echoed in Brock, 'Early Syrian Asceticism', 5–7.

they do, it suggests such households were not unusual in Edessa at this time. As such, this analysis of *Euphemia* has shed further light on the position of women within Edessa at the turn of the fifth century, perhaps even suggesting that the options for female-only living were better integrated than for women elsewhere in the Empire. Certainly, the position of mother and daughter on Euphemia's return to Edessa creates a picture in which, with the protection of family, Church, and state, and above all, the sponsorship of the Martyrs, a poor widow and her daughter could live together in peace, trusting in God as integrated members of something greater, the Blessed city of Edessa.

Bibliography

PRIMARY SOURCES

Acts of Paul and Thecla: R. A. Lipsius (ed.), *Acta Apostolorum Apocrypha*, Vol. 1 (Leipzig: Mendelssohn, 1891 [repr. Hildesheim: Olms, 1972]).

Acts of Perpetua and Felicitas: H. Musurillo (ed. and trans.), *The Acts of the Christian Martyrs* (Oxford: Clarendon Press, 1972), 106–31.

Alphabetical collection of *Apophthegmata Patrum*: L. Regnault, *Les sentences des Pères du désert, collection alphabétique* (Sablé sur Sarthe: Abbaye de Solesmes, 1970).

Ambrose, *Epistulae*: O. Faller and M. Zelzer (eds.), *Sancti Ambrosi Opera, Epistulae et Acta*, CSEL 82.3 (Vienna: OeAW, 1982).

Epistulae extra collectionem: O. Faller and M. Zelzer (eds.), *Sancti Ambrosi Opera, Epistulae et Acta*, CSEL 82.3 (Vienna: OeAW, 1982)

Anonymous collection of Apophthegmata: L. Regnault (trans.), *Les sentences des Pères du désert, série des anonymes* (Bégrolles-en-Mauges: Abbaye de Bellefontaine, 1985).

Antony, *Epistulae*: in S. Rubenson (trans.), *The Letters of St Antony: Monasticism and the Making of a Saint*, Studies in Antiquity and Christianity (Minneapolis, MN: Fortress Press, 1995).

Aristotle, *Nicomachean Ethics*: M. Ostwald (trans.), *Aristotle, Nicomachean Ethics* (Indianapolis: Bobbs-Merrill, 1962).

Rhetoric: J. H. Freese (ed.), *Aristotle, The Art of Rhetoric*, LCL 193 (Cambridge, MA.: Harvard University Press, 1926, 2000).

Athanasius, *Orationes contra Arianos*: K. Metzler and K. Savvidis (eds.), *Athanasius: Werke, Band 1. Die dogmatischen Schriften, Erster Teil, 2. Lieferung* (Berlin: de Gruyter, 1998).

Vita Antonii: PG 26:835–976; R. C. Gregg (trans.), *Athanasius. The Life of Antony and the Letter to Marcellinus* (Mahwah, NJ: Paulist Press, 1980).

Augustine, *Commentary on John*: J. Rettig (trans.), *Tractates on the Gospel of John 1–10*, FOTC 78 (Washington, DC: Catholic University of America Press, 1988).

De Catechizandis Rudibus: J. B. Bauer (ed.), CCSL, 46 (Turnhout: Brepols, 1969), 115–78; Joseph P. Christopher (trans.), *The First Catechetical Instruction* (London: Longmans, 1952).

Basil, *An Ascetic Discourse*: W. K. L. Clarke (ed. and trans.), *The Ascetic Works of Saint Basil* (London: SPCK, 1925), 133–9.

Another Ascetic Discourse: W. K. L. Clarke (ed. and trans.), *The Ascetic Works of Saint Basil* (London: SPCK, 1925), 141–4.

Letters: B. Jackson (trans.), NPNF 8 (Peabody, MA: Hendrickson, 1999).

The Longer Rules: W. K. L. Clarke (ed. and trans.), *The Ascetic Works of Saint Basil* (London: SPCK, 1925), 145–228.

The Morals: W. K. L. Clarke (ed. and trans.), *The Ascetic Works of Saint Basil* (London: SPCK, 1925), 101–31.

Preliminary Sketch of the Ascetic Life: W. K. L. Clarke (ed. and trans.), *The Ascetic Works of Saint Basil* (London: SPCK, 1925), 55–9.

Renunciation of the World: W. K. L. Clarke (ed. and trans.), *The Ascetic Works of Saint Basil* (London: SPCK, 1925), 60–71.

The Shorter Rules: W. K. L. Clarke (ed. and trans.), *The Ascetic Works of Saint Basil* (London: SPCK, 1925), 229–351.

Book of Steps: M. Kmosko, ed. *Liber graduum*. PS 1.3 (Paris: Firmin-Didot, 1926); R. A. Kitchen and M. F. G. Parmentier (trans.), *The Book of Steps: The Syriac Liber Graduum*, Cistercian Studies 196 (Kalamazoo, MI: Cistercian Publications, 2004).

Bradeen, D. W. (ed.), *The Athenian Agora. Volume 17* (Princeton, NJ: The American School of Classical Studies at Athens, 1974).

Chronicle of Edessa: B. H. Cowper (trans.), *Journal of Sacred Literature and Biblical Record*, Series 4, Vol. 5/9 (1864), 28–45.

Codex Justinianus: P. Krueger (ed.), *Corpus Iuris Civilis*, Vol. II (Berlin: Weidmann, 1877, repr. 1954).

Codex Theodosianus: P. M. Meyer, T. Mommsen (eds.), *Theodosiani Libri XVI cum Constitutionibus Sirmondianus et leges Novellae ad Theodosianum pertinentes* (Berlin, Hildesheim: Weidmann, 1905, 1954, 1990); C. Pharr (trans.), *The Theodosian Code and Novels and the Sirmondian Constitutions: A Translation with Commentary, Glossary, and Bibliography* (Princeton, NJ: Princeton University Press, 1952).

Dessau, H. (ed.), *Inscriptiones Latinae Selectae* (Berlin: Weidmann, 1906).

The Didache: in M. W. Holmes (ed.), *The Apostolic Fathers* (Grand Rapids, MI: Baker Academic, 2007).

Digesta: P. Krueger, *Corpus Iuris Civilis*, Vol. I (Berlin: Weidmann, 1895, repr. 1954).

Engelmann, H. and Merkelbach, R. (eds.), *Die Inschriften von Erythrai und Klazomenai*, 2 vols. (Bonn: R. Habelt, 1972).

Epiphanius of Salamis, *On Faith*: K. Holl and J. Dummer (eds.), *Epiphanius: Panarion haer. 65–80. De fide*, GCS 37 (Berlin: De Gruyter, 1985).

Panarion: K. Holl and J. Dummer (eds.), *Epiphanius*, III vols., GCS 10, 31, 37 (Berlin: De Gruyter, 1915 [2013], 1980, 1985).

Euphemia and the Goth: F. C. Burkitt (trans.), *Euphemia and the Goth, with the Acts of Martyrdom of the Confessors of Edessa* (London: Williams and Norgate, 1913).

Gregory of Nazianzus, *Epigrams*: W. R. Paton (trans.), *The Greek Anthology*, *VII–VIII*, LCL 68 (Cambridge, MA: Harvard University Press, 2000).
De Vita Sua: C. Jungck (ed.), *Gregor von Nazianz. De vita sua* (Heidelberg: Winter, 1974).
Gregory of Nyssa, *Encomium in xl martyres i*: PG 46:749–772.
Encomium in xl martyres ii: PG 46:772–788.
First Homily on the Forty Martyrs of Sebaste Ia and Ib: J. Leemans, W. Mayer, P. Allen and B. Dehandschutter (eds. and trans.), *'Let Us Die that We May Live,' Greek Homilies on Christian Martyrs from Asia Minor, Palestine, and Syria* (London: Routledge, 2003).
The Life of Gregory the Wonderworker: M. Slusser (ed. and trans.), *St Gregory Thaumaturgus, Life and Works*, FOTC 98 (Washington, DC: Catholic University of America Press, 1998).
Life of Saint Macrina, On Virginity: P. Maraval (ed.), *Grégoire de Nysse. Vie de sainte Macrine*, SC 178 (Paris: Éditions du Cerf, 1971); V. Woods Callahan (trans.), *Saint Gregory of Nyssa, Ascetical Works*, FOTC 58 (Washington, DC: Catholic University of America Press, 1967).
On Virginity: V. Woods Callahan (trans.), *Saint Gregory of Nyssa, Ascetical Works*, FOTC 58 (Washington, DC: Catholic University of America Press, 1967).
Gregory of Tours, *Libri historiarum* x: B. Krusch and W. Levison (eds.), *Gregorii Turonensis libri historiarum* x, MGH, SRM, 1.1 (Hanover: Hahn, 1951).
Heberdey, R. (ed.), *Tituli Asiae Minoris, III. Tituli Pisidiae linguis Graeca et Latina conscripti, I. Tituli Termessi et agri Termessensis* (Vienna: Imperial Academy of Sciences, 1941).
History of the Great Deeds of Bishop Paul of Qenṭos and Priest John of Edessa: H. Arneson, E. Fiano, C. Luckritz Marquis and K. Smith (trans.), *The History of the Great Deeds of Bishop Paul of Qentos and Priest John of Edessa*, Texts from Christian Late Antiquity 29 (Piscataway, NJ: Gorgias, 2010).
Ibn Ishāq (Ibn Hishām), *Life of the Messenger of God (Sīr. ras. All.)*: A. Guillaume (trans.), *The Life of Muhammad: A Translation of Ibn Ishaq's Sirat Rasul Allah* (Oxford: Oxford University Press, 2002).
Iamblichus of Chalcis, *Letters*: J. M. Dillon and W. Polleichtner (trans.), *Writings from the Greco-Roman World Number 19* (Atlanta, GA: Society of Biblical Literature, 2009).
Jerome, *Life of Malchus*: C. Gray, *Jerome, Vita Malchi: Introduction, Text, Translation, and Commentary* (Oxford: Oxford University Press, 2015).
John Chrysostom, *Against the Jews*: W. Pradels, R. Brändle and M. Heimgartner, 'Das bisher vermisste Textstück in Johannes Chrysostomus, Adversus Judaeos, Oratio 2', *Zeitschrift für antikes Christentum*, 5 (2001), 23–49; PG 48:843–942; P. Harkins (trans.), *Saint John Chrysostom, Discourses against Judaizing Christians*, FOTC 68 (Washington, DC: Catholic University of America Press, 1977).
Catechesis de Juramento: A. Papadopoulos-Kerameus (ed.), *Varia Graeca sacra* (St Petersburg: Kirschbaum, 1909), 154–66.

Catechesis ultima ad baptizandos: A. Papadopoulos-Kerameus (ed.), *Varia Graeca sacra* (St Petersburg: Kirschbaum, 1909), 166–75.
Commentary on Job: H. Sorlin and L. Neyrand (eds.), *Jean Chrysostome. Commentaire sur Job*, SC 346, 348 (Paris: Éditions du Cerf, 1988); and R. C. Hill (trans.), *St John Chrysostom. Commentaries on the Sages. Volume One. Commentary on Job* (Brookline, MA: Holy Cross Orthodox Press, 2006).
Commentary on the Psalms: PG 55:39-498; R. C. Hill (trans.), *St John Chrysostom: Commentary on the Psalms* (Brookline, MA: Holy Cross Orthodox Press, 1998).
De mutatione nominum: PG 51:113–56.
De regressu: A. Wenger (ed.), *Revue des études byzantines* 19 (Paris: Institut Français d'Études Byzantines, 1961).
Homilies on the Acts of the Apostles: PG 60:13–384.
Homilies on Colossians: Field 5.172–312; PG 62:299–392.
Homily on 'Concerning Perfect Love': PG 56:279–90.
Homilies on 1 Corinthians: Field 2.1–555; PG 61:9–382.
Homilies on 2 Corinthians: PG 61:381–610.
Homilia De capto Eutropio: PG 52:395–414.
Homilies on Ephesians: Field 4.104–365; PG 62:9–176.
Homily on 'For Fear of Fornication, Let Each Man Have His Own Wife' (1 Cor. 7:2): PG 51:271–302.
Homilies on Genesis: PG 53, 23–386, 54, 385–580; R. C. Hill (trans.), *St John Chrysostom. Homilies on Genesis*, FOTC 82, 87 (Washington, DC: Catholic University of America Press, 1990, 1992).
Homilies on Hebrews: Field 7.1–384; PG 63:9–236.
Homilies on 'I Saw the Lord' (Isa 6:1): J. Dumortier (ed.), *Jean Chrysostome. Homélies sur Ozias*, SC 277 (Paris: Éditions du Cerf, 1981); R. C. Hill (trans.), *St John Chrysostom, Old Testament Homilies. Vol. 2. Homilies on Isaiah and Jeremiah* (Brookline, MA: Holy Cross Orthodox Press, 2003).
Homilies on John: PG 59.23–482.
Homilies on Lazarus: PG 48:963–1054; C. P. Roth (trans.), *St John Chrysostom: On Wealth and Poverty* (Crestwood, NY: St Vladimir's Seminary Press, 1984).
Homilies on Matthew: PG 57:13–472, 58:471–794; G. Prevost (trans.), *NPNF* 10 (Peabody, MA: Hendrickson Publishers, 1994).
Homilies on Philemon: Field 6.325–53; PG 62:701–20.
Homilies on Philippians: PG 62:177–298.
Homilies on Romans: Field 1.1–495; PG 60:415–22.
Homilies on 1 Thessalonians: PG 62:391–468.
Homilies on 2 Thessalonians: PG 62:467–500.
Homily on 'Those Who Have the Same Spirit of Faith' (2 Cor. 4:13): PG 51:187–208.
Homilies on 1 Timothy: Field 6.1–161; PG 62:503–600.
Homilies on Titus: Field 6.264-324; PG 62:663-700.
In Praise of Saint Paul the Apostle: A. Piédagnel (ed.), *Jean Chrysostome: Panégyriques de S. Paul*, SC 300 (Paris: Éditions du Cerf, 1982).

Instructions to Catechumens: A. Wenger (ed.), *Catecheses ad Illuminandos*, SC 50 (Paris: Éditions du Cerf, 1958); PG 49:223–40; P. Harkins (trans.), *St John Chrysostom, Baptismal Instructions*, ACW 31 (New York, NY: Newman Press, 1963).

On the Priesthood: A.-M. Malingrey (ed.), *Jean Chrysostome: Sur le sacerdoce*, SC 272 (Paris: Éditions du Cerf, 1980).

On the Statues: PG 49:15–222.

On Vainglory and the Education of Children: A.-M. Malingrey (ed.), *Jean Chrysostome: Sur la vaine gloire et l'éducation des enfants*, SC 188 (Paris: Éditions du Cerf, 1972); M. L. W. Laistner (trans.), *Christianity and Pagan Culture* (Ithaca, NY: Cornell University Press, 1951).

On Virginity: B. Grillet (ed.), *Jean Chrysostome: La virginité*, SC 125 (Paris: Éditions du Cerf, 1966); S. Shore (trans.), *John Chrysostom: On Virginity; Against Remarriage* (New York, NY: Edwin Mellen, 1983).

Quales ducendae sint uxores (= De laude maximi): PG 51:225–42.

Sermons on Genesis: L. Brottier (ed.), *Jean Chrysostome: Sermons sur la Genèse*, SC 433 (Paris: Éditions du Cerf, 1998).

John of Ephesus, *Lives of the Eastern Saints*: E. W. Brooks (ed. and trans.), *John of Ephesus: Lives of the Eastern Saints*. 3 vols., PO 17–19 (Paris: Firmin-Didot, 1923–5).

Kern, O. (ed.), *Inscriptiones Graecae, IX, 2. Inscriptiones Thessaliae* (Berlin: de Gruyter, 1908).

Kirchner, J. (ed.), *Inscriptiones Graecae II et III: Inscriptiones Atticae Euclidis anno posteriores*, 2nd edn., 3 parts (Berlin: de Gruyter, 1913–40).

Lactantius, *Divine Institutes*: M. F. McDonald, *The Divine Institutes, Books, I–VII*, FOTC 49 (Washington, DC: Catholic University of America Press, 1964); A. Bowen and P. Garnsey (trans.), *Lactantius, Divine Institutes*, TTH 40 (Liverpool: Liverpool University Press, 2003).

Libanius, *Letters*: A. F. Norman (ed. and trans.), *Libanius: Autobiography and Selected Letters*, 2 vols. (Cambridge, MA, Harvard University Press, 1992); R. Cribiore (trans.), *The School of Libanius in Late Antique Antioch* (Princeton, NJ: Princeton University Press, 2007).

Orationes: R. Foerster (ed.), *Libanii opera*, 4 vols. (Leipzig: Teubner, 1903–8).

Oration 1: A. F. Norman (ed. and trans.), *Libanius' Autobiography (Oration 1)* (London: Oxford University Press, for the University of Hull, 1965).

Oration 3, To His Students about His Speech (= Foerster, III, 119–46): A. F. Norman (trans.), *Antioch as a Centre of Hellenic Culture as Observed by Libanius*, TTH 34 (Liverpool: Liverpool University Press, 2000), 185–92.

Oration 31, To the Antiochenes for the Teachers (= Foerster, III, 119–46): A. F. Norman (trans.), *Antioch as a Centre of Hellenic Culture as Observed by Libanius*, TTH 34 (Liverpool: Liverpool University Press, 2000), 70–83.

Oration 58, To His Students on the Carpeting (= Foerster, IV, 175–200): A. F. Norman (trans.), *Antioch as a Centre of Hellenic Culture as Observed by Libanius*, TTH 34 (Liverpool: Liverpool University Press, 2000), 170–81.

Oration 62, Against the Critics of His Educational System (= Foerster, IV, 342–83): A. F. Norman (trans.), *Antioch as a Centre of Hellenic Culture as Observed by Libanius*, TTH 34 (Liverpool: Liverpool University Press, 2000), 90–109.

Life of Febronia: P. Bedjan (ed.), *Acta martyrum et sanctorum*, Vol. v (Leipzig: Otto Harrassowitz, 1895); S. P. Brock and S. A. Harvey (trans.), *Holy Women of the Syrian Orient* (Berkeley, CA: University of California Press, 1998).

Maximus of Tyre, *Philosophical Dissertations*: G. L. Koniaris (ed.), *Maximus Tyrius: Philosophumena – ΔΙΑΛΕΞΕΙΣ*, Texte und Kommentare 17 (Berlin: De Gruyter, 1995).

Novellae: R. Schoell and W. Kroll (eds.), *Corpus Iuris Civilis*, Vol. 3 (Berlin: Weidmann, 1912, repr. 1954).

Pelagii I papae epistulae quae supersunt (556–561): P. Gassò and C. Batlle (eds.) (Barcelona: In abbatia Montiserrati, 1961).

Peter Damian, *In Praise of Flagellation*: PL 145.679–686c.

Philo of Alexandria, *De opificio mundi*: F. H. Colson and G. H. Whitaker (trans.), *Philo in Ten Volumes (and Two Supplementary Volumes)*, LCL (Cambridge, MA: Harvard University Press, 1981), Vol. 1, 6–137.

Possidius, *Life of Augustine*: F. H. Hoare (ed.), *The Western Fathers* (London: Sheed & Ward, 1954), 193–244.

Pseudo-Nilus, *Narrations*: F. Conca (ed.), *Nilus Ancyranus: Narratio* (Leipzig: Teubner, 1983); D. F. Caner (trans.), *History and Hagiography from the Late Antique Sinai*, TTH 53 (Liverpool: Liverpool University Press, 2010).

Socrates, *Historia ecclesiastica*: P. Maraval and P. Périchon (eds.), *Socrate de Constantinople, Histoire ecclésiastique* (Paris: Éditions du Cerf, 2004–7).

Theodoret, *History of the Monks of Syria*: P. Canivet and A. Leroy-Molinghen (eds.), *Théodoret de Cyr: Histoire des moines de Syrie*, 2 vols., SC 234, 257 (Paris: Éditions du Cerf, 1977, 1979); R. M. Price (trans.), *A History of the Monks of Syria by Theodoret of Cyrrhus*, Cistercian Studies 88 (Kalamazoo, MI: Cistercian Publications, 1985).

Zosimus, *New History*: F. Paschoud (ed.), *Zosime, Histoire Nouvelle* (Paris: Les Belles Lettres, 1971–89).

SECONDARY LITERATURE

Adkin, N., 'Ambrose and Jerome: The Opening Shot', *Mnemosyne*, 46 (1993), 364–76.

Alberici, L. and Harlow, M., 'Age and Innocence: Female Transitions to Adulthood in Late Antiquity', in A. Cohen and J. Rutter (eds.), *Constructions of Childhood in Ancient Greece and Italy* (Princeton, NJ: ASCSA, 2007), pp. 193–203.

Albrecht, R., *Das Leben der heiligen Makrina auf dem Hintergrund der Thekla-Traditionen* (Göttingen: Vandenhoeck & Ruprecht, 1986).

Aletti, M. and Alberico, C., 'Tra brainwashing e libera scelta. Per una lettura psicologica dell'affiliazione ai Nuovi Movimenti Religiosi', in M. Aletti and G. Rossi (eds.), *Ricerca di sé e trascendenza* (Turin: Centro Scientifico Editore, 1999), pp. 35–48.

Ali, K., 'Concubinage and Consent', *International Journal of Middle East Studies*, 49 (2017), 148–52.

Allen, P. and Bronwen N. (eds.), *Crisis Management in Late Antiquity (410–590 CE): A Survey of the Evidence from Episcopal Letters*, Supplements to Vigiliae Christianae (Leiden: Brill, 2013).

Altman, J. G., *Epistolarity: Approaches to a Form* (Columbus, OH: Ohio State University Press, 1982).

Amélineau, E. (ed.), *Monuments pour servir à l'histoire de l'Égypte chrétienne aux IVe et Ve siècles*, Mémoires de la mission archéologique française au Caire IV, 2 (Paris: Leroux, 1895).

Ando, C., *Law, Language, and Empire in the Roman Tradition* (Philadelphia, PA: University of Pennsylvania Press, 2011).

Archetti, G., 'Ildemaro a Brescia e la pedagogia monastica nel commento alla Regola', *Brixia Sacra*, 3 (2006), 113–78.

Arias, I., 'Complexities of Family Violence and the Need for Belongingness', in R. C. A. Klein (ed.), *Multidisciplinary Perspectives on Family Violence* (New York, NY: Routledge, 1998), 212–19.

Arjava, A., 'Paternal Power in Late Antiquity', *Journal of Roman Studies*, 88 (1998), 147–65.

Women and Law in Late Antiquity (Oxford: Clarendon, 1996).

Aslan, R., *No God But God: The Origins, Evolution and Future of Islam* (New York, NY: Random House, 2008).

Athanassiadi, P., *Vers la pensée unique, la montée de l'intolérance dans l'Antiquité tardive* (Paris: Les Belles Lettres, 2010).

Banaji, J., *Agrarian Change in Late Antiquity: Gold, Labour, and Aristocratic Dominance* (Oxford: Oxford University Press, 2001).

Barlow, J., 'Kinship, Identity and Fourth-Century Franks', *Historia: Zeitschrift für Alte Geschichte*, 45 (1996), 223–39.

Barnes, T. D., *Constantine: Dynasty, Religion and Power in the Late Roman Empire* (Oxford: Wiley-Blackwell, 2014).

'Ambrose and the Basilicas of Milan in 385 and 386: The Primary Documents and Their Implications', *Zeitschrift für antikes Christentum*, 4 (2000), 282–99.

'Angel of Light or Mystic Initiate? The Problem of the Life of Antony', *Journal of Theological Studies*, 37 (1986), 353–68.

Constantine and Eusebius (Cambridge, MA: Harvard University Press, 1981).

Barrier, J. W., *The Acts of Paul and Thecla. A Critical Introduction and Commentary* (Tübingen: Mohr Siebeck, 2009).

Barthes, R., *Criticism and Truth* (Minneapolis, MN: University of Minnesota Press, 1987).

'Death of the Author', in S. Head (ed. and trans.), *Image-Music-Text* (New York, NY: Hill & Wang, 1977).

Bateson, M., Nettle, D., and Roberts, G., 'Cues of Being Watched Enhance Cooperation in a Real World Setting', *Biology Letters*, 2 (2006), 412–14.

Beagon, P. M., 'The Cappadocian Fathers, Women, and Ecclesiastical Politics', *Vigiliae Christianae*, 49 (1995), 165–79.

Beaucamp, J., *Le statut de la femme à Byzance (IVe-VIIe s.)*, 2 vols. (Paris: De Boccard, 1990–2).

Becker, M., *Porphyrios, 'Contra Christianos'. Neue Sammlung der Fragmente, Testimonien und Dubia mit Einleitung, Übersetzung und Anmerkungen* (Berlin: De Gruyter, 2015).

Belche, J.-P., 'Die Bekehrung zum Christentum nach Augustins Büchlein *De Catechizandis Rudibus*', *Augustiniana*, 29 (1979), 247–79.

Bernstein, B., *Pedagogy, Symbolic Control and Identity: Theory, Research, Critique* (London: Taylor and Francis, 1996).

Class, Code and Control, Vol. IV: The Structuring of Pedagogic Discourse (London: Routledge, 1990).

Class, Code and Control, Vol. III: Towards a Theory of Educational Transmissions (London: Routledge, 1975).

Berzon, T. S., *Classifying Christians: Ethnography, Heresiology, and the Limits of Knowledge in Late Antiquity* (Berkeley, CA: University of California Press, 2016).

Betzig, L., 'Roman Polygyny', *Ethology and Sociobiology*, 13 (1992), 309–49.

Biedenkopf-Ziehner, A., *Koptische Schenkungsurkunden aus der Thebais. Formeln und Topoi der Urkunden, Aussagen der Urkunden, Indices*, Göttinger Orientforschungen IV Reihe: 'Ägypten' 41 (Wiesbaden: Harrassowitz, 2001).

Bloomer, W. M., 'Corporal Punishment in the Ancient School', in W. M. Bloomer (ed.), *A Companion to Ancient Education* (London: Wiley-Blackwell, 2015), 184–98.

'Schooling in Persona: Imagination and Subordination in Roman Education', *Classical Antiquity*, 16 (1997), 57–78.

Bond, S., 'Altering Infamy: Status, Violence and Civic Exclusion in Late Antiquity', *Classical Antiquity*, 33 (2014), 1–30.

Bonner, S. F., *Education in Ancient Rome: From the Elder Cato to the Younger Pliny* (London: Methuen, 1977).

Boon, A. (ed.), *Pachomiana latina. Règle et épîtres de St Pachôme, épître de St Théodore et 'Liber' de St Orsiesius. Texte latin de St Jérôme*, Bibliothèque de la Revue d'Histoire ecclésiastique 7 (Leuven: Universiteitbibliothek, 1932).

Bounoure, G., 'Eusèbe citateur de Diodore', *Revue des Études Grecques*, 95 (1982), 433–9.

Bourdieu, P., *Pascalian Meditations*, R. Nice (trans.) (Cambridge: Polity Press, 2000).

The State Nobility: Elite Schools in the Field of Power, L. C. Clough (trans.) (Stanford, CA: Stanford University Press, 1996).

The Logic of Practice, R. Nice (trans.) (Cambridge: Polity, 1990).

Distinction: A Social Critique of the Judgement of Taste (Cambridge, MA: Harvard University Press, 1984).

Bourdieu, P. and Passeron, J.-C., *Reproduction in Education, Society and Culture*, R. Nice (trans.) (London: Sage, 1990).

Bradbury, S., 'Constantine and the Problem of Anti-Pagan Legislation in the Fourth Century', *Classical Philology*, 89 (1994), 120–39.

Bradley, K. R., 'Sacrificing the Family: Christian Martyrs and their Kin', *Ancient Narrative*, 3 (2003), 150–81.

'The Problem of Slavery in Classical Antiquity', *Classical Philology*, 92 (1997), 273–82.

Slaves and Masters in the Roman Empire: A Study in Social Control (Oxford: Oxford University Press, 1987).

'On the Roman Slave Supply and Slavebreeding', in M. I. Finley (ed.) *Classical Slavery* (London: Routledge, 1987), 53–81.

Brakke, D., *Demons and the Making of the Monk* (Cambridge, MA: Harvard University Press, 2006).

Athanasius and the Politics of Asceticism, Oxford Early Christian Studies (Oxford: Clarendon Press, 1995).

Brändle, R., '"Gott wird nicht allein durch richtige Dogmen, sondern auch durch einen guten Lebenswandel verherrlicht." Zur Verhältnisbestimmung von Glaube und Werken bei Johannes Chrysostomus', *Theologische Zeitschrift*, 55 (1999), 121–36.

Bremmer, J. N., *The Rise of Christianity through the Eyes of Gibbon, Harnack, and Rodney Stark* (Groningen: Barkhuis, 2010).

'The Social and Religious Capital of the Early Christians', *Hephaistos*, 24 (2006), 269–78.

'Magic, Martyrdom and Women's Liberation in the Acts of Paul and Thecla', in J. N. Bremmer (ed.), *The Apocryphal Acts of Paul and Thecla* (Kampen: Pharos, 1996), 36–59.

Briggs, S., 'Can an Enslaved God Liberate? Hermeneutical Reflections on Philippians 2:6–11', *Semeia*, 47 (1989), 137–53.

Brock, S. P., 'Radical Renunciation: The Ideal of *Msarrqûtâ*', in R. Darling Young and M. J. Blanchard (eds.), *To Train His Soul in Books: Syrian Asceticism in Early Christianity* (Washington, DC: Catholic University of America Press, 2011), 122–33.

'Early Syrian Asceticism', *Numen*, 20 (1973), 1–19.

Brock, S. P., and Harvey, S. A. (trans.), *Holy Women of the Syrian Orient*, Transformation of the Classical Heritage 13 (Berkeley, CA: University of California Press, 1998).

Bromley, D. G. and Melton, J. G. (eds.), *Cults, Religions, Violence* (Cambridge: Cambridge University Press, 2002).

Brown, P., *Through the Eye of a Needle: Wealth, the Fall of Rome, and the Making of the Christian West, 350–550 AD* (Princeton, NJ: Princeton University Press, 2013).

Augustine of Hippo: A Biography, revised edn. (London: Faber, 2000; orig. published 1967).

Power and Persuasion in Late Antiquity: Towards a Christian Empire (Madison, WI: University of Wisconsin Press, 1992).

The Body and Society: Men, Women, and Sexual Renunciation in Early Christianity (New York, NY: Columbia University Press, 1988).

'The Rise and Function of the Holy Man in Late Antiquity', *Journal of Roman Studies*, 61 (1971), 80–101.

'Christianity and Local Culture in Late Roman Africa', *Journal of Roman Studies*, 58 (1968), 85–95.

'St Augustine's Attitude to Religious Coercion', *Journal of Roman Studies*, 54 (1964), 107–16.

Bryen, A. Z., *Violence in Roman Egypt: A Study in Legal Interpretation* (Philadelphia, PA: University of Pennsylvania Press, 2013).

'Judging Empire: Courts and Culture in Rome's Eastern Provinces', *Law and History Review*, 30 (2012), 771–811.

Burkitt, F. C., *Euphemia and the Goth, with the Acts of Martyrdom of the Confessors of Edessa* (London: Williams and Norgate, 1913).

Burrus, V., *Saving Shame: Martyrs, Saints, and Other Abject Subjects* (Philadelphia, PA: University of Pennsylvania Press, 2008).

Begotten, Not Made: Conceiving Manhood in Late Antiquity (Stanford, CA: Stanford University Press, 2000).

'Equipped for Victory': Ambrose and the Gendering of Orthodoxy', *Journal of Early Christian Studies*, 4 (1996), 461–75.

'Reading Agnes: The Rhetoric of Gender in Ambrose and Prudentius', *Journal of Early Christian Studies*, 3 (1995), 25–46.

Chastity as Autonomy: Women in the Stories of the Apocryphal Acts (Lewiston, NY: Edwin Mellen Press, 1987).

Cabouret, B., 'Libanius' *Letters*', in L. van Hoof (ed.), *Libanius: A Critical Introduction* (Cambridge: Cambridge University Press, 2014), 144–59.

Cameron, Al., 'A Misidentified Homily of Chrysostom', *Nottingham Medieval Studies*, 32 (1988), 34–48.

Cameron, Av., *Dialoguing in Late Antiquity*, Hellenic Studies Series 65 (Cambridge, MA: Harvard University Press, 2014).

The Later Roman Empire, AD *284–430* (Cambridge, MA: Harvard University Press, 1993).

Caner, D. F. (ed.), *History and Hagiography from the Late Antique Sinai*, Translated Texts for Historians 53 (Liverpool: Liverpool University Press, 2010).

Wandering, Begging Monks: Spiritual Authority and the Promotion of Monasticism in Late Antiquity, Transformation of the Classical Heritage 33 (Berkeley, CA: University of California Press, 2002).

'Notions of "Strict Discipline" and Apostolic Tradition in Early Definitions of Orthodox Monasticism', in S. Elm, É. Rebillard and A. Romano (eds.), *Orthodoxie, christianisme, histoire* (Rome: École Française de Rome, 2000), 23–34.

Canning, R., 'Teaching and Learning: An Augustinian Perspective', *Australian E-journal of Theology*, 3 (2004), 1–10.

Carriker, A., *The Library of Eusebius of Caesarea* (Leiden: Brill, 2003).

Cassin, M., Debié, M. and Perrin, M.-Y., 'La question des editions de l'*Histoire ecclésiastique* et le livre x', in S. Morlet and L. Perrone (eds.), *Eusèbe de Césarée. Histoire ecclésiastique. Commentaire, Tome 1: Études d'introduction* (Paris: Les Belles Lettres, 2012).

Chappell, A. T. and Lanza-Kaduce, L., 'Police Academy Socialization: Understanding the Lessons Learned in a Paramilitary-Bureaucratic Organization', *Journal of Contemporary Ethnography*, 39 (2010), 187–214.

Chevallier Caseau, B., 'Childhood in Byzantine Saints' Lives', in C. Horn and R. R. Phenix (eds.), *Children in Late Antiquity* (Tübingen: Mohr Siebeck, 2009), 127–66.

Chin, C. M., 'The Bishop's Two Bodies: Ambrose and the Basilicas of Milan', *Church History: Studies in Christianity and Culture*, 79 (2010), 531–55.

Grammar and Christianity in the Late Roman World (Philadelphia, PA: University of Pennsylvania Press, 2008).

'Telling Boring Stories: Time, Narrative and Pedagogy in *De Catechizandis Rudibus*', *Augustinian Studies*, 37 (2006), 43–62.

Clark, E. A., *Reading Renunciation: Asceticism and Scripture in Early Christianity* (Princeton, NJ: Princeton University Press, 1999).

'Holy Women, Holy Words: Early Christian Women, Social History, and the "Linguistic Turn"', *Journal of Early Christian Studies*, 6 (1998), 413–30.

'Antifamilial Tendencies in Ancient Christianity', *Journal of the History of Sexuality*, 5 (1995), 356–80.

'Ideology, History and the Constitution of "Woman" in Late Ancient Christianity', *Journal of Early Christian Studies*, 2 (1994), 155–84.

'Sexual Politics in the Writings of John Chrysostom', *Anglican Theological Review*, 59 (1977), 3–20.

Clark, G., 'Women and Asceticism in Late Antiquity: The Refusal of Status and Gender', in V. L. Wimbush and R. Valantasis (eds.), *Asceticism* (Oxford: Oxford University Press, 1995), pp. 33–49.

Women in Late Antiquity: Pagan and Christian Lifestyles (Oxford: Oxford University Press, 1993).

Clines, D. J. A., 'Reading Esther from Left to Right', in D. J. A. Clines, *On the Way to the Post-Modern: Old Testament Essays, 1967–1998*, 2 vols., Journal for the Study of the Old Testament Supplement Series 292–3 (Sheffield: JSOT Press, 1998), Vol. 1, 3–22.

'Women, Slaves and the Hierarchies of Domestic Violence: The family of St Augustine', in S. R. Joshel (ed.), *Women and Slaves in Greco-Roman Culture* (London: Routledge, 1998), 109-29.

Coleman, K. M., 'Fatal Charades: Roman Executions Staged as Mythological Enactments', *Journal of Roman Studies*, 80 (1990), 44–73.

Colish, M. L., 'Why the Portiana? Reflections on the Milanese Basilica Crisis of 386', *Journal of Early Christian Studies*, 10 (2003), 361–72.

Connolly, S., *Lives behind the Laws: The World of the Codex Hermogenianus* (Bloomington; Indianapolis, IN: Indiana University Press, 2010).

Coon, L. L., *Sacred Fictions: Holy Women and Hagiography in Late Antiquity* (Philadelphia, PA: University of Pennsylvania Press, 1997).

Cooper, K., 'Marriage, Law, and Christian Rhetoric in Vandal Africa', in S. T. Stevens and J. P. Conant, *North Africa under Byzantium and Early Islam* (Washington, DC: Dumbarton Oaks, 2016), 237–49.

Band of Angels: The Forgotten World of Early Christian Women (London: Atlantic Press, 2013).

'The Bride of Christ, the "Male Woman", and the Female Reader in Late Antiquity', in J. Bennett and R. M. Karras (eds.), *Oxford Handbook of Women and Gender in Medieval Europe* (Oxford: Oxford University Press, 2013), 529–44.

'A Father, a Daughter, and a Procurator: Authority and Resistance in the Prison Memoir of Perpetua of Carthage', *Gender and History*, 23 (2011), 685–702.

'Gender and the Fall of Rome', in P. Rousseau (ed.), *A Companion to Late Antiquity* (Chichester: Wiley-Blackwell, 2009), 187–200.

The Fall of the Roman Household (Cambridge: Cambridge University Press, 2007).

'Approaching the Holy Household', *Journal of Early Christian Studies*, 152 (2007), 131–42.

'Closely Watched Households: Visibility, Exposure and Private Power in the Roman *Domus*', *Past & Present*, 197 (2007), 3–33.

'Ventriloquism and the Miraculous: Conversion, Preaching, and the Martyr Exemplum in Late Antiquity', in K. Cooper and J. Gregory (eds.), *Signs, Wonders, Miracles: Representations of Divine Power in the Life of the Church*, Studies in Church History 41 (Woodbridge: Boydell and Brewer, 2005), 22–45.

'The Virgin as Social Icon: Perspectives from Late Antiquity', in M. van Dijk and R. I. A. Nip (eds.), *Saints, Scholars, and Politicians: Gender as a Tool in Medieval Studies* (Turnhout: Brepols, 2005), 9–24.

'The Voice of the Victim: Gender, Representation, and Early Christian Martyrdom', *Bulletin of the John Rylands University Library*, 80 (1998), 147–57.

The Virgin and the Bride: Idealized Womanhood in Late Antiquity (Cambridge, MA: Harvard University Press, 1996).

'A Saint in Exile: The Early Medieval Thecla at Rome and Meriamlik', *Hagiographica*, 2 (1995), 1–24.

'Of Romance and *Mediocritas*: Re-reading the Martyr *Exemplum* in the *Passio Anastasiae*', in G. Barone (ed.), *Modelli di comportamento e modi di santità* (Turin: Rosenberg & Sellier, 1994), 107–23.

'Insinuations of Womanly Influence: An Aspect of the Christianization of the Roman Aristocracy', *Journal of Roman Studies*, 82 (1992), 150–64.

Corbellini, C., 'Sesto Petronio Probo e l'elezione episcopale di Ambrogio', *Rendiconti dell'Istituto Lombardo, Classe di Lettere, Scienze morali e storiche*, 109 (1975), 181–9.

Cranz, F. E., 'The Development of Augustine's Ideas on Society before the Donatist Controversy', *Harvard Theological Review*, 47 (1954), 255–316.

Cremaschi, L. (ed.), *Basilio di Cesarea, Le regole* (Bose: Qiqajon, 1993).
Cribiore, R., *Libanius the Sophist: Rhetoric, Reality, and Religion in the Fourth Century* (Ithaca, NY: Cornell University Press, 2013).
The School of Libanius in Late Antique Antioch (Princeton, NJ: Princeton University Press, 2007).
Gymnastics of the Mind: Greek Education in Hellenistic and Roman Egypt (Princeton, NJ: Princeton University Press, 2001).
Writing, Teachers, and Students in Graeco-Roman Egypt (Atlanta, GA: Scholars Press, 1996).
Crislip, A., *Thorns in the Flesh: Illness and Sanctity in Late Ancient Christianity* (Philadelphia, PA: University of Pennsylvania Press, 2012).
Crook, J. A., 'Patria Potestas', *Classical Quarterly*, 17 (1967), 113–22.
Crum, W. E., Steindorff, G. and Schiller, A. A., *Koptische Rechtsurkunden des achten Jahrhunderts aus Djeme* (Leipzig: Zentralantiquariat der Deutschen Demokratischen Republik (reprint), original: 1912).
Dagron, G., *Vie et miracles de Sainte Thècle*, Subsidia Hagiographica 62 (Brussels: Société des Bollandistes 1978).
Dailey, E. T., 'Confinement and Exclusion in the Monasteries of Sixth-Century Gaul', *Early Medieval Europe*, 22 (2014), 304–35.
Dassmann, E., 'Archeological Traces of Early Christian Veneration', in W. S. Babcock (ed.), *Paul and the Legacies of Paul* (Dallas, TX: Southern Methodist University Press, 1990), 281–306.
Davies, S., *The Cult of Saint Thecla: A Tradition of Women's Piety in Late Antiquity* (Oxford: Oxford University Press, 2001).
Davies, W., *Small Worlds: The Village Community in Early Medieval Brittany* (Berkeley, CA: University of California Press, 1988).
Dawes, J., *The Language of War: Literature and Culture in the US from the Civil War through World War II* (Cambridge, MA: Harvard University Press, 2002).
De Bruyn, T., 'Flogging a Son: The Emergence of the *pater flagellans* in Latin Christian Discourse', *Journal of Early Christian Studies*, 7 (1999), 249–90.
De Certeau, M., *The Practice of Everyday Life*, S. Rendall (trans.) (Berkeley, CA: University of California Press, 1984).
De Jong, M., *In Samuel's Image: Child Oblation in the Early Medieval West* (Leiden: Brill, 1996)
De Wet, C. L., *The Unbound God: Slavery and the Formation of Early Christian Thought* (London: Routledge, 2017).
Preaching Bondage: John Chrysostom and the Discourse of Slavery in Early Christianity (Oakland, CA: University of California Press, 2015).
'The Discourse of the Suffering Slave in 1 Peter', *Ekklesiastikos Pharos*, 95 (2013), 15–24.
'Honour Discourse in John Chrysostom's Exegesis of the Letter to Philemon', in D. Francis Tolmie (ed.), *Philemon in Perspective: Interpreting a Pauline Letter* (Berlin: de Gruyter, 2010), 317–31.
'John Chrysostom on Slavery', *Studia Historiae Ecclesiasticae*, 34 (2008), 1–13.

Del Cogliano, M., 'The Literary Corpus of George of Laodicea', *Vigiliae Christianiae*, 65 (2011), 150–69.

Delehaye, H., *Les légendes hagiographiques* (Brussels: Société des Bollandistes, 1927).

Demacopoulos, G., *The Invention of Peter: Apostolic Discourse and Papal Authority in Late Antiquity* (Philadelphia, PA: University of Pennsylvania Press, 2013).

DesPlaces, E., *Études Platoniciennes, 1929–1979* (Leiden: Brill, 1981).

Dignas, B., and Winter, E., *Rome and Persia in Late Antiquity: Neighbours and Rivals* (Cambridge: Cambridge University Press, 2007).

Dixon, S. 'Conflict in the Roman Family', in B. Rawson and P. Weaver (eds.), *The Roman Family in Italy: Status, Sentiment, Space* (Oxford: Clarendon Press, 1997), 149–68.

The Roman Mother (London: Croom Helm, 1988).

'Womanly Weakness', *Tijdschrift voor Rechtsgeschiedenis*, 52 (1984), 343–371.

Dörries, H., *Die Vita Antonii als Geschichtsquelle*, Nachrichten der Akademie der Wissenschaften in Göttingen, Philologisch-Historische Klasse 14 (Göttingen: Vandenhoeck & Ruprecht, 1949).

Dossey, L., *Peasant and Empire in Christian North Africa* (Berkeley, CA: University of California Press, 2010).

'Wife Beating and Manliness in Late Antiquity', *Past & Present*, 199 (2008), 3–40.

Drake, H. A., 'Intolerance, Religious Violence, and Political Legitimacy in Late Antiquity', *Journal of the American Academy of Religion*, 79 (2011), 193–235.

Drijvers, H. J. W., 'The Persistence of Pagan Cults and Practices in Christian Syria', in H. J. W. Drijvers (ed.), *East of Antioch*, Collected Studies 198 (London: Variorum Reprints, 1984), 35–43.

Drijvers, J. W., 'Flavia Maxima Fausta: Some Remarks', *Historia*, 41 (1992), 500–6.

Dudden, F. H., *The Life and Times of St Ambrose*, 2 vols. (Oxford: Clarendon Press, 1935).

Duval, Y.-M., 'Ambroise, de son élection à sa consécration', in G. Lazzati (ed.), *Ambrosius episcopus: atti del Congresso Internazionale di Studi Ambrosiani* (Milan: Vita e Pensiero, 1976), 243–84.

'L'originalité du "De virginibus" dans le mouvement ascetique occidental: Ambroise, Cyprien, Athanase', in Y.-M. Duval (ed.), *Ambroise de Milan: Dix études* (Paris: Études augustiniennes, 1974).

Eastburn Boswell, J., *The Kindness of Strangers: Abandonment of Children in Western Europe from Late Antiquity to the Renaissance* (London: Lane, 1988).

Ellis, S., *Roman Housing* (London: Duckworth, 2000).

Elm, S., *Virgins of God: The Making of Asceticism in Late Antiquity* (Oxford: Oxford University Press, 1993).

Elsner, J., 'Late Antique Art: The Problem of the Concept and the Cumulative Aesthetic', in S. Swain and M. Edwards (eds.), *Approaching Late Antiquity* (Oxford: Oxford University Press, 2004), 271–309.

'From the Culture of Spolia to the Cult of Relics: The Arch of Constantine and the Genesis of Late Antique Forms', *Papers of the British School at Rome*, 68 (2000), 149–84.

Eltis, D. and Engerman, S. L. (eds.), *The Cambridge World History of Slavery: Volume 3, AD 1420–AD 1804* (Cambridge: Cambridge University Press, 2011).

Errante, A., 'Where in the World do Children Learn 'Bloody Revenge'? Cults of Terror and Counter-Terror and Their Implications for Child Socialisation', *Globalisation, Societies and Education*, 1 (2003), 131–52.

Evans Grubbs, J., 'Making the Private Public: Illegitimacy and Incest in Roman Law', in C. Ando and J. Rüpke, eds., *Public and Private in Ancient Mediterranean Law and Religion* (Berlin: Walter de Gruyter, 2015) 115–42.

'Marrying and Its Documentation in Later Roman Law', in P. L. Reynolds and J. Witte, *To Have and to Hold* (Cambridge: Cambridge University Press, 2007) 43–94.

'Parent–Child Conflict in the Roman Family: The Evidence of the Code of Justinian', in M. George (ed.), *The Roman Family in the Empire: Rome, Italy, and Beyond* (Oxford: Oxford University Press, 2005), 92–128.

Women and Law in the Roman Empire: A Sourcebook on Marriage, Divorce, and Widowhood (London; New York, NY: Routledge, 2002).

Law and Family in Late Antiquity: The Emperor Constantine's Marriage Legislation (Oxford: Clarendon Press, 1995).

'"Pagan" and "Christian" Marriage: The State of the Question', *Journal of Early Christian Studies*, 2 (1994), 361–412.

'"Marriage More Shameful than Adultery": Slave–Mistress Relationships, "Mixed Marriages", and Late Roman Law', *Phoenix*, 47 (1993), 125–54.

'Abduction Marriage in Antiquity: A Law of Constantine (CTh IX. 24. I) and Its Social Context', *Journal of Roman Studies*, 79 (1989), 59–83.

Eyben, E., 'Fathers and Sons', in B. Rawson (ed.), *Marriage, Divorce and Children in Ancient Rome* (Oxford: Clarendon Press, 1991), 114–43.

Fantham, E., 'Stuprum: Public Attitudes and Penalties for Sexual Offences in Republican Rome', *Échos du monde classique: Classical Views*, 35 (1991), 267–91.

Farnell, L. R., *The Cults of the Greek States*, 5 vols. (Cambridge: Cambridge University Press, 1896).

Ferguson, E., 'Catechesis and Initiation', in A. Kreider (ed.), *The Origins of Christendom in the West* (Edinburgh: T & T Clark, 2001), 229–68.

Finley, M. I., *Ancient Slavery and Modern Ideology* (Harmondsworth: Penguin, 1980).

Flint-Hamilton, K., 'Images of Slavery in the Early Church: Hatred Disguised as Love?', *Journal of Hate Studies*, 2 (2003), 27–45.

Flood, G., *The Ascetic Self: Subjectivity, Memory and Tradition* (Cambridge: Cambridge University Press, 2004).

Florence, M., 'Michel Foucault', in D. Huisman (ed.), *Dictionnaire des Philosophes* (Paris: Presses Universitaires des France, 1984), 942–4.

Foucault, M., *On the Punitive Society: Lectures at the Collège de France, 1972–1973*, A. I. Davidson (ed.) G. Burchell (trans.) (New York, NY: Palgrave Macmillan, 2015).

'The Subject and Power', *Critical Inquiry*, 8 (1982): 777–95.

Discipline and Punish: The Birth of the Prison, A. Sheridan (trans.) (New York, NY: Vintage, 1977).

Surveiller et punir. Naissance de la prison (Paris: Gallimard, 1975).

Frank, G., 'Macrina's Scar: Homeric Allusion and Heroic Identity in Gregory of Nyssa's Life of Macrina', *Journal of Early Christian Studies*, 8 (2000), 511–30.

Frankfurter, D., *Religion in Roman Egypt: Assimilation and Resistance* (Princeton, NJ: Princeton University Press, 1998).

Frazee, C. A., 'Anatolian Asceticism in the Fourth Century: Eustathios of Sebastea and Basil of Caesarea', *Catholic Historical Review*, 66 (1980), 16–33.

Frend, W. H. C., 'Edward Gibbon (1737–1794) and Early Christianity', *Journal of Ecclesiastical History*, 4 (1994), 661–72.

The Donatist Church: A Movement of Protest in Roman North Africa (Oxford: Clarendon Press, 1952).

Gaddis, M., *There Is No Crime for Those Who Have Christ: Religious Violence in the Christian Roman Empire* (Berkeley, CA: University of California Press, 2005).

Gallagher, E., 'Piety and Polity: Eusebius' Defense of the Gospel', in J. Neusner, E. S. Frerichs and A. J. Levine (eds.), *Religious Writings and Religious Systems* (Atlanta, GA: Scholars Press, 1989), 139–55.

García Landa, J. A. and Jaén, S. O. (eds.), *Narratology: An Introduction* (London: Longman, 1996).

Garnsey, P., 'Sons, Slaves – and Christians', in B. Rawson and P. Weaver (eds.), *The Roman Family in Italy: Status, Sentiment, Space* (Oxford: Clarendon Press, 1997), 101–21.

Ideas of Slavery from Aristotle to Augustine (Cambridge: Cambridge University Press, 1996).

Garnsey, P. and Saller, R. P., *The Roman Empire: Economy, Society and Culture*, 2nd edn. (Berkeley, CA: University of California Press, 2015).

Gaudemet, J., *L'Eglise dans l'empire romain (IV–V siècle)* (Paris: Sirey, 1958).

Geerard, M., *Clavis Apocryphorum Novi Testamenti* (Turnhout: Brepols, 1992).

Giannarelli, E., 'Macrina e sua Madre: Santità e Paradosso', *Studia Patristica*, 20 (1989), 224–30.

La tipologia femminile nella biografia e nell' autobiografia cristiana da IV secolo (Rome: Istituto storico italiano per il Medio Evo, 1980).

Gibson, J. T., 'Training People to Inflict Pain: State Terror and Social Learning', *Journal of Humanistic Psychology*, 31 (1991), 72–87.

Ginzburg, C., 'Microhistory: Two or Three Things that I Know about It', *Critical Inquiry*, 20 (1993), 10–35.

Il formaggio e i vermi. Il cosmo di un mugnaio del Cinquecento (Turin: Einaudi, 1976).

Giorda, M. C., 'Children in Monastic Families in Egypt at the End of Antiquity', in C. Laes and V. Vuolanto (eds.), *Children and Everyday Life in the Roman and the Late Antique World* (Oxford; New York, NY: Routledge: 2017) 232–46.

'I bambini nei monasteri dell'Egitto bizantino (v–viii secolo)', *Iuris Antiqui Historia, an International Journal of Ancient Law*, 4 (2012), 93–104.

"Il regno di Dio in terra". I monasteri come fondazioni private (Egitto v–vii secolo) (Roma: Edizioni di Storia e Letteratura, 2011).

'De la direction spirituelle aux règles monastiques. Péchés, pénitence et punitions dans le monachisme pachômien (ive–ve siècles)', *Collectanea Christiana Orientalia*, 6 (2009), 95–113.

Glancy, J. A., 'Slavery in *Acts of Thomas*', *Journal of Early Christian History*, 2 (2012), 3–21.

'Slavery and the Rise of Christianity', in K. Bradley and P. Cartledge, *The Cambridge World History of Slavery, Volume 1: The Ancient Mediterranean World* (Cambridge: Cambridge University Press, 2011), 456–81.

'Christian Slavery in Late Antiquity', in R. Hörmann and G. Mackenthun (eds.), *Human Bondage in the Cultural Contact Zone: Transdisciplinary Perspectives on Slavery and Its Discourses* (Münster: Waxmann, 2010), 63–80.

Slavery in Early Christianity (Oxford: Oxford University Press, 2002).

Gleason, M. W., *Making Men: Sophists and Self-Presentation in Ancient Rome* (Princeton, NJ: Princeton University Press, 1995).

Goldhill, S. (ed.), *The End of Dialogue in Antiquity* (Cambridge: Cambridge University Press, 2008).

Gray, C., *Jerome: Vita Malchi* (Oxford: Oxford University Press, 2015).

Greatrex, G., 'The Romano-Persian Frontier and the Context of the *Book of Steps*', in K. S. Heal and R. A. Kitchen (eds.), *Breaking the Mind: New Studies in the Syriac 'Book of Steps'* (Washington, DC: Catholic University of America Press, 2014), 9–31.

Greenfield, R., 'Children in Byzantine Monasteries: Innocent Hearts or Vessels in the Harbor of the Devil', in A. Papaconstantinou and A. M. Talbot (eds.), *Becoming Byzantine: Children and Childhood in Byzantium* (Cambridge, MA: Dumbarton Oaks Byzantine Symposia and Colloquia. Harvard University Press, 2009), 253–82.

Gryson, R., *Scolies ariennes sur le Concile d'Aquilée*, Sources chrétiennes 267 (Paris: Éditions du Cerf, 1980).

Haines-Eitzen, K., 'Engendering Palimpsests: Gender, Asceticism, and the Transmission of the Acts of Paul and Thecla', in W. Klingshirn and L. Safran (eds.), *The Early Christian Book* (Washington, DC: Catholic University of America, 2005), 177–93.

Haley, K. J. and Fessler, D. M. T., 'Nobody's Watching? Subtle Cues Affect Generosity in an Anonymous Game', *Evolution of Human Behaviour*, 26 (2005), 245–56.

Hall, D. E. (ed.), *Muscular Christianity: Embodying the Victorian Age* (Cambridge, Cambridge University Press, 2006).

Hall, S., 'Negotiating Caribbean Identities', *New Left Review*, 209 (1995), 3–14.

Hallett, J. P., *Fathers and Daughters in Roman Society: Women and the Elite Family* (Princeton, NJ: Princeton University Press, 1984).

Harkins, P. W., *St John Chrysostom: Baptismal Instructions*, Ancient Christian Writers 31 (New York, NY: Paulist Press, 1963).

Harmless, W., *Augustine and the Catechumenate* (Collegeville, MI: Liturgical Press, 1995).

Harper, K., *Slavery in the Late Roman World, AD 275–425* (Cambridge: Cambridge University Press, 2011).

Harries, J., 'The Empresses' Tale, AD 300–360', in C. Harrison, C. Humfress and I. Sandwell (eds.), *Being Christian in Late Antiquity* (Oxford University Press, 2014), 197–214.

Law and Crime in the Roman World (Cambridge: Cambridge University Press, 2007).

'Constructing the Judge: Judicial Accountability in and the Culture of Criticism in Late Antiquity', in R. Miles (ed.), *Constructing Identities in Late Antiquity* (London: Routledge, 1999), 214–33.

Harrill, J. A., 'The Vice of Slave Dealers in Greco-Roman Society: The Use of a Topos in 1 Timothy 1:10', *Journal of Biblical Literature*, 118 (1999), 97–122.

Harris, W. V., 'The Roman Father's Power of Life and Death', in R. S. Bagnall and W. Harris (eds.), *Studies in Roman Law in Memory of A. Arthur Schiller* (Leiden: Brill, 1986), 81–96.

Harrison, V., 'Male and Female in Cappadocian Theology', *Journal of Theological Studies*, 41 (1990), 441–71.

Hartmann, E., 'Das "schwache Geschlecht" im römischen Recht – Frauen und Rechtsprechung', in M. Reuter, R. Schiavone (eds.), *Gefährliches Pflaster, Kriminalität im römischen Reich* (Mainz: von Zabern, 2011), 269–79.

Hartney, A. M., *John Chrysostom and the Transformation of the City* (London: Duckworth, 2004).

Harvey, S. A., 'Revisiting the Daughters of the Covenant: Women's Choirs and Sacred Song in Ancient Syriac Christianity', *Hugoye: Journal of Syriac Studies*, 8 (2005), 125–49.

'Sacred Bonding: Mothers and Daughters in Early Syriac Hagiography', *Journal of Early Christian Studies*, 4 (1996), 27–56.

Asceticism and Society in Crisis: John of Ephesus and the Lives of the Eastern Saints (Los Angeles, CA: University of California Press, 1990).

Hatlen, J. F., 'Honour and Domestic Violence in the Late Roman West, c. 300–600 AD', unpublished PhD thesis Norwegian University of Science and Technology, Trondheim (2014).

Hays, R. B., *The Faith of Jesus Christ: The Narrative Substructure of Galatians 3:1–4:11*, new edn. (Grand Rapids, MI: Eerdmans, 2002).

Healey, J. F., 'The Edessan Milieu and the Birth of Syriac', *Hugoye: Journal of Syriac Studies*, 10 (2007), 1–34.

Heather, P., *The Goths* (Oxford: Blackwell, 1996).

Hen, Y., 'Martin of Braga's *De correctione rusticorum* and Its Uses in Frankish Gaul', in E. Cohen and M. de Jong (eds.), *Medieval Transformations: Texts, Power and Gifts in Context* (Leiden: Brill, 2001), 35–50.

Hendon, J. A., 'The Engendered Household', in S. M. Nelson (ed.), *Women in Antiquity: Theoretical Approaches to Gender and Archaeology* (Lanham, MD; Plymouth: AltaMira Press, 2007), 141–68.

Hermanowicz, E. T., *Possidius of Calama: A Study of the North African Episcopate at the Time of Augustine* (Oxford: Oxford University Press, 2008).

Herzberger, S., *Violence within the Family* (Boulder, CO: Westview Press, 1996).

Hezser, C., *Jewish Slavery in Antiquity* (Oxford, 2005).

Hillner, J., *Prison, Punishment and Penance in Late Antiquity* (Cambridge: Cambridge University Press, 2015).

'Family Violence: Punishment and Abuse in the Late Roman Household', in L. Brubaker and S. Tougher (eds.), *Approaches to the Byzantine Family* (Aldershot: Ashgate, 2013), 21–45.

'Gregory the Great's "Prisons": Monastic Confinement in Early Byzantine Italy', *Journal of Early Christian Studies*, 19 (2011), 433–71.

'Monastic Imprisonment in Justinian's Novels', *Journal of Early Christian Studies*, 15 (2007), 205–37.

'Domus, Family, and Inheritance: The Senatorial Family House in Late Antique Rome', *Journal of Roman Studies*, 93 (2003), 129–45.

Hollerich, M. J., 'Religion and Politics in the Writings of Eusebius: Reassessing the First "Court Theologian"', *Church History*, 59 (1990), 309–25.

Hombert, P.-M., *Nouvelles recherches de chronologie augustinienne* (Paris: Institut d'Études Augustiniennes, 2000).

Hopkins, K., 'Novel Evidence for Roman Slavery', *Past & Present*, 138 (1993), 3–27.

Howe, J., 'Voluntary Ascetic Flagellation: From Local to Learned Traditions', *Haskins Society Journal: Studies in Medieval History*, 24 (2012), 41–62.

Hübner, S. R., *The Family in Roman Egypt: A Comparative Approach to Intergenerational Solidarity and Conflict* (Cambridge: Cambridge University Press 2013).

Huisman, D. (ed.), *Dictionnaire des Philosophes* (Paris: Presses Universitaires des France, 1984).

Humfress, C., *Multi-Legalism in Late Antiquity (212–565 CE)* (Oxford: Oxford University Press, forthcoming).

'Thinking through Legal Pluralism: "Forum Shopping" in the Later Roman Empire', in J. Duindam, J. Harries, C. Humfress and N. Hurvitz (eds.), *Law and Empire: Ideas, Practices, Actors* (Leiden: Brill, 2013), 225–50.

'Law in Practice', in P. Rousseau (ed.), *A Companion to Late Antiquity* (Oxford: Blackwell, 2009), 377–91.

Hunter, D. G., 'Marrying and the *Tabulae Nuptiales* in Roman North Africa from Tertullian to Augustine', in P. L. Reynolds and J. Witte, *To Have and to Hold* (Cambridge: Cambridge University Press, 2007), 95–113.

'The Virgin, the Bride, and the Church: Reading Psalm 45 in Ambrose, Jerome, and Augustine', *Church History*, 69 (2000), 281–303.

Inowlocki, S., *Eusebius and the Jewish Authors* (Leiden: Brill, 2006).

Jacobs, A., *Remains of the Jews: The Holy Land and Christian Empire in Late Antiquity* (Stanford, CA: Stanford University Press, 2004).

Jacobs A. and Krawiec, R., 'Fathers Know Best: Christian Families in the Age of Asceticism', *Journal of Early Christian Studies*, 11 (2003), 257–63.

Jenkins, T. E., *Intercepted Letters: Epistolarity and Narrative in Greek and Roman Literature* (Lanham, MD: Lexington Books, 2006).

Jensen, A., *Thekla – die Apostolin. Ein apokrypher Text neu entdeckt* (Freiburg; Basel; Vienna: Herder, 1995).

Johannessen, H., *The Demonic in the Political Thought of Eusebius of Caesarea* (Oxford: Oxford University Press, 2016).

Johnson, A. P., 'The Implications of a Minimalist Approach to Porphyry's Fragments', in I. Männlein-Robert (ed.), *Die Christen als Bedrohung: Text, Kontext, und Wirkung von Porphyrios' Contra Christianos* (Stuttgart: Franz Steiner Verlag, 2016), 41–58.

'*Porphyry in Fragments: Reception of an Anti-Christian Text in Late Antiquity* by Ariane Magny (Review)', *Journal of Late Antiquity*, 8 (2015), 231–3.

Eusebius (London: I. B. Tauris, 2014).

'The Author of the *Against Hierocles*: A Response to Borzì and Jones', *Journal of Theological Studies*, 64 (2013), 574–94.

'Introduction', in A. P. Johnson and J. Schott (eds.), *Eusebius of Caesarea: Tradition and Innovations*, Hellenic Studies 60 (Washington, DC: Center for Hellenic Studies, Trustees for Harvard University, 2013), 3–10.

Religion and Identity in Porphyry of Tyre (Cambridge: Cambridge University Press, 2013).

'Eusebius the Educator: The Context of the *General Elementary Introduction*', in C. Zamagni and S. Inowlocki (eds.), *Reconsidering Eusebius* (Leiden: Brill, 2011), 99–118.

'Rethinking the Authenticity of Porphyry, *c.Christ.* fr. 1', *Studia Patristica*, 46 (2010), 53–8.

Ethnicity and Argument in Eusebius' Praeparatio Evangelica (Oxford: Oxford University Press, 2006).

'Eusebius' *Praeparatio Evangelica* as Literary Experiment', in S. Johnson, ed., *Greek Literature in Late Antiquity: Dynamism, Didacticism, Classicism* (Aldershot: Ashgate, 2006), 67–89.

Johnson, S., *The Life and Miracles of Thecla: A Literary Study* (Cambridge, MA: Harvard University Press, 2006).

Jones, A. H. M., *The Later Roman Empire 284–602: A Social Economic and Administrative Survey*, 2 vols. (Oxford: Basil Blackwell, 1964).

Jones, A. H. M. and Martindale, J. R., *Prosopography of the Later Roman Empire*, 3 vols. (Cambridge: Cambridge University Press, 1970–92).

Joyner, C., 'From Here to There and Back Again: Adventures of a Southern Historian', in J. B. Boles (ed.), *Shapers of Southern History: Autobiographical Reflections* (Athens, GA: University of Georgia Press, 2004), 137–63.

Kalligas, P., 'Traces of Longinus' Library in Eusebius' *Praeparatio Evangelica*', *Classical Quarterly*, 51 (2001), 584–98.

Kantorowicz, E. H., 'On the Golden Marriage Belt and the Marriage Rings of the Dumbarton Oaks Collection', *Dumbarton Oaks Papers*, 14 (1960), 1–16.

Kaster, R. A., 'Controlling Reason: Declamation in Rhetorical Education at Rome', in Y. L. Too (ed.), *Education in Greek and Roman Antiquity* (Leiden: Brill, 2001), 317–37.

Guardians of Language: The Grammarian and Society in Late Antiquity (Berkeley, CA: University of California Press, 1988).

Kelemen, D. and Rosset, E., 'The Human Function Compunction: Teleological explanation in adults', *Cognition*, 111 (2001), 138–43.

Kelemen, D. and Rottman, R., 'Is There Such a Thing as a Christian Child? Evidence of Religious Beliefs in Early Childhood', in P. McNamara and W. Wildman (eds.), *Science and the World's Religions: Origins and Destinies* (Santa Barbara, CA: Praeger Press, 2012).

Kelly, B., *Petitions, Litigation, and Social Control in Roman Egypt* (Oxford: Oxford University Press, 2011).

Kelly, C., *Ruling the Later Roman Empire*, Revealing Antiquity 15 (Cambridge, MA: Harvard University Press, 2004).

Kelly, J. N. D., *Golden Mouth: The Story of John Chrysostom – Ascetic, Preacher, Bishop* (London: Duckworth, 1995).

Kenny, A., 'Was St John Chrysostom a Semi-Pelagian?', *The Irish Theological Quarterly*, 27 (1960), 16–29.

Kitchen, R. A., 'Disturbed Sinners: In Pursuit of Sanctity in the *Book of Steps*', in K. S. Heal and R. A. Kitchen (eds.), *Breaking the Mind: New Studies in the Syriac 'Book of Steps'* (Washington, DC: Catholic University of America Press, 2014), 205–20.

Kitchen, R. A. and Parmentier, M. F. G. (trans.), *The Book of Steps: The Syriac* Liber Graduum, Cistercian Studies 196 (Kalamazoo, MI: Cistercian Publications, 2004).

Klijn, A. F. J., *The Acts of Thomas: Introduction, Text, and Commentary*, Supplements to Novum Testamentum 108 (Leiden: Brill, 2003).

Klostermann, E., *Eusebius Werke* IV. *Gegen Marcell, Über Die Kirchliche Theologie*, Die Griechischen Christlichen Schriftsteller 14 (Leipzig: J. C. Hinrichs'sche Buchhandlung, 1906).

Konstan, D., *The Emotions of the Ancient Greeks: Studies in Aristotle and Classical Literature* (Toronto: University of Toronto Press, 2007).

Sexual Symmetry: Love in the Ancient Novel and Related Genres (Princeton, NJ: Princeton University Press, 1994).

Kotsifou, C., 'A Glimpse into the World of Petitions: the Case of Aurelia Artemis and her Orphaned Children', in A. Chaniotis (ed.), *Unveiling Emotions: Sources and Methods for the Study of Emotions in the Greek World* (Stuttgart: Franz Steiner Verlag, 2012), 317–27.

'Papyrogical Perspectives on Orphans in the World of Late Ancient Christianity', in C. Horn and R. R. Phenix (eds.), *Children in Late Antiquity* (Tübingen: Mohr Siebeck, 2009), 339–73.

Krause, J.-U., *Gefängnisse im Römischen Reich* (Stuttgart: Franz Steiner Verlag, 1996).

Krawiec, R., '"From the Womb of the Church": Monastic Families', *Journal of Early Christian Studies*, 11 (2003), 283–307.

Kreider, A., 'Changing Patterns of Conversion in the West', in Alan Kreider (ed.), *The Origins of Christendom in the West* (Edinburgh: T&T Clark, 2001), 3–46.

Krueger, D., *Writing and Holiness: The Practice of Authorship in the Early Christian East* (Philadephia, PA: University of Pennsylvania Press, 2004).

'Writing and the Liturgy of Memory in Gregory of Nyssa's *Life of Macrina*', *Journal of Early Christian Studies*, 8 (2000), 483–510.

Kuefler, M., 'The Marriage Revolution in Late Antiquity: The Theodosian Code and Later Roman Marriage Law', *Journal of Family History*, 32 (2007), 343–70.

Kyle, D., *Spectacles of Death in Ancient Rome* (London: Psychology Press, 1998).

Laes, C., 'Kinship and Friendship in the Apophthegmata Patrum', in C. Krötzl and K. Mustakallio (eds.), *De Amicitia: Social Networks and Relationships in Ancient and Medieval World* (Rome: Institutum Romanum Finlandiae, 2010), 115–34.

Lakoff, G. and Johnson, M., *Metaphors We Live By* (Chicago, IL: University of Chicago Press, 2003).

Lakomski, G., 'On Agency and Structure: Pierre Bourdieu and Jean-Claude Passeron's Theory of Symbolic Violence', *Curriculum Inquiry*, 14 (1984), 151–63.

Lamberton, R., 'The Neoplatonists and Their Books', in M. Finkelberg and G. G. Stroumsa (eds.), *Homer, the Bible, and Beyond* (Leiden: Brill, 2003), 195–212.

Homer the Theologian (Berkeley, CA: University of California Press, 1986).

Larsen, L. I., 'Redefining Solitude: Monastic Registers of Fictive (and Factual) Family', *Forum*, 3rd Series, 9/1 (2020), 77–102.

'On Learning a New Alphabet: The Sayings of the Desert Fathers and the Monostichs of Menander', *Studia Patristica*, 55 (2013), 59–77.

Laurin, J.-R., *Orientations maîtresses des apologistes chrétiens de 270 à 361*, Analecta Gregoriana 61 (Rome: Université Grégorienne, 1954).

Lavan, L., 'The Agorai of Antioch and Constantinople as Seen by John Chrysostom', *Bulletin of the Institute of Classical Studies*, 50, S91 (2007), 157–67.

Layton, R. A., 'Plagiarism and Lay Patronage of Ascetic Scholarship: Jerome, Ambrose and Rufinus', *Journal of Early Christian Studies*, 10 (2002), 489–522.

Le Bohec, Y., *The Roman Imperial Army* (London: B. T. Batsford, 1994).

Le Roy Ladurie, E., *Montaillou, Village occitan de 1294 à 1324* (Paris: Gallimard, 1975).

LeDoux, J. E., *The Emotional Brain: The Mysterious Underpinnings of Emotional Life* (New York, NY: Simon and Schuster, 1996).

Leduc, F., 'Gérer l'agressitivé et la colère d'après l'oeuvre de Saint Jean Chrysostome', *Proche-Orient Chrètien*, 38 (1988), 31–63.

'L'eschatologie: une préoccupation centrale de saint Jean Chrysostome', *Proche-Orient Chrètien*, 19 (1969), 109–34.

Leipoldt, J., *Sinuthii archimandritae vita et opera omnia* (Paris: Imprimerie Nationale 1913).

Lendon, J. E., *Empire of Honour: The Art of Government in the Roman World* (Oxford: Clarendon Press, 1997).

Lenox-Conyngham, A. D., 'Juristic and Religious Aspects of the Basilica Conflict of AD 386', *Studia Patristica*, 18 (1985), 55–8.

Lenski, N., 'Captivity and Slavery among the Saracens in Late Antiquity', *Antiquité Tardive*, 19 (2011), 237–66.

Levine, D., 'Martial Arts as a Resource for Liberal Education: The Case of Aikido', in M. Featherstone, M. Hepworth and B. S. Turner (eds.), *The Body: Social Process and Cultural Theory* (London: Sage, 1991), 209–24.

Leyerle, B., 'Lot's Wife on the Border', *Harvard Theological Review*, 107 (2014), 59–80.

'"Keep me, Lord, as the Apple of Your Eyes": An Early Christian Child's Amulet', *Journal of Early Christian History*, 3 (2013), 73–93.

Theatrical Shows and Ascetic Lives: John Chrysostom's Attack on Spiritual Marriage (Berkeley, CA: University of California Press, 2001).

'Appealing to Children', *Journal of Early Christian Studies*, 5 (1997), 243–70.

Leyser, C., *Authority and Asceticism from Augustine to Gregory the Great* (Oxford: Oxford University Press, 2000).

Liebeschuetz, J. H. W. G., *Ambrose and John Chrysostom: Clerics Between Desert and Empire* (Oxford: Oxford University Press, 2011).

Ambrose of Milan: Political Letters and Speeches (Liverpool: Liverpool University Press, 2005).

Lightman, M., and Zeisel, W., 'Univira: An Example of Continuity and Change in Roman Society', *Church History* 46 (1977), 19–32.

Limberis, V., *Architects of Piety, The Cappadocian Fathers and the Cult of the Martyrs* (Oxford: Oxford University Press, 2011).

Lipsius, R. A., *Acta apostolorum apocrypha*. Vol. 1 (Leipzig: Mendelssohn, 1891 [repr. Hildesheim: Olms, 1972]).

Llewelyn, S., 'P. Harris 1 62 and the Pursuit of Fugitive Slaves', *Zeitschrift für Papyrologie und Epigraphik*, 118 (1997), 245–50.

Lofland, J., and Stark, R., 'Becoming a World-Saver: A Theory of Conversion to a Deviant Perspective', *American Sociological Review* 30 (1965), 862–75.

Longo, K., *Donne di potere nella tarda antichità. Le Augustae attraverso le immagini monetali* (Reggio Calabria: Falzea, 2009).

Looper-Friedman, S. E., 'The Decline of Manus-Marriage in Rome', in *Tijdschrift voor Rechtsgeschiedenis*, 55 (1987), 281–96.

Luck, G., 'Notes on the *Vita Macrinae* by Gregory of Nyssa', in Andreas Spira (ed.), *The Biographical Works of Gregory of Nyssa. Proceedings of the Fifth International Colloquium on Gregory of Nyssa (Mainz, 6–10 September 1982)* (Philadelphia, PA: The Philadelphia Patristic Foundation, 1984), 21–33.

Lynch, J. H., 'Monastic Recruitment in the Eleventh and Twelfth Centuries: Some Social and Economic Considerations', *American Benedictine Review*, 26 (1975), 425–47.

MacCoull, L. S. B., 'Child Donations and Child Saints in Coptic Egypt', *East European Quarterly*, 13 (1979), 409–15.

MacDonald, D. R., *The Legend and the Apostle: The Battle for Paul in Story and Canon* (Philadelphia, PA: Westminster Press, 1983).

MacMullen, R., 'The Preacher's Audience (AD 350–400)', *Journal of Theological Studies*, n.s., 40 (1989), 503–11.

'What Difference Did Christianity Make?', *Historia*, 35 (1986), 322–43.

Christianizing the Roman Empire (AD 100–400) (London: Yale University Press, 1984).

Malosse, P.-L., 'Libanius' *Orations*', in L. van Hoof (ed.), *Libanius: A Critical Introduction* (Cambridge, Cambridge University Press, 2014), 81–106.

Mansfeld, J., *Prolegomena: Questions to Be Settled before the Study of an Author, or a Text* (Leiden: Brill, 1994).

Mansfeld, J. and Runia, D. T., *Aëtiana: The Method and Intellectual Context of a Doxographer* (Leiden: Brill, 1997).

Maraval, P., 'La *Vie de Sainte Macrine* de Grégoire de Nysse: Continuité et nouveauté d'un genre littéraire', in G. Freyburger and L. Pernot (eds.), *Du héros païen au saint chrétien* (Paris: Études Augustiniennes, 1997), 133–8.

Grégoire de Nysse. Vie de sainte Macrine, Sources chrétiennes 178 (Paris: Éditions du Cerf, 1971).

Markus, R. A., *The End of Ancient Christianity* (Cambridge: Cambridge University Press, 1990).

Marrou, H. I., *A History of Education in Antiquity*, G. Lamb (trans.) (London: Sheed and Ward, 1956).

'Ammien Marcelin et les "Innocents" de Milan', *Recherches de science religieuse*, 40 (1952), 179–90.

Martens, J. W., '"Do Not Sexually Abuse Children": The Language of Early Christian Sexual Ethics', in C. Horn and R. R. Phenix (eds.), *Children in Late Antiquity* (Tübingen: Mohr Siebeck, 2009), 227–54.

Martin, D. B., 'The Construction of the Ancient Family: Methodological Considerations', *Journal of Roman Studies*, 86 (1996), 40–60.

Mathieu, J. E., 'A Causal Model of Organization Commitment in a Military Training Environment', *Journal of Vocational Behaviour*, 32 (1988), 321–35.

Matthews, J., *Western Aristocracies and Imperial Court AD 364–425* (Oxford, Clarendon Press, 1975).

Maxwell, J. L., *Christianization and Communication in Late Antiquity: John Chrysostom and His Congregation in Antioch* (Cambridge: Cambridge University Press, 2006).

Mayer, W., 'Poverty and Generosity toward the Poor in the Time of John Chrysostom', in S. R. Holman (ed.), *Wealth and Poverty in Early Church and Society* (Grand Rapids, MI: Baker Academic, 2008), 140–58.

'John Chrysostom as Bishop: The View from Antioch', *Journal of Ecclesiastical History*, 55 (2004), 455–66.

'Who Came to Hear John Chrysostom Preach? Recovering a Late Fourth-Century Preacher's Audience', *Ephemerides Theologicae Lovanienses*, 76 (2000), 73–87.

Mayer, W. and Allen, P., *John Chrysostom* (London: Routledge, 2000).

Mazza, R., *L'archivio degli Apioni. Terra, lavoro e proprietà senatoria nell'Egitto tardoantico* (Bari: Munera, 2001).

Mazzarino, S., *Storia sociale del vescovo Ambrogio* (Rome: L'Erma di Bretschneider, 1989).

McCurry, S., *Masters of Small Worlds: Yeoman Households, Gender Relations, and the Political Culture of the Antebellum South Carolina Low Country* (Oxford: Oxford University Press, 1995).

McGinn, T. A. J., *The Economy of Prostitution in the Roman World* (Ann Arbor, MI: University of Michigan Press, 2004).

Prostitution, Sexuality and the Law in Ancient Rome (Oxford: Oxford University Press, 1998).

'Concubinage and the Lex Iulia', *Transactions of the American Philological Association*, 121 (1991), 335–75.

McGuckin, J. A., *St Gregory of Nazianzus: An Intellectual Biography* (New York, NY: St Vladimir's Seminary Press, 2001).

McLynn, N. B., 'Genere Hispanus: Theodosius, Spain and Nicene Orthodoxy', in K. Bowes and M. Kulikowski (eds.), *Hispania in Late Antiquity: Current Perspectives* (Leiden: Brill, 2005), 77–120.

Ambrose of Milan: Church and Court in a Christian Capital (Berkeley, CA: University of California Press, 1994).

'The "Apology" of Palladius: Nature and Purpose', *Journal of Theological Studies*, 42 (1991), 52–76.

Mellon Saint-Laurent, J.-N., *Missionary Stories and the Formation of the Syriac Churches*, Transformation of the Classical Heritage 55 (Berkeley, CA: University of California Press, 2015).

Meyer, E. A., *Legitimacy and Law in the Roman World: Tabulae in Roman Belief and Practice* (Cambridge: Cambridge University Press, 2004).

Meyer, E. M., 'The Problems of Gendered Space in Syro-Palestinian Domestic Architecture: The Case of Roman-Period Galilee', in D. Balch and C. Osiek (eds.), *Early Christian Families in Context: An Interdisciplinary Dialogue* (Grand Rapids, MI: Eerdmans, 2003), 44–69.

Milgram, S., 'The Small World Problem', *Psychology Today*, 22 (1967), 61–7.

Millar, F., *The Emperor in the Roman World* (London: Duckworth, 1977).

'Emperors at Work', *Journal of Roman Studies*, 57 (1967), 9–19.

Miller, W. I., *The Mystery of Courage* (Cambridge, MA: Harvard University Press, 2000).

Misset-Van de Weg, M., 'A Wealthy Woman Named Tryphaena: Patroness of Thecla of Iconium', in J. N. Bremmer (ed.), *The Apocryphal Acts of Paul and Thecla* (Kampen: Pharos, 1996), 16–35.

Mitchell, M. M., 'Christian Martyrdom and the Dialect of the Holy Scriptures: The Literal, the Allegorical, the Martyrological', in R. S. Boustan, A. P. Jassen and C. J. Roetzel (eds.), *Violence, Scripture, and Textual Practice in Early Judaism and Christianity* (Leiden: Brill, 2010), 174–203.

The Heavenly Trumpet: John Chrysostom and the Art of Pauline Interpretation (London: Westminster John Knox Press, 2002).

Momigliano, A., 'The Life of St Macrina by Gregory of Nyssa', in J. W. Eadie and J. Ober (eds.), *The Craft of the Ancient Historian: Essays in Honor of Chester G. Starr* (Lanham, MD.: University Press of America, 1985), 443–58.

Mooney, J., *Gender, Violence and the Social Order* (New York, NY: St Martin's Press, 2000).

Morgan, L. H. *Ancient Society* (London: MacMillan, 1877).

Morgan, T., *Roman Faith and Christian Faith:* Pistis *and* Fides *in the Early Roman Empire and Early Churches* (Oxford: Oxford University Press, 2015).

'Assessment in Roman Education', *Assessment in Education: Principles, Policy & Practice*, 8 (2001), 11–24.

Morlet, S., 'L'Antiquité tardive fut-elle une période d'obscurantisme? À propos d'un ouvrage recent [P. Athanassiadi, *Vers la pensée unique, la montée de l'intolerance dans l'Antiquité tardive* (Paris, 2010)]" *Adamantius*, 16 (2010), 413–21.

La Démonstration Évangélique *d'Eusèbe de Césarée: Étude sur l'apologétique chrétienne à l'époque de Constantin* (Turnhout: Brepols, 2010).

'La *Démonstration évangélique* d'Eusèbe de Césarée contient-elle des fragments du *Contra Christianos* de Porphyre? À propos du fr. 73 Harnack', *Studia Patristica*, 46 (2010), 59–64.

Morrisson, C. and Cheynet, J. C., 'Prices and Wages in the Byzantine World', in A. Laiou (ed.), *The Economic History of Byzantium from the Seventh through the Fifteenth Century* (Washington, DC: Dumbarton Oaks Press, 2002).

Moutsoulas, E., ΓΡΗΓΟΡΙΟΣ ΝΥΣΣΗΣ, Βίος, Συγράμματα, Διδασκαλία (Athens: Eptalophos A.B.E.E., 1997).

Mras, K., *Eusebius Werke* VIII. *Die Praeparatio Evangelica* (Berlin: Akademie Verlag, 1954).

Murray, S. J., 'The Characteristics of the Earliest Syriac Christianity', in R. W. Thomson, T. Matthews and N. G. Garsoian (eds.), *East of Byzantium: Syria and Armenia in the Formative Period* (Washington DC: Dumbarton Oaks, 1982), 3–16.

Nasrallah, L., *Christian Responses to Roman Art and Architecture* (Cambridge: Cambridge University Press, 2010).

Nathan, G., *The Family in Late Antiquity: The Rise of Christianity and the Endurance of Tradition* (London; New York, NY: Routledge, 2000).

Nauroy, G., 'Le fouet et le miel. Le combat d'Ambroise en 386 contre l'arianisme milanaise', *Recherches Augustiniennes*, 23 (1988), 3–86.

Nissen, T., 'Unbekannte Erzählungen aus dem Pratum Spirituale', *Byzantinische Zeitschrift*, 38 (1938), 351–76.

Nolan, S., 'Narrative as a Strategic Resource for Resistance: Reading the *Acts of Thecla* for Its Political Purposes', in G. J. Brooke and J.-D. Kaestli (eds.), *Narrativity in Biblical and Related Texts* (Leuven: Peeters, 2000), 225–42.

Noonan, J., 'Marital Affection', *Studia Gratiana* 12 (1967), 479–509.

Nowak, M., 'The Fatherless and Family Structure in Roman Egypt', in D. F. Leão and G. Thür (eds.), *Symposion 2015: Vorträge zur griechischen und hellenistischen Rechtsgeschichte (Coimbra, 1.–4. September 2015)*, Akten der Gesellschaft für griechische und hellenistische Rechtsgeschichte 25 (Vienna: Österreichische Akademie der Wissenschaften, 2016), 99–114.

Nussbaum, M. C., *Upheavals of Thought* (Cambridge: Cambridge University Press, 2001).

The Therapy of Desire: Theory and Practice in Hellenistic Ethics (Princeton, NJ: Princeton University Press, 1994).

Ochberg, R. L., and Rosenwald, G. C., *Storied Lives: The Cultural Politics of Self-Understanding* (New Haven, CT: Yale University Press, 1992).

O'Donnell, J. J., *Augustine, Sinner and Saint: A New Biography* (New York, NY: Ecco, 2005).

O'Roark, D., 'Parenthood in Late Antiquity: The Evidence of Chrysostom', *Greek, Roman, and Byzantine Studies*, 40 (1999), 53–81.

Papaconstantinou, A., 'Child or Monk? An Unpublished Story Attributed to John Moschos in MS Coislin 257', *Bulletin of the American Society of Papyrologists*, 45 (2008), 171–84.

'Notes sur les actes de donation d'enfants au monastère thébain de Saint Phoibammon', *Journal of Juristic Papyrology*, 32 (2002), 83–105.

'ΘΕΙΑ ΟΙΚΟΝΟΜΙΑ. Les actes thébains de donation d'enfants ou la gestion monastique de la pénurie', in *Mélanges Gilbert Dagron, Travaux et Mémoires*, 14 (Paris: Amis du Centre d'Histoire et Civilisation de Byzance, 2002), 511–26.

Papageorgiou, P. E., 'A Theological Analysis of Selected Themes in the Homilies of St John Chrysostom on the Epistle of St Paul to the Romans', unpublished PhD thesis, Catholic University of America (1995).

Patterson, O., 'Slavery, Gender, and Work in the Pre-modern World and Early Greece: A Cross-Cultural Analysis', in E. Dal Lago and C. Katsari, eds., *Slave Systems: Ancient and Modern* (Cambridge: Cambridge University Press, 2008).

Slavery and Social Death: A Comparative Study (Cambridge, MA: Harvard University Press, 1982).

Payne, R. E., *A State of Mixture: Christians, Zoroastrians, and Iranian Political Culture in Late Antiquity* (Berkeley, CA: University of California Press, 2015).

Peacock, J. L. and Holland, D. C., 'The Narrated Self: Life Stories in Process', *Ethos*, 21 (1993), 367–83.

Pears, D., 'Courage as Mean', in A. O. Rorty (ed.), *Essays on Aristotle's Ethics* (Berkeley, CA: University of California Press, 1980), 171–87.

Perkins, J., *The Suffering Self: Pain and Narrative Representation in the Early Christian Era* (London: Routledge, 1995).

Perry, M. J., *Gender, Manumission, and the Roman Freedwoman* (Cambridge: Cambridge University Press, 2013).
Perrone, L., 'Eusebius of Caesarea as a Christian Writer', in A. Raban and K. Holum (eds.), *Caesarea Maritima: A Retrospective after Two Millennia* (Leiden: Brill, 1996), 515–30.
Pervo, R. I., *The Acts of Paul: A New Translation with Introduction and Commentary* (Eugene, OR: Cascade Books, 2014).
Peters, G., 'Offering Sons to God in the Monastery: Child Oblation, Monastic Benevolence, and the Cistercian Order in the Middle Ages', *Cistercian Studies Quarterly*, 38 (2003), 285–95.
Pharr, C., *The Theodosian Code and Novels and the Sirmondian Constitutions: A Translation with Commentary, Glossary, and Bibliography* (Princeton, NJ: Princeton University Press, 1952).
Phang, S. E., *The Marriage of Roman Soldiers (13 BC–AD 235): Law and Family in the Imperial Army* (Leiden: Brill, 2001).
Phillips, J. E., 'Roman Mothers and the Lives of Their Adult Daughters', *Helios*, 6 (1978), 69–80.
Piese, A., '"Something under the Bed Is Drooling": The Mediation of Fear through the Rhetoric of Fantasy in Literature for Children', in K. Hebblethwaite and E. McCarthy (eds.), *Fear: Essays on the Meaning and Experience of Fear* (Dublin: Four Courts Press, 2007), 145–57.
Pocock, J. G. A., *Barbarism and Religion*, 6 vols. (Cambridge, Cambridge University Press, 1999–2015).
Pohl, W., 'Introduction: Strategies of Distinction', in W. Pohl and H. Reimitz (eds.), *Strategies of Distinction: The Construction of Ethnic Communities, 300–800* (Leiden: Brill, 1998), 1–16.
Potter, D., *Constantine the Emperor* (Oxford: Oxford University Press, 2013).
Pradels, W., Brändle, R. and Heimgartner. M., 'Das bisher vermisste Textstück in Johannes Chrysostomus, *Adversus Judaeos*, Oratio 2', *Zeitschrift für antikes Christentum*, 5 (2001), 22–49.
Price, S. R. F., *Rituals and Power: The Roman Imperial Cult in Asia Minor* (Cambridge: Cambridge University Press, 1983).
Prinzing, G., 'Observations on the Legal Status of Children and the Stages of Childhood in Byzantium', in A. Papaconstantinou and A. M. Talbot (eds.), *Becoming Byzantine: Children and Childhood in Byzantium* (Cambridge, MA: Harvard University Press, 2009), 15–34.
Pudsey, A., 'Children in Late Roman Egypt: Family and Everyday Life in Monastic Contexts', in C. Laes, K. Mustakallio and V. Vuolanto (eds.), *Children and Family in Late Antiquity: Life, Death and Interaction* (Leuven: Peeters, 2015), 215–24.
Ramelli, I., 'Gregory of Nyssa's Position in Late Antique Debates on Slavery and Poverty, and the Role of Asceticism', *Journal of Late Antiquity*, 5 (2012), 87–118.
Rance, P., '*Simulacra Pugnae*: The Literary and Historical Tradition of Mock Battles in the Roman and Early Byzantine Army', *Greek, Roman, and Byzantine Studies*, 41 (2000), 223–75.

Rawson, B. (ed.), *Marriage, Divorce and Children in Ancient Rome* (Oxford: Clarendon Press, 1991 [repr. 2004]).

The Family in Ancient Rome: New Perspectives (London; New York, NY: Routledge, 1986 [repr. 1992]).

Rawson, B. and Weaver, P. (eds.), *The Roman Family in Italy: Status, Sentiment, Space* (Oxford: Clarendon Press, 1997).

Rebillard, E., 'Religious Sociology: Being Christian', in M. Vessey (ed.), *A Companion to Augustine* (Malden, MA: Wiley-Blackwell, 2012), 40–54.

Regnault, L., *Les sentences des Pères du désert, série des anonymes* (Bégrolles-en-Mauges: Abbaye de Bellefontaine, 1985).

Les sentences des Pères du désert, collection alphabétique (Sablé sur Sarthe: Abbaye de Solesmes, 1970).

Reid, C. J., *Power over the Body, Equality in the Family: Rights and Domestic Relations in Medieval Canon Law* (Grand Rapids, MI: Eerdmans Publishing, 2004).

Reynolds, P. L., *Marriage in the Western Church: The Christianization of Marriage during the Patristic and Early Medieval Periods* (Leiden, 1994).

Reynolds, P. L. and Witte Jr., J. (eds.), *To Have and to Hold: Marrying and Its Documentation in Western Christendom, 400–1600* (Cambridge: Cambridge University Press, 2007).

Richter, T. S., 'What's in a Story? Cultural Narratology and Coptic Child Donation Documents', *Journal of Juristic Papyrology*, 35 (2005), 237–64.

Rechtssemantik und forensische Rhetorik: Untersuchungen zu Wortschatz, Stil und Grammatik der Sprache koptischer Rechtsurkunden (Leipzig: H. Wodtke und K. Stegbauer, 2002).

Rives, J. B., 'The Piety of a Persecutor', *Journal of Early Christian Studies*, 4 (1996), 1–25.

Religion and Authority in Roman Carthage (Oxford: Clarendon Press, 1995).

Robinson, O., *The Criminal Law of Ancient Rome* (London: Duckworth, 1995).

Penal Policy and Penal Practice in Ancient Rome (London: Routledge, 2007).

Roth, U., 'Paul, Philemon, and Onesimus', *Zeitschrift für die Neutestamentliche Wissenschaft und die Kunde der älteren Kirche*, 105 (2014), 102–30.

Rousseau, P., 'The Pious Household and the Virgin Chorus: Reflections on Gregory of Nyssa's *Life of Macrina*', *Journal of Early Christian Studies*, 13 (2005), 165–86.

Basil of Caesarea (Berkeley, CA: University of California Press, 1998).

'Blood Relationships among Early Eastern Ascetics', *Journal of Theological Studies*, 23 (1972), 135–44

Rubenson, S., *The Letters of St Antony: Monasticism and the Making of a Saint, Studies in Antiquity and Christianity* (Minneapolis, MN: Fortress Press, 1995).

The Letters of St Antony: Origenist Theology, Monastic Tradition and the Making of a Saint (Lund: University Press, 1990).

Russell, F. H., 'Augustine: Conversion by the Book', in J. Muldoon (ed.), *Varieties of Religious Conversion in the Middle Ages* (Gainesville, FL: University Press of Florida, 1997), 13–30.

Sachers, E., 'Pater familias', in *Real-Encyclopädie der classischen Altertumswissenschaft*, 18 (Waldsee: Alfred Druckemüller Verlag, 1949), cols. 2121–57.

Saller, R. P., 'Symbols of Gender and Status Hierarchies in the Roman Household', in S. R. Joshel and S. Murnaghan (eds.), *Women and Slaves in Greco-Roman Culture: Differential Equations* (London: Routledge, 2001), 85–91.

'Pater Familias, Mater Familias, and the Gendered Semantics of the Roman Household', *Classical Philology*, 94 (1999), 182–97.

'Roman Kinship: Structure and Sentiment', in B. Rawson and P. Weaver (eds.), *The Roman Family in Italy: Status, Sentiment, Space* (Oxford: Clarendon Press, 1997), 7–34.

'The Hierarchical Household in Roman Society: A Study of Domestic Slavery', in M. L. Bush (ed.), *Serfdom and Slavery: Studies in Legal Bondage* (London: Routledge, 1996), 112–29.

Patriarchy, Property and Death in the Roman Family (Cambridge, Cambridge University Press, 1994).

'Corporal Punishment, Authority, and Obedience in the Roman Household', in B. Rawson (ed.), *Marriage, Divorce, and Children in Ancient Rome* (Oxford: Clarendon Press, 1991), 144–65.

'*Pietas*, Obligation, and Authority in the Roman Family', in P. Von Kneissl and V. Losemann (eds.), *Alte Geschichte und Wissenschaftsgeschichte: Festschrift für Karl Christ zum 65. Geburtstag* (Darmstadt: Wissenschaftliche Buchgesellschaft, 1988), 392–410.

'Slavery and the Roman Family', *Slavery and Abolition*, 8 (1987), 65–87.

'*Patria potestas* and the Stereotype of the Roman Family', *Continuity and Change*, 1 (1986), 7–22.

'*Familia, Domus*, and the Roman Conception of the Family', *Phoenix* 38 (1984), 336–55.

Saller, R. P. and Shaw, B. D., 'Tombstones and Roman Family Relations in the Principate: Civilians, Soldiers and Slaves', *Journal of Roman Studies*, 74 (1984), 124–56.

Salzman, M. R., 'Ambrose and the Usurpation of Arbogastes and Eugenius: Reflections on Pagan-Christian Conflict Narratives', *Journal of Early Christian Studies*, 18 (2010), 191–223.

'Symmachus and His Father: Patriarchy and Patrimony in the Late Roman Senatorial Elite', in R. Lizzi Testa (ed.), *Le trasformazioni delle 'élites' in età tardoantica* (Rome: L'Erma di Bretschneider, 2006), 357–75.

The Making of a Christian Aristocracy: Social and Religious Change in the Western Roman Empire (Cambridge, MA, Harvard University Press, 2002).

'Reflections on Symmachus' Idea of Tradition', *Historia*, 38 (1989), 348–64.

San Bernardino, J., '*Sub imperio discordiae*: l'uomo che voleva essere Eliseo (giugno 386)', in L. F. Pizzolato and M. Rizzi (eds.), *Nec timeo mori: atti del Congresso internazionale di studi ambrosiani* (Milan: Vita e Pensiero, 1998), 709–36.

Sandwell, I., *Religious Identity in Late Antiquity: Greeks, Jews and Christians in Antioch* (Cambridge: Cambridge University Press, 2007).

Sarris, P., *Economy and Society in the Age of Justinian* (Cambridge: Cambridge University Press, 2006).

Savon, H., 'Saint Ambroise a-t-il imité le recueil de lettres de Pline le Jeune?', *Revue des Études Augustiniennes*, 41 (1995), 3–17.

Schaten, S., 'Koptische Kinderschenkungsurkunde', *Bulletin de la Société Archéologie Chrétienne*, 35 (1996), 129–42.

Scheidel, W., 'Sex and Empire: A Darwinian Perspective', in I. Morris and W. Scheidel (eds.), *The Dynamics of Ancient Empires: State Power from Assyria to Byzantium* (Oxford: Oxford University Press, 2009), 255–324.

Scheidel, W. and Friesen, S. J., 'The Size of the Economy and the Distribution of Income in the Roman Empire', *Journal of Roman Studies*, 99 (2009), 61–91.

Schenke, G., 'Kinderschenkungen an das Kloster des apa Thomas', *Journal of Juristic Papyrology*, 37 (2007), 177–83.

Schott, J., *Christianity, Empire and the Making of Religion in Late Antiquity* (Philadelphia, PA: University of Pennsylvania Press, 2008).

Schroeder, C., 'Children and Egyptian Monasticism', in C. Horn and R. R. Phenix (eds.), *Children in Late Antiquity* (Tübingen: Mohr Siebeck, 2009), 317–38.

Monastic Bodies: Discipline and Salvation in Shenoute of Atripe. Divinations: Rereading Late Ancient Religion (Philadelphia, PA: University of Pennsylvania Press, 2007).

Schroeder, J. A., 'John Chrysostom's Critique of Spousal Violence', *Journal of Early Christian Studies*, 12 (2004), 413–42.

Seabourne, G., *Imprisoning Medieval Women: The Non-Judicial Confinement and Abduction of Women in England, c. 1170–1509* (Aldershot: Ashgate, 2011).

Segal, J. B., *Edessa, 'The Blessed City'* (Oxford: Clarendon Press, 1970).

Sellew, P., 'Paul, Acts of', in D. N. Freeman (ed.), *The Anchor Bible Dictionary*, 6 vols. (New York, NY: Doubleday, 1992), Vol. v, 202–3.

Sessa, K., 'Ursa's Return: Captivity, Remarriage and the Domestic Authority of Roman Bishops in Fifth-Century Italy', *Journal of Early Christian Studies*, 19 (2011), 401–32.

Shanzer, D., '*Avulsa a latere meo*: Augustine's Spare Rib – Confessions 6.15.25', *Journal of Roman Studies*, 92 (2002): 157–76.

Shaw, B. D., *Sacred Violence: African Christians and Sectarian Hatred in the Age of Augustine* (Cambridge: Cambridge University Press, 2011).

'African Christianity: Disputes, Definitions, and "Donatists"', in M. R. Greenshields and T. Robinson (eds.), *Orthodoxy and Heresy in Religious Movements: Discipline and Dissent* (Lampeter: Edwin Mellen Press, 1992), 5–34.

'The Family in Late Antiquity: The Experience of Augustine', *Past & Present*, 115 (1987), 3–51.

'Latin Funerary Epigraphy and Family Life in the Later Roman Empire', *Historia*, 33 (1984), 457–97.

Shepardson, C., 'Syria, Syriac, Syrian: Negotiating East and West', in P. Rousseau (ed.), *A Companion to Late Antiquity* (Chichester: Wiley-Blackwell, 2009), 455–66.

Sirinelli, J. and des Places, E., *Eusèbe de Césarée. La Préparation Évangélique*, Sources chrétiennes 206.1 (Paris: Éditions du Cerf, 1974).

Sivan, H., *Galla Placidia: The Last Roman Empress* (Oxford: Oxford University Press, 2011).

Slootjes, D., *The Governor and His Subjects in the Later Roman Empire* (Leiden, Brill, 2006).

Sogno, C., *Q. Aurelius Symmachus: A Political Biography* (Ann Arbor, MI: University of Michigan Press, 2006).

Sordi, M., 'I rapporti di Ambrogio con gli imperatori del suo tempo', in L. F. Pizzolato and M. Rizzi (eds.), *Nec timeo mori* (Milan: Vita e Pensiero, 1998), 107–19.

Spectorsky, S. A., *Women in Classical Islamic Law: A Survey of the Sources* (Leiden: Brill, 2010).

Stahlmann, I., *Der gefesselte Sexus. Weibliche Keuschheit und Askese im Westen des römischen Reiches* (Berlin: Akademie Verlag, 1997).

Stark, R., *The Rise of Christianity: A Sociologist Reconsidered History* (Princeton, NJ: Princeton University Press, 1996).

Steinwenter, A., 'Kinderschenkungen an koptische Klöster', *Zeitschrift der Savigny-Stiftung für Rechtsgeschichte* 42, *Kanonistische Abteilung* 11 (1921), 175–207.

Stewart, C., *'Working the Earth of the Heart': The Messalian Controversy in History, Texts, and Language to AD 431* (Oxford: Clarendon Press, 1991).

Stewart, R., *Plautus and Roman Slavery* (Malden, MA: Wiley-Blackwell, 2012).

Stock, B., *Augustine the Reader: Meditation, Self-Knowledge, and the Ethics of Interpretation* (London: Belknap Press, 1996).

Stoneman, R., *The Ancient Oracles: Making the Gods Speak* (New Haven, CT: Yale University Press, 2011).

Stratton, K. B. and Kalleres, D. S. (eds.), *Daughters of Hecate: Women and Magic in the Ancient World* (Oxford: Oxford University Press, 2014).

Szidat, J., 'Die Usurpation des Eugenius', *Historia*, 28 (1979), 487–508.

Taylor, D. G. K., 'Bilingualism and Diglossia in Late Antique Syria and Mesopotamia', in J. N. Adams, M. Janse, and S. Swain (eds.), *Bilingualism in Ancient Society: Language Contact and the Written Text* (Oxford University Press, 2002), 298–331.

Thissen, H. J., 'Kinderschenkungsurkunden. Zur Hierodulie im christlichen Ägypten', *Enchoria*, 14(1986), 117–28.

Thurmond, D. L., 'Some Roman Slave Collars in CIL', *Athenaeum*, 82 (1994), 459–78.

Tilley, M. A., 'Sustaining Donatist Self-Identity: From the Church of the Martyrs to the Collecta of the Desert', *Journal of Early Christian Studies*, 5 (1997), 21–35.

Tornau, C., 'Intertextuality in Early Latin Hagiography: Sulpicius Severus and the Vita Antonii', *Studia Patristica*, 35 (2001), 158–66.

Trakatellis, D., *Being Transformed: Chrysostom's Exegesis of the Epistle to the Romans* (Brookline, MA: Holy Cross Orthodox Press, 1992).

Treggiari, S., 'Ideals and Practicalities in Matchmaking in Ancient Rome', in D. I. Kertzer and R. P. Saller (eds.), *The Family in Italy from Antiquity to the Present* (New Haven, CT: Yale University Press, 1993), 91–108.

Roman Marriage: Iusti Coniuges from the Time of Cicero to the Time of Ulpian (Oxford: Clarendon Press, 1991).

'Digna Condicio: Betrothals in the Roman Upper Class', *Échos du monde Classique: Classical Views*, New Series, 3 (1984), 419–51.

'Consent to Roman Marriage: Some Aspects of Law and Reality', *Classical Views*, 26 (1982), 34–44.

Turner, B. S., 'Warrior Charisma and the Spiritualization of Violence', *Body & Society*, 9 (2003), 93–108.

Urbainczyk, T., *Theodoret of Cyrrhus: The Bishop and the Holy Man* (Ann Arbor, MI: University of Michigan Press, 2002).

Van Dam, R., *Families and Friends in Late Roman Cappadocia* (Philadelphia, PA: University of Pennsylvania Press, 2003).

Van den Hoek, A., 'The Concept of *sōma tōn graphōn* in Alexandrian Theology', *Studia Patristica*, 19 (1989), 250–4.

Van der Lof, L. J., 'The Date of the *De Catechizandis Rudibus*', *Vigiliae Christianae*, 16 (1962), 198–204.

Van der Meer, F., *Augustine the Bishop: The Life and Work of a Father of the Church*, B. Battershaw and G. R. Lamb (trans.) (London: Sheed and Ward, 1961).

Van de Paverd, F., *St John Chrysostom, The Homilies on the Statues: An Introduction*, Orientalia Christiana Analecta 239 (Rome: Pontificium Institutum Studiorum Orientalium, 1991).

Van Hoof, L. (ed.), *Libanius: A Critical Introduction* (Cambridge, Cambridge University Press, 2014).

Van Rompay, L., 'Syriac Studies: The Challenges of the Coming Decade', *Hugoye: Journal of Syriac Studies*, 10 (2007), 23–35.

Veyne, P., *A History of Private Life: From Pagan Rome to Byzantium* (Cambridge, MA: Belknap Press of Harvard University Press, 1987).

'La famille et l'amour sous le Haut-Empire romain', *Annales. Économies, Sociétés, Civilisations*, 33 (1978), 35–63.

Vööbus, A., *History of Asceticism in the Syrian Orient*, 3 vols. Corpus Scriptorum Christianorum Orientalium 184 (Louvain: Secrétariat du Corpus SCO, 1958).

Vuolanto, V., *Children and Asceticism in Late Antiquity: Continuity, Family Dynamics and the Rise of Christianity* (Farnham: Ashgate, 2015).

'Elite Children, Socialization, and Agency in the Late Roman World', in J. Evans Grubbs and T. Parkin (eds.), *The Oxford Handbook of Childhood and Education in the Classical World* (Oxford: Oxford University Press, 2013), 309–24.

'Choosing Ascetism: Children and Parents, Vows and Conflicts', in C. Horn and R. R. Phenix (eds.), *Children in Late Antiquity* (Tübingen: Mohr Siebeck, 2009), 255–91.

'Selling a Freeborn Child: Rhetoric and Social Realities in the Late Roman World', *Ancient Society*, 33 (2003), 169–207.

Wallis, I. G., *The Faith of Jesus Christ in Early Christian Traditions*, Society for New Testament Studies: Monograph Series 84 (Cambridge: Cambridge University Press, 1995).

Wallis Budge, E. A. (ed.), *Coptic Martyrdoms in the Dialect of Upper Egypt* (London: British Museum, 1914).

Ward, W. D., *Mirage of the Saracen: Christians and Nomads in the Sinai Peninsula in Late Antiquity*, Transformation of the Classical Heritage 54 (Berkeley, CA: University of California Press, 2014).

Watson, N., Weir, S. and Friend, S., 'The Development of Muscular Christianity in Victorian Britain and Beyond', *Journal of Religion & Society*, 7 (2005), 1–21.

Webb, M., '"On Lucretia Who Slew Herself": Rape and Consolation in Augustine's *De ciuitate dei*', *Augustinian Studies*, 44 (2013), 37–58.

Wemple, S., *Women in Frankish Society: Marriage and the Cloister* (Philadelphia, PA: University of Pennsylvania Press, 1981).

Wenger, E., *Communities of Practice: Learning, Meaning, and Identity* (Cambridge: Cambridge University Press 1998).

Wiles, M. F., *The Divine Apostle: The Interpretation of St Paul's Epistles in the Early Church* (Cambridge: Cambridge University Press, 1967).

Wilken, R. L. *John Chrysostom and the Jews: Rhetoric and Reality in the Late 4th Century* (Eugene, OR: Wipf and Stock, 2004).

Wilkinson, J., *Egeria's Travels* (London: SPCK, 1971).

Wilkinson, K., *Women and Modesty in Late Antiquity* (Cambridge: Cambridge University Press, 2015).

Williams, D. H., *Ambrose of Milan and the End of the Nicene–Arian Conflicts* (Oxford: Oxford University Press, 1995).

'Ambrose, Emperors and Homoians in Milan: The First Conflict over a Basilica', in M. R. Barnes and D. H. Williams (eds.), *Arianism after Arius: Essays on the Development of the Fourth Century Trinitarian Conflicts* (Edinburgh: T & T Clark, 1993), 127–46.

Williams, G., 'Some Aspects of Roman Marriage Ceremonies and Ideals', *Journal of Roman Studies*, 48 (1958), 16–29.

Williams, M. S., *Authorised Lives in Early Christian Biography: Between Eusebius and Augustine* (Cambridge: Cambridge University Press, 2008).

Wilson-Kastner, P., 'Macrina: Virgin and Teacher', *Andrews University Seminary Studies*, 17 (1979), 105–17.

Winlock, H. E. and Crum, W. E., *The Monastery of Epiphanius*, 2 vols. (New York, NY: The Metropolitan Museum of Art Egyptian Expedition, 1926).

Wipszycka, E., *Moines et communautés monastiques en Egypte (IVe-VIIIe siècles)* (Warsaw: Taubenschlag Foundation, 2009).

'Donation of Children', *Coptic Encyclopaedia* (New York, NY: Macmillan, 1993), Vol. III, 918–19.

Wood, P., 'Syriac and the "Syrians"', in S. Fitzgerald Johnson (ed.), *The Oxford Handbook of Late Antiquity* (Oxford: Oxford University Press, 2012), 170–94.

'We Have No King but Christ': Christian Political Thought in Greater Syria on the Eve of the Arab Conquest (c. 400–585) (Oxford: Oxford University Press, 2010).

Woolf, G., *Becoming Roman: The Origins of Provincial Civilization in Gaul* (Cambridge: Cambridge University Press, 1998).

World Health Organization, 'World Report on Violence and Health' (2002), www.who.int/violence_injury_prevention/violence/world_report/en/, accessed 11 August 2017.

Wright, W., *Apocryphal Acts of the Apostles* (Amsterdam: Philo Press, 1968).

Young, J., 'Risk of Crime and Fear of Crime: A Realist Critique of Survey-Based Assumptions', in M. Maguire and J. Pointing (eds.), *Victims of Crime: A New Deal?* (Milton Keynes: Open University Press, 1988), 164–76.

Zamagni, C., 'Eusebius' Exegesis between Alexandria and Antiochia: Being a Scholar in Caesarea – A Test case from Questions to Stephanos I', in S. Inowlocki and C. Zamagni (eds.), *Reconsidering Eusebius* (Leiden: Brill, 2011), 151–76.

Zangara, V., 'Eusebio di Vercelli e Massimo di Torino. Tra storia e agiografia', in E. Dal Covolo, R. Uglione and G. M. Vian (eds.), *Eusebio di Vercelli e il suo tempo* (Rome: Libreria Ateneo Salesiano, 1997), 257–322.

Zink, O. and Des Places, E., *Eusèbe de Césarée. La Préparation Évangélique, Livres IV–V, 1–17*, Sources chrétiennes 262 (Paris: Éditions du Cerf, 1979).

Index

Lightning Source UK Ltd.
Milton Keynes UK
UKHW020719300721
388018UK00004B/25